shift

INTERNET DIRECTORY 2001

TOP PICKS AND THE SKINNY FROM THE SHIFT LIST

SEARCH BETTER

SEARCH FASTER

SEARCH FARTHER

SCOTT MITCHELL

DARREN WERSHLER-HENRY

A Pearson Company
Toronto

Canadian Cataloguing in Publication Data

Internet directory: a Canadian guide to the best Web sites and tools

Annual.
1999–

ISSN 1490-8476
ISBN 0-13-031108-1 (2001 issue)

1. Web sites – Canada – Directories. 2. Computer network resources – Canada – Directories.
3. World Wide Web (Information retrieval system)

ZA4226.I5 004.67'8 C00-900743-1

ISBN 0-13-0311081-1

Editorial Director, Trade Division: Andrea Crozier
Acquisitions Editor: Paul Woods
Researchers: Lu Cormier, Emmet Mellow, Chris Sloan
Copy Editors: Gillian Scobie, Valerie Adams
Production Editor: Jodi Lewchuk
Art Direction: Mary Opper
Cover Design and Interior Design: Dave Murphy, Sarah Coviello/ArtPlus Limited
Cover Image: Masterfile
Production Manager: Kathrine Pummell
Page Layout: Heather Brunton, Steve Fyall/ArtPlus Limited

1 2 3 4 5 W 04 03 02 01 00

Printed and bound in Canada.

Visit the Prentice Hall Canada Web site! Send us your comments, browse our catalogues, and more. www.phcanada.com.

A Pearson Company

CONTENTS ▶

PART TWO: DESTINATIONS 191

ACKNOWLEDGMENTS ▶

Thanks to Grant Yoxon and Canadian Driver **<www.canadiandriver.com>** for help on all the thorny questions involved in the process of buying a car online. GameSpy and RadioSpy **<www.gamespy.com>** were ready with fast and effective user support for all of our finicky little questions. Lucas Mulder of [sic] **<www.sicmagazine.com>** provided invaluable information about Hotline, MAME and webcams, as well as an occasional duelling partner for Quake III and StarCraft (and thanks to all at id Software and Blizzard, respectively, for providing the ultimate in high-tech procrastination tools). Mark Surman of The Commons Group **<www.commonsgroup.com>** and Tonya Hancherow of Web Networks **<www.web.net>** provided sounding boards for many of the ideas in this book. Thanks to Liz Phillips for tolerating the many late-night cathode-ray tanning sessions involved in the research phase. Finally, thanks to Paul Woods and all at Prentice Hall Canada for expressing ongoing interest in this project.

INTRODUCTION ▶

Welcome to the new millennium.

A lot of computer users didn't think we'd get this far. By the middle of 1999, the bulk of the western world was firmly in the grip of millennial fever, as pundits everywhere delivered dire predictions of the mayhem that would result because the little clocks in our computers wouldn't roll over properly. Many computer users were rushing out to buy expensive Y2K crash-prevention software, hiring expensive Y2K consultants to make their networks "Y2K compliant," or worse, stockpiling food and supplies in their basement for that dreaded moment on New Year's Eve when the power was supposed to go out...

Oops. Though it might have been P.T. Barnum who first observed that no one ever became rich by overestimating the intelligence of the American public, Peter de Jaeger, the most prominent of the Y2K consultants, might well have been thinking the same thing on New Year's Day. De Jaeger's Web site, **<www.year2000.com>**, baldly states the obvious: "In the process of [spreading awareness of the Year 2000 problem], we accidentally created one of the most financially successful ventures in the world of online publishing. Year2000.com now has served its purpose well, and in the last year of the millennium we have made the domain name available to a new owner." Adding insult to injury, anyone out there with $10 million U.S. to spare is welcome to contact Mr. De Jaeger to discuss the purchase of the site.

Just because the Y2K bug fizzled out of existence and a handful of people had to sheepishly eat their way through their stockpiles of freeze-dried soybeans doesn't mean that the first half of the year 2000 has lacked for digital drama. However, the big stories have been somewhat anticlimactic, and the genuinely interesting stories have all started from very humble beginnings. In the online world, small actions can cause big ripples.

The most significant of the big Net-related stories of the year to date has been the final judgement in the United States vs. Microsoft antitrust case, calling for the breakup of the Microsoft empire into two companies: one that builds operating systems and one that builds applications. Now, the breakup of Microsoft shouldn't really come as a surprise to anyone, because there have been years of grumbling in the computing community leading up to this moment. And, in all likelihood, the appeals process and the messy business of balkanizing the company will drag on for a few years more. In other words, the Microsoft breakup isn't news, it's an ongoing fact of life. The viable alternatives to the Microsoft monopoly that are beginning to emerge are far more interesting.

One such alternative is the radical promise of a world of free software. Championed by members of the Open Source community—the people who volunteer their time and programming expertise to work on Linux and other free, generic versions of the Unix operating system—this cooperative effort has generated software that is arguably more stable and more powerful than anything produced by commercial software companies. One hacker Web site bears the following epigraph: "The software box said it required Windows 95 or better to run, so I installed Linux."

The big stumbling block to the widespread adoption of Linux remains the lack of availability of end-user applications, though that is changing rapidly as well. Corel Corporation has already produced a Linux version of its office suite, which includes the venerable WordPerfect word-processing program. Quake III, one of the world's most popular video games, runs on Linux, and other applications will surely follow. (To find out more about the Open Source movement, visit Slashdot **<www.slashdot.org>**, one of its liveliest watering holes.)

This is not to say that the events of the first half of the online year have all been related to utopian optimism and logical progress—far from it. Inevitably, as more people go online, more things will begin to go wrong. This is due both to increases in online traffic, which taxes existing systems to their limits, and to the fact that there will be greater numbers of people online whose only interest is in mischief and malice. The emergence of viruses such as "I Love You," which exploited the security holes in Microsoft's mail program Outlook Express, and the revelation that there are further security gaps in the Windows OS itself (such as the ironic vulnerability created by Microsoft's cloyingly cute "intelligent agents" help system), added fuel to the fires of anti-Microsoft sentiment. As a secondary effect, such events also create a significant amount of paranoia and low-level panic about the "evil" lurking in dark corners of the Internet, when the causes of said evil are far more complex than first appearances might suggest.

Consider the case of teen Montreal cracker Mafiaboy. While his February "Denial of Service" attacks against CNN.com, Amazon.com, E-Trade.com, Yahoo.com and other major Internet portals were undoubtedly annoying and expensive crimes, they're hardly the acts of "cyberterrorism" that were depicted by a panicked business community and an overly imaginative press. After Mafiaboy's arrest, when the hysteria had dropped a tone or two in pitch, Bruce Schneier, president of security service provider Counterpane Internet Security Inc., noted that Mafiaboy's actions were the digital equivalent of cow tipping. Far more ominous is the manner in which big business has assumed control of the agenda for public opinion about online events. How else to explain the inflation of a teenager with access to a few commonly available software tools into Internet Public Enemy Number One?

Napster is another case in point. Home duplication of recorded music is nothing new; nor are MP3s, for that matter, which Napster didn't invent. What Napster (the product of one college undergrad looking for an easy way of exchanging MP3s with his friends) has changed is the speed and efficacy with which music is exchanged. At the time of this writing, over 200,000 copies of Napster are downloaded each day. What is occurring is nothing short of a revolution in the use of the Internet, similar to the one that occurred with the World Wide Web when the first versions of Netscape became available. The RIAA and other parties may have legitimate concerns about the violation of musicians' copyrights, but that doesn't mean that the technology of peer-to-peer file exchange itself is something that should be eliminated. What the Napster phenomenon does mean is that the Internet is still a work-in-progress, and as new technologies to expand it continue to emerge, our world will change rapidly, and often in unexpected ways that will produce unforeseen results.

This is where *Internet Directory 2001* enters the picture.

Undoubtedly, there are many, many more changes in store for online culture over the coming years. The increase in overall Internet population, the advent of peer-to-peer computing, the breakup of Microsoft, and the ascendancy of Linux and the Open Source movement will all contribute to those changes, but so will the gradual increase in high-speed modem use, the rejuvenation of Apple as a major player in the computer industry, the AOL-Time Warner merger, the volatility of the NASDAQ tech-stock market, and many other factors that we can't even currently imagine.

Internet Directory is a tool that will evolve along with the Internet, helping you to understand and utilize new technology, and to understand the underlying social and cultural implications of that technology.

Stick around. Things are about to get *really* interesting.

TOOLS

PART ONE

ONE

PREPARING FOR THE TRIP ▶

> The Net is "an oracle," fostering an unprecedented dialog between human beings and the sum total of human knowledge.
>
> *Terence McKenna in Erik Davis's "Terence McKenna's Last Trip,"* Wired

Browser Basics and Beyond

The Web is a new world, a place where headspace links up with cyberspace, and the browser is its ever-changing tool of access and exploration. Although it's one of the newer pieces of Internet software, it's the one that you'll use most often. As connections become faster and people spend increasing amounts of time online, browsers have become increasingly sophisticated, and are, at least in the case of Microsoft's Internet Explorer, major components of the GUIs (Graphical User Interfaces) of entire operating systems. This increasing complexity has its pros and cons. On the plus side, today's browsers allow you to access Web sites featuring a wide variety of new media formats—animation, sound, and streaming video are now commonplace. The downside is that the latest browser versions require ever-increasing amounts of your hard disk and memory to operate. What's more, because of the demand to rush the software to market, the integrity of the releases can be questionable. Installing the latest version of a browser is a task you should approach with a great degree of caution, as it can cause severe system conflicts and crashes.

There are more browsers around than you might think, including Atomnet, Netcaptor, NetQuest, NeoPlanet, and Power Browser, to name a few (for a longer list, go to the BrowserWatch site **<browserwatch.internet.com>**—you'll be amazed). Overwhelmingly, though, most users end up using one of the three major browsers: Netscape's Communicator or Navigator, Microsoft's Internet Explorer, or Opera Software's Opera. What follows are descriptions of the major features of the most recent versions of these programs.

▶ARE WE THERE YET?

Futurelog

www.gyford.com/futurelog

Futurelog is the motherlode of technolological punditry: a running index of predictions about the brave new world to come, ranging in tone from breathless and uncritical ecstasy to the most cynical pessimism you can imagine. Check out Bruce Sterling's predictions about life in 2035: "Okay, here's my bottom line: By your standards, my world is fantastically advanced, but it's also gray, sagging, increasingly conservative, and visibly running out of steam."

Packing the Software: The Big Three Browsers

Netscape

home.netscape.com/browsers

In the halcyon days of the Web, Netscape was the hero, fighting the good fight of the small independent against the corporate giant. Then things changed: Netscape kept getting bigger, was bought by America Online (AOL), and began to think (and work) more and more like its foes. Adding insult to injury, Netscape invented the cookie, a device for tracking the surfing patterns of users (many longtime netizens—who believe online anonymity is a right—will curse Netscape for years to come because of this "innovation").

Nevertheless, Netscape is the only user-friendly alternative to the Microsoft monopoly, and many people continue to install Netscape on their machines as a statement of principle. Netscape is also better about bundling the state-of-the-art plug-ins with its product than Microsoft, which tends to simply invent its own version of everything.

Two problems. One, Microsoft Internet Explorer and Netscape Navigator don't play well together. Each wants to be the default browser on your system, and will continually pester you every time you start it up if it's not in control. Luckily, there's a tick-box that you can use to instruct the browser not to ask you this question again. Do so for your own sanity. (For more on this topic, see "Choosing a Default Browser" below.)

Two, and potentially more serious, is that installing new browsers on top of existing ones can cause system conflicts that are severe enough to crash your computer. (Since it's closer to being a part of the Windows operating system, Explorer is rarely the loser in the struggle for dominance between two browsers on a PC. Mac users usually have better luck running two browsers than their PC friends.) Most users are better off if they decide which browser they like best and stick to it rather than constantly adding the latest version of both browsers to their system. If you absolutely have to have both, install the latest update to Explorer first, then Netscape. As long as you let Explorer continue to operate as the default browser, everything should work fine. If you encounter problems, uninstall Netscape from the Control Panel and then delete all traces of it from the Registry (a scary but necessary step). If you do this two or three times, you might get lucky and arrive at something like a state of détente.

NUTS & BOLTS

4.72 Release Notes

home.netscape.com/eng/mozilla/4.72/relnotes/windows-4.72.html

These notes describe installation issues and known problems in Communicator 4.72.

Netscape Communicator 4.72

Everyone who's been on the Internet for more than a couple of years knows Netscape, the first really successful web browser. So what's changed with Netscape 4.72?

For starters, the program's creators have beefed up the implementation of Netscape's Internet keyword search function—you can now use it to find e-com-

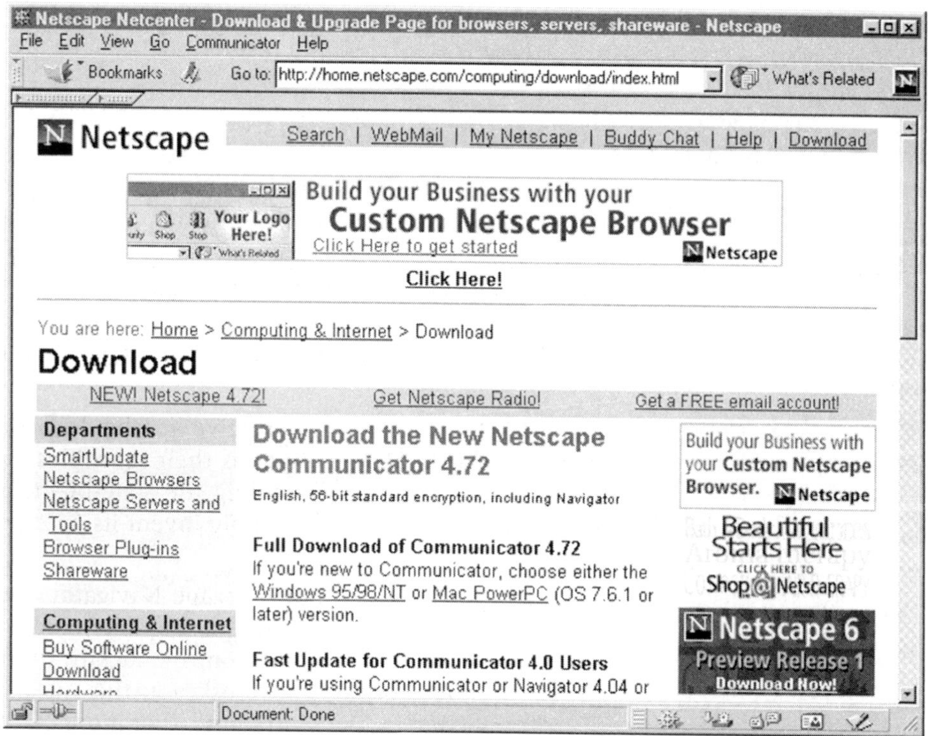

The Netscape Communicator download and upgrade page

merce sites by using the word "shop" before the product you want, or to get stock quotes from AOL by typing "Quote AOL." There's also a "Shop" button on the toolbar that takes you to the Shop@Netscape megamall page (which is okay, but frankly, there are better online malls). The bottom line is that with version 4.72, Netscape is trying to find new ways to get you to spend money on the goods manufactured by their eCommerce partners.

The appearance of the Netscape Radio and WinAmp features is a real sign of the times. Over the last year, interest in online music has exploded, largely because of the MP3 craze (more on that later—see the section on MP3s in Chapter 3 of this book), but also because of the rising popularity of high-speed connections (DSL and cable modems). These technologies make streaming audio (i.e., continuous audio that you can listen to immediately rather than having to wait for chunks to be downloaded to your hard drive) a viable technology; even on a 56K modem, streaming audio tends to sound kind of jerky. By bundling audio technology into your browser, Netscape is moving one step closer to providing a comprehensive, multimedia front end for your online surfing safaris.

In Netscape version 4.72, the mail program is fully integrated with a Usenet newsreader. Its three-frame interface is very easy to learn and use, and allows you to download newsgroup articles for later use. When you enable the program's Pinpoint Addressing system, it will complete the e-mail address you're typing if you've used it before. And if you want to e-mail an entire Web page to someone, just drag the page's bookmark to the Attachments tab of the e-mail, or select "Send page" from the

File menu if you have the page open in your browser, and follow the instructions. If you like to compose your e-mail in advance or on the road, you can send e-mail from your Palm Pilot to Netscape Messenger via the bundled PalmPilot Sync Tools.

Overall, Netscape 4.72 is a reliable package, and, with the proper plug-ins, will definitely accomplish anything you require of a Web browser... that is, as long as you can figure out how to get it to coexist peacefully with Explorer.

> **NUTS & BOLTS**
>
> **Netscape Navigator Plug-ins**
>
> **home.netscape.com/plugins**
>
> For a complete list of available plug-ins, visit the Netscape Browser Plug-ins page. For a list of the plug-ins currently installed in your copy of Navigator, type "about: plugins" in the browser's Location window.

Netscape 4.72 is available in two versions: 128-bit Strong Encryption, for the U.S.A. and Canada, and 56-bit Standard Encryption, for the rest of the world (U.S. law forbids export of encryption technologies beyond a certain degree of sophistication). The complete version of Netscape Communicator 4.72 includes Navigator (the browser), Messenger (the e-mail program), Composer (an HTML editor), AOL Instant Messenger 3.0, Netscape Radio (which rebroadcasts music and news from Spinner, the music netcast service that was recently absorbed into the giant AOL amoeba), WinAmp 2.5 (an MP3 player, included in the Windows version of Netscape only), PalmPilot Sync tools (Windows only), and multimedia plug-ins (Shockwave, Flash, RealPlayer G2, etc.).

A Note on Netscape Communicator 6

http://www.netscape.org/browsers/6/index.html

ZDNet's Netscape 6 Review and Guided Tour

http://www.zdnet.com/products/stories/pipreviews/0,8827,221080,00.html

Netscape 6? What happened to Netscape 5? Official version: Netscape 6 is built on Gecko, an entirely different engine than the one that powered older Netscape technology, including the stillborn Netscape 5. Unofficial version: In an effort to keep one step ahead of their beleaguered neighbours at Microsoft (in appearance, if nothing else), AOL Time Warner has skipped a grade, moving straight from release 4.72 of their browser to the brand-spanking new Netscape 6 (which is still in pre-release), pulling ahead of the tardy Internet Explorer 5.5 (which is still unreleased at the time of writing).

Now that Netscape has been assimilated body-and-soul into the biggest multimedia conglomerate in history, there's no longer any need to install it on your machine as a statement of principle. (If that's your game, see Opera, below, for a real alternative.) Still, if you're a believer in the KISS philosophy (Keep It Simple, Stupid), the latest version of Netscape may be right for you.

First of all, size matters. In an unexpected moment of good corporate citizenship, Netscape has actually struck back against software bloat. The program is now only 5.5 megs when compressed, and 8.5 megs when installed, which makes it 25-30% smaller than a comparable version of Explorer.

In the spirit of simpler-is-better, the Netscape interface itself has been pared down drastically. There are now only four big round buttons on the toolbar—forward, back, reload, and stop. Buttons to various Netscape NetCenter features, such as shopping and calendaring, have been reduced to tiny, unobtrusive text links along the top of the toolbar. (Note: This is the charitable, "good design" reading of the current version of Netscape. Our cynical, geeky inclinations, on the other hand, lead us to think that the overall simplification of Netscape has a lot to do with making the program more attractive to AOL users. With each new release, expect Netscape to be assimilated further and further, Borg-like, into the collective.)

Then there's the question of style. If user interface cosmetics make you feel all sweaty and breathless, Netscape's slick new design will really get your motor running. Netscape has ditched the traditional rectilinear grey window frame for blue streamlined curves. When prerelease 2 hits the Net, you'll be able to change the browser's skin similar to the way you can change NeoPlanet or WinAmp skins.

The biggest structural changes in this latest version of Netscape have to do with the browser's new sidebar. The sidebar houses a customizable series of tabs, which include the search function, the What's Related list, your chat buddy list, news, stock quotes, and tabs for high-content sites like CNN. You can add your own tabs for other Web sites with a single click (don't worry, your bookmarks haven't disappeared. Tabs are more appropriate for high-use sites, like search engines or shop bots).

Netscape's search capabilities, which appear as a tab in the sidebar, are much improved over previous versions. As with IE5, you can now run a search in your sidebar from one (or several) engines. The search results appear in a scrollable window in the sidebar, and the entire list remains visible when you pick a link to follow. If you don't want or need the control over your search that the sidebar offers, you can type your search string straight into the browser's address window and wait for the results to appear. The catch is that when using the browser's built-in search facilities, you're limited to Borg (um, I mean AOL) engines like AOL Search, CompuServe and Netcenter, which don't hold a candle to serious search tools like Northern Light and HotBot.

The inclusion of a Buddy List tab in the sidebar represents the integration of AOL Instant Messenger into Netscape itself. Well, *part* of Instant Messenger... you can send messages to your friends, but this release includes none of the other features of messaging programs, such as file transfer and real-time chat. KISS strikes again.

Instant Messenger isn't the only thing that's being assimilated in this version of Netscape. The browser's mail program has been tied into both the general AOL mail system and Instant Messenger. You can now use Netscape to check AOL accounts without having to log into the service. If you receive e-mail from one of your friends who's still online and logged into AOL Instant Messenger, an icon appears in your mail program, indicating you have the option of sending an Instant Message instead of an e-mail.

At the time this was written, Netscape 6 was still in the preview stage. Many of the most serious nuts-and-bolts questions, such as the browser's claim that its Gecko engine fully supports XML and DHTML, remain unanswered. Hopefully, the first full release of Netscape 6 will iron out the remaining technical kinks, and allow users to customize the program to operate beyond the narrow parameters of the Internet according to AOL.

NUTS & BOLTS

AltaVista Does a Google

www.raging.com

Tired of everything-but-the-kitchen sink portals? Raging Search, the newest search engine on the block, is as bare-bones as they come: a search window and a button. AltaVista, which operates the site, claims Raging is 20 percent faster than the competitors and that its 350-million-item index is free of dead and redundant links. Maybe, but so far, it's no match for Google.

Microsoft

www.microsoft.com/windows/ie

www.microsoft.com/mac/ie

If you've got hard disk space and memory to burn, plus a fast connection, and you aren't planning on running any other browsers, IE5 is the logical choice. The truth is that Internet Explorer is probably a part of your life whether you want it to be or not, since it ships with almost all PCs and Macs as the default browser. Though you can choose not to install it, or try to uninstall it, Explorer is an integral part of the Microsoft software universe, and virtually every other major product that they make calls on it in some way. Mac users have it a little easier, because the MacOS exists autonomously from all browsers (for now). For PC users, though, entirely removing IE from your system is like cutting off your nose to spite your face. If you uninstall Explorer, there's no telling which obscure but totally vital files might vanish in the process, or when MS Office or some other key program might go looking for a piece of it.

> **NUTS & BOLTS**
>
> **Exploring IE**
>
> Internet Explorer 5 Tour
>
> **www.microsoft.com/windows/ie/tour**
>
> Internet Explorer 5 Companion Site
>
> **www.netmag.co.uk/ie5**

If you don't have Internet Explorer 5 on your system and are considering downloading it, brace yourself: the download can be anywhere from 6 to 45 megabytes in size. Fully installed, the program is huge: 56 MB for browser-only installation, 72 MB for standard installation, and 98 MB for full installation (larger than the entire Linux operating system). For an average download of about 26 MB, which would include most of the plug-ins, but not the Web page construction software, you're looking at a solid hour and a half download time at 56 Kbps. Make sure you have a good book handy.

Downloading IE5 proceeds with the help of an "agent," a smaller program that you download first to allow you to select the components that you wish to install, then to select the fastest local file server, as well as initiating the download. IE also allows multiple file downloads through "Download Merger."

Users who've already installed a recent version of Netscape but still want IE5 should consider uninstalling Netscape, and manually deleting all traces of it from the directory tree and the Registry, before installing IE5. Why? Netscape probably won't work properly after you install IE due to system conflicts, and may even crash your entire system. You can try to reinstall Netscape after you've successfully loaded IE5, but even that may take several attempts before you meet with success.

So why bother installing both browsers? Well, the IE5 general interface has been reworked to make it look and function more like Microsoft's other programs. If you have more than one Internet connection, you'll find it much easier to make IE5 go where you want when you want. There have been some real improvements to error handling: IE5's error messages are now much more intelligible, making it easier to figure out what's happening when (not if) something goes wrong. When IE5 returns a "404 File not found" message, it also displays a simple explanation and some suggestions on how to proceed.

For those of you who like cruise control, IE5's auto-complete, auto-correct and auto-search features are now much more useful. Auto-complete provides a drop-down menu of URLs you've visited that share the same opening characters with whatever you happen to be typing; if you've been to the site already, all you have to do is pick it from the list. Auto-correct watches for common keying errors, like leaving out one of the "t"s in "http://," and adjusts your entry accordingly. Auto-search turns your address window into a search engine. All you have to do is type "?" or "go," followed by your search terms, into the address window of the browser, hit the return key, and the browser will conduct your search.

Explorer is gradually becoming as functional as some of the more specialized Internet utilities, such as Web rippers (programs capable of downloading entire Web sites to your hard disk with the page and directory structure intact) and dedicated FTP programs. In IE5, you can now save individual Web pages with all the graphics in place, and its FTP Folders feature allows for much easier handling of return visits to your favourite FTP sites.

▶NUTS & BOLTS

Web Accessories for IE5

www.microsoft.com/windows/Ie/WebAccess/default.asp

If all the extra options for IE5 still aren't enough to satisfy your need for gadgetry, check out the Web accessories available on this page:

- wallpaper for your Explorer toolbar
- "power tweaks" (additional buttons, mouse options, etc.)
- a package of developer tools including a very cool "view partial source code" option that allows you to highlight a section of a Web page, right-click on your mouse, and view the HTML for that specific piece of the page
- a number of customized "Explorer Bars" that sit at the bottom of your IE5 screen and provide you with information about the site you're visiting (the Alexa bar), stock quotes (the Bloomberg bar), news from the *New York Times*, or instant access to the AltaVista search engine

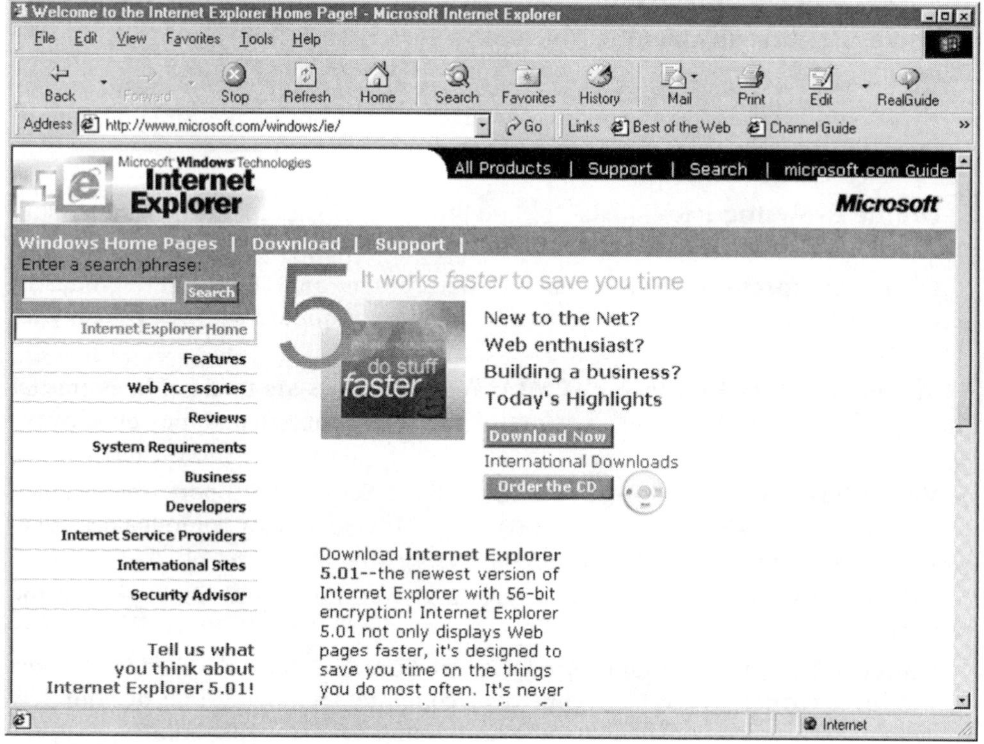

The Internet Explorer home page

One of the reasons IE5 is so huge is that it comes with a lot of luxury options that may or may not enhance your experience of the Internet. These smaller programs are briefly described below, so you can decide which components to specify for download.

Agent 2.0: Those annoying little animated characters (the smirking paperclip, etc.) that Microsoft uses in its interactive guides and entertainment features are now available on some Web sites. These "agents" are actually a massive security risk ... we knew there was a good reason to hate them. You can download the security patch at **<www.microsoft.com/technet/security/bulletin/msøø-ø34asp>**.

Chat 2.5: Microsoft's own chat utility. The optional "comic-strip" mode is kind of cool, because it lets you choose your own character and its facial expressions from a roster created by weirdo underground comic artist Jim Woodring.

DirectAnimation: This feature increases your computer's animation and multimedia capabilities both on the Web and in certain software products.

Dynamic HTML Data Binding: Data binding eliminates the need to reconnect to the Web server each time you query a page to display different information, which means that the amount of time it takes to sort information online will drop.

FrontPage Express 2.0: FrontPage Express is an elementary WYSIWYG Web-page editor, and the Web Publishing Wizard 1.61 is a step-by-step program that will walk you through posting your first Web pages. These tools might be useful for rank beginners, but everyone else should give them a pass.

Internet Explorer Core Fonts and Additional Web Fonts: Typography on the Web is finally becoming a possibility, thanks to protocols like this, which allow Web authors to specify fonts other than serif or sans serif.

Microsoft Virtual Machine: Microsoft's Java engine. You need this, but the reliability of Java implementation still varies a lot from browser to browser, so be prepared for the odd crash.

NetMeeting 2.11: This program works with your desktop computer's camera to allow videoconferencing.

Offline Browsing Pack: Makes offline browsing of sites in your cache, or sites that you've snagged for later viewing, a more pleasant experience.

Outlook Express 5: Outlook handles both e-mail and Usenet newsgroups. It has reasonably good spam filters, and now allows you to jazz up your e-mail with "stationery."

Vector Graphics Rendering (VML): Vector graphics are made of lines (rather than pixels). This is Microsoft's version of the technology that drives Shockwave and Flash.

Visual Basic Scripting Support: Visual Basic Scripting Support was installed on your computer when you installed Windows. This updated version makes Visual Basic scripts run faster, so you should probably download it.

VRML 2.0 Viewer: An acceptable VRML viewer, but Cosmo Player is still the standard.

Wallet 3: This little program stores your credit card numbers and address information in a virtual "wallet" on your own computer, removing one of your few remaining excuses for not shelling out vast amounts of cash while online.

Windows Media Player 6.0: The Media Player can handle most multimedia content formats you'll encounter on the Internet or elsewhere, including Advanced Streaming Format (ASF), Real Audio/RealVideo 4.0, QuickTime, AVI, WAV, MPEG, and MP3.

A Note on Internet Explorer 5.5

Upgrades, upgrades upgrades . . . there's no avoiding them. Sneak previews of Internet Explorer 5.5, scheduled to ship with Windows Millennium Edition sometime in 2000, indicate that the next generation of the browser isn't really all that different from IE5. In the wake of the big Microsoft trial, you can bet that there'll be some improvements to IE's compliance with HTML, DHTML, Java and JavaScript standards, which means that you'll be able to see a greater range of pages in IE without it returning errors. The only real new feature that's been announced so far is a Print Preview option, which will allow you to get an idea of what a Web page will look like if you choose to run it out on your printer. Two previous components of the browser package, Microsoft Wallet and Microsoft Chat, will be dropped from the new release. The failure of Wallet isn't really a surprise, as a workable, secure system for rapid online payment is evidently years away, and Microsoft has been pushing its MSN Chat hard through a series of TV ads as an alternative to ICQ or AOL

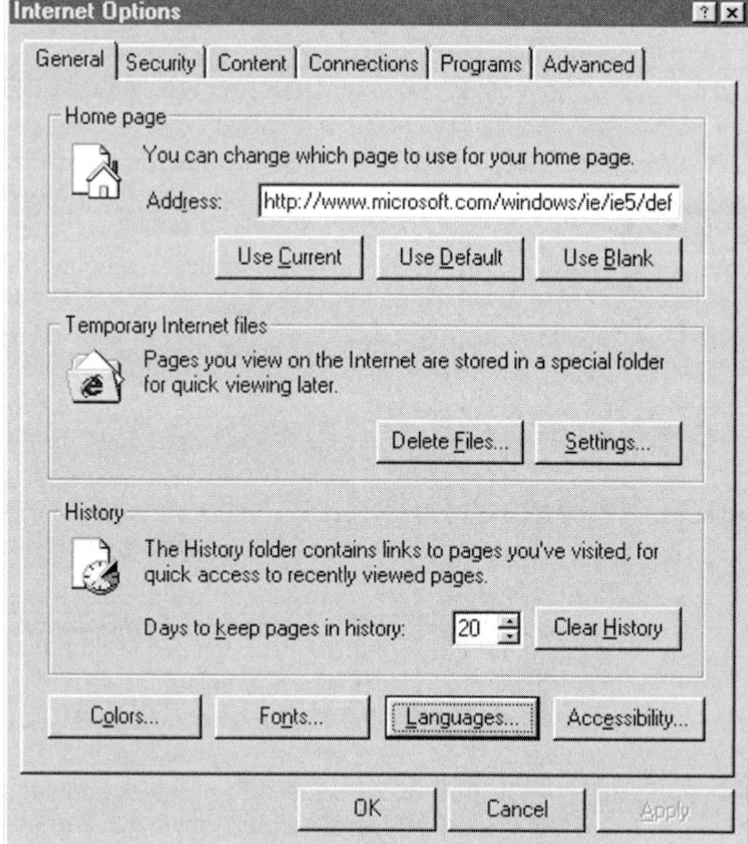

The Internet Options dialog box

Instant Messenger. Still, a lot can happen between the beta stage and the next release, so whatever ends up in the final version of IE5.5 remains open to conjecture.

Opera

www.opera.com

If you're a no-nonsense, power-user type who's not afraid to tinker with the default settings of your software, or if you're fed up enough with the neverending Netscape/ IE wars to want to become a no-nonsense, power-user type, Opera is for you.

Why bother? First of all, Opera is tiny. When zipped, version 3.62 for Windows 95/98 is only 1.4 MB, and installed, only requires between 3 and 7 MB (the beta of Opera 4 isn't much larger). Compare that to the 56 to 98 megabytes of your precious hard disk that Internet Explorer 5 requires, and think about how long it's going to take to download in comparison. But Opera's diminutive size contains a surprising amount of strength. Even though installing Opera takes less than a minute, it contains a basic newsreader program and an e-mail program, and can link to external mail programs like Eudora. It appeals chiefly to people who do research online rather than pleasure-surfers seeking the latest in multimedia thrills, because it excels at handling text information quickly and efficiently. If you choose, you can navigate entirely from the keyboard, speeding up your search process even more.

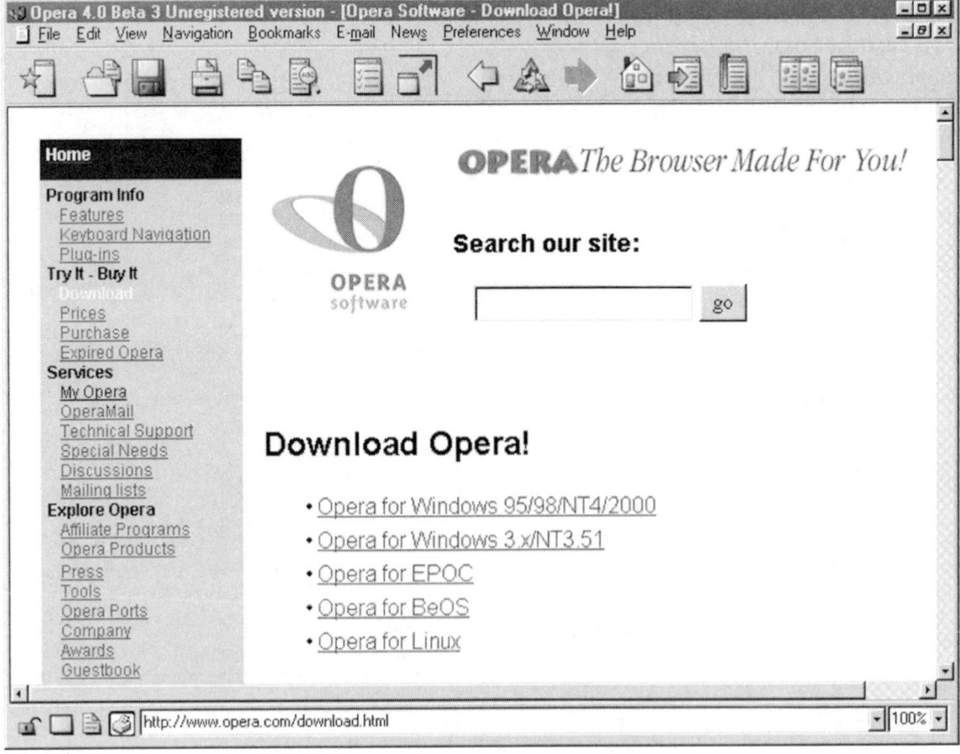

Opera, the little browser that could

Opera's basic structure is built around a series of open "windows," which operate without tapping into all your free memory. So what? Well, for example, you can designate multiple home pages for your startup, such as your home site and several search engines. You can run a query on a Web search engine, then open new documents in the background without losing the screen containing your search results. Or redirect output from one window to another. Opera also retrieves multiple documents and images at the same time: while you have a document downloading in one window, you can browse in another. And you can conduct multiple synchronous downloads, which the program manages in a single download window.

Opera is also a good tool to have for Web developers concerned with accessibility issues, because, unlike either Netscape or Internet Explorer, it adheres strictly to the current HTML standard. If you can view a page properly in Opera, it'll appear in pretty much anything.

Users of older PCs may also want to consider Opera as a first resort. The software's makers state that a 386SX with 8 MB of RAM (read "boat anchor") is sufficient to run the Opera browser, which may well be true, but you'd have to find a computer that old in working condition before you could verify the claim (look in schools or nonprofit organizations).

At present, Opera is only available for PCs running Windows, but the good folks at Opera are working on versions of their browser for various flavours of Unix (including Linux), the MacOS, the BeOS, and EPOC. The Opera for EPOC browser can be used on devices such as smart phones, screen phones, and communicators.

The other major difference between Opera and its two larger competitors is a philosophical one. While Netscape and Internet Explorer are nominally both freeware, Opera sells for $35 U.S. The developers have a reasonable, well-developed argument for this fee, which you can read online at **<www.opera.com/whypay.html>**.

Until you get a chance to view the Opera site for yourself, though, ponder this nugget of rhetoric for a moment:

> The CEO of one of our competitors once said: "Every six-year-old knows that FREE doesn't mean 'free.'" We leave that uncommented, but want to point out that the very same CEO has now made his own product available for free, cutting off about 18% of his company's income, slashing hundreds of employees, and . . . giving up his own salary because of the miserable situation he has led his company into—all in the name of "market share and domination." Hmmm . . .

Hmmm, indeed.

NUTS & BOLTS

NeoPlanet

www.neoplanet.com

NeoPlanet is not a browser per se, but rather an "interface-lift" that integrates a Web browser, e-mail client, instant messaging, chat, Web directory, search engine, and discussion groups into a single interface. Because it allows you to choose from a number of custom surfaces or "skins," NeoPlanet is bound to be a big hit with designers and other fashionable types (as long as they don't use Macs—sorry, this is a Windows-only application), but power users will likely conclude that it's just more tinsel between them and their applications. Still, NeoPlanet is free, and a fast download (less than 2 MB, which takes about five minutes with a 56 Kbps connection), so check it out for yourself.

Browser Updates

People who feel compelled to keep up with the latest technology belong to a minority group known as "early adopters." At the other end of the spectrum—barring self-proclaimed Luddites, who take perverse pride in living an unwired lifestyle—are those who happily peck away on old computers running ancient browsers. The rest of us are somewhere in between, upgrading occasionally as the need arises, as time permits, or as fancy strikes.

In the browser arena, cost is not the primary issue. Both the major browser manufacturers at one time or another flirted with selling their software, but Navigator and Internet Explorer are both currently available free of charge. As browser software continues to bloat, and the minimum requirements for memory, speed, and disk space continue to rise, you may not have a choice about upgrading—your computer may simply be incapable of complying. Or you may be tired of fixing problems caused by every new installation.

The only upgrades you should always be concerned about are security patches. Otherwise, it all depends on your own needs and desires. Serious content providers are usually mindful of their market—they want to present a contemporary look, or make use of new delivery technologies, but they can't afford to lose their lag-behind customers.

▶NUTS & BOLTS

SmartUpdate

With recent versions of Navigator and Communicator, Netscape has introduced a service called SmartUpdate. When you visit the SmartUpdate page—choose Help > Software Updates from the browser menu, or key in the URL **<www.netscape.com/smartupdate>** and then click on "Select Software," the site automatically detects which version of the Netscape browser you're using and what components are missing. You select the updates you want, and the site downloads and installs the necessary bits. This avoids the traditional long, long wait required to download and reinstall the entire browser every time you want to upgrade.

But if you've got the space on your hard drive, a souped-up processor, and buckets of RAM (the bare minimum is probably 32 MB, although 64 MB is quickly becoming the de facto entry level), the truth is that browsers just keep getting better. For Web searching, the built-in technology is making it faster and simpler to find what you're looking for. And the Web is just way more fun when the pages dance.

To update your favourite browser, visit the company page of your choice. How do you know when it's time to update? Well, if you regularly read any of the major online Internet news publications, it's pretty hard to avoid the marketing announcements when a new version of Navigator or Internet Explorer is released. Alternatively, you can sign up for e-mail alerts from the company itself. The Opera Newsletter **<www.opera.com/cgi-bin/mailman/listinfo/opera-newsletter>**, for example, is a low-volume mailing list that notifies Opera users about items of interest, typically new releases. The Internet Options menu in Internet Explorer includes a tick-box that directs IE to automatically check for updates every thirty days or so and then notify you if an update is available.

▶ARE WE THERE YET?

The Industry Standard

www.thestandard.com

If you really want to know the dirt about what's happening in the online universe, The Standard is essential reading. This is a deep-content site: not only does it present in-depth articles on the latest online trends, there's a Metrics section with enough stats about online growth to satisfy the most meticulous of researchers. (Bonus geek points: if you want to really impress your coworkers with your next presentation, download some of The Standard's ready-made PowerPoint slides, which feature plenty of impressive charts and graphs.)

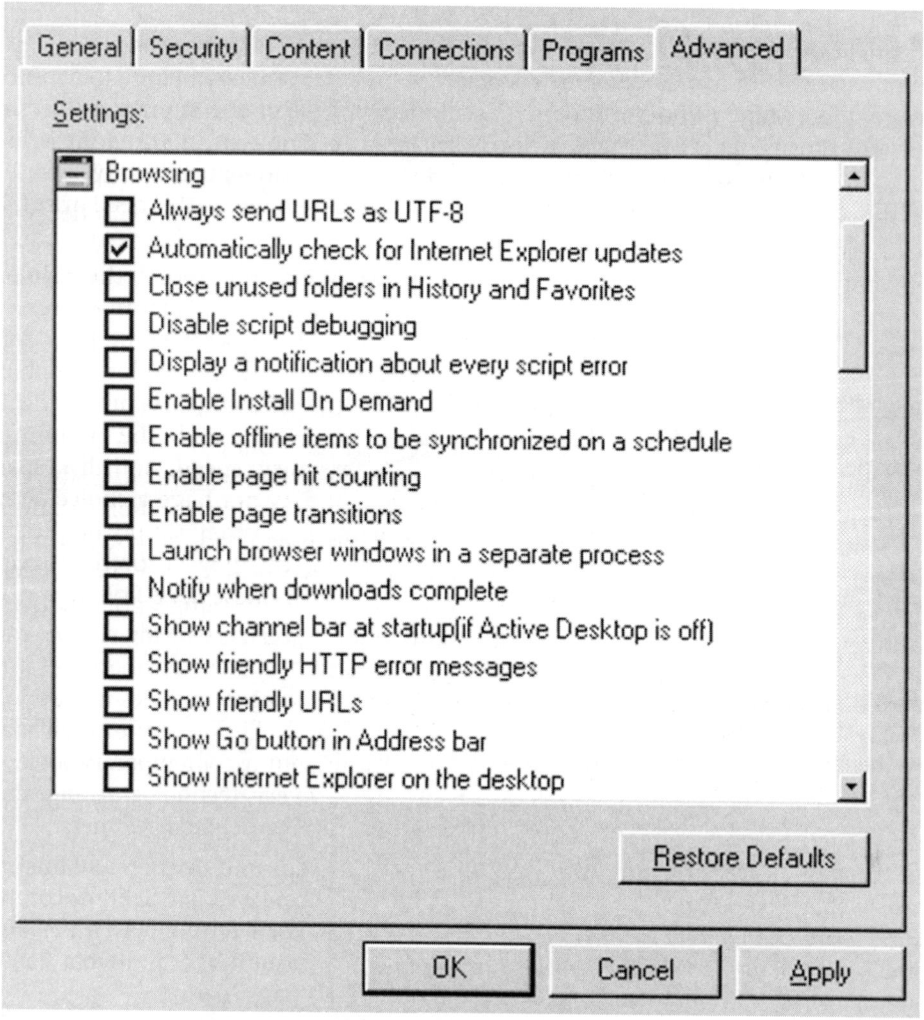

Setting the Updates option in Internet Explorer

Alternative Methods of Browsing

There are other methods of exploring the brave new world of the Internet, but they're more in the line of supplements than replacements. The following two types of browsers, offline browsers and browsers for handheld devices, are options you might want to consider to suit special situations (or just to satisfy your raging technophilia).

Offline Browsers

Offline browsers (or "Web site rippers," as they're affectionately known) have two major uses. For users with limited amounts of Web time at their disposal, offline browsers allow you to save a particular Web site and view it at your leisure. They also let Web designers study the construction of a particularly interesting site up close.

In theory, offline browsers download Web pages, including source code and all graphics, and save them on your hard drive for later viewing. In practice, many of them will miss some elements, or will crap out on particular Web pages for mysterious reasons. Many offline browsers let you specify the depth that you wish to save (i.e. how many layers of clicking you want to preserve—you don't want to pull down the whole Web, now, do you?) and will follow the links that you specify.

NOTE: When using an offline browser, remember that Web sites, like any other publication, are protected by copyright. Don't redistribute someone else's Web site or remount an unmodified version of it without express permission from the site's owner.

BlackWidow

www.softbytelabs.com/BlackWidow

BlackWidow is a Swiss Army knife for the Internet: an offline browser/site ripper/site scanner/site mapping and mirroring tool. It uses an Explorer-like interface, which presents you with a file listing that allows you to select the individual files you want to download from the site (or you can just download the whole thing at one go). You can run multiple instances of BlackWidow to work with different Web sites simultaneously, or download from one site while profiling another. BlackWidow is shareware with a 15-day evaluation period. Cost is $39.95 U.S.

WebWhacker 2000

www.bluesquirrel.com/products/whacker/whacker.html

WebWhacker was one of the first offline browsers, and has enjoyed considerable critical success. You can use it to "whack" an entire site or a single Web page, schedule automatic whacks, filter, print, and monitor Web sites, and so on. You can automate WebWhacker to check for changes to your favourite Web sites and notify you about those changes on a daily, weekly, or monthly basis. WebWhacker is available as a 15-day demo, while the full version costs $49.95 U.S. and is available for the MacOS as well as Windows 95/98/NT.

WebZip

www.spidersoft.com

Here's a new and interesting approach to Web ripping. WebZip not only downloads entire Web sites, it compresses them into a single archived zip file. It also has an add-in tool which will generate a compressed HTML-Help file, complete with a table of contents, index, and full-text search capabilities for the captured Web site. WebZip costs $39.95 U.S. for the regular version, or $64.95 for the one that generates the table of contents and index.

Browsers for Handheld Devices

Browsers for handheld PIMs (Personal Information Managers) like the PalmPilot and, yes, your cell phone, are rapidly making the transition from novelty item to useful addition to your online arsenal. The programs for these tiny computers are marvels of clean, efficient coding that allow you to do serious work with minuscule resources. Sure, they're no match for their full-scale PC cousins—yet—but they've already evolved past the ability to access core information (such as e-mail, stock quotes, news items, and the yellow pages) to include more frivolous services, such as ordering movie tickets or buying items online. If you're a techno-hipster with a desperate need to maintain that all-important air of gadget-based superiority, here are the most powerful current options for mobile browsing.

Bell Canada Mobile Browser

www.bellmobility.ca

Dick Tracy's wristwatch videophone is looking pretty feasible right about now. Within the next three to five years, cell phones will become one of the most common forms of Internet access. Bell Canada's Mobile Browser service is now included free with their RealTime Digital PCS phone service in Ontario and Quebec, and is coming soon to other cities across the rest of the country. The RealTime package allows you to send and receive e-mail anywhere, do your banking, trade stocks, book tickets for sports and entertainment events, and so on, all through your phone. If you still feel the need to lug along your laptop, Bell's Digital Data To Go package will turn your cell phone into a wireless modem (you can also use this package with a Windows CE palmtop or a pre-Palm VII PalmPilot).

Palm VII Connected Organizer

www.palm.com/products/palmvii

The Palm VII, which includes a built-in wireless modem, is looking more and more like transitory technology. Like Bell's Mobile Browser service, Palm.net provides "Web clippings" rather than real Web pages—bare-bones information extracted from a variety of online services, such as e-mail, stock quotes, telephone numbers from the yellow pages, news stories, and so on. The old computing adage that "It's not a flaw, it's a feature!" really applies here; Palm's bumph says that Web clippings give you the information you want "without the graphics, links, or decorations to slow you down." Whatever. The punchline is that you can't use Palm.net outside of the U.S.A. (even OmniSky **<www.omnisky.com>**, the company that built a kick-butt wireless modem system for the Palm V, doesn't work anywhere in Canada yet). By the time online service for PalmPilots is available in Canada, your phone will have absorbed your PIM whole-hog, so the Palm is living on borrowed time. For eventual dominance of the mobile Web access market, the smart money is on Ma Bell.

> **NUTS & BOLTS**
>
> **Palm Gear HQ**
>
> **store.yahoo.com/pilotgearsw/faxemail.html**
>
> Here's a one-stop spot to buy fax, e-mail, and Web software for your Palm.

Casio Cassiopeia

www.casio.com

In January 2000, America Online and Casio announced that AOL members will soon be able to to access their AOL e-mail via Casio's Cassiopeia, the top-selling

Windows CE PIM. The Cassiopeia is a slick little machine—it's full colour, and you can use it as an MP3 player *and* a Windows Media Player, as well as an electronic organizer. The drawback here, of course, is that you'll have to be an AOL user to take advantage of Cassiopeia's e-mail service, and most computer geeks (the target market for high-end PIMs) would rather crawl over a kilometre of broken glass than use AOL for anything other than a cheap source of CD-ROM coffee-cup coasters.

Getting the Most from Your Browser

Fine-tuning the browser to suit your own needs is a little like adjusting your car's rearview mirrors and shifting the seat for comfort—it makes for a better driving experience. So take some time to explore all the options. You can change the appearance settings (including the face and size of display fonts, the colour of text, links, and page backgrounds, and the look and placement of toolbars), enable (or disable) the various "smart browsing" features, specify the default character set for reading pages in other languages, and alter the security settings to match your personal feelings of well-being or paranoia, as the case may be.

Most browsers allow you to muck around with the controls, tweaking the browser to look and act the way you want it to. In Internet Explorer 5, choosing Internet Options from the Tools menu will open a dialog box that allows you to manage everything from fonts and colors to security certificates. Similar controls in Navigator are called Preferences. They're located under the Edit menu, where you'll find most of the controls for fine-tuning your browser in the ways described below.

Setting Your Start-Up Page

A good place to begin personalizing your browser is to change the start-up page. Why wait for the default home page—usually the browser company's home page—to load every time you launch the browser, only to surf away again to somewhere you really want to go? (And why help the company sell banner ad space by artificially increasing their hit count?) Change the home page URL to the site you tend to visit most often—your favorite search engine or news site, for example—so that you immediately land on that page whenever you fire up the browser. It'll save you time, and whenever you click on the Home button, you'll be returned to that page.

If you aren't stuck on a particular site, then starting with a blank page is even quicker, and both Navigator and Internet Explorer make that option available.

Choosing a Default Browser

Both Navigator and Internet Explorer display the personality traits of schoolyard bullies, toughing it out for control of your desktop. When you click on a desktop shortcut, try to open an HTML file by double-clicking in the file manager, or click on a Web-enabled link in another application, your operating system looks for a browser to launch—but what happens when you have more than one browser installed? Only one browser at a time can be registered as the default application, and so the struggle begins. When you install or upgrade your browser, you will probably be asked whether you want to register it as the default browser. And if you

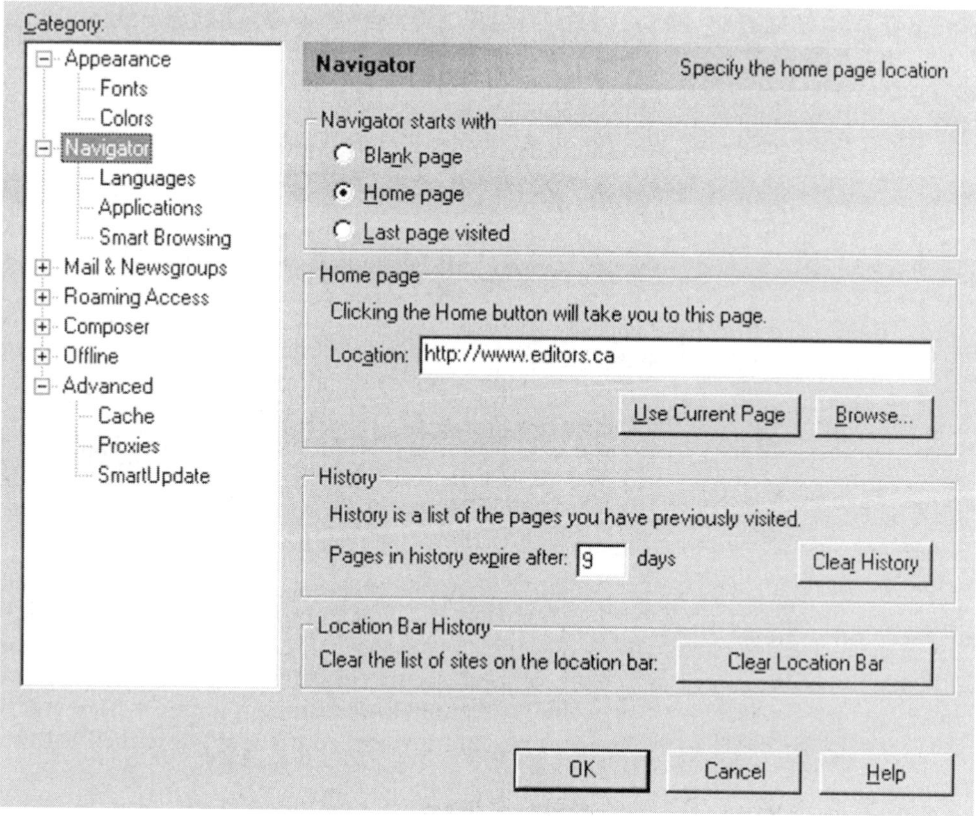

Setting the start-up page in Navigator

register one browser and then run its competitor, the competitor will likely ask you the same question, hoping you'll choose to displace the original contender. But sometimes it won't ask—it'll just go ahead and assume.

So, how do you settle the question once and for all?

The procedure will vary, depending on your platform (Windows 3.1+, Windows 95/98/NT, or Macintosh) and which versions of the browser you have installed. Netscape provides online instructions on "How to Make Communicator Your Default Browser" **<www.netscape.com/download/netscape_now.html>**. Of course, they're geared to making the Netscape browser your first choice, but you can reverse that decision by reversing the instructions. Netscape also reminds you that the best way to declare an end to the conflict is simply to remove the offending browser altogether, and gleefully provides step-by-step instructions for deleting Internet Explorer. The browser war continues.

▶ARE WE THERE YET?

Looking Good in 2010

www.businessweek.com/2000/00_10/b3671021.htm

IDEO, the firm that designed the sexy, streamlined Palm V, has taken a guess at what sorts of toys the geek who has everything will be playing with a decade from now. This article has lots of snappy renderings of digital pens, artificially intelligent personal assistants, featherweight phones that perch delicately inside your ear, roll-up LCD screens.... Gee, if our stationery looks this good, we might not have to worry about war, famine and disease at all.

Graphics and Multimedia Display Settings

Pictures are definitely worth a thousand words when it comes to how long they take to download and how much space they consume on your hard drive. Despite file compression schemes and the best efforts of Web designers to optimize graphics—that is, shrink the file size as much as possible without entirely compromising the quality of the image—pictures will always slow you down. So, instead of twiddling your thumbs while a giant JPEG trickles onto your screen, why not turn the graphics off? The idea of surfing the Web without images may sound like watching TV without the picture on, but you'd be surprised how much time you can save. And properly designed Web pages will display <alt> text in place of the images to let you know what you're missing.

Both Navigator and Internet Explorer give you the choice of whether or not to automatically load images (as well as other multimedia files). If you shut them off and then come to a page that looks interesting, you can load the images for that particular page. In Navigator, choose Show Images from the View menu to display all the images on the page, or right-click on the image icon and choose Show Picture to see an individual image. In IE, only the right-click option is available, so you'll have to load the images one by one. Or go back and change the overall setting, then click on Refresh.

▶NETHEADS

World Wide Web Consortium (W3C)

www.w3.org

Created in October 1994 by Web-inventor Tim Berners-Lee "to lead the World Wide Web to its full potential by developing common protocols that promote its evolution and ensure its interoperability," the W3C now has more than 400 member organizations around the world. Although the role of the W3C is to set standards for the Web, the trouble is that certain too-big-for-their-britches browser makers don't seem to take the idea of standards very seriously, which is why Web pages often look very different from one browser to another. Still, the W3C soldiers on, working towards its three stated long-term goals:

1. *Universal Access:* To make the Web accessible to all by promoting technologies that take into account the vast differences in culture, education, ability, material resources, and physical limitations of users on all continents;
2. *Semantic Web:* To develop a software environment that permits each user to make the best use of the resources available on the Web;
3. *Web of Trust:* To guide the Web's development with careful consideration for the novel legal, commercial, and social issues raised by this technology.

Good luck, Tim!

Styles, Scripts, and Dynamic HTML

Cascading Style Sheets

When HTML was invented, it was intended as a vehicle for sharing content in an organized way across platforms, not to make content look snazzy. Which is fine for academic essays, but it drove graphic designers crazy. So, Cascading Style Sheets were developed by the World Wide Web Consortium (W3C) **<www.w3.org/Style/CS/>** to give creators better control over type, page positioning, and other aspects of visual design. And yet, browser implementation of Cascading Style Sheets (CSS) remains spotty—which means a Web page may look different, depending on which browser is being used to view it.

Java and JavaScript

First things first. JavaScript has almost nothing to do with Java. They're both programming languages, and their names sound alike, but the resemblance stops there. Java, invented by Sun Microsystems (see sidebar), is mostly used to write small, portable programs called applets, which are supposed to run equally well on any platform, including Unix, Windows, and Macintosh. Java-enabled browsers can run Web-based applets that make chat rooms, stock tickers, animation, and other good stuff possible.

JavaScript, on the other hand, is a much simpler language that's not far removed from HTML. Whereas HTML is the authoring language used to create basic Web pages, JavaScript is written as part of the Web document, nestled inside the HTML, and does a few tricks to make Web pages more dynamic. One of the most common effects is the rollover—rolling your mouse over an image, such as a navigation button, causes the old image to be replaced by a new one. JavaScript also allows Web designers to make forms that can do calculations, or verify that all the fields have been filled in correctly before the form is submitted—actions that would otherwise require a CGI (Common Gateway Interface) script running on the server. JavaScript can make things easier and quicker, since the checking and calculating can be done on your computer, rather than remotely.

> **NETHEADS**
>
> **Sun Microsystems**
>
> **www.sun.com**
>
> The first global software company, Sun calls themselves the dot in com. They started out with a vision of computers talking to each other no matter who built them, the beginnings of Java. CEO Scott McNealy says, "The network is our DNA." Not *too* self-conscious.
>
> For more about Java, visit the Sun site **<java.sun.com>**, or Gamelan: The Official Java Directory **<www.gamelan.com>**.

JavaScript is supported by most popular Web browsers, including all versions of Netscape Navigator 2.0 and later, Microsoft Internet Explorer 3.01 and later, and Opera 3.0. That said, you should know that more recent browsers are better—though still not perfect—at handling both Java and JavaScript. If your computer is new enough to handle the upgrade, your surfing will be smoother.

Of course, JavaScripts don't always run smoothly. Sometimes you'll encounter a pop-up box informing you of a JavaScript Error. When this happens, it's usually the fault of the Web-page developer, who hasn't written correct code, so there's nothing you can do about it (except complain, if you're feeling cranky). Just click on OK. On the other hand, different Web browsers support different JavaScript features, and here the fault resides with the browser manufacturers. No browser has achieved perfect and complete JavaScript implementation.

VBScript

A relatively simple scripting language invented by Microsoft, VBScript enables the presence of interactive Web controls, such as buttons and scrollbars. It is Microsoft's answer to Netscape's widely used JavaScript. The name is short for Visual Basic Scripting Edition, since it was built on the foundation of Visual Basic, a much more powerful programming language. For an overview, visit the Microsoft Scripting Technologies page **<msdn.microsoft.com/scripting>**.

ActiveX

Rather than a single, well-defined entity, ActiveX is a loosey-goosey set of Microsoft technologies that grew out of OLE (Object Linking and Embedding) and COM

(Component Object Model). ActiveX has since found its way—or rather, their way—into almost everything the Redmond giant makes, from Microsoft Office to the Windows operating system. For an in-depth propellor-head explanation, read *Byte* magazine's special issue, "ActiveX Demystified" **<byte.com/art/9709/sec5/sec5.htm>**.

Dynamic HTML

For the most part, HTML documents are static. Once a Web page is loaded into your browser, the content or look doesn't change unless the page is reloaded. Dynamic HTML, or DHTML, enables more design flexibility. Web content becomes more malleable—text, images, and other objects can be hidden, revealed, and pushed around on the page, visual effects such as screen wipes, dissolves, and morphs can add colour and movement, and so on.

DHTML uses a combination of technologies, including Cascading Style Sheets (CSS), the Document Object Model (which provides scripting access to Web page elements), JavaScript, VBScript, ActiveX, and Java. Using CSS, for example, Web authors can define fonts, margins, and line spacing, as well as absolute positioning of content. A z-index even allows elements to overlap.

Unfortunately—and predictably, given the history of the Web so far—a standard for DHTML has not yet been decided on. Although both big browser makers have pledged future support for W3C standards, Netscape and Microsoft currently have different implementations of DHTML in their browsers. Netscape even made up its own tags, or "extensions"—principally the <LAYER> tag, which provides a mechanism for organizing content into layers with strict orders of precedence, transparency, and visibility. IE has its own non-W3C tags as well. Until a standard is agreed on, therefore, cross-browser compatibility will continue to be an issue and sites designed to do tricks in IE may not perform reliably when viewed in Navigator, and vice versa.

Cache Management

The cache (pronounced just like the stuff in your wallet) is a reserve area on your computer that temporarily holds data downloaded from the Net. Each page you visit is automatically stored on your hard disk. If you call up a page that you've looked at before, the browser will check to see if it's available to load from the cache, rather than fetching it from the network again—speeding up your surfing significantly.

There are actually two types of cache: memory cache and disk cache. The memory cache uses RAM (random access memory), and holds information only while your browser is running. Retrieving data from the memory cache is much faster than from the disk cache, but when you close the browser, all data in the memory cache disappears. The disk cache, on the other hand, stores information on your hard disk. It remains on disk even after you close your browser or shut off the computer, so that cached pages are still available when you reopen your browser. While the data stored in the disk cache is "persistent" (stays around for a long time), it will eventually be erased when the cache fills up and old files are removed to make way for the new.

Both Navigator and Internet Explorer let you customize your cache settings. Changing the size of your cache may improve the performance of your browser, depending on your computer and your surfing habits. Emptying the cache once in a while may also speed up overall computer performance by freeing up the hard drive, particularly if you've been online for a long time, or if you tend not to revisit the same pages very often. You can also change how often your browser compares cached pages with the online version. The Navigator controls are located under "Edit > Preferences > Cache". The IE Internet Options dialog box is located under the View menu in IE4 and the Tools menu in IE5.

A larger memory cache may make downloading from the network a bit faster. However, while Navigator lets you change the size of the memory cache (IE lets you change only the disk cache size), it doesn't always make sense to increase the RAM for the memory cache. The Navigator default setting is 1024 K on Windows. On the MacOS, memory requirements can be specified in the application's Info box (from the Finder, select the Navigator icon and choose Get Info from the Finder's File menu). But unless your computer has 32 MB of RAM or more, you probably shouldn't set it any higher. And if you tend to run other programs simultaneously, such as a word processor, you're better off keeping the memory cache low—say, 600 K—so that all programs have enough RAM to run efficiently. But if you have lots of RAM and you run only the browser, why not crank up the size of the memory cache and see if your cruising speed doesn't increase?

Both Navigator and IE let you determine how much space is devoted to the disk cache. The default size is usually between 7 MB and 10 MB. Be aware, however, that a large disk cache will likely slow the performance of your computer. Naturally. It takes more time to search the cache. If you notice your browser getting sluggish, particularly after being online for awhile, it may be time to clear your cache. The buttons for clearing both types of cache are located in the same dialog box where you set the cache sizes.

The other option you can control is how often the browser compares a document in the cache with the original document on the Web. The default setting is "Once per session," which means that the documents will be compared only one time during the period you have your browser open. This level is usually okay, unless you're checking a news site, for example, and want to retrieve a page that is constantly being updated. The other options are "Every time" and "Never." Every time checks for changes whenever you request a particular document, which means you'll always get the most current version, even though your system will slow down a bit with the extra work. But the cache size becomes less of an issue because the key information is what would be updated anyway. Choosing Never means that you'll always be given the page from your cache, if it's there, without any verification. Fast, but risky if you care about updates.

When you use the Back button or click on a History item, the browser doesn't bother to check the network for updates, since you are explicitly asking for a previously viewed page. The browser first tries to retrieve the cached copy—it returns to the network only if the cached copy has been trashed.

Whatever setting you've chosen, pressing Reload will always cause Navigator to go back to the network to look for a fresh version of the page. If the page has been updated, it will be downloaded. If the page hasn't changed, the cache version will be reloaded. This is useful if you're revisiting a site to look for new information, and you want to make sure you have the latest version of the page. If you hold down the Shift key (Option key on the Mac) while pressing Reload, Navigator retrieves a fresh version from the network regardless of whether or not the page has been updated, and the cache is ignored altogether.

Internet Explorer performs the same function when you press the Refresh button. (Just to confuse matters, Navigator also has a Refresh button, but it means something different. When you press the Refresh button, Navigator redraws the current page on your screen using the cached information. IE doesn't provide an option for simply redrawing the screen from the cache.)

If you want to go poking around in your cache, you can find it using your file manager. Netscape keeps its cache safely tucked away inside the browser directory. By default, Microsoft for PC puts the IE cache in the Windows directory, in a folder conveniently labelled Temporary Internet Files. Recent versions of IE let you look at this folder through the Internet Options box.

Various plug-in applications called cache viewers are available for working with cache files. They make it easier to organize and view cached files offline, perform full text searches, look at thumbnails of all the images, export and import files, create multiple cache folders for better management, and so on. Cache viewers are often combined with cookie managers (see the "Handling Cookies" section below). See the "Plug-Ins and Add-Ons" section for a list of Web sites where you can download cache viewers (among other things).

Plug-Ins and Add-Ons

Plug-ins and add-ons are software applications that work with your Web browser to extend its capabilities, allowing you to play movies, listen to sound files, watch animations, explore 3D worlds, participate in live conferences, listen to radio programs, and other nifty tricks. Some of the most popular applications now come bundled with your browser, so you don't need to worry about getting up to speed right away. (In addition, Internet Explorer now supports ActiveX controls, which accomplish the same thing as plug-ins in a slightly different way.) But there are hundreds more plug-ins that can be downloaded from the Web, often at little or no cost. You can pick them up as you go along, whenever you trip over a site that needs something new.

If you try to download a page that requires a plug-in, but you don't have the proper plug-in installed, you'll soon know about it. You're likely to be confronted by a little icon that looks something like a puzzle piece, followed by a dialog box that opens to tell you what's missing and to ask if you'd like to download it. Do you want the full Web experience? Just say yes.

The only restriction may be your computer platform. Many plug-ins are developed to run on a

> **NUTS & BOLTS**
>
> **Plug-ins**
>
> If you can't find the Web accessory you need, here are a few online repositories worth visiting:
>
> - Plug-In Plaza **<www.browserwatch.com/plug-in.html>**
> - Tucows **<www.tucows.com>**
> - Plugins.com **<www.plugins.com>**
> - Macdownload.com **<www.macdownload.com>**

specific platform, or may work only with the latest operating system. If you own a PC and you want to run the Talker plug-in, for example—a speech synthesis program by MVP Solutions **<www.mvpsolutions.com/PlugInSite/Talker. html>** that lets Web pages talk (and sing) to Macintosh users—tough luck.

Most plug-ins fall into a few general categories: image viewers, 3D and animation, audio, video, business applications and utilities, and presentations. More recently, with the rising popularity of online shopping, we're seeing new plug-ins to help consumers with essential tasks such as comparison shopping. Click The Button **<www.clickthebutton.com>** will appeal to book lovers, for example, as it instantly compares the price of any book offered by a list of online retailers such as Amazon.com.

Created by third-party software developers—that is, by companies other than the browser maker—each small plug-in is dedicated to performing a specific function, so you need only install the one you need. Of course, in a competitive marketplace like the Web, it's tempting for software makers to keep adding more and more features, until a plug-in that began life as a dedicated player of one file type becomes a bloated, megabyte-chewing monster that plays hundreds of file formats and wants desperately to be all things to all people. This strategy of building everything into one big plug-in relies on the theory that Web users don't want to install dozens of plug-ins when a single application will do the same work.

You may already own another piece of standalone software that will let you play the same file type as a plug-in, but the important difference with true plug-ins is that the file will play within the browser window, seamlessly integrated with the Web page you're viewing. Helper applications, like standalone software, are not integrated within the browser window, but can still be launched automatically whenever you encounter a particular file type on the Web.

Helper applications can be virtually any other piece of software installed on your system. Aside from not appearing inside your browser window, helper apps are usually installed in separate directories, whereas plug-ins are installed in a special subdirectory within the browser directory. If you want to use a standalone program in conjunction with your browser, say, GhostView for viewing PostScript files on PCs **<achille.cs.bell-labs.com/cm/ms/who/wim/ghost/index.html>**, you'll need to tell your browser where to find it. Open the helper applications dialog box, choose the file type, and show the browser where to look for the executable file (.exe) that launches the application.

If you have a choice between using a plug-in and using a standalone software program as a helper, is there any good reason to go with the standalone? Well, if you already own the standalone, why clog up your hard drive with something you don't really need—especially if the plug-in's not free? And a helper application often provides you with more features than a plug-in. For example, you can find a plug-in to display spreadsheet data in your browser, but you can accomplish a lot more if you simply open the spreadsheet in Excel.

Anyway, downloading and installing plug-ins is pretty much a no-brainer. Click on the download link and wait for the files to be deposited on your machine, run the installer or move the files to your browser's plug-ins folder, then quit and restart your browser. Take note: If you use more than one kind of browser, you have to install the plug-in separately for each browser, if the plug-in resides in a plug-in subdirectory of the browser. Add-ons such as Adobe Acrobat Reader, however, live in their own folder, and a single copy can be shared by more than one browser.

What happens when you want to update your browser after spending all that time downloading and installing plug-ins? Don't worry, you can keep the stuff you've already accumulated. Just install the new browser over the old version, instead of uninstalling the old one first. And if the new browser now incorporates what used to be a plug-in, or includes a newer incarnation, the installation program will recognize your earlier plug-in and automatically replace it.

The plug-ins too are getting a little brighter about updates. Some programs, like Shockwave, will detect whether you're up to speed with the most current version. If you're not, the newest release will be automatically downloaded and installed. Of course, other plug-in makers go too far by reminding you that you're still only using the free version and repeatedly asking whether you want to "upgrade" to the version with a pricetag. In general, however, plugging in is a pretty painless affair.

To find specific plug-ins for Netscape Navigator, visit the plug-in page on the Netscape site **<home.netscape.com/plugins/index.html>**. They currently list more than 200 available plug-ins, including a few plug-in extras—that's right, plug-ins for plug-ins.

Following is a short list of some of the most common helper applications. Installation instructions and troubleshooting tips for each plug-in are available online at the maker's Web site. If you're eager to try out your new toy, the download site will probably offer a few links to Web sites that make good use of the technology.

Adobe Acrobat Reader

www.adobe.com/prodindex/acrobat/readstep.html

Acrobat is a software program that converts DOS, Windows, Macintosh, and Unix documents into a proprietary file format, called Portable Document Format (PDF), for viewing on other machines. While Acrobat costs money, the helper program, Acrobat Reader, is free and lets you view, navigate, and print PDF documents.

A PDF file preserves the layout, colours, and fonts of the original document, so that any user, on any platform, can see it the way the designer intended. Think of it as a universal translator. It's also the ideal format for distributing electronic documents because it transcends the usual problems of electronic file-sharing. The format is widely used in the magazine industry for sharing proofs, avoiding PostScript problems with printers, and rapidly converting print-based publications for electronic distribution, with complete control over how the pages look on the Web—something you can't do with standard HTML.

And just to cover all bases, Adobe has recently developed a new version of Acrobat Reader written entirely in Java which runs on any platform

ARE WE THERE YET?

The Future Gets Fun Again

www.wired.com/wired/archive/8.01

Wired magazine's first issue of the millennium, which focused entirely on gee-whiz technological predictions for the coming decade, is now available online. As is usual for *Wired*, the content ranges from hard science to whimsy to outright garbage, often within the span of a single article. Our favourite bit is about the patent attorney who's worried that "doctors in the former Soviet Union will go ahead with a head transplant under less-than-optimal conditions, which could queer the procedure's entire future." Don't lose any sleep over this one.

that has a Java Virtual Machine (JVM) installed. You can download Acrobat Reader (and other Adobe plug-ins) from the Adobe site.

Beatnik

www.headspace.com/beatnik

The Beatnik plug-in manages the playback of Rich Music Format (RMF) and other music and sound files (such as MIDI, WAV, AIFF, and AU). Even though it is entirely software-based, Beatnik's high-fidelity sound quality is comparable to high-end soundcards. Using JavaScript functions, it can also create interactive music, allowing a Web page to play music not only when it first loads, but also on events such as a "mouseclick" or "mouseover."

Crescendo

www.liveupdate.com

The free Crescendo plug-in by LiveUpdate delivers high-quality stereo MIDI music to the Web. MIDI stands for musical instrument digital interface, and is a standard adopted by the electronic music industry for controlling devices, such as synthesizers and sound cards, that emit music. Although other plug-ins can handle MIDI files, Crescendo does it exceedingly well. Shockwave, for example, will play MIDI files in a serviceable manner, but Crescendo is less program- and memory-intensive. Enhanced versions, including Crescendo Plus and Crescendo Max, add real-time streaming, automatic upgrades, technical support, and other benefits, but you have to pay for the "plus."

Media Player

www.microsoft.com/windows/windowsmedia/download

Microsoft Windows Media Player plays most local media file types, including MIDI, MPEG, WAV, AVI, and MP3, as well as Advanced Streaming Format (ASF) content streamed with Windows Media Services, and competing formats like RealAudio (RA, RAM, etc.), Apple QuickTime (QT, MOV, etc.), and so on. That means you can listen to live news updates, watch sports replays, review music videos, or preview clips from a new movie.

Now that streaming technologies have improved, the big media companies are making more multimedia content available online. CBS, for example, is now encoding all its video in the Windows Media format. You can view a selection of recent video from CBS News by visiting **<www.cbs.com>**. This is a great improvement over the cheesy background music and sound effects that infested early Web sites and passed for "multimedia."

Media Player is available for Windows 95, Windows 98, Windows NT 4.0, and Windows 3.x, and if you use one of those platforms, you probably already have a copy, since it ships with the operating system. Mac users can download Microsoft Media Player for Macintosh, while a Unix player has been promised for the near future. Check for Media Player updates at the Microsoft site.

QuickTime

www.apple.com/quicktime/index.html

QuickTime files can be movies, sound, animation, or virtual reality environments. The format was invented by Apple Computer, so it's no surprise that every Mac comes with the QuickTimePlayer installed with its operating system. There's a player for the PC too, but it's not automatically bundled with Windows. It's free, however, and easily available for downloading at the Apple site.

QuickTime offers a reasonable alternative, or an addition, to RealPlayer, since it will handle all the popular video, music, 3D, and other formats, as well as QuickTime files. In fact, the most recent release, QuickTime 4, claims over 200 digital media capabilities, including live video and audio streaming, support for Macromedia's Flash file format, and support for MP3 audio files. Apple claims that well over half of Web sites using video use QuickTime.

When Lucasfilm released a trailer for *Star Wars: Episode I, The Phantom Menace,* they made it available online exclusively in QuickTime 4 format, impelling more than a million fans to install the new QuickTime 4 viewer. Other downloadable clips included a music video for "The Duel of the Fates" from the movie soundtrack, TV commercials, and a game preview of the *Star Wars* simulation "The Gungan Frontier." Keeping up with pop culture is one of the incentives for keeping up-to-date on plug-ins.

▶INFOHAZARDS

Webopedia

www.webopedia.com

Napster? What's Napster? For the definitions of any scary technobabble or netspeak that you encounter while online, check out Webopedia. This is a glossary that can answer pretty well any question you've got.

RealPlayer G2

www.real.com

RealNetworks has been creating online multimedia tools for years, and RealPlayer G2 is the latest version of their free plug-in player. It supports RealAudio and RealVideo, as well as most other multimedia formats. The omnipresent RealAudio is a super-compressed streaming sound format that makes it possible to listen to live concerts, press conferences, and other events on the Web. Check out the Showcase page for current offerings from all corners of the Web, including online zines, music videos, animations, and film previews. Don't forget to investigate the latest creations from animation companies like Camp Chaos **<www.campchaos.com>**, the twisted minds behind The Telefuglies (a weird blend of Star Wars and Teletubbies).

▶NUTS & BOLTS

Shockrave

www.shockrave.com

The Shockwave phenomenon is so successful, Macromedia devotes a full site, called Shockrave, to showcasing the latest and greatest games, cartoons (from *Peanuts* to *South Park*), music, and animated postcards. If you spent your youth, and your allowance, playing coin-operated video games at the local arcade, don't miss the Arcade section at Shockrave, where you'll find scaled-down versions of old-time favourites like Galactic Marauders.

Shockwave

www.macromedia.com/shockwave

Macromedia, makers of Director and other top-rated authoring software, rule the Web with their free

Streaming video footage of Mount Usu erupting in March 2000 on the Japanese island of Hokkaido, from Fuji TV <**www.fnn-news.com**> via RealPlayer G2

plug-in players Shockwave and Flash (see below). Shockwave Player lets you view interactive Web content such as games, business presentations, entertainment, and advertisements. It quickly became a hot technology among Web developers, adopted by everyone from Disney to IBM. Shockwave Player ships with Windows 95, 98, MacOS, Internet Explorer CD, America Online, and Netscape Navigator. If you somehow missed it, you can download a free copy at the Macromedia site.

Flash Player

www.macromedia.com/flash

Known as FutureSplash until 1997, when Macromedia bought the company that created it, Flash is a vector-graphic animation technology—that is, images are represented by geometrical formulas, rather than a pattern of dots (bitmaps). Bandwidth friendly and browser independent, vector-oriented images outperform bitmapped images in several ways: they can be resized and stretched, they look better on high-res monitors, and they require less memory. These advantages contributed to the rapid rise of Flash,

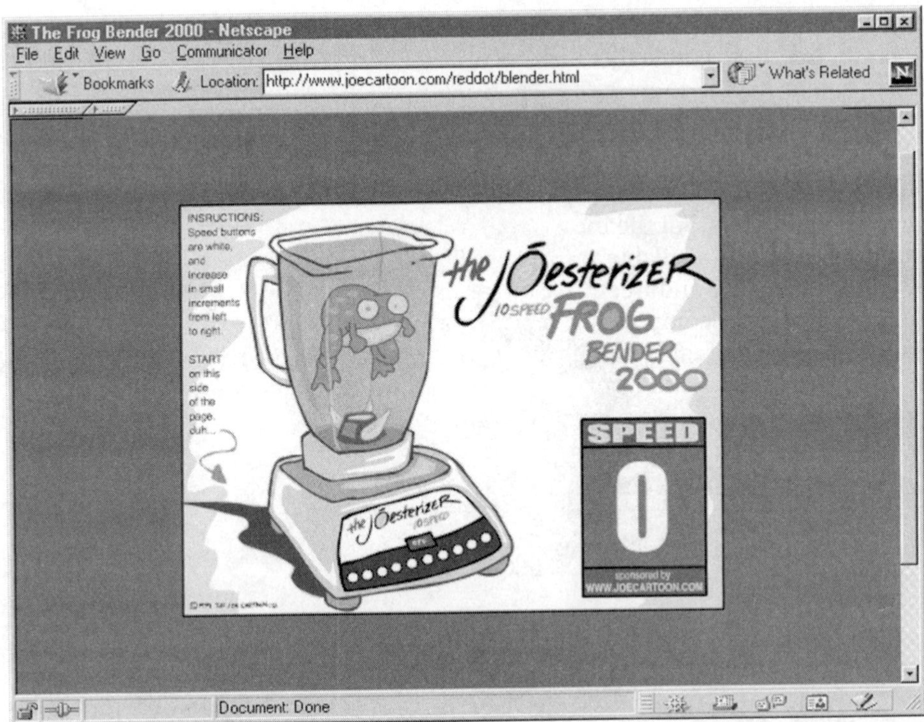

A popular Shockwave animation from Joe Cartoon

to its current status as de facto leader in Web animation. A study conducted in March 2000 by MediaMetrix parent NPD Research determined that for 89.9% of Web users, Flash Player (the required plug-in) came pre-installed with their browser.

File Compression and Decompression

Almost any file you download from the Internet, whether it's software, documents, or pictures, will be compressed or archived. For our purposes, these terms are synonymous—both refer to files that have been encoded in such a way that they occupy the absolute minimum amount of disk space.

File compression is a vital part of the information storage and retrieval process. Think about it: if a software vendor can, without much trouble, create a compressed version of a file that occupies 50% to 90% of the disk space required to store the uncompressed version of the same file, it can cram up to twice as many digital products into the same space. And compressed files provide a convenient method of gathering many associated bits of information, such as Help files and plug-ins for a software program, or all the versions of a single typeface in a font family.

Compression techniques are also useful for individual users: they're great for keeping your fonts, smaller pieces of software, and old documents organized, as well as for creating small, efficient files to e-mail to friends and associates. This latter use is quite important, because even if you can manage to successfully send an e-mail with an attachment over 1 MB in size there's no guarantee that the person on the receiving end will be able to download it successfully. Large attachments can cause mail servers to crash, freeze, or garble the message, resulting in either the system administrator or the recipient having to purge the document and attachment through the Unix shell (that's not as bad as it sounds, but it is annoying). As an act of courtesy, then, you should compress any file(s) over 500 K that you plan to attach to an e-mail.

The upshot of all this is that you'll need some software to do your compressing and decompressing. All the most popular compression software is either freeware or shareware, and is available on major shareware sites. You can find a list of over 300,000 shareware and freeware programs at the Jumbo site **<www.jumbo.com>**. Some examples of compression shareware are WinZip, DropStuff for Windows, and PKZip. (Note: The registration price for compression software is always very reasonable, so there's no reason not to shell out a few bucks for the people who've made the lives of computer users everywhere more tolerable.)

Common Compression Formats

Though there is a bewildering variety of file compression formats, most of the archived files that you encounter will be one of the following types:

.exe

For PC users only. Although .exe is technically not a compression format (it simply denotes an executable program), many of the compressed files you download will be self-extracting and tagged with the .exe extension. You don't need any decompression software to open them. All you have to do is click on them and they'll automatically extract themselves and begin their installation routine. No muss, no fuss.

.zip

The .zip compression format, not to be confused with the Iomega Zip disk, was created in 1989 by PKWare (see below). There are probably more .zip files on the Internet than any other type of compressed file. You can use PKZip, Winzip, or pretty much any of the competing compression utilities on the market to open these files.

.sit and .sea

These file formats are produced by Aladdin's Stuffit software (see below). The .sea file (self-extracting archive) is the Mac user's equivalent of the .exe file: just click on it and let it do its thing. The .sit file is the compression standard for Mac files on the Internet. PC users who share files with Mac users should be prepared to deal with these file types. Stuffit Expander will open .sit files for you, and DropStuff for Windows will let you make both .zip files and .sit files.

.hqx

Another common Mac compression format. Macs have a two-fork file system: .hqx combines the two forks into a single data file for storage on other system types. Winzip and Stuffit Expander can both handle .hqx files.

E-mail Encoding Formats: UUencoding, XXencoding, BinHex, and MIME

Believe it or not, the Internet wasn't designed to carry anything other than text files (i.e. files made up of printable ASCII characters). A number of formats were created in order to bypass these limitations, allowing people to e-mail programs and other binary file types to each other (the specific encoding format was determined by the particular e-mail provider; for example, documents sent through CompuServe would be UUencoded).

These formats all do the same job: they encode the non-binary files into ASCII characters that can then be e-mailed and decoded on the receiving end to recreate the original file (they're not compression formats either; in fact, sometimes files encoded for e-mailing get larger).

These days, because most of the encoding and decoding in these formats is handled by your e-mail software or browser, the process is completely transparent. If you somehow end up with one of these file types in your download directory, though, Stuffit Expander, Winzip and other decompression programs can open them for you.

ARE WE THERE YET?

Retrofuture

retrofuture.web.aol.com

The future isn't what it used to be. I mean, where's all the great stuff that we were promised over the last hundred years, like the personal flying belts and transporters and phasers and tall, beautiful people in diaphanous silver togas? Answer: they're on Retrofuture. This hilarious site covers every misguided piece of past futurology from flying cars and Star Trek uniforms to the meal-in-a-pill (As the late Phil Hartman said, "Soylent Green is people! It's made out of PEEEEEPULLLLL!").

Unix Compression Formats

In days of yore, when the Internet was a text-based environment and accessing it required at least a smattering of Unix, these file formats were part of everyday Netlife. You may encounter one of these file types from time to time on a university or other Unix-based site, but Winzip and StuffIt Deluxe will open all of them with ease (though they won't create them). Of course, these files can all also be opened by the appropriate Unix utilities, but why would you bother? (Unless, of course, you're running Linux, and if that's the case, you're too smart to need our help.)

.z and .gz

.z is a Unix compression format created with either the compress or the gzip utility. Another common compression format, .gz, is a distant cousin of the PC .zip file. Neither .z nor .gz compressed files can contain multiple files, though they can contain a .tar file (see below).

.tar, .taz, .tgz

The .tar file format's name is an acronym for "Tape Archive." A .tar file doesn't actually do any compressing; instead, it gathers multiple files together into one group. A .tar file will sometimes also have a .z extension following it, indicating that the .tar file has to be uncompressed before its contents can be de-archived. Files with either the .taz or the .tgz extension are .tar files that have been compressed using .z or .gz.

Other File Compression Formats

Unless you're poking around some of the more obscure corners of the Internet, such as FTP sites that have fallen into disuse, you probably won't encounter too many of these files. Though they were created by programs that have more or less fallen out of favour, the common decompression packages will usually support them through the use of external applications.

.arc, .arj, .lzh and .zoo

DOS formats .arc and .arj are created by programs called (surprise) ARC and ARJ. Another DOS compression format, .lzh, was created by the LHA program. In 1991, LHA was pretty hot stuff, so you may still stumble across the odd .lzh file on an old floppy disk every now and then. Created by a program of the same name, .zoo files were once common in DOS, Unix and Vax environments.

> **INFOHAZARD**
>
> **Toss Your Cookies**
>
> **www.peacefire.org/security/iecookies**
>
> After the "I Love You" virus, which only affected users of MS Outlook, many people are starting to wake up to the unpleasant fact that there are massive security holes in many Microsoft products. This site demonstrates that any Web site that uses cookies to authenticate users could have its cookies exposed and intercepted by a third-party Web site because of flaws in Internet Explorer. This means, among other things, that your name, address, postal code, Webmail accounts, and other information commonly stored in cookies are up for grabs. The solution? Well, you can continue to use Explorer and disable JavaScript (which will prevent you from using many features on the majority of Web sites), you can change browsers, or you can wait for Microsoft to release a patch for the hole. You're all adults; we're sure you'll do the right thing.

.lha

Remember the Commodore Amiga? The .lha file was the dominant Amiga archiving method, created by either the lha or the lz program.

(De)Compression Software

Though there are many file compression formats, and almost as many software packages that will deal with most of them, the following programs will deal with almost anything you come across on the Internet.

Winzip

www.winzip.com/tucows

Winzip is the most popular compression utility for Windows, and has won a haystack of awards that testify to its excellence. The program features support for compression formats including Microsoft's cab files; and Internet file formats such as .tar, .gzip, Unix compress, UUencode, XXencode, BinHex, and MIME. External programs support .arj, .lzh, and .arc files. In addition, Winzip will interface with most virus scanners so that you can scan your files before you open them, and with your browser, so that you can download and decompress with one click.

StuffIt

www.aladdinsys.com

Aladdin Systems is the maker of StuffIt Deluxe, the de facto Internet compression standard for Mac users. Other than StuffIt Deluxe, which is currently available for Mac only, Aladdin makes DropStuff (a compression utility) and Expander (a decompression utility) for both Windows and the MacOS. Expander, which is freeware, allows users to decompress, decode, convert and access file formats including .sit, .zip, UUencoding, MacBinary, and BinHex. Aladdin Expander for Windows also supports Mime/Base64, .arc, .arj, and .gzip. With the addition of the StuffIt Engine (included with DropStuff and StuffIt Deluxe), StuffIt Expander for Mac supports MIME/Base64, .arc, .arj, .gzip, .lha, .tar, CompactPro, AppleLink, and more. Aladdin products are particularly easy to use because of their drag-and-drop interface; on a Mac with StuffIt Deluxe, decompression after Internet downloading is totally effortless.

IMPORTANT NOTE: As if sorting out compression standards wasn't complicated enough, the later versions of StuffIt (release 5 and higher) are a proprietary format that is not fully compatible with earlier versions of the program. This means that you can use Stuffit 5 to open older .sit files, but the ones that you produce with it cannot be opened by earlier versions of the program.

ZipMagic

www.ontrack.com/ZipMagic

This amazing little program makes compressed zip files act like folders. In other words, because ZipMagic works transparently, at the OS level, you can open a zip file like any Windows folder, modify and save documents within zip files, and even run many programs from inside a zip file. $39.95 U.S. and worth every penny.

PKZip

www.pkware.com

PKWare, the company that actually invented the .zip file format in 1989, has been around since 1986. Its archiving utility, PKZip, is still very popular among Windows users, and will open many file compression formats as well as create .zip files. The latest version of PKZip (2.70), which boasts a sophisticated set of abilities, is available for download as shareware, or you can get the registered version for $39 U.S. ($29 if you download it). On a morbid note, Phillip W. Katz, the creator of the .zip protocol was just found dead in a filthy hotel room with a bottle of creme de menthe and a suitcase full of sex toys; evidently, he was a chronic alcoholic. A sad ending for a brilliant young mind.

Testing Your Browser

Now that you've tinkered with your browser settings, it's time to go for a test drive. If you just want to try out a new plug-in, the company's home page will typically offer links to other sites that use the technology. It may also provide its own showcase, and some will even offer a test page to give you direct feedback. Shockwave and QuickTime are examples.

But what if you want to know whether everything else is working as it should? *Windows Magazine* provides browser test and tune-up pages at BrowserTune 2000 **<www.browsertune.com/bt2kfast>.** BrowserTune will test your browser's ability to handle a wide range of standard, "legal" HTML functions and features, from fonts and colours, through tables, forms, and various other layout attributes, to multimedia applications, scripting languages, style sheets, and more. You can work your way through the three progressively more detailed test levels, stopping at any point. The whole process can take anywhere from 15 to 40 minutes, depending on your connection speed and your familiarity with the tests. And it's free. Although the tests are browser independent—that is, they're not designed specifically for one type of browser or another—they do begin with one underlying assumption: that your operating system is Windows. That doesn't mean you can't try it out if you're using a Mac, although some tests are specifically designed to check the browser's compatibility with Windows standards.

If you simply want to know at a glance whether your particular type of browser does what a good browser should—in theory, at least—check out the Webmonkey Browser Chart **<www.hotwired.com/webmonkey/browserkit>** from Hotwired, a handy page that keeps track of which browsers support what features. So, if you're cruising with CyberDog 2.0 on a Mac, for example, you'll see that frames and tables are within your grasp, but Java, dynamic HTML, stylesheets, and (gasp) plug-ins are a no-go.

> **NETHEADS**
>
> **Fred McLain's Internet Exploder**
>
> **www.halcyon.com/mclain/ActiveX/Exploder/FAQ.htm**
>
> In 1997, in response to the release of Microsoft's Internet Explorer, programmer Fred McLain put up a Web page that has become known in the annals of Net folklore as the Internet Exploder page. Exploder is an ActiveX control that demonstrated security problems with Microsoft's initial release of Internet Explorer. What the Exploder does is simple: it downloads a control onto your machine that uses ActiveX to shut down Windows 95, and turns off the power on machines that have a power conservation BIOS (basic input output system).
>
> Fred's FAQ explains that Exploder is not dangerous in itself, but demonstrates that ActiveX could be dangerous if a misguided person misused ActiveX in some way that the developers of the software didn't foresee.
>
> In Fred's opinion, an "ActiveX control is essentially a Windows program that can be distributed from a Web page. These controls can do literally anything a Windows program can do. That means you could write an ActiveX control to erase a hard drive. A control containing a virus or trojan can be written, distributed, and activated from a Web page, and the viewer of the control might never know. A control could even scan your drive for tax records or documents the control's author was interested in, and e-mail them off to some other person. All this can be done in a control that pretends to be something interesting, like a video game."
>
> After a phone call from VeriSign, the company that holds the code-signing certificates for controls developed with Microsoft's ActiveX technology, and a discussion with his lawyers, Fred removed the Exploder from his Web page in order to avoid possible litigation. The demonstration did its job, though, alerting both consumers and Microsoft to potential difficulties with the ActiveX software.

Privacy and Security

How dangerous is the Web?

Short answer: Not very.

Long answer: In general, the possibility of a Web page causing you to experience anything worse than boredom or moral indignation is extremely low. This is because, most of the time, surfing the Web is a lot like watching television: you view a page until you lose interest in it, then move on with a click of your mouse. The older the Web page you're viewing, the more passive the experience will be; smooth vector-based animation, sound, and streaming video are all fairly recent additions to Web functionality.

The more sophisticated Web pages designed during the last few years are another matter: many of them can be downright pushy in their insistence that you modify your hardware or software before viewing them. Web designers have learned how to write scripts that can determine what kind of hardware and software you're using as soon as you access their site. If your equipment is dated, or made by a competing manufacturer, the page may respond in a number of ways: it might refuse to give you access to the site altogether, it might shunt you to a simpler version of the site, or it might provide you with instructions about how to upgrade your current equipment.

In the first two cases, you don't have a lot of choice in the matter, but no harm has been done. The third case isn't necessarily a bad thing, but it can be a little intimidating for neophytes. If you're the kind of person who obsessively updates your software and hardware, you probably won't run into this problem very often, because the latest versions of Navigator and Explorer are usually bundled with all major plug-ins, which install along with the program itself. Problems can and do arise with the installation of any new software, though, so it's worth your while to take a few precautions.

The key rule to remember when dealing with the "dangers" of online culture is that nothing can physically harm your hardware or your software as long as you're paying attention to what the site in question is trying to send to you. You can set your browser to query you before it accepts downloads of any sort; while this may slow down your surfing in the short term, it will prevent real frustration and possible financial loss in the long run.

Familiarize yourself with the major browser plug-ins (Shockwave, Flash, RealPlayer, QuickTime, etc.) and ensure that you have the latest versions installed. If a site offers to install something on your machine that you've never heard of, click on the "No" option, do a little research, and, if the product looks legitimate, download it from the manufacturer's site, or a major shareware site such as Tucows, and install it yourself while you're offline.

▶INFOHAZARD

Um... Your port is open

grc.com

www.zonelabs.com

Got a DSL line or a cable modem? Lucky you. If you want to stay lucky, you need a firewall to render your computer invisible to hackers and data thieves. Not worried? Visit the Gibson Research Corporation's site **<grc.com>** and run Shields Up!, a series of diagnostics that will tell you exactly how vulnerable your computer is to outside attacks. Once you've got the results of the test, take a moment to calm down, then head over to ZoneLabs **<ww.zonelabs.com>**. Zone makes a nifty shareware firewall that installs in seconds, and will have you feeling all cozy and smug again in no time flat (Attention Quake players: no, it doesn't mess up your ping, either).

Using this strategy will help you to avoid two potential problems. The first is virus infection. The closer the supplier of a program is to its origin, the less likely it is that the copy you download will be infected. Before you install any new software obtained online, scan the file with your virus detector, then proceed to install it, cautiously. (See below for the scoop on antivirus programs.)

The second, and sadly far more likely scenario, is that new software may conflict with the software that's already on your machine. Your computer is like a terrarium. It contains a very delicate little ecosystem, and every time you introduce a new critter into it, all hell can break loose . . . especially if the critter in question is the product of a company that competes for the same market with some of the software already on your system. Far be it from us to suggest that such conflicts are deliberate, but one does begin to wonder when any browsers or plug-ins other than those coded or authorized by A Certain Software Giant That Supplies Your Operating System regularly cause entire systems to crash without even the flicker of a bluescreen error.

File conflicts can cause anything from the simple failure to receive a file to a total system crash. Usually these conflicts are caused by different versions of shared files, such as .dlls, overwriting each other—two programs may require different versions of the same file. Tracking down such conflicts is tedious and difficult work, and may require you to uninstall the software you've just installed and begin again (which can cause even more difficulties, because sometimes uninstalling a piece of software may remove shared files from your system that other programs require in order to operate . . .). It's all enough to make you long for the days when the most sophisticated writing technology available was wet clay tablets and pointed sticks.

Problems with software conflicts aren't going to go away as long as software manufacturers remain contemptuous of the consumers that they've cornered with their various monopolies—if there's no alternative to poorly coded software, you can complain until you're blue in the face and it won't do you any good. However, you can minimize the occurrence of possible conflicts by doing the following:

- Back up your system while it still works, and, if disaster strikes, you can always revert to the previous system. Programs like Norton Utilities can be extremely helpful in this regard.
- Before you install anything new, turn off all the software that you may have running in the background, such as antivirus checkers, system monitors, toolbars, and programs associated with peripherals like scanners. With luck, you'll at least make it to the end of the installation process that way.
- After installation, read the Readme and Help files for your program before running it, and check to see if you can avoid any of the last-minute bugs that the software manufacturer has discovered (there are always some) by ensuring that you have the proper .dlls, all files are in their proper directories, and so on.
- If the software manufacturer provides free support, whether by telephone or e-mail, don't be afraid to use it. You may solve your problem, and, by alerting the manufacturer to existing difficulties, you may help to eliminate the problem for future users.

Fear of the Unknown

Surveys show that privacy and security are the most worrisome issues for Internet users. Indeed, about 40 percent of people who don't use the Internet say these issues are their primary reason for staying offline.

The biggest concern seems to be the vulnerability of transmitted data—credit card numbers or personal e-mail, for example. And those concerns are not entirely unjustified: eavesdropping is possible on the Internet. After all, it's a public communications network, where information is shared between millions of computers, travelling over a mixture of public and private lines and across countless connections. Someone could intercept and view that data along the way. It's hard to say how likely that is, but the possibility exists. In reality, however, most cases of Internet theft don't happen during transmission. Rather, the information is stolen sometime afterwards from a company computer where it is stored without adequate protection. The thief is likely to be either someone on the inside—a disgruntled employee, for example—or a hacker who tunnels under the company's firewall.

Computer viruses, Internet fraud, personal privacy, protecting children: there will always be an element of risk when using the Internet. For new users, fear of the Internet is a little like the fear of getting mugged on your first visit to New York City. However, you can significantly reduce the risks through a combination of built-in security measures and safe surfing practices.

Security Standards

The simplest way to keep private information private, of course, is not to send sensitive data over the Internet. But if you do, you can use your browser and Internet data-security features to thwart prying eyes. Security standards have been established for encrypting data and keeping it secure during transmission. Both major browsers support Secure Sockets Layer (SSL), a protocol that was originally developed by Netscape. SSL is a set of rules that govern the conversation between your computer and other computers connected to the Internet. It uses public key encryption to prevent eavesdropping, data integrity rules to make sure your messages aren't tampered with during transmission, and authentication procedures to verify that the computer receiving your data is who it claims to be.

Most Web browsing doesn't require the use of SSL, since the vast majority of Web pages are "insecure" and the only "information" you send out is your request for Web pages, when you type in a URL or click on a hyperlink. If you try to send any other type of unencrypted information—when you fill out an online form with your name and e-mail address, for example, on a Web site that's not using SSL—your browser pipes up with a warning before it sends. The warning doesn't mean the site is not legitimate, it's only a reminder to think twice, because your data will be unprotected as it travels from here to there. You can turn the option off so that the warning never shows again (there's a checkbox on the warning screen), but leaving it on is a useful precaution.

You should only transmit truly sensitive information, such as your credit card number, when connected to a secure site. How do you know it's secure? Both Navigator and Internet Explorer display an icon, a small image of a closed lock, to indicate that you are connected to a secure server. (In Navigator 3.0 and earlier, the icon was a solid key symbol in the lower-left corner of the browser window, which showed as a broken key when you connected to an insecure site.) Check the site's URL in your browser location window for additional evidence: if the first part of the address includes an extra "s" (https) instead of the usual "http," then SSL is in effect.

Along with encryption, SSL offers something called site certification. Anyone who sets up a secure server must also be issued a special digital certificate

▶INFOHAZARD

Geek Culture

www.geekculture.com

Guess what? Being shunned is now a marketable commodity. The Geek Culture site ensures that even "normal" people can feel like part of the information revolution by accessorizing their life with the trappings of geekdom (download the screensaver! Buy the shirt!). Strangely, there's no mention of the downside of geek life here.... For that *real* geek feeling, maybe the site owners should offer to call you names, refuse to dance to "Stairway to Heaven" with you or give you wedgies in the locker room.

by the appropriate certifying authority. When you enter a secure site, you can check the certificate using your browser's security features. In recent versions of Netscape Navigator, the View Certificate button is located under Encryption in the Security Info window. If there is no View Certificate button, the site does not have a certificate. In Internet Explorer, open the File menu and click Properties, then click Certificates. Checking for this digital stamp of approval is like looking on the wall at your doctor's office for graduation diplomas and licences to practice. Personal certificates work the same way, to verify your identity when you're dealing with a secure Web site. Of course, they cost money.

Security technology continues to improve, but like the proverbial chain, it's only as strong as its weakest link. To make sure you have access to the most up-to-date security technology, always use the latest version of your browser. Don't let your browser be the weak link.

The U.S. government has set export restrictions on encryption technology, meaning that browsers exported from the U.S. must use a weaker level of encryption than the U.S.-only version. Fortunately, Canada falls under the "U.S.-only" definition, so Canadians can download Web browsers that use 128-bit encryption, rather than the standard 40-bit or 56-bit encryption. In fact, you will be required to use the 128-bit version if you plan to conduct certain kinds of financial business online, such as Web banking or stock trading.

Security Patches

Whenever new software is released, sooner or later someone finds a hole in it, either a glitch that prevents it from working as promised, or a security problem that opens the back door for malicious intruders. It may be a problem with the browser itself, or a bug in the underlying operating sytem. Software makers frequently issue security patches and service upgrades, so it pays to stay in tune with recent releases.

If you provide an e-mail address when you register your software, you may be sent e-mail alerts whenever a new bug is found or a new patch is released. Similarly, if you subscribe to free e-mail news services that cover Internet stories, such as CNET News Dispatcher (sign up at **<www.news.com>**), you'll hear about security issues as they arise. Otherwise, you should periodically check the company's Web site for announcements about upgrades and patches.

Privacy

If you're concerned about privacy, you should be cautious about what personal information you divulge. If a site asks you for information, typically by filling out a site registration form, entering a contest, or subscribing to a free e-mail newsletter, be sure to check the site's privacy policy first. Find out what the site plans to do with your good name and whether they're likely to share it with others. Reputable sites will have an easy-to-find policy that clearly states how your information will be used, and includes a guarantee that the details you provide won't be used for other purposes. Watch for a contact phone number or e-mail address in case you have questions about security.

A small group of privacy advocates, prompted by the knowledge that many users don't trust the Web, in conjunction with the CommerceNet Consortium (whose mission is to accelerate electronic commerce), launched an independent, nonprofit organization called TRUSTe **<www.truste.org>**. The TRUSTe mission is "to build users' trust and confidence in the Internet by promoting the principles of disclosure and informed consent." Watch for the TRUSTe icon. It's displayed on any Web site that buys into the program by following established privacy principles and allowing TRUSTe to review its privacy practices and audit them for compliance. Called a "trustmark," the icon functions like the Good Housekeeping seal of approval.

Anonymous Surfing

Can Web sites gather information about you without your knowledge? When you click on a link or type in a URL for a Web page, you send a request to the Web server that hosts the page you're looking for. That request contains information about you, including your IP address—that is, the network address of your computer, or at least the address of your Internet service provider. After all, the Web server needs to know where to send the page you asked for. Other information that may be gathered by the Web site includes the type of browser and operating system you're using, what pages you look at during your visit, and what links you click on. However, the site has no way of finding out your name, e-mail address, where you live, or anything else about you—unless you willingly provide that information.

You can reduce the amount of tracking and information gathered by telling your browser not to accept cookies (see "Handling Cookies" below). You can prevent intrusion by malicious code (Java, JavaScript, or ActiveX programs designed to exploit security holes in your software and gather information or inflict pain and misery by deleting files) by telling your browser not to run those applications. At the very least, if you don't want to turn them off, you should use the most recent version of your browser (that is, the most recent final release, not the most recent beta) and make certain you have all security patches installed.

New search utilities, such as the What's Related button on recent versions of Netscape Navigator and the Alexa plug-in, use tracking technology to suggest Web pages similar or related to the one you're viewing. Despite reassurances to the contrary, these devices could be used to create user profiles. You can choose to disable them or turn them off.

If you want to go one step further and surf anonymously, you can use a service such as the Anonymizer **<www.anonymizer.com>**, which hides your identity completely by passing all your URL requests through its own server first and scrubbing away details like your IP address and browser type. A similar service called ProxyMate **<www.proxymate.com>** lets you browse anonymously, set up anonymous personalized accounts at Web sites, and combat junk mail.

Handling Cookies

Cookies are small, unobtrusive text files that some Web servers deposit on your hard drive to track your activity on their Web site. They get on your hard drive by being transmitted through an HTTP header (HTTP [HyperText Transfer Protocol] is the communications protocol between Web servers and browsers). Cookies are generally benign and can even be helpful in some cases. For sites that require registration, for example, the cookie stores information so you don't have to re-register or remember a password every time you visit. With sites that allow you to "personalize" the page, the cookie keeps track of your interests so the site can give you what you asked for—or the ads it thinks you ought to see.

▶NUTS & BOLTS

Disabling Cookies

www.junkbusters.com/ht/en/cookies.html#disable

Instructions for turning off cookies can be found at the Junkbusters Web site.

There are several common uses for cookies. E-commerce sites are fond of using cookies so they can note what books, CDs, or other hot merchandise you put into your virtual shopping basket. My Yahoo! **<my.yahoo.com>** and other sites that offer personalization options—such as picking the news headlines you want to see, tracking investments, or arranging the page layout the way you like it—use cookies to remember your content and design choices. Web-site tracking enables Webmasters to more accurately count the number of unique visitors and know what paths people follow as they navigate the site—all in the interest of better site design, of course. And ad companies such as DoubleClick **<www.doubleclick.com>** use cookies for targeted marketing to build up a profile of what pages you look at and what ads you click on so they can guess what your interests are and show you more relevant ads.

While cookies make the experience of browsing the Web a little more interactive, you might not be thrilled about the idea of a remote computer putting stuff on your hard drive without your knowledge, and knowing things about you and your surfing habits. But only information you choose to provide, or the choices you make while visiting a Web site, can be stored in a cookie. For example, your e-mail address can't be captured in a cookie, unless you type it in at the Web site. Permitting a Web site to put a cookie on your computer does not give that site, or any other site, access to the rest of your computer—that is, it can't read data off your hard disk. How do you know a cookie is even there? If you see a welcome page with your name on it instead of a generic welcome page, that's a pretty good clue. But you can delete cookies at any time—just remember to turn off your browser first. One good thing: at least cookies don't carry viruses.

Nonetheless, concerns about personal privacy online prompted a number of software developers to create applications specifically for identifying and keeping track of the cookies on your computer, easily deleting them, or blocking them altogether. Inevitably they have cute names, such as Cookie Cutter, Cookie Crusher, and Cookie Pal, but if you're worried about your privacy or you simply object on principle, they offer an easy and inexpensive way to keep your eye on the cookie jar.

If you don't want to invest time in yet another piece of software, both Navigator and Internet Explorer now provide you with a few basic options, built right into the browser, for monitoring the cookie trade. It's easy to set up your browser to not accept cookies, or you can simply sweep them away by deleting the cookies.txt file (or magiccookie on the Mac) in your browser subdirectory each time you log off. (Recent versions of

▶INFOHAZARD

Cookie Central

www.cookiecentral.com

For more information about cookies, check out Cookie Central, home of the Unofficial Cookie FAQ.

> **INFOHAZARDS**
>
> **PGP International**
>
> **www.pgpi.com**
>
> Worried about your privacy? Visit the International PGP home page and fret no more. PGP (Pretty Good Privacy) is nearly unbreakable public domain encryption software for your e-mail. Version 6.5.3 is now available for Windows, Macintosh, and Linux. The PGP download wizard helps you access the latest freeware PGP version.

Internet Explorer put cookies in separate files in the Windows/Cookies folder.) Keep in mind, however, that blocking or restricting the use of cookies will limit the way many sites work, and may slow you down.

Navigator users will find the cookie controls in the Preferences dialog box, under the Advanced category. The choices are to accept all cookies, to accept only cookies that get sent back to the originating server, or to disable cookies. Option number two may be the best compromise: it allows a certain level of functionality but sets security restrictions. A checkbox in Preferences also lets you decide whether you want to be warned every time a server tries to set a cookie—but you may find this option more annoying than helpful, as warnings constantly pop up and require your approval. It's educational for a while to see just how many sites try to send cookies, but eventually you'll prefer to make a blanket decision and let the browser handle the cookie business in the background.

IE5 puts the cookie controls under the Security tab in Internet Options. Click on Custom Level to open the Security Settings dialog box, where you can set preferences for cookies as well as other things, such as Java and ActiveX controls. To see what kinds of cookies are already in your jar, choose the General tab in Internet Options, click on Settings under Temporary Internet Files, then click on View Files. From here, you can read source and date information about cookies—and you can manually delete them.

One final note. Even after you've changed the cookie settings in Navigator and Internet Explorer to prevent new cookies from being accepted, the browser will still send out existing cookies. You must manually delete any cookie crumbs cluttering up your hard drive.

Sunscreen and Mosquito Repellent: Utilities and Antivirus Software

Virus Updates and Internet Hoaxes

The Trojan horse e-mail message is, of course, a joke, but it does point to several real, and quite important bits of information about both the handling of e-mail attachments, and the handling of hoaxes and "urban legends" associated with e-mail attachments.

By now, most Internet users have either sent or received a document attached to an e-mail message. Most users have also learned that it is possible to write a virus using the macro language native to Microsoft Word and other word processors, and that when an infected document (whether received over the Internet or through other means, such as on disk) is opened, the virus will rewrite the normal.dot file associated with all blank word processing documents to redistribute itself and hamper the functioning of the word processing software itself.

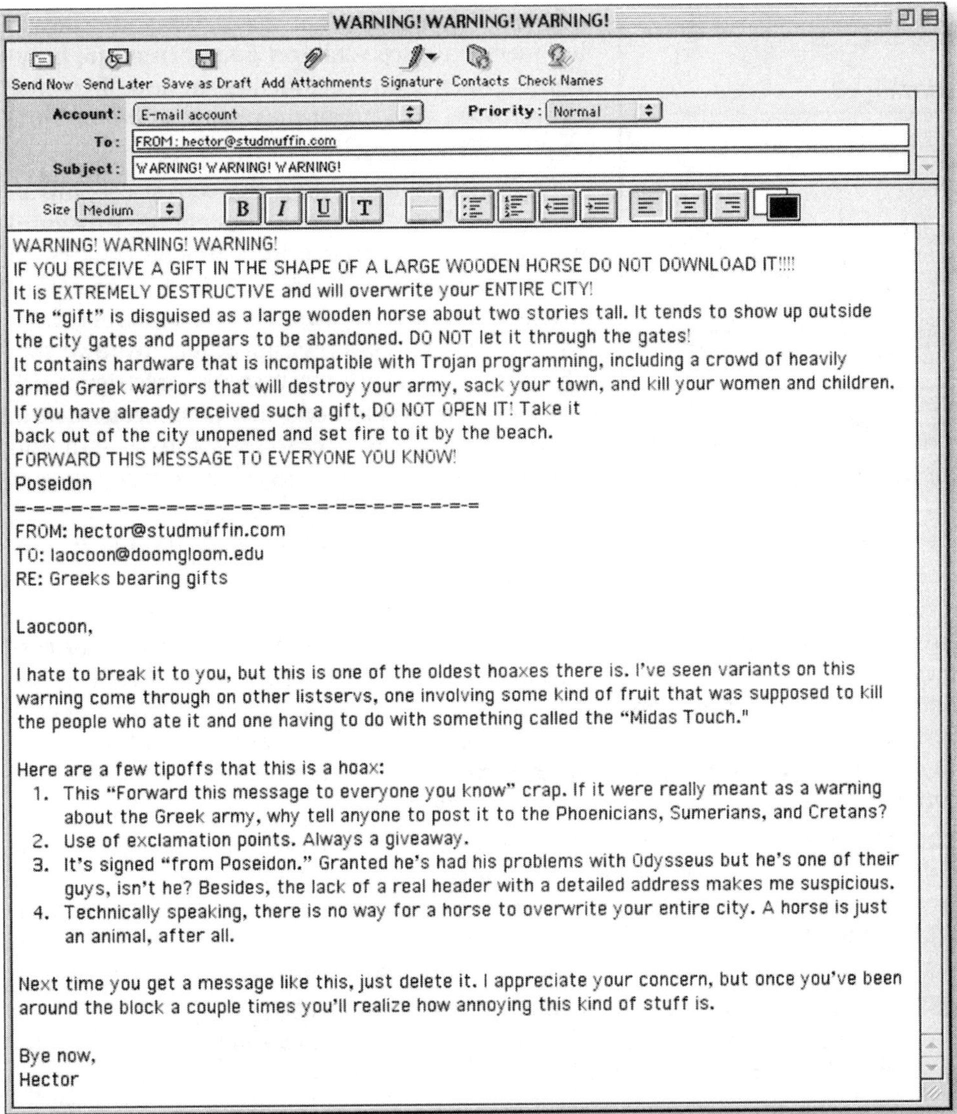
WARNING! WARNING! WARNING!

Send Now Send Later Save as Draft Add Attachments Signature Contacts Check Names

Account: E-mail account
Priority: Normal
To: FROM: hector@studmuffin.com
Subject: WARNING! WARNING! WARNING!

Size Medium

WARNING! WARNING! WARNING!
IF YOU RECEIVE A GIFT IN THE SHAPE OF A LARGE WOODEN HORSE DO NOT DOWNLOAD IT!!!!
It is EXTREMELY DESTRUCTIVE and will overwrite your ENTIRE CITY!
The "gift" is disguised as a large wooden horse about two stories tall. It tends to show up outside the city gates and appears to be abandoned. DO NOT let it through the gates!
It contains hardware that is incompatible with Trojan programming, including a crowd of heavily armed Greek warriors that will destroy your army, sack your town, and kill your women and children.
If you have already received such a gift, DO NOT OPEN IT! Take it back out of the city unopened and set fire to it by the beach.
FORWARD THIS MESSAGE TO EVERYONE YOU KNOW!
Poseidon
=-=
FROM: hector@studmuffin.com
TO: laocoon@doomgloom.edu
RE: Greeks bearing gifts

Laocoon,

I hate to break it to you, but this is one of the oldest hoaxes there is. I've seen variants on this warning come through on other listservs, one involving some kind of fruit that was supposed to kill the people who ate it and one having to do with something called the "Midas Touch."

Here are a few tipoffs that this is a hoax:
1. This "Forward this message to everyone you know" crap. If it were really meant as a warning about the Greek army, why tell anyone to post it to the Phoenicians, Sumerians, and Cretans?
2. Use of exclamation points. Always a giveaway.
3. It's signed "from Poseidon." Granted he's had his problems with Odysseus but he's one of their guys, isn't he? Besides, the lack of a real header with a detailed address makes me suspicious.
4. Technically speaking, there is no way for a horse to overwrite your entire city. A horse is just an animal, after all.

Next time you get a message like this, just delete it. I appreciate your concern, but once you've been around the block a couple times you'll realize how annoying this kind of stuff is.

Bye now,
Hector

Until the advent of word processor viruses, only software packages obtained under questionable circumstances, or unprotected disks used on more than one computer, were potential sources of contamination. Word processor viruses forever blurred the distinction between documents and programs as the lowly document became more complex. So far, no one has figured out how to infect an e-mail message itself with a virus, so the mere act of reading your e-mail can't harm your computer in any way, even if that e-mail contains an attachment, as long as you don't open the attachment. If you receive an e-mail with an attachment that you find suspect (for example, one that arrives as part of a mass mailing, in an anonymous e-mail, or from a party whose name you don't recognize), check it out before you open it. Most antivirus software can now detect word processor viruses, and there

> **NUTS & BOLTS**
>
> **How Fat Is Your Pipe?**
>
> **www.computingcentral.com/topics/bandwidth/speedtest.asp**
>
> Now don't get offended: A "fat pipe" is what we geeks call a fast Internet connection. This page will measure your current line speed, then show you how you measure up to other connection types. Guaranteed to instil feelings of inadequacy in one and all.

are some programs that have been specifically designed to do so. When in doubt, copy the originating e-mail address, then delete both the message and the attachment, and try to contact the sending party yourself to verify its legitimacy.

The Trojan horse e-mail message also points to the plague that results from the relatively insignificant problem of infected attachments: the chain letters warning e-mail users about such potential threats. Usually, the letters themselves are a hoax. How can you tell? As "Hector" notes, you can spot a hoax e-mail warning through tell-tale signs such as the lack of a proper originating address, poor or hyperbolic punctuation and grammar, technological inaccuracies, and the exhortation to "forward this message to everyone you know."

If you receive such a warning and feel that it might nevertheless have some truth to it, do yourself a favour and wait a day or two before inundating your friends and co-workers with forwarded copies. A sheepish apology will almost always follow in the wake of the original message. If no such apology comes, check out the Norton Antivirus Research Center's Virus Hoax page **<www.norton.com/avcenter/hoax.html>**, or check the recent postings in one of the Usenet groups interested in such problems for verification.

Popular Antivirus Programs

Okay, worst-case scenario time. Whether you downloaded something that was a little dodgy, took an unprotected Zip or floppy disk to a service bureau or copy shop and didn't check it for viruses afterwards, whatever, you have a virus on your computer. What happens next?

If you've already got updated antivirus software installed, you'll probably be all right. Your antivirus software, which usually runs unobtrusively while you're doing other things, may actually do its job, detecting and alerting you to the presence of the virus, perhaps even automatically deleting the virus for you.

On the other hand, if you haven't updated your virus definitions recently, or (gasp) haven't actually installed the software, you may not realize you have a problem until things start to go wrong (your computer won't boot properly, files begin to disappear, et cetera).

If you suspect you have a virus on your machine, do the following immediately:

- Determine the type of virus. There are two broad categories of viruses: macro viruses, which attach themselves to Word and Excel documents, and exe/com/boot sector viruses.

Macro Viruses

Macro viruses are a recent phenomenon, but are, if anything, more common than their exe/com/boot sector ancestors. The good news is that macro viruses are easier to remove than exe/com/boot sector viruses. The bad news is that they're much more infectious.

Macro viruses spread when you open infected Word documents or Excel spreadsheets that you have received through e-mail, downloading or shared storage media (CD-ROM, floppy or Zip disk). Once you open an infected document, all documents currently on your hard drives will likely become infected. If you think your computer has a macro virus, do the following:

- DON'T insert any writable storage media (floppies, Zip disks) into any drives unless they're locked to avoid spreading the virus.
- Use your antivirus software to scan all hard drives for macro viruses. After ensuring that your hard drives are virus-free, scan all your storage media and all drives on any networks to which you regularly connect.
- Practice safe computer sex: tell everyone you exchange Word or Excel documents with that you've just had a virus attack and that they may already be infected.

Exe/Com/Boot Sector Viruses

These virus types are less common than macro viruses, but are much harder to remove from your system once it's been infected. Many of these viruses can load themselves into the memory of your computer, which makes them highly resistant to your anti-virus software. The following steps will help you to ensure that the virus doesn't skip from memory back onto your drives:

- Disconnect your computer from the local network (if you have one) and/or the Internet, if you have a continual connection (exception: if you're using an Internet-based utilities service, such as the McAfee Clinic [see below], connect to your service and follow their instructions).
- To avoid the possibility that there's a virus lurking in your computer's memory, you'll have to reboot from a clean, locked system disk (a system disk is a floppy disk that contains core system files, and sometimes additional files from your antivirus applications. System disks with such extra files are often referred to as "Rescue Disks"). Note: Because it's possible for a virus to modify your CMOS to prevent you from booting from your floppy drive, it's important to make sure your CMOS is set to boot from your floppy drive before you reboot (see your system manual for more information).
- Run your antivirus software to disinfect your hard disk's boot sector and all files on your drives. At this point, you should be able to remove your system disk from your floppy drive and reboot your computer normally. It's always a good idea to run your antivirus software again after your regular reboot; viruses can be amazingly persistent.
- Once your system is clean, it's time to check all of your storage media for possible infection. Run your antivirus scanner on all

floppies, Zip disks, CD-and other media types (yes, ALL of them—the virus could have lain dormant for a long time).

- If you have a network, repeat the above steps for all of the machines connected to the network.
- When all else fails, reformat the drives you suspect are infected, and reload all your software from your last clean backup. We know, it's a royal pain, but it beats having to deal with sustained damage to your data or your hardware.

Once you've got your system up and running again, here are a few hints to help minimize damage from virus infections in the future.

- Scan every incoming file you receive, and every piece of storage media you are given before you copy any files from it.
- If you haven't done so already, you may also want to install a virus scanning program such as the Norton Antivirus, which constantly runs in the background, checking your system for signs of infection.
- Antivirus software recognizes individual viruses by comparing them to a set of files called virus definitions. The software manufacturer updates these files regularly so that their software can recognize and defend against all of the latest viral strains. Get into the habit of checking the manufacturer's site to see if new virus definitions are available for download. Some programs, such as the Norton Antivirus, will automatically remind you to check if new definitions are available, and will even download and install them for you (see below). A subscription fee may be required.
- Always back up your data regularly. You can reload your software from the original disks (which, of course, as a law-abiding computer user, you own, have registered, and always have close at hand), but if your non-archived data is damaged, it's gone forever.
- Whenever possible, keep your data on a separate physical drive from your software in order to minimize the possibility of it being infected.

NUTS & BOLTS

Featherweight Sites

www.sylloge.com:8080/5k/home.html

Tired of bloated, ungainly Web pages that take forever to load? So are these people, who started the 5k Award for Excellence in Web Design and Production. Take a look at these sites and revel in what can be done with a mere 5 kilobytes of space. Small is beautiful.

Major Antivirus Resources

These are the major players. They will usually be able to deal with any viruses that raise their pestilent little heads on your system.

Norton Antivirus

www.symantec.com/region/can/eng/product/nav/index.html

Symantec Canada, makers of the Norton Antivirus, the best-selling antivirus software in the world, maintains this page. Features in Norton Antivirus 2000 Version 6 let you quarantine infected files, access online support, schedule regular virus definition downloads, and protect yourself from dangerous ActiveX and Java applets as well as traditional viruses. If you've already got the software, you can download your virus definition updates from here; if you don't, you can purchase the Norton Antivirus or other programs through their e-commerce engine.

The Antivirus Research Centre on this site provides useful up-to-the-minute information on the latest viruses sweeping the Net (which include, at the time of this writing, the I Love You, Kill98.Trojan, PrettyPark.Worm, The Fly, and W97M.Vale viruses), and special tools dedicated to their removal. There's also useful information about other hazards of online life, such as the recent wave of "Denial of Service" attacks against major online etailers.

McAfee

www.mcafee.com

McAfee has joined the ranks of those companies moving to Web-based software services. Their Web-based applications protect, maintain, and optimize your computer any place you happen to be, at any time, as long as you can get on the Net. Because the apps are Internet-based, updates are free, and less hassle for you. There are two groups of applications: The McAfee Clinic, a yearly subscription service (usually $49.95 U.S., but available for $29.95 U.S. at the time of this writing) which provides access to their award-winning antivirus and other applications (a hard drive cleaner, an application remover, an update wizard, and so on), and a suite of free applications (a software finder, a PC book finder, a system info report generator, and free online file storage) that will help you identify, research, and upgrade your PC components.

There are two catches. First, on older versions of Windows 95 that didn't ship with ActiveX, you must install Internet Explorer as well as Netscape to use this service, because the McAfee site requires ActiveX controls to operate (Netscape can be your default browser, though). Second (and this is the big problem), remember that in order to use the Clinic, you have to be able to get online. In many instances of virus attack, you won't even be able to get your computer to boot properly, let alone dial into the Net. If you're a cautious user who likes to have all your software on your hard drives, $29.95 U.S. will still get you version 5 of the venerable McAfee VirusScan program. The software has some nice features, including e-mail X-Ray, which catches viruses in your e-mail even before you've opened your messages.

Ontrack

www.ontrack.com/virusinfo/index.asp

Ontrack (formerly Mijenix) is the new kid in town. They make the amazing ZipMagic compression/decompression utility and a very efficient, very compact set of systems utilities called Fix-It Utilities ($49.95 U.S.), which includes antiviral software. The Virus Information Centre that Ontrack has established contains a lot of useful resources, including a virus FAQ, a tutorial, recommended procedures for disinfecting an infected system, corporate virus policy guidelines, information on hoaxes, and all sorts of other useful information.

F-Secure

www.f-secure.com

Another well-respected antivirus program, F-Prot, was also recently combined with another product, AVP, to produce F-Secure, an antivirus package that uses both sets of antivirus technology to provide extra protection. Its special feature is F-Secure Gatekeeper, a product designed to protect PCs against viruses transmitted over the Internet. When files are transferred via e-mail or downloaded from Web pages and FTP sites, F-Secure Gatekeeper automatically scans them for viruses as they arrive on your hard drive.

False Alarms

No antivirus program is foolproof. Occasionally, they'll miss a really new virus, but more often, they'll alert you to a virus that isn't actually there. Why? Because virus detection programs use a set of protocols called heuristics to identify virus-like behaviour. On installation, most virus detection programs take a kind of snapshot of all the files on your computer. While running in the background, they check the current status of your files against that snapshot. If there are any changes, they will usually set off their alarms. This means that if you regularly update a program through online downloads, your virus detection software will usually go off. Don't panic: check the name and location of the suspect file before you delete it. If the file is in a directory that houses a recently updated program, it's probably safe to instruct your antivirus software to validate the file, and carry on with your business.

INFOHAZARD

hacker, n.

1. A person who enjoys exploring the details of programmable systems and how to stretch their capabilities, as opposed to most users, who prefer to learn only the minimum necessary. 2. One who programs enthusiastically (even obsessively) or who enjoys programming rather than just theorizing about programming. ... 7. One who enjoys the intellectual challenge of creatively overcoming or circumventing limitations. 8. [deprecated] A malicious meddler who tries to discover sensitive information by poking around. Hence "password hacker," "network hacker." The correct term for this sense is *cracker.*

The term "hacker" also tends to connote membership in the global community defined by the Net. . . . Hackers consider themselves something of an elite (a meritocracy based on ability), though one to which new members are gladly welcome. There is thus a certain ego satisfaction to be had in identifying yourself as a hacker (but if you claim to be one and are not, you'll quickly be labeled *bogus*). See also *wannabee.*

cracker, n.

One who breaks security on a system. Coined ca 1985 by hackers in defence against journalistic misuse of *hacker* (q.v., sense 8). An earlier attempt to establish "worm" in this sense around 1981–82 on Usenet was largely a failure.

Use of both these neologisms reflects a strong revulsion against the theft and vandalism perpetrated by cracking rings. While it is expected that any real hacker will have done some playful cracking and knows many of the basic techniques, anyone past larval stage is expected to have outgrown the desire to do so except for immediate, benign, practical reasons (for example, if it's necessary to get around some security in order to get some work done).

Thus, there is far less overlap between hackerdom and crackerdom than the mundane reader misled by sensationalistic journalism might expect. Crackers tend to gather in small, tight-knit, very secretive groups that have little overlap with the huge, open poly-culture this lexicon describes; though crackers often like to describe themselves as hackers, most true hackers consider them a separate and lower form of life.

Source: Hacker Jargon **<www.antionline.com/features/jargon>**

The Dangers of DSL and Cable

Big bandwidth (relatively speaking) is finally within reach of the average consumer, as telcos and cable giants roll out competing schemes for high-speed connections at home. Phone companies are offering DSL (digital subscriber line), which can potentially deliver T1 speeds and better over regular copper telephone wires. ("Potentially" because the speed of DSL varies according to your distance from the telco's Central Office, and, sadly, because some suppliers have decided to kneecap their customers by downgrading from the Ethernet protocol to PPPoE (Point-to-Point Protocol over Ethernet), and providing only a 1-Meg modem. For more on this issue, read the FAQs at SympaticoUsers.org **<www.sympaticousers.org>**). Cable has its own problems, including connection speeds that tend to plummet as more people in your neighbourhood log on to share the same piece of pipe.

But the one thing both DSL and cable have in common is their promise of an "always on" connection—and, consequently, the vastly greater security risk that goes with it. If you're connected to the Internet, you're connected to a slimy sea of unknown fellow travellers who may decide to crawl back up the wire into your computer. The more time you spend online, the greater the odds are that someone—i.e. the computer-age bogeyman known as The Hacker, or more accurately, The Cracker—will find you. You need protection.

If you haven't already traded in your dial-up modem, don't let this warning scare you away from acquiring high-speed access. (High-speed rocks!) Remember, even if you're only connecting to the Net via (gulp!) a 14.4 Kbps dial-up modem, you're still at risk. The chances of being infiltrated are significantly lower, since you don't have a static IP address (that is, a permanent Internet address that stays the same whenever you log on) and you probably don't stay online for extended periods of time, but you're still vulnerable. Hacking tools are getting faster and more sophisticated, and they're remarkably easy for anyone to acquire. If you need convincing, take a quick peek at the arsenal archived at AntiCode **<www.AntiCode.com>**. The list includes everything from network scanners, rootkits, and Ethernet sniffing tools to e-mail bombers, system exploits, and distributed attack utilities.

Parent company AntiOnline, a computer security information portal, finds itself under constant attack by would-be crackers—"For some STRANGE reason," reports the AntiOnline network administrator, "malicious hackers just LOVE trying to break into our network." AntiOnline's mocking

▶NETHEADS

Kevin Mitnick

www.kevinmitnick.com

First arrested when he was seventeen, for stealing computer manuals, Kevin Mitnick (a.k.a. Condor) may be the world's most famous hacker. Following his teenage exploits as an L.A. "phone phreak" and several mid-80s run-ins with the law, Mitnick was arrested by the FBI in 1988, at the age of twenty-five, for scooping source code from Digital Equipment Corp. Released after a year in prison, he was charged in 1992 for violating the conditions of his supervised release (he made contact with one of his teenage hacker pals), but he went underground and started cracking computers at places like Motorola, Fujitsu, and Sun Microsystems. Captured by the FBI in February 1995, with the help of security expert Tsutomu Shimomura, Mitnick served another five years before his release in January 2000. Banned by court order from touching any kind of computer or cell phone for three years without written permission from his probation officer, Mitnick complains that he's not even allowed to own a pocket organizer: "I have to live as if I'm part of the Amish." Meanwhile, Mitnick made headlines again when he was engaged by a panel of U.S. senators to offer advice as an expert in the art of hacking. Visit the official Kevin Mitnick Web site to read all about his continuing troubles with justice. While you're there, buy a "Free Kevin" bumper sticker from his grandmother.

NUTS & BOLTS

Disable Windows File and Print Sharing

Step 1: Open Control Panel > Network.

Step 2: Click on File and Print Sharing, uncheck the two options for files and printers, and click OK twice to close the Network dialog boxes.

Step 3: Restart your computer if prompted to do so and close the Control Panel.

INFOHAZARD

Password Tips

Here are a few suggestions for choosing a good password and keeping it secure:

- Use a unique combination of characters (with a mix of upper and lower case), numbers and, if possible, symbols.
- Don't use a password that someone who knows you can easily guess, like your Social Insurance Number, your birthday, your mother's maiden name, or a word that's currently newsworthy.
- Don't use words that can be found in dictionaries of any language—these are easily cracked by hackers using powerful programs that systematically run through a long list of English and foreign words and phrases.
- Don't use words spelled backwards—password-cracking programs can flip words back and forth.
- Avoid using proper names, especially names of spouses, friends, pets, or the local sports team.
- Don't use the same password for all applications.
- Never divulge your password to strangers.
- Don't write your password on a sticky note and paste it to your computer, or store it in an unencrypted file on your hard drive. If you must write it down, do it somewhere discreet.
- Change your passwords regularly.

response is to publish its own computer logs **<www.AntiOnline.com/NetworkOperations/hacks.html>**, along with the IP address of the would-be attackers, so that visitors to the site can "take a peek at the different types of hack attempts and strange activity that we see on a daily basis." The logs are updated in real time, and if you're curious about any of the activity types, you can get details from Ask Bub, "the virtual security expert"—an underground version of Ask Jeeves!

The point being, you may feel invisible to the world when you're surfing the Net, but you're not. Your cable or DSL modem attaches directly to a network card inside your computer, and this makes you a node on the network. If you can "see" and talk to other computers—which is the whole point of being on a network—then they can see you too.

The first step towards making your computer secure is understanding your operating system and how to control your network connection (heads up if you use Windows, but if you run MacOS or Linux or some other operating software, keep reading anyway). Here are a few steps you should take to help protect yourself. There is no such thing as being 100% secure, but at least you can prevent the most common types of vandalism.

Use Passwords

Passwords are your first line of defence—and they're absolutely free. It doesn't cost you a penny to protect your files, computer drives, and applications with a code word that can keep everyone else out. A password is an unspaced sequence of characters—typically between four and sixteen characters in length, depending on how the system is set up—used to determine whether a user requesting access to a computer system is really that particular person. However, passwords can be compromised by various methods, including brute force attacks by password-cracking software and the less technical method known as "social engineering"—that is, being tricked into giving away your password. A sneaky hacker may call you, for example, posing as the system administrator from your ISP or a computer technician from a company you have dealings with, telling you that your file was accidentally wiped out by a computer glitch and asking you to help him restore the account. Don't laugh—it happens, and people fall for it. Famed cracker Kevin Mitnick penetrated as many computer security systems by charming people as he did through technical prowess.

Turn Off Windows File and Print Sharing

If you don't need to share files and printers over a local area network (LAN), simply turn off this option altogether (see sidebar on previous page).

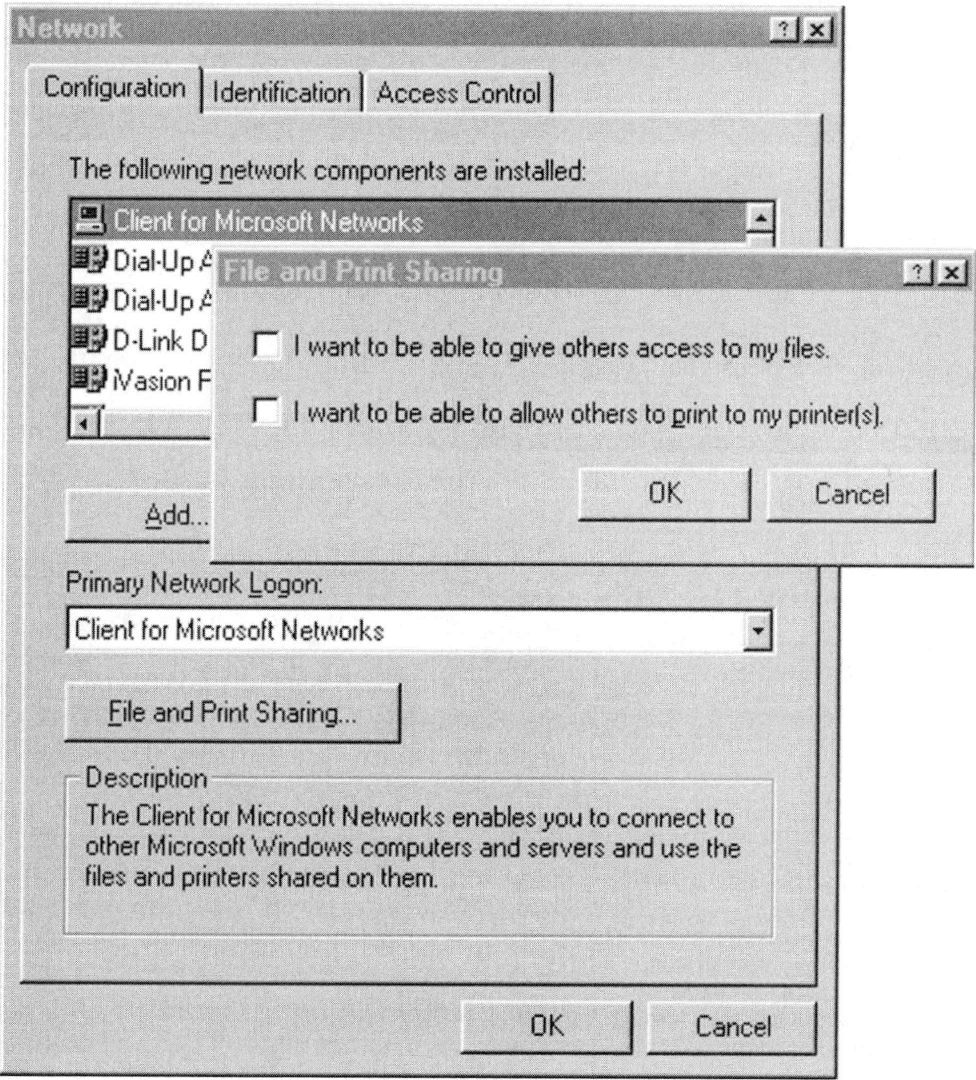

Turn off Windows file and print sharing in the Network options dialog box

Properly Configure Your Network Protocols

If you do want to share files and/or printers on a LAN, disable NetBIOS over TCP/IP—NetBIOS is an unsafe Microsoft networking protocol—and use NetBEUI instead. (You may need to install NetBEUI in the Configuration list.) Unbind TCP/IP from Microsoft Networking for all instances of TCP/IP that point to a network adapter, including any dial-up adapters.

If you need file and printer sharing over TCP/IP using NetBIOS, then set a Scope ID. Computers running NetBIOS over TCP/IP with a Scope ID are invisible to other computers that don't have the same Scope ID. (For more information on Scope ID, see Microsoft support documents Q138271 **<support.microsoft.com/support/kb/articles/Q138/2/71.asp>** and Q138449 **<support.microsoft.com/support/kb/articles/Q138/4/49.asp>**.)

For detailed instructions about configuring network protocols in Windows, and lots of other useful information, visit Gibson Research Corporation's ShieldsUP page **<grc.com/x/ne.dll?bh0bkyd2>**. Steve Gibson, a California-based software programmer and tech journalist, offers step-by-step directions for safeguarding your Windows computer from intruders. While he seems overly fond of bold italics and big headlines, and his rhetoric sometimes gets a little, um, overexcited—his site reads like a late-night infomercial—he nevertheless writes clearly and provides well-illustrated, in-depth information. His site also offers a free security check—just hit the Probe My Ports button to launch the service.

What's a port? A computer running TCP/IP software has 65,535 potential access points—or ports—each with its own logical address. Upper-level applications that use TCP/IP have ports with preassigned numbers, designated by the Internet Assigned Numbers Authority **<www.iana.net>**. Port 80, for example, is typically where Web server software running HTTP (HyperText Transfer Protocol) connects to the outside world, while port 21 is the access point for FTP (File Transfer Protocol). Other applications are given port numbers dynamically for each connection. Network ICE (makers of the firewall software BlackICE Defender) provides a list of common ports and the programs that are likely to run on them **<www.netice.com/Advice/Exploits/Ports/default.htm>**. Trojan horse programs like Back Orifice, DeepThroat, and Happy 99, which can be installed on unprotected computers without the owner's knowledge, open their own ports to communicate with invasive scanners. For a list of known Trojan horses and the ports they commonly use, see the SANS Institute Intrusion Detection FAQ **<www.sans.org/newlook/resources/IDFAQ/oddports.htm>**. Any antivirus program worth its salt should be able to detect and expunge most Trojan horses, but if you run a security check and notice any of the commonly used ports open

INFOHAZARD

The Box Network

astalavista.box.sk

If you ever need the feeling that there are a whole bunch of people on the Internet that are younger and smarter and far, far more cavalier about the legalities of information technology than you, drop by the Box Network. This series of search engines, directories and archives focuses mostly on hacking and security-related matters (AstaLaVista, NewOrder), but also delves into computer music (Thrax), MP3s (MP3 Box), the open source movement (Linux Box), Gaming (Gameguru) and graphic design (Eye).

for no apparent reason, you may have an unwanted gift horse hiding within your gates.

Port scanners—used by online security checkers and popular within the hacker community—are programs that send TCP/IP requests to a range of ports on the target computer, hoping to find ports that are open (that is, "listening" for such requests). Open ports respond to the probe with an acknowledgement that they're ready and waiting to conduct business. Open ports are like unlocked back doors—sooner or later, someone will try the handle, and if they find the door open, they'll come inside for a look around.

Other free online security checkers for home computers include the HackerWhacker Remote Network Security Scan **<hackerwhacker.com>**, the E-Soft My Security Desktop Audit **<secure1.e-softinc.com/cgi-bin/session/slogin?service=mysecure>**, and the WebTrends Online Security Scan **<www.webtrends. net/tools/security/scan.asp>**. As well as checking for various known vulnerabilities (such as open file sharing), all of these services perform TCP port scans, although the level of scrutiny varies from basic (10 ports) to intense (2,000+). Commercial versions provide even more thorough inspection.

You can't really prevent port scans by snooping hackers, but you can make your computer a lot less interesting to them by pulling the plug on sharing and by shutting down open ports. You can also get software that detects suspicious activity on particular ports or a range of ports. Two common programs for Windows are Genius and Nuke Nabber.

▶NETHEADS

Løpht Heavy Industries

<**www.Løpht.com**>

Founded in the early 1990s, Løpht is a Boston-based organization of freelance computer hackers who became famous for cracking private security systems and then publicly announcing the security flaws that enabled the break-ins. Once feared as a menace to society, Løpht is now revered as a "hacker think tank," and their news releases have assumed the status of Consumer Reports for the security world. In January 2000, Løpht announced that it was coming in out of the cold: the hacker collective, lured by the call of real cashflow, has merged with a new company called @Stake **<www.atstake.com>**. Founded by former computer industry executives, including top guns from Compaq, Forrester Research, and Cambridge Technology Partners, @Stake is devoted to providing businesses with "computer security solutions."

The hacker who goes by the name of Mudge (a longtime Løpht member best known for his development of Løpht Crack, an NT password auditing tool) is now vice-president of research and development. Commenting on how the once-lofty domain of the true hacker has been overrun by "script kiddies"—young crackers who make mischief with scripts and programs written by others, often without understanding the code itself—Mudge complains: "The media actually encourages them. If you read about someone breaking into a high-profile Web page, it's 'a 16-year-old, brilliant misguided kid.' If a 16-year-old walks into a liquor store and shoots the clerk to get the money, they never say, 'a brilliant juvenile expert in spontaneous combustion.'"

Use a Firewall

A firewall controls access to your computer by examining information associated with TCP/IP packets—including the port addresses being used and the source and destination IP addresses—and using a defined set of rules to allow or deny the packet or session. Various firewalls differ in the amount and type of information they examine—in general, the more data they examine, the better security they can provide. There are also three types of firewall architecture: packet filter firewalls, proxy servers, and hybrids that combine both features. Firewalls that act as application-level gateways (proxy servers) are considered more secure than packet filter firewalls. But any firewall is better than none at all, so home users who don't want to set up a second computer to act as the proxy should at least consider installing a personal firewall program to monitor their system. Following are a few of your options.

ZoneAlarm toolbar

ZoneLabs makes a free firewall worth considering, the easy-to-use ZoneAlarm **<www.zonelabs.com/zonealarm.htm>**, which monitors activity in and out of your computer. You can define the level of security you're comfortable with, specify which programs can access the Internet, create customized zones where specific computers and networks can be predefined as trustworthy or not, or use the Internet Lock to block *all* traffic while you're not using the Net or you step away from your computer.

Norton Internet Security 2000 **<www.symantec.com/sabu/nis>**, by the folks who bring you all those other fine products, stops viruses, uninvited access, and malicious Java applets and ActiveX controls. If you've got young'uns at home, you can use NIS to play the role of censor, by preventing access to specified Web sites, newsgroups, and other evilness. You can stop the kiddies from submitting personal information through Web forms without your paternalistic approval. Best of all, you can kiss annoying banner ads and pop-up windows goodbye.

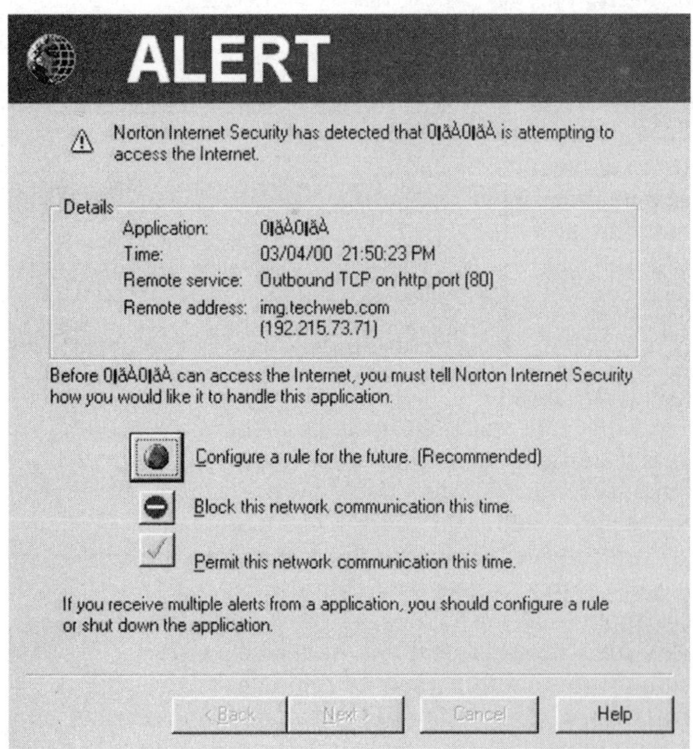

Norton Internet Security nabs a suspect

ConSeal PC Firewall and ConSeal Private Desktop move beyond Winsock-based applications to provide network security for your operating system, network, and applications, as well as encrypted chat, voice over IP, and other communications through ConSeal Private Links, a PC-to-PC VPN (Virtual Private Network). ConSeal Private Desktop is certified under the Canadian Common Security Scheme (CSS) **<www.cse-cst.gc.ca/cse/english/cchome.html>**, an independent third-party evaluation and certification service for measuring the trustworthiness of IT security products and systems. ConSeal was developed by Signal9 Solutions **<www.signal9.com>**, a Canadian company acquired in February 2000 by McAfee **<www.mcafee.com>**, who morphed ConSeal Private Desktop into the McAfee Personal Firewall.

For Mac users, Open Door Networks **<www. opendoor.com>** offers DoorStop Firewall, which provides packet filtering for all TCP-based services, along with other programs such as ShareWay IP that supplement OS9's built-in Internet file-sharing features.

PGP inventor Phil Zimmermann visiting Red Square

Source: Computerworld Russia

NETHEADS

Phil Zimmermann

<**www.pgp.com/phil**>

PGP (Pretty Good Privacy) is the world's most widely used e-mail encryption software, and Phil Zimmermann is the guy who invented it. He's also the guy the U.S. government hounded for years with legal threats after Zimmermann released PGP as freeware, violating U.S. export restrictions on cryptographic software. The case was dropped in 1996. Since then, Zimmermann has been showered with awards for his pioneering work, including the 1999 Louis Brandeis Award from Privacy International and the 1996 Norbert Wiener Award from Computer Professionals for Social Responsibility for promoting the responsible use of technology.

For More Information

The Navas Cable Modem/DSL Tuning Guide **<navasgrp.home.att.net/tech/cable_dsl.htm>** offers an excellent collection of "tips on increasing speed, enhancing security, fixing problems, sharing a connection, and more." Other sites to stir the imagination include the following:

Phrack

<www.phrack.com>

SecurityFocus

<www.securityfocus.com>

Hacker News Network

<www.hackernews.com>

Internet Security News Archive

<www.landfield.com/isn>

Now that you've chosen a browser and primped it to suit your own idiosyncrasies, installed the necessary plug-ins, and strapped on some security gear, let's take a look at the road ahead.

TWO

READING THE ROADMAPS ▶

> I like serendipity and not being sure what I'm looking to find, and one of the most positive aspects of the Internet is its very openness. I think the Internet holds the potential for revolutionary change and leaps of imagination, even as it holds an infinite quantity of spam.
>
> *Sallie Tisdale, "I've got homework, Ma,"* Salon

How Wide Is the Web?

If you looked at every currently existing Web page one by one, even at the impossible rate of one per second, it would take you almost fifty years. And by then, you'd be further behind than when you started. Much further. According to the latest metrics—a joint study by Inktomi and NEC Research Institute, published in February 2000 **<www.inktomi.com/webmap>**—there are over 1 billion unique, indexable Web pages, and that number is growing by 2 million pages a day. (Okay, so some Web surveys are educated guesses at best, but they're still helpful for understanding how quickly the online universe is expanding.) International Data Corporation **<www.idc.com>** estimates that by the year 2002, the number of Web pages will hit 8 billion, surpassing the entire population of the planet.

How Big Is Your Database?

When you look at the numbers, it's clear that even search engines—robotic hunters and gatherers of information that index millions of pages and store the results in their databases—aren't keeping up with the onslaught. The actual scope, size, and accuracy of search engine databases varies considerably, but even the biggest engines capture barely 30 percent of what's on the Web. The numbers are still impressive, though: relative newcomer FAST **<www.ussc.alltheweb.com>** has quickly climbed past 340 million pages, followed by AltaVista **<www.altavista.com>**, Northern Light **<www.northernlight.com>**, and Excite **<www.excite.com>**, with 250, 240, and 214 million pages respectively. Google **<www.google.com>** weighs in at 200 million pages, but because of the unique way it captures intelligence about links between pages, Google's coverage extends to 350 million. Lower down on the scale, Lycos **<www.lycos.com>** and InfoSeek **<infoseek.go.com>** check in at 50 million, HotBot **<www.hotbot.com>** hovers below 40 million, and Web-

ARE WE THERE YET?

What's Old

Back in the early days, when most Web pages sported grey back grounds and the text was either Times or Courier, you could actually manage to keep up with the developing universe by visiting the What's New page at the National Center for Super computing Applications. NCSA is where a young Marc Andreesen and several other student programmers invented Mosaic, the first inline graphical browser for the World Wide Web, released in early 1993. Andreesen went on to develop a commercial version of the browser, known as Netscape Navigator. Internet nostalgia buffs can relive history by visiting the NCSA What's New Archives **<www.ncsa.uiuc.edu/SDG/Software/Mosaic/Docs/whats-new.html>**. Stored in monthly installments, the What's New announcements reveal all that was new and cool on the Internet between June 1993 and June 1996, when the service was discontinued.

The very first entry in the What's New list, dated June 14, 1993, reports that "An experimental WWW physics preprint server at Los Alamos is coming along nicely." Unfortunately, most of the links are way out of date, so you can't visit the actual pages. Instead, you get a big mouthful of Error 404 messages. But it's entertaining and touching to see what the Web pioneers were busy building. There's even a link to the NCSA Mosaic Home Page, where you can read about this antique piece of equipment and download a copy—albeit a later version—for your own software museum. Here are a few highlights from December 1993:

- "The FBI and NASA have been working together to make information on the UNABOM investigation available to the users of the Internet. The information is also accessible via FTP and Gopher."
- "Take a hop to what could be the world's first virtual holiday greeting." (The outdated URL **<baldrick.cecer.army.mil/hyplans/rewerts/christmas.html>** points to a server belonging not to Hallmark but to those other greeting card specialists, the U.S. military.)
- "Norwegian Telecom Research have put the last issue of their technical journal "Telektronikk" online—a special issue named "cyberspace." It contains 14 articles with more than 100 images. The Web version beat paper by about one week."
- "Our favorite magazine ***Wired*** now is running a Web server."
- "The Canadian Federal Government's Communications Research Centre now has a Web server. Interesting things include CBC Radio information including online audio for some radio shows, Industry Canada documents, and a Canadian Coat of Arms display."
- "The University of Limerick now has a map of Ireland complete with links to all known Irish World Wide Web sites."
- "A new Web server is running at the University of Cambridge Computer Laboratory. The server includes the first coffee machine on the Web."
- "NTT Basic Research Labs in Japan has made a set of modifications to Mosaic 2.0 to support various national character sets, including Greek, Hebrew, Chinese, Korean, and Japanese."
- "A J.R.R. Tolkien information page is now online at University of Waterloo."

Crawler **<www.webcrawler.com>** has a measly 5 million.

So far, no individual search engine comes close to indexing the entire Web, much less the whole Internet. (In April 2000, Inktomi announced that its database had broken the 500 million mark—about half the known Web—but the funny thing is, you can't search that database directly. Inktomi is the power behind many of the Web's major portals and content sites, and each one has its own tunnel into Inktomi's data mine. Search results are filtered and ranked according to each partner's preferences.) But among the major search engines, the amount of overlap is less than you might think—all the major databases contain many URLs that don't appear in any other database. Which may be good news if your favourite search engine doesn't turn up the page you're hunting for, since there's a good chance that a different search engine will have found it. (For a detailed look at the relative sizes and how they overlap, see Search Engine Showdown **<www.searchengineshowdown.com>**.)

If you think you can get around the limitations of individual engines by querying a metasearch engine—which sends your query to multiple search engines and collates the results—think again. You're actually searching less of the Web, not more. Since most metasearchers retrieve only the top 10 to 50 hits from each search engine on their list, the total number of hits retrieved may be considerably less than if you conduct a direct search on a single search engine. For example, a search for the phrase "cream cheese" in Savvy-Search **<www.savvysearch.com>** returned 113 links, whereas the same search in AltaVista turned up 40,671 links. Of course, you're probably not going to look past the first page or two of results anyway, so the real test is how accurately the results are ranked—that is, how good the search engine is at putting the right pages at the top of the list. (See "Understanding Search Results" below for more on this topic.)

Some search engines are better than others at keeping up-to-date and eliminating dead links. The number of outdated URLs can run as high as 20 percent, despite the ceaseless toil of Web spiders (robot software that explores the Web by retrieving a document and following all the hyperlinks in it). Your chances of finding a Web page are considerably reduced if it has recently changed or moved, since the search engines may be slow keeping up. AltaVista, for example, will return every month or so to a site it has already indexed.

Helpful Webmasters will leave a forwarding address—that is, a page at the old URL announcing the new location—and will manually register the site's new location with the search engines, instead of waiting for the spiders to discover the change. But evidence suggests that most Webmasters are either forgetful or woefully overworked, so you can't rely on their efforts.

> **NUTS & BOLTS**
>
> **Does Size Matter?**
>
> Search Engine Showdown
>
> **www.searchengineshowdown.com**
>
> Billing itself as "The Users' Guide to Web Searching," this site by Greg Notess could also be called the Battle for the Planet of the Search Engines. It's packed with stats about useful things like which engine produces the most dead links (if you hadn't noticed yet, it's poor old AltaVista). In the Unique Hits section, the site states that FAST produces the most unique results (i.e. pages that aren't listed in any other search engine), followed distantly by AltaVista and Excite. Visiting this site regularly will help to ensure that your searches produce the results you need.
>
> Search Engine Watch
>
> **www.searchenginewatch.com**
>
> Danny Sullivan's Search Engine Watch is one of those essential Web sites that every new user (and all serious searchers) should visit on a regular basis. It provides detailed reviews of the major search engines, charts and graphs that compare engine performance, instructions for Webmasters on how to code search-engine-friendly pages, and links to many engine-related articles and services. Nice crisp design too.

Different search engines also vary in how deep they'll venture into a particular site. Spiders are supposed to follow every link they find, but it's unusual for a search engine to actually index every page on a large site, especially if the site is built with many layers. So, if your search results are only close, and not dead on, don't rule out finding what you need. If you can use a search engine to get to the home page of a site that looks promising, or some other page within the site that managed to get indexed, you can take your search to the next level by scouring the site yourself.

Of course, there are some things that search engines are just unable to index in the first place. What's likely to be missing from search engine databases? Here's a list of some of the AWOL items:

- sites that deliberately prevent search engines from indexing certain files and/or directories, through the use of a robots.txt file
- password-protected sites that require users to log in
- dynamically generated content, such as information pulled from a database by CGI scripts
- intranet sites

- orphan pages that aren't linked to from anywhere else, and can't be found by wandering bots
- commercial sites that want cash up front and clearly don't understand that information wants to be free

What's Not Online?

What's *not* online? Frankly, most of the world's accumulated knowledge. Many libraries have begun the time-consuming process of digitizing their collections—the Library of Congress **<lcweb.loc.gov>**, for example, is a pioneer in this field—but there's still a long way to go. The Library of Congress possesses more than 17 million books, as well as nearly 95 million maps, manuscripts, photographs, films, audio and video recordings, prints and drawings, and other special collections, comprising "the world's most comprehensive record of human creativity and knowledge," according to their own publicity. Those physical objects occupy some 532 miles of shelf space, and new materials are added to the library at a rate of 7,000 items per working day. That's a lot of information, and the majority still resides in the physical, rather than the virtual, world.

The Web is a good place to look for current news and information—the American Journalism Review **<ajr.newslink.org/news.html>** provides links to almost 5,000 online newspapers around the world, including more than 230 in Canada—but old information, such as journalism that was written long before the Web made its appearance in the early 90s, is harder to find—unless you're willing to pay for it. Commercial services like Lexis-Nexis **<www.lexis-nexis.com>** and Infomart Dialog **<www.infomart.ca>** make a business of electronically archiving news stories, financial and corporate information, legal documents, scientific and technical publications, and other research material in their immense databases. There are limits here as well, since these services have only been operating since the advent of electronic data storage, so truly historical information will not be available. Microfilm at the reference library may still be your best bet. You can read the *Globe and Mail*, for instance, as far back as 1849 on film.

Many of these commercial services, at one time available only through direct dial-up accounts, are now accessible via the Web. However, their vast holdings are not catalogued by Internet search engines, and in most cases you'll need to open a paid account before you can find out whether they have what you need.

Similarly, privileged information and confidential documents are not, as a rule, made available online—except by mistake or through malicious intent. In May 1999, Richard Tomlinson, a 37-

ARE WE THERE YET?

How Many People Use the Internet?

According to estimates by Nua Internet Surveys **<www.nua.ie/surveys/how_many_online/index.html>**, there were over 304 million people online as of March 2000. Nua acknowledges that the figure is inexact at best, but calls it an "educated guess" based on their analysis of many surveys published over the last two years. Here's their breakdown by geographical region:

Africa: 2.58 million

Asia/Pacific: 68.9 million

Europe: 83.35 million

Middle East: 1.9 million

Canada and USA: 136.86 million

South America: 10.74 million

Chiming in with a similar count, Computer Industry Almanac **<www.c-i-a.com>** reported over 259 million Internet users at year-end 1999. They peg Canadian usage at 13.2 million. However, other estimates are more conservative. Nielsen//NetRatings **<www.nielsen-netratings.com>**, the new media offshoot of the folks who measure TV viewing audiences, estimate the size of the "current Internet universe" at 129.6 million users. So, take your pick.

year-old New Zealander and former officer with the British Secret Intelligence Service (formerly known as MI6) who was jailed on secrecy charges two years earlier, made international headlines when he threatened to out British agents and reveal the location of MI6 offices around the world. According to reports, he used the Web to publish more than 100 names of alleged spies, until the British government obtained a court injunction to shut the sites down. (See Spy Corner **<www.mcs.com/~klast/www/tomlin.html>** for links to news coverage, as well as links to the official spook sites and resources.) Also rarely available on the Web are in-depth studies and market surveys that some company paid big bucks to produce—you may find the title and an executive summary online, but you're likely to face a hefty price tag if you want to see the full monty.

> **NUTS & BOLTS**
>
> **Direct Search**
>
> **gwis2.circ.gwu.edu/~gprice/direct.htm**
>
> Search engines don't know everything. In fact, a huge chunk of the Web—material that's in databases—is completely invisible to them. Librarian Gary Price has compiled a list of direct links to these resources, which you probably wouldn't even know existed otherwise. Don't you just love librarians?

The bottom line is that you shouldn't expect to find everything on the Web. It's an extremely rich resource, but a long way from perfect.

What Are Portals?

In fantasy games and science fiction, a portal is a gateway leading to a past, present, or future world, or to an expanded state of consciousness. If you have an active imagination, you can easily stretch that definition to fit the Web, where browsing can surely be considered a consciousness-rasing activity. In businessland, however, *portal* generally means a Web site that wants to be your primary access point, or gateway, to the Internet—the page that loads up first when you start your browser, or the first place you go when you need to shop. When the portal concept cropped up, most of the major search engines transformed themselves from mere switching stations to become destinations in and of themselves. These engines now offer free home pages, free Webmail, and other customizable services, like local news, weather, stock quotes, telephone directories, and horoscopes. They have their own discussion forums, and they offer proprietary content in special directories. And, yeah, there's still a search function. Of course, a well-organized set of bookmarks will give you access to the same information and services. But everyone needs to start somewhere, and portals offer all-in-one convenience.

Personalization is also a hot option, especially if you own stocks or like to read your daily horoscope. News headlines can be tailored to the topics you choose, and even the page layout on some portal sites is flexible, if you feel like doing a little

> **ARE WE THERE YET?**
>
> **History Lessons**
>
> For a list of major milestones in the history of the Internet, visit Hobbes' Internet Timeline **<www.isoc.org/zakon/Internet/History/HIT.html>**. A potted history of the Web, written in 1997, can be found at CERN—European Laboratory for Particle Physics **<www.cern.ch/Public/ACHIEVEMENTS/WEB/history.html>**, where the World Wide Web was invented by physicist Tim Berners-Lee. The CERN page is notable for the snapshot of Berners-Lee seated in front of his computer and having an extremely bad hair day. Berners-Lee is now director of the World Wide Web Consortium, which maintains its own archive of significant documents **<www.w3.org/History>**. Other sites worth visiting include NetHistory **<www.geocities.com/SiliconValley/2260/index.html>** and The Roads and Crossroads of Internet History **<www.Internetvalley.com/intval.html>**.

interior decorating, but overall, the options tend to be rather limited. A word of warning: if you want to "personalize" your portal page, you'll need to register. When you do, watch out for the little check boxes that say something like, "Yes, I do want to clog up my mailbox with wads of information on new stuff to buy." Quite often they're checked by default, which means you'll start getting e-mail, just like they promised, about new products or services. If you don't want more junk mail, remember to uncheck these boxes before you finish registering.

While you're at it, take a few minutes to read the site's privacy policy to find out what it plans to do with the personal info you provide when you register. If you don't like what you see, find another portal. As an example, customizing your own My Yahoo! page **<my.yahoo.com>** has been made as simple as possible. After plugging in some basic information about yourself, you can pick news headline categories and fiddle with the layout a bit, let everyone in on your personal philosophy and your interests, add some links, et voilà: your own home page with the barest minimum of energy spent.

More recently, several portals have ventured into the community-building business, with services that allow you to create your own online community space with integrated features such as message boards, live chat, group calendars, online photo albums, and shared contact lists.

Best of all, these services are free. But how do you choose? Overall, Yahoo! probably offers the most complete and reliable combination, with particularly good games, guest chats, weather, and personalization features. Excite is a good pick for finance, due to its close connection with Quicken **<www.quicken.com>**. If you're interested in real estate, MSN.com stands out with the content provided by Microsoft HomeAdvisor, while AltaVista My Live!**<live.altavista.com>** wins in the search department.

There are only a few portal contenders north of the border, none offering as extensive an array of services as their American counterparts. More information is available on these sites in the "Foreign Affairs" section of Chapter 3. While the big search-engine-cum-everything sites are the most visible contenders, there are no hard-and-fast rules about what constitutes a portal. Localized sites like MyBC **<www.mybc.com>** and city-specific spots like Toronto.com **<www.toronto.com>** are becoming popular because they provide news and information more immediately relevant to users.

A portal site usually captures the coveted spot of home page in one of two ways: by offering enough services so the user will change the browser settings to make that URL the default home page, or by delivering a preprogrammed browser to the user, as Sympatico does, with its site already ensconced. Pursuing the latter strategy, the large portals are continually getting into bed with Internet service providers and equipment manufacturers. Is there any cause for concern? Keep reading.

Portal Combat

Market is the key word in the portal phenomenon. Portals attract serious attention on the stock market because they are capable of providing potential advertisers with large captive audiences. Portals know a lot about you, because when you fill out the forms that generate your custom home page, custom e-mail account and whatnot, you're creating a detailed profile of your likes, interests, and spending habits. Thanks to the magic of computers, advertisers are able to use the profile you generated to pitch taste-specific ads to your home page in order to increase the possibility that you'll buy.

To those of us outside the corporate grind, highly targeted marketing may be annoying, but ultimately it's pretty innocuous. The emergence of portal sites points towards a more serious issue: the growth of vertical monopolies that span every level of Internet interaction, from client software (your browser) to your search engine, to the content itself.

Consider America Online. When AOL bought Netscape and Mirabilis ICQ (the grassroots competitor to its AOL Netfind), many people were worried that suddenly one company controlled a huge swath of the total sum of Internet content, plus the tools necessary to access that content. Those fears were amplified when AOL took AT&T to court to attempt to block them from using common Net phrases like "You Have Mail" (yes, this really happened). After the judge rejected AOL's suit, AT&T's counsel stated that "we feel this sort of overreaching by one company raises serious concerns about whether AOL is truly committed to keeping the Internet an open platform, or whether it intends to leverage its dominance to make the Net more proprietary." Now that AOL owns all of Time Warner—content, cable networks, the whole nine yards—corporate attempts to totally control vast chunks of cyberspace will probably continue unabated.

Even though AOL and Time Warner signed a "memorandum of understanding" in March of 2000, promising to allow rival Internet Service Providers access to their cable networks in the interest of promoting competition, members of a U.S. Senate panel investigating the merger have already expressed their skepticism. Committee Chair, Senator Orrin Hatch said, "Given that this [agreement] lacks both enforceability and specificity, this committee remains to be convinced of its value beyond the boardroom and public relations office of AOL Time Warner." While the senators didn't pull any punches, bluntly asking why "AOL's Version 5.0 software appears to hijack users' computers and prevent them from accessing competing services" (*Washington Post*), it's unlikely that anyone at AOL even broke a

NETHEADS

Tim Berners-Lee

If anyone asks you where the name World Wide Web came from, or tries to tell you that you're writing it the wrong way, you can quote the voice of authority: Tim Berners-Lee. After all, he's the guy who invented the Web, so he has a say in the matter. In his own online FAQ, he sets the record straight:

Q: How in fact do you spell World Wide Web?

A: It should be spelled as three separate words, so that its acronym is three separate "W"s. There are no hyphens. Yes, I know that it has in some places been spelled with a hyphen but the official way is without. Yes, I know that "worldwide" is a word in the dictionary, but World Wide Web is three words. I use "Web" with a capital W to indicate that it is an abbreviation for "World Wide Web." Hence, "What a tangled web he wove on his Web site!" Often, WWW is written and read as W3, which is quicker to say. In particular, the World Wide Web consortium is W3C, never WWWC.

Q: Why did you call it WWW?

A: Looking for a name for a global hypertext system, an essential element I wanted to stress was its decentralized form allowing anything to link to anything. This form is mathematically a graph, or web. It was designed to be global of course. (I had noticed that projects find it useful to have a signature letter, as the Zebra project at CERN which started all its variables with "Z." In fact by the time I had decided on WWW, I had written enough code using global variables starting with "HT" for hypertext that W wasn't used for that.) Alternatives I considered were "Mine of information" ("Moi," c'est un peu egoiste) and "The Information Mine" ("Tim," even more egocentric!), and "Information Mesh" (too like "Mess" though its ability to describe a mess was a requirement!).

Source: Tim Berners-Lee, "Press FAQ" **<www.w3.org/People/Berners-Lee/FAQ.html>**

NETHEADS

Buckminster Fuller

www.bfi.org

Bucky Fuller has been dead since 1983, long before the Web was born, but if anyone deserves the title of Nethead Emeritus, it's him. Author of 28 books and 25 U.S. patents (including those for the most famous of his inventions, the geodesic dome) and the recipient of 47 honorary doctorates, this engineer, inventor, and philosopher circled the globe 57 times with the goal of using technology to provide more and more life support for everybody, with fewer and fewer resources. The Buckminster Fuller Institute has placed the full text of some of his most influential books online, along with the transcript of his 42-hour lecture, "Everything I Know." Amazing.

sweat, because the Senate has no jurisdiction over the merger. Thus, the newly born multimedia juggernaut lumbers onward ...

This sort of corporate greed is omnipresent in portalspace. In June 1999, shortly after Yahoo! bought GeoCities, they changed the GeoCities Terms of Service in an incredibly draconian way, specifying that any content a user placed on GeoCities or any other of Yahoo!'s properties was Yahoo!'s to use, royalty-free, forever. Users weren't even allowed to take their content off the network without agreeing to the new terms. After a seven-day boycott of Yahoo! and an accompanying media maelstrom, Yahoo! backed off, changing the Terms of Service to something more equitable. But until that point, Yahoo! had been one of the Internet Good Guys . . . just like Netscape had been, once upon a time.

The point to all of this is that the Internet is a volatile environment—politically and financially. An act as innocuous as obtaining a custom Web page on a portal site can have enormous implications, for yourself and for others. This is not to say that you shouldn't ever use portals; that's both impractical and unnecessary. But pay close attention to who owns your favourite Internet services, and be prepared to complain loudly and often if anyone does anything to restrict your right to use what's left of the "free" Internet.

Keeping Up with the Online World

"Keeping up" is really just a figure of speech, since there's just too much happening on the Web to stay truly informed about more than just a tiny fraction. But keeping in touch with new developments will at least give you a sense of where to start looking when you need to find something.

Plenty of print sources point to new Web sites and compile lists of the Top 100. Computer magazines have been something of a growth industry, although many popular titles such as *Windows* and *Byte* have stopped producing paper versions and now publish strictly online. And as Internet culture seeps into society at large, URLs have become so visible—splashed on everything from bus shelters to billboards—they are just about unavoidable. But the best place to keep up with the online world is . . . online.

NETHEADS

Salon

www.salon.com

Question: Has the Internet come of intellectual age when the *Globe and Mail* starts printing articles from *Salon* in their editorial section? *Salon* is a sprawling landscape of features on art, music, books—anything that resembles the idea of culture in the digital age. And with maybe only a little irony, trying to be an arbiter of culture on the Web, getting its cachet from the great salons of history.

Many large Web sites will gladly send you regular updates by e-mail about new additions and services to their own site. It's a good way of reminding you they exist. Watch for newsletter sign-up options on the home page. Hotwired **<www.hotwired.com>**, the online version of *Wired* magazine, is a good example. Their weekly e-newsletter provides brief synopses of new articles and special features, and includes links to the full stories. Technology news sites send out regular bulletins to keep readers informed of the latest developments. Red Herring **<www.redherring.com>**, for example, which bills itself as a "conduit of information, analysis and opinion, between the vision of Silicon Valley and the power of corporate America," offers a choice of more than a dozen e-mail bulletins, from daily news analysis in Catch of the Day, behind-the-scenes gossip in The Red Eye, and occasional announcements in Red Herring Events Update, to the quarterly newsletter Red Alert.

CMP Net **<www.cmpnet.com>** offers a variety of free e-mail newsletters, from TechWeb News to TechShopper Savvy. Fred Langa **<www.langa.com>**, former editorial director of *Windows Magazine* and editor-in-chief of *Byte Magazine*, writes a twice-weekly e-mail newsletter called LangaList that covers the technology beat. Following are a few other e-mail announcement services that offer regular reports, not about themselves, but about new and newly discovered Web resources. Many of these newsletters are compiled by librarians and other information specialists. (To keep up with developments in search technology, see "Where to Learn More about Search Engines" below.)

CIT Infobits

Intended primarily for educators, CIT Infobits **<www.unc.edu/cit/infobits/infobits.html>** is an electronic service of the University of North Carolina at Chapel Hill Academic & Technology Networks' Center for Instructional Technology. Each month, the e-newsletter reports on selected information technology and instructional technology sources. Visit the home page for subscription details (it's free), or to read back issues.

Edupage

Edupage **<www.educause.edu/pub/edupage/edupage.html>** is a free e-mail service that summarizes developments in information technology. Stories are culled from newspapers and magazines and sent to subscribers three times a week. It's published by Educause, an American association that focuses on the management and use of computer, network, and information resources in support of higher education. Find subscription details and online archives at the Web site.

Internet Resources Newsletter

Intended for academics, students, engineers, scientists, and social scientists, the monthly Internet Resources Newsletter **<www.hw.ac.uk/libWWW/irn/irn.html>**, produced by the Heriot-Watt University Library in Edinburgh, is full of information on new and newly discovered Internet sites, many (but not all) of them British. The newsletter also tracks new information about the Internet that appears in print. In addition, the "Get a Life" section offers a few entertaining tidbits, such as the Loch Ness Webcam **<www.lochness.scotland.net/camera.htm>**, where you can keep an eye out for the fabled Nessie. The Internet Resources Newsletter is available only on the Web site, and not by e-mail.

Netsurfer Digest

Netsurfer Digest **<www.netsurf.com/nsd>** has been delivering free e-mail snapshots of the ever-expanding Web since 1994. Each issue announces a couple of dozen new sites, with the particulars described in short, witty paragraphs. Their motto promises "More Signal, Less Noise," but the ratio is about 50-50— a new site doesn't have to be useful to be mentioned. Being weird or unusual is sometimes enough. A recent issue included news about the world's biggest game of Tetris **<bastilleweb.techhouse.org>**, a 12-storey installation on the side of a building orchestrated by a clutch of engineering students at Brown University in Rhode Island, death-row stats from the Texas Department of Criminal Justice **<www.tdcj.state.tx.us/statistics/stats-home.htm>**, and the online home of the *Underdog Show* **<www.theunderdogshow.com>**, a resurrected 1960s cartoon about a crime-fighting canine.

The Digest is delivered as HTML-formatted text suitable for viewing with any Web browser or HTML-enabled e-mail reader. A plain-text version is no longer available. The HTML version has embedded links to all the sites named so you can connect directly to anything that catches your interest. Back issues of the Digest are available on the Web site. Geeky types can also subscribe to Netsurfer Science **<www.netsurf.com/nss>**, an e-mail announcement focusing on "neat" science and technology sites. Mostly serious stuff, but sometimes not, and the newsletter style is still cheeky. Netsurfer Books **<www.netsurf.com/nsb>** and Netsurfer Education **<www.netsurf.com/nse>** provide a similar services for readers, educators, and others.

▶INFOHAZARD

FreedØm

www.freedom.net

Have you got what it takes to be a Zero-Knowledge Internet Freedom Fighter? A bastion of techno-libertarianism, Freedom is the source for all the latest privacy-related news and resources. If you're serious about protecting your privacy online (if you aren't yet, you will be after reading the privacy breach stories on their site), you'll want to consider downloading their product, Freedom 1.1, which encrypts all of your outgoing e-mail, hiding both the source and destination addresses, as well as encrypting the data flow. Somehow it all makes more sense when you realize these guys are from Montreal...

Netscape: What's New and What's Cool

Netscape keeps Netcenter visitors up to date with two columns, What's New **<home.netscape.com/netcenter/new.html>** and What's Cool **<home.netscape.com/netcenter/cool.html>**. The commentary is usually brief—sometimes just two or three words—but each entry comes with a 1-to-10 rating (from "Don't bother" to "Don't miss") for both content and design. The "best of" both new and cool listings are arranged under a handful of categories, and the archives are accessible by date, as well as through the Randomizer, a link that picks a past date for you. If you use Navigator, a link to the new and cool pages is built into the browser toolbar (Communicator > Bookmarks > Guide > What's Cool).

The Scout Report

The Internet Scout Project **<www.scout.cs.wisc.edu>**, located in the Computer Sciences Department of the University of Wisconsin–Madison, provides regular updates about the best resources on the Internet to the U.S. research and education community—and it's free for everyone else, too. The service uses librarians and educators to read hundreds of new site announcements each week and do the filtering for you. Their tag line is "Surf smarter, not longer." Published every Friday both on the Web and by e-mail, the regular report includes research and education sites, general interest pages, network tools, and news. Three other reports focus on business and economics, science and engineering, and social sciences.

The Scout Project also offers several "current awareness services." Net-Happenings distributes individual e-mail announcements about Internet resources, and postings number between 40 and 60 per day. The postings are also available via the USENET newsgroup **<comp.internet.net-happenings>**. Net-Newsletters combines in one place the best of the Internet's regularly published e-zines. New-List provides prompt notification about new mailing lists. And K-12 Newsletters combines the best of 25+ newsletters for K-12 educators. You can subscribe to any or all of these newsletters at the Scout Project site, or search the online archives. Another resource available at the Web site is the Scout Toolkit, which includes an annotated list of meta-sites that are meant to be used as starting points for further exploration of academic Internet resources, a collection of links to searchable indexes, subject catalogues, annotated directories, subject guides, and specialized directories, articles focused on using the Web, and a list of links to help you stay up-to-date on browsers, plug-ins, and Web development tools.

Spyonit

Why wait for a newsletter to discover and write about a site, when you can activate your own Web spy? Using webcrawler technology, Spyonit **<www.spyonit.com>** watches for new sites that match the keywords you supply, and then notifies you right away. The nifty twist is that you can choose to get your alerts not only by e-mail, but via pager, ICQ, and AOL Instant Messenger, among other options. And there's even a Palm VII version for PDA fans. The Spy Catalog covers popular topics like finance, auctions, sports, and TV, while the various Swiss Army Spies keep track of specific services, like UPS and Fedex package tracking. The Vanity Spy will let you know whenever your name is discovered by the top search engines. And Spyonit members can make their personal spys available for public use—not unlike the early trend of publishing your personal bookmarks.

Search Engines and Directories

Search engines are the pivot around which the World Wide Web turns. Imagine a library with no catalogue. What good would all that information do you if you had no idea where to begin looking? Domain names and file names aren't a lot of help,

NETHEADS

Bruce Sterling

www.well.com/conf/mirrorshades

Cranky Texan SF writer and cultural pundit Bruce Sterling has many soapboxes, and the MIRRORSHADES conference on the WELL is among the best of them. If it's in MIRRORSHADES, it'll be science fiction in a year. In two years it will be in *Wired* magazine. In three years teenage girls will be wearing it. In four years it'll be mentioned on CNN **<www.cnn.com>**. In five years it'll be "discovered." If you aren't a WELL member, the conference's home page has some pretty neat stuff too.

▶NUTS & BOLTS

Botspot

www.botspot.com

Spiders, bots, or intelligent agents—call them what you will, they're changing the way we think about, and look for, information. Parts of this site, which discusses the subject of bots with fanatical intensity, will only appeal to serious propellerheads. On the other hand, the article on how "intelligent agents" are taking over the world of commerce should really scare the pants off your technophobic friends.

because they can vary wildly from the name of the company, program, or person you're seeking, and common-sense guesses will only get you so far (on the Web, sometimes not very far at all).

Thankfully, a number of patient and enterprising souls got together and began to catalogue, well, everything on the Internet. In the early days, searching the Net involved learning to use a bewildering variety of cranky programs with whimsical names: gophers, Archie, Veronica. Today, there are a wide variety of search engines. At first glance they look similar, but they differ substantially in purpose, the size of their catalogue, the speed and accuracy with which they return results, and how current their information is. Some engines will routinely return dead links because they don't update their database regularly enough. As you begin to use search engines, you can decide for yourself which ones work best for your purposes.

Using a search engine can be as simple or as sophisticated a process as you like. Engines like AskJeeves **<www.askjeeves.com>** will take "plain English" questions and produce search results that are reasonably accurate. Or you can go a step further and use the sophisticated search forms at HotBot to delimit the terms of your search, which will produce better results. Finally, power users will want to learn about search syntax, which will allow you to specify the exact terms of your search, and enter them manually into almost any search engine window. Be sure to look at the Help section of each engine for pointers on the site's particular search syntax, because what works in one search engine may not work in another.

Anatomy of a Search Engine

So, what's inside a search engine? Two sets of components—the parts that are almost entirely automated, and those that rely on human judgement.

The automated parts of the search engine are the interface, the catalogue, and the bot or spider. The interface is the part that your computer interacts with, allowing you to perform searches on the catalogue. The interface then sorts and ranks the results to make them usable. The bot is the program that ranges around the Internet cataloguing Web sites. Different spiders do different kinds of work. Some only look for home pages, while others will follow all links leading from a given page and catalogue them as well. You probably know by now that the accuracy of the automated parts of a given search engine depends on how well the spider performs, and on how often it runs. An engine whose spider follows too few links is going to provide really thin search results. If the spider doesn't repeat its trail very often, the engine is going to return results that are full of dead links, because many Web sites change URLs from time to time. The other, human, part of the search engine is the directory. A directory is organized into a series of nested topics, which are initially very broad, and become more specific as you click down through the hierarchy. Directories often contain brief summaries of site contents as well as URLs, which will often help you speed up your search time.

Directories and search engines used to be totally separate entities, and many old-time nerds still get all persnickety if you confuse the two. Yahoo! was (and still is) the primary Internet directory, and took real pride in its difference from the "dumber" engines. But times have changed. In addition to automated search capabilities, almost all search engines now have built or acquired directories of their own (many use material supplied by the volunteer-driven Open Directory Project **<dmoz.org>**), so the distinction between a directory and a search engine is now more of an internal rather than external identifying characteristic.

So what should you use: a directory or an engine? Depends on the task at hand. If you're looking for an exemplary site on a particular topic (say, in-depth information on Labrador retrievers), use a directory. If you're looking for a number of sites on a topic, use an engine.

How Search Engines Work

How does a search engine interface deal with your query? When you enter a string into a search engine and hit the "Go" button, it looks for two things: the places on the page where the string appears (priority), and the number of times it appears on a given page (recurrence). Search engines operate the same way. If your string appears in the page's meta tags (see below), in the page title, or near the top of the page, and/or if the string reappears frequently throughout the page, the engine will rank the page highly and return it near the top of the search results. The more a page varies from those criteria, the lower the ranking it will receive.

Of course, this basic system varies considerably from engine to engine, which means that no two engines will return the same results for the same search string. Google, for example, also takes into account the number of links that lead to a site from the other popular sites in its database.

Some engines won't even return the same results if you search them through different interfaces, which has led to allegations of search engines "dumbing down" the services they sell to other sites. There's also a nasty new element to searching: some companies now pay particular engines for the privilege of having their sites listed at the top of any search results (GoTo is the largest engine that accepts payment for result placement; this doesn't necessarily make it a bad engine, but if you use GoTo, it's worth remembering that this factor will partially determine the kinds of results you get). For these reasons, it's a good idea to run any search on several different engines. As in the real world, information is never neutral.

A Note about Meta Tags

Inside the <HEAD> tags of an HTML document, it's possible to create a special type of tag called a meta tag. Meta tags have different parameters that allow the author of a Web site to specify descriptions of their pages, lists of keywords, and notes to spiders about whether or not a particular page should be indexed. You can see them if you use the "View Page Source" command in your browser when a Web page is loaded.

Some search engines (like HotBot) will give a page a slightly higher ranking if it has meta tags, on the assumption that a more careful programmer put the page together, making it, as a result, of higher quality.

```
www.terriwelles[1] - Notepad
File  Edit  Search  Help

<html>
<head><title>Terri Welles Erotica</title>

<META NAME="description" CONTENT="Playboy Playmate Of The
Year 1981 Terri Welles website featuring erotic nude photos,
semi-nude photos, softcore and exclusive Members Club">

<META NAME="keywords" CONTENT="terri, welles, playmate,
playboy, model, models, nude...">

<META NAME="rating" CONTENT="adult only"><meta
http-equiv="PICS-Label" content='(pics-1.1
"http://www.rsac.org/ratingsv01.html"  l gen true comment
"RSACi North America Server" by "terri@terriwelles.com" for
"http://www.terriwelles.com" on "1997.09.09T14:02-0800" r (n
3 s 0 v 0 l 0))'>
```

Here's a peek at the tags (edited) that got Playboy all hot and bothered (Rating: PG13)

▶INFOHAZARD

Playboy vs. Terri Welles

When Terri Welles, *Playboy*'s 1981 Playmate of the Year, launched a Web site in 1997 promoting her personal virtues, Hef and company launched a lawsuit. Welles had embedded the trademarked terms "Playboy" and "Playmate" in her meta tags, as well as using them on her site, and *Playboy* cried "infringement." The judge, however, refused to grant a preliminary injunction against Welles, feeling that the former Bunny had a legitimate excuse, and besides, the meta tags were essential to properly register her site with search engines. *Playboy* appealed, and in January 1999 Welles countersued over the company's continued attempts to curtail her use of the terms. In December 1999, the court finally tossed out the *Playboy* suit. Welles has generously revealed all the legal details on her site <**www.terriwelles.com/legal/counterclaim.html**>.

Meta tags' usefulness is limited, though. Only some engines bother to look at a page's meta tags (Lycos doesn't look at them at all), and there are no real standards for proper tag syntax. The Web is full of unscrupulous programmers who use unrelated terms or brand names and trademarks belonging to others in their meta tags in order to increase traffic on their sites (some engines are smart enough to actually rank sites lower for doing this). But meta tags do help to explain why you get some of the otherwise inexplicable results that show up in your searches.

Comparing Search Engines

Choose the Best Search Engine for Your Purpose
www.nueva.pvt.k12.ca.us/~debbie/library/research/adviceengine.html

Introduction to Search Engines
www.kcpl.lib.mo.us/search/srchengines.htm

For the purposes of this book, we've divided search engines into several different categories: major search engines (the big ones that everyone uses regularly), metasearch engines (engines that perform and combine searches from several different engines simultaneously), in-browser and plug-in search engines (a relatively new phenomenon, and one that has yet to produce a service that can match the performance of the major engines), Canadian search engines (proving once and for all that there's more to Canada than Terrance and Philip), and specialty search engines (engines for kids, news engines, multimedia engines, fee-based engines, and so on). Descriptions of each engine and its URL follow.

Major Search Engines

Like everything else in the new electronic frontier, search engines wax and wane in popularity. This is due partly to the frenzied world of e-commerce, where search engine companies are bought and sold at a dizzying rate. Sales can result in either a rise or fall in service quality. (How much does a search engine cost? On June 26, 1999, CMGI bought 83 percent of AltaVista from Compaq for about $2.3 billion. Save your pennies, kids.) The emergence of new ideas about how to conduct searches effectively is also a factor. FAST Search, Northern Light, and Google, all recent additions to the Internet, are consistently among the top five or so search engines.

The following search engines are, in approximate order of quality, the best of the lot. Any one of them will be sufficient for most applications. If you have more specific requirements, see the Specialty Search Engines section below.

> **NETHEADS**
>
> **The Haddock Directory**
>
> **www.haddock.org**
>
> A kind of alternative Yahoo!, the Haddock Directory was built by a bunch of self-described cynical British geeks. Haddock is your one-stop source for links to celebrity death pools, the Elvis Index (a scale for rating anything on the Internet against the King), gold foil-wrapped excrement, and crisp packet triangle shrines (it's too hard to explain—look it up).

Yahoo!

www.yahoo.com

Yahoo! is not only one of the oldest search sites, it's still the most popular. They believe in the human touch, employing over 150 people to catalogue and sort through the billion-plus page nightmare that is the Web. From this mess, they've extracted about a million listings that they think will be of use to you and other Web surfers. If your search string doesn't turn up any results from the Yahoo! database, the engine will supplement its listings with results from Inktomi, so in a sense, Yahoo! gives you the best of the mechanical search process as well.

Though its ability to specify search parameters is not as sophisticated as HotBot's or Northern Light's, a Yahoo! search will almost always produce a higher quality (if smaller) set of results. Why? Yahoo!, which is actually a directory rather than a search engine, is a marvel of organization. Its heavily cross-referenced collection of nesting categories allows you to move in either a more general or a more specific direction from your initial search results, so that you zoom in on your target rapidly. Moreover, Yahoo! lists entire sites rather than specific pages, so there's less redundancy to deal with than on other search services. If you're looking for one site that will contain focused information on your topic, Yahoo! is the engine that'll help you find it.

HotBot

www.hotbot.lycos.com

There's no doubt that HotBot is one of the best search engines on the Web. If you have a list of keywords that are likely to appear in the Web pages you're searching for, try HotBot first.

> **NUTS & BOLTS**
>
> **Search Engine Terms**
>
> **www.cadenza.org/search_engine_terms**
>
> The good people who run the I-Search Discussion list (an ongoing conversation about search engines, which you can subscribe to from this page) have built this useful glossary of terms relating to all aspects of search engines. They've even provided translations in French, Italian, German, Spanish, Dutch, and Serbian.

Powered by Inktomi (a massive search engine that you can't access directly, which also powers MSN Search) and Direct Hit (a service that helps search engines increase the accuracy of their results by monitoring the popularity of those results with actual users), HotBot provides more options for delimiting a search than any other service. HotBot's results tend to be markedly better than most other engines because, like Google, Inktomi uses relevance as a measure of which pages it indexes (i.e., a page's ranking is determined by how many other pages link to it).

HotBot's main page allows you to choose between various search possibilities, including logical combinations (all the words, any of the words, exact phrase), page titles, people, links to a particular URL, date, language, and multimedia content (images, video, MP3, JavaScript). If you still can't find what you want, HotBot has an advanced search page as well, which allows you to filter out unwanted content, specify page depth, limit domain types, and so on. HotBot can return from 10 to 100 results at a time.

Staying on top in the search engine business is hard work, and the busy techgnomes at HotBot are not content to rest on their laurels. If you're feeling civic-minded, help them work the kinks out of the beta version of the new HotBot at **<beta.hotbot.com>**, by running a few searches and then sending an e-mail to **<betabot@wired.com>** to let them know how well your search succeeded.

Google

www.google.com

Feeling lucky? Give Google a shot. It's not the biggest search engine, and it's a long way from providing the most sophisticated search options, but it's uncannily accurate because of the revolutionary search technology it employs.

Originally a Stanford University research project, Google uses a complicated mathematical analysis, basing the popularity (and therefore usefulness) of a Web site on how many other sites link to it. Thanks to its link relevancy system, Google can actually return results for pages that it's never spidered itself—a stunt no other major search engine can accomplish. The payoff for all the math is that you don't have to sift through mountains of bunk after every search.

The Google programmers are so cocky about the success of their engine that they've included an "I'm Feeling Lucky" button, which takes you directly to the top-ranked search result (ranking is based on how many links from other highly ranked pages point to a site).

Google also maintains cached copies of many of the Web pages it returns. Hitting the cached version will often be much faster than following the regular link, so as long as the site you're looking for isn't full of time-sensitive information, like the daily news, the cached version is the better option. There's also a neat function called GoogleScout, which will automatically scour the Web for pages similar to the result it's already turned up. All in all, Google is an excellent engine that's ideal for quick-and-dirty Web searches.

FAST Search

www.ussc.alltheweb.com

FAST Search launched in May of 1999, and has been going like gangbusters ever since. FAST was the first engine to index 200 million Web pages, and as of April 2000, has about 340 million pages listed, second only to Inktomi's 500 million. They also claim to have the fastest search time, returning results in under half a second.

Aside from the huge database and blistering speed, FAST offers a couple of other services that make it an engine you'll want to use regularly. They've got an excellent MP3 search engine, with over 1 million listings (they also built the Lycos MP3 search engine), and an FTP search engine, which will help you avoid long waits and possible interruptions when attempting to download files. What's more, they expect to have natural language search facilities soon: move over, Jeeves.

Northern Light

www.northernlight.com

One of the new kids on the block, Northern Light is already much more powerful and accurate than many of its predecessors. Northern Light will search over 240 million Web pages, which makes it number four in size after Inktomi, FAST, and AltaVista. And it's very comprehensive, burrowing deep into the sites it indexes, and re-indexing those sites once a month or so.

In addition to the basic search page, and a Power Search page that provides advanced features (including Boolean operators, nested queries, and wildcard characters), Northern Light has special search facilities dedicated to industry, news gathered from 33 different newswires, and financial investment resources. For a fee, you can also search the Northern Light collection of over 4,500 journals, periodicals, and news services. Because Northern Light is capable of grouping results into folders of related hits to help you focus your search, it's a good place to start if you have a general topic in mind and need to get down to specifics.

AltaVista

www.altavista.com

Not all that long ago, AltaVista was THE search engine: nothing could match its huge database and sophisticated search tools. It's still the third largest, with over 250 million pages indexed. Because it offers such a wide range of search possibilities—everything from high-powered Boolean searches to natural language searching supplied by Ask Jeeves—many people still swear by AltaVista, and it remains one of the busiest engines on the Web.

However, over time, the accuracy of AltaVista's search results has dropped. AltaVista searches are infamous for containing everything but the kitchen sink, making the process of sifting through the results long and tedious. Though it is capable of advanced searches, its interface still depends on the user typing long character strings rather than using a system of drop-down menus, check boxes, and buttons.

Excite

www.excite.com

Though Excite isn't as powerful as its competitors (with around 214 million pages indexed, it ranks about fifth in size, and has been in that same rank for a long time by Net standards), it returns good results in all three search modes: Basic, More (which allows you to specify language and category), and Advanced (which has some of the functionality of Boolean operators, though you can't enter them yourself). Excite's particular strong point is its accuracy—after HotBot and Google, it's more likely to find what you want than most other engines. It also helps that the results Excite returns from your search all have useful and detailed summaries of the page contents. There's also an option after every result summary that allows you to "search for more documents like this one," which allows you to focus your search with one click.

Lycos

www.lycos.com

Although it's consistently at the low end of the major search engine ratings, Lycos has made a lot of aggressive moves to improve its service over the last couple of years. They bought HotBot in October 1998, and in April of 1999, they switched over to a Yahoo!-style directory structure. Their latest move is a new partnership with FAST, which powers their advanced search page, Lycos Pro **<lycospro.lycos.com>**, and feeds some information into the main search page's results. The results are tangible, but Lycos still doesn't get to sit with the Big Boys.

Metasearch Engines

And for those of you who aren't afraid of overkill, there are the metasearch engines. These monsters will take the string you've entered into their window and submit it to a number of other search engines (including the ones listed above), then return all the results that the various engines produce.

Metasearch engines can be both a blessing and a curse. For a research project in its initial stages, they're very useful devices. If, on the other hand, you're doing a quick-and-dirty search for a common piece of shareware, HotBot, Northern Light, or even Google should be able to do the job without having to resort to a metasearch. Also, keep in mind that because search syntax differs from engine to engine, even the most carefully constructed Boolean search string may be garbled when it hits one of the sub-engines. On the other hand, if you're using a metasearch engine in the first place, you'll be sifting through so much data that you may not even notice.

Go2Net MetaCrawler

www.go2net.com/search.html

Bookmark this one right away. MetaCrawler is a Web search engine that was developed at the University of Washington in 1994, and is now operated by Go2Net. When you submit a search to MetaCrawler, it queries other search engines (including AltaVista, Infoseek, WebCrawler, Thunderstone, Google, Excite, Lycos and LookSmart), organizes the results, and ranks them according to relevance. There's also a Power Search option, which allows you to specify which of the engines you want MetaCrawler to search, and how many results you'd like returned (both per page, and per source engine). If you have a browser with cookies enabled, you can even customize your favourite MetaCrawler settings so they'll be the same on return visits.

For those who spend extended periods of time online and want rapid access to a search engine without having to clutter up their desktop, there's MiniCrawler. Only a fifth the size of a regular search interface, MiniCrawler sits unobtrusively in a corner until you need it.

You can also use MetaCrawler to search the Go2Net channels, or to access other resources, such as weather, horoscopes, map databases, and people finders.

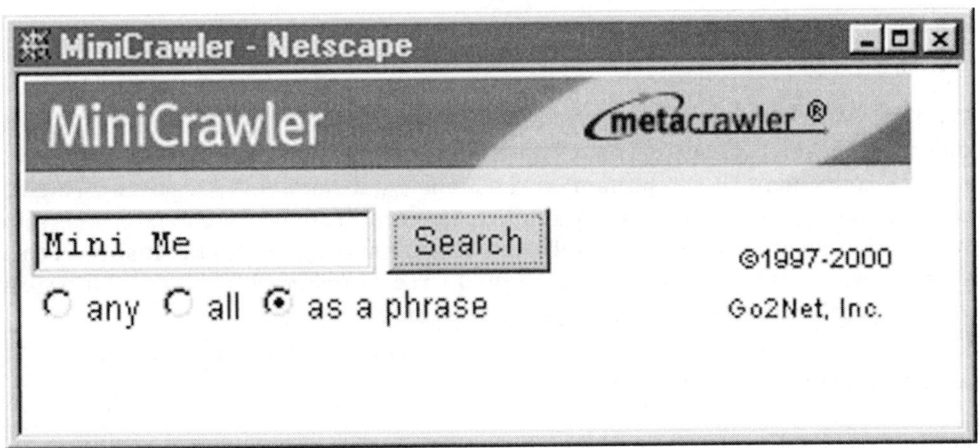

Dogpile

www.dogpile.com

In the case of Dogpile, there's truth in a name. This engine, also part of the Go2 network, searches the Web via other engines (with a list of engines very similar to MetaCrawler's), but doesn't sort the results for you as neatly as MetaCrawler does. However, you can also use Dogpile to search Usenet, FTP sites, newswires, business news, stock quotes, weather forecasts, the yellow and white pages, and a map database. As with MetaCrawler, you can customize Dogpile to use any combination of the 18 services it searches. Dogpile also has a remote mini-searcher called Arfie, which is similar to the MiniCrawler but not as tiny.

InFind

www.infind.com

Like most metacrawler sites, InFind canvasses a number of other search engines (currently WebCrawler, Yahoo, Lycos, AltaVista, InfoSeek, and Excite) for its results. What makes it especially useful is that it groups its results together thematically, in a manner similar to the way that Northern Light makes folders. When searching through the huge number of results that a metasearch engine will generate, this feature can be a lifesaver.

All-in-One Search Page

www.allonesearch.com

All-in-One scours over 500 search engines, databases, indexes, and directories (which you can also access individually). The main reason to visit All-in-One now is not to do a huge, generic search, but to get an idea of the range of specialized search engines that exist. All-in-One connects to engines that will locate all manner of things, including video game cheats, genealogy information, drug product information, business articles, online bookstore prices, and available rental properties. The mind boggles.

Searching from Your Browser

With the newer generations of Explorer and Netscape, it's also possible to search directly from the browser without first having to access an engine site. While this may be convenient, it's important to remember that neither Netscape nor IE can provide all the power or accuracy that the major search and metasearch engines can with their Advanced options. If you make a bookmark folder that contains all the search engines that you use regularly, you'll have a greater range of possibilities at your disposal, with as much convenience as in-browser searching.

That said, here's a little information on the search capabilities of your browser, which are useful for quick queries if you configure them properly.

Internet Explorer Search

When you press the Search button on the IE toolbar, a simple Search window opens on the left side of your browser window, which allows you to search for Web pages, addresses, businesses, maps, and previous searches. Pressing the "More" button will add words, pictures, and newsgroups to that list, but doesn't improve your search capabilities beyond a basic keyword search.

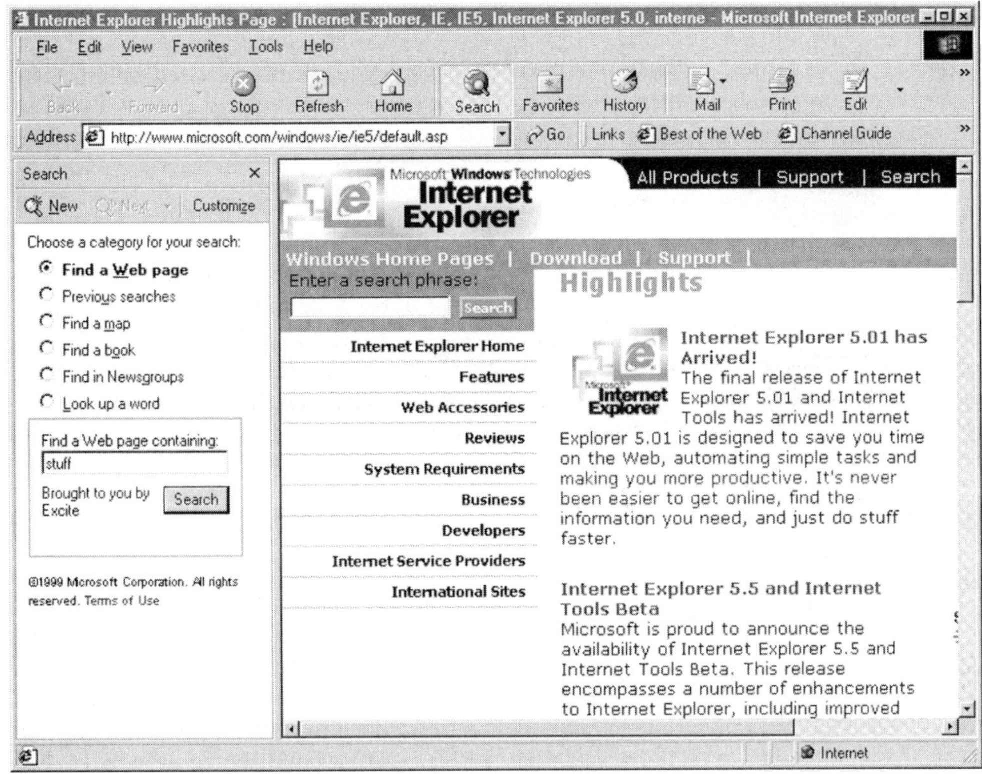

The IE5 search window

If you're going to use Explorer search, customize it first. The default setting is for the GoTo engine, but you can change that to one of 16 major engines (including AltaVista and Yahoo!), or to Microsoft's Search Assistant, which will guide you through the search process (note: if you want to search quickly, the assistant can be extremely annoying). The Customize window also contains a button that lets you control which engine powers your Autosearch settings. An Autosearch works like this: simply type the word or string you're seeking into the browser's address window, then hit "Go." The results will be displayed in your main window.

Netscape Search

With version 6, Netscape's Search capabilities are much better than they were in previous versions, but they still leave a lot to be desired. As with IE5, you can now run a search in your sidebar from one (or several) engines (unfortunately, they're all anemic, AOL-owned engines like AOL Search, CompuServe and Netcenter). The search results appear in a scrollable window in the sidebar, and the entire list remains visible when you pick a link to follow. If you don't want or need the control over your search that the sidebar offers, you can type your search string straight into the browser's address window and wait for the results to appear.

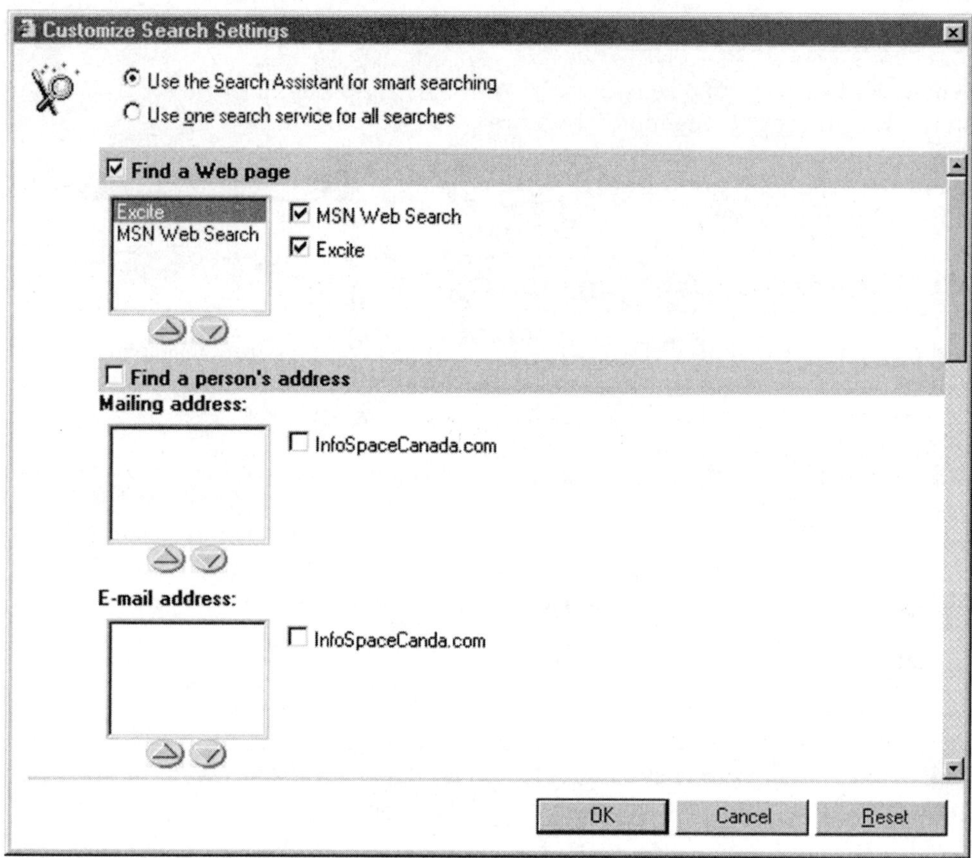

IE5 offers limited options for customizing your search

Alexa

www.alexa.com

Alexa is a free Web navigation service available for Internet Explorer. It works like Netscape's What's Related and Explorer's Links buttons, but has greater functionality. Alexa provides detailed information (such as the number of pages and links) for every site you visit, as well as ratings and reviews based on the opinions of other Alexa users. As if that weren't enough, Alexa has integrated access to stock quotes, news, the Merriam-Webster Dictionary and Thesaurus, and the Encyclopaedia Britannica. And it's freeware.

So what's the catch? Well, despite the utopian rhetoric of Alexa's founders, somewhere on the other end of your copy of Alexa (deep in the heart of the San Fransisco Presidio, no less) is a computer that's logging your surfing habits very carefully, and adding them to a database that's eventually going to be sold to whoever has the cash. It's really no more Orwellian than anything else on the Web, and the program's makers swear up and down that they don't log the surfing habits of individual users, only trends of larger groups. Like the man said, no one rides for free.

Specialty Search Engines

Why mess around with a generic search when you can sharpen your focus immediately? The Internet is teeming with search engines dedicated to special purposes. Some of them, such as search engines for kids, you may want to bookmark for frequent use. You may not use many of the others every day, but it's good to know where to start looking if you need one.

Multimedia Search Engines

There's a lot more to the Web than text, so it's only logical that someone would have figured out how to sort through the other stuff. While most of the major search engines mentioned earlier have multimedia search capabilities as well as their text search functions, there are also engines that specialize in audio, video, and still images (for information on MP3 search engines, see Chapter 3). Whether you're looking for something to spark up your Web site (check for copyright notices before you swipe something!), or are just killing time, these engines will put you on the right track.

Scour

www.scour.com

Scour is an engine that will locate a wide variety of audio, video, and image types, including MP3s, streaming Internet radio stations, and animations. You can conduct a keyword search, browse by genre, or have a look at their lists of top videos, downloads, Web sites, and features. Scour also has a good collection of downloadable

media tools, including their own proprietary formats. One of the best things about Scour is their featured videos. "Cannibalism and Your Teen," for instance, is chock-full of useful facts, such as "Some cannibals can run very fast. Others are good at math." Need we say more?

StreamSearch

www.streamsearch.com

StreamSearch is devoted solely to categorizing and indexing streaming and downloadable media files. It organizes media into channels including Music, Movies, Sports, Radio, News, Politics, Finance, Horoscopes, live events, and pay-per-view. The advantage that StreamSearch has over regular search engines is that most Web spiders do not locate actual media files, just pages that include the words requested in your search parameters. The result is usually a huge swath of non-relevant results. In addition, StreamSearch uses its proprietary technology as well as hundreds of content experts to add, modify, and update their listings and to provide accurate descriptions of their content.

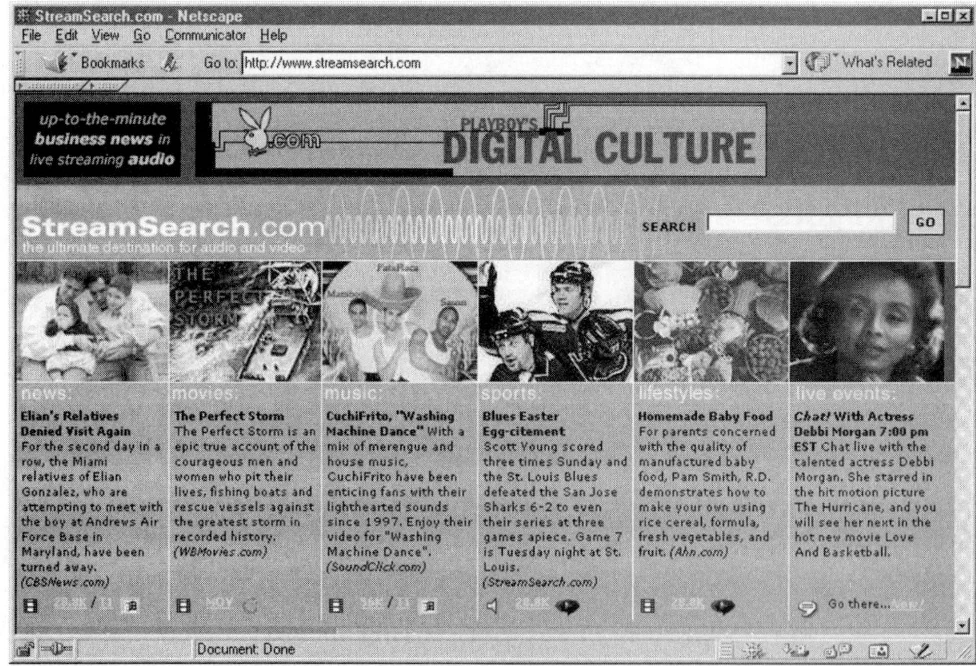

Stream Search indexes downloadable media files

WebSEEk

disney.ctr.columbia.edu/webseek

What is WebSEEk? This is the official Columbia University story: "It came in a vision—a man appeared on a flaming pie and said unto them, 'From this day on you are WebSEEk with a capital SEE.' Thank you, Mister Man, they said, thanking him."

Cheesy Beatles references aside, WebSEEk is a content-based search tool that will allow you to search for videos, colour or black-and-white photos, and graphics on any topic you specify. It returns a series of thumbnails, which you can then sort through and view at a larger size if you wish. Neat.

MovieFlix.com

www.movieflix.com

The first Web site of its kind, MovieFlix.com boasts the largest collection of online feature films that are viewable for free. Action films to Westerns, it's all here: Bruce Lee, Gumby, and other cultural icons are waiting to compete for your attention in streaming RealPlayer video. You have the option of viewing at "narrowband" (for slow modems) or "broadband" (for speedy DSL-type people), but even at high speed, it's a lot like watching one of those late-night infomercials that refreshes its image every ten seconds. Still, MovieFlix is one step closer to full video content on demand.

Kids' Search Engines

If you have kids over the age of eight and a computer, odds are they know more about it than you do. If you've got younger kids and are already bracing yourself for the time when you'll have to pry their grubby little fingers off the keyboard in order to get any work done, you'll be looking for some tools to help introduce them to online culture. Look no further—here are some of the best kids' engines on the Web.

Searchopolis

www.searchopolis.com

Designed specifically for K-12 school use, the Searchopolis engine provides a number of useful teaching aids, including tutorials on how to conduct searches, and an index of Web terms. You can also use Searchopolis to access the Microsoft Encarta Learning Zone—a slick online implementation of the Encarta CD-ROM encyclopedia.

Ah-ha

www.ah-ha.com

This filtered search engine is powered by FAST search, which guarantees quick, relevant results. Still, there's no option for anything other than a keyword search here.

Ask Jeeves for Kids

www.ajkids.com

Ask Jeeves for Kids is a "natural language" search engine whose answers have been vetted for appropriateness (i.e. it won't display anything on SurfWatch's block list **<www.surfwatch.com>**). If Ask Jeeves can't answer the question itself, it kicks into metacrawler mode and pulls results from various other engines. It's even got a voyeur window that displays "what kids are asking right now."

Yahooligans!

www.yahooligans.com

You guessed it: this is a simplified, sanitized version of Yahoo! for the 7 to 12 set. The Help files are very clear, and there's lots of basic information about the Internet in the FAQ, but you'd think that part of the function of a kids' search engine would be to teach them how to use a more sophisticated searching tool. Not a chance: it's keywords all the way here.

AltaVista Family Filter

www.altavista.com

You can configure AltaVista to filter searches for multimedia only (images, video, and audio), or for everything, including Web pages and news. This is a good option for older children who are learning how to do more sophisticated searches. The filter settings are password protected, so the little monkeys can't change them when you're not looking.

NUTS & BOLTS

What a Voyeur Sees

Here's an unedited sampling of search strings from Magellan's Voyeur.

where can i find softwaredrivers for a HP laser printer?

erectile dysfunction

+pokemon +codes+and+cheats

When was St Peter's church, Wolverhampton, built?

How can I meet Eminem?

'body jewelry'

Who invented writing?

Who makes the drug called ritalin?

Cathy Rigby

Where can I learn to speak Mohican and follow trails?

Fishnet +legs

Can I charge admission for a club and not have a public restroom?

(It's a little like going through someone's sock drawer, eh?)

Voyeur Engines

If you've ever wondered what sorts of things other people search for, here's your chance to find out. Several major engines have built "voyeur" sites, which display a constant stream of the strings that have been entered into the engine by other users. By turns hilarious, pathetic, and insightful (it's actually a reasonably good way to learn about proper search syntax as well as human nature), voyeur engines are a great device for wasting five minutes of your day.

Magellan Search Voyeur

voyeur.mckinley.com/cgi-bin/voyeur.cgi

Displays 12 randomly selected real-time searches that users like you are performing. In level two or higher browsers, the page refreshes every 15 seconds to give you a new glimpse of the myriad questions that need answering—everything from "Where can I find listings on chow chows?" to "How can I make money without working?" If something intrigues you, you can follow along and find out how Magellan responded by clicking on the item. The big question for us is, where do people learn to spell so poorly?

Metaspy and Metaspy Exposed

www.metaspy.com

Metacrawler's voyeur window has two options, one for the prudish, and the other (Metaspy Exposed) a no-holds-barred, unfiltered view of the information economy at its seediest and most venal (actually, the former isn't really all that different from the latter, but it does add a little frisson to the experience by forcing you to click through the "I promise I won't get all huffy and offended" disclaimer). Expecting the worst, however, has the curious side effect of making you think twice about even the most benign search terms.

Excite Search Voyeur

www.excite.com/voyeur_xt

This one is a little different, and therefore more interesting. The voyeur page on Excite is actually a little popup Java window that streams by the search strings ticker-tape style. Leave it open on your desktop. Read out loud from it as an exercise in Dadaist performance poetry. Amaze your family and housemates.

Other search engines offering the same trick are WebCrawler Search Voyeur **<webcrawler.com/SearchTicker.html>**, byteSearch Agent 007 **<www.bytesearch.com/cgi-bin/agent007.pl>**, which returns the last 20 submitted URLs as well as the last 20 search terms, InfoTiger Voyeur **<infotiger.com/cgi-bin/voyeur>**, and SavvySearch SavvySnoop **<www.savvysearch.com/snoop>**. For most of these voyeur sites, your browser must support Java. WebCrawler and Excite, for example, open a separate Java applet window, where the terms flow past in a fast-flowing stream of big green type, with a handy Pause button. (During the height of the Clinton/Lewinsky scandal, this question went by in the Excite window: "Did Bill Clinton sleep with Monica?" It was reassuring to know that people turn to the Web for the truth about important issues.)

Is this information useful? Perhaps not, but at the very least this brand of voyeurism offers a narrow glimpse of the online zeitgeist. Then again, people are curious by nature—if you see a crowd gathered around to look at something, chances are you'll try to catch a glimpse of it too. Randomly following someone else's lead might answer questions you didn't know you even wanted to ask. After all, asking the right question is 90 percent of the task when you're searching for something.

Advertisers, of course, are extremely interested to know what people are looking for. So are Webmasters seeking to improve their ranking on search engines. Knowing the top search terms allows them to seed their meta tag keyword lists. The Web site Searchterms.com **<www.searchterms.com>** lists the top 100 search terms from GoTo, and also allows you to search Amazon.com for related books, movies, and videos. The top word every time is "sex," though "MP3" is now right behind it. Are you shocked and appalled? Mall-Net **<www.mall-net.com/se_report>** publishes weekly search engine keyword statistics, including the top 100 query phrases. On their list, MP3 is now number one, and sex, well, it doesn't make it on the list until the number 7 slot. Times are changing.

Voyeur technology can be put to better use than seeding search engines or just plain peeping, however. By compiling search requests, tracking users, and extracting patterns of behaviour, it becomes possible for search engines to make educated guesses about your interests. When you search for a word or phrase, the engine can suggest related searches based on similar words or phrases.

Ask Jeeves **<www.askjeeves.com>** includes a window on its home page to display "What people are asking Jeeves right now." It's only a brief sample, but pushing the Ask button takes you to the Ask Jeeves to Peek Through the Keyhole page. (At the bottom, a discreet checkbox allows you to filter out objectionable questions—it's checked by default. Purely for the purposes of research, we unchecked it. The questions didn't change. Oh well, guess no one asks objectionable questions anymore.) Forgive us for being suspicious, but all the questions on Ask Jeeves are unusually articulate, always written as complete, grammatically correct sentences, and no typos. A few minutes of watching any other voyeur engine reveals how unlikely this is. And a few minutes of watching Jeeves reveals that the same questions begin to reappear. Not surprisingly, a little poking around confirms that Ask Jeeves exerts firm editorial control over its listings, so that the questions onscreen are really template versions of commonly asked questions.

Various search engines have adopted a similar strategy of posing questions for you, albeit without pretending they're random samples by other users. AltaVista **<www.altavista.com>**, for example, will sometimes suggest related searches based on the keywords you entered. Sometimes it will offer to answer a very specific question, also based on your query—in essence, the software is rephrasing your question so that it can provide a predetermined answer. That is, if you accept AltaVista's question, you will be directed to a single site (presumably that of a business partner). Another simple example can be seen at Amazon.com **<www.amazon.com>**. When you search for and find a particular title, a list of recommended books is also shown. That list is compiled on the basis of all the shoppers who shopped before you and bought the book you searched for. The recommended books are related titles that those previous shoppers also bought.

News Search Engines

Searching for news on the Internet used to mean searching through the Usenet "newsgroups," a rat's nest of rhetoric that often weighed far too heavily on the "noise" side of the signal-to-noise ratio. Now that the major newspapers are all online, and the newswires are available for searching, there's a lot more "signal" out there—if you know where to look. The following engines, which specialize in news searches, will help you pare away the dross from the relevant data.

Excite NewsTracker

nt.excite.com

This is one of the best features of Excite, an otherwise unremarkable search engine. NewsTracker doesn't just search for news, it allows you to create topics for which it will return clippings. You can rate each clipping as it comes in, which helps NewsTracker to "learn" the type of news that you're after.

Newsbot

www.newsbot.com

HotBot's news service searches any or all of eight different categories of news: business, politics, technology, culture, health, sports, world, or U.S. You can specify that your results be from the last six hours, day, week, or month, then sort it by day or relevance. There are also direct links to Wired's technology news, ESPN.com, and Mr. Showbiz entertainment news.

Northern Light Current News

www.northernlight.com/news.html

Current News provides a search of the last two hours, last day, or last two weeks of news gathered from over 70 sources, including 33 newswires and online publications. Current News also includes continually updated real-time headlines, weather, and sports. If you're interested in something more than two weeks old, it's not news, it's history, and is available through the Northern Light pay-per-document search system.

AltaVista Canada News

www.altavistacanada.com

Searching for Canadian news just got a whole lot easier. Enter your search terms as always, then click the little "News" button right below the search box.

Usenet/Web Forum Search Engines

As we were saying a moment ago, Usenet is a mess. Even if it weren't, there's so much of it (a full newsfeed is over 500 MB a day) that picking the relevant needles out of the digital haystack would prove almost impossible without some sort of search engine. If you have a question about the minutiae of a particular piece of software, mechanical device, Hollywood film, or what have you, the answer might be lurking out there on Usenet. Rather than having to go through the tedium of hunting it down, you can sometimes simply scoop what you need out of one of Usenet's many endless conversations. It's worth a shot, anyway. Most of the major search engines (including AltaVista, MetaCrawler, HotBot, and Infoseek) now let you search Usenet as well as the Web, but some of the sites listed below offer additional advantages.

deja.com

www.deja.com/usenet

Deja.com has pared away many layers of commercial crap and hopelessly convoluted pages choked with search windows, polling windows, surveys and bar graphs to provide you, the surfer, with this simple, elegant method of searching Usenet. Wasn't that nice of them?

Remarq

www.remarq.com

The former Supernews engine tracks over 38,000 different online communities, which you can search by category or through their search engine. Remarq also allows you to set up a Webmail address at their site, so that you can post to any newsgroup using their e-mail address. Why is this a good idea? Because it will keep your main e-mail accounts spam-free (Usenet is constantly being combed for e-mail addresses by all manner of bots looking to add you to their spam lists).

Forum One

www.forumone.com

The Forum One Index is not a Usenet search engine. Rather, it catalogues over 310,000 separate Web forum topics in current events, public policy, entertainment, finance, sports, society, and so on. Their database is divided into a "topic" section, which simply lists the names and URLs for forums related to your search, and a "discussions" section, which tracks many of the largest forums on the Web, including those at the *New York Times, Washington Post, Salon, The Utne Reader, Time, People,* Yahoo!, Excite, and *Slate*.

Natural Language Search Engines

Not feeling up to Boolean logic and search engine math? Well, with the following engines, you can enter your search query in normative English syntax.

AltaVista

www.altavista.com

In its quest to become all things to all people, AltaVista has picked up the natural language gauntlet. It works fairly well, too, but not as well as an Advanced Search.

Ask Jeeves

www.askjeeves.com

Ask, and you shall receive. When you pose a question—any question, not just one related to the Internet—Ask Jeeves returns answers in a framed window, and a list of similar questions with drop-down menus allows you to refine your query. In addition, Jeeves is a metasearch engine of sorts: it will include the top ten answers that it collects from other search engines along with information drawn from its own knowledge base. With every additional question, Jeeves gets "smarter," because the searches themselves have been archived. Con-

ARE WE THERE YET?

Interview with the Search Engine

www.fnwire.com/features/satire-jeeves interview.html

Natural language technology is heading in the right direction, but the horizon's a long way off. If you've ever been amused by the answer Jeeves comes up with to a simple question, you'll be howling with laughter when you read this "interview" with Jeeves by Treat Warland, editor of SatireWire.

ducting a search with Ask Jeeves is kind of a stress-free public service then: you get what you wanted, and you've added to the pool of common knowledge. Makes you feel all tingly, doesn't it?

Regional Search Engines

searchenginewatch.com/facts/regional/index.html

Ever notice that the so-called "worldwide" search engines overwhelmingly return results from the U.S.? If you haven't, trust us, it's true. If you're looking for information pertaining to a particular section of the world that's outside of the continental U.S., you might want to try using a regional search engine.

Regional engines work by filtering out all content except for material from sites with particular domain name suffixes. For example, Yahoo! Canada returns results that are primarily from sites with the .ca suffix in their domain names. Of course, not all domains in a region will end with the appropriate suffix—there are plenty of .net, .org, and .com domains in Canada as well. These sites have to be added to the database by humans—which means that a regional search engine is ultimately only as good as its search staff. Of the major search engines, Excite, HotBot, Infoseek, and Lycos all offer regional searching capabilities.

For more on this topic, see "Foreign Affairs" in Chapter 3.

Canadian Engines

Philosophical puzzler of the day: why is it that a profoundly diverse and multicultural country like Canada relentlessly asserts its national identity on the Web, that most post-national of spaces? Talk amongst yourselves. If you need more information to fuel your discussion, take a look at some of the following engines.

AltaVista Canada

www.altavistacanada.com

AltaVista now offers access to more than 14 million pages of Canadian Web content—which is 50 to 90 percent more Canadian pages than any other engine has indexed. You can use AltaVista Canada to access Canadian sites, Canadian government sites, and Canadian news. When you add access to the 150 million pages that AltaVista has catalogued worldwide and a Usenet search capability, you have an impressive database. What's more, AltaVista Canada offers search and translation capabilities in both of Canada's official languages, English and French, as well as others. You can filter search results so that you see only documents published in a selected language.

NUTS & BOLTS

Babel Fish

babelfish.altavista.com/cgi-bin/translate?

This is a good tool, and an even better toy. Remember the Babel Fish in Douglas Adams's *The Hitchhiker's Guide to the Galaxy*? All you had to do was stick one in your ear and you could instantly understand anything anyone said to you in any language. The AltaVista version lets you cut and paste text into its window, which it then translates to (and from) a variety of European languages: English, French, Italian, Portuguese, Spanish, and German. Parents with children in foreign language classes take note: this has the smell of a classic homework dodge about it.

Yahoo! Canada

ca.yahoo.com

The Canadian cousin of the perennial Internet favourite, Yahoo! Canada is the best of both worlds. You can use it to search regular Yahoo!, or Canadian sites only. As always, check out the Options, which allow you to refine your search (specify some Boolean operators, or whether to search Yahoo! Categories or Web sites). There are also links to news, weather, sports, entertainment, and other topics of national interest. Yahoo! Canada est en anglais ou en français, lequel que vous préférez . . .

Canada.com

www.canada.com

Owned by the Southam newspaper chain, Canada.com has a database of over 110 million Internet and Web documents, making it the largest Canadian search engine. Canada.com provides powerful full Boolean support, phrase and adjacency searching, date restrictions, recognition of multimedia files and other embedded objects in Web pages, and inclusion of other document meta-data, which makes it a serious contender for your regular search engine. Its access to Southam's newswires doesn't hurt either.

Excite Canada

www.excite.ca

In May of 1999, Rogers Media and Excite@Home announced the creation of Excite Canada. Excite spends a lot of time and effort on personalization technology, so it's easier to adapt the interface of this engine for your own needs than many of the other Canadian portal sites. And unlike Canada.com, which is an unapologetic part of the Southam chain, Excite Canada's news draws from a balanced selection of newsfeeds, including the Associated Press, Canadian Press, Reuters Limited, and United Press International.

The Rest of the World

Well, we can't talk about every search engine. However, the Search Engine Watch site contains links to many regional engines around the world—both independents and expansions of major engines like AltaVista and Yahoo! Nip over to **<www.searchenginewatch.com/facts/regional>** and you'll be searching the far corners of the earth before you know it.

Online Encyclopedias

Electric Library Encarta

www.iac-on-encarta.com

In one of the countless Internet mergers of the last year, Encarta, Microsoft's online library and encyclopedia, merged with Electric Library to form Electric Library Encarta (an inspired choice of name). The good news is that the resulting database of

150 full-text newspapers, hundreds of full-text magazines, two international newswires, two thousand classic books, hundreds of maps, thousands of photographs, major works of literature and pieces of art is (gasp) free to search—well, for 30 days, at least. Moreover, eLibrary Tracker will search their database for new articles on topics you select, and deliver the headlines to your e-mail address, also for free.

Encyclopedia.com

www.encyclopedia.com

Another branch of Electric Library, Encyclopedia.com provides free access to over 14,000 articles from the *Concise Columbia Electronic Encyclopedia*, Third Edition, supplemented with information from Electric Library itself. You can do keyword searches or browse through a volume-by-volume directory. Once you've found your entry, you'll notice that pictures, maps, and "premium resources"—serious articles from academic journals and magazines—will cost you extra. Which brings us to our next subject...

Fee-Based Services

The days of the door-to-door encyclopedia salesman may be numbered. The established encyclopedia companies are migrating to the Internet, and there are plenty of upstarts like (who else) Microsoft who want a piece of the action. Prices for online encyclopedias are competitive, and they all offer free trial periods, so look at both pricing and interface before you decide on a service.

Electric Library Canada

www.elibrary.ca

Electric Library Canada contains hundreds of full-text magazines and newspapers, along with newswires, books, transcripts, maps, and pictures. Some of the publications they carry in digital form are *Maclean's, Canadian Business, Chatelaine, TIME, Sports Illustrated, People*, the *Toronto Star, USA Today*, the *Canadian Encyclopedia, The Complete Works of Shakespeare*, and *Collier's Encyclopedia*. The site also houses more than 50,000 pictures, hundreds of maps, 2,000 books, and tens of thousands of transcripts from TV programs, radio shows, and government sources. This material is searchable either with natural language strings or Boolean strings, and you can specify whether you want Canadian content alone, or content from the entire Electric Library collection. If you decide to investigate, ELC will give you a free 30-day trial. After that you can pay $12.95 per month, or $89.95 for a full year subscription.

Encyclopedia Britannica Online

www.eb.com
www.britannica.com

Even the old guys are getting in on the act. The venerable *Encyclopedia Britannica* is now online, and you've got a choice: pay $5 U.S. per month or get it for free. Hmmm. The paid site **<www.eb.com>** offers a free 30-day trial period and a sample search so you can get a feel for the engine. You can search the encyclopedia itself and/or Britannica's Internet Guide, which is free anytime. Advanced searches (including Boolean operators) are possible in both the encyclopedia and the guide (but not on the sample search). The free site, a newer incarnation, offers the full text of the encyclopedia, the Internet Guide, and more. Go figure.

Northern Light Special Collection

www.northernlight.com/docs/specoll_help_catlook.html

Along with its free search engine, Northern Light has a pay-per-use document database called the Special Collection. It includes over 16 million individual full-text documents, gathered from a variety of sources including *American Banker, ENR: Engineering News Record, The Lancet,* PR Newswire, and ABC, NPR, and Fox News transcripts. The first step in using the Special Collection is searching for your article, which you can do by category or alphabetically (assuming you know the title of the article you want—the Title List can be downloaded for free and dumped into a spreadsheet or database for sorting). Before you order a Special Collection item, Northern Light will send you a free abstract of the article. If you like the abstract and decide to purchase the whole article, you can initiate a secured online credit card transaction. Most Special Collection documents range in price from $1 to $4 U.S. per article, with a few that are slightly more expensive.

. . . and the Kitchen Sink Search Award goes to . . .

We just had to throw this one in. There are search engines and services that specialize in finding just about anything you can imagine, and a few that you can't. Rather than risk further exposure to Repetitive Stress Injury from typing our fingers to the bone, we thought we'd leave you with this:

GoGettem

www.gogettem.com

In addition to being a metasearch engine, GoGettem contains links to over 2,600 search engines and searchable databases. That's 2,600 search engines, not Web sites. Revel in your choices—the freedom you demanded is now mandatory.

Search Techniques

Now that you know what search engines are and a little about how they operate, you'll be itching to put them to use. If you've been on the Internet for even a brief time, you probably already know most of the information in the Basic Search section. You can either bear with us, or skip to the Advanced Search section. Remember that search syntax does differ from engine to engine, though, so before you begin entering long, meticulous Boolean strings, check the Help page of the engine you've chosen.

Basic Search Techniques

Basic Internet searching is really a no-brainer: just type the words that you're looking for into the search engine window and hit the "Search" button. You can perform searches like this until the end of time, and at some point the engines may actually become complex enough to be able to figure out "what you really mean" despite typos, spelling mistakes, and bad grammar. However, you'll save yourself a lot of grief by learning more about how the search process works, and how you can make it work to your advantage. Read on.

What's a String?

A string is the sequence of letters and other characters that you enter into a search engine window. It contains both the words or phrases that you're searching for, and operators that instruct the engine about how to treat those words. "Who is Doctor Evil," "Doctor Evil," "evil doctor," and "doctor AND evil" are all strings.

Natural Language Queries

Confused already? Don't be. An increasing number of search engines will accept strings that take the form of a simple sentence, with or without punctuation marks. These are called natural language queries, and "Who is Doctor Evil?" is a good example. The Ask Jeeves engine specializes in answering natural language queries, and AltaVista is the other major engine that accepts them. (There are lesser contenders as well.) Though natural language queries have the advantage of allowing the timid to enter the world of searching with relative ease, they don't have the muscle that Boolean searches possess. After you've tried a few natural language queries, try a Boolean search on the same subject and compare the results.

Automatic Assistance

As search engines become more sophisticated, they've developed features that automatically assist you in your searches. These automatic features include things like the ability to search for variations of the word you entered (stemming), the display of only one page per Web site at the top of your search (clustering), and the display of related searches or the option to search for more pages like the one you've located. If you want to learn more about these features, and how you can modify them, see Search Engine Watch **<searchenginewatch.com/facts/assistance.html>**.

Burrowing

Sometimes you'll need to follow links from the results of your first search to get to the content you wanted in the first place. This act of searching from within a search you've just performed is called "burrowing" because, with each added click, it involves moving further into a search engine's data hierarchy. Sometimes you'll have to burrow more than once, or back up and follow different "tunnels" of information if you take a wrong turn. Burrowing is most common in search directories, but engines that allow you to perform related searches or look for similar pages are also good contenders for burrowing. Don't be afraid to look at some alternative possibilities during a search. You can always use the Back button or your History list to return to former locations, and you might just find that extra-special nugget of information in some place just around the digital corner from where you thought it would be.

Advanced Search Techniques

Advanced search techniques are easier than anything you'd ever encounter in an introductory Logic class, and will yield substantial rewards out of all proportion to the tiny amount of time you spend learning about them. In effect, what these techniques do is limit the number of dud sites that an engine will return by providing exact instructions about how a search is to be conducted as well as what the engine is searching for.

Quotation Marks

The first thing you can do to improve your searches is simple: surround exact phrases with quotation marks. This will ensure that the search returns pages containing the exact phrase rather than pages that contain the words in a different order, or pages that just contain both words. A search for

"Dr. Evil"

will fare better than a search for

Dr. Evil

which will also return pages about Evil Doctors in general (Doctor Doom, Doctor Phibes, Doctor Moreau, etc.), some pages that are exclusively about Doctors, some that are exclusively about Evil, and some pages discussing Doctors and Evil, which might even be about Doctors that fight Evil. Oh, the irony of it all. All the major search engines support quotation marks. Consult the Help sections of other engines for more details.

Math Symbols

The + Symbol

Adding the plus symbol (+) to the beginning of every word or phrase in your string will ensure that the engine returns only pages containing all the words and phrases in the string. Note that plus signs don't do anything to establish word order. The string

+Dr. +Evil

will ensure that both words are on every page, but it won't keep those other pesky Evil Doctors from turning up to ruin the party. To narrow things down, you might try

+"Dr. Evil" +"Mini-Me"

which will return pages concerning both the E-man and his diminutive clone. (Geek trivia: Ever notice how much Dr. Evil's logo looks like the F-Secure logo? F-Secure makes very good antivirus software, so they're far from Evil, but... Visit **<www.fsecure.com>** and see for yourself).

The – Symbol

If you're repeatedly getting something you don't want to appear in your search results, using the minus symbol (–) will ensure that it doesn't appear in any of the pages the search engine returns. For example, if Doctor Moreau and Doctor Who keep turning up in your searches for information on Doctor Evil, try the following:

+"Dr. Evil" –"Doctor Moreau" –"Doctor Who"

All the major search engines support the + and – symbols. If you're not sure about whether they'll work with other engines, consult the Help files on the engine's home page for more information.

Boolean Searches

Boolean Searching on the Internet

www.albany.edu/tree-tops/docs.library/internet/boolean.html

Boolean searches are named after George Boole, the logician (if you want to know more than that, go search for the information yourself). They consist of strings containing Boolean Operators (such as AND, NOT, OR, NEAR), which allow you to construct more powerful searches than you could with the plus and minus symbols. They're also more difficult to use and aren't supported by all major engines. They can sometimes be annoying because they don't always behave according to the dictates of common sense (that's logic for you). Most of the time, you can get by with quotation marks, + and –. But for the record, here's how Boolean operators work.

AND

Works just like the + sign, except you don't have to put it in front of the first word or phrase in your string:

Dr. AND Evil

will produce the same results as

+Dr. +Evil

Strangely enough, while all the major search engines support +, Yahoo!, Google, and Infoseek do not support AND.

NOT

As you'd expect, NOT works just like the – symbol, except you don't have to put it in front of the first word or phrase in your string:

"Dr. Evil" NOT "Doctor Moreau"

The major search engines listed in this book all support NOT, except for Yahoo!, Google, and Infoseek (they support the – sign). At AltaVista and Excite, you have to use AND NOT instead of simply NOT.

OR

The OR command does pretty much what most search engines do already: it specifies that any phrases or words in the string that appear on any page should count as a hit. So

Dr. OR Evil

will return pages with either or both words on them. You can't use OR on Google or Infoseek, but it's fine on all the other major search engines.

NEAR

Of the major search engines listed in this book, only AltaVista supports NEAR. This is too bad, because NEAR allows you to specify that a page should contain two or more phrases that appear in the same general area. At AltaVista, the words have to be within 10 words of each other:

"Dr. Evil" NEAR "Bigglesworth"

will find you plenty of links for pages mentioning the bald Doctor and his equally hairless pussycat.

( ) Creating Complex Queries with Parentheses

Using parentheses enables you to create queries with an even greater degree of complexity. Items within parentheses form a subset, as in the following example, which should return information about Scarborough's favourite son and two of his best-known characters:

("Dr. Evil" OR "Wayne Campbell") AND "Mike Myers"

Excellent! You can even nest brackets within brackets:

(("Dr. Evil" OR "Austin Powers") NOT "Wayne Campbell") AND "Mike Myers"

The mind boggles, doesn't it? The trick with Boolean commands is determining in which order the search engine will process the various operators, because it varies from the left-to-right order you'd expect. If a Boolean search isn't proceeding the way you think it should, check the Help files of individual search engines for more details.

Wildcards and Stemming

Characters that can represent any other characters are called wildcards. The usual wildcard character is *, the asterisk. HotBot, Northern Light, Yahoo! and AltaVista all support wildcard searches. You can use wildcards in the middle of a word, if you're not sure how to spell the word, or are looking for variant spellings. Remembering that Americans have a strange habit of dropping the second "u" out of "humour," you might hedge your bets with the following string:

(humo*r AND Canadian) AND movies

You can also use a wildcard at the end of a word, to cover all words formed from the same root. The following string will search for words including "Canada" and "Canadian":

Canad*

Using wildcards at the end of a string to cover all possible suffixes is called stemming. Some search engines now do it automatically, so it may not be necessary to actually use the asterisk. Check the engine's Help files for more details.

Title Searches

Because the title of an HTML document sits inside a special set of tags, it's possible to do searches for strings that appear only in the page's title. All you have to do is type "title:[page title]," as in the following example:

title:"Dr. Evil"

HotBot, Northern Light, AltaVista, Infoseek, Lycos, and some other engines support title searches (Yahoo! does as well, but requires you to use "t:" instead of "title").

URL Searches and Domain Searches

With some engines (AltaVista, Northern Light, Infoseek), you can also perform a search for strings within the site's URL similar to the way in which you can search titles. This string will search for "austinpowers" in any URLs that the engine has catalogued:

url:austinpowers

As with a title search, you can also search for URLs on Yahoo! if you use "u:" instead of "url:".

Once you've found a particularly good site, you can use a domain search to display all of the pages that the search engine has catalogued from that site. The name of this command varies from engine to engine. On HotBot, you use "domain:"; on AltaVista, "host:"; and on Infoseek, "site:" See the Help files of other engines for more details.

host:www.austinpowers.com

Shagadelic! You can also delimit a domain search by including keywords after the domain name, along with plus or minus signs to indicate whether you want pages with these words to be included or excluded from the search results:

host:www.austinpowers.com +"Dr. Evil"

You can also include or exclude particular domain names from your search:

"Dr. Evil" –"host:ca"

This string will search for pages that contain the phrase "Dr. Evil," but will exclude all sites that end with the .ca (for Canada) extension.

Link Searches

If you want to measure the popularity of a site you've built yourself, or any site for that matter, you can instruct HotBot, AltaVista, Google, or Infoseek to search for all pages that link to that page. On AltaVista and Google, you can use the "link:" command:

link:www.austinpowers.com

On HotBot, the command is called "linkdomain:" but it does the same thing. (If you have a level 4 or 5 browser, remember that you can also get this information from the "Links" or "What's Related" buttons, or through the Alexa plug-in.)

Geographical Region Searches

Most engines now let you specify particular geographic regions for your search. On the Advanced Search page at HotBot, the location/domain box will allow you to delimit your search by continent or by domain extension (MetaCrawler's Power Search page has a similar function). Northern Light's Power Search page lets you specify a particular country for your search, as does Infoseek. Check the Help files of other engines for more details.

Language Searches

Sometimes you can specify the language of the document you want as well as its region of origin. HotBot, Northern Light, and Lycos all allow you to specify a particular language. AltaVista lets you enter keywords in a number of languages other than English (and its Babel Fish option will even translate between languages for you). Check the Advanced Search page of other engines for language search capabilities.

Other Special Filters

Suffice it to say that there are lots of other filters. Every engine has its own specialties, and they're all constantly being improved, so watch for new features when you visit your favourite engines, and check their Advanced Search pages for options that you might have missed.

Understanding Search Results

Okay, fine. You've conducted your search using Boolean characters, math symbols, quotation marks, blah blah blah, and you're sitting there staring at a screen full of the entries that have been returned by your search engine of choice. Now what? The machine has done its job. Now it's time for you to do yours. You have to manually sort through the lists of results and decide what's worth investigating and what isn't. That task will be a lot less painful if you understand how the engine has organized those results, and how to extract the information that you need.

Ranking

We've already discussed how search engines rank pages (see "How Search Engines Work" above), but sometimes there's also a more literal indication of an entry's rank in your search results. When you look at a list of search results, there is often a percentile ranking that describes how closely the page in question matches the specifications of your search. The more the page varies, the lower the percentage will be. Simple enough. Of the major search engines listed in this book, HotBot, Northern Light, Excite, and Infoseek provide percentile ratings, while Lycos, Yahoo!, and (surprisingly) AltaVista do not. Google uses a bar graph, which is actually more useful than a number. Who cares if a page is a 97 percent or a 98 percent match? Remember also that in a Google search, a page's ranking has nothing to do with how well it matches your query; it's a measure of overall "worth" against the other pages in the Google Archive.

Reading URLs

The core of each search result entry is a URL (Uniform Resource Locator), or Web address. Usually, you don't have to pay a lot of attention to the URL, especially for the first few entries on your results list—just click on it and boom, you're at the site. As you move deeper into your search results, though, you'll discover that the pages listed may well be from some of the same sites that you've already examined. This is because most search engines will only place one page from a site at the top of the results list, and put the rest in later (the home page usually comes first). If you're paying attention to the URLs of the sites as you examine them, though, you can usually avoid redundancies. Try pages that have relatively short URLS first, such as:

www.austinpowers.com

Home pages usually have no subdirectories listed, or will be identified as /index.html or /home.html, depending on the server. Reading subdirectories can also help you to find exactly what it was you were looking for in the first place:

www.austinpowers.com/EVIL/EVILINDEX.HTML

Summaries

While some search engines return only URLs, most will give you a snippet of text as well, called a summary. A quick glance at the summary will often tell you if the context for your string is correct or not. The quality of summaries varies in significant ways from engine to engine. On Yahoo!, the summary has been written either by the site's creator or by a Yahoo! employee, but on most other search engines, the summary will be a reproduction of the portion of the page text that included your search string. Some engines, such as HotBot, allow you to specify whether you want full descriptions, brief descriptions, or URLs only. (The latter is a good option if you're compiling a list for someone else to investigate later, or if you have a particular site in mind, but just can't remember the URL syntax.)

Dates and File Sizes

A lot of the information on the Internet is well past its prime. How much is "a lot"? Visit Ghost Sites of the Web **<www.disobey.com/ghostsites>** and take a good long look. Suffice to say that there are more than enough abandoned Web sites and obsolete pages to clog up your searches big-time, so you should always check out any Web site's "last modified" date before you bother to surf it. This is particularly true for pages about time-sensitive or repeated events—if you're looking for information on how to get to your high school reunion and accidentally grab the page from last year that no one's bothered to take down yet, you could find yourself standing in an empty gymnasium in your best threads. Or worse. The page's date will usually appear after the summary information, indicating the last time a new version of that page was posted. Some sites (including HotBot and Yahoo!) don't include a date in their summary, but allow you to specify how recent the page must be in their Advanced Search options.

Along with the date, you'll usually find the page size indicated in kilobytes (K). This indicates how quickly the page will load—the smaller the page size the faster the loading time. Keep in mind that page size usually doesn't include any graphics on the page, which will always slow down your load time. Usually, though, page size won't be of any real concern, unless you're planning on ripping down a copy of a site for later reference, and need to fit it onto a zip or floppy disk.

Related Searches

Sometimes you don't know exactly what you're searching for, and are trying to establish how much material exists over a range of topics. Search engines can tell you that too. Most of them have a function that allows you to search for topics related to the one you've specified. AltaVista, Excite, and Infoseek all include related search links after every summary. Northern Light's Custom Search Folders are more useful. Each folder contains a number of links on a topic related to your search. A search for "Dr. Evil," for example, produces folders on subjects including Mike Myers, movies, Rob Lowe (who plays Number Two, one of Dr. Evil's henchmen), and, oddly, the British royal family. Yahoo!'s related search feature is unusual in that it returns links to recent news stories pertaining to your search. Once again, its slight difference from what everybody else is doing makes Yahoo! a truly useful service.

Refining Your Search

Often you won't get exactly what you wanted the first time you run a search query, even if you're an experienced Net researcher. Nearly all engines give you an opportunity to refine your original search after the first results have been returned. Sometimes there will be an actual button saying "Refine Your Search" or something similar. On other engines, the search window will appear at the top of your results list, with your original string still entered. Usually all you need to do is tweak your original string with quotation marks or plus/minus signs, or add an extra word or phrase. Still, you'll appreciate not having to retype your string (on that note, it's a good idea to highlight your string and hit the Control key and the C key to copy your string onto your computer's clipboard before you search, in case it gets lost or you want to enter the same string into another engine later).

Dead Ends

The Tao of Error Messages

If you went to the bookstore and asked for a book by the wrong title—say, *Peace and War*—you might be told that such a book doesn't exist. But chances are that a helpful and knowledgable bookstore employee would lead you to the Russian literature section, stop at the T's for Tolstoy (or Tolstoi, depending), and reach for a thick volume entitled *War and Peace*. But if bookstore clerks were anything like network computers, they would listen to your polite request and then simply spit out an error message: "404 – Not Found." Big help, eh? Do computers always have to speak in code? The online magazine *Salon* **<www.salon.com>** challenged its readers to improve on the soulless nature of error messages by writing something more humane. *Salon* suggested that such messages be written in the form of haiku. Readers happily responded, using simple English to convey the unfortunate truth in clear terms and to invest the message with the appropriate sentiment—"two things," *Salon* commented, "that engineers rarely provide."

Respondent Joy Rothke's haiku could well replace the ubiquitous Error 404:

> The Web site you seek
> cannot be located but
> endless others exist

While it does little to help you find the missing site, the poem offers at least a glimmer of consolation.

Translated for the real world, the message "404 – Not Found" means that the Web page you asked for has been moved, deleted, renamed . . . or never existed in the first place. Maybe you just got the address wrong. Since the most common cause is a misspelled URL, bad typists will always get their unfair share of Error 404 messages.

Unlike bookstore clerks, however, computers generally don't try to guess what you really meant. They literally take you literally. So, if they spit back the number 404, check your typing first. If your keyboard skills can't be blamed, then perhaps someone else's skills can be called into question. For example, if you didn't actually key in the URL but simply clicked on a link, then maybe the URL was incorrectly specified in the HTML code. Point your mouse at the link and the URL will be displayed in the destination bar at the bottom of your browser. If you spot a potential error, try typing in the URL yourself.

If you can't find the page by guessing at the correct URL, use a search engine to find out if the site has moved to a new location. Choose a search engine that lets you specify a date range and shows information about when the Web page was last modified, so you don't waste your time chasing down old URLs. AltaVista Advanced Search, HotBot, and Northern Light Power Search all provide this option. If all else fails, and you really need to find the missing page, then try the Archive function on Alexa **<www.alexa.com>**. You'll have to download and install the free software first. Alexa began archiving the Web in July 1996 and now contains over 13 terabytes of data stored on tape— approximately 1 billion Web pages. The Archive button lets you retrieve stored copies of Web pages that no longer exist or have changed since you last visited them—as long as the page you need was archived in the first place.

Plain Error 404 messages are less common now than they were in the early days of the Web—not because there are fewer bad typists today or because there are fewer "missing" pages (in fact, there are likely to be more of both), but because Web developers and network administrators are providing more helpful information for lost and wandering souls. You're more likely to get something a little friendlier, such as the following: "Oops! We're sorry, but the page you requested no longer exists or is in a new location." It's not haiku, but neither is it engineer-speak. If the page you were looking for was part of a larger site that still exists, then the error message may also include a site navigation bar. Instead of starting from scratch, you can now narrow your search to the present site. At the very least, the browser Location box will show you how much of the URL is still valid, and you can back up along the path name until you find a legitimate page. To back up, put your cursor in the Location box and start deleting the last part of the URL, from right to left, until you come to a slash. Then press Enter. Or go straight to the top-level address by deleting everything else, and then start looking for the page you want.

Error messages come in two flavours: numerical and non-numerical. Following is a list of the most common messages and a brief description of what they mean.

Numerical Error Messages

400 – Bad Request

The server doesn't know what the heck you're talking about. You may have typed the wrong URL or there may be a problem with the page itself. What to do? If it's really important, contact the webmaster.

401 – Unauthorized

Evidently, you don't know the secret word. You may encounter this error message if you tried to enter a site that requires a password, but you didn't give the right answer. Either you didn't fill in the blank or you typed in the wrong code word. If you're supposed to be on the guest list and you've got your invitation, try typing in the password again, carefully. If it still doesn't work, get in touch with the site administrator to find out if anything's wrong at that end. (You might also see this message if you were presented with a password screen but changed your mind and just closed the dialog box. In this case, use the Back button to retrace your steps back to the previous Web page, or blithely forge ahead by typing in a brand new URL. Whatever you do, just try not to look suspicious.)

403 – Forbidden

What part of "no" don't you understand? You aren't among the privileged few who are allowed access to the particular place you tried to go. A password won't do any good—you need the key and you'd better be a good friend of the boss. You may run up against this error message when you try the trick mentioned above, about moving backwards up the file path by deleting one section at a time.

404 – Not Found

Check your typing. The most common cause of this error message is an incorrect URL. Then again, if your keyboarding is flawless, it may mean the page you requested has been deleted, renamed, or moved to another location. Try looking for the information you need elsewhere on the same site, or try a search engine. But be prepared to accept the possibility that the page you're looking for is extinct.

500 – Internal Server Error

At least you can be reasonably certain that whatever happened, it wasn't your fault. It also means there's not much you can do except try again and hope the server was just experiencing a temporary hiccup. If the problem persists, however, and you desperately need the page, then contact the site administrator and let them know what's up.

501 – Not Implemented

You're asking too much. The server simply isn't capable of executing whatever command you've issued. The site may need to upgrade its equipment.

502 – Service Temporarily Overloaded

Come back later. The server is way too busy processing other requests to even think about handling yours. There may be too many other people visiting the site, or there may be someone behind the scenes doing site maintenance. Your best bet is to try again when server traffic is lighter—say, four in the morning. Or you could be persistent and keep repeating your request until you get through. Keep your fingers crossed.

503 – Service Unavailable

Three possibilities: your ISP's server may be down, the connection between your Local Area Network (LAN) and the Internet is broken, or your own system is malfunctioning. Wait a minute and try again. If the error doesn't go away, identify the problem (access provider, gateway, or your system) by process of elimination.

Non-numerical Error Messages

Failed DNS Lookup

Oops! Not only is the page you want not available, the whole damn site's missing. DNS stands for Domain Name System, and it's the way that computers on the Internet find each other—it's the *uber* address book. When you ask for a Web page by name, as in **<www.sympatico.ca>**, the URL is submitted to the DNS server, which translates it into the numerical IP address of the computer you're looking for. If you get this error, try retyping the URL. If that doesn't work, try again later, in case the problem is a non-responsive server. If you still hit a dead end, the site may indeed not exist anymore. It happens.

As a last resort, you can check the DNS database yourself through the Web interface at Network Solutions **<www.networksolutions.com/cgi-bin/whois/whois>**. This is the company that used to hold the monopoly on handing out the .com (as well as .net and .org) IP addresses. Now they share that honour with a few other companies, but they still keep track of things in their database. Just type the address (without the "http://www" part) in the box, and you can find out when the URL was registered, who owns it, and the name and e-mail address of a contact person.

File Contains No Data

You've come to the right place, but there's nothing to see. That is, the URL works, but the file's empty. Perhaps the data was moved somewhere else, but the site administrator forgot to change the navigation. Or you caught the webmaster in the midst of uploading new files. Try again.

Gateway Timeout

You've been disconnected, probably due to inactivity. Use it or lose it, as the saying goes. Many ISPs set a time limit—say, 20 minutes—and if you don't use your connection during that period, by requesting a Web page or sending e-mail, for example, the server assumes you're asleep at the wheel or you've gone for a walk, and it hangs up your modem for you. Once in a while, this event could be the result of server or network troubles, rather than a timeout.

Helper Application Not Found

You're trying to open a file that your browser can't handle by itself—a PDF file or a QuickTime movie, for example—but you don't have the proper plug-in. Either that, or the browser doesn't know where to look for it on your hard drive. Download and install the program you need, then restart your browser and try again. If you know you've got the program installed but it's not launching when it should, then you may need to specify the helper application in the browser settings (see "Plug-Ins and Add-Ons" in Chapter 1).

Unable to Locate Host/Server

The Eucharist and the dinner party both suffer without the host. Similarly, your Web search may falter if you can't make contact with the computer that holds the Web site you're looking for—a computer known as the host (or server). Again, your typing may be at fault, if you've misspelled the URL. Often, the server itself is offline. Otherwise, try the usual tricks for tracking down missing sites.

Site Unavailable

Pretty straightforward, although it would be nice to know *why* the site is unavailable. As always, check the URL or try again later.

TCP Error Encountered While Sending Request to Server

Transmission Control Protocol (TCP) is one of the fundamental Internet protocols, created to enable communication between dissimilar systems. This error message means your computer and the site you want to connect with are having trouble talking to each other. If the problem persists, contact your Internet service provider.

Too Many Users

Just what it says. Take a number and get in the queue (figuratively speaking), or come back later when the crowd thins out.

Finding the Wrong Page

A database programmer we know has the same name as a famous Canadian actor. When he created a Web site to promote his business, our friend registered a domain name, using, well, his own name. When the TV series *Due South* became a hit, fans of the lead actor went looking for him online, but instead of fulfilling their fantasies, they found a page by some database geek. Sympathetic to their search, the not-famous guy published a picture of their idol, with a polite notice saying that, no, this Paul Gross and that Paul Gross are not the same guy at all. The actor still doesn't have his own Web page, so our friend Paul still gets adoring, though misdirected, e-mail.

Similarly, anyone looking for the Magellan search directory, a once highly regarded site, might guess that the URL was **<www.magellan.com>**. It's not, in fact, but the owner of that URL—a major supplier of voice services to the telecom industry—has taken pity on hapless searchers and provided a link on the front page pointing visitors to a list of "Other Magellans." Alongside an image of the Portuguese navigator, a note explains:

> One problem that the New World explorer Ferdinand Magellan did NOT have was other explorers naming themselves after him and causing brand confusion. In today's world, however, his name has many positive connotations: exploration, successful discovery, new territory, being first. . . . In the spirit of exploration, here are links to a few of our better known namesakes.

Five alternative links are provided, including a mutual fund, a spacecraft from NASA, and the search engine. Unfortunately, these two scenarios are rare cases, and don't reflect the common experience of Internet searchers. More often, search queries turn up a big zero. Then what?

Alternative Routes

Maybe you're just not asking the right way (and we don't mean using the magic word—you can try saying "please" if you like, but search engines generally aren't swayed by politeness). It's like using an index at the back of a book. If you're looking for "cars" and the indexer decided to list them under "automobiles" or "motor vehicles," searching only under the letter "c" won't help. Try searching under as many synonyms as you can think of.

If you can't think of another way to ask for what you want, try the Visual Thesaurus **<www.plumbdesign.com/thesaurus>**, which creates a spatial map of related words. By clicking on words, you follow a thread of meaning and linguistic associations. Although not created specifically for Web researchers, it's an entertaining tool for finding alternative search terms. A more traditional, text-based, and less Java-intensive source for synonyms is the free online version of *Roget's Thesaurus* **<www.thesaurus.com>**, where you can browse alphabetically or categorically, in one of the six broad categories by which Mr. Roget classified the entire vocabulary of the English language: abstract relations, space, matter, intellect, volition, and affection.

Maybe you're just looking in the wrong place. If one search engine doesn't turn up the right answer, try a different one. No single search engine indexes the entire Web. Each one indexes a different subset of pages and each engine offers a different set of tools for narrowing your search. But don't stop at general search engines. You may need to find a specialty engine that indexes only the type of resource you're after, or delve into subject catalogues that cater to special interests. Looking for MP3 files? Try Lycos MP3 Search **<mp3.lycos.com>** or MP3 Box **<mp3.box.sk>** or MP3.org **<www.mp3.org>**. Searching for sailboats, swimwear, or fishing news? Try Aqueous **<www.aqueous.com>**, the search engine devoted to water-related sites. Hack and crack fans (and the authorities trying to catch them) will be interested in Astalavista **<astalavista.box.sk>**, number junkies will adore MathSearch **<www.maths.usyd.edu.au:8000/MathSearch.html>**, while DIY Search **<www.diysearch.com>** caters to underground culture vultures. As the Web expands, search resources grow more specialized. And don't forget the human element—the Internet isn't just a collection of documents, it's a community of millions of people. If you don't know the answer, someone else will. Shared knowledge abounds in newsgroups and discussion forums. E-mail makes anyone accessible.

Knowing When to Stop

The ideal time to stop is when you find what you're looking for, of course. But unless you're absolutely convinced that the information you're looking for exists online—or you're being paid by the hour to find it—you should be prepared to call off the cyber-dogs at some reasonable point, before your behaviour blurs into obsession. Some experienced researchers suggest that if you can't find the object of your search after 10 minutes, your time will be better spent looking elsewhere. If you lose your patience or find that your eyes don't focus properly anymore, then you should probably pack it in. If you start to go around in circles, seeing the same data over and over again on different sites, then you should consider it closing time.

NUTS & BOLTS

You Be the Judge

Evaluating Quality

www.delphi.com/navnet/quality.html

Here's a little essay by Walt Howe providing pointers on how to tell whether the results that the search engine has produced for you are useful or just plain trash.

Evaluating Quality on the Internet

www.tiac.net/users/hope/findqual.html

Librarian Hope Tillman's essay offers an even more thorough discussion of the topic.

Evaluating Web Sites

Faced with an impossibly large sea of information, search engines make it possible to locate pages that match your request, but they do nothing to ensure the accuracy of the sites you find. And the sites that rise to the top of the list, usually through some mathematical algorithm, aren't guaranteed to be the best ones for your needs.

Almost anyone can put anything up on the Internet. How do you know whether the information you find is accurate, well-researched, reliable, truthful? Where did it come from? Is it original? Has it been plagiarized?

Has it been "filtered" in any way—that is, reviewed by peers, verified by an authority, or edited by an editor? Measuring the "quality" of a site means more than just determining its accuracy. If the information is stale, if the design interferes with your reading, or if it's hard to find your way around a site, then its usefulness is greatly diminished.

A combination of common sense and critical thinking skills will help you separate the wheat from the chaff on the Web. Skepticism is a healthy trait, and it serves just as well online as it does in the real world. Never accept anything at face value—take the time to judge a site's reliability, credibility, and perspective. Following are a few guidelines.

- Ask yourself whose site it is. Who is the author and what are her or his credentials? Check for ownership information, including copyright, to clarify who's responsible for the content. Is contact information provided for the author? What does the URL extension—.edu, .com, .gov, .org, .net, .ca—tell you about the publisher? (Remember that anyone can hold a .com, .net, or .org URL.) Being misled in matters of fact may not have any serious consequences. On the other hand, real harm could result from following inappropriate medical or legal advice posted in a newsgroup or on a Web site. Even if the author means well offering the information, you can risk a great deal by trusting blindly.
- Does the author have a bias or express a particular point of view? Sites that seem to present information objectively might turn out to be sponsored by commercial, political, or other organizations that have a particular message to push.
- Why is the author publishing this information? Who is the intended audience? Is the site written for a popular or a scholarly reader?
- Is the material well organized and written coherently? Are the writing style, vocabulary, and tone of voice appropriate? Is it serious or satirical?
- Is the information up-to-date? Do you have the latest version of the document? How do you know? The Web can be great for getting the most recent news, often beating traditional media to the punch, but it's also common to encounter pages that haven't been updated for years.
- Does the author cite reliable sources? Are the facts accurate? Is sufficient evidence provided? What conclusions are drawn?
- How does the information compare with that given elsewhere? Can you find secondary independent sources that confirm the first? Don't hesitate to look for confirmation offline—libraries are still a good place to find useful information. Not everything has been put on the Web, and print publications often carry more intellectual authority.
- How easily can users navigate through the site? Is it well-structured to provide easy access to content? Does it have a searchable index, a site map, or help pages?
- If the site uses new multimedia features, are they used to help convey information or only to display the Web designer's abilities? Are there clear instructions for downloading and installing any required plug-ins or helper applications?

- Has this site been reviewed by a professional publication, such as a library journal or publication that specializes in the topic? Has the site been rated by a commercial rating service? Search sites like Lycos Top 5% **<point.lycos.com/categories/>** try to save you the trouble of sifting through dreck by showing you only the "best sites on the Web." The topic directory contains a selective list of "top-shelf sites rated by the Web's most experienced reviewers." Of course, there's no guarantee you'll find the information you're looking for among these highly rated sites, and it's a given that no rating service that hand-picks the top pages will ever have enough time to review even a fraction of the entire Web. So, if you go beyond those safe borders, you'll have to rely on common sense and your own critical skills.

For more information about evaluating online resources, visit Evaluation of Information Sources **<www.vuw.ac.nz/~agsmith/evaln/evaln.htm>**, a collection of links maintained as part of the World Wide Web Virtual Library.

Organizing Information

The Art of Bookmarking

Originally called Hotlinks or Quicklinks in early browsers like Mosaic, they became Bookmarks in Netscape Navigator, and the name stuck as the generic label of choice. "Favorites," the equivalent term favoured by America Online and Microsoft Internet Explorer, just doesn't cut it. "Bookmark" works better as a noun, a verb, and a concept. I mean, how do you "favoritize" a site? And besides, the term "Favorites" is too judgmental (we bookmark a lot of sites that aren't favourites, just useful), and perhaps just a little too prissy.

That said, both major browsers provide basic support for keeping track of places you want to revisit, although Netscape's bookmarking tool has at least one advantage over Microsoft for serious Net users—space for keeping detailed notes attached to each bookmark.

Why Bother with Bookmarks?

A well-maintained list of bookmarks can save you time and frustration. Rather than combing through search engine results or burrowing into subject directories again and again, you can go straight back to a site that you know has the answer because you've been there before. You might think it's easy enough to find something again simply by typing the same query into the same search engine, so why bother bookmarking it? But the truth is, you may not get the same search results, even if you repeat your search an hour later, let alone a few days or weeks later.

Because thousands of new pages flood the Web every day, and thousands more disappear or relocate to a new URL, the relevance of a particular document in relation to a specific search query is constantly in flux. Whereas the site you found the first time around may have popped up in the top 10 hits, the second time around it may plummet in the rankings, as compared to other documents added to or removed from the index. Or the page may disappear from the listings altogether. Search engines sometimes "misplace" parts of their indexes, although you'll never hear them confess to it. In mid-1998, for example, both Lycos and HotBot were rumoured to have lost millions of pages. They just went AWOL. Some of those pages have returned, but many have not. So don't trust search engines to always turn up what they turned up before. Besides, it's simply more efficient to keep a list of resource sites close at hand. Why walk all the way to the library when you can keep an encyclopedia on your desk for quick reference?

Maintaining Your Bookmarks

Here are a few tips for keeping your bookmark list in order.

- Be Organized—Rather than leaving your bookmarks in one long and gangly string, use the folder and divider options to organize your bookmarks into logical categories. You can also make drop-down menus on your browser's toolbar, make shortcuts on the desktop, make aliases in other folders, and add bookmarks to the start menu. All these options make it easier to find the link you need, and to get to it more quickly.
- Do Your Filing Now—Use your browser's quick filing option to save a bookmark in its proper folder immediately, instead of adding it to the "to be filed" pile.
- Edit and Annotate—When you bookmark a site, take a minute to edit the information. Edit the default title to make it short and meaningful. Delete initial articles so you can take advantage of the browser's alphabetical sorting function. Add a few descriptive lines about the site so you'll remember why you bookmarked it in the first place. (This option is not available in Internet Explorer.) Instead of writing the description from scratch, click on the "About this site" link that most sites provide, copy relevant lines from the site description, and paste them into the Properties box.
- Practise Restraint—Don't feel compelled to bookmark every cool site you find. Your bookmark list will start to balloon out of control, and you won't be able to find an important bookmark when you need it. And be honest with yourself—are you really going to go back and spend time at that site? Do you also collect newspapers and magazines in huge piles around the house, telling yourself that one day you'll catch up on your reading?
- Purge—Set aside time to give your bookmark list a good dusting. If you've accumulated too much junk, bite the bullet and hit the Delete key. If you can't bear to bid adieu, save your little-used bookmarks in a separate file. It's easy to reopen and search your archives later.
- Make Backups—Months of surfing and bookmarking can go down the drain if your bookmark file corrupts. Make regular backups in a separate directory.

Bookmarks or Favorites?

Why not both? If you use both Microsoft Internet Explorer and Netscape Navigator, you can easily access the other browser's bookmarks. To use Navigator Bookmarks in Internet Explorer, start IE and open the HTML file called bookmark.htm, usually located in the Netscape directory. You can access any link in the file by clicking on it. And while you have the bookmark.htm file open in IE, simply add the page to IE Favorites for fast access later. Using Internet Explorer Favorites in Navigator is slightly less straightforward, since IE doesn't store its Favorites as an HTML file. Using the File Manager, locate your Favorites folder and create a shortcut to this folder on your desktop. When you want to access any of the links, open the shortcut folder and drag the link into the Navigator window.

Later, Baby

Don't be distracted by alluring but off-topic links during a search. Stick to what you're doing, or you'll find yourself an hour later deep in the middle of a Web site that's utterly irrelevant to where you were heading in the first place. If you see a link to something you want to investigate, you can add it to your bookmark list and go back later, instead of wasting time by visiting the page now. Put your mouse over the link and right-click (hold the mouse button down on a Mac), then choose Add Bookmark (or similar command) from the pop-up menu. If you really need to take a quick look before you decide to add a site to your bookmark list, open the link in a new browser window by using the same right-click technique and choosing Open in New Window. That way, you can carry on with what you were supposed to be doing and sneak a peek at the site that sidetracked you while you're waiting for sites to load in your main browser window.

Bookmark Software

The bookmarking (or favouritizing) function on your browser works pretty well for basic record-keeping, but if you're a serious bookmarker, you may want to use a more powerful program to manage your collection. There are numerous tools available, mostly shareware, that will help you organize and make better use of your list. One popular program for Windows 95/NT users is Powermarks **<www.kaylon.com/power.html>**, which works with Navigator, Internet Explorer, or Opera. Powermarks lets you include a lot of additional information with your bookmarks, either manually or by scanning Web pages automatically, and then provides useful search tools. For example, whenever you add a new bookmark to your collection, it automatically captures keywords and descriptions from the HTML meta tags on the page, and then creates a dictionary of these words. When you click on any keyword in the dictionary, you're shown all related links in your collection. There's also a form that lets you search your bookmark collection by title, URL, or phrase. In addition, Powermarks lets you import and export bookmarks in various formats, checks for changes to bookmarked pages, and supports proxies and firewalls, including authentication. Try it for free, and if you like it, Powermarks will set you back a mere $25 U.S.

History Lessons

Remember the story of Hansel and Gretel? When the children were led into the dark wood to be abandoned by their woodcutter father, Hansel cleverly left a trail of white pebbles (and, not so cleverly, bread crumbs the second time out) behind them, so they could find their way back home again. Learning their lesson from this fairy tale, browser makers included their own version of the white pebbles. Whether or not you choose to bookmark a site, your browser remembers where you've been. By automatically keeping a list of all the pages you've viewed, the History list lets you to retrace your steps. To view the entire History list in Navigator, look under Window > History. In Internet Explorer, the menu path is View > Explorer Bar > History. The browser's Location or Address bar also contains a shorter drop-down History list of sites you've keyed or cut-and-pasted into the address field. And a list of sites you've visited only during your current browser session is accessible via the Go (or View > Go To) menu.

When you want to retrace your steps without backing up one site at a time, the History list lets you jump directly to a previously visited spot. It's also helpful if you forget to bookmark a site—both major browsers allow you to add the URL to your bookmark list without actually revisiting the site. You can easily search, sort, and edit the History list. You can also specify in your browser preferences how many days you want items to stay on the list before thay are automatically deleted—that is, before your white pebbles turn into bread crumbs and get eaten by hungry birds.

Saving Web Pages

Sometimes you may want to save a copy of a Web page to disk, so that you can read it offline and cut down on connection costs. Unless it's 100 percent text, the page you see in your browser is made up of many different elements, held together by HTML. You need to save each item in order to reconstruct the entire page when you look at it later.

All the different bits, including images, style sheets, audio and video files, and even Java and ActiveX applets, are linked to the main page through the HTML. These elements may be stored individually in different directories, on other computers, and perhaps even other Web sites, so saving a local copy of a single page can be complicated. Even if you capture the HTML and images from a simple page, the HTML references probably won't point correctly to the image files you've saved.

However, there are several ways to grab a whole working page. Version 5 of Internet Explorer will do the work for you, with a new Save As feature that puts all the components in a separate file and rewrites the HTML so all the references point the right way. The Favorites feature lets you specify how much content you want to download—just a single page or a page and all its links—and choose how you want to update that content on your computer. If you have Outlook Express 5 or later, you can also choose Web Archive to save all the information needed to display the page as a single MIME-encoded file, which takes a snapshot of the current Web page.

If you're not completely up-to-date with the latest browser, you should still be able to save Web pages both as plain text (all the words without the formatting) or

HTML. If you want the images as well, you must save them individually. Right-click (or hold the mouse button down on a Mac) on each one, and choose Save Image As or Save Picture As from the pop-up menu. You'll have to edit the HTML file to point to whatever folder you save the images in. This process is a little too labour-intensive for most people, and not everyone wants to go as far as learning how to edit HTML just to save a few Web pages. Luckily, there are software programs that will capture whole Web pages and even entire Web sites. More powerful than the built-in features on Internet Explorer 5, these utilities let you annotate, organize, search, and send archived sites to other users. Among the dedicated offline offerings are CatchTheWeb **<www.catchtheweb.com>**, WebWhacker **<www.bluesquirrel.com>**, and WebZip **<www.spidersoft.com>**.

Similarly, some Web creation tools, such as recent versions of Microsoft FrontPage, Macromedia's DreamWeaver, and Allaire's HomeSite, will import entire sites for you, although they aren't designed for research purposes or equipped with the same functionality as offline browsers.

Printing Web Pages

Web pages weren't designed for printing. They were designed to look good in your browser. Nevertheless, if you have a fetish for the paper object, you can still print most Web pages. And, of course, both major browsers give you a handy Print button. Just don't be surprised if the resulting output isn't an exact replica of what you see on screen. Some sites acknowledge the problem and help you out a little by providing a second, printer-friendly version of their articles. But this nicety is not common enough to rely on. If you're interested only in the basic information, you can highlight, copy, and paste the text into a word processing program and print from there. This won't work on some pages that use Java or ActiveX applets to display text. In this case, you may be able to use View Source to reveal the raw HTML, and simply highlight and copy the text from that window. To print the original Web page, click the Print icon on your browser toolbar, or choose File > Print from the menu. This is just like printing out a text document from a word processing program. Some pages, however, don't print very well, particularly if they use coloured type on patterned backgrounds. You may have to set your Preferences to black type on a white background.

Other common printout problems can be fixed by adjusting the settings in your browser's Page Setup dialog box. Netscape offers several options, including support for printing beveled lines, black text, and even backgrounds. The same Netscape dialog box provides useful options for including page headers (document title and URL) and footers (page number, page total, and date printed), as well as setting margin widths. Internet Explorer's Page Setup options also allow you to set margin widths and to specify header and footer information, although the latter requires you to use code. The default header code, for example, is "&w&bPage &p of &P," which means window title, current page number, and total number of pages, along with instructions to centre the page numbers and include the words "Page . . . of." The system certainly permits a greater level of control over header and footer information, but you must master the geekspeak first. Look in the Help file for detailed instructions, or click on the tiny question mark in the top-right corner of the Page Setup dialog box, then click on the headers and footers feature to bring up a chart.

Printing is a bit trickier when the Web page uses frames. With Netscape, you can print only one frame at a time, which means you can't reproduce the whole framed document as it appears in your browser. Click on the frame you want to print, then choose Edit > Print Frame from the menu. Alternatively, you can right-click on the frame, choose Open Frame in New Window, and then print it as you would a regular Web page. Recent editions of Internet Explorer offer more sophisticated options for dealing with frames. When you choose Print, the dialog box includes three options under Print Frames: as laid out on screen, only the selected frame, or all frames individually. All three choices are nicely illustrated with a coloured diagram. Two other Internet Explorer options allow you to print a table of links or print all linked documents. Choosing the latter could be dangerous, depending on how big the Web site is. Finally, IE also lets you print to file. That means creating and saving a .prn or .ps file, which can later be physically printed by sending it to your printer.

Citing Internet Sources

At a minimum, Internet sources should be identified in formal citations by author, title, and date, as well as location (URL) and/or document type. But there are many variations on how this information can be presented, just as there are many style options for citing printed material. Since the Internet is always in flux and documents can change frequently, the citation date is particularly important. A Web page may include the date when it was last updated, equivalent to the publication date. If it doesn't, you should use the date you looked at the page. In either case, clearly state which date you're using.

The University of Alberta Libraries provides a discussion of style issues and a list of both print and online resources in Citation Style Guides for Internet and Electronic Sources **<www.library.ualberta.ca/library_html/help/pathfinders/style/style.html>**. The list points to style guides that follow various recognized authorities, including the Modern Language Association (MLA), American Psychological Association (APA), and International Organization for Standardization (ISO).

Another excellent resource is Library and Information Science: Citation Guides for Electronic Documents **<www.ifla.org/I/training/citation/citing.htm>**, published by the International Federation of Library Associations and Institutions.

Copyright Concerns

Contrary to popular belief, publishing something on the Internet doesn't mean relinquishing copyright—it only makes it easier for someone else to abuse that copyright. Online publications are just like any other creative work, which means that it's illegal to republish them without getting permission from the copyright holder. This rule applies to writing, graphics, music and sound files, and any other element of a Web page. For more information about Canadian copyright, visit the Canadian Intellectual Property Office **<cipo.gc.ca>**. CIPO is responsible for the administration and processing of the greater part of intellectual property in Canada. CIPO's areas of activity include patents, trademarks, copyrights, industrial designs, and integrated circuit topographies. Copyright and Fair Use **<fairuse.stanford.edu>** is a comprehensive information site sponsored by the Council on Library

NETHEADS

Copyright Champions

www.terla.com

TERLA, The Electronic Rights Licensing Agency, is the proverbial Good Guy of the Internet. TERLA's mandate is to ensure that Canadian writers, photographers, illustrators, journalists, and other content creators don't get screwed by big corporations out to make a fast buck.

Resources, FindLaw Internet Legal Resources, and the Stanford University Libraries and Academic Information Resources.

It is important to note here that Canadian copyright law uses the term "fair dealing" rather than "fair use" when referring to the copying of material. The two terms are not identical. U.S. use is far broader than Canadian use. In fact, the Canadian definition is more like a defence to be used in a copyright violation suit, rather than terms under which material can be used. For Canadian information about copyright law, check out the site maintained by Lesley Ellen Harris **<www.copyrightlaws.com>**, author of *Canadian Copyright Law.*

Where to Learn More about Search Engines

Search engines are as competitive as any other marketing- and technology-driven business on the Web, and so they are constantly in flux—adding new features, forming new partnerships, primping themselves to be your portal-of-choice. They continue to be essential tools for navigating the online world, so the more you know about them, the better. Following are a few tips for improving your knowledge of search engines and staying abreast of the constant changes.

Help Files

If you have questions about a particular search engine, the first place to look for more information is the help file provided by the engine itself. After all, who should know more about how a particular tool works than the toolmaker? All the same, the help files of the major search engines are not equally helpful. Here's a brief outline of what to expect.

AltaVista **<www.altavista.com>** advises you on using its two search windows, Basic and Advanced, as well as its Refine Results feature (a tool that dynamically sorts your results into different topics to help you polish your keyword searches). The Basic instructions include an intro to using keywords, phrases, and some of the radio-button options, natural language searching, special characters and punctuation, and the various "fancy features" that let you look for matches in page titles, domain names, and other aspects beyond the regular text. Advanced help explains Boolean operators, relevance ranking, and date ranges.

Deja.com **<www.deja.com>** offers a very generous collection of help pages, from general FAQs about Deja and Usenet to specific search advice, as well as a glossary and a new user tour.

Excite **<www.excite.com>** provides brief answers to simple questions, rather than in-depth explanations. There are a few General and Advanced Tips, guidance for interpreting Search Results, a very short list of Error Messages, and an introduction to the Search Wizard, a tool that suggests words closely related to your search subject. Not much to get excited about.

FAST Search **<www.ussc.alltheweb.com>** doesn't pander to new users. The word "help" doesn't appear anywhere on the home page. Instead, a four-line set of examples immediately below the search box illustrates the available operators for key word and phrase searching. The FAQ files provide a few clues, as well as a fair amount of background information about the technology, including their Pattern Matching Chip, but aren't intended as user guides. FAST MP3 and FTP searches conducted as part of the Lycos network are supported by more extensive help files, although they read like an engineering manual.

HotBot **<www.hotbot.com>** offers both basic search tips and extensive help for its advanced searching features, including Boolean operators, query modifiers, meta words, wildcards, and case-sensitive searches. The language is hip and friendly.

Infoseek **<www.infoseek.com>** provides very detailed How to Search instructions, complete with examples, a couple of Quick Reference tables, explanations of Advanced search options, definitions, help with interpreting search results, an overview of search features, advice on dealing with "inappropriate content," and a searchable help database.

Lycos **<www.lycos.com>** walks you carefully through the basics of searching, helps you interpret Search Results, instructs you on finding and using pictures and sound, and provides pointers on building search expressions in Lycos Pro Search Tips. In addition, there are links to help files for other specialized searches offered through the Lycos Network (people finder, yellow pages, roadmaps, and so on).

The Optimize Your Search page provided by Northern Light **<www.northern light.com>** delivers straightforward advice on Boolean operators, search symbols, truncation, wildcards, and field searching, as well as tips on power searching. Three versions of a Quick Reference Card are provided for viewing onscreen or printing out. Help files are also available for each of the special content areas, and for using Northern Light's custom search folders.

WebCrawler **<www.webcrawler.com>** offers basic tips and shortcuts, advice for improving your results, and a few examples of Boolean queries for "advanced" searches.

The Yahoo! **<www.yahoo.com>** help pages are presented as an entire how-to-use-the-Internet guide **<howto.yahoo.com>**, including a How to Yahoo section with general search advice aimed at novices. Help Central **<help.yahoo.com>** covers all the portal features that Yahoo! has to offer, from Address Book to Yellow Pages.

Web Sites and Newsletters

Newsletters are an invaluable resource for staying alert to the ever-evolving world of search engines. Most newsletter authors also maintain a Web site where you can sign up for e-mail delivery, read back issues, and find other resources. Following are a few of the top tipsheets.

The helpful Glossary of Search Engine Terms **<www.cadenza.org/search_engine_terms>** covers the full range of specialized language used by search engines. There are links to all the major search sites on the Web, and the glossary is available in English, Dutch, French, German, Italian, Serbian, and Spanish.

The I-Search Discussion List **<www.audettemedia.com/i-search>** is a free twice-weekly e-mail discussion list moderated by Detlev Johnson, Director of Search Engine Optimization Services at Outrider. The discussion focuses mostly on issues of concern to Web developers—methods to improve relevancy rankings, problems with listings, search engine news, and so on—but the information is helpful for searchers too. The site maintains a searchable archive.

Online Inc. **<www.onlineinc.com>** has a regular feature called "Internet Search Engine Update," outlining new search features, developments, and content. It's written by librarian and Web researcher Greg Notess, who also maintains Search Engine Showdown **<www.searchengineshowdown.com>**, a review site covering search features, statistics, and comparisons.

ResearchBuzz **<www.researchbuzz.com>** started in April 1998 as a companion site to *The Official Netscape Guide to Internet Research*. The book's author, Tara Calishain, includes a handful of Quick Tips and longer articles, and a searchable collection of research resources. The ResearchBuzz newsletter (formerly Internet Research News), which delivers fresh gossip every Thursday, can be read onsite or delivered to your e-mail box.

Search Engine Report **<www.searchenginewatch.com/sereport/index.html>** is a monthly newsletter edited by journalist and consultant Danny Sullivan. It's the companion to Sullivan's news and information site Search Engine Watch. Sign up at the site, or read back issues online.

Web Search Newsletter **<websearch.miningco.com/library/blnl/current.htm>** is published twice monthly by Chris Sherman. This free newsletter, available on the Web site or by e-mail subscription, features highlights of current search-related news stories, reviews search software and tools, and updates on new Web search links. Sherman is the author of Guide to Web Search on About.com (the reincarnation of the Mining Company), and his site offers an extensive collection of articles and resources, as well as a Web Search Forum for talking about search issues and sharing tips. You can read the forums anonymously, but you must register (for free) to participate in the discussions.

Online Tutorials

The Teaching Library at UC Berkeley offers Finding Information on the Internet: A Tutorial **<www.lib.berkeley.edu/TeachingLib/Guides/Internet/FindInfo.html>**, with beginner, intermediate, and advanced sections.

Despite the apparent simplicity of Boolean logic, it's all too easy to write poorly constructed queries and produce totally useless results. Boolean Searching on the Internet **<www.albany.edu/library/Internet/boolean.html>** serves up an illustrated introduction to narrowing and refining your search with Boolean operators.

The developers of Mata Hari, a sophisticated offline metasearching agent, provide an in-depth, 12-part tutorial called Power Searching 101 **<thewebtools.com/searchgoodies/tutorial.htm>**, which includes the use of keywords, advanced operators and query construction, pitfalls to avoid, and a comparison of the major search services.

Future Trends

Talk about information overload. The Web is swelling by roughly 2 million pages a day. How can you retrieve relevant, high-quality pages using today's limited search engines from the unstructured, chaotic soup of knowledge, propaganda, and complete nonsense that is the Web? The next generation of search engines must find more effective methods for focusing on the most authoritative documents. Used at its full potential, search technology, coupled with an intelligent navigation system, can take users beyond the current list-generating technologies into the brave new world of "knowledge discovery." Here are a few new ideas in development.

> **ARE WE THERE YET?**
>
> **Universal Soldiers**
>
> **www.darpa.mil/baa/baa00-34.htm**
>
> Science fiction is the new social realism. The Defense Advanced Research Projects Agency (DARPA) is now soliciting innovative research proposals on Exoskeletons for Human Performance Augmentation (which, in their own inimitable way, they call EHPA). The overall goal of this program is to develop self-powered, wearable exoskeletal devices for soldiers in combat environments. If you aren't all that you can be, don't worry: DARPA will just weld some stuff onto you and everything will be fine.

Text Mining

Text mining examines textual information to discover structure and implicit meanings buried within the text. By identifying this structure and meaning, it can create a useful index that allows information to be retrieved through search technology.

To address the problem of information overload, Semio Corporation **<www.semio.com>** developed a tool that lets you navigate through mountains of text using a concept map. SemioMap **<demo.semio.com/public/discover.cgi>** creates a three-dimensional representation of individual topics in the source material, represented by nodes in a visual map. Related topics are linked by lines between nodes, which may in turn be linked to several different maps. These shared nodes connect the maps into a "world."

SemioMap has already been deployed by big business for research and development, competitive intelligence, and customer service applications. Turning to the Web, Semio has built a new text-mining tool called Semio Taxonomy **<demo.semio.com/semio3/cattaxonomy.cgi>**, which enables portals and corporations to automatically create browsable directories from their content, so they can find what they want more easily.

Information Topography

Cartia **<www.cartia.com>** takes the information "mapping" idea literally. Their ThemeScape software automatically organizes document collections into an interactive landscape of information—a topographical map—that shows you what's inside documents and Web pages. The greater the similarity between any two documents, the closer together they appear on the ThemeScape map. Peaks appear where several documents about the same topic are concentrated, and the distance between peaks shows how closely the topics are related.

Its developers claim that ThemeScape gives you the ability to scan 1,000 daily news articles in less than a minute. In truth, ThemeScape is visually reminiscent of map-based board games like Risk, and learning to effectively navigate these new

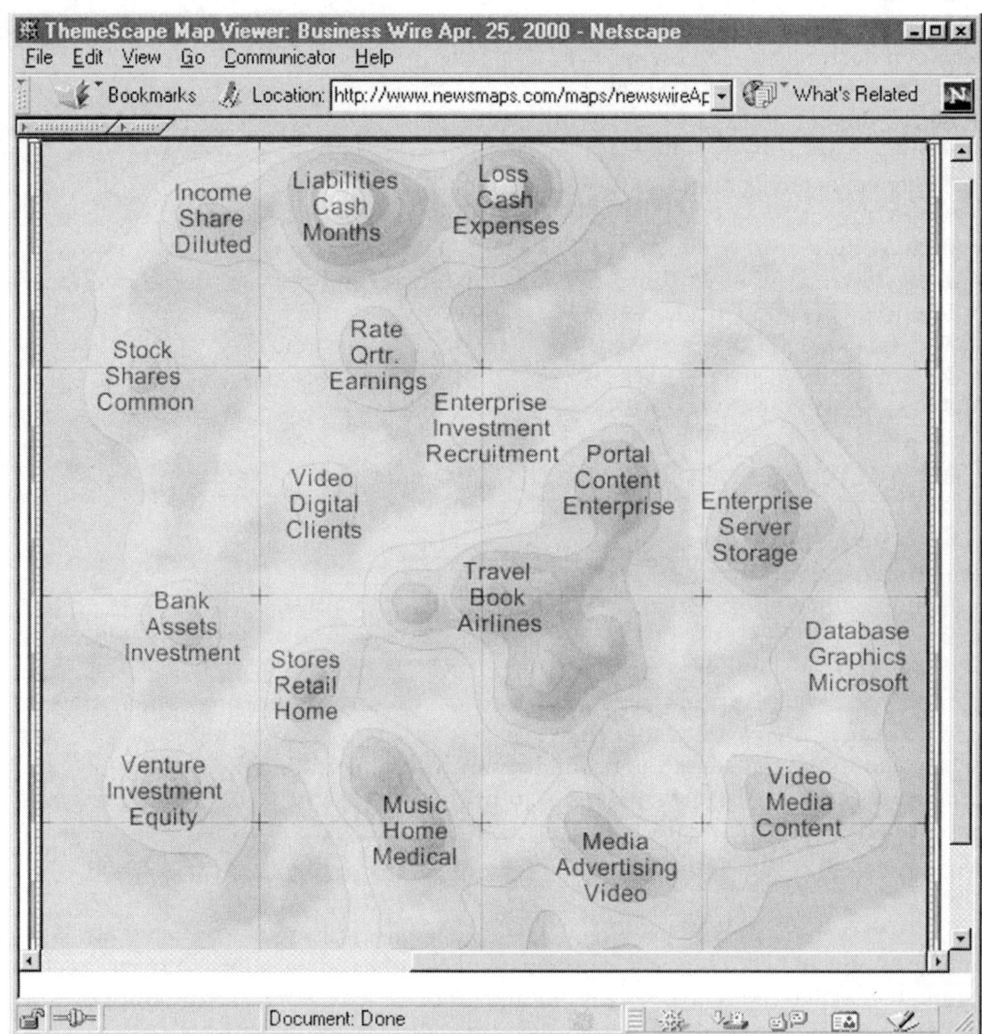

The NewsMaps rendition of daily updates of technology, business, and finance press releases from Business Wire

information landscapes will require a similar grasp of strategy and knowledge of the ground rules. A Quick Tour and two demonstration maps are available on the company site, but if you want to see the technology in action on a live site, visit NewsMaps **<www.newsmaps.com>**.

Relativity Theory

The Web's staggering volume of information is loosely bound together by billions of hyperlinks, and scientists at the IBM Almaden Research Center in San Jose, California, have come up with a way to exploit this structure of interconnections. They call it the Clever Project **<www.almaden.ibm.com/cs/k53/clever.html>**. Current search engines use indexing and retrieval schemes that rely solely on the text and largely ignore the hyperlinks. But it's the hyperlinks that reveal relationships between documents. The Clever approach relies on the underlying assumption that every link is an implicit endorsement of the page it points to. The Clever engine analyzes the connections and automatically locates two types of pages: authorities and hubs. Authorities are the best sources of information on a particular topic, and hubs are collections of links to those locations. This method enables users to quickly pinpoint the information they need. The approach is similar to that of Google! **<www.google.com>**, which also draws on the power of hyperlinks to impose a ranking system, although there are some significant algorithmic and philosophical differences between Google! and Clever. The Clever Project is still in development, so you can't take it for a test spin yet, but you can read more about it in the Scientific American article "Hypersearching the Web" **<www.sciam.com/1999/0699issue/0699raghavan.html>**.

Semantic Space: The Final Frontier

Oingo **<www.oingo.com>** approaches the problem of inaccurate returns through something called "meaning-based search." Going beyond simple text character matching, Oingo attempts to narrow the context by first running your search terms through their own database-enabled lexicon of word meanings and relationships. When you enter your keywords, alternate and/or refined choices are offered, and you pick the most appropriate match. Rather than maintain its own directory of indexed pages, however, Oingo draws on Netscape's Open Directory Project for its demo, and hopes to license the technology to other sites. Still in beta, Oingo asks for user feedback to assist their team of lexicographers. Another engine still in beta, Simpli **<www.simpli.com>**, works on a similar premise.

Beyond Words

You probably noticed, but the Web ain't just words and pictures anymore. Audio and video files are a regular feature on news sites, not to mention the sea of music samples and full-length recordings available in the wake of the MP3 revolution. The experimental SpeechBot **<speechbot.research.compaq.com>** is an audio search engine from Compaq that indexes popular U.S. radio shows via speech-recognition technology. Less reliable perhaps than indexing written transcripts, it nonetheless augurs well for the multimedia-intense Web of the future. The search results include a text sample and a link to the precise audio segment. Pretty cool.

Next up: Now that you know how to rev your search engines, let's take a look at some of the sites worth finding. Chapter 3 recommends a few itineraries for your online travels.

THREE

ITINERARIES ▶

> The rise of the MP3 is a watershed event in net history, revealing the ways in which the Internet is transforming both culture and commerce.
>
> *Jon Katz in "i want my mp3,"* Shift

Now that you can operate your browser, and you have a solid grip on how to conduct searches, you're ready to venture out onto the Net. But if you don't know what's out there, where will you start? This chapter steers you towards some of the more popular destinations on the Internet—sites that will in turn lead you on to other sites. So: pick a heading that interests you and start surfing.

Information

Canadian Portals: CanConLine

Part of the problem with being a Canadian on the Internet (or anyone other than an American, for that matter) is figuring out how to work around all of the "universal" content that inevitably turns out to be U.S.-specific: newswires, zip code and telephone search services, weather, maps, et cetera. If you're a Canadian and you want any of this sort of information to pertain to you in a direct way, you'll need to use a Canadian portal. Here are a few of the major Canadian portals, and some information on the services they offer.

CANOE

www.canoe.ca

Since its launch on March 4, 1996, CANOE (the CANadian Online Explorer) has developed into one of Canada's leading news and information sites. In addition to their brand-name news services (SLAM! Sports, JAM! Showbiz, CNEWS, Money, CHealth, and AUTONET.CA), CANOE offers exclusive online editions of many daily newspapers from across the country. You can also check out national TV and movie listings, daily weather, stock market and sports scoreboard updates, horoscopes, lottery results, comics, crosswords, concert listings, and travel information. If you feel like participating directly, CANOE has reader forums, polls, and regular contests.

▶INFOHAZARD

Big Mother Is Watching You

www.kola.net

Kids Online America, or KOLA, is concerned about what your children will find on the Internet (did anyone see the MadTV "I Love Lucy" parody where Lucy ends up murdering one of Ricky's musicians because she thinks he's "The Internet Pedophile"?). KOLA's CEO, Steve Valerie, says, "I'm an eligible bachelor. The Internet is so fraught with risks that I've hesitated to bring my own kids into the world." While we think he's overstating the case just a touch in order to shill his wares, there are those who believe there's an argument to be made for limiting your children's access to the Net. KOLA's answer is a system that replaces your regular user interface with a standard, locked proprietary connection to five different "worlds" for different age groups, with restricted parameters governing Internet content. The software also allows parents to add acceptable sites and e-mail buddies to their children's online experience. Sounds like AOL.

You can also personalize CANOE through the "My CANOE" feature, which allows you to specify that particular services will be available instantly as soon as you open your browser. Overall, CANOE is the best Canadian portal choice for people who already have dial-up, and are after fairly conservative (sports and light news-focused) content.

CANOE also has great Web search capabilities, allowing you to quickly and easily toggle between AltaVista, AltaVista Canada, Infoseek, Yahoo!, Yahoo! Canada, Excite, and HotBot. Access to the Canadian yellow and white pages is also on the same page.

Canada.com

www.canada.com

Canada.com quaintly bills itself as "Your Canadian Search Engine," but its Inktomi-powered database holds 10+ million documents. Canada.com also provides free e-mail, news from the far-reaching Southam chain, weather from The Weather Network **<www.theweathernetwork.com>**, financial information, TVTimes, travel services, lottery results, horoscopes, career and car resources, a people finder and business directory (both via InfoSpace **<www.infospace.com>**), and plenty of shopping. Canadian business community, take note: in addition to the site's specialization in financial news, Canada.com maintains the Hello Yellow business directory, which has about 1.2 million records, and is updated twice a year. No chat or discussion forums, though. At least, not yet.

Sympatico

www.sympatico.ca

Unlike the other portals listed here, Sympatico is also an ISP (Internet service provider), with over half a million subscribers. If you don't have dial-up service yet, and are after an approach to content that's more liberal than CANOE, Sympatico is a compelling portal choice. Only subscribers get access to e-mail, Webspace, and customized home pages, but anyone can access the Sympatico sites and use most of their facilities, which include access to national and international news, yellow pages and directory assistance, digital greeting cards, weather, horoscopes, and discussion forums.

The real test of a portal is its search facilities, and Sympatico passes with flying colours. Sympatico's built-in Web search will let you choose between HotBot, Canada.com, Looksmart, or Lycos.

Yahoo! Canada

www.yahoo.ca

Do you consider yourself a Yahoo? If the GeoCities story didn't turn you off Yahoo! completely, Yahoo! is still a great choice for a portal. In addition to instant access to the phenomenal Yahoo! directory, you can get a customized start page, free e-mail, a personal online address book, access to the Yahoo! Messenger (which pages your friends and lets you chat with them if they're online), and opportunities to bid on items in the Yahoo! auction. There's also the usual news, sports, and weather.

Foreign Affairs

English-speaking Internet users currently account for 54 percent of people online. By the year 2005, six out of ten Internet users will speak a language other than English, according to a June 1999 report by Computer Economics **<www.computereconomics.com>**. And while the number of English-speaking Internet users is predicted to rise by 60 percent within the next five years, the number of non-English-speaking users will jump by 150 percent. That means an increase in the number of multiple-language sites. On many sites, English will not be the default language—it may not even be offered as an option at all.

What does the internationalization of the Web mean for users and developers?

From a technical standpoint, the online world has a lot of catching up to do. HTML is the lingua franca for publishing hypertext on the World Wide Web, and to be truly international it must support all the characters and symbols of all the world's languages, which number in the tens of thousands. Until very recently, however—up to and including version 3.2—the official HTML standard was ISO 8859-1 (or Latin-1), an eight-bit character set that supports only the 200-odd characters common in Western European languages. Not quite enough for a supposedly "global" communications Network, to say the least.

Fortunately, the most recent "definitive" iteration of HTML, version 4.0, has adopted a new character set, which includes a 16-bit (65,536-character), Unicode-equivalent subset called the Basic Multilingual Plane that will do the trick nicely. This is one of many steps being taken by the computer industry to internationalize the Internet, a coordinated effort led by the World Wide Web Consortium **<www.w3.org/International/Overview>**.

▶NETHEADS

Mahir "I Kiss You!" Cagri

members.xoom.com/primall/mahir

Last year's 15 minutes of Netfame went hands-down to Mahir Cagri, Turkey's answer to Forrest Gump. After his homespun home page was posted, featuring shots of Mahir lounging around in his red Speedo, playing the accordion and describing his hobbies in broken English—"I like to take foto-camera (amimals, towns, nice nude models and peoples) . . ."—the site received millions of hits simply due to people circulating his URL e-mail. Mahir fan clubs sprang up all over the world, and the parody sites, such as the Bill Clinton "I Kiss You" page **<www.geocities.com/Athens/Ithaca/4637/kissyou.html>**, began to appear shortly thereafter. Flash-forward a year, and Mahir has hooked up with a tour company to start the official Mahir tour of Turkey: see the sights and have dinner with Mahir! Who needs real celebrities when you can just build one yourself?

Browser Encoding

Conscious of the international market, browser makers have created versions in various other languages. Netscape Navigator and Internet Explorer are both available in upwards of 20 international flavours. Most users interested in non-English Web content already have the necessary fonts installed. They are often supplied with localized versions of operating systems and use encodings that are popular for that particular language. Many browsers allow the use of such fonts for viewing Web pages.

> **NUTS & BOLTS**
>
> **Unicode Consortium**
>
> **www.unicode.org**
>
> The Unicode Consortium is the source of the Unicode Standard, a path-breaking universal 16-bit character encoding method used for representation of text for computer processing. Reaching far beyond ASCII's limited ability to encode only the Latin alphabet, Unicode provides a consistent way of encoding multilingual plain text. With more than a million characters, the standard defines codes for characters used in today's major languages, including Latin, Greek, Cyrillic, Armenian, Hebrew, Arabic, Devanagari, Bengali, Gurmukhi, Gujarati, Oriya, Tamil, Telugu, Kannada, Malayalam, Thai, Lao, Georgian, Tibetan, Japanese Kana, the complete set of modern Korean Hangul, and a unified set of Chinese/Japanese/Korean (CJK) ideographs, in addition to many historic and archaic scripts. Many more scripts and characters will soon be added, including Ethiopic, Canadian Syllabics, Cherokee, additional rare ideographs, Sinhala, Syriac, Burmese, Khmer, and Braille. The official Unicode Web site provides extensive information and resources for programmers, implementers, and others involved in computer globalization work.

English-language versions of Navigator and Internet Explorer include support for documents encoded using character sets other than ISO Latin-1. You can set the preferences in your browser to render documents in such languages as Chinese, Cyrillic, Japanese, Greek, and Turkish, as well as others that use various Unicode sets. Netscape 4 offers 18 encoding options, while IE5 offers 16, and both provide for user-defined settings. Of course, this option doesn't translate those languages into English, it merely allows your browser to understand and show them correctly, as their authors intended. (The newest incarnation of Netscape, version 6, includes AutoTranslate, enabling the automatic translation of Web pages courtesy of Alis Technologies' Gist-In-Time online translation software. Fourteen language pairs are currently available.)

In most cases you will need to download and install the appropriate browser support files or fonts to render the international characters properly. If you select Japanese encoding in IE5, for example, you must download and install a 2.7 MB file. The support file for Hebrew, on the other hand, is only 422 KB. The Internet Explorer Install on Demand option makes this operation relatively painless. Or you can go directly to Microsoft's Download page **<www.microsoft.com/ie/download>** and install Internet Explorer's Multi-Language Support add-on for each language you wish to view.

Choosing a Language

When you ask for a Web page, your language priorities are automatically included as part of the request. If the page is available in more than one language, the server will respond by sending you the preferred version. If nothing matches your request, then you may be presented with an error message and a list of alternative encodings.

Your request consists of a language code and sometimes a region code. For example, the code "fr-CA" represents the French language in the region of Canada. These language tags are ISO standards. Your browser preferences allow you to specify your language of choice, as well as other secondary choices. Netscape 4 offers a range of 55 language choices, while IE5 gives you 140 (due to a greater variety of regional variations, including 17 varieties of Arabic, 13 flavours of English, and 20 takes on Spanish).

Let's say you read Japanese and you want to access Web pages in that language. The professional route would mean installing the Japanese version of both your operating system and your browser. The amateur method would be to download and install the appropriate fonts and then set your browser preferences. Here's the routine in Navigator 4 for Windows 95: Select Edit > Preferences from the menu. In the Appearance | Fonts area, set the encoding to Japanese, select MS Gothic for both variable and fixed width fonts, and select "Use my default fonts, overriding document-specified fonts." In the Languages area, add Japanese (ja) to the list. Open the View > Encoding menu and select Japanese (Auto-Detect). And you're all set. (Except that English-language pages will now look a little funny . . .)

▶NUTS & BOLTS

International Fonts

Yamada Language Center Font Archive

<babel.uoregon.edu/yamada/fonts.html>

If you're having trouble locating fonts for foreign languages, try this page where you'll find 112 free fonts for 40 languages. (Looking for a Morse Code font, or perhaps Klingon, Romulan, or Tolkien? Look no further.) In addition, the Yamada Language Guides contain information about 115 languages, including mailing lists and Web resources.

Adobe.URL

<www.adobe.com/supportservice/custsupport/NOTES/c9c6.htm>

Adobe offers suggestions about where to buy international language fonts (including their own).

Frequently Asked Questions about Fonts

<www.nwalsh.com/comp.fonts/FAQ/index.html>

Although it hasn't been updated since August 1996 (with apologies from the author), this page is still a good source of basic technical information.

Many browsers still have problems related to document character encoding. For example, even when the text of a document is correctly displayed, its title may appear broken in the window title bar, since the font used in that window is determined by the operating system rather than by the encoding of the document. Other elements that may not display correctly include ALT texts in place of inline images, button labels in forms, and text-oriented Java applets.

For detailed information about viewing international pages with Netscape, see Basic Setup Information for International Users **<home.netscape.com/eng/intl/basics.html>**.

Macintosh users can display various non-Western languages by installing Apple's Language Kits **<www.apple.com/macos/multilingual>**, or by installing the Mac operating system for the language in question. To properly display international fonts, Mac users may also require two other system components: WorldScript II and a separate script bundle for each language.

Speaking in Tongues

How do the major search engines fare in the new world order? Here's a brief rundown.

AltaVista

www.altavista.com

AltaVista has partnered all over the world, with sites in Asia, Australia, Canada, Latin America, Northern and Southern Europe, as well as the United States. Links are provided from the International Search Network page **<doc.altavista.com/international.shtml>**. The search page accepts queries in 25 languages, from Chinese and Czech to Icelandic, Russian, and Swedish. And queries can be restricted to pages within a specified domain. For example, you can use "domain:fr" to find pages from France. For our French Canadian cousins, AltaVista has launched AltaVistaCanadien.

HotBot

HotBot offers to limit your search results to pages in any one of nine European languages. The advanced search options allow you to narrow your search by location or domain, including whole continents or individual countries (by using country codes, such as .ca for Canada, which limits the search to Canadian sites that actually make use of our national top-level domain).

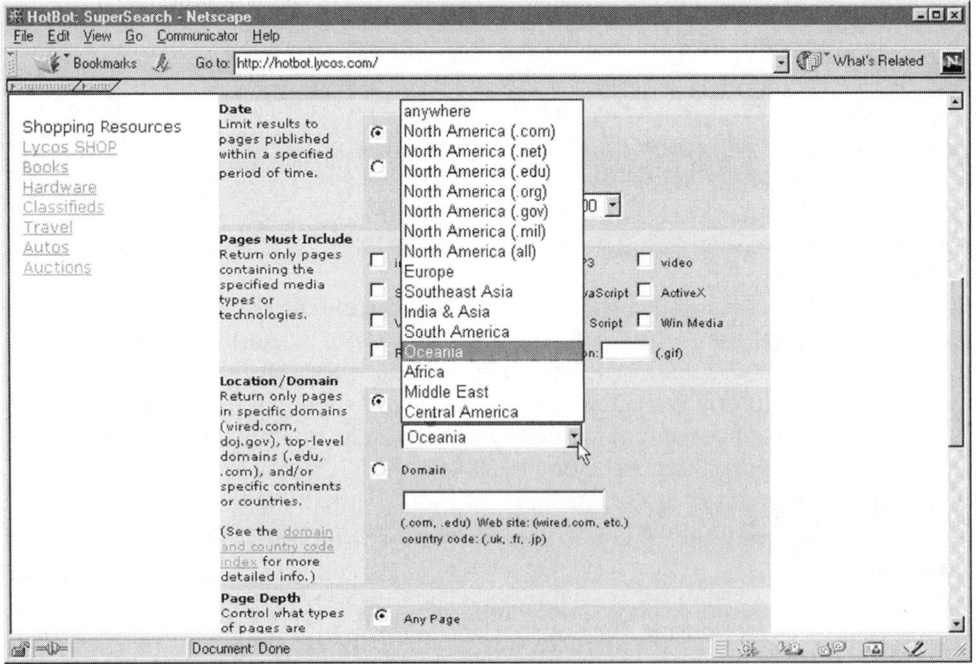

SuperSearch options on HotBot include the ability to specify a geographical region

Lycos

Lycos has spawned sister sites in Belgium, Denmark, France, Germany, Italy, Japan, Korea, Netherlands, Norway, Spain, Sweden, Switzerland, and the U.K. The Lycos advanced search options include a choice of 15 languages.

Yahoo!

Yahoo! has built an extensive network of regional sites in Europe (Denmark, France, Germany, Italy, Norway, Spain, Sweden), the U.K. and Ireland, the Pacific Rim (Asia, Australia, New Zealand, Hong Kong, Japan, Korea, Singapore, Taiwan), and the Americas (Brazil, Canada), as well as a Spanish-language site and support for Chinese.

Excite

Excite allows searching in 11 languages and provides search pages for Australia, France, Germany, Italy, Japan, Netherlands, Sweden, and the U.K., plus Excite in Chinese. In each case, the search can cover the whole Web or be restricted to sites in the host country (or at least sites using the top-level country domain).

Infoseek

Infoseek International covers Brazil, Denmark, Germany, Spain, France, Japan, Mexico, the Netherlands, Sweden, and the United Kingdom, with each site offered in its own language. The Advanced Search page **<www.go.com/find?pg= advanced_www.html>**—which,with its many options, is only available on the U.S. site—provides the ability to narrow your search to one of 20 countries, 17 broader geographical areas, or simply "Earth" ;-).

> **NUTS & BOLTS**
>
> **How Do You Say "Search Engine" in . . .**
>
> Danish—Søgenmaskine
>
> Dutch—Zoekmachine
>
> Finnish—Hakukone
>
> French—Moteur de recherche/Engin de recherche/Outil de recherche
>
> German—Suchmaschine
>
> Hebrew—Manoa Khipus
>
> Italian—Motore di ricerca
>
> Portuguese—Ferramenta de procura/ Mecanismo de procura
>
> Spanish—Motore de busqueda
>
> Swedish—Sökmotoer
>
> Source: Search Engine Watch **<searchengine watch.internet.com/facts/sprechen.html>**

Northern Light

The Northern Light Power Search allows searches for documents written in English, French, German, Italian, or Spanish, or published in one of 25 countries.

Translating the World

For those of us with a limited repertoire of languages (one?, two, of course, if you're Canadian), AltaVista offers a free, on-the-spot translation service called Babel Fish **<babelfish.altavista.com>**. Users can instantly translate a search query, Web page, or any other body of words, such as e-mail, by cutting and pasting the full text, or simply the URL of a Web page, into the translation window. Bidirectional translations are available between English and a choice of five other languages: French, German, Italian, Portuguese, and Spanish.

AltaVista advises that the technology works best when the text is grammatically correct and does not use too many idioms. Otherwise you're liable to end up with a dog's breakfast—or, as the French might (not) say, courtesy of Babel Fish: "Vous êtes exposé à terminer vers le haut avec le petit déjeuner d'un chien." (Or, translated back into English: "You are exposed to finish upwards with the breakfast of a dog.") Oh well, it's the thought that counts.

To be fair, Babel Fish can do an impressive job of translating entire Web pages (although there are limits on length). And it works very quickly. Inevitably the result will read as though written by someone with just enough grasp on the language to create an amusing turn of phrase but convey their meaning nonetheless. The translation option is actually offered with every search result in AltaVista: just press the Translate link. Or you can add an AV translation button to your browser toolbar for instant access (JavaScript required).

Similar services in word wizardry are offered by the Babylon Dictionary and Translator **<www.babylon.com>**, which transmutes text from English to Spanish, German, French, Italian, Dutch, Japanese, and Hebrew. An online version and a downloadable software version are both available for free. FreeTranslation.com **<www.freetranslation.com>** is an easy-to-use site "for rapid translations where you can get the 'gist' of foreign-language text and Web pages." The same warnings about idioms and grammar apply ("Vous êtes responsable pour finir par avec un petit déjeuner du chien," d'après FreeTranslation.)

SYSTRAN **<www.systransoft.com>**, the software company that supplied AltaVista with its Babel Fish translation technology, also sells SYSTRANET, a piece of personal software that works with Internet Explorer and Netscape to translate Web pages "on the fly."

A Glimpse of the Future

For unilingual Web users who want to access foreign-language resources, e-Lingo (formerly WorldBlaze) **<www.elingo.com>** has married translation technology with search technology to provide language-independent access to the Internet. E-Lingo enables on-the-fly translation of search queries and Web pages between any of the five supported languages: English, French, German, Italian, Portuguese, or Spanish. The translation is seamlessly integrated into the search process.

The e-Lingo company site offers several demonstration pages. All you have to do is enter your search term, choose a language, and press Translate. E-Lingo translates the term, finds the relevant pages, and returns the link along with a translated abstract (plus the original text). Search options include keyword and phrase searching, domain searching, and media searching. In addition, e-Lingo follows in the footsteps of Babel Fish (or should we say "finsteps") with its browsing service: just enter a URL and you can browse the translated page, which includes clicking on hyperlinks and having the next page automatically translated.

E-mail and text translation are also available. Although individual visitors are free to use the demo pages, this is a business service aimed at portals, e-tailers, content sites, and Web-based e-mail providers. The ePALS Classroom Exchange **<www.epals.com>**, for example, uses the e-Lingo service to enable translation on its site, which connects 1.7 million students and teachers from more than 25,000 classrooms in 130 countries. Other adopters include Spanish search engines Yupi **<www.yupi.com>** and Lycos Latin America **<espanol.lycos.com>**.

The Old-Fashioned Way

If you'd rather muddle through with your own translations, you'll find numerous dictionaries on the Web to help out. The best place to start is A Web of Online Dictionaries **<www.facstaff.bucknell.edu/rbeard/diction.html>.** Make sure you bookmark this site. Maintained by Robert Beard, director of the Russian and Linguistics program at Bucknell University in Pennsylvania, the site links to more than 800 dictionaries in 160 different languages. Included are thesauri and other language aids, pronunciation and rhyming dictionaries, and sites that identify (or guess) languages that you type into them. You'll also find links to the Web of Grammars and the Web of Linguistic Fun.

For a comprehensive catalogue of language-related Internet resources, check out the Human Languages Page **<www.june29.com/HLP>**. It boasts over 1,900 links to language resources on the Web, including online language lessons, translating dictionaries, native literature, translation services, software, and language schools. A handy menu allows you to translate the page into German, Italian, French, Spanish, or Portuguese.

International Portals

There are many regional portals that provide access to other countries and other cultures, including a healthy variety of European access points.

The interface on search engine EuroSeek **<www.euroseek.net>** defaults to the language specified in your browser, but you can change it to one of 40 other European languages. Two drop-down menus on the query form let you limit your search results to specific regions or to documents in specific languages. If you'd rather browse, EuroSeek provides a subject directory, also available in any of its many languages.

Europe Online **<www.europeonline.com/guide.htm>** serves as an information portal with links to news, weather, stocks, business directories, and chat, as well as thematic channels and 25 country channels, while the Voila **<www.voila.com>** search engine is available in eight languages.

Life Is Elsewhere

Online since 1995, Russia on the Net **<www.ru>** lays claim to the title "the original Russian Web directory," with searching in English or Russian. In the Middle East, ArabiaWeb **<www.arabiaweb.com>** covers Saudi Arabia, Jordan, Palestine, Yemen, United Arab Emirates, Lebanon, Qatar, and Oman, while iGuide **<www.iGuide.co.il>**, searchable in English or Hebrew, indexes Israeli sites.

GlobePage **<www.globepage.com>** provides an English-language interface for searching Web sites in Mainland China, Hong Kong, and Taiwan. GlobePage also offers you the ability to search using Chinese words and phrases. It currently supports two language encodings: Big5, which is used in Hong Kong and Taiwan, and GB, the encoding for Mainland China and Singapore. Complete instructions, with relevant links, are provided for downloading the necessary fonts for Windows, Macintosh, and Unix.

At least 20 search engines offer access to India, including 123 India.com **<www.123india.com>**, Jadoo **<www.jadoo.com>**, and SouthAsia.Net **<www.southasia.net>**, which includes resources from India, Nepal, Bangladesh, Pakistan, Sri Lanka, Bhutan, and Maldives.

The WoYaa! **<www.woyaa.com>** search engine and site directory focuses on digital Africa. Zebra **<www.zebra.co.za>** is an African search engine developed in South Africa featuring a database of over 100,000 Web pages and a further 120,000 "earmarked for indexing." Playing on both its own name and the racial geography of Africa, Zebra bills itself as "The Black and White Search Engine." It embodies the moniker by presenting all its imagery in black and white (and grey). No colour means smaller file sizes, so Zebra is strategically "optimized for speed," according to its creators.

You can also scour the Maltese Islands with Search Malta **<www.searchmalta.com>**, investigate Hong Kong with Search HK **<search.hk.org>**, or discover more than 5,000 Icelandic sites in The Web Collection **<www.hugmot.is/ssafn/english>**. As you might expect, the latter site encompasses half a dozen other Scandinavian countries and encourages searching in nine languages, including Faroese (a Scandinavian dialect with roots in Old Norse, spoken mainly on Denmark's Faroe islands).

Think Globally, Search Locally

Orientation **<www.orientation.com>** is "dedicated to developing and connecting Internet communities in the cyberworld beyond North America and Western Europe," and they do an impressive job. At last count, they had opened doorways to more than 190 countries. Jump off from their central site to Asia (29 countries), Africa (54), Central and Eastern Europe (22), Latin America and the Caribbean (49), the Middle East (15), and Oceania (22)—and to a growing list of individual country sites that currently includes Bulgaria, Colombia, Costa Rica, Hungary, Kenya, Philippines, Romania, Russia, Sri Lanka, Tanzania, Thailand, Uganda, and United Arab Emirates—all with chat, classifieds, weather, Web site reviews, searching and browsing by subject or country, and links to related newsgroups. The primary sites are all in English, while the local sites offer both English and the host language. Hoping to build the most comprehensive directories of their kind, Orientation sends forth its own robot crawler, known as The Black Bot, to not only index sites with country codes that fall within each region but also to search the entire Internet for sites that are about the region or countries within it.

Many smaller, country-specific search engines and directories are available only in their native language. France, for example, offers at least half a dozen, including Eurêka **<www.eureka-fr.com>** and Nomade **<rechercher.nomade.fr>**. The latter engine forms part of a mini network known as AllEurope **<www.alleurope.com>**, which also includes Italy's Virgilio **<www.virgilio.it/home/index.html>**, Germany's Web.de **<web.de>**, and UK Plus **<www.ukplus.com>** in the United Kingdom (with sub-channels for Scotland, Ireland, and Wales). Spain's Terra **<www.terra.es>** covers the Old Country, with New World relatives in Argentina, Chile, Colombia, Peru, Uruguay, and Venezuela.

For a list of other English and non-English country-specific search engines, visit AllSearchEngines **<www.allsearchengines.com/foreign.html>**, Beaucoup **<www.beaucoup.com>**, or Search Engine Colossus **<www.searchenginecolossus.com>**.

The latter collection lists more than 1,000 search sites, arranged by country or category (academic, business, medical, etc.), with colour-coded commentary for each one that reflects the type of search engine (directory, spider-driven, or "unusual").

News on the Net

The information landscape has changed dramatically in the last five or six years. Radio and TV stations are no longer the only free sources of news. All forms of media—newspapers, magazines, television (both broadcast and cable Networks), and radio—have migrated to the Internet and now offer plenty of breaking stories online. New, entirely Web-based entities have arisen, while search engines and directories that began life as mere finding aids are now flashing and hopping with top headlines, sports scores, and stock quotes. It's almost impossible to find a major portal that doesn't have a news ticker somewhere on the front page.

But readers want access to more than just the headlines. In fact, online news sites have grown so popular with Internet users that they have long displaced search engines as the primary port of call, according to a survey conducted in late 1998 by Media Metrix **<www.mediametrix.com>**.

A more recent study by *Editor & Publisher* **<www.mediainfo.com>** (see Joe Strupp, "Local News Wins Popularity Contest on Newspaper Web Sites," 30 June 1999) confirmed that news sites win top billing. E&P reports that 82 percent of people surveyed log on to read newspaper Web sites (after checking their e-mail, of course). Most readers said they were disappointed with local online newspapers, even though local news was deemed the most desirable content. For national or international coverage, more than 50 percent said they turn to a major online news source, not their regional outlet. After local news, the most sought-after information online was news about the weather, followed by national news, and then classified ads.

NETHEADS

Ananova

www.ananova.com

Created by an English news agency, Ananova is a computer-generated character designed to read the news. RealPlayer video clips feature the green-haired virtual news babe badly lip-synching to the computer-generated soundtrack—text-to-speech translations from news stories. The A-Files offer a behind-the-pixels peek at Ananova, including technical drawings (e-baby pictures, so to speak), a recording of her "historic first words," a series of outtakes, and even a couple of bad celebrity impressions, including the famous line from Clint Eastwood in *Dirty Harry*. For a shot at 15 minutes of cyberfame, you can e-mail a message for Ananova to read (she picks one a day). Or better yet, send in your picture if you think you might have been separated at birth from Ananova—among the dozen or so lookalike pictures posted on the site, sixteen-year-old Canadian Victoria Molner comes pretty close. Not surprisingly, Ananova has also inspired fan clubs and imitators, including the feebly satiric AndyNova **<www.liketelevision.com/web1/classictv/andynova/index.html>**, a guy with an empty six-pack on his head who claims to be "the first real-life human simulating a 3-D virtual newscaster." Some people have way too much time on their hands.

A typical (lack of) expression from virtual newscaster Ananova

Extra, Extra: The Latest Headlines

If you gotta know, where do you go? The following sites act as aggregators, gathering the top news stories from a variety of sources. If you're looking for local news, forget it. But if you want to quickly scan the top headlines, try these spots. Keep in mind that the news sources are almost exclusively American. For Canadian news, visit the Canadian portals discussed earlier or the sites named below under "Newspapers Online," "Local News," and "Broadcast News."

NewsHub **<www.newshub.com>** is updated every 15 minutes. You can browse headlines or search 90 papers, including a 45-day archive for some.

Updated several times a day, TotalNews **<www.totalnews.com>** lets you search 1,200 news sources and provides access to a few months' worth of archives.

Search current editions of 250 news sources at NewsIndex **<www.newsindex.com>**, updated hourly.

The HotBot News Channel **<www.newsbot.com>**, a subdirectory within HotBot, lets you search multiple news sources for articles published within the last 6 hours, 24 hours, week, or month. In addition, the News and Media directory **<directory.hotbot.lycos.com/news>** provides annotated links to thousands of sites.

The useful search tools at Northern Light Current News **<www.northernlight.com/news.html>** provide access to the past two weeks of news stories from over 70 sources, as well as weather and sports.

NETHEADS

Blame Canada, or, the Compleat Mafiaboy Saga

www.mafiaboy.com

Meticulous Web archive of articles related to the antics of Montreal's Mafiaboy, the 15-year-old wannabe hacker who was magnified by an alarmist U.S. press into a "cyberterrorist."

Newspapers Online

The worst part about online newspapers is that you can't use them for the cat's litterbox when you're finished reading. The best part is that you don't have to worry about recycling the rest of the paper. (Think of all the trees you're saving.)

Rather than reinvent themselves to reflect the new medium, some major newspapers, such as the *New York Times* **<www.nytimes.com>,** retained the look of their paper products when they migrated to the Web. That's not necessarily a bad thing if you're already accustomed to the way a print publication looks. But after they launched, the *New York Times* discovered that half of the 3 million registered users of its Web site had never bought a copy of the paper.

The original version of the *New York Times* on the Web tried a little *too* hard to look like the original, even providing a daily front-page scan of the actual paper. (Why?) Not one to avoid new media, the *New York Times* now provides multimedia treats and recommends a number of browser plug-ins for the full experience. All the regulars are here—RealPlayer, Shockwave, Flash, Acrobat Reader, and Quicktime Player—along with the IPIX PhotoBubbles viewer from Interactive Pictures Corp. **<www.ipix.com>**, required to "step inside" special spherical photographs in the paper's Gallery in the Round.

While the regular crosswords are premium priced, java-powered junior versions are offered through the New York Times Learning Network

The *New York Times* publishes the day's top stories, and keeps a 365-day archive of the entire printed paper (sans photographs and illustrations), including the *Sunday Magazine* and Sunday regional weeklies. The archive is also padded out with 60,000 articles from Britannica Online. Searching is free, but the full article will set you back $2.50 U.S. A special free archive contains book reviews back to 1980, film and theatre reviews, recent articles and columns from particular sections (CyberTimes, Technology, Circuits, Science—deemed to be of special interest to cybergeeks, we guess), recent Op-Ed columns, specials on politics, and automobile articles. Access to the online paper is free, but you need to register.

Other major international newspapers have also "established a presence" on the Web. Online since January 1996, the *London Times* **<www.londontimes.com>** carries virtually the complete content of their printed edition. *Le Monde* **<www.lemonde.fr>** from France, Germany's *Die Welt* **<www.welt.de>**, *El Pais* **<www.elpais.es>** from Spain, and many others have spiffy Web editions, albeit only in their original language.

The major Canadian players also have an online presence. National newspapers The *Globe and Mail* **<www.theglobeandmail.com>** and the *National Post* **<www.national post.com>** both deliver digital versions, along with the big local dailies such as the *Toronto Star* **<www.torontostar.com>**.

The Sun chain of newspapers was one of the first in Canada to reinvent itself online, spawning the Canadian Online Explorer, or CANOE **<www.canoe.com>**.

Almost 30 Canadian newspapers and a dozen magazines belonging to press baron and *National Post* publisher Conrad Black have leapt online. Many have their own URL and there are links from the Southam site **<www.southam.com>**, but the most convenient gateway is the Canada.com News Cafe **<www.canada.com/newscafe>**. It crawls about 80 Canadian and international newspaper and media sites every six hours and contains roughly 15,000 news-related documents. Daily headlines are presented from the full spectrum of Southam papers, with continuous newswire updates from Canadian Press.

But heck, why not go directly to the source? All the major wire services have Web sites of their own: Associated Press **<www.ap.org>**, Bloomberg **<www.bloomberg.com>**, Canada Newswire **<www.newswire.ca>**, Canadian Press **<www.cp.org>**, Reuters **<www.reuters.com>**, and so on.

Reports of My Death Have Been Greatly Exaggerated

Are people who read online news abandoning their old ways in the "real" world? *Editor & Publisher* found that at least one quarter of online readers consume less of the offline variety. But another survey, conducted around the same time by the Newspaper Association of America **<www.naa.org>**, suggested that 82 percent read the print edition as often, or more often, since going online.

Are newspapers an endangered species? In "Fear.com," an article about interactive newspapers trying to define their role within new media culture (part of a special report on "The State of the American Newspaper"), reporter Chip Brown gives us a useful reminder:

> Pundits have been predicting the death of newspapers for more than 100 years. In 1880, the assassin was supposed to be photography. In the 1920s, newspapers were going to be destroyed by radio; in the 1950s, TV was going to destroy newspapers and radio. In the 1990s the Web was going to destroy . . . well, you get the idea, and it is a misleading one because the main theme of media history is not extirpation of one form by another, but mutual accommodation among forms. Old Media has shown a remarkable resilience. As Roger Fidler, one of the pioneers of electronic distribution, observes in his book Mediamorphosis, even parchment scrolls, the preferred medium for 5,000 years, are still used in some tradition-conscious religions.
>
> Source: AJR Newslink **<ajr.newslink.org/special/part12.html>**

Print reading aside, other activities have suffered even greater abandonment by the Web public. *Editor & Publisher* reports that the greatest decline has been in video consumption, cited by 35 percent of respondents. Thirty percent use the telephone less, 29 percent watch less TV, and 25 percent listen to less radio.

Local News

The Canadian Community Newspapers Association **<www.ccna.ca>** represents almost 700 small papers, and provides links to a third of them from the CCNA site. Not surprisingly, given the meagre resources of most small newspapers, many sites are just plain pitiful. "Under construction" signs abound, still up from the fateful day last year when they decided to go virtual. And the quality of journalism is inconsistent, to put it kindly. Nevertheless, there are numerous sites that manage to look professional. Among the more successful ventures are North and West Vancouver's *North Shore News* **<www.nsnews.com>**, the *Thunder Bay Source* **<www.tbsource.com>**, the Northern News Service **<www.nnsl.com>** in Yellowknife, and Robinson-Blackmore Printing and Publishing **<www.rb.nf.ca>**, which combines the resources of 15 community newspapers throughout Newfoundland and Labrador.

Need to know what's happening a little farther north? The *Nunatsiaq News* site **<www.nunatsiaq.com>** features the Nunavut and Nunavik editions of this Iqaluit-based publication. The site is bilingual—English and Inuktitut—but you'll need to download the Nunacom font (available at the site) if you want to view the Inuktitut text.

Broadcast News

If you're a TV news junkie, you'll find your favourite station online, too. They're all there: ABC **<www.abcnews.com>**, CBC **<www.cbc.ca>**, CBS **<www.cbs.com>**, CNN **<www.cnn.com>**, Fox **<www.foxnews.com>**, NBC **<www.nbc.com>**, and everything else up to XYZ. Read the top stories, listen to audio interviews, watch video clips and live news feeds, customize the site to see only the news you want, or stick a scrolling news ticker on your desktop so you can carry on surfing with the latest headlines always in view.

The BBC **<news.bbc.co.uk>** does a particularly fine job of presenting the news—and they offer it not only in English, but also Arabic, Cantonese, Mandarin, Russian, Spanish, and Welsh. The BBC World Service provides a choice of 44 languages.

One of the best things about the Net is the way it erases geography. Listen to local radio programs from faraway places, tune in to nonprofit, independent outlets like National Public Radio **<www.npr.org>**, or catch up on all things Canadian, coast to coast, at CBC Radio **<www.radio.cbc.ca>**.

Pirate radio is a natural for the Net—for a guide to the underground waves, visit About.com **<pirateradio.about.com>** or the Free Radio Network **<www.frn.net>**. If you want to tap into shortwave radio stations funded and operated by guerrilla groups, opposition parties, and intelligence agencies around the world—from Radio Free Iraq to the Voice of East Timor—you'll find everything you need to know at Clandestine Radio Intel Web **<www.qsl.net/yb0rmi/cland>**.

For a comprehensive list of live and archived radio channels worldwide, visit Live Radio **<www.live-radio.net>**.

ARE WE THERE YET?

News on Demand

www.cbc.ca/news/live/newscast.html

Visitors to CBC Newsworld's News on Demand can now watch the latest newscast within minutes of its appearance on the Newsworld TV network.

Unfortunately, half the news clip is used up by unasked-for commercials. RealPlayer or QuickTime is required.

Top News Sites

Where do the mainstream masses get their news? The slick Microsoft Network/NBC News joint venture known as MSNBC holds the current title as the Web's most popular news destination, at least according to mid-1999 results from PC Data Online. And the number two spot? The Weather Channel. (Confirming that people really do care about the forecast, the number 20 spot is occupied by Intellicast, serving up "Weather for Active Lives.")

Here's the full line-up:

Top 20 News Sites—June 1999

Rank	Web Site	Average Time Spent (hour:minute)
1	MSNBC **<www.msnbc.com>**	00:35
2	The Weather Channel **<www.weather.com>**	00:24
3	CNN **<www.cnn.com>**	00:51
4	Time**<www.pathfinder.com>**	00:26
5	ESPN **<www.espn.com>**	00:58
6	ABC News **<www.abcnews.com>**	00:19
7	Sportsline **<www.sportsline.com>**	00:34
8	PC World **<www.pcworld.com>**	00:17
9	USA Today **<www.usatoday.com>**	00:28
10	CNET News **<www.news.com>**	00:09
11	CNN/Sports Illustrated **<www.cnnsi.com>**	00:43
12	Washington Post **<www.washingtonpost.com>**	00:22
13	NASCAR Online **<www.nascar.com>**	00:41
14	New York Times **<www.nytimes.com>**	00:45
15	APB Online **<www.apbonline.com>**	00:13
16	Slate **<www.slate.com>**	00:17
17	Wired **<www.wired.com>**	00:10
18	NBA.com **<www.nba.com>**	00:20
19	TodaysSports **<www.todayssports.com>**≈	00:02
20	Intellicast **<www.intellicast.com>**	00:10

Source: PC Data Online **<www.pcdataonline.com/press/pcdo71499.asp>**

Yes, the survey is heavily biased towards U.S. sites, but the mixture—"traditional" sources (online editions of print newspapers and magazines), major cable news stations (CNN), and wholly online ventures (CNET and Slate)—is revealing. Also interesting (and open to interpretation) is the average time spent on each site, ranging from the two-minute quickie at TodaysSports to almost an hour on ESPN. The average time spent is 26.2 minutes. (The top-20 ranking, by the way, is based on the number of readers, not the time spent online.)

For a broader appraisal of the top news sites, visit 100hot.com **<www.100hot.com>**, which lists the top 100 Web sites in numerous categories, including newspapers and magazines. Both categories actually include news sources that are definitely not newspapers or magazines, such as the BBC Online **<www.bbc.co.uk>**. And once in a while they completely miss the mark with listings like the Lifesaver Candystand **<www.candystand.com>**, a Shockwave gaming site. Oops! Nevertheless, the 100hot rankings, which are based on a reading of daily server logs, cast a much wider Net to include many international news outlets. When I last looked, Indonesia's Astaga **<www.astaga.com>** was number 8 on the list, *Express India* **<www.expressindia.com>** was 22, and the *Globe and Mail* was down at 97.

The Truth (or at Least the News) Is Out There

One notable newcomer to PC Data top 20 is APB Online, originally subtitled "The Source for Police and Crime News, Information and Entertainment." Recently renamed APBnews.com: Crime, Justice, Safety **<www.apbnews.com>**, this site reflects the North American public's appetite for lurid true-crime stories dished up as entertainment. Current news headlines mingle with "Most Wanted" and "Missing" lists, a special section on serial killers, a registry of sex offenders, and behind-the-scenes profiles of law-enforcement officials. And for that lifelike feeling of sitting in the front (or back) seat of a police cruiser, APB Online connects you to live audio feeds from police scanners in 29 major U.S. cities. There's even a list of radio codes to help you decipher the transmissions, and a chat function so you can connect with others who share your hobby. Scanning requires either Windows Media Player or RealPlayer.

APB Online also offers a section called "Unsolved," described as an interactive true-crime mystery. Something about it seems to blur the boundary between news and entertainment.

> Unsolved is . . . a new online journalism genre combining law enforcement source documents, enterprise reporting by APB's reporters and contributors, compelling narratives, interactive analytical tools and the legendary profiling skills of ex-FBI Special Agent John Douglas [the psychological profiler portrayed as a character in *Silence of the Lambs*].
>
> Unsolved is not a game. It is the multidimensional exploration of a real-life crime that has not yet been solved. You can navigate the case, learn its facts, see its sites, read its documents, and then use interactive methods to analyze relevant details in the same way

that elite federal investigators do. Your hunches, conclusions and tips can then be posted on the "Unsolved, with John Douglas" bulletin board where they will be discussed by Douglas and other law enforcement authorities and buffs.

Source: APB Online **<www.apbnews.com/unsolved/index.html>**

Eavesdropping on the action on New York's mean streets via the APBnews.com police scanner.

Browsing the Newsstand

Looking for something new to read? Cruise any of the following directories, and you'll find links to more news than you can consume in a lifetime.

The American Journalism Review keeps a lengthy list of more than 9,000 online newspapers, magazines, radio/television broadcasters, and other news services worldwide at AJR NewsLink **<ajr.newslink.org>**.

The Newspaper Association of America **<www.naa.org>** presents Newspaper-Links **<www.newspaperlinks.com>**, a geographically organized collection of, you guessed it, U.S. newspapers. A handful of Canadian sites snuck onto the list, too.

Editor & Publisher's Media Links **<emedia1.mediainfo.com/emedia>** extends to magazines, radio and television, news services, city guides, and media associations.

NewsDirectory.com **<www.newsdirectory.com>**, formerly known as Ecola Newsstand, provides logically organized links to more than 8,400 English-language newspapers and magazines worldwide, all of which have paper-based equivalents. The list extends to U.S. television networks with an online presence, archives of U.S. news and computer publications, and a few Bonus Guides (U.S. travel planners and college locators). The interface is remarkably clean and efficient, and beyond the U.S. favouritism, you'll find a reasonable selection of international publications.

If you prefer editorial opinion to plain old facts, Opinion-Pages **<www.opinion-pages.org>** points the way to current editorials, opinions, commentaries, and columnists from more than 650 English-language newspapers and magazines on the Web. For other news directories, try Yahoo! **<dir.yahoo.com/News_and_Media/Newspapers/Web_Directories>**.

Alternative News

The Association of Alternative Newsweeklies **<www.aan.org>** runs headine news from its member publications and links to more than 110 online papers. Most are American, such as the *LA Weekly* **<www.laweekly.com>** and the *Village Voice* **<www.villagevoice.com>**, but the AAN has half a dozen Canadian members too, including Toronto's *NOW* **<www.nowmagazine.com>** and Montreal's *Voir* **<www.voir.com>** and *Mirror* **<www.montrealmirror.com>**.

The subculture search engine Disinformation **<www.disinfo.com>** serves as a guide to "extreme" information that's usually ignored or suppressed by media conglomerates. Run by Richard Metzger, who refers to himself as a "subculture tour guide," the site's motto updates the famous Timothy Leary mantra: "Tune In, Turn On, Freak Out."

NUTS & BOLTS

CRAYON

Can't decide what newspaper to read? Why not make your own? CRAYON **<www.crayon.net>** stands for "CReAte Your Own Newspaper," and that's exactly what this site encourages you to do. Started in 1995 by Bucknell University student Jeff Boulter, CRAYON lets you pick and choose from close to a thousand free online sources to assemble your own news concoction. Beyond the long string of local, national, and international news outlets, there are OpEd columns, business briefs, weather reports, science and technology columns, health, religion, lifestyle, sports, tabloids, snippets and tidbits (quote of the day, lottery results, tips from the Farmer's Almanac, etc.), and a long, long list of funny pages. The whole smorgasbord. Beside each source on the newslinks page is a number that shows the percentage of CRAYON subscribers (now numbering more than 245,000) who've included that particular publication. It's not as slick as the big-name portals—in fact, it's a bit like comparing a crayon drawing to an oil painting—but when you sign up for the service, you get to name your own paper (naturally), write a suitable motto, and choose a layout. And you thought Yahoo! invented the idea of personalized pages!

AlterNet **<www.alternet.org>** is the world's only syndication service for independent and alternative content. Launched in 1987, the nonprofit organization is devoted to promoting and strengthening the independent press.

And of course there's always the well-known Mother Jones **<www.motherjones.com>**—or MoJo Wire, as the online version is called—publisher of "daily news for the skeptical citizen." Along with its own interactive political exposés, MoJo uncovers and reprints stories from elsewhere on the Web in its "Must Reads" column. A pioneer in Web publishing, Mother Jones startled industry naysayers by reporting that their online venture actually caused a growth in paper subscriptions to their magazine.

A Grain of Salt

Let me remind you of what your parents (should have) taught you: don't believe everything you read. Following are a few sites whose purpose is to give you a new perspective on the news.

Published out of Vancouver, British Columbia, by the Media Foundation, *Adbusters* **<www.adbusters.org>** is a not-for-profit magazine whose goal is "to galvanize resistance against those who would destroy the environment, pollute our minds and diminish our lives."

The Media Awareness Network **<www.media-awareness.ca>** supports media education at home and in the community, and provides French and English Canadians with information and food for thought about media culture.

The Media Literacy Online Project **<interact.uoregon.edu/MediaLit/HomePage>**, from the University of Oregon, houses a comprehensive database of articles on media literacy and education, and provides a gateway to numerous other resources on the Web.

Online Investing

The financial world has stormed the Web. There are about a gazillion sites for everyone from accountants and brokers to venture capitalists. The Canadian Financial Network **<www.canadianfinance.com>**, a searchable, descriptive guide to the world's online financial resources, is one place to find a comprehensive, annotated list of links.

But before you run off and start burning up Bay Street, take some time to learn the ins and outs. The Investor Learning Centre **<www.investorlearning.ca>**—founded by the Canadian Securities Institute **<www.csi.ca>**, Canada's only recognized authority for training investment advisors (stockbrokers)—is an independent, not-for-profit organization devoted to teaching plebes like us about the world of investing. Their free online course, Investments 101, walks you through the market system.

The Investment FAQ **<www.invest.faq.com>** is a thorough collection of answers to frequently asked questions about investments and personal finance, including stocks, bonds, options, discount brokers, information sources, retirement plans, and life insurance.

Do Your Homework

Before you start buying and selling, you'll need up-to-the-minute facts and figures, as well as a healthy dose of opinion and analysis from the experts.

Business news abounds on the Net. For a Canadian slant, try CANOE Breaking Business News **<www.canoe.ca/MoneyNews/home.html>**, *Report on Business* **<www.theglobeandmail.com/hubs/rob.html>** from the *Globe and Mail*, and the *National Post*'s *Financial Post* **<www.nationalpost.com/financialpost.asp>**.

Bloomberg **<www.bloomberg.com>** is one of the world's best providers of real-time data and analysis. Offering investment information from around the world, this well-organized site is the place to catch the story the minute it breaks.

News, market data, charts, stock screening, quotes, columns, and more are all free at CBS MarketWatch **<cbs.marketwatch.com>**, a comprehensive U.S. source that features lots of solid Canadian content.

Carlson Online Services **<www.carlsononline.com>** is the site for Canadian public company information, plus today's headlines (searchable by exchange and/or industry group), quotes, charts, and market stats.

And these guys win for scoring the best domain name: The Street **<www.thestreet.com>**. Some people say it's the top spot for financial intelligence—and a lot of it's free, including some basic guides for getting started.

Wait a minute . . . maybe *this* site should win the Best URL award: The Motley Fool: Finance and Folly **<www.fool.com>**. Their motto is "Educate, Amuse, Enrich," and that's pretty much what they do.

The Feeling Is Mutual

Brill's Mutual Fund Interactive **<www.brill.com>** delivers a complete set of tools for the mutual fund investor—free quotes, portfolio tracking, news, corporate earnings charts, and Value Line fund screening.

The Fund Library **<www.fundlibrary.com>**, designed to educate and inform investors about Canadian mutual funds, provides company information, a personal fund monitor and portfolio tracker, a discussion forum, and a learning centre.

To Market, to Market

Visit the Toronto Stock Exchange **<www.tse.com>** to check fundamental ratios like Price/Earnings and Dividend Yield for stocks and other financial instruments listed on the TSE. Its Investor Centre is another good place to educate yourself about the stock market: learn how to trade, try different strategies using the TSE's online Investment Challenge, or paper trade a $100,000 portfolio. The nifty Market Landscape feature generates 3-D graphics every 15 minutes throughout the trading day, showing how each of the TSE 300's 14 different subgroups move up and down.

The International Federation of Stock Exchanges **<www.fibv.com>** will direct you to its member sites.

CNN World Stock Markets **<cnnfn.com/markets/world_markets.html>** provides U.S. and world stock market indexes updated every three minutes.

Ready to trade? Open an account at an online brokerage firm like Ameritrade **<www.ebroker.com>**, Daytek **<www.datek.com>**, or E*Trade **<www.etrade.com>**.

Caveat Emptor

But just to be on the safe side, read this article from Ameritrade about "Avoiding Online Fraud" **<www.ebroker.com/html/articles/regular/article_fraud.art>**. It's brief, but it points to a few other sites with cautionary advice.

Before you buy stocks, pay a visit to the StockDetective **<www.financialweb.com/stockdetective>** for the latest dirt dished up "from the underbelly of Wall Street." Read about stock schemes and scams, study the guide to pseudo-research and phony financial reports, and don't miss the Stinky Stocks Roundup.

The Small Investor Protection Association **<www.sipa.to>**, a nonprofit consumer organization that meets regularly in Markham, Ontario, is devoted to raising awareness of how the investment industry works, providing guidance for making complaints, and improving regulation and enforcement. The SIPA site is a rich resource with plenty of eye-opening articles.

Okay, now go and get rich.

Online Services

Internet Storage

You can't win when it comes to having a big enough hard drive. Sure, 20 gigabytes sounds like acres of open country, but just wait until the next version of your favourite office suite starts fencing off a parcel here and a parcel there. Pretty soon you'll be back to borrowing space on your overcrowded Zip disks, just to save a few text files.

Luckily, the next brainwave has arrived: online storage. Several companies are begging to give you free space on their servers. How come? So your inner packrat can happily continue to collect MP3s and shareware and photos and ripped Web pages and every other digital file you desire—and the storage company can support itself through partnerships with the companies that provide MP3s and shareware and so on. Why bother paying for a second hard disk or a backup drive when you can keep your files for free at an off-site location? These sites not only act as extensions of your hard drive—hence the fondness for the word "drive" in many of the names—they also let you access stored files from anywhere else, via a Web browser, and let you share them with others.

The following sites are best suited for personal use, rather than heavy-duty corporate accounts. If you need an enterprise-level service, you'll need to check out places like SkyDesk **<www.skydesk.com>** (formerly known as @Backup) or Connected **<www.connected.com>**.

i-drive

www.idrive.com

Promising "infinite Internet space," i-drive offers 50 megabytes of online disk space for your own desktop files (word processing documents, spreadsheets, etc.), but unlimited space for anything you collect from the Web. Several tools are available for collecting stuff on the Web: Filo helps you gather Web pages, Sideload lets you save music files from Scour **<www.scour.com>**, and Sync keeps files on i-drive synchronized with local copies, as well as letting you schedule backups and other file uploads. These must be installed locally, but the files are relatively small. Functioning like your personal FTP site, i-drive lets you share files with others and set password restrictions on private areas.

driveway

www.driveway.com

Driveway works very much the same way as i-drive, but it's stingier with free space. You get 25 MB free to start, but you'll have to work or pay to get more. The options for adding extra space include 5 MB the first time you share files with a friend, 2 MB for every friend who opens a Driveway account (up to 20 friends), and 10 MB for filling out one of the surveys (there are three in total)—which adds up to 100 MB free. Beyond that, you'll have to start renting: 100 MB costs $29.95 U.S. for 90 days and an additional 100 MB can be had for $107.95 a year. Definitely a scheme dreamed up by some dweeb in the marketing department. Now, you tell two friends, and they'll tell two friends ...

FreeBack

www.freeback.com

This no-frills service lets you save files (up to 50 MB free) and get to them from anywhere, but you can't share your files with friends or create new folders online (although it mirrors the folder structure on your hard drive). The site design is kind of rinky-dink, barely a step above early 1995 home pages, complete with bad clip art. But hey, it's free. In addition to the regular storage service, you can use a variation called BackOnline that requires a locally installed Java applet to compress your files before uploading them for backup.

X:drive

www.xdrive.com

The best feature of X:drive—for Windows users, at least—is that it integrates with Windows Explorer (small download required), letting you add, move, rename, and delete Web-based folders and files directly within the Explorer window, as though X:drive were truly local. Non-Windows folks can still access X:drive through a regular browser. If you're a Palm VII or WAP device owner, you can download a little app that lets you manipulate your X:drive files remotely. Users get up to 100 MB of free space to store and share files, but it comes in increments, similar to the Driveway scheme: sharing files, telling all your friends, and simply coming back to use the service repeatedly after you open an account.

Mailing Lists

It's hard to find an Internet Service Provider these days that supports mailing list software, such as Majordomo or Listproc. You need to belong to an educational institution or use an ISP with a social conscience, such as Web Networks **<www.web.net>**, where the idea of "community" still exists, with no marketing strings attached. Usenet newsgroups don't engender the same sense of group discussion. They're more like free-for-all bulletin boards. A couple of Web-based mailing list services, however, leapt in to fill the gap. They come with a few strings attached, but they provide a much-needed service.

eGroups

www.egroups.com

Anyone can start an e-mail group, and it's absolutely free. There are multiple options for the type of list—private or public, moderated or unmoderated, two-way or broadcast only—and the management interface is easy to use. What's the "but"? Tiny text ads unobtrusively inserted at the bottom of every message. And when you become a "member" of eGroups (formerly OneList), you are encouraged to sign up for lots of marketing newsletters. Still, it's a small inconvenience, as long as you just say No ... or Yes, if you like that sort of thing. Most of the groups are listed in a searchable directory, organized Yahoo-style, and you can choose to get e-mail or just read messages online (postings are archived and accessible to group members).

ListBot

www.listbot.com

Microsoft's answer to eGroups isn't quite up to snuff yet. ListBot offers much the same package for free, but the user interface isn't as friendly, and they clearly intend to woo you into upgrading from ListBot Free to ListBot Gold. For $99 U.S. a year, you don't see any ads, you can import existing lists, send larger messages (up to 250 KB), and the demographic questionnaire can be customized to your liking. ListBot is one of the small-business services from Microsoft's bCentral **<www.bcentral.com>**, aimed at entrepreneurs. It's a marketing tool, not a coffee club.

Shopping

Welcome to the Big Mall, formerly known as Planet Earth. Forrester Research predicts that in the year 2000, 28.4 million U.S. households will shop online, up from 17.4 million the previous year. U.S. online retail revenues will hit $38.8 billion, up from $20.3 billion in 1999.

Odds are, then, that you'll be spending a little money online yourself. The following section will help to ensure that you get the best stuff in exchange for your hard-earned dollars. In the spirit of eating the vegetables first so you can enjoy the good parts of dinner at your leisure, let's start with sales taxes and some details about secure servers. After that, it's time to get out your credit card.

Sorting Out Sales Tax

When you shop online, what happens to Provincial Sales Tax (PST), Goods and Services Tax (GST), or Harmonized Sales Tax (HST)? Good question. Since you're not actually visiting a province when shopping online (like Gertrude Stein said about Oakland and William Gibson said again about cyberspace, "There's no there there"), you don't have to pay sales taxes, right?

Well, not really. Sort of. The answer is, no one knows the answer. So how do you know what you're going to end up paying? You don't. Isn't online shopping fun?

The best you can do is to understand how Canadian sales tax structure is supposed to work, and then deal with what *really* happens.

This is how it's suppposed to work: On the Internet as in the real world, the Canadian Goods and Services Tax (GST) is an annoying fact of life: 7% of the total of almost everything that you can buy in Canada goes to the feds. When you're bringing an item into your home province for personal use, whether you bought it by mail order or over the Internet, you are also required to pay Provincial Sales Tax (PST) on that item to the provincial government. In Newfoundland and Labrador, Nova Scotia, and New Brunswick, instead of paying separate PST and GST, you pay the Harmonized Sales Tax, which is 15%. The Yukon, the Northwest Territories, and Nunavut have no PST equivalent, so if you're a northern resident, all you pay is GST.

In practice, there's absolutely no consistency in the way sales tax works online. Some sites will charge you PST and GST, as you'd expect from the information above, but many commercial sites won't charge you *any sales tax at all.* How is this possible? Canadian laws stipulate that merchants are only responsible for collecting sales tax in provinces where they're registered to operate as a business. So if you live in Ontario and you buy an item from a merchant in Manitoba that isn't registered to operate in Ontario, no sales tax appears on your bill. In theory, you still owe PST on the item to the government of your province, and the onus is on you as a consumer to pay that tax. The people who work at your local Retail Sales Tax Office will be more than happy to tell you how to remit that payment, but at present, there's really no mechanism in place to monitor transactions and ensure that consumers actually pay PST.

In the U.S.A., things get even wilder and woolier. South of the border, tax laws stipulate that businesses only have to collect tax from consumers who live in a state where that company has "established offices." An established office has to be an actual physical presence, so a U.S. business that exists entirely online really only has to pay tax on items bought in the state where its server is located. There's no way of telling whether this situation is going to change in the immediate future. Some judgements have allowed state governments to sue or criminally indict companies that sell prescription drugs and alcohol online, but the bulk of online businesses remain unscathed by the taxman.

As a Canadian buying from the U.S., whether or not you'll have to pay tax is a crapshoot that usually depends on the company's shipping method. If you're ordering from a small company that uses surface mail, you probably won't be asked to pay any tax at all. Larger U.S. retailers will bill you for the duty and applicable GST and PST (or HST) due on your order, and remit the proper amount to Revenue Canada. With some online retailers, when you place your order, you authorize them to appoint a Canadian customs broker to act on your behalf to obtain customs clearance of your merchandise, and, if necessary, to remit applicable duty and taxes to Revenue Canada. You may grumble a little about such arrangements being *too* efficient for your liking, but it's ultimately far simpler and more convenient than asking you to figure out the details of importing merchandise yourself.

Until the various governments sort out the problems of Internet sales tax, the pragmatic thing to do is to act as though the site itself is providing you with the correct tax amount when you place your order (if it's not, you're probably being underbilled, and most likely, you won't be inclined to complain). As with other hidden charges (like shipping and handling), getting sales tax information requires some burrowing: find the Help, Ordering, or FAQ page, and look for details about taxes. As with shipping charges, you may not find out that you'll have to pay taxes until you get to an ordering page. And, as with shipping charges, if you decide you don't want to pay the total plus tax, you can always back out of the order by continually hitting the Back button on your browser until you're away from that page.

Secure Servers

When conducting financial transactions online, it's crucial to ensure that you're inside a secure server. Let's just say that again: NEVER, EVER, release your credit card number or other personal information online unless you're on a secure site.

So: how do you identify a secure site? There's usually a small banner somewhere on the home page identifying the site's secure server, or linking to something like a "Securities and Guarantees" page. There will often be additional logos from organizations such as TRUSTe **<www.truste.org>** or the Better Business Bureau to bolster your confidence. You can confirm this information by checking two locations in your browser. First, look at the page URL. If the page you're on has an ".shtml" extension instead of an ".html" extension, you're on a secure site. Secondly, both Netscape and Explorer display a lock icon in the program's bottom bar if the site is secure. If no lock appears, or the lock is open, the site is not secure. If you're feeling paranoid, you can adjust your browser's default Security level to alert you when you're entering an unknown site.

Consumer Information Sites

So now you know about online taxation (or lack thereof) and secure servers. As Harvey Feirstein said on *The Simpsons*, "Let's go shopping!"

[Pause. Think of your mom's voice when you read this next bit.] Hold on just one minute. Before you go charging off to buy something, do some research first. You might find some real bargains, you know. And change your shirt! I frankly don't know how you manage on your own. [End mom's voice.]

Actually, there are some useful consumer information sites out there. Some provide their own ratings, others poll their users. Here are a couple of the best.

Productopia

www.productopia.com

Productopia provides product information and advice that will help you find products from over 450 categories, from appliances to toys. Once you've decided on an item, their where-to-buy links and listings provide on- and offline tips for tracking down your stuff. (Of course, none of the links are for Canadian merchants. Get used to it.)

Deja.com

www.deja.com

Deja.com was overly encrusted with excess menus and polls and other useless crap for a long time, but we are glad to report that the site managers have stripped away everything but the essentials, and it's usable once again. Deja will perform all kinds of tasks for you that will increase your ability to make informed decisions while shopping online. The left-hand side of the Deja.com home page contains a directory of categories: Arts & Entertainment, Sports, Travel, etc. Each category in turn has a flyout menu full of subcategories. Following the links takes you to a page of the top products in that category, as rated by other users. And, of course, there are links to retailers that sell the product. If you want more information about a particular product before you buy it, use Deja.com to look for material in Usenet discussion groups.

Shopping Engines

The Internet is lousy with retailers who want to sell things to you. Many of the major search engines we've already discussed have shopping directories, and, of course, you can always just enter the brand name or retailer you're looking for into the engine itself and run a normal query. But what if you want to save a little money, or do some consumer research?

Enter the shopping engines, or shop bots. Shopping engines are sites that do some sort of price comparison for you, based on searches that they perform of the online retailers in their database. Of course, there aren't any Canadian shopping engines to date, so the prices that the existing engines return won't be in Canadian dollars, but they can still save you some money.

Most shopping engines have other features as well, like consumer rating services and discussion groups. Doing a little research with the help of these services can help you ensure that the device you're buying isn't going to crap out on you a week after you've taken it out of the box.

DealTime

www.dealtime.com

DealTime's 17-category engine, which catalogues over 7,300 merchants, will take a lot of the tedium out of your search for the best deals on the things you want to buy. You specify the model, manufacturer, price range, and keywords of the item you want, then wait for DealTime to search for matches. DealTime remembers what you're looking for and continues searching the Web for the latest deals, transmitting updates to you instantly via your choice of e-mail or pager. You can also download a free DealTime Notifier—a 300 K icon that sits on your taskbar and keeps you informed of new deals by flashing and emitting a real-time chime. Hmmm... Just like Pavlov's dog.

mySimon

www.mysimon.com

Don't let Simon, the site's so-bland-it's-scary mascot, frighten you away (check out the Borg version of Simon in the computer software section, which is even worse). mySimon is a quick, efficient shopping directory that provides prices for and links to consumer goods from over 2,000 different online merchants and auction sites. The results are listed by merchant, so you can compare prices for the same item at different retailers. If you're seriously into the whole mySimon shopping experience, they also have a variety of tools that sit on your desktop so that you can buy, buy, buy whenever the impulse hits.

EvenBetter

www.evenbetter.com

The former DealPilot.com has morphed (again) into EvenBetter, which is, as the name suggests, even better. This engine works for books, music, or movies. Its database has expanded to contain the inventories of 43 bookstores (including Chapters and Indigo, which are recent additions), 15 music stores, and 11 movie stores. Like every other shopping site, they have a little widget that you can download to your desktop for enhanced services. That's fine if you only use one or two shopping sites, but it's not hard to imagine your desktop encrusted with annoying little bits of code, all booping and chiming and bleeping for you to spend more money...

Excite Shopping Directory

shopping.excite.com

Excite maintains a reasonably good shopping assistant whose only major shortcoming is that it doesn't allow for comparisons. Its operation is standard: click on the category of product you're looking for, and you'll gradually burrow down to a specific item. If you're not happy with the result, scroll down the page to the "Still Looking?" box, which will allow you to search online classifieds, auctions, Excite channels, or the Web in general.

Online Shopping Canadian-Style

Paying in the coin of the realm is a relatively new experience for Canadian online shoppers. There are substantially greater numbers of Canadian retailers online this year than there were last year, and more directories of said retailers, but so far, there's only one Canadian comparison engine on the horizon: eZuz. Following are your best bets for locating Canadian online merchants.

Sympatico Shopping

www.shopping.sympatico.ca

While Sympatico's directory of online Canadian vendors is on the skimpy side, they do provide links to some useful tools. The site connects to Active Buyer's Guide **<www.activebuyersguide.com>**, a directory of consumer information which will teach you about a selected product, help you decide between products based on criteria you select, then search for prices like a comparison engine. They also have a currency converter, a present picker, and an archive of product reviews.

Canada.com Shopping

www.canada.com/shopping

The Canada.com Shopping directory is a pretty accurate reflection of which major Canadian retailers currently have more than a token online presence. Everything is still listed on one page, so the selection isn't huge, but it's much bigger than it was even a year ago. If you can't find what you're looking for in the Canadian retailers directory, Canada.com also maintains a list of U.S. retailers that ship to Canada.

AltaVista Canada Shopping Guide

www.altavista.ca/en/shopping/shopping.htm

The shopping section of this site is fairly new, but because of AltaVista's brand name recognition, you can be sure that it'll grow quickly. You browse by category here, and for every link, the site will tell you whether or not the merchant bills in Canadian dollars and ships from Canada. There are a number of links to services here as well: banking, insurance, real estate, travel, and so on.

Excite Canada Shopping

www.excite.ca/shopping

Excite Canada Shopping looks more like a conventional shopping engine than the Canada.com directory, but doesn't have much more to offer in terms of content. No bells, no whistles, just links, folks.

Canadashop.com

www1.canadashop.com

Canadashop.com is an online mall with one cash register—you're actually buying from the mall, which buys thousands of items from individual retailers. You can search the site by product, or by store, or do a general book search. Shopping at Canadashop has a kind of flea-market feel. There are some good retailers here, but the selection of goods is haphazard, and can take you in unexpected directions (for example, the only subcategories under Electronics are "Educational Software" and "Videos").

Coming Soon: Comparison Shopping, At Last

eZuz Canada

www.ezuz.ca

What promises to be Canadian online retail's most sophisticated site to date will actually do U.S.-style comparison shopping, providing multiple retailer listings for a single product, complete with prices. Right now, all you get is a long series of Flash screens based on the opening of *The Matrix*, so here's hoping the site lives up to the hype.

Online Auction Houses

Auction sites have passed rapidly from novelty status to a part of everyday culture, never mind Net culture. William Gibson's article in *Wired* about buying Swiss watches from EBay certainly helped; anything he mentions instantly gains huge amounts of credibility in the online community. There's more to the success of EBay than one person's endorsement, though: people are losing their fear of credit card fraud and are learning how to spend money online. If you want to join in the fray, visit EBay or one of its many imitators (even Yahoo! has an online auction now). Remember: other peoples' junk can be your goldmine.

EBay

www.ebay.com

Right now, EBay stages over 2.5 million auctions a day, for items in over 2,000 categories. It is the number one e-commerce site in the world, with an average of 1.782 million vistors a day, as of January 2000. Registering is free. Selling an item costs you a small insertion fee, plus a tiered final fee based on the final selling value of your item (if you want to know the exact formula, take a look at EBay's FAQ page **<pages.ebay.com/aw/faq.html>**. There are a number of different auction types to choose from: Reserve Prices, Restricted Access Auctions, Dutch Auctions, and Private Auctions (it may sound complicated at first, but once you get into it, everything becomes clear). If you get tired of browsing or buying, you can always just hang out and chat with the other constituents of this brave new digital shopping mall.

Bid.Com Canada

www.bid.com/storefronts/canada

Bid.Com provides Canadians with the opportunity to participate in auctions for brand-name merchandise direct from the manufacturer. If you know the EBay system, you're in luck, because Bid.Com works in a similar fashion (if you don't, their Help files are more than adequate). The main difference (other than the pleasure of being able to conduct transactions in your own currency) is that Bid.Com's focus is more narrow than EBay's, sticking to high-tech items—computers, monitors, office equipment, camera equipment—that are in as-new condition, and are backed by full warranties. (Actually, there are also some ticky-tacky gift and jewelry items, and some sporting goods, but there are better online sources for these things.)

BidStream

www.bidstream.com

Want more auction sites? Okay. BidStream is an auction site search engine. Its search parameters are quite specific: you can send BidStream out to find items that fall within a given price range, or stipulate that the search results must contain pictures or descriptions, and that they must be for either fixed-price items or auction items. If you're in a browsing mood, just search through their directory (12 major categories and thousands of individual items).

Major Shareware Sites

There are thousands of shareware sites out there, ranging from huge commercial interests to sites run by hyper adolescents for their friends. If you're running a search for a particular type of shareware program, an engine could return any of them as results. So before you pick a site at random and begin your download, you need to consider a couple of factors.

First, who is hosting the site? If it's not the creator of the software or a reputable shareware company, you run the risk of downloading a corrupted or virally infected program. There's also the possibility that a smaller "shareware" site may be offering illegal downloads of commercial software packages (called "warez"), which may or may not have been tampered with. Check to see if the site guarantees the reliability of its downloads before you begin. Hint: if the site is covered in ads for porn sites and requires you to click through any of them before downloading (this generates revenue for the site owner—most warez sites support themselves with porn ads), you're probably on a pirate site.

Second, where is the site relative to you? If it's on a different continent, your download may take longer, and may be interrupted. To avoid headaches, download from the geographically nearest shareware site. Many of the large shareware sites have mirror sites that duplicate their content in different locations in order to avoid slow downloads. Bookmark a couple of the closer ones and you're in business.

> **INFOHAZARD**
>
> **Warez Sites**
>
> If you're ever tempted to follow a link offering to connect you to a site full of "warez" (stolen and occasionally password-stripped or "cracked" commercial software), pause for a minute and consider this: downloading unlicensed, unauthorized copies of commercial software is illegal, but simply visiting a warez site will usually cause you more grief than you expected. Why? Warez sites make money by linking to porn sites—they get paid for every click-through they send from their own page. When you hit a warez page, your screen will begin to fill with browser windows full of porn ads, windows that you'll sometimes find you can't close without terminating the application. Occasionally, you'll have to reboot to get rid of them all. It's almost impossible to tell where the warez are at all, if they're really there (and usually they aren't). So save yourself the embarrassment and the annoyance (not to mention the possible arrest)—just buy your software in the first place.

You might want to begin your shareware search at one of the following sites.

TUCOWS Canadian Mirror Sites

www.tucows.com/Canada.html

TUCOWS (an acronym for "The Ultimate Collection Of Winsock Software") is a class act. In addition to providing rated, reviewed, and virus-free downloads of all the major shareware products for every conceivable operating system (including Linux and BeOS), they also have a site featuring free desktop themes and screensavers, and a free newsletter you can subscribe to if you want to keep apprised of the newest shareware releases.

There are over 480 TUCOWS mirror sites on six continents. This URL links to all of the TUCOWS mirror sites in Canada, and even rates the frequency with which the various mirrors update their software.

Winfiles.com

www.winfiles.com

One of the original Windows 95 shareware sites, Winfiles.com is now a division of CNET, the computer and technology information network. In addition to a plethora of shareware for Window 95/98, NT, and CE, they've also got Windows drivers (oh, you THINK you have all the drivers you need to run your hardware, but the time will come, my friend . . .), software reviews, bug fixes, tips and tricks, a hardware price comparison section, high-tech equipment auctions, and all sorts of other useful and interesting things. If you use IE, you can even add Winfiles.com as an active channel, or simply plop a link onto your active desktop (which raises an interesting point: does anyone out there use active desktop?).

What Is Betaware?

In your search for useful and interesting shareware, you've probably come across the term "betaware." Betaware is the generic term for software that's still in the testing stage. Software companies routinely release betaware to a group of people called (predictably) beta testers, who use the software as much as possible in as many ways as possible, in an attempt to locate bugs that overstressed engineers may have missed. Sometimes beta testers even help to fine-tune the software's interface design. During the beta test period, testers provide feedback to the designers and to each other via e-mail, Web forums, and mailing lists. The reward for beta testing is usually a copy of the final program and small amounts of street credibility among the propellerhead set.

Sound like fun? Be warned: betaware can and will cause system crashes—that's why it's betaware. If you use any products while they're still in beta, make sure you back up your system regularly.

PDA Software

If you've already made the migration from a paper address book to a personal digital assistant (PDA) like the PalmPilot, a Windows CE machine, or the late (but not so lamented) Newton, you know that your little digital buddy can do a lot of things other than find addresses for you. If you haven't, finding out that PDAs can do everything from running a sophisticated spreadsheet or database program to playing extremely accurate copies of old arcade favourites like Asteroids and Pac-Man may be enough to persuade you to make the change.

Using a PDA can be a genuinely pleasurable experience. The software is tiny and efficient, and, when it's not freeware, rarely costs more than $15 U.S. to register (and registering usually results in a regular flow of updates to your e-mail box—can you say the same for the software you've bought for your desktop box?). As an added bonus, you get that feeling of technological superiority every time you walk into a meeting and casually place your PDA on the desktop while everyone else fidgets with their pens and papers.

With Apple no longer supporting the Newton OS, PDAs generally fall into two categories: PalmPilots or Windows CE machines (recently reborn as Pocket PCs). PalmPilots resemble miniature writing tablets and require you to enter text by writing on the screen with a special stylus. Most have monochrome displays (the recently released Palm IIIc ushered in a new era of colour screens, but you won't get the full effect unless your applications support colour too, and most are still written for monochrome Palms), but are fast and easy to use, thanks to the well-designed Palm OS. Windows CE machines tend to resemble miniature laptops, and are sometimes called palmtops. Many of them have colour screens and run stripped-down versions of the major Microsoft apps, like Word, Excel, and Explorer. Because of the power demands of their colour displays, they tend to be slower than Pilots, and trying to type on their minuscule keyboards can be frustrating.

Many of the major shareware sites have large collections of PDA software, but there are also a few first-rate Internet sites that specialize in PDA software. Here are a few of the better PDA sites to get you started.

CEcity

www.wincecity.com/index-pc.html

CEcity is the most complete resource on the Internet for information relating to Microsoft's Windows CE and Pocket PC operating systems. They've got shareware, but they also have news, reviews, support, and information on where to buy new hardware.

PDACentral Canadian Mirror Sites

www.pdacentral.com/Canada.html

Operated by TUCOWS, PDACentral offers freeware, shareware, and commercial software for Pilots, Newtons, Windows CE machines, and Psions, as well as the latest news about your handheld system of choice.

Palm Gear HQ

www2.viaweb.com/pilotgearsw/index.html

This site offers freeware, shareware, and commercial products for your PalmPilot.

ARE WE THERE YET?

His Boy Elroy, or The Extropians

www.extropy.org

The Extropians are a fun-loving bunch of regular folks with their collective technologically enhanced eye on the future. Here's their mission statement:

> Extropy Institute acts as a networking and information center for those seeking to foster our continuing evolutionary advance by using technology to extend healthy life, augment intelligence, optimize psychology, and improve social systems. Through its networking function, the Institute brings together the finest critical and creative minds to challenge conventional thinking about human limits and to develop, critique, and implement new ideas about the use of technologies of all kinds to improve the future. As an information center, the Institute acts as a repository and portal for detailed information on advanced technologies, their positive potentials, their challenges, and their possible dangers.

Good rhetoric, but the deeper you delve into the site, the more these people start to sound like the bastard offspring of George Jetson and Ayn Rand.

Books

Isn't it ironic? One of the hottest-selling items in the world of digital commerce is . . . the book.

In Canada, Chapters and Indigo are duking it out for dominance of the online bookselling market. Chapters, the clear Canuck frontrunner, has been wheeling and dealing its way around the Net, first launching Chaptersglobe.com with the *Globe and Mail,* then Chapters.ca when it became evident that there would be complaints if the site used *Globe* book reviews without adequately compensating the paper's columnists. Chapters has been aggressively inking deals with other high-profile portals, including AltaVista Canada and ChumCity Online, as well as starting to acquire other properties, beginning with GardenCrazy **<www.gardencrazy.com>**.

All this effort still hasn't brought Chapters within spitting distance of their Yankee competitors, although Canadian consumers are now tending to shop in their own digital neighbourhood. In the U.S., Barnes and Noble is the closest analogue to Chapters, but the real heavyweight is Amazon.com. The truly amazing thing about

▶NUTS & BOLTS

Bookwire

www.bookwire.com

Book publishing is big business, and Bookwire provides an in-depth online guide for industry professionals. Created by R.R. Bowker **<www.bowker.com>**, the company that produces Books in Print, the site is both rich in content and heavily slanted at the U.S. market. Home to Publisher's Weekly Online, Library Journal, the Book Industry Study Group, and various industry associations, the site offers news, book reviews, guides to literary events, author interviews, and thousands of annotated links to book-related sites.

Amazon.com is that they've managed to dominate the Internet book market without any physical stores (yet). Amazon operates entirely on a "just in time" model, ordering books from the publisher as the orders arrive. It seems to work well, but one wonders how long the Amazon.com boom will continue. If anyone can sell books online, why not go to the publisher's Web site and buy your books direct? Hmmmm . . . .

Amazon.com

www.amazon.com

Amazon.com now runs online auctions and sells toys, electronics, music, and videos as well as their ostensible specialty, books. You can browse their stock by category, or use their sophisticated search tools (which include Boolean operators and the ability to search by ISBN numbers) to locate a specific title. If you're looking for suggestions, they maintain a Top 100 sellers list that's updated hourly, as well as providing the *New York Times* bestseller list and Oprah's picks.

One of the best features of Amazon.com is that the books are often reviewed. The reviews can come from the Amazon.com staff, the book's publisher (who can also add cover art, flap copy, etc.), the author, or fans, so it's easy to quickly gather a wide range of opinions.

If you buy regularly, you might want to open a personal account page, so you don't have to enter all your identification information every time you visit the site (this will require you to enable your browser cookies).

Barnes and Noble

www.barnesandnoble.com

www.bn.com

Barnes and Noble is working hard to catch up to Amazon.com—they're now selling software and music as well, and have streamlined their URL and their ordering service to get you through the purchasing process as quickly as possible.

Features of note include their bargain book section (6,000 titles under $10 U.S.), their huge used, rare, and out-of-print book selection, and a link to textbooks.com **<www.textbooks.com>**, the world's largest buyer and seller of new and used college textbooks (yes, you CAN get rid of that Biology 101 book that's mouldering under your table).

Borders

www.borders.com

Although it lacks the bells and whistles of Amazon or Barnes and Noble, the Borders site makes up for its plain presentation by providing strong customer service and prompt delivery. Queries and cancellations are handled promptly, and if you're not happy with your purchase after you get it, you can even return your book at any of their bricks-and-mortar stores.

Chapters

www.chapterglobe.com

www.chapters.ca

Chapter maintains two independent Web sites, Chaptersglobe.com, which they run in partnership with the *Globe and Mail*, and Chapters.ca. The latter site opened second, and is a no-nonsense retail site. The former site contains reviews, interviews, and customer forums as well as access to the Chapters database. Their search system is competent, if not as complex as Amazon's, and the selection of titles is excellent. The online database lists more than 2.5 million book titles, as well as over 46,000 music CDs and 28,000 videotape and DVD titles.

Chapters Online has entered into marketing agreements with AltaVista Canada, AOL Canada, Bid.Com, CANOE, ChumCity, Infospace Canada, MSN Canada, Toronto-Dominion Bank, TSN.ca, and Yahoo!Canada, among other leading Canadian portal and Web content sites. For a while, Chapters Online resisted the urge to expand beyond books, CDs, and software, but in January 2000, Chapters acquired e-tailer GardenCrazy.com, signalling the start of their transformation into an online megamall. Chapters Online president Rick Segal—who, incidentally, led the first-generation development of MarthaStewart.com and BarnesandNoble.com while employed by Microsoft—has declared the company's intention to keep on sucking up successful online enterprises.

If you live in Canada and you feel the need to buy from a megabookstore rather than your neighbourhood independent, this is where you should do your shopping. You can pay in Canadian dollars, and delivery will be faster. (Sneaky hint: if you can't find what you're looking for in the Chapters database, run a search for it on Amazon, copy the author, title, ISBN, and publisher, then special order the book through Chapters, or someone else.)

▶NETHEADS

Jeff Bezos

Glamour boy of the digital bookselling world, and widely hailed as a Wall Street wunderkind, Jeff Bezos is the founder of Amazon.com, the first online bookstore to make a big splash—but not, as some mistakenly believe, the first online bookseller. There were at least three e-tailers already hawking books online when Bezos launched Amazon in July 1995, including Computer Literacy (which eventually morphed into Fatbrain) and Book Stacks (acquired by Barnes and Noble). Bezos, however, was definitely the first to become a billionaire—not bad for a guy who spent at least one youthful summer flipping burgers at McDonald's.

Indigo

www.indigo.ca

Indigo Books and Music leapt into the online book business by buying out a prebuilt site—developed by Guelph, Ontario-based independent retailer The Bookshelf, who had already secured a spot on Sympatico—and then giving it a facelift. Indigo.ca has created an online "editorial team" to select and review books, much like a literary magazine. The list of high-profile contributors includes political author Stevie Cameron, bad-boy book reviewer Bert Archer, designer Bruce Mau, *Shift* cofounder Evan Solomon, and digital guru Don Tapscott.

Positioning itself as an elegant highbrow boutique for the gift shopper, Indigo.ca quickly moved beyond books to offer everything from flowers and home-decorating doodads to bath products, spa services, and garden goods. Shortly after Chapters.ca bought GardenCrazy.com, Indigo one-upped the competition by going directly to the source and acquiring Cruikshanks, a respected and long-established garden supplier. Indigo's other partners include Holt's and Roots. After a slow start on the bookselling side, with a poorly maintained database, Indigo is working hard to bring its catalogue up to scratch, although basic elements such as cover scans are still absent in many cases.

Used Bookstores and Independents

There are alternatives to the online megabookstores. Many of the independent book dealers of the world (and even a few publishers) have realized that their survival necessitates getting their inventories online. If you like your literature Oprah-free, check out some of the following sites.

Advanced Book Exchange

www.abebooks.com

This site is the world's largest source of out-of-print books, with over 13 million titles listed. Once you conduct a search, you are presented with detailed results describing the state of each copy of the book that's in the database. Beyond the usual title, author, publisher, and keyword search (based on AltaVista technology), you can query the database using book attributes (type of binding, whether or not it's a first edition, whether it's signed or has the orginal dust jacket—a glossary of attributes is helpfully provided), search by geographical region, or browse by subject.

Based in Victoria, B.C., ABE represents a network of over 5,000 used and antiquarian booksellers—it's also the official out-of-print search engine for Barnes and Noble—and you can search the entire stock or browse the inventory offered by individual stores. The cool thing about ABE (pronounced "Abe," in case you wondered) is that you can then link to the individual bookstore that stocks the copy you want, and order directly by e-mail rather than dealing with a middleman. Alternatively, ABE provides an e-commerce option for many (though not all) titles.

Canadian Online Bookseller List

ca.yahoo.com/Regional/Countries/Canada/Business_and_Economy/Companies/Books/Shopping_and_Services/Booksellers

Yahoo! Canada's list of Canadian booksellers with Web sites.

CBAbook.com

emall.netmerchant.net/cba

Launched by the Canadian Booksellers Association **<www.cba.book.org>**, CBAbook.com is a half-baked attempt to provide Canadian independent booksellers with an online presence, but the amateur storefront and clumsy interface can't hold a candle to Chapters or Indigo. It's too bad, because the 1,300 stores represented here deserve a fighting chance. The problem starts with the conceptual model: the store is visualized as a three-storey building offering something different on every floor. It's an idea that was attempted and that quickly failed in the early days of the Web when people were still trying to wrap their minds around the idea of an online mall. The three options are described as Express Lane Shopping (featuring a searchable database and e-commerce shopping cart), Local Shopping (where users can "read about their local bookstore ... and hot-link to their Web site"—an area that was still "under construction" more than a year after the site launched), and the Main Floor (a store locator—searchable by city, store name, postal code, or specialty, though not in combination—that gives you nothing more than an address, contact information, and a URL if one exists).

The biggest problem is the poorly maintained database, which appears to be badly out of date. The site claims that it holds a million titles, but a few random searches on not-so-rare books turned up mostly blanks, and when the right books do turn up, there is little or no supplementary information, often no cover scan, and, worst of all, never a discount on the retail price.

Coach House Books

www.chbooks.com

Coach House is the only book publisher in the world with its entire front list on the Internet, unexpurgated—and they're Canadian. If you like what you read, you can purchase their titles directly, or just leave a tip for the authors.

Powell's Books

www.powells.com

With a constantly rotating inventory of more than 1.5 million new, used, and out-of-print books in their seven bricks-and-mortar stores located in and around Portland, Orgeon, Powell's has pretty good support for its online operation. And they manage to maintain the feel of a traditional independent bookseller, even while providing an efficient and powerful search engine. Browse the Rare Book Room (recently showcasing an 1814 first printing of Lewis and Clark's *History of the Expedition*), download Rocket eBook editions, read interviews, book news, and reviews from the *Utne Reader*, join the discussion in Powell's Cafe, browse the bestseller lists, and more. Powells.com offers both rich content and deep discounts.

E-Books

When Isaac Asimov was asked what the characteristics of the ideal entertainment cassette would be, he responded that it should be small, lightweight, cheap, accessible at any point, and capable of generating different experiences for different users. He then noted, somewhat wryly, that the object closest to fulfilling this definition is a paperback book.

Years later, no one is really sure exactly what an "e-book" is. On top of HTML, standalone programs, and CD-ROMs, there are also a number of competing proprietary hardware devices that require specially coded downloads. The situation is sort of like

▶NETHEADS

Patricia le Roy

Liverpudlian by birth and Parisian by domicile, novelist Patricia le Roy's *The Angels of Russia* was nominated in 1998 for Britain's esteemed Booker Prize. What's geeky about that? Well, for one thing, her novel was published only in digital format, making it the very first e-book to win a Booker nomination. The e-publisher was Online Originals **<www.onlineoriginals.com>**, a joint venture by American writer/editor David Gettman and British professor Christopher Macann that launched in January 1997 with 16 original books. OO continues to produce about 20 new titles each year, which sell for $7 U.S. apiece.

Le Roy, who has worked as a journalist, a translator, and a research editor for Radio Free Europe, set her spy novel/love story in Gorbachev's Russia during the age of perestroika. When the *Times Literary Supplement* swooned over *Angels* and recommended it as a Booker submission, the Booker committee resisted the idea, claiming that *Angels* was not a "real book." Gettman countered: "Is this a prize for writing or for printing?" *The Angels of Russia* didn't make the Booker shortlist, but in May 1999 it was issued by London-based Piatkus Books **<www.piatkus.com>** in an unusual new format—print.

the early days of home VCR use, when Betamax and VHS first appeared, only worse. Choosing one format over the other is a gamble, and technological superiority no guarantee of long-term success.

For the techophiliacs out there, though, following are a few options if you decide that your life would be incomplete without a library of e-books. If worst comes to worst, you can always put your e-book in the basement with your Newton, your Colecovision, your Commodore 64, and your Pong game.

Hoping to avoid a repetition of history, a group of hardware and software companies, publishers, and e-book users launched an association in January 2000 called the Open eBook Forum (OEBF) **<www.openebook.org>**, intending to create standards and promote the successful adoption of electronic books. Members include Microsoft, IBM, Random House, NuvoMedia, Palm, Nokia, McGraw-Hill and other high-profile players. The OEBF will build on prior work by the Open eBook Authoring Group, who in September 1999 released version 1.0 of the Open eBook Publication Structure, a set of specs based on HTML and XML defining the format that content takes when it is converted from print to electronic form. That standard received overwhelming support, but the big issue going forward will concern security and encryption efforts. Keep your fingers crossed.

E-Book Readers

Only a couple of dedicated hardware devices for reading e-books have so far reached the market, while half a dozen other devices wait in the wings. Several software platforms have also emerged for PalmPilots and other PDAs, as well as PCs and Macs.

Rocket eBook

www.rocket-ebook.com

NuvoMedia's Rocket eBook is a 22-ounce handheld device that holds the equivalent of 10 paperback novels or 3,200 pages. It's a little larger than a PalmPilot and competitively priced at $199 U.S.—a sharp drop from its prohibitive initial pricetag of $499 U.S. With a 32 MB memory upgrade, it can store another 190 books, or 36,000 pages of text and graphics. Unknown to many, there's also a little speaker, just in case a RocketEdition comes with audio files. The device comes pre-loaded with *Alice in Wonderland* and the *Random House Dictionary*. Anything else you'd like to read has to be downloaded (and paid for, unless it's in the public domain), but you'll need a computer with an Internet connection, since the Rocket doesn't have its own modem.

Barnes and Noble **<www.barnesandnoble.com>** has a good selection of Rocket titles, as does Powell's **<www.powells.com>**. "Good selection" is a relative term, of course, unless your reading list consists entirely of bestsellers and public domain literary classics. It'll be a while before you can count on reading all your favourite books in Rocket format. If you prefer periodicals, you can visit the eNewsstand for subscriptions to mags like *Fast Company, Salon,* and *The Industry Standard*. And with the new RocketWriter and Rocket-Librarian software, users can download and read files other than e-books, including Microsoft Word documents and Web pages, as well as share their documents on Rocket-Library **<www.rocket-library.com>**, an e-book community Web site.

SoftBook Reader

www.softbook.com

SoftBook Press produces this handheld reader, featuring a 6″ x 8″ greyscale screen, a built-in 33.6 Kbps modem or Ethernet connection for downloading from the SoftBook online shop, enough memory to store about 5,000 pages (capable of expanding to 50,000 pages with optional Flash Memory cards), and a leather cover for that touchy-feely effect. The device weighs in at just under three pounds (1.3 kg). The file format allows searching, bookmarking, and hyperlinking, and the reader comes with a stylus for marking and highlighting the text. The pricing model offers two options: you can fork over a one-time payment of $599.95 U.S. and then pay as you go for SoftBook titles, or pay $299.95 U.S. with an agreement to buy newspapers, magazines, or books worth $19.95 per month for 24 months. Either way, you get 100 free literary classics to start you off.

EveryBook

www.everybk.com

EveryBook's EB Dedicated Reader is still on the drawing board. EveryBook is bigger and more powerful than the Rocket—it has two colour screens, can store a thousand volumes, and is about the size of a large hardcover. And EveryBook has worked out a deal with Adobe to use the Acrobat PDF file format, which does away with the problem of yet another proprietary file type. But will it sell? Your guess is as good as ours. EveryBook will eventually be available in two versions, one for consumers and one for professionals—EveryBook has gone for the green by signing an agreement to publish *Pediatrics*, the journal of the American Academy of Pediatrics, and other professional markets are sure to be targeted. The larger professional version, measuring 11″ x 8 1/2″, is anticipated toward the end of 2000, and will cost somewhere between $1,600 and $2,000 U.S. (gulp!). The somewhat smaller (6″ x 9″) consumer version will follow along about six months later, with a TBA price tag.

TealDoc for PalmPilot

www.tealpoint.com

If you've already got a Pilot, this should scratch your e-book itch while you wait for a standard to emerge. TealDoc is a full-featured reader for standard PalmPilot documents with the capability to handle embedded images and to conduct advanced content searches. It only costs $16.95 U.S., and there's a fair amount of stuff out there for you to download, including Jim Munro's indie hit "Angry Young Spaceman" **<www.nomediakings.org>**.

Glassbook Reader

www.glassbook.com

The Glassbook Reader is a free software program that supports both PDF and the Open eBook Publication Structure. It comes with a built-in browser for buying and downloading books and keeping track of your e-library. Amazon.com partnered with Glassbook to offer a free electronic copy of Stephen King's 16,000-word ghost story *Riding the Bullet* in March 2000, setting off an online feeding frenzy among rabid King fans. The Glassbook Plus Reader ($39 U.S.) includes an *American Heritage Dictionary* and allows you to lend your copy of an e-book to your friends. A word of warning: if you don't own a fast PC, you may find that Glassbook responds a little sluggishly. It also wants to be your primary PDF reader, which opens the door to potential conflicts if you have Acrobat Reader installed.

MS Reader

www.microsoft.com/reader

Arriving late to the party, as usual, Microsoft unveiled its own version of e-book software in April 2000. MS Reader ships with Pocket PC for Windows, Microsoft's new operating system for palm-sized computing devices. Pocket PC replaces Windows CE and is designed to support e-books, digital music, games, Web surfing, and other applications. Text files are searchable, the reader allows highlighting, bookmarking, and annotations, and it comes with a built-in dictionary. The difference from other e-book devices is ClearType, a display component that Microsoft claims will provide sharply focused type akin to the paper experience. At press time, Hewlett-Packard and Compaq were producing the first handheld devices for Pocket PC, although only the HP unit was available, priced at $500 U.S. Thirty free titles accompany new Pocket PC devices, and e-books for MS Reader will be available through the Barnes and Noble eBook Store **<www.bn.com/ebook>**. MS Reader also supports audio books, available from Audible.com **<www.audible.com>**.

netLibrary

www.netlibrary.com

What does the age of e-books mean for the traditional concept of borrowing books freely from the public library? Well, netLibrary thinks the concept works just fine online. Create an account, find the book you want, and choose between viewing it online or "borrowing" it. During the period you have the book checked out, it's unavailable to other netLibrary patrons, just like a real library. When your checkout period expires, however, the book automatically checks itself back in—hey, no more overdue fines! Offline consumption requires the netLibrary eBook Reader, which provides the ability to search, bookmark, and annotate text, as well as zoom in. The copy-and-paste function lets you insert selected passages into another document, and automatically creates a citation (author, publisher, and page number).

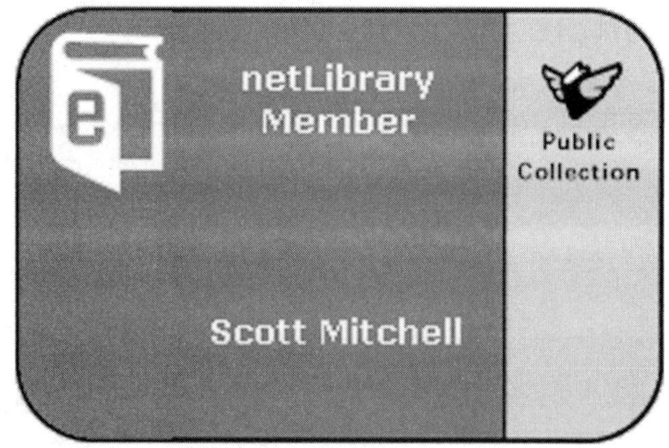

Not one to overlook the important details, netLibrary even provides a digital library card.

The Public Collection offers e-texts free of charge (courtesy of Project Gutenberg, Bibliobytes, and other sources—free because they're in the public domain), while the Library Collection holds copyrighted titles that have been purchased by a library and made available to its patrons. You also have the option of buying e-books, either at the netLibrary site or, for handheld devices, through Peanut Press **<www.peanutpress.com>**, although unlike other e-book schemes, they're not downloadable. Instead, they're stored indefinitely on your own private e-books page. Recently, netLibrary announced that it would be making PDF-version e-books available for Glassbook Readers. More than 18,000 titles from 200 publishers are available from netLibrary.

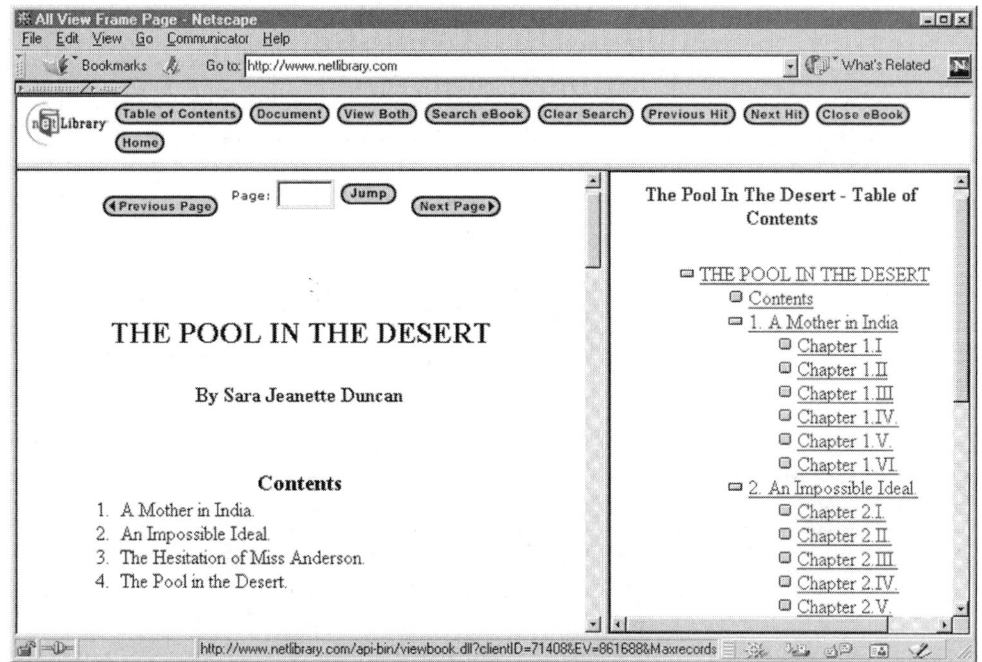

netLibrary uses a framed reading window for viewing books in the Public Collection reading room

> **ARE WE THERE YET?**
>
> **Buying Your "Entertainment Content" Online**
>
> **www.forrester.com**
>
> Forrester Research reports that the electronic delivery of software, music, books, games, and video accounted for a mere 3 percent of online sales in 1999, but that by 2004, digital downloading will amount to 22 percent of online sales for these categories, to make a grand total of $2.9 billion U.S. That's a lot of copies of Quake.

Music

Maybe literature isn't your thing. Fine. There's a lot of music on the Net too.

Music E-tailers Online

In the last two years, music industry retailers have taken to the Internet like pigs to mud. Bricks-and-mortar retail giants HMV **<www.hmv.com>**, Tower Records **<www.towerrecords.com>**, and homeboy Sam the Record Man **<www.samscd.com>** are all hawking their wares online, cheek by jowl with Yankee Internet-based sites such as CDNow **<www.cdnow.com>**. You'd think this would be good news for you, that all that competiton for your dollar would lead to low prices. Once you factor in shipping costs (plus currency conversion, if you're ordering from the U.S.A.—use the Quicken Canada Foreign Exchange Calculator **<www.quicken.ca/eng/banking/calculators/currency>** to figure out your totals)—and the time it takes for a CD to reach your house through the mail, though, it's a different story.

CD costs vary much more from site to site than comparable items like books. As an example, consider the following costs for ultracool cowpunk diva Neko Case's *Furnace Room Lullaby* album:

E-tailer	Cost US	Cost CDN	Shipping & Handling	CDN Total
HMV		$15.99	$3–$15, depending on the level of service. Free shipping on four or more titles.	$18.99
Sam		$14.99	$3 for one item. (Costs go UP with more items.) From $4 for 3–4 items, all the way to $17 for 29–32 items.	$17.99
Tower	$11.99	$17.44	$7.20	$24.64
CDNow	$13.99	$20.35	$4 to $22, depending on location and method.	$24–$44

There's a $25 CDN difference between the lowest and highest price here, which should tell you that it's always worth your while to shop around. What you should be looking for are sales and special promotions—online music stores regularly suspend shipping costs, or offer you free stuff, or some sort of point system for free goodies down the line. Unfortunately, the existing comparison shopping engines do a crummy job of finding low music prices, especially in Canada (they often don't take Canadian e-tailers into account at all), and they won't tell you about sales incentives, so if you're dedicated to the premise that you have to buy your music online, bookmark the major music sites and do your own comparisons.

Remember, whatever difference you find between online prices, the low-end prices are all at par with what you'll find at your local record store. Unless you live in a small town or out in the country, or you find some sort of amazing short-term offer, you'll probably continue to do your CD shopping by sneakernet (i.e. on foot).

Your Best Bets for CD Shopping

There are plenty of companies online that want to sell you music (see for yourself at Yahoo!—look in the "Business and Economy/Companies/Music/CDs, Records and Tapes" directory). Many of them are highly specialized, catering to particular slices of the music market, like junglists or Deadheads (Q: What did the Grateful Dead fan say when she ran out of drugs? A: Hey, this band sucks!). Other online outfits like Chapters, Indigo, and Amazon carry music, but their inventory tends toward MOR (music industry weaselspeak for "middle of the road"), and their prices are high. For access to the greatest range of commercial, major-label music of all genres, the following sites are your best bets.

HMV

www.hmv.com

Like the bricks-and-mortar store, HMV online is generally better organized and better stocked than Sam's site. The collection of sound clips is extensive—you'll find excerpts from at least half the tracks on many of the albums for sale. The site's notes on musicans and albums are intelligent and useful, too. As a general rule, HMV.com is only cheaper than Sam's if you buy at least four discs to wipe out shipping costs. HMV.com is reasonably good at filling orders, though sometimes they'll back-order an obscure import that's difficult to obtain. If you're not happy with the results of an order, their customer service people will fall all over themselves to make you happy.

Sam the Record Man

www.samscd.com

Nobody ever shopped at a Sam's retail store because of the carefully maintained inventory or customer service. Shopping at Sam's has always been about the price, and even on the Net, the pricetags are generally lower than the competition's (unless you buy in bulk).When you've decided what you want to buy, always check Sam's price before you commit yourself, but do your research elsewhere.

Tower Records

www.towerrecords.com

While Tower has stores inside Canada, they still ship from the U.S. when you buy online. Nevertheless, their prices are very competitive.

CDNow

www.cdnow.com

CDNow's CD prices are usually prohibitive for Canadians. The main reason to visit the site is to experience the paradigm of what ethical online music retail will look like if all of the various copyright infringements suits against MP3.com and Napster succeed. CDNow has a "digital download" section, but you pay for all your downloads, and the band receives a royalty as a result. Similarly, CDNow will also assemble a custom CD for you (from a small selection of tracks, listed on the site) for $19.99 U.S. Once again, everybody gets paid, and everyone goes away happy.

Streaming Audio

PC Magazine Streaming Audio Review

www.zdnet.com/products/stories/reviews/0,4161,2313783,00.html

Streaming audio is the Internet equivalent of radio, with all the checks and balances that radio entails. On the plus side, streaming audio content is available to you for nothing, as long as you have the proper software (usually shareware or freeware), and you've paid for some decent hardware—i.e. a good sound card, stereo speakers, and a reasonably fast connection. With a high-speed line (cable or DSL), streaming audio works pretty well. On anything slower, it's all hiccups and jerks, particularly if your computer is doing something labour intensive in the background. Even if your connection is lightning-fast, you'll probably be listening to the content through crappy little PC speakers, so the resulting sound will remind you of your dad's factory-shipped car stereo circa 1985. In other words, streaming audio is the perfect mood-setting device for those late-night cathode-ray tanning sessions.

Another sad-but-true fact is that Internet radio, which used to be relatively commercial-free like FM radio in the 80s, is slowly being ruined by advertising. Now that the honeymoon for Internet startups is over and cold, hard reality is setting in, there'll likely be more ads everywhere as companies used to giving everything away for free scramble madly to establish revenue streams.

Streaming Audio Software

There are three major players in the world of streaming media: Real Networks, Apple's QuickTime, and Microsoft's Windows Media Player. Following the pattern that should be familiar to everyone by now, Microsoft invented its own proprietary format, Windows Media, in an effort to quash the dominant protocol (RealAudio/RealVideo). Though many developers prefer to work with QuickTime or WMP rather than RealPlayer (because Real charges broadcasters for the use of its audio streams), so far, Microsoft hasn't caught up to the competition. According to the Industry Standard **<www.thestandard.com>**, in December of 1999, there were 9.1 million RealPlayer users, 4.8 million QuickTime users, and 3 million Windows Media Player users. In March of 2000, the RealPlayer was still the norm, with about 12% of all netizens using it.

In order to view all the streaming media you're likely to encounter, you'll need to install all three players. Installation is easy, but downloading is a grind—with a 56 K modem, you'll need about an hour to download RealPlayer. This is the price you pay for techno-hipness—spending vast amounts of your time watching the little blue download bar creep across your screen.

Real Networks

www.real.com

RealPlayer 7 is the leading streaming audio player. Depending on your level of audiophilia, you'll want either its free basic version, or the souped-up RealPlayer Plus with built-in equalization, which costs $29.95 U.S. but delivers higher quality audio and video than the freebie. Once you've got your player, you can access content from within the player itself, or from sites like RealGuide **<realguide.real.com>**, which list the most popular streaming audio and video clips of the moment.

> **INFOHAZARD**
>
> **Weasel Warning**
>
> **www.real.com**
>
> Though RealNetworks may look good by comparison when standing next to Microsoft in the corporate lineup, it isn't exactly a knight in shining armour. Last fall, it became clear that despite what it claimed in its online privacy policy, RealNetworks was tracking and storing user profiles. Whether they were intended for Real's own use or possible resale remains unclear. Subsequently, two class-action lawsuits were filed citing unfair business practices and consumer protection laws. The outcome of these cases could set important precedents for the privacy rights of netizens.

Windowsmedia.com

windowsmedia.microsoft.com

Windows Media Player comes bundled with IE5, but you can download WMP alone from this site if you don't have a full set of plug-ins. This page provides direct webcasts for a number of audio and video sources, as well as Windows Media downloads, and a Broadband section for users with DSL, cable, T1, or T3 connections.

QuickTime

www.apple.com/quicktime/download

QuickTime 4.1.1 is the latest version of Apple's media player, which handles everything from virtual reality to MP3s. Like RealPlayer, the basic version of QuickTime is free, but you'll have to pay more to control bass, treble, and balance. You won't encounter as many clips for QuickTime as you will for RealPlayer and WMP, but a lot of high-profile sites, like the official home of Star Wars **<www.starwars.com>**, use QuickTime exclusively.

Streaming Audio Portals

While each media player has built-in shortcuts to various streaming audio portals and Net radio stations, they may not necessarily be to your taste. Most of the major search engines and directories have extensive listings of streaming audio portals or webcasters, mostly drawn from Open Directory's "Webcasts" category **<dmoz.org/Arts/Music/Webcasts>**. When snooping around for streaming audio online, make sure you try Lycos MultiMedia Search **<richmedia.lycos.com>**, which allows you to search for audio streams. If you want to save yourself a little search time, though, the following sites will help you locate whatever flavour of music gets your mojo working.

NetRadio

www.netradio.com

Netradio, the only music-related site to win *Forbes* magazine's "Best of the Web" label, is over 120 channels of uninterrupted music, in every genre that you can imagine. The stations play through your RealPlayer or WMP (the required player varies, depending on which channel you choose). If you like what you hear, you can click on a "Buy" button, and the CD will be winging its way to your door before you know it. There are other reasons for visiting NetRadio, too. The site's "Learn" section features in-depth articles on many genres, subgenres, and musicians, and their daily list of 10 CDs, which sell for $9.88 U.S. each (plus $3 shipping to Canada), features some real bargains.

Scour Radio

www.scour.com/Radio

Scour.com's streaming audio search facilities, um, rock. Check out their featured picks, search by genre, by station location, even download Scour Caster and start your own Internet radio station. They've also got all the major streaming audio tools available for download, if you find that you're missing something.

Yahoo! Broadcast

www.broadcast.com

Yahoo! Broadcast is actually much more than a streaming audio source: it's a whole network of streaming media of every genre and description (radio and TV stations from around the U.S., movies, news, sports events, lifestyle programs, business and finance programs, you name it). The main page works like a TV guide, telling you which programs in your genre of choice are available, and when. This site requires more of your active attention than NetRadio, because when one clip runs out, you'll have to switch to another. Coolest feature: the CD Jukebox, which lets you listen to an entire album, like Fu Manchu's bongwater-soaked masterpiece *King of the Road*.

ChannelSeek

w2.channelseek.com/dial-up

ChannelSeek claims to be "the most comprehensive guide for streaming audio and video on the Net," but mostly it's an overdesigned, slightly inferior version of Yahoo! Broadcast. ChannelSeek has a broadband channel as well as their regular skinny pipe, but it's choked up with a lot of second-rate Flash animation. Forewarned is forearmed.

Proprietary Players and Networks

Liquid Audio

www.liquidaudio.com

Liquid Audio is the first Internet music player to feature a built-in system to manage the digital rights for any given music file on their network. When you install the software, you provide a credit card number as part of the registration process. When you click on a Liquid Audio file, it downloads to the player, along with album art, lyrics, and credits. Some songs are free, but you'll have to pay for more than a 30-second preview of many of them. The Liquid Player plays a number of types of files, including MP3s, and its own proprietary format, LQT. Unlike MP3s, LQT files have permissions attached to them, and the publisher can determine in advance whether or not a particular track is burnable to CD.

Spinner

www.spinner.com

Spinner is like NetRadio in that it features over 130 channels of music, but the service requires the use of its own proprietary player. The Spinner player is available in two free versions: Spinner Plus, a downloadable (Windows/NT only) player, and Spinner Lite, a Web-based player (Mac or Windows/NT).

For downloaded music (including Playlist-to-Go™), the Spinner Music Download Player is also available, which will play MP3s and other forms of downloadable music. Spinner is a fine service, but the big question is, why would you want one more piece of software cluttering up your hard drive when you can get all the streaming audio you'd want without it?

MP3

Remember "Home taping is killing music—and it's illegal"? That phrase used to appear routinely on LP sleeves (remember LPs?), along with a skull-and-crossbones logo with a cassette tape for a skull. Well, compared to the MP3 phenomenon, home taping was a Sunday walk in the park with Grandma.

▶INFOHAZARD

Pay Lars

www.paylars.com

This is too good. In the wake of Metallica vs. Napster, the San Fransisco–based e-commerce development company August Nelson has built a site called Pay Lars, which allows any good-hearted people out there to make direct donations to Metallica to help offset the losses they feel they've incurred at the hands of their own fans trading in their music. Here's a chunk of their explanation for this cheeky act:

> At August Nelson, we think that industry fears of rampant piracy ruining the music business are nothing but paranoid propaganda. Industry representatives have failed to point to any data that shows the extent to which MP3s and CD burners, by making copying music so easy, have hurt industry revenues. That's because there are no such data, because sales keep going up!
>
> We don't believe that it's a mere coincidence that as copying has gotten easier, more people have had the chance to try out more music, and as a result they've ended up buying more music. Here are some numbers from Soundscan that show CD sales are way up in the 1st Quarter of 2000, against the 1st Quarter average from 1995-1999:
>
> Jan 2000 change from Jan 95-99 average +07.3%
>
> Feb 2000 change from Feb 95-99 average +19.4%
>
> Mar 2000 change from Mar 95-99 average +20.7%
>
> Q1 2000 change from 95-99 average +15.8%
>
> So, sales are up, copying is easy, everybody is suing everybody for millions of dollars in lost revenue that actually weren't lost. Metallica is seeking $10,000,000 in damages and may try to put their fans in jail. Has the whole world turned upside down?

Mark Erickson, the author of the piece, writes in summation, "Until I can pay for my groceries with a pirated MP3 file, I think that Q Prime [Metallica's management company]'s position is nothing but hype, and does nothing to endear Metallica or its associates to their fans." For your shopping convenience, Paylars.com takes Visa, Mastercard, American Express, and Discover.

MP3, which stands for "MPEG Audio Layer 3," is a storage and compression standard for audio files. Its popularity stems from the fact that MP3s require relatively little space to produce near-CD quality sound (about one meg per minute of sound, as compared to CDs, which require 11 times as much space). MP3 is a "lossy" compression standard, which means that it actually removes part of the original sound, so audiophiles tend to sneer at it, but the majority of people haven't noticed the difference, or just don't care (the reason for this should be obvious: the subtleties of the musical stylings of Puff Daddy and his ilk don't require tube amplifiers to be fully appreciated).

MP3 isn't just a static format; there are also streaming MP3 servers, which work pretty much like other streaming audio servers. The difference is that while streaming MP3s aren't as crisp as MP3 files themselves, they sound noticeably better than other streaming media. They still skip around a bit when you save a file or run another program with MP3s streaming in the background, but they represent a major improvement nonetheless.

Like we said, "MP3" replaced the word "sex" as the number one search string on Internet search engines last year. Market Tracking International **<www.marketfile.com>** estimates 3 million tracks are downloaded daily. In other words, many, many people are constantly combing the Internet, scooping up files by the dozen, downloading them to their computers and portable MP3 players, burning custom CDs, and "ripping" content off their own CD collection to upload for others to download, regardless of whether the artists who created the music received any payment for the digital version.

So are MP3s illegal? No. At least, not the file format itself, but many of the files you'll find on the Net violate copyright, and are therefore illegal. Major sites like MP3.com (which, by the way, didn't invent the MP3 format and doesn't own it) make formal agreements with artists to circulate their work in digital format in exchange for the exposure and/or (rarely) a royalty of some sort. MP3s from such sites are perfectly legal, but many of the files you'll find on smaller sites or in MP3 newsgroups, which trade in encoded binary files, are pirated.

There's a lot of poorly articulated rhetoric on the Net left over from its *Whole Earth Review* techno-hippie phase about how "information wants to be free." That may have been true at one time, but these days, information wants to get paid. The current flurry of lawsuits over various issues surrounding online music (Recording Industry Association of America vs. MP3.com, everybody vs. Napster) should be enough to convince anyone that times have changed, and open piracy will not be tolerated by the recording industry. (Interesting fact: despite all the arm-waving and shouting, online music is a tiny slice of the music industry pie. Karen Solomon of *The Industry Standard* writes that "Only 10 percent of the $46-billion-a-year music industry that's projected by 2005 will consist of online sales, and only $635 million of that will be derived from online-download sales, according to a study by Music Business International, a consultancy in Hollywood, Calif. An even smaller percentage will be in the MP3 format.")

Whether the record labels will be able to keep up with the kids exchanging the music is a moot point. File formats come and go, but the relentless biological drive to make tapes (or CDs) for one's girlfriend or boyfriend will continue unabated.

As for you, gentle reader, here's the dirt on MP3 players, portals, and newsgroups. Take a look at the issues, do some research—there are many good articles on the MP3 controversy at The Standard **<www.thestandard.com>** and ZDNet **<www.zdnet.com>**—and make your own decisions.

MP3 Players

While WMP, RealPlayer, and QuickTime will play your MP3s (and even streaming MP3 radio) for you, their basic (free) versions don't allow for fine adjustments such as equalization, and they don't have cool toys like "skins" (custom interfaces) and plug-ins (which usually allow for different kinds of music visualization—the new millennium's equivalent of a lava lamp). The latter goodies may not be all that important to you, but it's surprising how much sound quality you can squeeze out of an MP3 player by tweaking the equalization. Downloading one of the following players will enhance your online listening experience considerably.

WinAmp

www.winamp.com

By many accounts, NullSoft's WinAmp is the slickest MP3 player around. Even in its full-sized version, it's only a 2 MB download, and it installs quickly and easily. The equalization makes a huge difference—after listening to MP3s or MP3 radio through WinAmp, you'll never go back to your old streaming audio player. The WinAmp site features a large variety of skins (our favourite is 1914, which looks like something Fritz Lang might have whipped together in a spare moment), and access to WinAmp's SHOUTcast radio network. Attention budding DJs: the SHOUTcast network allows you to broadcast as well as listen... all you need is the free SHOUTcast server, and huge amounts of time to waste.

MusicMatch

www.musicmatch.com

MusicMatch, another excellent player, is sparring with WinAmp for its long-held, number one MP3 player slot. MusicMatch supports Windows Media files and WAVs as well as MP3s, but not RealPlayer files. Like WinAmp, it allows you to change skins and add plug-ins (although both are currently in short supply), but its real strength is its file-management capabilities. If you have a lot of MP3s on your hard drive, you'll appreciate the 17 different organization criteria the program allows. There's also a Plus version for $29.95 U.S. that allows you to record CDs at higher bit rates than the free version.

Sonique

www.sonique.com

Sonique is an MP3 player that will appeal instantly to fans of Kai's Power Tools. Its skins can make it look like just about anything, and some of them approach the threshold of utter incomprehensibility. Like MusicMatch, it supports a wide range of

Computing in the age of steam: WinAmp, a popular MP3 player, allows you to change its look and feel to almost anything you can imagine, including this design, call "Old Timey"

audio formats, including Windows Media, and it has an impressive 17-band equalizer, as well as standard balance and pitch controls. It won't encode MP3s or rip CDs, but if all you're looking for is a player, Sonique is a definite contender.

MP3 Search Engines

What a difference a year can make. Web-based MP3 search engines used to be pretty reliable when it came to ferreting out MP3s, but most of them have been gutted by their operators for fear of being sued. While they will return results when searching for artists and songs, the results are usually amateur musicians who *sound like* what you're searching for rather than the real deal. If you're lucky enough to get hits for your search term, you'll likely find that the FTP servers you want are almost always either busy or down. The following MP3 search engines are better than most, but their results are still inconsistent.

Scour

www.scour.com

Wow... an MP3 search engine that actually works. The results aren't always plentiful, but at least the results that you find are usually accurate. As well as MP3s, Scour will find WAVs, RealAudio, midi, MOD, AU, Liquid Audio, and Net radio results for your search, as well as a variety of video and still image formats. Expect Scour to continue operating smoothly until someone decides to sue them.

Listen.com

www.listen.com

Listen.com, a division of ZDNet, has over 60,000 legal MP3s on its Web site, and the good news is, you'll know who many of the bands are. The bad news is, you have to pay to download some of them. But the price is a small one to pay for a legal MP3 search service that does what it's supposed to do.

FindSongs

www.findsongs.com

The Change Music Network maintains FindSongs, a metasearch engine which queries the current top 30 MP3 search engines on the MP3Now list **<www.mp3now.com>**. Also provides reviews of albums by the artist you're seeking, plus a list of "Related Artists." If FindSongs can't locate the music you're after, nothing that's Web-based will do the job.

MP3Meta

www.mp3meta.com

MP3Meta saves you some time by querying several other engines for MP3s (as well as music sites, cover art, and lyrics, if you like). Because they start with more information, you'll find fewer dead links.

Lycos MP3 Search

mp3.lycos.com

Lycos MP3 Search lists over 1 million MP3 files, but the question is, how many of them will be there when you go looking for them? We spent 10 minutes looking for files for a number of artists from different genres before we gave up, after having drawn a total blank. There are few other features to the site than the MP3 engine: a few downloadable players, rippers, encoders, and so on, and a "Music Listening Room" that's suffered the same fate as MP3.com.

MP3.com

www.mp3.com

MP3.com has changed a lot over the last year, mostly because of the various lawsuits leveled against it (you can read all about it at **<stations.mp3s.com/stations/23/your_music_your_rights.html>**). Right now, the content of the site is mostly streaming MP3s from various struggling musicians; entering the name of a well-known rock band, say, Black Sabbath, will return a list of MP3 stations playing music "by bands influenced by Black Sabbath" and another list of the artists themselves, but nary a tune by England's finest. Great for A&R men and college radio programmers, but what about the rest of us?

MP3 Newsgroups

Besides Web sites, you can also get MP3 files from newsgroups in the alt.binaries category, which carry files. There are currently several dozen newsgroups for MP3 files, including **<alt.binaries.sounds.mp3.1970s>**, **<alt.binaries.sounds.mp3.1980s>**, **<alt.binaries.sounds.mp3.1990s>**, and **<alt.binaries.sounds.mp3.bootlegs>**, and more are being created all the time. The MP3 files you get from newsgroups are almost always unauthorized. Even if you have no intention of downloading illegal MP3 files, you can still use MP3 newsgroups to find out more information about MP3.

MP3 Search Tools

This is the real deal. If you want to find MP3s on the Internet, you need a software client for a service like the infamous Napster, the nearly infamous Gnutella, and the soon-to-be-infamous Scour Exchange.

Why all the infamy? In April of 2000, Metallica launched a suit against Napster (and several universities, for refusing to curtail their students' use of the software) for copyright infringement and racketeering. Metallica seem hell-bent on reinforcing the stereotype of heavy metal musicians as knuckleheads; motormouth drummer Lars Ulrich says in their press release, "It is sickening to know that our art is being traded like a commodity rather than the art that it is." As Michelle Goldberg asked in a recent article in *The Industry Standard*, "Wait a minute—isn't Metallica's problem that its music *isn't* being treated as a commodity, i.e., as something that needs to be paid for?" Given the fact that Metallica has increased its fan base by actively encouraging bootleg taping of its live shows for years, the lawsuit seems more than a little hypocritical.

Metal musicians haven't got the market cornered on greed and stupidity, though (for one thing, there are a lot fewer of them than there used to be): gangster rappers exhibit both qualities in abundance. Dr. Dre (probably not a real doctor), aka Andre Young, followed in Metallica's wake with a suit of his own, sending a letter to Napster demanding that the company delete all of his recordings from the directory. Napster responded by pointing out, as they did for Metallica, that any Dr. Dre MP3s are not actually on their server, but on the hard drives of individual users, and asked Dr. Dre and his attorney to identify the individual users of the system who are violating the rapper's copyrights before proceeding.

The Napster boys probably laughed themselves to sleep that night, too—until Metallica found a hacker of their own who figured out how to track individual Napster users. Shortly thereafter, Metallica's lawyers produced 13 file boxes containing the names of some 300,000 users alleged to have traded Metallica's songs online. True to their word, Napster promptly banned the users from their service, though banned users can either appeal the ban or simply reinstall their software and reregister with another user name to continue service. Last time we checked, there were still a lot of Metallica songs being traded on Napster, no doubt as a form of protest.

[Totally unrelated but interesting fact: George Lucas's Lucasfilm Ltd. has filed a copyright and trademark infringement lawsuit against Dr. Dre, Aftermath Entertainment, and Interscope Records, based on the contention that the good doctor uses Lucasfilm's trademarked "THX Deep Note" sound to open his current album, *Dr. Dre — 2001*, without Lucasfilm's permission. It takes a thief . . .]

> **▶INFOHAZARD**
>
> **Hotline Central**
>
> **www.hotlinecentral.com**
>
> In order to find anything on Hotline, you first need to go to Hotline Central on the Web and grab the current addresses of some of the trackers. There's also a good basic tutorial there, as well as a search engine for files on the Hotline itself. Technical note: To make Hotline work properly, you'll probably have to turn off your firewall, if you have one. There's a setting under options that asks the program to "tunnel through" your firewall, but it's not necessarily going to work. And a word of warning: Because Hotline is a fairly new phenomenon, there's a lot of questionable content on it. If you take the time to look, though, you'll find some genuinely interesting and totally wholesome stuff as well.

With belligerent teenage hackers on one side and rich, ignorant musicians on the other, this lawsuit business could drag on for years. Some high-profile musicians, such as Limp Bizkit and Chuck D, have actually come out in favour of Napster. Legally, the situation is still cloudy. At the time of this writing, the case was in full swing; Napster's argument under the U.S. Digital Millennium Copyright Act (passed in 1998) that it is simply a "dumb pipe"—a network that conducts information but has no responsibility for it—failed to hold water with the judge. Their best hope for avoiding certain corporate death is the so-called Betamax case, which established that technologies such as the VCR (and potentially Napster) can't be banned as long as they have possible legal uses as well as illegal uses.

But Napster is just a distribution protocol, and MP3 is just a file format. There will be (and already are) other services springing up, hydra-like, to take their place if Napster and MP3 disappear. The Gnutella network, the Hotline, and the Scour Exchange already have a head start. Gnutella, originally a rogue AOL project that has continued to develop among the open source community in unauthorized releases, has the potential to be unstoppable, because unlike the other services mentioned, Gnutella is a distributed service, with no central servers. Be very afraid, and/or rock on.

Napster

www.napster.com

This is what the fuss is all about, and no wonder: Napster is like a magic window into the music collections of everyone you know—a window that allows you to reach in and grab the tunes that you like. This tiny little piece of software (640 K

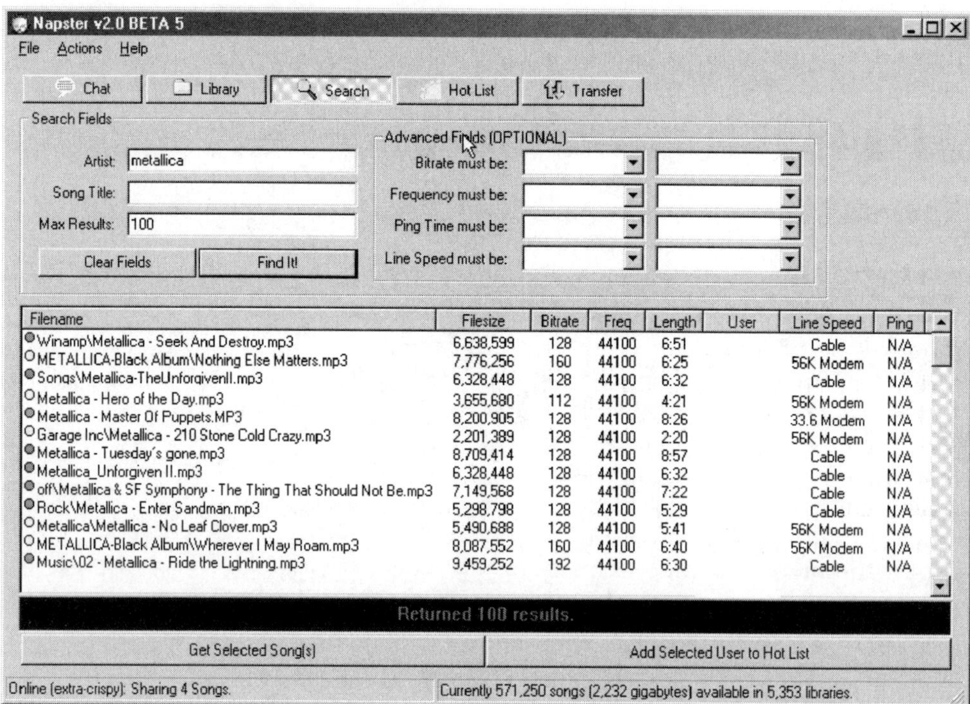

Napster: a whole lotta tradin' going on, Metallica lawsuit or no...

compressed) turns a section of your hard drive into a file server, and allows you access to the corresponding section of the hard drives of everyone else who happens to be connected to the network. From the client, you can search by artist or song title, with advance options specifying connection speed. When you locate your MP3, the file is added to your download list. Multiple downloads happen simultaneously, and very quickly, but people still like to hang out in one of the chat channels when trading music. Note: Napster is betaware, and therefore slightly buggy. Expect the odd crash to happen while running it. If you are a cable or DSL user and you're operating behind a firewall, you may have to temporarily disable it for your Napster sessions.

> **INFOHAZARD**
>
> **The Anti-Napster Cometh**
>
> **mediaenforcer.tripod.com/enforcer/index.html**
>
> Enter Media Enforcer, the security guard of the file-sharing universe. This program (which is available as freeware) lurks on the Napster network, quietly gathering the names of any users sharing files matching any string you specify, say "Metallica" or "Dr. Dre." The program's creator, who wishes to remain anonymous to avoid the wrath of the file-sharing community, is confident that if you're a musician who wishes to protect your intellectual property, Media Enforcer will provide you with enough identifying information to either submit a petition to ban the offending users from the service, or to hold them responsible in a court of law. While Media Enforcer currently only runs on Napster, its next version will add support for the CuteMX, iMesh, and Scour.net networks. Zeropaid.com features an interview with Net Enforcer's creator at <**www.zeropaid.com/9online/media0531.shtml**>.

Scour Exchange

www.scour.com/Software/Scour_Exchange

SX, or Scour Exchange, is Scour.com's Napster clone. It operates according to the same basic principles as Napster, but allows users to share video and image files as well as music. SX hasn't been around very long, but the record industry lawyers are already looking for blood. Scour maintains that they're simply adding functionality to their search engine, and that they've taken adequate precautions to protect the interests of copyright holders, but only time will tell whether or not their head is next on the block after Napster's.

RadioSpy

www.radiospy.com

We can't recommend this highly enough. One fine day the makers of the excellent GameSpy online video game server locating tool realized that they could apply their technology to streaming MP3s as well. RadioSpy locates all of the SHOUTcast (MP3), Windows Media, and RealAudio streaming audio servers on the Internet, sorts them by genre, number of listeners, bandwidth, and other pertinent information, then plugs the tunes into WinAmp for you (its custom WinAmp skin is pretty good, too). RadioSpy also has built-in chat, news, and bulletin board services—what more can you ask for? If you're too lazy to download the software, the RadioSpy Web site itself also has an excellent directory.

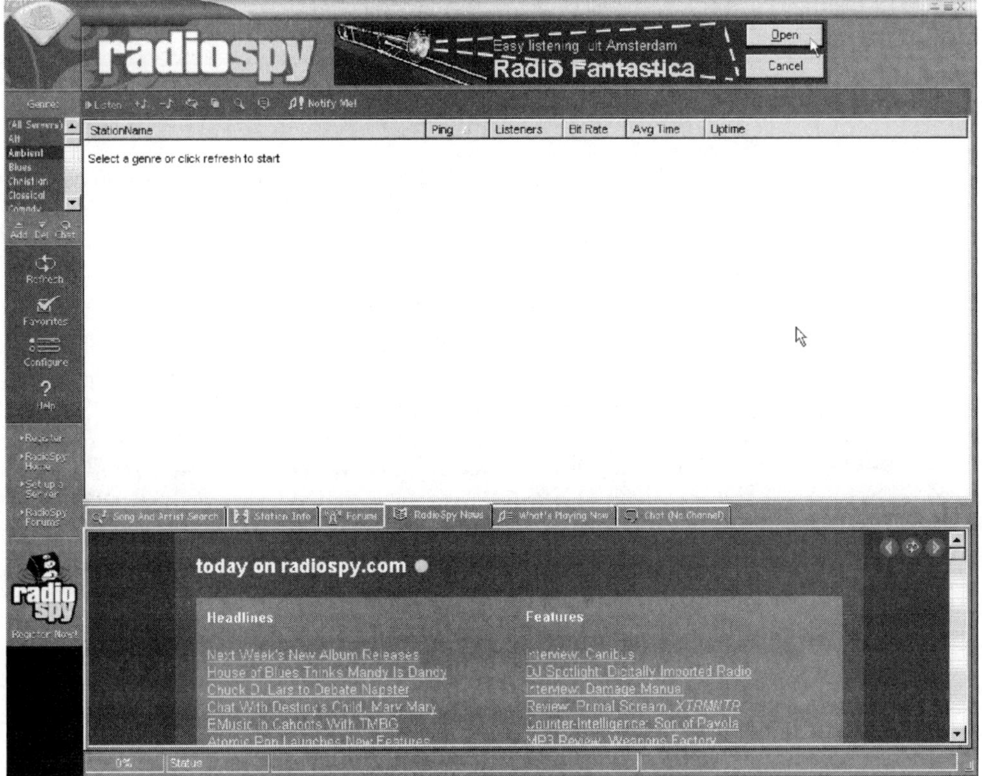

For serious listeners of Internet radio, RadioSpy is an indispensable tool

Gnutella

gnutella.wego.com

GNU (from the open-source Unix clone, GNU) + Nutella, a tasty hazelnut-flavoured breakfast spread beloved by Europeans = Gnutella, a distributed, file-sharing network championed by the open-source community. This is the *uber*-geek version of Napster, more raw and potentially much more powerful because there's no central server to sue or to shut down. If one of those stray Russian nukes accidentally takes out New York, too bad—you lose your Gnutella buddies in New York, but hey, the network will still be running. If you're the kind of person who's a regular Slashdot **<www.slashdot.org>** reader, you'll take to Gnutella like a duck to water. If you're thinking to yourself "Slashdot? What's Slashdot?" you should probably steer clear for the time being.

Spinfrenzy

www.spinfrenzy.com

SpinFrenzy is a hybrid, halfway between Napster and a Web-based search engine. Users share files using SpinFrenzy Xchange, a little piece of software called a "download helper." Anyone can see the available files by running a search on the Web page, but you can't download without the helper app. SpinFrenzy is a useful site, but its target audience seems to be 15 year olds, so you may not get all the references (are *you* more ambitious than your GF/BF?). Don't let the little monsters generation-gap you.

Props to the Old School

Resources for Tape Trading

www.resourcesfortapers.com

Tape-trading networks existed long before the Internet, but they've really adapted to take advantage of the new technology. For those who don't know, tape traders trade noncommercial music and "live concert" (aka bootleg) tapes of their favourite bands. As in the world of MP3s, this is sometimes illegal, but many bands (including the Grateful Dead and Metallica) encourage the trading of live tapes because it increases the loyalty of their fan base. If you're curious, this site is a good place to go for more information.

ARE WE THERE YET?

alt.culture's Jaundiced Retrospective

www.altculture.com

Alt.culture is a searchable online Devil's Dictionary (What? Never read Ambrose Bierce? Shame on you.) that turns its jaundiced eye back on where we just were (i.e. the 90s). The site's clipped, acerbic tone occasionally makes The Onion **<www.theonion.com>** (What? You don't read The Onion either? What kind of cynic are you, anyway?) looks positively sunny by comparison. Sample entry: "Stone Temple Pilots: Southern California band that could, at one point, claim to be the most hated quintuple-platinum rock act in America."

Buying Cars Online

Let's say, just for laughs, that you want to haul your pale carcass away from the computer screen for a few hours, maybe even leave the city. Uh oh. You'll need a car... unless you're one of those insane bicycle-riding people.

Buying a new car has always been a headache (don't get us started about used cars—that's a whole other conversation), but whether you buy from a dealer, or direct over the Web, the Internet can help you get a better deal than if you just march into a showroom. At the very least, you can do some research (there's that mom voice again), print everything out, and walk into the dealership with printouts in hand. Hopefully, the dealer will believe you know your business and won't be quite so eager to pull a fast one. The following sites will tell you everything you need to know.

General Automotive Information

Canadian Driver

www.canadiandriver.com

CanadianDriver is the best online guide to Canadian automotive resources, with over 1,700 links to Canadian automotive Web sites, including car dealers, parts retailers, automotive services, consumer information, government organizations and industry associations, magazines and e-zines. Their editorial staff is keenly aware of the differences between the Canadian and U.S. online environment, and their articles often discuss how you can use U.S. information to your advantage.

Edmund's

www.edmunds.com

Edmund's is the definitive car information site, hands down. It contains much information of value to any car owner, or prospective car owner: reviews, road tests, consumer advice, and a "town hall" of discussion forums packed with people who can answer just about any question you can ask about automobiles. The only drawback is that the prices are all in American dollars, and are indexed to U.S. markets, so they can't easily be converted for Canadian use.

Car and Driver

www.caranddriver.com

If you care about cars, the online version of the venerable auto magazine is a site you'll want to bookmark. The people who write these incredibly detailed and informative reviews love driving for its own sake, kind of like the way you love your computer. Hard to comprehend, but true.

Dealer Invoice Price Suppliers

In the U.S.A., buying a car is a very different matter than it is here, for one particular reason: you can head to the Internet and find out exactly how much the dealer paid for the car. This amount, called the dealer invoice price, comes from an extensive network of contacts, all of whom provide information to several organizations that track the invoice prices for all current models, and then make this information available for free to the public. Having access to the dealer invoice price is the only sure way of knowing how much the car has been marked up for retail.

While it's true that there's no *free* source of Canadian dealer invoice prices online, that doesn't mean that the information is totally unavailable. The following sites are the first to offer Canadian dealer invoice prices for sale. The prices they charge are actually very reasonable, when you consider that they could save you hundreds of dollars.

CarCost Canada

www.carcostcanada.com

The people who run the Auto Hotline (1-800-805-2270)—a telephone service that provides dealer invoice costs—launched CarCost Canada late in 1999. Their Standard plan (there are others—check the site for details) costs $39 plus GST. For that sum, you get detailed dealer cost pricing for up to two vehicles (must be in the current year, or already-released models from next year), plus telephone and e-mail support, and the assistance of CarCost Canada in locating a cooperative dealer who'll give you a good price. This last item may be harder than you'd think—a lot of car dealers are hopping mad about the availability of dealer invoice prices online.

Automobile Protection Agency

www.apa.ca

The Automobile Protection Agency provides two options for obtaining Canadian dealer invoice prices (they'll also tell you which domestic automakers sell cars *below* the invoice price). The first option, for non-APA members, is a flat fee of $25 plus tax per dealer cost quote. The second option, which makes sense if you're doing any comparison shopping, is to take out an APA membership, which only costs $52 plus GST per year. As a member, you get two quotes free, along with a lot of other great stuff, like a subscription to *Lemon-Aid*, the APA magazine, lists of recommended dealers, garages, etc., and discounts on rustproofing, repairs, and other services.

Canadian Car-Buying Sites

TD Autoexplorer

www.tdautoexplorer.com

TDAutoExplorer maintains a database of over 500 new cars, has a good engine for locating dealers near you, and will help you with their financing, but the best reason to visit the site is to use their Compare tool. Select one car make and model from their database, then hit the "Compare" button at the bottom of the left-hand menu. The tool will display the cars—and their stats—side-by-side on the same screen, grouping comfort, safety, technical, and exterior features together and indicating whether they are standard equipment or options (you can select which options you want from a set of check-boxes).

Carclick

www.carclick.com

Brought to you by the Southam people, Carclick can be a useful resource ... if you're a potential auto buyer who lives in Vancouver, Edmonton, Calgary, Montreal, Ottawa, Kingston, St. Catharines, or Windsor (the areas for which they currently track car service information). If you're anywhere else, note that they do maintain the largest online database of Canadian car profiles from 1993 on, and of cars for sale in this country. You can also use their online insurance or financing malls to apply for insurance (from CIBC, Believer Plus, Insure Explorer, or the Vector Insurance Network) or for financing (from mbanx, Excelease, TD, or the Royal Bank).

Autobuytel Canada

www.autobuytel.ca

Autobuytel has a headlock on the U.S. online car-buying racket, and is coming up fast in Canada. They've got a large database of info on new cars, and some simple but useful tools to help you narrow your choices. If you'd like to buy direct from the Web, you can do that too—just remember that if you ask them for a quote, they're unlikely to haggle over it with you because they're starting with a lower pricing scheme.

Autonet Canada

www.autonet.ca

Autonet has been around since 1996, and offers all the basic services you'd expect: information on new and used cars, and links to the CIBC loan site and insurance site. If you're having trouble locating a dealer, their Search option will help you locate either a bricks-and-mortar or online auto dealer anywhere in the country.

Real-Time Internet Communication

Though we aren't quite at the Dick Tracy wrist-videophone yet, person-to-person communications are moving rapidly in that direction. Real-time multi-person communication on the Internet is now commonplace, thanks to programs like ICQ. Actually, almost every new client program, regardless of its use, now has its own chat system, and a light version of AOL Instant Messenger has been built right into Netscape. The problem that results from this proliferation is the need to convince all of your friends to use the same chat software. The major programs are listed below. Find out what your friends use, and get it.

IRC

Internet Relay Chat (IRC) is the CB radio of the Internet: a series of global channels full of people talking about . . . stuff. Science fiction writer Bruce Sterling once noted that IRC is a vast, complex machine whose sole purpose is to put you in touch with the most boring guy in Bolivia, but hey, who knows? You might have some fun with it. First, though, you'll need an IRC client.

mIRC

www.mirc.com

mIRC 5.7 is the standard chat client for Windows users, rated by ZDNet as one of the top 50 shareware/freeware programs of the millennium (mIRC is *way* better than the medieval IRC programs, and noticeably superior to the IRC programs of the Italian Renaissance). It's shareware, and only $20 U.S. to register—a real bargain. For serious geek-world credibility, you can join the mIRC SETI (Search for Extra-Terrestrial Intelligence) **<www.mirc.co.uk/seti.html>**, a scientific experiment that harnesses the power of hundreds of thousands of Internet-connected computers and uses them as a massive parallel processor. All you have to do is run a small but incredibly cool-looking screensaver that downloads and analyzes data from the Arecibo Radio Telescope when you're not using your computer yourself. (Our theory about all of this is that the mIRC people are simply getting bored chatting with each other and are looking for some better conversation.)

IRCle

www.ircle.com

Not Urkel, IRCle. A good IRC client for the MacOS.

AOL Instant Messenger

www.aol.com/aim/home.html

AOL Instant Messenger is now the number one chat software on the Net, with over 50 million users. A lite version has been incorporated into Netscape 6, but you can get the full-featured version here.

ICQ

www.icq.com

ICQ, the predecessor to AOL Instant Messenger, still exists as a separate product, even though AOL bought the company. Feature for feature, this program kicks AOL IM's bloated corporate butt. It's primarily used by online gamers, but given the chance, even your mom will love it. (Weirdest fea-

NUTS & BOLTS

IRC Fun Facts

www.geocities.com/~mirc/ircintro.html

The mIRC FAQ is a goldmine of trivia, including the following: "IRC gained international fame during the Gulf War in 1991, when updates from around the world came across the wire, and most IRC users who were online at the time gathered on a single channel to hear these reports. IRC had similar uses during the coup against Boris Yeltsin in September 1993, where IRC users from Moscow were giving live reports about the unstable situation there." Apparently, people have also been married over IRC. Whatever.

ture: the manual typing noise that the program makes when you enter a message. How utterly 20th century.)

MSN Messenger

messenger.msn.com

Despite what the conmmercials would have you believe, MSN Messenger is not the chat software of choice for workplace rebels. Or for anyone who doesn't work for Microsoft, actually. Compared to ICQ or AOL IM, MSN Messenger looks pretty skimpy. Once it's bundled with Windows, though, everything else is doomed. Sigh.

Internet Telephony

You may not have realized it yet, but your telephone and your television are in a race to see which one will get to consume the other first. Your computer is just the thingy attached to the end of the network, and is, in many respects, inconsequential. The folks at MIT (Massachusetts Institute of Technology) know all about it, and, in fact, are directly responsible in some ways for the innovations that make such a convergence possible.

One of those innovations is Internet Telephony. A few years ago, some bright light out there realized that the Internet could theoretically carry a telephone voice signal as well as textual data, and that, after dial-up costs, long-distance phone calls would be free, and of no fixed length. There are drawbacks, of course. You have to talk to someone who has an IT client, and you have to take turns talking, like on two-way radio. Otherwise, it's a pretty neat idea.

To learn more about Internet Telephony, visit the MIT Internet & Telecoms Convergence Consortium site **<itel.mit.edu>**. Their Lists and Resources section features links to a plethora (that's right, a plethora) of sites that make IT software for the PC, Mac, and Linux operating systems.

CU-SeeMe

www.wpine.com/Products/CU-SeeMe

Despite the name, this piece of software has nothing to do with the horrifying Lionel Ritchie song from the 1980s. CU-SeeMe is the most popular videoconferencing and video chat software available for the Internet. It used to be free, but is now shareware that costs $69 U.S. (or $99 with a webcam included, which you also need if you don't have one already). Unfortunately, and predictably, the people who've gotten the most usage out of this type of software are porn enthusiasts, but there are undoubtedly wholesome uses for it as well . . .

Another Roadside Attraction: Fun and Amusement

Okay, enough about work. Though it was built by the military, and is rapidly being taken over by multinational corporations, at its core the Internet is about wasting perfectly valuable time in as many different ways as you can imagine, and a few you can't. If humanity really is *homo ludens*, the creature who plays, then welcome to the biggest and best toy ever created.

There are games all over the Net—games you can download, games you play through your browser, games you play against others in real time. As connection speeds get faster, the level of detail and rapidity of movement increase, and the games themselves become more sophisticated. It's a truism of computer culture that all the real advances in hardware development are due to pressure from gamers and gaming companies. After all, you don't need a huge 19″ monitor, 128 megs of video memory, a 64x CD-ROM, and a 32 MB Diamond Viper 3D graphics accelerator to run a spreadsheet, do you? Heck no—your PalmPilot can do that. It can't, however, display really cool exploding full-colour alien battlecruisers . . . yet. And God help the working world when it can.

Now. Time to start wasting time. Here are a few excellent places to begin.

Free Stuff

Let's start you off slowly, so you don't have to invest any more money in your computer than you already have. The first one is always free ;-).

Shockwave Games Directory

shockwavegames.hypermart.net

This page is a list of links to arcade sites featuring Internet games running on Macromedia's Shockwave plug-in. It's included with Netscape 4.x, but if you don't have it yet, you can get it from **<www.macromedia.com/shockwave/download>**. While you're at the Macromedia site, swing by Shockrave **<www.shockrave.com>** and check out their collection of primo time-wasting devices.

FreeArcade.com

www.javaarcade.com

Java is a programming language that allows for a degree of interactivity not possible in HTML. If it's level three or higher, your browser can handle it (in theory, at least—be prepared for the odd crash). Here's a site full of 100 different Java games, some that closely resemble old arcade faves, most totally new.

Excite Online Games

www.excite.com/games/online_games

Excite maintains a large collection of traditional games that have been ported to the Web, such as chess, checkers, crosswords, bridge, and so on, plus a few simple arcade games. You can play by yourself, or against others. These games are incredibly addictive—at any time we've checked, there are about 35,000 people playing.

Riddler

www.riddler.com

This popular site features a number of puzzle-type games—trivia, crosswords, and jigsaws—that you can play by yourself or against others. There are hourly tournaments too.

File Mine Game Directory

www.filemine.com/Games

File Mine, a popular shareware site, has a large selection of downloadable shareware games, ranging from trivia to arcade action. Dig it.

Game Emulators

Do you often think fondly of the good old days when videogames came one each, in a case as large as your refrigerator? Or even of your monochrome Game Boy? You're not alone. The latest craze in online gaming is emulation software, which creates a virtual machine inside your computer capable of running the ROMs (programs stripped off hardware chips) that ran those original games. From a legal perspective, emulation is a grey area. It's (usually) legal to make or own an emulator, but lately the owners of the software on the original ROMs have been tracking down the distributors of the ROMs and forcing them to cease their activities. You'll probably be able to locate emulators, then, but you may not be able to locate any software for them.

bleem!

207.71.8.31

bleem! is a Sony PlayStation emulator for the PC. Install the software, drop the PlayStation disc into your CD-ROM drive, and away you go. It's a nifty bit of coding: for a long time, it was generally considered to be impossible to write a PlayStation emulator because play would be too slow. What's more, bleem! is fully legal: it'll cost you $29.95 U.S., but all future updates are free. bleem! has thoughtfully provided a compatibility list on the site as well, so that you can check to see if the game you want to buy will work with the current emulator version before you buy it.

MAME (Multi Arcade Machine Emulator)

arcadeathome.efront.com

MAME lets you play over 1,300 classic arcade video games on your PC. These are not recreations, but the actual arcade games that appeared in arcades in the 70s and 80s. MAME is an anthropological enterprise: it was designed to digitally preserve games and gameplay that would otherwise be forgotten in the modern-day rat race of console games and computers. This site, Arcade at Home, will provide the emulation software, plus its history in an extended FAQ. It also links to several ROM sites, including a page at Top-25.com, that keeps track of the top 25 emulation sites on the net. **<www.top-25.com/emu/index.html>**

The Hard Stuff: Commercial Games

This is the big league of online gaming. It's actually possible to make a living now as a professional video game player (just not probable). All of the major games have their own forums, tournaments, and ranking systems. Some, like Quake and Starcraft, even have their own culture: literature, art, music, humour, and language.

The whole point of gaming online is that you get to play with other humans, or with other humans against a computer. Though there are many different kinds of online games, the most popular ones capitalize on the unpredictability of human vs. human play. They fall into three basic types: first-person shoot-em-up, real-time strategy (or RTS), and role-playing adventure. In a first-person shoot-em-up game, your character runs down dark hallways and kills everything it encounters. RTS gaming is more cerebral, but usually no less bloody. Your perspective is third-person, and you must construct a small civilization in order to produce combat units, whose job is to venture out into the unknown (RTS games typically employ something called "the fog of war," which hides terrain until you explore it) and kill everything they encounter. Either way you slice it, there's darkness and killing. Quake, with its various sequels, mods and spinoffs, rules over the first-person shoot-em-up universe with an iron fist, and Blizzard Games' Starcraft and Starcraft Brood War is the current RTS favourite. Role-playing and adventure games are more meditative and have a larger text component. Some of the new ones,

NETHEADS

Clan Culture

Gamers are an odd and fractious bunch. As soon as you gather them together (which you have to, in order to play), they start splitting off into little subgroups, each with its own particular likes, dislikes, and playing styles. Each clan, as these groups are called, usually has its own rankings, its own Web site, and its own chat forum on their gaming network of choice. You can usually tell a clan member by some sort of odd insignia that appears as part of their user name, and by their incessant attempts to recruit you to join. Dakota's Gamer's Guide **<www.bluesnews.com/guide>** has the following to say about clans:

> The Quake clan is an interesting sociological experiment. The clan usually begins with five single nomadic players joining forces. At this stage, there usually aren't any set policies and only a rudimentary administrative structure. As the clan grows, stratification among the membership also grows and policies increase in size and complexity. Typically, the "government" of the clan evolves from either a despotism or a pure democracy into either a representative form of government or a plutocracy. It is rare for a large clan to have not redefined its governmental structure at least once, and most have revised the government several times.

You can also read "Twenty Minutes Later: The History of the Clanring" at **<www.mpog.com/clanring/history>**. Whew! There's a whole Cultural Studies doctoral dissertation in the offing here.

such as Baldur's Gate and its sequel, Planescape: Torment, are worthy heirs to the complex role-playing games of the 80s.

Careful: if you get started down the path of hardcore gaming, there may be no turning back short of professional deprogramming or aversion therapy.

Gaming Assistants

Every game that's playable online includes software that will connect you to its master server, at which point you can select a game and begin playing. Trouble is, the connection software often isn't very complex—all of the programming attention goes into the game itself. A whole industry has sprung up that's dedicated solely to making software that provides you with the best connection available for the gaming options you want.

Gaming assistants do different things: some put you onto a separate network, others allow you to filter out particular game types, and to locate your friends. Descriptions of the better ones follow.

GameSpy

www.gamespy.com

GameSpy is a sophisticated filtering program for gaming servers. It allows you to set up customized lists of the servers you use regularly, and to search for servers on those lists without having to sit through the refresh for an entire game's network. You can also use it to locate individual players online, which is a nice feature if you like to game with your friends. And, like every other piece of client software that's come down the pipe in the last few years, it has a chat network.

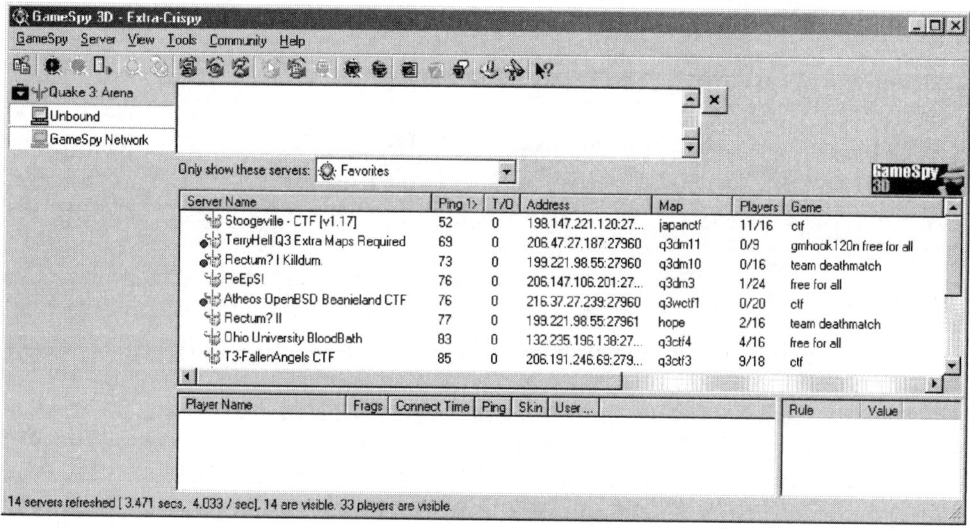

Gamespy—the best way to increase your gib counts

Kali

www.kali.net

Kali (named after the Hindu goddess of creation and destruction) is the largest gaming network on the Internet, allowing over 275,000 players on more than 350 servers in 40 countries to beat the virtual tar out of each other. The most popular games on Kali include Starcraft, Warcraft II, Quake II, Quake III Arena, Duke Nukem 3D, Mechwarrior 3, Descent 1 & 2, Diablo, Age of Empires, and many others (the list is endless). $20 U.S. registers you for life, and lets you download the Kali client software for Windows 95/98, MacOS, DOS or OS/2 (OS/2??). There's also news, a huge Games Resource Centre, a download site for patches and demos, and a series of ladders so you can put a numerical value to just how good you are. Still not ready to part with your 20 bucks? (Well, it is American currency after all . . .) There's a demo version of the Kali software, but it only lets you stay online for 15 minutes at a time. You either have to be really good or really bad to play in that time, so be prepared to pony up.

Heat

www.heat.net

Heat is Sega's online gaming network. It functions like Kali, but has more membership options. Anyone can join as a "Perimeter member" and play for free, but there are also "Premium members." Premium membership is $5.95 U.S. a month, $15.99 for three months, $29.99 for six months, or $49.99 a year for unlimited access. What do you get for your dollars, aside from an illusory feeling of superiority? Frequent player points, or "Degrees," along with sneak previews of new games, a Web page, e-mail account, etc. In other words, save your money on membership and buy more games.

Quake: Official Sport of the Internet

It's 5 p.m. on a weekday, and you're in any office on the continent with a LAN. Suddenly, all productive work comes to a halt. All you can hear are explosions and horrible tortured alien screaming noises. No, it's not a terrorist attack—it's just the sound of Quake.

Japan has mandatory after-work drinking sessions for salarymen. Quake isn't all that different. It's nearly ubiquitous, and man, is it addictive.

The Quake phenomeon began in the early 90s, with a scrolling videogame called Castle Wolfenstein. It was a good game for the time, and spawned a sequel, Beyond Wolfenstein. Then something interesting happened—the developers added, literally, a new dimension to their product, and released Wolfenstein 3D. (We think we still have it on floppy somewhere. That's right, it all fits on one disk.) Wolfenstein, whose plot centered around the breakout from a castle turned into a Nazi prison, placed the player in the role of the protagonist in a 3D-world.

In retrospect, Wolfenstein was a fairly flat and boring affair, not all that different from the 3D Pac-Man games that had been floating around for years. Then along came the sequel, Doom, which changed everything. Not only was the Doom graphics engine infinitely superior to Wolfenstein's, it allowed for live, interactive play over the Internet—the first deathmatch. At one point, Doom was actually out-distributing Microsoft: there were 27 million official copies of Windows in circulation, and 30 million copies of Doom. Doom II, the sequel, sold more than 500,000 copies for Christmas 1994 according to its Texas-based creator, id Software **<www.idsoftware.com>**. Quake, the sequel to Doom, beefed up the graphics engine yet again, though game play remained essentially the same. By January 1997 there were over 5 million Quake players, busily constructing their own culture, complete with humour, art, language, and social structures (called clans). Quake II, with its rumbling soundtrack by Trent Reznor, spawned countless imitators, some even better than the original (like Valve's Half-Life, and, arguably, Unreal). Quake III was released in late 1999, which established Quake as the undisputed ruler of the FPS universe.

John Carmack, the technical director at id and the creator of the Quake 3D engine, is now a very, very rich man. If you want to know what he looks like, stop by level 15 of Quake III: his severed, bloodied head sits in the corner of a room in the basement, down by the lava. Happy fragging.

Quake3World

www.quake3world.com

The official home of Quake 3 is the best place to start looking if you want to know more about Quake III. Aside from all of the latest patches and modifications to the game, there are also extensive discussion forums, stats, events listings, and articles about id and the Quake phenomenon.

PlanetQuake

www.planetquake.com

Part of the GameSpy network, PlanetQuake has sections for Quake, Quake II, and Quake III Arena (yes, people still play the earlier versions of the game; some even prefer them). Aside from downloadable mods, skins, and levels, there's discussion, news, and a good set of scripting tutorials for neophytes. This is where things get really geeky: Quake has its own scripting language, and to play the game effectively, you need to (gulp) do some programming. No one said this was going to be all fun and games, did they?

Blue's News

www.bluesnews.com

This venerable fan-run site is focused around the Quake universe, but reaches out to cover many aspects of online gaming in general. Mandatory reading.

Team Fortress

PlanetFortress and Q3Fortress

www.planetfortress.com

www.q3f.com

One of the most popular mods (short for "modifications") of Quake has consistently been Team Fortress: a virtual version of capture the flag. Team Fortress was originally built for Quake II, then modified into team Fortress Classic for Half-Life, and, most recently, Quake 3 Fortress, which is still in beta-testing, but playable (Team Fortress 2, a stand-alone game, is still in development). Team Fortress features unique character classes with special abilities and their own weapons, and it presents a much more cerebral gaming experience than straight Quake. If this intrigues you, the PlanetFortress site will guide you through the various flavours of Team Fortress that are available. If you want to have a say in the development of the mod, start playing Q3F and jump into the discussions on the site. Heated debate is the order of the day.

RTS (Real-Time Strategy) Gaming

RTS is like playing chess with living pieces. And explosions. Overall, a significant improvement, then.

Battle.net

www.battle.net

Though there are many companies competing for the RTS demographic, Blizzard Entertainment **<www.blizzard.com>** makes the most consistently interesting games, with detailed fictional worlds and gorgeous visuals. Battle.net is Blizzard's game network, and this is the official Battle.net Web site. If you buy Starcraft, Brood War, Warcraft, Diablo (and soon, Diablo II—are you ready to fight against evil, bipedal, halberd-wielding cows? Judging from the screenshots Blizzard releases on a weekly basis, that's what in store), you can play online for free. B.net also features discussion forums, a new downloadable Starcraft map every week, and seasonal tournaments for their games.

Offroading: The Untamed and Abandoned Internet

There's a lot more to the Internet than the World Wide Web. Most people don't see the other "places" anymore because many of them, like FTP sites, IRC, and Usenet, have Web front ends now. They still exist, though, and people still use them for purposes legal, quasi-legal, and illegal.

Another recent development, in the wake of Napster, is the popularity of peer-to-peer servers. Client software programs like Napster and Gnutella can turn any hard drive into a file server, making it possible for anyone to make any type of file available for a short period of time. Peer-to-peer servers could change the whole nature of the Internet in the same way the Web did: there could be far fewer static servers, and a lot more people on the move, turning on their wireless modem-equipped laptops, exchanging files, and moving on. Of course, government officals and legal authorities will be filling their pants when they figure out the full implications of this trend, because it means that criminals as well as hobbyists can distribute materials and remain virtually untraceable, especially on a decentralized network like Gnutella.

The Web also has some pretty strange corners itself. The sites that follow are just the top layer of the weirdness that you'll find online if you look hard enough, but on one of those days when watching RealPlayer channels just isn't going to cut it, try out one of the following options.

Webcams

The sudden explosion of cheap little cameras that sit on top of your computer monitor created two interesting situations at once. The first was that anyone could suddenly be a broadcaster. The second was that all these fledgling broadcasters were limited to displaying things that could be seen from within a one-yard radius of their PC (the average length of webcam cord). Necessity being the mother of invention, people came up with all sorts of solutions, such as the following.

The Public 8 Ball

8ball.federated.com

This is not a cheesy simulation program: this is a real Mattel-manufactured model number 3048AA Magic 8 Ball, housed in a custom-built Lego Mindstorms shaking cradle, triggered and watched by a Linux computer. As the site operator says, 50,000 years of technological advancement has culminated in a system to bring you mysticism on demand. The Public 8 Ball currently only works with Netscape, and wins our vote for the "Guy with Too Much Free Time" award for 1999 and early 2000, hands down.

Jennicam

www.jennicam.com

This is the one that cracked webcams in the real world. Jenni is Jennifer, a Web designer who lives in Washington, D.C., and Jennicam is an uncensored look into her life. If you're a guest, you get a new picture of Jenni's apartment every 20 minutes; if you're a paying member, you get a new picture every two minutes (membership costs $15 U.S. a year). See Jenni watch TV. Have sex. Lay around a lot. Read. Narcissism + Voyeurism = E-commerce.

Earthcam

www.earthcam.com

This Web site lists thousands of webcam sites worldwide, pointing at anything and everything you can imagine. We like the Ashtray Cam **<www.ashtraycam.com>**, located right here in Toronto, which sort of says it all.

File Servers: The Dark Side?

The Hotline

www.bigredh.com

Hotline is a kind of net within the Net that works like a hybrid of FTP and ICQ. Users sign on the Hotline as either a client or a server. The server provides news, chat, and file areas where clients can interact, while users download this shareware and connect to any server listed in its directory. Hotline also tracks currently accessible servers for you, providing a description and number of users logged in.

The Hotline client software enables you to connect to a server, chat with other users, read and post news, and simultaneously transfer files (including MP3s). The client incorporates cutting-edge features such as resumable downloads and uploads, private personal messaging, news, and real-time chat. The downloadable evaluation version of the Hotline client is classic nagware: every 15 minutes it displays a message notifying you that you are using an evaluation version. After one hour of concurrent use, it will disconnect you. To register the client, you'll need to shell out $44.70 Canadian.

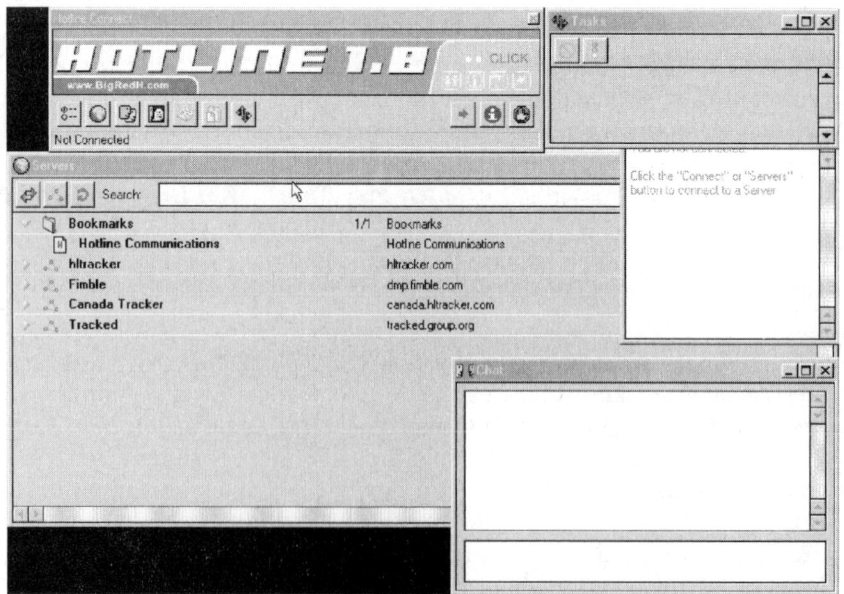

Hotline is one of those programs that scatters confusing little windows all over your desktop. Keeping track of which window is telling you what is half the fun.

Retro-Fun

Times change quickly online. But surprisingly, many of the institutions of the online community persist. The cosmetics of many of these sites change over time—most now have a Web-based front end—but the underlying purpose remains the same. The following sites are offered both as a kind of Netculture history lesson, and because they still have much to offer.

MUD Resource Collection

www.godlike.com/muds

MUDs, or Multi-User Dimensions, were the killer app on the Internet about eight years ago. Imagine a fantasy role-playing game taking place over ICQ, only without a Dungeon Master. That's a MUD (there are other "flavours" of MUD, called things like MOO and MUSH, but the differences are all technical). Because MUDs are text-based, they've fallen out of favour, but one day, when full-motion video in customizable virtual worlds is a reality (We mean, worlds where the object is not solely to kill everyone else), MUDs will rise again and be reborn. Until then, visit the The MUD Resource Collection to learn more about MUDding.

One of the downfalls of MUDding is that it's insanely complicated if you want to do it well. Of course, this means that anyone who bothers to learn enough about them to participate fully becomes insanely loyal to their particular MUD. This page will tell you all you need to know about MUD culture. To find a MUD running now, visit The MUD Connector site **<www.mudconnect.com>**. Last time we checked, there were over 1,500 still in existence.

The Internet Oracle

www.cs.indiana.edu/~oracle

If you can't find the answer you want on the Public 8 Ball, you might consider consulting the venerable Internet Oracle. This site, formerly known as The Usenet Oracle, has been around since about 1989, and the roots of its code go all the way back to 1975–76. Basically, the Oracle is a collective effort at humour by the denizens of the Internet. Questions mailed to the Oracle are forwarded to other Oracle users, who serve as an "incarnation" of the Oracle by providing an anonymous, witty answer to the question. The funniest and cleverest answers are selected by the Oracular Priesthood for inclusion in the famous Oracularities, which are posted periodically to the newsgroup **<news:rec.humor.oracle>**. Discussion of the Oracularities occurs in the newsgroup **<news:rec.humor.oracle.d>**. To submit your question, go to the gateway form at **<www.cs.indiana.edu/hyplan/oracle/gateway.html>**.

No questions? Okay, go forth and surf.

DESTINATIONS

PART TWO

PART TWO

Arts & Entertainment

ACTORS

Canadian Celebrities

Okay, so this site is lo-fi and text heavy but did you know that Colin Mochrie is Canadian? Do you care? Get your nose out of the latest *Entertainment Weekly* and start appreciating some homegrown stars!

www.geocities.com/canadiancelebs

Celebrity Directory

This star-struck listing of links brings fans everything from "Birth Certificates of the Rich and Famous" to web pages for actor Billy Zane. Brought to you by HotBot.

dir.hotbot.lycos.com/Arts/Celebrities

Keanu Reeves Ring of Fire

Seventy, yes 70, different people have created web sites dedicated Keanu Reeves. Maybe this internet thing isn't such a good idea after all ...

members.aol.com/romeornbow/keanurng.htm

Miketown

Does Mike Myers really need any more exposure? Apparently ... yes.

redrivel.com/miketown

Molly Parker

An adoring fan pays tribute to the Canadian star of the controversial *Kissed* and the hilarious *Twitch City*.

www.angelfire.com/on/mollyparker

Sarah Plain and Short: The Unofficial Sarah Polley Homepage

Another Canadian-based actor who deserves more attention at home and abroad. A tempting combination of singing, social activism, directing, and acting! How can you resist?

cs.wilpaterson.edu/~led/Polley/Polley.htm

Screen Trade Canada

Tired of reading about the stars in the firmament called Hollywood? Look north to find such luminaries as Sandra Oh, Megan Follows, and Callum Keith Rennie. Screen Trade Canada cultivates Canadian celebrity status with news and bios on all your favourite actors from north of the border.

www.screentradecanada.com

The Unofficial Don McKellar Web Site

While most media outlets glom onto the latest sitcom actor who lived in Moose Jaw for two months as a baby, real home-grown talent is largely ignored. Don McKellar deserves to be a great big star and this little site is a tech-savvy and whip smart resource for his adoring fans.

surf.to/Don McKellar

The Unofficial Jim Carey Fan Page

This tribute to that elastic thespian, Jim Carey, brings you more photos than you could possibly have any use for, as well as links to about a billion other fan pages.

w3.goodnews.net/~jhenn

The William Shatner Experience

Experience the glory that *is* William Shatner at this web site dedicated to one of Canada's "greatest thespians." Relive such career highs as *T.J. Hooker* and Bill's brief foray into pop music with "The Transformed Man."

www.geocities.com/Area51/Zone/8865

ARCHITECTURE

ADAM, the Art, Design, Architecture, and Media Information Gateway

A straightforward search engine of almost three thousand different architecture, design, and media-related sites. Hundreds of professional librarians can't be wrong!

adam.ac.uk

Architecture and Historic Preservation

The Digital Librarian brings you this ready-made list of links that covers archives, search engines, and various other architecture-related resources.

www.servtech.com/~mvail/architecture.html

Building Canada

Based on Professor Emeritus John Bland's course on the history of Canadian architecture, this page features a digitized selection of slides of buildings from across the country. Take an introductory course in Canadian architecture, brush up on the architectural lingo, or learn about John Bland himself.

blackader.library.mcgill.ca/cac/bland/building

Canadian Centre for Architecture

The CCA's collections contain over 42 000 prints and drawings, 50 000 photographs, and a library of over 180 000 volumes. Not a bad place to start for research and related queries.

cca.qc.ca/default.htm

Green Building Information Council

The Green Building Information Council is a Canadian nonprofit organization that provides information about energy and environmental issues in the building sector. Find out what simple upgrades to older buildings can help you save energy and money. It's about time that movements like this one were taken seriously.

greenbuilding.ca

Plan Net

An online resource for those interested in architechture and design. Plan Net is a great starting point for those who would like to learn more about the field, or students curious about programs at various universities.

www.plannet.com

R. Buckminster Fuller: Thinking Out Loud

This well-packaged page based on the PBS television program gives the basics for any would-be followers of this architectural guru. Heady subject matter that is well worth the time to investigate.

www.pbs.org/wnet/bucky.cgi

World's Tallest Buildings

It's the way of the world. Bigger is synonymous with better in a culture that adores SUVs, home theatre systems, and two-litre slurpees. It only makes sense that someone would eventually create a web site dedicated to those monolithic, sun-blocking, skyscrapers that dot the cityscapes of the world's urban centres. See what's already out there and what has been proposed for the world of high-altitude architecture.

www.worldstallest.com

ART

A Momentary Vignette

Here's a beautifully presented and frequently updated look at architechture, art, and design.

www.logia.com/vignette/99714b.html

Artcyclopedia

An extremely useful tool for locating online exhibitions of the work of over 5000 fine artists. Lets you see which artists are the most popular for each month.

www.artcyclopedia.com

Artengine

Strictly non-commercial, and absolutely free, Artengine provides an online forum for discussion and viewing of new visual art pieces. With funding provided by various government institutions, exhibitors need only apply and provide the necessary picture files to make their work available to thousands of would-be critics.

www.artengine.ca

Artists for Kids Gallery

The Artists for Kids Trust was established in 1989 thanks to the cooperation of some of Canada's finest artists and the North Vancouver Board of School Trustees. Its mission, achieved by the sale of original prints by its artist patrons, is to build a lasting legacy for visual and performing arts programs for the children of British Columbia. Browse through the online art gallery and find out about the Summer School of Visual Art.

www.artists4kids.com

artnet

As with everything on the internet, it is probably better to provide the uninitiated with the general so they can search for the particular. Here it is in the form of artnet, a collection of links and feature articles concerning art, artists, and galleries from all over the world.

www.artnet.com

Canartscene.com

Canartscene is a collective of artists who live in Canada and wish to make their work available for the world to see. The options on this site allow visitors to communicate with other artists around the world and to discuss or contribute to the artwork on the site.

www.canartscene.com

Council for the Arts in Ottawa

Red tape and political meanderings aside, this site provides a useful arts and heritage directory, including sections with local and national appeal.

www.arts-ottawa.on.ca

shift

Hello?

If a phone booth rings in the desert, will anyone pick it up? Read the history of the ill-fated Mojave Phone Booth project and its global repercussions.

www.deuceofclubs.com/moj/mojave.htm

Inuit Gallery

Not only does this site provide a great deal of its collection of masterwork Inuit art for online viewing, but visitors can also use contact information to arrange for purchase and shipping worldwide.

www.inuit.com

MangaArt Archive

Anime fanatics, head here for your fill of Manga images, wallpaper, and themes. Updated weekly.

www.mangaart.com

Visual Orgasm

An online community of self-proclaimed aerosol artists that encourages contributions of written work, photos, and digital design. A site that is both visually stunning and socially relevant.

www.graffiti.org/vorg

Words of Art

Words of Art is the online project of Okanagan University College, which is working to provide a glossary of major terms and ideas from the world of art criticism. Students will appreciate this alphabetical listing of terms with hypertext cross-references to provide illustration or clarification.

www.arts.ouc.bc.ca/fiar/glossary/gloshome.html

ARTISTS

Artist Info

With listings for over 60 000 artists from 90 different countries, this should be your first stop when searching for online information on your favourite master. The worldwide listings for gallery and museum web pages might be useful as well.

www.artist-info.com/artisthtml/index.asp

Emily Carr: At Home and at Work

Browse the galleries for hundreds of digitized images of Emily Carr's paintings. Her autobiographical writings also provide valuable insights into her life and work.

www.tbc.gov.bc.ca/culture/schoolnet/carr/index.htm

Group of Seven

Though represented in digital form, the paintings at this web site are no less beautiful for having been pixelated. A good resource for desktop wallpaper.

www.tomthomson.org/g7room.htm

Twentieth Century Artists

And you thought Fauvism wasn't getting enough attention! This aesthetically sparse but information-rich site breaks down all the important movements of the past century with sections for all the major players.

www.1001.org/20th

Wet Canvas: Virtual Museum

Here's a nice introduction to the great master painters of the modern era. Those who have any background in art history would do well to avoid this overly didactic site—unless you're looking for cool .jpg's.

www.wetcanvas.com/Museum/

ARTISTS — GROUP EXHIBITS

CCCAnet

This site is a project of the Centre for Contemporary Canadian Art to promote professional artists. It houses a bank of over 6085 images by 125 artists. It also contains a directory of links to over 320 visual art sites.

www.ccca.ca

Glass Works

This exhibit by Canada's Museum of Civilization is as much a history of the art of glass blowing and sculpture as it is an exhibit of the artists and their works. An interesting tour of a beautiful art form.

www.civilization.ca/membrs/canhist/verre/veintooe.html

shift

ParkBench

In 1994, artists Nina Sobell and Emily Hartzell staged the web's first live performance piece. Subsequent work at ParkBench, their web site, treats the net as public theatre. The duo's video series, *ArTisTheater*, includes more than 80 performances, the latest of which meld web video with streaming RealAudio. Amazing.

www.cat.nyu.edu/parkbench

Women Artists in Canada

This site houses images of nearly 1500 works of art in a wide range of media. Well over 100 artists are represented, each with a brief biography.

collections.ic.gc.ca/waic

ARTS & CULTURE — INDICES

Exploring Ancient World Cultures

As a wired global citizen one must be versed in the diverse and compelling history of all the world's countries. Though perhaps a little too egg-headed for some, this page provides a varied resource for students of ancient history or the curious few who want to learn more. Everything from ancient Greece and Rome to Medievel Europe is explored.

eawc.evansville.edu/index.htm

Festival Seeker

Though a clunky and unattractive government site, Festival Seeker gives a good excuse to get out of your respective town or city to enjoy plays, concerts, and other special events.

www.festivalseeker.com

Virtual Library of Museums

An overly comprehensive, searchable index of museums from all over the world. Care to visit the Oceanographic Museum and Marine Aquarium in Gdynia?

www.chin.gc.ca/vimp

World Wide Arts Resources

This interactive arts gateway will give you access to artists, museums, galleries, high-quality art, art history, arts education, antiques, performing arts, classified ads, resume postings, arts chats, arts forums, and much more.

www.world-arts-resources.com

ARTS & CULTURE — NEWS

Arts & Letters Daily

Arts & Letters Daily is a densely packed, text-heavy collection on subjects ranging from poetry and literary theory to gossip from artistic circles. A collection of links to major publications, columnists, and news sources will help visitors find anything that has not already been compiled here.

www.cybereditions.com/aldaily

CBC Infoculture

You have to give the CBC credit. In spite of yearly cutbacks and a programming agenda that is geared toward Canadians in their post-60s, they still manage to produce an informative and interesting web site like Infoculture. All the major, and minor, topics in the world of the arts news are covered here.

www.infoculture.cbc.ca

Hissyfit

Born from the fertile mind of ex-pat Canadian Wing Chun, Hissyfit is a collection of rants, raves, and miscellaneous gripes. Read articles, book and movie reviews, and travelogues, or drop in on several different ongoing forums at this site. Laced with just the slightest hint of vitriolic wit.

www.hissyfit.com

shift

Platform Network

No one is more loyal to the spirit of New York's underground than Platform Network. A pioneering portal site with loads of street cred, it porvides one-stop access to the best magazines, clothing, and music of alt culture. Listen to the latest from the Jungle Brothers while you purchase fresh new streetwear from the Triple 5 Soul clothing company.

www.platform.net

tulevision

Weekly arts news with an eye on the avant-garde. This site leads the post-contemporary arts movement with online galleries of art, photos, and essays. The film gallery screens independent features and allows submissions from visitors.

www.tulevision.com

ARTS & CULTURE — ORGANIZATIONS

Alliance of Canadian Cinema, Television and Radio Artists

ACTRA's mission has always been to negotiate, safeguard, and promote the professional rights of its members. Read about ongoing labour negotiations, browse through the ACTRA talent directory, or check out links to local chapters in major cities across Canada.

www.actra.com

Association of Canadian Publishers

Writers! Get published, get distributed, get publicity through the slick new site for the Association of Canadian Publishers. The ACP web site includes membership information, postings on ACP marketeing enterprises, and links to affiliated organizations.

www.publishers.ca

Canada Council

Another boring, government-sponsored site? Wrong! This is where starving writers, painters, filmmakers, and other artists go to get funding so that they can afford food. Here you'll find information on grants, endowments, prizes, and much more.

www.canadacouncil.ca

Canadian Publishers' Council

Look up copyright information, hook up with Cancopy, or read up on the legalities of web publishing at this site. There are also sections for Council news and events, as well as information on the web-related topic of intellectual property.

www.pubcouncil.ca

Common Knowledge

A journal brought out by Oxford University Press that covers topics ranging from psychology to popular fiction. Dedicated to undermining all foundational structures that impede agreement.

www.utdallas.edu/research/common_knowledge/

Editors' Association of Canada

"Let us now be told no more of the dull duty of an editor." A geographically indexed list of professional editors (with resumes) and a variety of other resources.

www.editors.ca

League of Canadian Poets

A smooth and aesthetically pleasing site awaits visitors to this site that keeps you abreast of the activities of Canadian poets. This site's best attribute is the immediate availability of many new and classic poems for online reading.

www.poets.ca

Open Space

Open Space is a collective of artists dedicated to freedom of expression and the rights of individual artists. Visit their web space to view online exhibits in media art, visual art, song, and performance, or find out how to get your own work onto the internet.

www.openspace.ca

ASTROLOGY

Canoe Horoscope

Read daily astrological news at this collection of horoscopes by Eugenia Last. Unfortunately, she was predicting some earth-shattering events for May 5, 2000, so if you're reading this now you may have to question her advice.

www.canoe.ca/Fun/home.html

Chinese Astrology and Feng Shui

An introduction to relevant concepts in the realms of Chinese astrology, such as "The Four Pillars of Destiny" and "Zi Wei Dou Shu." Update your luck or take online courses through this site.

www.astro-fengshui.com

Free Will Astrology

Rob Brezsny's Free Will Astrology dares to be poetic in a world of banal predictions. Don't expect the usual "life for you is a dashing bold adventure" type projections here, where advice runs more along the lines of "I dare you to become obsessed with all the shades of red this week." Not the place for easy answers.

www.freewillastrology.com

Your Daily Zodiac Forecast

What lies in the stars for you today? Jonathan Cainer sees all, tells all.

stars.metawire.com/webstars

AUTOMOTIVE

Autonet.ca

Links to online financing, insurance, maintenance, and auto shows, coupled with a search engine for new and used vehicles, make this a worthwhile tool for the car consumer.

www.autonet.ca

Canadian Automobile Association (CAA)

Formed in 1913 when Canadians were making the change from horses to cars, the CAA is probably the best organization of its kind for emergency roadside assistance and travel information. Sign up here before you find yourself stranded in the middle of nowhere.

www.caa.ca

Canadian Driver

A good resource for new and used car listings, as well as online discussion groups. Plenty of belligerent advice on how to take care of your car too!

www.canadiandriver.com

Cartrackers

Yet another site with new and used car listings from across Canada and the U.S. Features nonpartisan reviews of previously owned cars.

www.cartrackers.com

Electric Vehicle Association of the Americas (EVAA)

Here's a car-related site that cares about the impact of fossil fuels on the environment. Find out about the latest developments in fuel-cell and battery-powered cars.

www.evaa.org

Greasergrrls

Though dedicated solely to female motor enthusiasts, Greasergrrls is a welcome change for anyone who's tired of the testosterone and tires set. Features range from advice on tuning up your ride to photos of cars from around the world. Those who are particularly enthusiastic will find information on joining their local offline chapter of the organization at this site.

www.greasergrrls.com

Maplerace.com

This site offers free web space to all racing tracks and racers across Canada. Features include a newsroom and a classified section.

www.maplerace.com

Ontario Federation of Vanners

Included here not for its amazing design but for its completely surreal atmosphere. Read "Vanner" newsletters while listening to Casio-synth versions of Iron Butterfly.

www.tcn.net/~ofv

Raceline Radio Network

Gentlemen start your browsers! This weekly radio-magazine devoted to motorsports is heard in various regions around the country.

www.raceline.on.ca

BOOKS

Amazon.com

Thousands upon thousands of new businesses have emulated Jeff Bezos's model for selling goods online using a customer-friendly interface and multiple suppliers. In case you hadn't heard, they sell books, among other things. Some even use Amazon's comprehensive database of book titles for research purposes.

www.amazon.com

Bibliofind

Comparison shopping at its easiest, Bibliofind is an invaluable free service for anyone who can't track down that hard-to-find title anywhere. It searches the catalogues of thousands of online booksellers and then presents the results so you can easily compare prices.

www.bibliofind.com

Book Club Canada

Book Club Canada provides Canadian readers with book reviews, author information, publishers, book history, and a literary site of the week.

www.bookclubcanada.com

Bookwire

Dive into the business of publishing with this in-depth online guide. Bookwire brings you the best in news, reviews, guides to literary events, author interviews, and links to different publishing-related resources.

www.bookwire.com

Canada Book Day

Tired of burning your retina in front of a computer screen? Here's an excuse to go try the old-school version.

www.canadabookday.com

Canadian Bookbinders and Book Artists Guild

All right, so books are obsolete and will eventually be a thing of the past, but hey, you bought this one didn't you? Check out the latest workshops, exhibitions, publications, and mailing lists made available at this web site for anyone who's still interested in making books.

www.cbbag.ca

Canadian Bookclubs

Visit this site for info on starting, maintaining, and conducting discussions for book clubs. Everyone wants to join a book club, right? Hello? (Cue sound of crickets.)

www.canadianbookclubs.com

Canadian Bound

Created by a Can-lit fan (without any corporate advertising!), this site rounds up reviews on the most recent novels, plays, and poetry by Canadian authors.

www.canadianbound.com

Chapters

Order books and music in (gasp!) Canadian dollars! Search through Chapters' online inventory for thousands of books, videos, and CDs that can be mailed right to your home.

www.chapters.ca

Crime Writers of Canada

Amateur sleuths will appreciate the listings for mystery authors and sources provided at this web site. Hard-core crime fighters may even want to investigate the forensic entomology page. Not for the squeamish!

www.crimewriterscanada.com

Evenbetter.com

A search engine that helps consumers look for books, CDs, and movies. Lets you see not only how much the same item costs at different retailers, but even who delivers faster. As a bonus for Canucks, searches can be customized for Canadian location and currency.

www.evenbetter.com

Impressions: 250 Years of Printing

It's nice to see that this site provides a tribute to the role that print has played in the history of Canada. It's deeply ironic that this tribute appears on that scourge of print culture, the internet. Books aren't dead yet, but sites like this one are certainly hurrying them along their way.

www.nlc-bnc.ca/events/twofift/eimprint.htm

Indigo

Did everyone just suddenly decide to take up reading in their spare time or is this book store boom a little out of hand? Here's that other major book retail site that's competing for your hard-earned toonies. You might not find more books or better deals, but there certainly is more of the colour blue!

www.indigo.ca

Project Gutenberg

Don't buy that Penguin edition just yet! Unless you need all the extraneous notes for what you are reading, you can probably find the plain text version of what you're looking for here. This site hopes to eventually have all materials in the public domain available online for free. Here's hoping they don't get carpel tunnel syndrome in the process!

www.gutenberg.net

The Writers' Union of Canada

Writers unite! Fight bourgeoisie publishers—or just get some free legal advice and find out about funding information.

www.swifty.com/twuc

Wired for Books

Poetry, fiction, essays, and lectures all brought to you in RealAudio. Like having a library of virtual books on tape that cover all kinds of literary ground.

www.tcom.ohiou.edu/books

CANADIANA

An American's Guide to Canada

An expatriate American explains Canada to our friends south of the border. Handy tips include a list of particularly Canadian peccadilloes, an explanation of Canadian history, and a guide on how to immigrate. "We'll explain the appeal of curling to you if you explain the appeal of the National Rifle Association to us."

www.icomm.ca/emily

Canadian World Domination

Fall in, take up arms ... and pick up some donuts. The time has come for Canada to take over the world! Yes, Generals Claire and Jenny are here to lead us to our destiny of complete world domination! Imperialist satire aside, the best part of this web site is the incredibly large archive of hate-mail from Yanks who don't seem to get the joke.

www.standongaurd.com

Early Canadiana Online

Early Canadiana Online is a full-text online collection of more than 3000 books and pamphlets documenting Canadian history from the first European contact to the late 19th century. The collection is particularly strong in literature, women's history, native studies, travel and exploration, and the history of French Canada.

www.canadiana.org

Grave Sites of Canadian Prime Ministers

We certainly don't seem to pay much attention to them when they're alive, or in office, so maybe Canadians will be interested in their PMs now that they're dead and in pretty cemetaries. Dance on or pay homage to the graves of everyone from John A. Macdonald to Lester B. Pearson, you morbid freaks.

parkscanada.pch.gc.ca/pm/english/GraveSites_e.HTM

MyCanada

Though perhaps a little bit heavy on the flag waving, this site provides an interesting overview of the country from the perspective of a recent immigrant. Available in English and Russian.

members.tripod.com/alex-net/canada/

No! Canada

Created by a vigilant American, this site professes to be "watching our northern neighbours" who are "a bit too much like us." Discover the dark underbelly of Canadian society or read a proposed solution to the Canadian problem. Help root out Canadian infiltrators in the beloved United States!

www.lanset.com/hrs/bill/nocanada

The Displaced Canadian

A virtual home away from home for Canadians living in the U.K. Get involved in local Canuck events or join the chat line to see if you recognize anyone from home.

www.canadian.demon.co.uk

The National Atlas of Canada Online

One more reason not to run out and by the multivolume print version—this online atlas provides kids and adults alike with an accurate resource for geographical queries.

atlas.gc.ca

TVO Great Canadian Challenge

First play an amusing game of Canadian trivia in which you hunt our unofficial national animal, the mosquito. Then make your own web page explaining what you think it means to be Canadian, or read the pages made by others. Great fun for kids, or anyone who enjoys cartoon animals.

www.tvo.org/eh

CENSORSHIP

A Chronicle of Freedom of Expression in Canada

This online archive of censorship and violations of the Charter of Rights and Freedoms stands as a stark reminder of the precariousness of any free society. Divided into sections covering pre- and post-1994, the chronicle is coupled with links to other relevant sites, such as the Freedom to Read organization and resources for teachers and librarians.

www.efc.ca/pages/chronicle/

Canadian Association for Free Expression

Dedicated to maximizing the freedom of speech and freedom of expression provisions in the Canadian Charter of Rights and Freedoms, the CAFE web site provides the latest on one of Canada'a foremost civil liberties groups.

www.canadianfreespeech.com

Free Expression Clearinghouse

Keep abreast of the latest issues involving censorship and free speech at this U.S. organization's site. Items are updated daily and cover everything from books in schools to the more current issues involving censorship on the internet.

www.freeexpression.org

The Electronic Frontier Foundation

The EFF acts as a watchdog for issues of censorship related to the internet. The section on "Defining Digital Identity" may be a wake-up call to those who haven't considered the ramifications of privacy issues in the electronic media.

www.eff.org

CINEMA

Absolute Authority on Film Studies

Contrary to what the self-aggrandizing title may suggest, this site is meant to inform rather than intimidate its visitors. Those who are looking for more than a thumbs-up synopsis of the latest blockbuster will be pleased to dig through this collection of resources for the theoretical and technical background of film production. Sections on Eisenstein's basic montage principles and the films of Akira Kurosawa will keep visitors well informed.

www.absoluteauthority.com/Film_Studies/

shift

Ain't It Cool News

Wanna know who's playing Aragon in the upcoming *Lord of the Rings* flick? Or maybe you need to verify the rumour that Sarah Michelle Gellar's going to appear in *Hannibal*. Whatever dirt you're looking for, odds are that Ain't It Cool News, the internet's premier source for Hollywood insider info, has it.

www.aint-it-cool-news.com

Alliance Communications

A major creator, broadcaster, and distributor of filmed entertainment in Canada, Alliance Communications has produced such critically praised films as *The Sweet Hereafter* and *The Red Violin*. Geared more towards the prospective investor than the casual film buff, this web site provides detailed financial data for the company. Skip to the Shockwave-run Web Cinema section which screens the latest trailers for Alliance-distributed films.

www.alliance.ca

shift

AtomFilms

While you await the day when Hollywood films are regularly broadcast over the internet, check out AtomFilms, a beautifully designed site bent on reviving the lost art of the short film by running four new mini-epics a week.

www.atomfilms.com

shift
Bad Movie Night

Considering that irony is one of the defining attributes of contemporary culture, it's no surprise that the web hosts a number of pages dedicated solely to singing the praises of the cinematic food-chain's bottom-feeders. While similar sites focus primarily on low-budget B-grade flops, Bad Movie Night casts its critical net a little wider, going as far as taking the piss out of *Schindler's List*.

www.hit-n-run.com/

Cinema Clock

Movie listings, reviews, and showtimes for every major urban centre in Canada. Visitors can download movie trailers, submit their own reviews for movies, or link to web sites for specific theatres.

www.cinemaclock.com

Darth Maul Estrogen Brigade

Here's a site authored by female fans totally devoted to the menacing, phantom-like villain from a certain popular film.

dmeb.net

David Cronenberg Home Page

A comprehensive fan site that features a spooky picture of Cronenberg morphing into one of his mugwumps. Long live the new flesh!

www.netlink.co.uk/users/zappa/cronen.html

shift
Film Threat

When the revered underground journal *Film Threat* went belly-up in 1997, cinema lost one of its greatest dissenting voices—until it was reborn courtesy of the web, that is. While the site itself is not particularly comprehensive, the weekly e-mail updates—chock-full of reviews, interviews and news (all delivered with patented *FT* snarkiness)—are required reading for the true alternative cineast.

www.filmthreat.com

Genie Awards

See who's been nominated this year or browse through listings of past award winners at this site for the best in Canadian film.

www.academy.ca/Academy/Awards

shift
Hollywood Stock Exchange

Forget that wimpy day-trading action. Head to the Hollywood Stock Exchange for some wheeling and dealing in celebrity futures. You won't make any dough, but the sublime pleasure of dumping overvalued Sean Connery bonds in order to pick up some bargain-basement Rick Schroeder stocks is one of those things you can't put a price tag on.

www.hsx.com

IFILM

Ten bucks a ticket? Why bother when you can view the best of independent cinema online for free? IFILM features hundreds of different short-form films for viewing and, if you don't like what you see, you don't have to walk out, just close the window. Includes the online hit "Black People Hate Me and They Hate My Glasses."

www.ifilm.com

Northern Stars: The Canadian History of Hollywood

Formerly a site dedicated solely to tracing the history of Canadian actors in popular film and television, Northern Stars now follows current events surrounding Canuck movies and TV as well.

www.northernstars.net

The Canadian Movie Guide

The *Toronto Sun*'s movie critic Bruce Kirkland has found the time to compile a comprehensive collection of reviews for Canadian cinema's best, worst, and obscure moments. These are Canadian films, not films starring Canadians or shot in Canada. Don't expect *Titanic, Police Academy,* or *Back to the Future* to be found in the Guide.

www.canoe.ca/JamMoviesCanadian/home.html

shift
The Internet Movie Database

You have a question about a film. There is an answer. In fact, there are more answers than you ever dreamed of. And they're all on the Internet Movie Database, meticulously linked to hordes of other answers, enabling you to trace the career of your favourite actor, director, or gaffer. At press time, IMDb had 170 479 movie titles listed and 2 462 516 filmographies available online. Those figures have since risen, given that IMDb is updated constantly by armies of faithful users, who also determine the site's best-of and worst-of film lists. *The Shawshank Redemption* was No. 1 for eons, while *Track of the Moon Beast* pulled up the rear, despite stiff competition from three *Police Academy* movies.

www.imdb.com

Arts & Entertainment

The Matrix

Set to eclipse *Star Wars* as an institution in the realms of sci-fi, *The Matrix* web site will provide the movie's rabid fans with just enough computer-generated Flash effects to tide them over until the next instalment in the trilogy is finished.

www.whatisthematrix.com

shift

Trailervision

Rarely exciting, often annoying, and always derivative—if there's one aspect of the film world that's due for a serious undressing, it's the trailer. Enter Trailervision, a Toronto-based production house that churns out nothing but trailers—albeit for films that don't, nor ever will, exist (think *Moon Attacks* and its sequal, *Moon Attacks 2000*). By simply co-opting the form's hyperbolic narration, hamfisted plot synopses, and overly intense line deliveries, Trailervision exposes the laziness and paint-by-numbers nature of Hollywood's hype machine. Sure, its a classic case of shooting fish in a thimble, with a howitzer, but Tineltown had it coming.

www.trailervision.com

Tribute

A Canadian magazine about Hollywood movies, this online version mirrors the print run that is given away in theatres. The site includes promo-type stuff on some of the latest releases.

www.tribute.ca

Web Guide to Atom Egoyan

A well-designed fan site specializing in one of Canada's most celebrated directors. The "Egoyan Nucleus" keeps tabs on past and present film projects, a history of the director's achievements, and the company Mr. Egoyan keeps.

www2.cruzio.com/~akreyche/atom.html

CINEMA — FILM FESTIVALS

Canadian Film Festivals

Simply put, links to all the major film festivals across Canada.

www.canfilm.co.kr/html/filmlink.fest.html

Film and Video Festival Index

Globe-trotting film aficionados will appreciate this month-by-month listing of film festivals occurring all over the world.

filmland.com/festivals/festcalendar.html

CINEMA — ORGANIZATIONS

ACTRA

The Alliance of Canadian Cinema Television and Radio Artists (ACTRA) is a "national organization of performers banded together to pursue common professional, cultural and economic goals." Check their web site for a history of the organization, an updated newsletter, talent directory, and an extensive list of related links.

www.actra.com

American Film Institute

The breeding ground for some of the most talented names in American film, the AFI is also dedicated to preserving the history of Hollywood movies. Find out about the institute's programs or take advantage of their online archive of film facts.

www.afionline.org

Canadian Film Centre

Founded in 1988 by director Norman Jewison, the Canadian Film Centre is dedicated to developing and promoting the artistic, technical, and business skills of emerging creative professionals working with the moving image. Flash effects make for interesting visuals at this site, home to some of the greatest minds in Canadian film.

www.cdnfilmcentre.com

National Film Board of Canada

Not just responsible for all those grainy 16 mm films you saw in grade school, the NFB has been producing award-winning motion pictures for most of the past century. Read about the Film Board's latest kudos and releases at this site.

www.nfb.ca

Sundance Institute

The Sundance Institute is a nonprofit organization dedicated to the support and development of independent film-makers, screen-writers, playwrights, composers, and other film and theatre artists. Read the latest on the wildly popular Sundance Film Festival or find out about international programs that develop film programs all over the world.

www.sundance.org

Telefilm Canada

Financed by the federal government, Telefilm Canada is an organization working with independent film producers to help finance their projects. Read up on past and present projects and financing at this site, or look up Canadian film festival listings and a history of this organization.

www.telefilm.gc.ca

The Academy of Motion Picture Arts and Sciences

Yes their awards show is ridiculously long, and they always nominate the wrong movies, but you watched all four hours. Admit it! Read exclusive fashion commentary on the show's attendees, or find out who actually won the awards.

www.oscars.org

COMICS & ANIMATION

Atomic Cartoons

This sampling of Flash-induced dementia may rival even John K.'s Spumco for visual kicks. Visitors can only browse developing concepts, though a web serial is in the works, or wait for one of their features on the *Cartoon Network*.

www.atomiccartoons.com

Bob the Angry Flower

The virtual version of a weekly *Edmonton Journal* comic by Steven Notley. Follow the lives of Bob, Stumpy, and the floating foetus as they control angry bees, argue with invisible cows, and purvey other assorted weirdness.

angryflower.com

Chilly Beach

Chilly Beach is a Flash-animated series about a bunch of stereotypical, Bob-and-Doug-type Canadians who do nothing but play hockey, drink beer, and get eaten by polar bears. Strictly an internet production.

www.chillybeach.com

Comic Art & Graffix Gallery

A virtual museum and encyclopedia and also a conveninent shop. You will be able to learn about the history of the medium from the days of cave art onwards. View classic covers and read bios of artists and authors.

www.comic-art.com

Comics

Too lazy to run down the street and buy a newspaper? Read the latest editions of comic strips like "Adam," "Mister Boffo," and "Bizarro" at this collection of virtual funnies.

www.canoe.ca/PlanetSun/canoecomics.html

Deparment H

Those unfamiliar with the Marvel Comics series on the Canadian superheroes, *Alpha Flight*, will be confused by the collection of assorted super dudes on display at this site. Read all about this now-defunct comic book that was the first to introduce an openly homosexual superhero.

kirk.prohosting.com/department_h

Flash Zone

Those looking to create a little Flash-fuelled mayhem of their own will find these resources useful. Features the latest developments in Flash programming, news about the latest versions, and tips for would-be animators.

www.flashzone.com

shift

Joe Cartoon

The ultimate in interactive, animated madness. Home to the infamous frog and blender game, visitors can also nuke hamsters, or watch Joe implode.

www.joecartoon.com

Machinima.com

Short-feature animated movies featuring the first person shooter. A combination of video game geeks and avid cinephiles makes for interesting footage.

machinima.com

Macromedia

Every web animation that you will come across is powered by either Shockwave or Flash. Come straight to the Macromedia homepage and download the latest versions of these plug-ins so you don't have to interrupt your internet cartoons.

www.macromedia.com

Spumco

If the ground-breaking online 'toon "Babysitting the Idiot" is not quite to your taste (and why wouldn't it be?), there's still plenty of mind-soothing eye-candy of other kinds at the Spumco web page, run by the infamous John Kricfalusi. Download comics, read interviews, or just gape at neat doodles at this site.

www.spumco.com

shift

StanLee.net

From the creator of the *X-men* comes a web toon about six video game beta-testers who are called on to save the world from monsters jumping through the "7th Portal," a doorway into our universe.

www.stanlee.net

The Thing

Sample Shockwave-powered animation from all over the world at this web site featuring everyone from Happy Smackett to Mr. Lunch.

www.word.com/thething

shift

Tripping the Rift

Meet Darph Bobo, the evilest fallen Jedi since Mel Brooks's *Spaceballs*. Had George Lucas been inspired by *Frtiz the Cat*, he still wouldn't have come up with something this crass—or this funny.

trippingtherift.com

CRAFTS

Crafters Network

Over 100 crafty web sites all rated and ranked by the people who use them. Put away your macaroni and cardboard collages, and get serious about something like ... decorative sponge faux wall painting!

www.topcraftsites.com

Crafts Search

Those who feel the urge to do something new with their hands will find everything they need here at this collection of online resources. Topics range from woodworking and baskets to shell crafts and polymer clay.

www.craftssearch.com

Get Crafty—Making Art out of Everyday Life

The philosophy espoused by the anonymous Jean is not just a technique for creating new and unusual art, but a lifestyle that will rule your world. Shop at thrift stores! Learn to decoupage! Dream of picnics! Get Crafty!

www.getcrafty.com

Pottery Making Illustrated

Plenty of links, recipes, and tips for the pottery enthusiast in you. Submissions are also accepted here for those potters who would like to share their secrets.

www.potterymaking.org

DANCE

Breakdance.com

You've been dying to learn how ever since the '80s and now you can—without having to embarrass yourself in public. Breakdance.com gives you descriptions for hundreds of moves accompanied by animated illustrations with ratings for difficulty level and phat level. Kick it!

www.breakdance.com

Bustamove

Now you can learn to dance on the Web. Bustamove will show you how to salsa, East Coast swing, West Coast swing, and do basic wedding dances. You'll be tripping the light fantastic in no time.

www.bustamove.com

Canadian Alliance of Dance Artists

Find out what's happening with the various chapters of the CADA around the country or follow links to related dance sites.

www.mcsquared.com/cada/index.htm

Canadian Children's Dance Theatre

Check out this site if there's a budding Karen Kain in your family. You'll find a listing of programs and a newsletter at the site for this dancing troupe that's been described as a "national treasure."

www.ccdt.org

Dancebot

A cutting-edge web site that allows dancers to find ... one another, funding, work, performances, and dance resources.

www.dancebot.com

Dancescape

Warning: this is not your mother's ballroom dancing. A notch above the achy-breaky dances that are all the rage, competitive ballroom dancing is popular with legions of new fans who revel in its blend of nostalgic charm, physical exertion, and social interaction. Now an Olympic-recognized sport, its stature is reflected in this comprehensive web site.

www.dancescape.com

National Ballet of Canada

With more than 45 dancers and its own full symphony ochestra, the National Ballet of Canada ranks as one of the world's top international dance companies. Read all about the latest activities and performances of the company here at their official web site.

www.national.ballet.ca

DESIGN ARTS

A Graphic Designer's Guide to the Galaxy

Here's a valuable resource for graphic design books, magazines, and software. You'll find 120 different links on categories ranging from print to web design.

www.icenter.net/~huebs/gdlinks/

Design Exchange

This site's home page molecule allows you to choose from which orbit to begin exploring the multi-faceted Design Exchange. Find out how design has influenced our culture, economy, and daily life at this virtual tour. You can also follow links to special events, a design encyclopedia, the permanent collection, and much more.

www.dx.org

Design Glossary

A plethora of graphic and web design terms are featured at this site to help make the uninitiated feel well informed. Netiquette for newbies!

www.grantasticdesigns.com/glossary.html

shift

Famewhore

A few things to know about Famewhore: 1) There is no real reason to visit the site; 2) If you go, you won't find anything that warrants a second visit; and 3) You shouldn't look for meaning in the content—there isn't any. That said, go to the site immediately. You'll love it.

www.famewhore.com

shift

Jodi.org

The splash page looks like an air traffic controller's worst nightmare writ large. Luminescent ASCII text tumbles over a black background, crashing into a chaotic storm of lines and circles. Hyperlinks abound, but they all point outward, leading to some of the net's finest design sites. With no content of its own, how did Jodi become the most recognized design site on the web? The answer can be found at oss.jodi.org. Here, Jodi mocks the conventional desktop. Schizophrenic windows open at random and careen across the screen, elduing even the deftest mouse. The whole thing looks like a massive CPU hemorrhage, but that's the point.

www.jodi.org

shift

Kaliber 10000

K10k, a.k.a. The Designer's Lunchbox, is an online gallery and design annual compressed into one very funky and elaborate web site. If you haven't been, you haven't used your Flash plug-in to its full potential.

k10k.com

shift

RamRaver

You can't beat German Flash engineering. Give your brain a break while you zone out to some of the finest visuals the web has to offer.

www.ramraver.de

Random Media Lab

Picture bunnies somersaulting in a field of ripe hibiscus; a place that is equal parts Marshall McLuhan and Chuck Jones; a story written through the combined efforts of Gertrude Stein and Elmore Leonard. All of these, and more, from the bowels of Random Media Lab.

www.random.ca

Snail TV

The fact that snails, when eaten, can act as a kind of aphrodisiac may be well known, but the effect that a 24-hour channel devoted entirely to snail observation has heretofore been unexplored. The result of optical exposure to these gods of the fishbowl, and subsequent study of the mathematics of their shells, is almost immediate. Snail TV = snail love.

www.snailtv.com

shift

Superbad

Descend into the Shocked realms of *Superbad* and let your eyes enjoy the ride. Tagging the virtual canvas.

www.superbad.com

The Italian Futurist Book

Though the site is not a stunning example of web design, it is still worth a look to see examples of this short-lived movement. The Futurist movement lasted less than 40 years, but the style of the book covers reproduced at this site seems to suggest it was a source of inspiration for modern-day advertising and graphic design.

www.colophon.com/gallery/futurism/index.html

shift

Thevoid

Like Volumeone, Thevoid is an online design company determined to prove its mettle. In what is arguably the net's most elegant use of Flash, Thevoid's stark black-and-white images slide across the screen in simulated 3D. On their own, the images are brilliant; when coupled with soundscape soundtracks, they're hypnotic.

www.thevoid.co.uk

Arts & Entertainment

shift

Volumeone

Like many online design companies, Brooklyn-based Volumeone maintains a web site to attract new clients. But because a portfolio sometimes isn't enough, the firm adds four cutting-edge Flash applications to its site every three months. Scroll through the archives and marvel at the rapid evolution of web technology.

www.volumeone.com

shift

www.uploading.com

Because pouring sugar on your eyes hurts.

www.uploading.com

ENTERTAINMENT

Chick Stars

All the best reviews on the latest in television, books, music, movies, and other miscellaneous celebrity ephemera. How can you resist a web site with empowering features like "Women Kick Ass!"?

chickstars.chickclick.com

Claptrap

Idle talk for the idle masses or a meeting ground for media pundits? Claptrap leans more toward the fizzy pop side of popular culture, but that doesn't mean that there isn't some serious commentary on all things from the world of Hollywood entertainment.

www.claptrap.com

shift

Fametracker

Subtitled "The Farmer's Almanac of Celebrity Worth," Fametracker cuts through the *Entertainment Tonight* fluff with a wickedly catty sense of humour. You needn't be a celebrity-gossip junkie to enjoy such populist fare as the Claire Danes Fame Audit or the Baldwin Brothers Obscurity Clock.

www.fametracker.com

Hip Online

Why visit Hip Online? Where else are you going to get serious coverage of ephemeral issues? The premier entertainment site for interviews, reviews, fashion, and much more.

www.hiponline.com

Scour

A comprehensive search engine for all things entertaining. Browse through ready-made categories for music, movies, radio, mp3s, videos, and images. Well designed with current content.

www.scour.com

ENTERTAINMENT — EVENTS

Culture Finder

Use this Lycos-fuelled search engine to track down events all over the world. Covers everything from theatre and opera to popular music and poetry.

culturefinder.lycos.com/cgi-bin/culturefinder/lycos

Just for Laughs Festival

The world's largest comedy festival is housed in Montreal and every year boasts international stars, as well as up-and-coming comics. Whether you're interested in attending the event in July or visiting the permanent museum, point your browser here first.

www.hahaha.com

Raves.com

Head to the "Find a Party" section of this site for listings of raves in Canada or some other international locale.

www.raves.com

The Junkie

The Junkie endeavours to help you feed your addictions (as if you needed any help!) by providing doorways to all the major entertainment web sites. Warning: the "Adrenalin" section may lead you to self-inflicted bodily harm!

www.thejunkie.com

Ticketmaster Online

Yes, six dollar service charges are ridiculous but sometimes there's just no other option ...

www.ticketmaster.ca

Toronto Rave Connection

Find out about the parties going on in the metro area or read up on some of Toronto's DJs at this web site maintained by local rave attendees.

members.home.com/raver4life

ENTERTAINMENT — MAGAZINES

Access Magazine

Access tries to be a hip publication while bringing readers the latest in Canadian music (often an example of working at cross purposes). Retuned to suit "lifestyles of the young and reckless," *Access* is making an obvious appeal to the high school set, but still manages to provide interesting music news.

www.accessmag.com

Chart Attack

Based on *Chart Magazine*, the new music monthly *Chart Attack* is a cornucopia of online data about the latest in popular music. There is a daily music news feature, an updated listing for industry events, and a plethora of band sites, interviews, and downloadable goodies.

www.chartnet.com

Exclaim Magazine

Aside from being the best print source for new music in Canada, *Exclaim* is the glue that holds a tenuous national independent music scene together. A lively and credible read.

www.shmooze.net/pwcasual/exclaim

Frank Magazine

The web site is as titillating and infuriating as its lawsuit-prone print counterpart. From Cynthia Dale naked, to infuriating rumours from the halls of government and business, and the requisite Mike Duffy name-calling, *Frank* keeps the establishment huffing and puffing.

www.achilles.net/frankmag

Jam!

Powered by the mighty Canoe, Jam! is one-stop shopping for all your entertainment news and reviews. Track down the latest info on movies, television, theatre, and books at this web site.

www.canoe.ca/Jam/home.html

Moxie

A virtual magazine geared towards women, this site's topics range from recaps of the latest *Sex and the City* episodes to financial advice. Join in on the Moxie online forums or visit the *Sway Magazine* section for the music reviews and news.

www.moxie.ca

Raygun

An exercise in surrealist visuals and nonlinear text, *Raygun Magazine* has always been as likely to turn readers on to great new music as to drive them to distraction. This new web site carries on the tradition with great visuals and all the usual attempts to make the reading experience just a little bit more challenging.

www.raygun.com

TV Guide Live

This site is banal and has an overwhelmingly American focus ... but the same could be said of most television shows. Useful for those who want the inside scoop on such topics as why Gil Bellows left *Ally McBeal*. See the *Adbusters* for the cure to this seemingly inescapable syndrome.

www.tvguidelive.com

Vice Magazine

Vice is rude, politically incorrect, degrading ... and hilarious. Great pop-cult commentary from the young and debauched. The minute the writers start taking any of their subject matter seriously, is the minute that everyone should stop reading.

www.viceland.com

FASHION

Aldo Shoes

Check out the latest men's and women's shoe fashions at this site that comes replete with "funky" tunes and "groovy" visuals. (Note: quotation marks denote sarcastic tone.)

www.aldoshoes.com

BeautyNet

Whether you want to maximize your small eyes, prevent swimmers hair, or stop biting your nails, BeautyNet will tell you how to do it. Or you could come to the realization that you are beautiful the way you are and put web sites like this one out of business.

www.beautynet.com

Bodytalk Magazine

The anti-fashion site for those who don't identify with certain rail-thin body types featured by the mainstream media. Articles on health and "beauty" issues are designed to cultivate personal happiness rather than unquenchable desire, and the writing style is unpretentious. No fashion police allowed!

www.bodytalkmagazine.com

Clothing for Big Folks in Canada

Those needing a size or two larger than what's available on the racks of the average department store will appreciate this resource of catalogues, retail stores, sewing patterns, and more.

www.bayarea.net/~stef/Fatfaqs/canada.html

Corporate Watch's Favorite Sweatshop Links

Make a more informed decision when shopping at the mall by visiting this collection of links. Corporate Watch is a no-nonsense site that brings a straight-up list of links to the consumer who is concerned with labour rights.

www.corpwatch.org/trac/feature/sweatshops/link.html

Estroclick

An online magazine for women's fashion, health, and finance, minus the *Cosmo*-type how-to-please-your-man-and-be-ultra-skinny shtick. Because there is life after *Sassy*.

estroclick.chickclick.com

Fashion Icon

Though geared towards a younger, female audience anyone could benefit from the latest "edgy" fashion news that is offered here by Fashion Icon. From street style, to the deepest trend-savvy crevices of pop culture, to backstage at the shows, there is no detail too small to escape her gimlet eye in giving you the complete story as it unfolds.

www.fashion-icon.com/index.html

Fashion Live

For those who follow the movements on catwalks around the world, Fashion Live Magazine porvides a Flash-enhanced site with all the latest news and photos. Surprisngly enough, there is a focus on the clothes rather than the models who wear them.

www.worldmedia.fr/fashion

Girlie Style

Browse this *ChickClick* affiliate for a monthly theme issue on various fashion topics or hop over to the ChickShops section for fashions available only online.

www.girliestyle.com

John Fluevog Shoes

Search for your sole! Buicks, Safetyvogs, Rounders, and Swingers shoes are available from this Vancouver company at a store near you. Resists alkali, water, acid, fatigue, and Satan.

www.fluevog.ca

La Dolce Vita

La Dolce Vita covers the basics of fashion, "beauty," and health in this magazine that comes in a print or online form.

ladolcevitacanada.com

The History of Costume

Colour reproductions from nineteenth-century German publications on dress throughout the ages. Some nifty morphing effects in the title page.

www.siue.edu/COSTUMES/history.html

Toronto Fashion Incubator

The Fashion Incubator offers comprehensive support to fashion designers in their early start-up stages. Get the low-down on the group's services and everything else that a young designer might need to know when starting out in this business.

www.fashionincubator.on.ca

FOLKLORE

Folklore Studies Association of Canada

Yes it sounds dry, but for those in the know the association's publication *Ethnologies* is the place the publish and read about folklore and its effect on culture. Students in the field can submit papers or apply for study grants at this site.

www.fl.ulaval.ca/celat/acef/index.htm

Myth/Folklore

A collection of academic links to various mythology-related programs at world-renowned universities. Topics range from classical and Germanic myths to fairy lore.

www.wcsu.ctstateu.edu/library/h_myth_folklore.html

Origin of the Rocket Car in the Cliff Legend

The origin of a popular urban myth or the mad ravings of a high school biology teacher? You be the judge.

www.cardhouse.com/rocketcar

The AFU & Urban Legends Archive

The alt.folklore.urban discussion group brings you this searchable database of those ever-popular urban legends. Find out the basis in fact for all the popular hook-on-the-car-door-type tales.

www.urbanlegends.com/

HUMOUR & FUN

Black Envy

As in Conrad Black, the wealthy Canadian media mogul. His willingness to share what's on his mind has provided plenty of material for this satirical site packed with quotes straight from the horse's mouth.

www.blackenvy.com

Blue Mountain Arts

Here you'll find a huge selection of animated greeting cards for every occasion, national holiday, denomination, or relative. All free, with cards as tasteful or as bawdy as you please.

www.bluemountain.com

Brunching Shuttlecocks: Alanis Lyric Generator

Stop wishing you were as brilliant a songwriter as Alanis Morissette and start pretending! It's easy with the help of the Brunching Shuttlecocks lyric generator. With snappy song titles like "Will to Live" and "Why?" you'll have a top-ten hit in no time. Now start practising your wail.

www.brunching.com/toys/toy-alanislyrics.html

shift

Center for the Easily Amused

Take out your cubicle-induced resentment on a goldfish (torture methods include the kitty-paw and good old electroshock). Follow the crazy comedic links to shtick galore. Use the Amuse-o-matic 2000 to generate pre-fab pop songs (simply fill in the blanks and prepare to whine your way up the charts). Are you starting to get the idea?

www.amused.com

Cool Jargon of the Day

Get your daily dose of lingo and underused words at this site, which provides visitors with definitions of jargon, common or otherwise. The Jargon File Resources allow you to browse past words entry by entry, wasting hours of your day at the office.

www.jargon.net

shift

Doodie.com

Yeah, it's juvenile. And kinda gross. And not exactly cutting-edge social satire. But if you can't see the humour in a Flash-animated Satan expelling a huge turd from his butt-chin, then I guess we can't be friends.

www.doodie.com

Eve

Personable feminist humour. "Bringing down the patriarchy one flip flop at a time."

www.eve.com

Humor Project

Humour consultant Joel Goodman operates this site, because in the corporate world that he serves, laffs is a serious business. So if you want to get more (gag) "smileage" out of your life ... practise Goodman's prescribed techniques.

humorproject.com

Interactive Fridge Poetry

Too lazy to appease your muse at the fridge? Click over to this web site and you can create fridge poetry without leaving your desk.

www.prominence.com/java/poetry

shift

Java on the Brain

Karl Hörnell, a Swedish programmer, is happy to share his nifty bag of Java tricks with you. Most of the applets are versions of classic time-wasters, like Solitaire or the Rubik's cube. There are some more complex games as well, presented with honest admissions about what's ripped off.

www.javaonthebrain.com/brain.html

shift

Leo's Big Day

What is Leo to do after his house is destroyed by a mudslide? Walk him to a new home in this slow-paced, whimsical Shockwave game.

pepworks.com

Lipstick Librarian

How does one become a lipstick librarian? Visit this site to see if you qualify. Hint: you don't if "your idea of sexy shoeware is Birkenstocks with a sling on the back" or if "an erotic evening for you would be trying to wash 10 of your long-haired cats while listening to National Public Radio."

www.teleport.com/~petlin/liplib

shift

Mullets Galore

The mullet haircut—short at the front and the sides, long in the back—epitomized late-70s style (and remains de rigeur among hockey players). Now, thanks to Mullets Galore, there's no need to visit a trailer park.

mulletsgalore.com

Nardwuar the Human Serviette

Our intrepid reporter asks the questions that demand to be asked. Read illustrated transcripts of his interviews with Jello Biafra, Mickey Dolenz, Beck, and Gorbachev. See video of his conversations with Michael Moore and Ron Jeremy. Thrill to the audio files of chats with Pierre Berton and Randy Bachman! But whatever you do, beware the MP3s of his band the Evaporators. You have been warned.

www.nardwuar.com

shift

Newgrounds

"The seal population is over overpopulated! The seals are starving and hungry. That's right, starving and hungry." The ramblings of a tree-hugger who has seen too many *Nova* specials? No. It's a justification for bashing a seal over the head with a club. Calm down, it's only a game. Don't give your bleeding heart a coronary like Scots People Against Child Abuse did last year, claiming that "this game abuses a child's innocence. The man who made this game has a disgusting and perverted mind." That man is 20-year-old Tom Fulp, the creator of games in which you kill or maim an assortment of lovable creatures—The Spice Girls, Jenny McCarthy, and Bill Gates, to name a few. Plus, you can page Jesus to ask him the meaning of life. Is that so wrong?

www.newgrounds.com

shift

Outerworlds

A 3D chat room that allows players to try on different avatars and then go interact with others. It's your world. Go play.

www.outerworlds.com

Punch Captain Kirk

Who doesn't have a reason to give the famous starship captain a quick left jab? Whether it's for *T.J. Hooker, Tekwars,* or Shatner's inimitable rendition of "Lucy in the Sky with Diamonds." In any case, here's your chance to smack him one. Other targets available: Bill Gates, Martha Stewart, John Tesh, and Michael Jackson.

www.well.com/user/vanya/kirk.html

Retrofuture

The future isn't what it used to be. I mean, where's all the great stuff that we were promised over the last hundred years, like the personal flying belts and transporters and phasers and tall, beautiful people in diaphanous silver togas? Answer: they're on Retrofuture. This hilarious site covers every misguided piece of past futurology from flying cars and *Star Trek* uniforms to the meal-in-a-pill.

retrofuture.web.aol.com

shift

Save the Humans

Shock therapy for planet earth. Because, y'know, they're, like, endangered.

savethehumans.com

Scottland

Sign up for citizenship now and worship the all-powerful Prime Minister ... um ... comedian, Scott Thompson. Yes, life was a little dull for this Canadian comic after *The Kids in the Hall,* so he started his own virtual country where he could be supreme ruler! And thank goodness he did! Join in the bureaucratic shenanigans of the Zen Ministry or relax in the cheekily titled "Bottoms UP" cafe.

www.scottland.com

shift

Shockwave

How many work hours have been wasted on this site? Millions? Hundreds of millions? Trillions? Clearly, small things amuse small minds, and well, you know the state of our education system. So first it's the games, from *Donut Boy 2* to *Waterballoon Drop 3.* Play for an hour. Master the technique. Play for another three hours and move on to the 'toons, from *Dilbert* to *South Park* to ... well this is a family publication.

www.shockwave.com

Sissyfight

Those who fell victim to the slings and arrows of the schoolyard can now, finally, seek revenge on their tormentors. Sissyfight allows you to customize the look of your bratty little girl (mohawk optional), and pit her against other sadistic peers. Taunt, scratch, and cower your way to victory!

www.sissyfight.com

shift

Smash Regis

Need we say more?

www.smashregis.com

SoundAmerica

Select from over 25 000 different sound files from movies, television, and cartoons. Download the software you will need to play the different sound files or follow the links to related sound clip pages. How can you resist wav.files from old *Laugh-In* episodes?

www.soundamerica.com

shift

Stickdeath.com

One nice thing about the web is that there's something for everyone. This particular something is for folks who find short animated films about stick figures killing/maiming/snowblowing other stick figures intrinsically hilarious—in other words, not to be missed.

www.stickdeath.com

The Gallery of the Absurd

The many-splendoured world of advertising revealed. In case there was any lingering doubt, this look into the imagery of popular culture proves once and for all that truth is stranger than fiction.

www.absurdgallery.com

The Hamster Dance

Nothing helps you get through the day like hundreds of twirling rodents dancing to the most delightful little tune. Exposure of longer than a few minutes to this site is not recommended.

www.hamsterdance.com

Unbearably Cool

This youth-oriented site is run by the Northwest Territories government. Find out about the plants, animals, and people of the NWT, and visit a special section on the myths and tales of the North. Plus, you'll find various links for young people, including arts, sports, clubs, and health.

www.gov.nt.ca/kids/kidshome.htm

Virtual Flowers

Too cheap to send the real thing? Try this free service that lets you send a virtual bouquet to anyone with web access.

www.virtualflowers.com

Webpedia Animated GIFs Online

An alphabetical listing of animated GIFs you can grab and stick on your own web pages. They even have an entire category devoted to *Star Wars*! 'Nuff said.

www.webdeveloper.com/animations

What's in Your Name?

Blame your parents and their ill-conceived name for you with the help of this web site. Names can be held responsible for everything from low self-esteem to liver and kidney trouble (and you thought it was just the heavy drinking!). Stop here before you make the same mistake with your kids!

www.kabalarians.com/gkh/your.htm

LITERATURE

Alex Catalogue of Electronic Texts

Writing that essay the night before it's due? Zip over here to get a quick list of reference materials to pad that anemic Works Cited. Or, use it for leisurely research beforehand.

sunsite.berkeley.edu/alex

Brick

This twice-yearly magazine, edited by Linda Spalding and Michael Ondaatje, consistently publishes fascinating non-fiction by some of the most interesting writers in Canada and around the world. Past conrtibutors have included Salman Rushdie, bp Nichol, Margaret Atwood, and Marilynne Robinson.

www.brickmag.com

Canadian Authors Association

Future scribes might want to consider a membership in the Canadian Authors Association. The CAA web site provides information on topics like copyright and electronic rights licensing, while listing the requisite events and writerly links.

www.canauthors.org/national.html

CanLit

Jennifer Anne Evans is your host at this site which opines and rants about literature, Canadian and international. Find out what Ms. Evans has been reading lately or check out her list of recommended Canadian authors. Critiques are well-written and as objective as possible, providing links to pages and articles with opposing points of view.

jenevans.com/geocities

Cherrysucker

More sour than sweet, this candy-coated journal of essays, poetry, and fiction posts submissions from mainly female contributors. As an off-shoot of the Spacegirl web page, readers can expect content that is honest and intelligent but never boring.

www.cherrysucker.com

Children's Literature Web Guide

The Children's Literature Web Guide is an attempt to gather together and categorize the growing number of internet resources related to books for children and teens. This site rates the best books from the last year with listings of award winners and best sellers, while providing enough links to make any book-buying decision difficult. Look for books that are not just spin-offs of the latest television craze!

www.ucalgary.ca/~dkbrown

Coach House Books

A world-renowned source for new writing, and the only publisher that allows visitors to read whole books online (though "tipping" for the author is encouraged). Those fetish objects (books) are also available for online ordering.

www.chbooks.com

Cool Poem of the Week

When was the last time you read a poem? Read past and present poems of the week brought to you by the York University Electronic Writers in Residence program.

www.wier.yorku.ca/~wier/CoolPoem.html

Douglas Coupland

No other author is as involved in electronic culture as Canada's own Douglas Coupland. He is resposible for the creation and the content of his own web site, which includes tour diaries, interviews, and writing created strictly for the web. This visually engaging site takes advantage of all the latest web-based toys.

www.coupland.com

Harlequin Romance Books

This famed publisher of bodice-rippers has a web site—"But please don't stop buying our books!" Actually, you can buy them online. The source for your romantic books ... and your romantic life?

www.romance.net

Inkspot

An online publication exploring current issues in the world of writing. Polls and career advice abound at this site, which also pays lip-service to the much-maligned role of the editor.

www.inkspot.com

Arts & Entertainment

It's Still Winter

This self-proclaimed journal of contemporary Canadian poetry and poetics is spare but does provide full text of interviews and articles from current and past issues, as well as a list of useful links.

quarles.unbc.ca/winter

Literature Links for the High School and College Student

Over 3000 links to various resources around the web, including hundreds of online texts, means a valuable tool for students and readers of all kinds.

www.teleport.com/~mgroves/index.shtml#Home/

Margaret Atwood

Though decidedly low-tech (do writers not use the internet?) and visually spare, this web site provides a tonne of online text related to Ms. Atwood's life and writings. A useful source for literature students or curious fans.

www.web.net/owtoad/index.html

Online Library of Literature

A handy collection of online texts in the spirit of Project Gutenberg. Includes Balzac, Poe, Tolstoy, Voltaire, and others.

www.literature.org

Poetica

Though most had their fill of this kind of thing (and ignored it) back in high school, Poetica provides a valuable online tutorial on poetry for those who are interested. Topics include the finer points on stress, metre, and historical poetic theories, and the site also features some easily accessible reference guides.

www.random.ca

Proof It

For common proofreading symbols, check out this web page. It gives the meaning of each symbol and provides an example of how it should be used.

webster.commnet.edu/writing/symbols.htm

Reader's Robot

Tired of deciding what you should read? Let someone else do the thinking at this site that divides poular books up into convenient genre categories. Includes a section for current works by or about Canadians.

www.tnrdlib.bc.ca/rr.html

Squiffy Ether Jag

Squiffy? Yes, there could not be a more apt name for this literary journal geared toward the etherized set. Read nonlinear poetry and prose in conveniently packaged modules with names like "nowhere" and "anywhere."

www.ethernaut.com/zine

The Art of Writing

A web zine about writing for writers, AOW covers all aspects and genres of writing: fiction, non-fiction, poetry, journalism, etc. With articles such as "*Star Wars: The Phantom Menace*— What's Missing in the Script?" how can a budding writer go wrong?

www.artofwriting.com

The Elements of Style

Unlimited online access to traditional reference books at no charge.

www.bartleby.com/index.html

shift

Timothy McSweeney's

In a world where gimlets like Tim Allen define humour, the arrival of *Timothy McSweeney's* is like the coming of the messiah. The site is a tornado of absurdist bliss, proffering scathing social commentary on the irony-deficient masses. Considering the site was conceived by Dave Eggers—one of the driving forces behind the satirical (yet sadly defunct) *Might Magazine*—it's no surprise that *McSweeney's* is the funniest and smartest publication on the net. Admittedly, the site's skewed take on life ain't for everyone. But for those who would rather eat glass than endure another fart joke, *McSweeney's* is nothing less than a sanctuary from cultural chaos.

www.mcsweeneys.net

Writer's Block

Writer's Block is your connection to professional writers and editors, and the secrets that have made them among the best in their field. Read featured articles or peruse fiction and poetry at this online magazine.

www.wrtitersblock.ca

MAGAZINES

Adbusters

Adbusters promotes its mission to redirect our existing commercial media culture towards ecological and social awareness through everything from "TV Turnoff Week" to "Buy Nothing Day." Find out how to stop economic progress from killing our planet, here!

www.adbusters.org

AfterHour

This hip and savvy Montreal-based new media magazine tackles everything from cutting-edge technology to the latest in underground music. Spiked with personal commentary and sharp wit, this site keeps you in the know about local and global issues.

www.hour.qc.ca

Alberta Report

The online version of popular newsmagazine *Alberta Report* provides a sampling of the articles from the latest print issue. Articles range from book reviews to opinion pieces on current events. You can also check out the indispensable feature "Who's Suing Whom."

albertareport.com

Alternative Press Review

Equal parts *Broken Pencil* and *Utne Reader, Alternative Press Review* compiles reviews and excerpts from publications that can't afford the prime space on the magazine rack of your local Chapters. Focused mainly on politics, this magazine does not pull its punches, holding a critical mirror up to the left and the right.

www.altpr.org

shift

Atlantic Unbound

The *Atlantic Monthly* magazine has been dishing out thoughtful commentary for 142 years, so one might think it wouldn't be eager to jump on the web-wagon. Wrong. The folks at Atlantic have been Unbound since 1993, offering learned web-only articles on the arts, books, and digital culture. Be sure to check out Post/Riposte, one of the more interesting egg-head bulletin boards on the net.

www.theatlantic.com

Bad Subjects

A collective that publishes a magazine (Bad Subjects: Political Education for Everyday Life) discusses current issues on a large and vital internet mailing list, and provides access to both via a public-access web site. In 1998, BS founded a small educational nonprofit corporation, also called Bad Subjects, which promotes the progressive use of new media and print publications.

eserver.org/bs/

Broken Pencil

Brought to you by the fertile mind of Hal Niedzviecki, *Broken Pencil* reviews alternative zines from around the country. How else are you going to keep up with the underground?

www.brokenpencil.com

Bust

The self-proclaimed voice of the new girl order is as empowering online as it is in print. Sample articles from the latest issue or browse features unique to the web page like the "Lounge" discussion forums or the *Bust*-approved travel guide. One of the highlights on the girl wide web.

www.bust.com

Canadian Geographic

What's in the latest issue of *Canadian Geographic*? Find out at their web site and take advantage of all kinds of resources designed for the online explorer.

www.cangeo.ca

Canadian House and Home Magazine

Get a free preview of Canada's magazine of home and style. Read "Ask a Designer" for decorating advice, or e-mail your own questions in, courtesy of this web site.

www.canadianhouseandhome.com

Canadian Living Magazine

Check out the banquet of online articles covering all kinds of home, health, gardening, and culinary issues. If the magazine itself is not your interest, you can follow the links to sites for *Canadian Living* radio and television programs.

www.canadian-living.com

Canadian Magazine Publishers Association

Lovers of Canadian magazines will want to bookmark this site for its alphabetical listing of CMPA links and "the Skimming Pool" of selected articles.

www.cmpa.ca

Chatelaine Connects

Among the recipes, lifestyle articles, and quizzes that one would expect at a web site for *Chatelaine*, there are also some other interesting tidbits. Internet 101 provides a how-to guide for people just learning to negotiate the web, and Ask an Expert allows visitors to e-mail advisors on topics such as car repair, law, and sex.

www.chatelaine.com

Factsheet5

Read descriptions of, and then follow links to, almost every zine, e-zine, online or print magazine represented on the web.

www.factsheet5.com

shift

Feed

It's about big questions (or is that esoteric questions?). Questions like, "What's the most important invention of the past 2000 years?" Things like an examination of how video games are rewiring the populace (or is that polis?). If you don't have time for discourse, you can check out Feed Daily—short bits of cultural criticism that are refreshed each morning. Then there's the discussion area called The Loop. Warning: all ye who enter, abandon hope of ever leaving.

www.feedmag.com

Giant Robot

Finally! A magazine for you, covering all the topics that you want to know about: masked wrestling, skateboarding, cooking, and Hong Kong films. Wondering where to find that photo of Sam who worked in the lab on TV's *Quincy*? Look here.

www.giantrobot.com/main.html

shift

IndiePlanet

IndiePlanet brings you the best of DIY art, music, humour, theatre, and film. Just say no to the corporate agenda. After all, it's your culture that you're consuming.

www.indieplanet.com

shift

Nerve

Proof positive that there is a connection between the brain and the genitals, Nerve serves up literate smut for the masses. The content is unabashed, dirty but not dumb, with sexperts like Susie Bright and Sallie Tisdale covering topics that even hard-core porn sites won't touch. Where else would you find STD etiquette, a defence of screamers, a polygamist manifesto, and an argument against foreplay?

www.nervemag.com

Pig Latin

"Messing with words" is probably the most accurate description of the goings-on at the Pig Latin web site. Writing subjects range from personal fame to girl scout cookie alternatives, with a healthy dose of customized magnetic poetry thrown in for good measure.

www.piglatin.net

Realm

Realm offers not just a web site, but a print magazine, and a digital version of the publication for online subscribers. This strictly Canadian publication is the source for entrepreneurs living in the world of digital culture.

www.realm.net

shift

Salon.com

Salon was once the smartest zine on the web. It no longer is—a zine, that is. In April 1999, it dropped the "magazine" and became Salon.com. It then acquired venerable online community The Well and, in July, partnered with TheStreet.com to provide improved business coverage. But its interest in money matters isn't strictly editorial: Coinciding with Salon's recent IPO was an ad campaign that sported the tagline "Makes You Think"—a rare example of truth in advertising. Now that Zippergate is mercifully over—Salon was Clinton's most vocal defender during Monica mania—Salon is back to being one of the few places on the web where you don't have to shift your brain to idle.

www.salon.com

Shift Online

Unlike most magazines that simply post a few select articles and subscription information on their web site, the creators of *Shift Online* have created a completely new animal. Though readers of the print monthly will recognize sections such as the "Shift List" and "Raw Shift" features, there are a number of essays and activities that can only be experienced by net viewers. Check out streaming video connections to the *Shift* offices or dig into the vault to explore past issues.

www.shift.com

Spank! Magazine

Apparently the first youth lifestyle mag in cyberspace, Spank! still packs a lot of punch. Drop by and read about entertainment, recreation, fashion, education, employment, and pop culture.

www.spankmag.com

Tao

An acronym for The Anarchy Organization, Tao is, in their own words, "a regional federation of local autonomous collectives and individuals involved in communications and media, radical activism and social work" interested in public interest research and education. Resistance is fertile! Anarchists unite and organize!

www.tao.ca

This Magazine

Over 30 years and still going strong, *This Magazine* is one of Canada's longest-publishing alternative journals. *This* focuses on Canadian politics, literature, and culture, but, in keeping with its radical roots, never pulls punches. Subversive, edgy, and smart, *This* is the real alternative to that.

www.thismag.com

Tomato Nation

Tomato Nation is organic commentary on print, film, and the myriad other forms that make up modern media. The "Ketchup" section archives past articles for easy, squeezable consumption.

www.tomatonation.com

Utne Reader

This *Utne Reader*'s compiliation of articles from various alternative media is a great guide for those who like to take the road less travelled. With sample articles from hundreds of different publications, readers will get a manageable helping of current events from the left-of-centre viewpoints that undermine the status quo of mainstream print. Join in on the lively discussions at Cafe Utne, which are based on topics raised in the latest issue.

www.utne.com

Vow

An online magazine that encourages its readers to save their money rather than spend it. Vow provides an advertising-free oasis in the midst of an increasingly money-hungry world wide web.

www.vow.com

Witty Banter

One man's rants and raves over current political issues. Readers may find fault in his banal subject matter, but you have to be impressed with the fact that he adds new articles every day, without the benefit of a major sponsor. Unusual slogan: "My mom is the best mom I have ever had."

www.wittybanter.com

shift

Word

A compendium of the new and strange, *Word* is one of the oldest online magazines. If you aren't now, or never have been, a regular *Word* reader, then you suck.

www.word.com

MUSEUMS, GALLERIES & EXHIBITS

Art Gallery of Nova Scotia

Forget about the usual hours and special events information, and head straight to this gallery's section for online exhibits.

www.agns.EDnet.ns.ca

Art Gallery of Ontario (AGO)

Art lovers cannot ignore the second-largest permanent collection in the country (even if they do hate Toronto). Though mainly filled with information that will only be relevant to visitors, this site does include some interesting images and articles on current exhibits.

www.ago.net

ArtSource

Check the Feature Exhibition section or artist archives to see works in paint, intermedia, sculpture, glass, printmaking, and photography at this online gallery.

artsource.shinnova.com

Artwave

I would be suspicious of any organization that overtly boasts about its connections to Rogers Communications and Sun Microsystems, but those less cynical (or more gullible) may be interested in this site that provides virtual connections to galleries across the country.

www.artwave.rogers.com

Calgary Science Centre

A web source for locals and visitors with all the usual exhibit, hours, and school program information.

www.calgaryscience.ca

Canadian Museum of Civilization

Those who cannot make the trip to Ottawa will appreciate this virtual tour of the museum's displays, replete with images and informative bits of text.

www.civilization.ca

Canadian Museum of Flight

A great web page for kids who are beginning to show interest in aviation. Lots of activities and history lessons that are succinct enough not to put the average reader to sleep.

www.canadianflight.org

Canadian Museum of Nature

Though Canada likes to emphasize its untamed wilderness and virgin forests as a lure for prospective tourists, we are mainly city dwellers who huddle near our southern border with the U.S., and are one of the world's worst offenders in terms of environmental destruction. Perhaps if more of us made trips, even virtual ones, to institutions like this one we would be more likely to reform our self-destructive ways.

www.nature.ca

Edmonton Space and Science Centre

Though the casual reader may not be interested in the museum's hours of operation, science enthusiasts will appreciate the extensive links provided at this site.

www.planet.eon.net/~essc/start.html

Glenbow Museum

This museum/art gallery/archive has a little bit of everything for the historically inclined. The uninitiated will appreciate the online exhibits that cover different periods in Canadian history, and with an endorsement form David Suzuki (possibly the coolest person in the country) how can you go wrong?

www.glenbow.org

Le Musée Des Beaux Arts

Not that you need an excuse to visit Montreal, but le Musée des Beaux Arts (along with the jazz festival, and the food, and the atmosphere ...) is one of the best going. A great deal of the permanent collection can be viewed online at this site available in both official languages.

www.mbam.qc.ca

Manitoba Museum of the Titanic

Why a museum dedicated to the Titanic? Why in the prairies? The curators may justify their existence all they like but, though they do have over 150 artifacts from the infamous ship available for online viewing, visitors to this site may wish they had gone down with the ship.

www.titanicconcepts.com

McMichael Art Gallery

Oh sweet Kleinburg, so close and yet so far removed from the sewer that is Toronto. One of the most picturesque art galleries on the planet resides here on several acres of farmland, and houses a substantial number of paintings by the Group of Seven to boot.

www.mcmichael.com

MOMA

The venerable Museum of Modern Art brought to you in all its pixelated glory! Browse selections from the world-renowned collection or take advantage of fly-wheel technology at the gift shop with one of the best selections of books on the only art that counts.

www.moma.org

National Aviation Museum

It's just plain fun at one of the world's greatest aeronautical collections. Kids can read articles on Canada's aviation history, try out the online aviation research tools, or follow instructions to build paper airplanes at this site.

www.aviation.nmstc.ca

National Gallery of Canada

Though not quite the same as an actual visit, this web site runs a close second with 24-hour access to the Gallery's collection of art and artist bios, the library, and assorted publications. Those expecting a select few paintings by popular artists will be astounded at how extensive the online gallery is.

national.gallery.ca

National Museum of Science and Technology

Get plugged into a virtual tour of Ottawa's Museum of Science and Technology. Boasting the largest collection of its kind in the country, the museum's web site provides background information and online displays of selected exhibits.

www.science-tech.nmstc.ca

Naval Museum of Alberta

Why does Canada insist on giving land-locked provinces the privilege of hosting museums dedicated to sea-faring vessels (see the Manitoba Museum of the Titanic)? Hey, prairie folk are interested in boats too! Defend the right to display ships on dry land at this web site.

www.navalmuseum.ab.ca

Newfoundland Museum

Even snappy titles like "Viking Millennium" cannot jazz up this woeful web site. Though still useful for visitor information, one may have to wait another thousand years before the next site update.

www.nfmuseum.com

Nova Scotia Museum

Actually, there are 25 smaller museums and historic sites around the province, all incorporated under the one title. They include mills, houses, farms; museums of geology, firefighting, and the fishery; and a planetarium.

www.ednet.ns.ca/educ/museum

Ontario Science Centre

Bouncing brains! Exploding zits! Concentration constipation! You'll also find information about the centre's current exhibits, education programs, memberships, and a kids' camp.

www.osc.on.ca

Royal Ontario Museum

Check out the various online tidbits about some of the most interesting things that Canada has stolen from other parts of the world.

www.rom.on.ca

The Nickle Arts Museum

"It's your Nickle!" All the news that's fit to print about numismatics and contemporary art.

www.ucalgary.ca/~nickle

The Royal British Columbia Museum

The RBCM web site provides a healthy collection of online research papers and project listings. Visit this page for exhibit information and detailed descriptions of the collection, or take a look at a live image from Victoria's inner harbour.

www.rcbm.gov.bc.ca

The Royal Tyrrell Museum

Located near some of greatest discoveries of dinosaur bones in the world, the Tyrell is *the* place in Canada for information on the Jurassic period. Apropos of such a boast, this site will hook you up to research materials and other interesting online information.

www.tyrellmuseum.com

The Tom Thomson Memorial Art Gallery

Owen Sound's tribute to the famous painter holds one of the largest collections of his work. This substantial web site lets visitors view a number of Thomson's paintings, and also includes many works by other members of the Group of Seven.

www.tomthomson.org

MUSIC

2look4

This music search "exchange" provides a search engine for MP3s and links to reviews and other related sites.

www.2look4.com

54.40 Online

Everything you need to know about one of Canada's most popular and well-respected rock groups. You can find out about their latest tour, help create their set list, and possibly even join them on stage.

www.sonymusic.com/artists/5440

88HipHop

Big pants, phat beats, and a live videostream. Pretty fly for any guy.

88hiphop.com

shift

Beatnik GrooveGrams

Remix a catalogue of songs—from Britney Spears to David Bowie—using a nifty app developed by Thomas "She Blinded Me with Science" Dolby Robertson. Then e-mail your sonic creations to your friends.

beatnik.com/groovegrams

Blues Access Online

Woke up this mornin'
Surfed to this site
I browsed and I clicked
It's got the blues alright!

www.he.net/~blues/ba_home.html

Blues and Race Relations

An online thesis that speculates on the effect blues music had on the improvement of race relations through the 19th and 20th centuries. It's interesting for both the political and musical aspects, and blues fans can follow an evolution of the genre from early minstrel shows to the British Invasion.

www.angelfire.com/sc/bluesthesis/

Buzzwords

Check out this promotional site for the heavy-hitting lineup of artists and bands signed to Sony Canada, including Leonard Cohen, Our Lady Peace, Chantal Kreviazuk, and Prozzak. Subscribe to their weekly newsletter, look through their contests, or read up about appearances by their artists.

www.buzzwords.com

Canadian Bootleg Traders Index

Though not so frequently updated, this site still has relevant information on the mad world of bootleg tapes. Go here for postage rates and e-mail addresses of fans for almost every band imaginable.

www.wincom.net/~gsawhney/boots

Canadian Classic Rock Page

If you happen to be looking for the lyrics to Trooper's "Raise a Little Hell" or perhaps a sound clip of "Cinnamon Girl" or "Patio Lanterns," your troubles are over my mullet-headed friend. Visit some links to your favourite artists or vote for them in an online poll.

www.ilos.net/~denden/CCRP.html

Canadian Musician

This online version of the leading music-industry magazine provides links to home pages of Canadian artists and bands, from Lee Aaron to Zero Degrees Kelvin. It features big-name acts as well as indie bands, and provides a guide to Canadian recording studios by province.

www.canadianmusician.com

Canadian Musician

Enter at your own risk! This online version of the music-industry magazine has been known to provide links to artists such as (shudder) Lee Aaron. The site does provide a nice listing for indie bans as well, though, and a guide to Canadian recording studios by province.

www.canadianmusician.com

CanEHdian Music Online

A patriotic look at music, "Canada's third official language." Fans of the regular top-forty schlock (Twain, Dion, et al.) will have a field day at this site.

www.geocities.com/SunsetStrip/Stadium/3968/first.html

Canmusic.com

Though updates seem irregular and every review gets the same five maple leaves out of five rating, there are still a few sections of this web site that may be of use to purveyors of indie rock.

www.canmusic.com

Canuck Punk

Though the concept of a patriotic punk rock page seems to go against the whole anarchy aesthetic, this page is chock-full of all the rawk labels, radio shows, and concert listings that any young rabble-rouser will need. Oi!

www.geocities.com/SunsetStrip/Alley/8941

Cape Breton Music Online

A well-maintained, intelligent, and sober site with all the necessary information on the likes of the Barra MacNeils and Natalie McMaster (no trace of Ashley MacIsaac for some reason?). The old-school radio interface is also a nice, quaint, addition.

www.cbmusic.com

Clever Joe's Musician Resource Centre

Though the odd article here may be of interest to the casual music fan, this site is mainly for guitar geeks only! Exhibit A: book feature on *The Best of Eric Clapton* and an article on guitar soloing techniques. A great page for the budding Steve Vai.

www.cleverjoe.com

shift

Clock Din

You're the DJ. You program the beats, hit the samples, and plug some loops. Now start dancing.

clockdin.com

Country Wave

Are you ready for the country? It's time to go to the home page for Canada's premier country music magazine, bringing you fan clubs, reviews, events, fashions, and back issues in an online format.

www.countrywave.com

Domenic's Accordian Beatles Page

Sacrilege or high art? Domenic Amatucci doesn't care because he's getting away with one of the best self-promotion schemes on the web. Do people *really* want to download an accordian-fuelled interpretation of Paul McCartney's "My Love"? Apparently, yes.

home.ican.net/~domenic/accordion.html

Early Music Vancouver

Founded in 1970, Early Music Vancouver was the first organization established in North America to foster and promote music from various periods in a historical context, using appropriate instruments and performance practices. A great page for those interested in Canadian music before the advent of rock and roll.

www.earlymusic.bc.ca

Eatsleepmusic.com

Formerly an MP3 archive for independent music, Eatsleepmusic.com has gone the more lucrative route of karaoke! Transform your PC into a karaoke machine and gather 'round the cubicle for an old-time sing-a-long.

www.eatsleepmusic.com

Fine Balance

A recent addition to the idependent music scene in Canada, Fine Balance brings you the best in local and international talent. Ground-breaking music in the tradition of such indie icons as Matador and Kranky.

www.finebalance.com

HipHopCanada

HipHopCanada brings you the northern touch with rap acts from north of the border. Check out the latest news on your favourite hip hop artists, read reviews of shows and CDs, download MP3s and videos, or sign up for free e-mail.

www.hiphopcanada.com

HMV Canada

Soundclips abound at this store's web presence. Prices are reasonable—and in Canadian dollars—with frequent sales and deals on shipping. An incredibly extensive listing of music is provided for visitors to browse, read reviews, and find out about the history of almost any band.

www.hmv.com

shift

Hookt

Streaming audio, an online store that sells the dopest wears, and a whole lot of attitude. The *Vibe* magazine of the web.

hookt.com

Internet Underground Music Archive

Visitors to the IUMA will be forgiven for not recognizing a single artist—most bands listed here are completely unknown. Though this policy is great for the bands themselves, it may make life difficult for the prospective music fan.

www.iuma.com

Juno Awards

A much-improved web site that provides a live netcast of the annual Canadian music awards. No longer a source page just for Celine Dion, there are links and features on almost all of the artists nominated.

www.juno-awards.com

KickInTheHead.com

KickInTheHead.com is a comprehensive, searchable web database that lets artists add and update their own information for free. A great opportunity for independent bands to get some free publicity.

www.kickinthehead.com

shift

Listen.com

The genius of Listen.com is that it will save you lots of time. A download directory of MP3s, the site tracks songs available on the web and tells you where to get them. If its engine can't find anything from, say, the Chemical Brothers, its intelligent agent will suggest something similar, like a Fatboy Slim track. There are also mini-reviews for each artist and a listening booth for previews. Vital.

www.listen.com

MP123

MP123 is a network set up to connect the people who want certain MP3s to the people who have them so they can share. All perfectly legal. Kind of.

mp123.com

shift

MP3 Control

The curse of free music is having to somehow organize the thousands of MP3 files that litter your hard drive. This free download will help you keep track of your pirated treasure chest.

hotfiles.zdnet.com

MP3.com

A comprehensive resource to MP3-formatted music on the web. Features established-label acts and unkown indies, with a great deal of the music available for free. Those with the proper technology are saving a bundle on CD costs thanks to this format.

www.mp3.com

shift

MP3.com

In case you've been living in outer space for the past year, MP3.com has become the *Buy & Sell* of net-based indie music by providing free server space for garage bands to post their tunes. A sure sign of its influence is that biggie labels and mainstream artists have caught on, offering their own tunes for free download from the site.

www.mp3.com

Napster

What is Napster? Some hail it as a revolutionary means of obtaining free MP3 files. Others, and their lawyers, maintain that it's a violation of copyright laws and musicians' rights. So, if you're looking for the newest music, or the latest litigation, check this site.

napster.com

Arts & Entertainment

Northern Journey Online

This celebration of Canadian folk music provides links to the sites of folk artists, music and book reviews, a calendar of performing arts events in Ontario, and an online journal.

wwww.northernjourney.com

Rockrgrl

The online companion to the *Rockrgrl* magazine has almost all the features of its bi-monthly sister. This DIY publication carries intelligent interviews with female musicians, advice on how to start a label, tips on booking your own tour, legal issues, gear reviews, studio tips, and more. Don't just read about rock stars—be one!

www.rockrgrl.com

Sam the Record Man

That old standard of Canadian retail is online and featuring as many sales and low-priced new releases as one would find in the store.

www.Samscd.com

shift

Sonicnet

Venerable Sonicnet continues to be a no-brainer music bookmark, delivering quality cybercasts of music festivals like Tibetan Freedom and the Warped Tour. Recently, Sonicnet partnered with Macromedia's Shockrave to form Flashradio (www.flashradio.com), which broadcasts tunes in tandem with abstract images. Bonus: the site also allows you to view new videos and chat with your favourite artists.

www.sonicnet.com

Teenage USA

Don't let the label name fool you—this is the home of some of the finest independent music in Canada. Visit such luminaries as Lonnie James, Mean Red Spiders, and the dearly departed Pecola. Digital seven-inches mean plenty of free music for the kiddies who just want to rawk!

www.teenageusarecordings.com

The Anti-Hit List

Interested in good music that will never grace the top-ten charts? John Sakamoto, a music fan's music fan, has the anti-hit list for visitors who want the low-down on music that's not judged by sales alone.

www.sunmedia.ca/JamMusicAntihit

The Blues MP3 and Lyrics Server

This online magazine from Germany brings blues fans a great resource for MP3s and lyrics to obscure songs.

www.blooze.de

The Canadian Choir Index

This site promises to be the most comprehensive and up-to-date listing of Canadian choirs on the web. Though hopelessly lo-fi, there is a useful list of links to organizations, events, and over 280 choirs in their database.

is2.dal.ca/~slide/camerata/resource.html

The Ultimate Band List

The home of indie rock on the web features some more widely acclaimed acts but, mostly, this MP3 site features unknown bands. Check out this comprehensive web site for reviews, discographies, concert news, and contests.

www.ubl.com

Tribe Magazine

A reliable source (in print and online) for the nation's news in rave and DJ culture. Visitors will appreciate event listings from across the country and various DJ profiles.

www.tribe.ca

Turntablism.com

Chock full of news and reviews on the latest in DJ culture. Those looking to try their hand at the world of scratch artistry will appreciate the only online version of the operating instructions for the legendary Technics 1200 MkII turntable system.

www.turntablism.com

MUSIC — ARTISTS

Alanis Morissette Sites

Disappointing sales of her latest record seem not to have diminshed the creation of web sites dedicated to Ms. Morissette. Yahoo provides a comprehensive listing of the best of them (as well as some anti-Alanis sites) on this page.

ca.yahoo.com/Entertainment/Music/Artists/By_Genre/Rock_and_Pop/Morissette__Alanis/

Beck

When everyone else was trying to figure out just how this whole internet thing worked, Beck already had himself one of the best sites on the net. These days he's still one of the best, with great Flash animations, strange collage art from Beck himself, and all those kind of news items and archival info that fans go crazy for. A recent news bulletin reported a bruise that Beck sustained when he was bumped by his bass player during a concert. Now that's thorough!

www.beck.com

Blue Rodeo

It's a diamond mine of information, news, and press on Toronto band Blue Rodeo. Sample the recipe for Blue Rodeo chili, listen to albums, or get lost together with other fans in the "Tales from the Road" section.

www.bluerodeo.com

Boards of Canada

Not boards and not even Canadian, these lads from Scotland swiped their moniker from the NFB films they saw so much of as children. Read all about this duo's unique brand of electronic music and liten to audio clips from their many recordings at their official web site.

www.boardsofcanada.com

Bryan Adams

All the latest news and releases from the forever 18-year-old musician, including exclusive fan-club news.

www.bryanadams.com

Celine Dion

If there's something you need to know about Celine Dion that has not already been overexposed in the mass media then you'll probably find it here. Fans of the Quebec songstress can sign up for "Team Celine" to receive exclusive information on all things Celine.

www.celineonline.com

Chantal Kreviazuk

As touchy feely as the artist herself, this web page will give fans something to do while they mope and wait for the next record. The Watermarks section even posts RealAudio reports from Chantal so she can stay in touch with her fans. Isn't she the greatest?

www.chantalkreviazuk.com

Cowboy Junkies

Instead of packing it in after parting ways with their record label, the Cowboy Junkies decided to take the DIY approach. Their web page, which is run by the band, acts as a sales outlet for recordings on their Latent label, and also provides the requisite tour info and band news. Benefiting from the lack of major-label gloss, the site provides a more intimate view of the group, with personal photos and comments about shows provided by the band members.

www.cowboyjunkies.com

Crash Test Dummies

Fans of eccentric rock/pop group Crash Test Dummies will enjoy this collection of band news, discographies, FAQs, lyrics, and a dummy-centric chat group.

www.crashtestdummies.com

Da Slyme

Here's the online residence of one of Canada's first punk rock acts where they shamelessly flog their latest trashy records. You probably remember them for such classics as "Speedballin' with Granny."

www.slyme.com

Elevator Through

Psychedelic stoner rock from the band formerly known as Elevator to Hell. Need we say more?

www.subpop.com/bands/elevator/website

IndieCanada.com

Check out this online index for information on relatively unknown acts. You can also find club listings, RealAudio song samples, and the IndieCanada online record store.

www.indiecanada.com

Julie Doiron

Read the bios and listen to the records of this recent Juno award winner and Eric's Trip alumnus.

www.subpop.com/bands/juliedoiron/website

Kid Koala

The web site for Montreal's Kid Koala is visually spare but adds a personal touch with drawings done by the man himself. Worth a visit if only to download an edited version of the coveted *Scratchcratchratchatch* tape.

www.kidkoala.com

Len

With influences ranging from the Buggles to Curtis Blow, these funky white boys (and a girl) from Canada have a buffet of beats to satisfy any musical craving. You can't stop the bum rush!

www.lensite.com

My Brilliant Beast

Explore this visually stunning Flash-enhanced site by Toronto band My Brilliant Beast. A mix of indie-cred and celebrity status (MBB member Byron works for MuchMusic's *The New Music*).

mybrilliantbeast.com

Ninja Tune

We could give you the URLs of all their separate artists, but why not just give you the home base? One of the best labels with some of the best artists (Coldcut, Kid Koala, and DJ Vadim) and some of the best web content. Everything from downloadable samples to remix software.

www.ninjatune.net

Our Lady Peace

Chill out to lyrics, audio and video clips from OLP albums, get tour news, read a band bio, or send a digital postcard of the guys to a friend. Features overly earnest audio reports from band members (whoopee!).

www.ourladypeace.com

Radiohead

A band site that isn't designed just to sell records? Those are few and far between, but Radiohead probably has the best. Chock-full of strange drawings, personal photos, and stream-of-consciousness reportage, even those who don't like the music will be compelled to explore.

www.radiohead.com

Rascalz

Representing the best in hip hop from Canada, the Rascalz web site will not disappoint web aesthetes or music fans. With all of its great Flash animations and tons of info on albums, band members, and tours, visitors may be tempted to just sit back and enjoy the visual and aural experience.

www.rascalz.com

Sarah McLachlan

Read all about the latest recordings and performances by the world-famous singer/songwriter, or browse through the vaguely titled "Things" section for related miscellany.

www.sarahmclachlan.com

Sloan

Hey you! This is the official site of one of Canada's favourite bands. Features pictures, releases, tour information, a fan chat section, and links to fan pages.

sloan.a-d-n.com

The Glenn Gould Archive

This site, developed by the National Library of Canada, contains extensive material on Canada's greatest classical musician. The late piano virtuoso's papers are exhibited here, along with audio files, biographical information, databases, related links, and Gould-inspired writings and art.

www.gould.nlc-bnc.ca/egould.htm

The Leonard Cohen Files

This is the only web site with input from the man himself, so fans should visit this page for updates and news on new writings and recordings. Check here for photos, poetry, and song lyrics that have yet to be published.

www.leonardcohenfiles.com

The Tragically Hip Home Page

Do fans of the Tragically Hip need to be told where to find the official web site? Probably not, but here it is anyway, filled with more recordings, tour news, and more input from the band than anyone really has any use for.

www.thehip.com

MUSIC — CLASSICAL

Classical Music Dictionary

One great thing about classical music—as opposed to pop—is that almost everything is in the public domain, so fans won't find the legal restrictions that affect other music sites. At this page there are hundreds of free MP3s and Midi files available to download, ranging from Bach to Shostakovich.

www.karadar.it/karadar.htm

Classical Music Links

Globe trotters and home bodies alike will enjoy this collection of links to fine music from all over the world. Visit this directory for links to Canadian and internationl orchestras, classical music pages, instrument sites, and music-related organizations.

www.tsomusicians.com/whatsnew/links.html

Classical Music Net

Everything a fan could want to know is either at this site or linked to it. There are composer bios, CD reviews, a detailed classical music buying guide, and over 2600 different links to related resources.

www.classical.net

Tafelmusik

Tafelmusik is a Toronto-based orchestra of international stature that specializes in Baroque music played on period instruments. The web site includes background on the ensemble and their director, as well as kudos from the venerable *New York Times*.

www.tafelmusik.org

Toronto Symphony Orchestra

Toronto's world-renowned symphony may very well be the best music that the city has to offer. Under the direction of conductor Jukka-Pekka Saraste and with regular visits from such luminaries as Yo-Yo Ma, the symphony has earned its high status. The web site keeps pace with the requisite concert information and provides a browser-based music selector to let visitors program sweet sounds to enhance the experience.

www.tso.on.ca

Toronto Symphony Orchestra Musicians

A unique opportunity where fans of the TSO can hear from the musicians themselves and learn a little about their background. Find out what's going on behind the scenes at the symphony, or get in touch with teachers who can help you learn how to play any number of musical instruments featured in the orchestra.

www.tsomusicians.com

Vancouver Symphony

This site allows you to consult season schedules, get ticket and subscription details, and check out performance reviews and profiles of conductors. Or you can browse through the VSO discography.

sitegeist.com/VCC/home.html

MUSIC — EVENTS

Edgefest

It may be over for another year, but fans can still relive the glory that was Edgefest at this web site full of photos, interviews, sound clips, and info on your favourite bands from the tour.

www.edgefest.net

Festival Seeker

Here's a searchable catalogue of festivals from across the country. You can limit your search by province, month, performer, or type of festival. Prepare to be festive.

www.festivalseeker.com

MUSIC — JAZZ

All About Jazz

As the title suggests, it's a great site covering all styles and periods of jazz music. Read reviews on the latest records or sample new tunes from Discovermusic.com.

www.allaboutjazz.com

Central Park North

Central Park North was created primarily to promote Canadian jazz music and musicians. Updates are few and far between, but this site may be one of the few Canuck jazz representatives on the web.

www.geocities.com/BourbonStreet/5580

du Maurier Downtown Jazz Toronto

Not just an institution for old-school, freestyle jazz (past performers have included Chicago's Tortoise), this site posts jazz news and festival updates all year.

www.tojazz.com

Jazz Clubs Worldwide

Not just a great source for finding local clubs, this site provides a comprehensive review of festivals, tours, and online magazines while listing venues from over 60 different countries.

www.jazz-clubs-worldwide.com/index.htm

Montreal International Jazz Festival

Don't judge this jazz festival by it's dated web site. Here is yet another excuse to pack up and head for Montreal (as if you really needed one). The Montreal Jazz Festival adds another jewel to the crown of this city's nightlife, with over a week's worth of the best jazz music in the world.

www.montrealjazzfestival.com

Saskatchewan Jazz Festival

Artist, schedule, and venue information, along with sample audio files of many of the acts, make up the web site for this annual event sponsored by SaskTel.

www.saskjazz.com

The Red Hot Jazz Archive

Go back to the beginning and read all about the origins of jazz music at this web page that covers jazz before 1930. Find out about the musicians and their songs through text and audio files, or follow links to essays and related films.

www.redhotjazz.com

MUSIC — ORGANIZATIONS

Canadian Disc Jockey Association

Need someone to DJ your dance or party? The web site for the Canadian Disc Jockey Association provides listings for professional DJs across the country, as well as trade information for those in the business. Just don't expect any of these vinyl monkeys to play the latest cuts from the clubs.

www.cdja.org

Canadian Independent Record Production Association (CIRPA)

The CIRPA web page provides a useful international marketing database for independent record producers looking to sell product overseas. Check this site for conference dates, research results, and a Canadian Music Industry Primer for those who are new to the business.

www.cirpa.ca

Canadian Musical Reproduction Rights Agency

The CMRRA is a nonprofit music licensing agency that represents the vast majority of music copyright owners. On their behalf, the CMRRA issues licenses to users of the reproduction right in copyrighted music. Musicians visiting this site can check up on various licensing policies, search the affiliated publishers directory, or contact the CMRRA with questions and comments.

www.cmrra.ca/default.html

Country Music Northern Ontario

Though filled with questionable vocabulary and cheese-ball graphics, this site does harbour a solid collection of links to country music sites. Make a quick visit and then depart for some other part of the web.

www.cyberbeach.net/~country

Foundation to Assist Canadian Talent on Records (FACTOR)

This nonprofit group was founded by a consortium of broadcasting standards bodies and large private companies like CHUM Ltd. and Rogers Communications. They provide grants to assist in the development of Canadian recording talent. Of course, with the CRTC still legislating a certain percentage of "Cancon" on the radio, it only makes sense to spend a bit of money finding and promoting "Cancon" that you might actually want to listen to. This dull web site includes news updates and application forms, and is essential for independent musicians.

www.factor.ca

SOCAN

Though this clunky site may turn off some visitors, the importance of the organization to musicians across Canada cannot be overemphasized. These are the people that make sure artists actually get paid for playing shows or having their music played in a public forum. Essential information for those in the industry.

www.socan.ca

Songwriters Association of Canada

The goal of this organization is to imporve the creative and business environment for songwriters in Canada and around the world. The association puts out a newsletter, gives workshops, and maintains a depository of Canadian songs to help with copyright issues. Professionals and amateurs can apply for membership online.

www.songwriters.ca

The Glenn Gould Foundation

Created in 1983, the Glenn Gould Foundation is a charitable organization that seeks to support the world of music and encourage its greatest talents. Check out this site for details on the various prizes and programs offered by the foundation, or read a biography of the great Canadian musician whose life inspired all those short films.

www.glenngould.ca

PERFORMING ARTS

Canadian Opera Company

Help stave off the seemingly imminent demise of the opera house with a visit to the COC web page. Valiant, operatic crusaders will find all the usual information about shows, programs, and, most importantly, how to donate money to this worthy cause.

www.coc.ca

Cirque du Soleil

Look up the features of this spectacular show's latest lineup or find out when the Cirque will be coming to a city near you. The site also features an online club for particularly rabid fans.

www.cirquedusoleil.com

Stage Hand Puppets

Not just a collection of hands in socks, this site contains a catalogue of puppets and books, a list of puppet links, and an activity page for kids.

www3.ns.sympatico.ca/onstage/puppets

PHOTOGRAPHY

Canadian Association of Photographers and Illustrators in Communications (CAPIC)

Those not interested in CAPIC's membership news may still want to check out the stylish design of their web page, complete with cool member photos and illustrations.

www.capic.org

Canadian Museum of Contemporary Photography

This Ottawa museum contains over 150 000 different images by some of the finest photographers in Canada. Online visitors can catch a glimpse of this staggering collection of photographic works and find out about upcoming exhibits.

www.cs.mcgill.ca/~raven

Floria Sigismondi

One of the most innovative and unconventional photographers of her time, Floria Sigismondi's fantastic and macabre photographs and videos have been created for such rock luminaries as Tricky, Marilyn Manson, and David Bowie. Who would have guessed that the creator of these "entropic underworlds" hails from Hamilton, Ontario?

www.floriasigismondi.com

Get the Picture

Learn the basics of photography technique by following the step-by-step process that seven different photographers went through to create their specific photos.

www.artsmia.org/get-the-picture

How to Make and Use a Pinhole Camera

A great site for would-be DIY photographers that breaks down the construction and use of a 126-cartridge pinhole camera in explicit detail. Illustrations are clear and easy to follow, and the site includes links to related resources.

www.toptown.com/nowhere/kypfer/pinhole/pinhole.htm

The American Museum of Photography

An informative site covering the first 75 years of photography in the U.S. Includes an excellent online gallery, a helpful research centre for information on various techniques, and links to other online resources.

www.photographymuseum.com

The World Map of Live Webcams

Click on the map at this web site to view real-time photos from every continent in the world. There are even webcams set up for special events, such as England's Glastonbury Music Festival.

dove.mtx.net.au/~punky/World.html

Yousef Karsh

Read this detailed account of the life and career of Canada's world-famous portrait photographer Yousef Karsh. Responsible for photographing seven Canadian prime ministers and nine U.S. presidents, Karsh seems to have taken pictures of everyone from Leonard Cohen to Winston Churchill, and there are links at this site to some of his most famous portraits.

www.jetcity.com/~azdarar/karsh.htm

RADIO

Amateur Radio WWW Bookmark File

An incredibly comprehensive listing of ham operators and resources. Book off several hours to explore this page or avoid it entirely.

wharax.hartford.edu/disk$userdate/faculty/newsvhf/www/ham-www.html

Canadian Amateur Radio on the Internet

An online central station for ham radio operators in Canada, this web site provides an e-mail database for over 5000 members. Amateur hams can follow links to other like-minded radio pages, look up local equipment dealers, take an online rules and regulations quiz, or check out the Canadian regulations for radio operators.

ve2m.net

Canadian Association of Broadcasters

Strictly an industry site, though links provided to Canadian television and radio sites may be of interest to others.

www.cab-acr.ca

Canadian Broadcast Standards Council

Do you think that there's too much sex and violence on television? Or not enough? Either way, you can complain about it here, at the Canadian Broadcast Standards Council web site.

www.cbsc.ca

Canadian Campus, Community and Non-Commercial Stations Online

The best programming is usually found off of the regular stops on the radio dial, and this listing of nonprofit stations gives visitors access to a world of new music. Fewer commercials mean fewer restrictions and better music at this site that provides the best in radio—online or otherwise.

www.web.net/csirp/stations.html

Canadian Radio-television and Telecommunications Commission

Interested in the people behind such strangeness as Canadian content rules and attempted internet regulations? Look no further than the CRTC. Their web site provides current news issues surrounding their fascist ... I mean civilized policies and regulations.

www.crtc.gc.ca

CBC Radio

Here you'll find listings of show times and descriptions for absolutely every program that CBC radio broadcasts. Also available are RealAudio connections for local CBC stations across the country, as well as community announcements, audio software, and links to all the other information from the larger CBC site.

www.radio.cbc.ca

CBC Radio News

CBC Radio has the largest news-gathering network in Canada and if you don't have the time to catch one of the 40 news broadcasts every day, you'll be able to update yourself at this site. There are links to specific news shows such as *The World at Six*, live internet radio feeds, and text listings for top stories.

www.radio.cbc.ca/news

Civil Air Search and Rescue Association

The CASARA is a Canada-wide volunteer aviation association dedicated to aviation safety and air search support services for the National Search and Rescue Association. Look up training information and publications, or join the SAR mailing list at this site.

www.casara.ca

Definitely Not the Opera

A weekly Saturday afternoon show on CBC, *Definitely Not the Opera* covers all aspects of pop culture, from music and film to technology and philosophy. Find information on the program, read entertaining features, or pitch ideas for the show at the DNTO web site.

www.opera.cbc.ca

Friends of Canadian Broadcasting

Friends of Canadian Broadcasting is a Canada-wide voluntary organization supported by 48 000 households, whose mission is to defend and enhance the quality and quantity of Canadian programming. Wonderful! But who cares? Apparently, more people listen to *Cross-Country Checkup* than you may have guessed.

friendscb.org

Radio Amateurs of Canada

A not-for-profit association representing the interests of licensed amateur radio operators.

www.rac.ca

Radio Canada International

"Canada's voice to the world" is accessible over the internet in RealAudio. A good source for world news from a Canadian perspective, this decidedly multicultural site is navigable in English, French, Chinese, Russian, Ukrainian, Spanish, and Arabic.

www.rcinet.ca

SPEAKERS

CanSpeak Speakers Bureau

If you need a speaker for an upcoming event, CanSpeak will help you find the one most suited to your group. Search for a speaker by name, topic of speech, or budget range, and then screen them through Real Player videos.

www.canspeak.com

Toastmasters

Those looking to improve their public speaking skills will find online tips as well as links to local organizations at the Toastmasters web site.

www.toastmasters.org

TELEVISION

Academy of Television Arts and Sciences

The official site for television's Emmy Awards contains news and updates from the world of TV in its handy online magazine. Fans will also find trivia games, results from the daytime awards, and general information on what the academy is all about.

www.emmys.org

Banff Television Festival

The Banff Television Festival takes place each summer in Canada's favourite national park. Mainly focused on project development within the industry, the festival attracts TV companies from all over the world. Here you'll find all the necessary registration and event information—as if you needed an excuse to go to Banff!

www.banfftvfest.com

Canada's TV Zone

Couch potatoes of the world unite! This site is for the hard-core tube-aholic, with a section on channels that carry your favourite shows, schedules of season finales, and info on ratings systems. Ah, the sweet idiot box! A great resource for planning time-wasting hours in front of its deathly glow.

tvzone.channelcanada.com

Canadian Cable Television Association

Visit the spine-tingling world of Canadian cable regulatory interventions!

www.ccta.ca

ClickTV

Look up your local broadcast, cable, and satellite television listings, or browse through a selection of TV-related news items.

www.clicktv.com

Cult Television

Look up favourite lost classics such as *The A-Team* or *The Incredible Hulk*, and then whine to other nostalgic viewers about how much you miss them in the chat forums.

www.cult-television.com

Free Speech Internet Television

Freedom is more than just another word for nothing left to do. Check out this site for all those stories that just don't seem to get picked up by major networks. Available in text, video, or audio formats.

freespeech.org

Gemini Awards

See the best of Canadian television honoured at this site for the Gemini Awards, and download pretty pictures of Ken Finkleman.

www.academy.ca/gallery.html

Media Technology

Keep up with the latest in television and home entertainment technology at this site. Also covers relevant news stories such as the proposed break-up of Microsoft.

www.mediatechnology.com

Mighty Big TV

Is there anything that the mighty ChickClick sisterhood hasn't covered? Mighty Big TV takes the piss out of prime time with episode summaries for the most popular shows, tinged with the usual sarcastic wit and black humour. All this and it's interactive to boot. Fans can join in on the discussion at any one of the online forums provided for each show.

www.mightybigtv.com

Museum of Television

Read an online history of the tube at this site brought to you by the MZTV Museum of Television. Point of interest: Moses Znaimer's extended rant to justify his television fetish.

www.mztv.com/mztvhome.html

Screen Trade Canada

Read the latest news from the world of Canadian television and film at this web site. Look up your favourite Canuck actors or browse through sections dedicated to various television shows and movies.

www.screentradecanada.com

Simpsons, Eh?

Q: Do we really care what Americans think about Canada? A: Damn straight, judging by this obsessive chronicle of every single Canuck reference on the Simpsons! Q#2: Who feels that strongly about these things to devote a web site to it? A: Find out here.

ccr.ptbcanadian.com/simpsons

Toon Tracker

Though your days of Froot Loops and Saturday morning cartoons may be long gone, you can relive the glee you felt upon hearing those catchy little theme songs, all in the comfort of your own cubicle. Transport yourself back to simpler times with songs from *Mr. Magoo*, *Mighty Mouse*, and the short-lived *Rubik the Amazing Cube*.

www2.wi.net/~rkurer/ttra.htm

TV Guide Live

Schedules are available by viewing area and include listings for the next two weeks. Plus, you can check out those must-have *TV Guide* features "Star News and Gossip" and "Celebrity Chef"! (Note mock enthusiasm.)

www.tvguidelive.com

TV Trivia

An engaging diversion in the form of a television trivia game. Also features links to humourous TV sites like *The Benny Hill Show*.

home.earthlink.net/~paulywogg/index.htm

TELEVISION — CHANNELS

Bravo! Canada

Artists will want to take advantage of Bravo!Fact, a foundation established to provide financial assistance and incentives for the production of Canadian shortform art videos. Oh yeah, these guys also have a TV station or something like that.

www.bravo.ca

Canadian Broadcasting Corporation (CBC)

Proof that your tax dollars can be used effectively, the CBC web site is one of the most extensive and up-to-date pages on the web. There are links to all programs related to Newsworld, CBC television, and CBC radio. The site is smooth, efficient, and current. Now if only we could say the same for all government-sponsored agencies.

cbc.ca

Arts & Entertainment

CBC Newsworld Online

View video clips of major events from the Newsworld channel, or take advantage of the extensive daily news coverage and archived information available at this page.

cbc.ca/newsworld

Comedy Central

The choppy, animated Jon Stewart that greets visitors to this site is enough to make anyone want to forget about taking the latest *South Park* quiz and surfing over to *Spumco* instead. Those who brave these trying graphics will find all kinds of news about their favourite shows.

www.comedycentral.com

Country Music Television

Mosey on over to the web site of the cable channel dedicated to country and western music. Peruse the program schedule, artists' birthdays, concert listings, video charts, and news. Yee haw!

www.cmtcanada.com

CTV News

Visit this site for the finest resolution video and sound broadcasts from the CTV News1 channel ... that is, if you have a high-speed connection. The rest of us will just have to be happy with choppy pictures and text versions of updates from around the globe. Look up news items by category or just stare at Lloyd Robertson's hair in awe-struck wonder.

ctvnews.sympatico.ca

Family Channel

The good news: this is a Flash-filled, entertaining site for the kids. The bad news: almost all the programming is brought to you by the evil empire (a.k.a. Disney)!

www.familychannel.ca

History Television

The web site of this specialty channel provides the usual schedule information and offers resources for teachers to use along with specific shows. The Fun and Games section allows you to send a friend a birthday card that lists events from that day in history.

www.historytelevision.ca

Life Network

Purporting to relate "real life stories," this network should probably be subtitled "television you wouldn't need if you got out and talked to people instead of staying home watching television." Home of the wildly popular cooking show "What's for Dinner?".

www.lifenetwork.ca

MTV

Whether you're looking for the latest on Britney Spears or airtimes for *The Tom Green Show,* MTV Online is the source for American pop music and pop culture.

www.mtv.com

MuchMusic

You're not really interested in checking out the number one song on the MuchMusic countdown or browsing through artist profiles, interviews, and videos. You just want Bradford How's e-mail address. Admit it!

www.muchmusic.com

Space

The web site of Canada's "imagination station" gives the run-down on all of its science fiction/fact programming. Visitors will be happy to find the section for daily science news that may hold their attention for longer than ten seconds.

www.spacecast.com

TVOntario

For literary types there's *Imprint,* for teachers there are educational resources, and for the rest of us there's *TVO Kids*. Plus, you can get TVO's programming schedule, become a member and support public television, or send Shelagh Rogers fan mail.

www.tvo.org

Vision TV

"Canada's faith network," which broadcasts religious programming for diverse faiths, now has a presence in cyberspace. The site contains schedules, contests, and a boutique, and allows you to send them feedback. No e-mail for the messiah though...

www.visiontv.ca

Women's Television Network Online

The web site of WTN offers feature stories, details of their programming schedule, and synopses (in case you missed an episode of your favourite drama). You can also submit reviews of movies soon to be broadcast.

www.wtn.ca

YTV

A great site for kids, with more focus on wacking green aliens than on program information. Just as it should be.

www.ytv.com

TELEVISION — SHOWS

CBC Television Series

An alphabetical listing of programs produced by the CBC between 1952 and 1982. Who can forget classics like *Outdoors with Hal Denton*?

www.film.queensu.ca/CBC

Dotto's Data Café

A popular technology TV series with a personable host. A good resource for tech-wary folks making tentative steps into the world of computers.

dotto.bc.sympatico.ca

Episode Guides

Miss the last few episodes of *Ally McBeal*? Need to catch up on *Frasier* plot lines? Have no fear, About.com has a handy reference that will lead you to plot summaries for these and other popular TV shows.

tvschedules.about.com/entertainment/tvschedules/library/shows/blepgd.htm

Fashion Television

While this site is supposedly intended to cater to the fashion-conscious woman looking to browse the runways of the world, the focus on scantily clad models would seem to indicate otherwise. More appropriate for lonely college boys than the connoisseur of haute couture.

www.fashiontelevision.com

Free TV Studio Audience Tickets

Does this really need an explanation? Your key to studio audience tickets for everything from *Friends* to *That 70s Show*.

www.tvtickets.com

Hammy Hamster's Homepage

This legend of Canadian children's television first took to the airwaves in 1959. Recently revived, the show is attracting a new generation, so naturally Hammy now has a web site. Who could forget all the adventures in the balloon invented by madcap G.P., or how about the Lizard Jamboree? But that's another story ...

www.hammyhamster.com

lookenpeepers

Weekly summaries and reviews of your favourite TV shows, a look at the evils of early-morning television, and an open invitation for writing submissions. A great site for TV-addicted shut-ins!

gmetropolis.com/lookenpeepers

Red Green Show

Apparently this show is a huge smash with viewers in one of our neighbouring countries, where they think it perfectly represents Canada. Pass the duct tape!

www.redgreen.com

Royal Canadian Air Farce

From radio comedy to TV stardom to the net, the RCAF keeps on going. The site includes video clips of Mike (from Canmore) and lets you suggest a target for the chicken cannon.

www.tv.cbc.ca/airfarce

The Canadian Travel Show

For those of you who don't get the Prime TV Network, rekindle your love of Canada through the archived episodes of this show. Follow host Holly Gillanders as she travels to such exotic locales as James Bay or Whistler, B.C. If you think there's a place the show's been neglecting, e-mail them and say so!

www.canadian-travel.com

The Littlest Hobo Page

Yes, it was a low-budget, made-in-Canada, video-only show, but for some reason *The Littlest Hobo* is as firmly ingrained in the Canadian TV-psyche as *Front Page Challenge* and *The King of Kensington*. I guess no amount of money spent on effects and production can beat a well-trained dog for pure entertainment value. Read this extensive tribute to this greatest of Canadian TV achievements, which has featured such actors as Mike Myers and Al Waxman.

members.tripod.com/kevinmccorrytv/hobo.html

The Tom Green Show

A surprisingly sober site for the king of dead animal mutilation and roadkill revival. Conscientious fans will want to make a quick donation to Tom's Nuts Cancer Fund.

www.tomgreen.com

Theodore Tugboat

Here's the site for the young children's TV show about a tugboat and other characters in a harbour. You can listen to sound effects from the show, download audio files of stories or the theme song, and read about the large cast of characters. Also includes a progressive media literacy guide. They're never too young!

www.cochran.com/theodore

This Hour Has 22 Minutes

Skip this dry Salter Street run site and head straight to 22online.com. Unless you want photos of Rick Mercer (and who wouldn't?).

www.salter.com/22minutes/22hour.htm

Twitch City

Flash animations inspired by old-school TV images abound, making visitors nostalgic for the days when they could do nothing but watch the tube (i.e., first year university). Read a synopsis of episodes you missed or get real-life advice from Rex Reilly.

www.twitchcity.com

THEATRE

OnStage Canada

A compendium of exclusively Canadian theatrical web sites. Check out this page for listings of theatre groups and shows across the country, a regular newsletter, and links to backstage notes and various newsgroups.

kenrussellassociates.bizland.com/onstage.htm

Playwrights Union of Canada

This web site provides a searchable database of Canadian plays, a directory of members (with bios and photos), and other items of interest for the theatre crowd.

www.puc.ca

Playwrights' Workshop Montreal

Founded 35 years ago, this is a professional centre for developing contemporary work for the Canadian stage. They offer a public reading program, and their web site houses an online resource library of playwright portfolios and scripts.

www.playwrightsworkshop.org

Second City

The theatre troupe that launched some of the biggest Canadian names in comedy (Candy, Short, Ackroyd, etc.). You can get tickets for the Toronto performances here, read about their history, or even find out about the audition process.

www.secondcity.com

Shaw Festival

This festival based in picturesque Niagara-on-the-Lake, Ontario, is the only festival in the world specializing in the works of George Bernard Shaw and his contemporaries, writers of "plays about the beginning of the modern world." Check out the behind-the-scenes photos of the production work and don't miss the contest to identify famous Victorians by their beards.

www.shawfest.com

Stage Business

Membership to this online forum is free for actors, directors, and theatre technicians. Post or read messages from theatre professionals across the country or take advantage of this site's other related resources.

www.stagebusiness.com

Stratford Festival

The official home page of the Stratford Festival is as attractive as the theatre productions it represents. Visitors to the site can read about the plays, find out background info on each production, see schedules, buy tickets, and even book accommodations at local inns.

www.stratford-festival.on.ca

The Canadian Improv Games

Improvisational theatre groups from high schools across the country receive training and compete in regional and national tournaments. Read here how to join in on the fun.

www.improv.ca

The Monster Makers

You were probably wondering where people go when they're stuck on techniques for making monster masks, or when they need a source for McLaughlin Micro-Cellular Theatrical Latex Foam. Wonder no more. There's plenty of info and ghoulish wares here in the Monster Shop.

www.monstermakers.com

The Plays of Shakespeare

The Electronic Literature Foundation presents a collection of Shakespeare's plays for online viewing. Each play comes with its own concordance and a search engine to help readers with unfamiliar details.

www.theplays.org

Theatre Link

A useful collection of links to playwrights, plays, productions, festivals, and theatre groups from all over the world.

www.theatre-link.com

TheatrePedia

The ELAC Internet Theatre Library brings you an online listing of theatre documents, history, craft, and other online resources.

www.perspicacity.com/elactheatre/library/library.htm

Winnipeg Fringe Theatre Festival

Information for those who want to attend, perfom, or volunteer at the annual Winnipeg event that draws Manitoba, national, and international companies. The site contains a complete listing of members of the Canadian Association of Fringe Festivals, with links to those with web sites of their own.

www.uwinnipeg.ca/academic/as/theatre/thefring.htm

TOYS

Barbie Links on the Web

She has impossible measurements, she's a bad role model for little girls, and, as this web site surely proves, she's still a worldwide fetish.

www.fau.edu/library/barblink.htm

Canadian Toy Collectors Society

Why are you hoarding all your mint-condition rubber Smurf figurines when you could be selling them? The Canadian Toy Collectors Society web site gives you links to all the possible outlets this side of eBay.

www.ctcs.org

Floaty Pens of the World

Some people collect spoons when they travel and others collect floaty pens. Visitors to this collector's online display may develop a case of (ahem) pen envy.

www.interlog.com/~aguila/home.html

Tamagotchi Cemetery

Sharing your grief is the first step to healing, and a tasteful interment for your virtual pet is only a click away at this site. Circuits to circuits, dust to dust ...

www.geocities.com/EnchantedForest/Cottage/2605/Cemetery1.html

VIDEOGAMES

shift

Classic Gaming

It's retro night for the joystick set. If *Quake* or *Zelda* leave you too confused to master your technique, you can now lumber back to simpler times. Classic Gaming lets you kick it old school with the cave-graffiti graphics of your favourite Atari, Commodore 64, Colecovision, and Intellivision games. Check out the museum, which begins with Pong, the home console that started it all.

www.classicgaming.com

shift

Gamasutra

How many virtual positions have you tried? With the help of this online resource for game developers, you could be contorting prospective players in all kinds of different ways. Topics cover music, visual arts, and programming(example: "Implementing subdivision surface theory").

www.gamasutra.com

shift

Gamecenter.com

CNET's Gamecenter is just that: a one-stop video game site. With endless (and nonpartisan) reviews, useful tips and tricks, sneak peeks at upcoming games, and snappy feature articles, this is nirvana for the true gaming junkie.

www.gamecenter.com

shift

GameDealer.com

Some games are well worth the 75 bones you drop on them. Most aren't. Take the sting out of game buying with GameDealer.com, an online video game mall with bargain-basement prices on everything from *WWF Attitude* to *Monster Truck Madness 64*. The bad games won't suck any less, but at least you won't feel quite as cheated.

www.gamedealer.com

shift

GameGirlz

Despite the oversexed vixens and rampant violence that fill so many video games, there are some girls out there who (gasp!) actually play them. For those unusual few—and anyone else looking for a distaff viewpoint—there's GameGirlz, the internet's best x-chromosome gaming zine.

www.gamgirlz.com

shift

Happy Puppy

The name and cartoony design of Happy Puppy may suggest the all-too-common wowee-zowee, ain't-this-fun, online video game zines that cover the web like poppy seds on a bagel. But on closer examination, you'll discover this gaming destination is anything but vapid. The site's pick of the litter is the fantatic Pawprint Press section, where you can feast your brain on the smartest and most lucid video game articles and reviews anywhere on the web. Just because you're playing like a kid doesn't mean you have to think like one.

www.happypuppy.com

Arts & Entertainment

shift

Myvideogames.com

In-depth features on the latest hoopla surrounding not only the games but issues surrounding them (e.g., connection between video game prowess and the shooters at Columbine). Don't Bogart that joystick.

www.myvideogames.com

shift

PC Game

If life is a video game, then this is your Yahoo!

www.pcgame.com

shift

Rockstar Games

From the swankiest bunch of video game designers ever to fly a Union Jack. Yeah, it's a promotional site. But man, does it have panache. Dig it.

www.rockstargames.com

shift

Sims: The Movie Challenge

The Sims teach you that there's more to being a happy family than owning a house in the burbs. If that's not hard enough, try using it to re-create the plot of a movie—*any* movie.

wrongwaygoback.com/thesims

shift

Videogames.com

Much like its name, Videogames.com is simple and straightforward. It's nothing more than a good old-fashioned, all-purpose console gaming site, complete with walk-throughs, plenty of non-boosterish reviews, and interesting articles that chart the continuing history of video games.

www.videogames.com

Women Gamers

Though available for both men and women, this site mainly caters to the needs of video game addicts who identify with Lara Croft rather than ogle her. But who needs Tomb Raider when you have access to all the latest video game reviews at this self-described "Girl's Guide to Gaming Etiquette"?

www.womengamers.com

shift

Xcheater

Everyone cheats. Accept it as a basic failure of human nature and you'll be free to indulge your basest, most Machiavellian appetites at Xcheater, a well-laid-out, incredibly extensive list of cheats for every game and system imaginable. Go on—you know you want to.

www.xcheater.com

VISUAL ARTS

Animated GIFs for Free Download

For animated GIF files, you just can't beat this site run by Webdeveloper.com. You can search the list of available files alphabetically.

www.webdeveloper.com/animations/

Blackwalk Productions

If you've ever watched videos by Canadian bands, then chances are you've seen a Blackwalk clip. With over 400 videos created so far and two feature films on the horizon, this is an independent production company to watch.

www.blackwalk.com

Image Paradise

A fine page of clip art resources organized by category. Useful for student projects or your next PowerPoint presentation.

desktoppublishing.com/cliplist.html

Leonardo Online

The web site for the International Society for the Arts, Sciences and Technology is a meeting place and exhibiting area for those working in all kinds of contemporary art.

mitpress.mit.edu/e-journals/Leonardo

Rhizome

Equal parts art critique and eye candy, Rhizome provides everything from language poetry to Flash animations. Multimedia artists will find a place to display their work, and art lovers will find a place to view, and provide commentary, on current online exhibits.

www.rhizome.org

WEBCASTING

shift
3wk

"Music as Art" is the way 3wk tags its content. And if you're a serious alternative rock fan, it'll be your saviour. The site's live-streaming radio is guaranteed to be better than anything you'll hear on the commercial wasteland of FM. 3wk also transmits regular e-broadcasts featuring everyone from the High Llamas to the Donnas.

www.3wk.com

Atomic Radio

Links to sites providing drum and bass, dub, trip hop, and your regular pop music. Added bonus: features the portal for Chuck D's *Bring the Noise*.

atomicpop.com/radiobrain

shift
B92

When the United States bombed Iraq in the early 90s, only CNN was on top of the action at ground zero. In this day and age, neither the American military nor its Middle Eastern adversary would have been so lucky. Just look at the Balkans. After having its transmitter shut down, Belgrade's politically minded radio station B92 turned to the web to promulgate its message. Picking up the site's netcast, the BBC re-broadcast B92 programming to Yugoslav listeners as well as the rest of the world. On its homepage, B92 posted personal diaries of petrified civilians enduring the NATO bombs, which were read by millions. On April 2, 1999, the site was shut down. The final words posted that day: "We will never surrender." True to its word, B92 was netcasting again just three months later.

www.b92.org

shift
Brave New World

Brought to you by the folks at the Ultimate Band List, Brave New World provides streaming audio that you program. Choose from your favourite indie rock artists like Sleater Kinney, Lamchop, or Buffalo Daughter. College radio without the education.

bravenewworld.net

Digitalnoise.com

All the best in online electronic music, featuring drum and bass, trance, hip-hop, house, and jungle. Urban hymns done dirt cheap.

digitalnoise.com

shift
Dublab

Before ambient, there was dub. Now you can experience the forgotten soul of electronic music online, in impressively high-quality sound. Don't dance—just chill.

dublab.com

shift
Heavy.com

Shows and toons range from *You Suck* to *Munchyman and Fatty* (take one cup of *Batman*, two cups of *Fat Albert*, and add a dime bag. Mix in blender). Kind of like Pseudo.com, only it's cool.

www.heavy.com

InterneTV

Visitors can choose and immediately view any number of music videos, comedy programs, dance prodcutions, short films, or InterneTV original shows at this web site. A number of A/V players are also available to facilitate the viewing experience.

www.internetv.com

shift
Jerkyvision

There's nothing jerky about this site's vision. So sit down, relax, and enjoy the ride. Who would have ever thought that the net could broadcast a videostream so crisply?

www.jerkyvision.com

Like Television

Watch classic TV shows, music videos, sports features, or live broadcasts on this virtual channel. Broadband video streams are surprisingly clear and easy to download.

www.liketelevision.com

shift
Neurofunk

Three live radio channels of the freshest beats in cyberspace, including "Oldskool Jungle '92-95."'Nuffsaid.'

neurofunk.com

shift
On2

Broadband has never been streamed like this before. Now if only they'd release a Mac version of the plug-in. Fascists!

www.on2.com

shift

Pixelon

Pixelon's proprietary format for distributing video on the web provides broadband users the highest quality video experience on the web. Convergence is no longer a buzzword.

www.pixelon.com

Pseudo

A completely internet-based TV station that creates all of its own programming instead of carting it in from other sources. The music shows are probably the best bet, but other topics include sports, science, and video games.

www.pseudo.com

shift

Pseudo

MP3.com may have heralded the net's beat-down on the record biz, but as this site shows, there's more to web music than buying and downloading. Exploiting a number of sites to form a network, Pseudo provides some of the best streaming media content on the web. From Streetsound's killer radio and video shows that weekly pump out hip hop, dance, jazz, and reggae tracks, to netcasts of 40 different interactive TV shows that represent almost 200 hours of original programming each month, Pseudo is the undisputed bleeding-edge innovator of music on the web.

www.pseudo.com

Radio Free Underground

Choose music by category or set up your own song-by-song playlist at this virtual juke box. There's also a regularly updated section for different DJ mixes and links to software sites to help you make your own music.

www.stitch.com

Spike Radio

Amazing animations, stellar graphics, and well-streamed tunes abound at this online radio station from Australia. Fans will come for the music and stay for the great effects, archival interviews, and multimedia reviews.

www.spikeradio.com

The Iceberg

A collection of variously themed music channels and magazines that allow you to choose the programming. Selection is current and the music is great, but the trouble it takes to find and actually hear what you're looking for may not be worth the trouble.

www.theiceberg.com

The Pipeline Network

The Pipeline Network is a great online source for 24-hour streaming hip-hop. Get your fix of daily live broadcasts, prerecorded mixes, and plenty of archival music. Especially good for fans from Canada, where non-top-40 radio is almost non-existent on the regular airwaves.

tpln.com

shift

The Sync

Enough original streaming video programming to make you forget about television for a while. Like the site says, "Stuff you won't see on TV." And then some.

www.thesync.com

shift

www.imagineradio.com

As big as MTV's presence is on the web, Imagine Radio is probably the only interesting site the network owns. Imagine's brilliance is that it allows you to build your own playlist, which is then streamed to your PC in RealAudio. And because it is a branch of MTV, there are plenty of tunes to keep you interested.

www.imagineradio.com

Yahoo! Broadcast

A healthy selection of live events in video and audio. Though everything is free, visitors should expect at least a few "special" messages from event sponsors.

www.broadcast.com

Sports & Recreation

BIRDING

Audubon Online

The mission of the National Audubon Society is to conserve and restore natural ecosystems, focusing on birds and other wildlife for the benefit of humanity and the earth's biological diversity. Audubon Online is a great resource for birders or curious kids who want to learn more about these creatures and their natural habitat.

www.audubon.org

Birdfeeding 101

Everything you need to know about attracting birds to your feeder, from types of seed to online shopping resources.

www.birdfeeding101.com

Birding in British Columbia

Though the focus of this web page is the practice of outdoor birding in B.C., a convincing argument is made for staying inside. Offering a duck pond screensaver with over 45 photographs, and a Virtual Birding Experience with sound and visuals, bird watching can be enjoyed from the comfort of your living room.

www.islandnet.com/~boom/birding/bc-home.htm

Birding in Canada

A collection of information including books, events, global links, reviews of different optics, and bulletins on rare sightings around the country.

www.web-nat.com/bic/

Birding on the Web

A great resource for birding web pages and ornithological information in general. Visitors will find scientific facts, a birder's code of ethics, and tips for those heading out into the wild.

www.birder.com

Birdnet

A site dedicated to the science of ornithology that contains a great deal of relevant information for bird lovers and birding enthusiasts.

www.nmnh.si.edu/BIRDNET/

Birds of Quebec

A site for amateur and professional ornithologists, Birds of Quebec provides valuable information for tracking down your favourite birds in la belle province. Articles and interactive checklists are posted alongside links to other Canadian bird-watching sites and resources from all over the world.

www.ntic.qc.ca/~nellus/quebangl.html

BODYBUILDING

A to Z Bodybuilding

A comprehensive collection of internet resources for fitness and bodybuilding enthusiasts. Over 700 sites to help you feel the burn!

www.atozfitness.com/indexnetscape.html

All About Anabolic Steroids

Anabolic steroids, which can cause bones to stop growing prematurely, can also lead to acne, testicular atrophy (the balls shrink and become inactive), liver tumours, mood swings, female breast development in men (gynecomastia), and several other side effects. Read about any muscle-enhancing drugs at this comprehensive site.

www.nutritionalsupplements.com/steroids140q.html

Canadian Bodybuilding Showcase

Check out the photos of really, really muscular people (you know, the kind who look all veiny and greased up).

www3.ns.sympatico.ca/swanson.noyes/bodybuild.htm

Cyberpump

A common-sense source of weightlifting information for those who've figured out that quick fixes don't work. Nutrition, training tips, and classic articles from old geezers in the iron game.

www.cyberpump.com

Fifteen Muscle Building Rules

An interesting collection of information on building muscle, with quicker results through high-intensity training and increased recuperative ability.

members.aol.com/infomuscle

Fig's Natural Weightlifting

A less intense option for those looking to add muscle but avoid the vein-popping, well-oiled route. Contains sample workout options and links to other bodybuilding resources.

members.surfsouth.com/~figarola/

The Female Bodybuilder

A lo-fi, no-nonsense site that delivers the straight goods on weightlifting for women. Matchups of different female bodybuilders are presented with commentary on technique, nutrition, and routine.

members.aol.com/hatour/fbbpix.html

BUNGEE JUMPING

Bungee Clubs Around the World

A useful index of sites for bungee opportunities around the globe.

www.bungeezone.com/clubs

Bungee Zone

An online collection of all things bungee, including a history of the "sport," a listing of bungee disasters, and a description of the equipment involved. Bonus feature: links to practically every bungee club or company on the web.

www.BungeeZone.com

Bungee.com

Check here for legal issues, safety tips, competition information, and an in-depth look at the engineering behind bungee cords.

www.bungee.com

Great Canadian Bungee

Throw yourself off the highest legal bungee jump in North America (200 feet) with this Ottawa company. Check out the equipment, rides, and package deals that you'll need to jump off a cliff!

infoweb.magi.com/~bungee

CARS

Carguide

This virtual companion to the print magazine provides Canadian motorists with information about the purchase, service, operation, and enjoyment of automobiles. Regular features include road tests, driving impressions, a historical look at cars, and the "Best Buys" guide to new vehicles.

www.carguideca.com

FIREARMS

Allen's Biathalon Page

Here's a use for guns that's not only responsibly conducted and fun, but also a great source of exercise. Check out the latest events in the world of biathalon or read a description of this sport and why any one would have thought to combine cross-country skiing and target shooting.

www.slip.net/~allenbt/

Dominion of Canada Rifle Association

If NRA members think that they will be able to bring their "recreational" M-16s over the border for "hunting," think again! A more civilized approach to firearms ownership is represented at this web site.

www.dcra.ca

Get the Facts About Gun Control

In one year 153 children were killed by firearms in Canada. In the same year 5285 children were killed by firearms in the United States. Hmmm ... I wonder if gun control is a good idea?

www.handguncontrol.org

Scientific American: A Scourge of Small Arms

An online article that examines the global deluge of surplus light weapons, such as pistols, machine guns, and grenades, and the marked increase in their use in local conflicts. Unbiased and informative.

www.sciam.com/2000/0600issue/0600boutwell.html

Universal Directory of Canada's Recreational Firearms Community

Guns, guns, guns! An unrepentant right-wing representative of the firearms community sounds off at this site. Why do they love their guns so much? I think Dr. Freud would have had a theory to explain that ...

magi.com/~mayfair/cdnguns

GAMES

A History of Traditional Games

Ever wonder what the origins of chess were? Well wonder no more, thanks to this site of games history that gives a detailed evolution of over 40 different board, table, pub, and lawn games.

web.ukonline.co.uk/james.masters/TraditionalGames/index.htm

Best Crosswords

Try your hand at a different crossword puzzle every day without ever picking up a pen. Bonus: you don't have to worry about all those eraser marks when testing out possible combinations of letters.

www.bestcrosswords.com

Chess 'n Math Association

Though chess and math are as offensive to children as the much-despised lima beans and Brussels sprouts, parents will find encouragement to introduce these subjects at the Chess 'n Math web site. Start early with links to books, equipment, and lessons to help create a love for these two topics that are so commnoly reviled.

www.chess-math.org

Chess Federation of Canada

Check out the home page for the country's national chess organization. Manoeuvre your way to a list of clubs across the country, ratings, and tournament information. In the Federation's efforts to preserve the healthy state of the game, the site makes resources for schools freely available.

www.chess.ca

Chinese Checkers

A Java-powered version of the popular board game that allows two players to compete or one player to match wits with the computer.

home-cgi.ust.hk/~wwkin/ccheckers.html

Email Games

If you don't have enough to do in life, here's another diversion: e-mail games. Stop by the Hasbro site to check it out. Numerous classics, such as Monopoly, are also offered in interactive online formats.

www.hasbro.com/home.html

Excite! Chess

A free, giant chess tournament that allows you to play against players at your own level. Just watch out for the taunts. A lot of wired teens like to play two-minute timed games, and even in a longer game they will rant and rave if you take longer than 30 seconds to think about a move.

www.excite.com/games

Fantasy Sports Guide

Those looking to try their hand at simulated sport leagues would do well to stop by this comprehensive guide. Games are rated and divided by sport to let you choose where you'd like to coach. There are also links to sites featuring console games and software that can be purchased for Mac or PC.

www.fantasysportsguide.com

shift

I Should Be Working

You really should ... but how can you with this collection of online games, jokes, contests, and other such mindless, time-wasting distractions?

ishouldbeworking.com

MSN Gaming Zone

The old favourites, like backgammon and chess, are availble for free. Premium games, such as "Hercules and Xena," are available for a price.

www.zone.com

TEN

TEN is the source for the board games and other popular diversions that most people access through larger providers, such as Netscape, Excite, GO Network, Lycos, or Prodigy. Since not all portals carry all the games, you should come here for a full list.

www.ten.net

Uproar!

For those who can't make it on *Who Wants to Be a Millionaire?*, Uproar offers false fame and illusory winnings in the form of an online game show network.

www.uproar.com

Yahoo! Games

Play everything from chess and pinochle to dominoes and mahjong at this online game site by Yahoo!

games.yahoo.com

OUTDOORS

Great Outdoor Recreation Pages (GORP)

Though ostensibly an American site, GORP covers possibilities for outdoor activities on every part of the globe. Biking, fishing, mountain climbing, and camping are just a few of the areas covered here, where health concerns even merit a large section to themselves. Includes a page of Canadian resources as well.

www.gorp.com

Great Outdoors

A good starting point for those interested in outdoor activities of all kinds. Sponsored by the Outdoor Life Network, this site has info on mountain biking, paddling, skiing, snowboarding, diving, and just about anything else that people do outside.

www.greatoutdoors.com

Out There

This site provides information on many different outdoor activities, from birding and adventure racing to orienteering and sea kayaking. Check out the site for travel resources, nature information, a guide to gear, and more.

www.out-there.com

Outdoor Review

Before buying new gear or booking that hiking trip, check here for reviews on all the latest products and most popular trails. It's a terrific resource if you're beginning to get outfitted for the great outdoors.

www.outdoorreview.com

Outside Online

The popular print mag brings international content and engaging articles to its web incarnation. More useful for reviews of possible destinations than practical advice for particular sports, *Outside*'s incredible photography and solid writing make the trip worthwhile.

www.outsidemag.com

Virtual North

An outdoor holiday resource searchable by region or type of activity. Read messages from fellow campers or post your thoughts on the "Outdoor Post."

www.virtualnorth.net

Virtually There

An odd photo tribute to the great Canadian outdoors that requires 3D glasses.

www.virtualnorth.com/vn3dgallery.html

Women's Only

A British Columbia-based club and web resource for women moutnain bikers. The site provides a photo gallery, product reviews, information about courses, a tip of the month, and more links than you can shake a stick at.

www.womensonly.com

OUTDOORS — CAMPING

AdventureZine

A useful camping news and resource page, if a little skewed toward the American trailer set (their main advertiser is Hitches 4 Less). Includes reviews of new camping equipment, vacation destinations, and a detailed guide to U.S. campgrounds.

www.adventurezine.com

Building an Igloo

An illustrated, step-by-step guide to building an igloo for camping or for fun.

wnyliving.com/outdoors/winter_camping_manual.htm

Camp Clueless

Those thinking of taking up camping should stop here for a useful intro to the activity. Focusing on inexpensive vacations, anyone can appreciate the low-cost, safe, and well-tested options presented at this site.

www.totalescape.com/tripez/clueless.html

Camp Creations

A searchable directory listing over 2000 campgrounds all over the world.

www.camp.ca

Canadian Camping Guide

A handy guide to camping that includes feature stories by campers from all over the country. There are links to local camping web pages, tips for those going to the States, and a useful summary of Canadian gun laws for our American friends.

nyquist.ee.ualberta.ca/~schmaus/camp.html

Equipped to Survive

Unbiased, independent reviews of all kinds of camping gear, as well as useful safety and survival information should your weekend trip turn into a scene from *Deliverance*.

www.equipped.com

Great Outdoor Food

A compilation of recipes, tips, and cooking techniques to help make your camping meals a little more palatable. Includes a guide to catching and preparing wild fowl and fish.

www.gorp.com/gorp/food/main.htm

Internet Guide to Camping in Canada

CampSource provides a useful forum for campers and backpackers with this listing of campgrounds, site reviews, maps, brochures, and guides. There are also sections for online discussion forums about camping and feedback for the webmaster.

www.campsource.com

Roy's Canadian Camping Guide

A noncommercial site that provides detailed, annotated links to descriptions and reviews of camp grounds. Focuses mainly on sites in western Canada.

nyquist.ee.ualberta.ca/~schmaus/camp.html

Seven Steps to Environmentally Friendly Wilderness Canoe Camping

Before you head out, read up. Some concise advice in the spirit of "leave nothing but your footprints."

www.wilderness.mb.ca/7steps.html

Solar Cooking FAQ

Everything you need to know about box, panel, and parabolic cookers that let you cook using only the energy of the sun.

solarcooking.org/solarcooking-faq.htm

Winter Camping Manual

A simple guide to the gear, clothing, sleeping bags, cooking equipment, and shelter-building techniques needed to have an enjoyable camping trip in the dead of winter.

wnyliving.com/outdoors/winter_camping_manual.htm

OUTDOORS — CLIMBING

Alpine Club of Canada

Strategically based in Canmore, Alberta, the web site for the Alpine Club of Canada provides information on membership, mountain expeditions, and mountaineering publications. Not for beginners.

www.alpineclubofcanada.ca

Bivouac Mountaineering Directory

A trek into the Canadian Rockies my not be quite what you're looking for, so the Bivouac Mountaineering Directory has provided listings for many different activities, including bike and canoe trips, for the more faint of heart. There are also news sections, avalanche warnings, and an online guidebook for visitors to peruse.

www.bivouac.com

Discover Alberta's Rockies

Though this site is more interested in tourism than mountain climbing, those planning an expedition into the Alberta Rockies will still find valuable resources on choosing their destination.

www.discovertherockies.com

Grant MacEwan Mountain Club

A lively collection of info about climbing in the Canadian Rockies. Written by experienced climbers, this site provides interesting insight into the mechanics of mountaineering.

www.ualberta.ca/~tjellard/gmmc.html

Mountain Web

A great source for articles on gear and climbing. Also includes features on related activities like winter camping and backcountry skiing.

www.mountainweb.com

Mountain Zone

Focusing mainly on events surrounding climbing and hiking, this site also covers mountain biking, snowboarding, and skiing. More useful for the seasoned pro than the beginner, visitors will find plenty of useful articles coupled with great multimedia features.

www.mountainzone.com

Rock List

Possibly the largest collection of rock-climbing links on the web, Rock List provides information for beginners or seasoned pros with sections devoted to women climbers, equipment, surveys, and even poetry.

www.rocklist.com

The Canadian Rockies Climbing Guide

This is the authoritative site for sport, multi-pitch rock, ice, and alpine climbing in the Canadian Rockies and Bugaboos. You'll also find photos, maps, links, info on weather, geology facts, facilities, and important telephone numbers.

www.ualberta.ca/~gbarron/index.html

Tree Climbing

Not for preschoolers, and anyway, why not try a sport that anyone with a backyard can attempt? Easy? Of course not. You'll need all the information on gear and safety that this site provides, as well as tips on tree conservation.

www.treeclimbing.com

OUTDOORS — HIKING

Backpacker

Claiming to be the web site for wilderness travel, Backpacker lives up to its claim for outbound hikers. Read articles on gear repair, maximizing the space in your pack, or reviews of hikes and camping opportunities.

www.backpacker.com

Backpackers Hostels Canada

A useful guide to the cheaper forms of accommodation across the country.

www.backpackers.ca

Bruce Trail Association

The Bruce Trail is an 800-kilometre path stretching from Niagara Falls to Tobermory, Ontario. Hikers can visit this site for information on featured hikes, a weather watch, and the Bruce Trail discussion group.

www.brucetrail.org

Cabot Trail

This trail in the Highlands of Cape Breton is named for the 15th-century explorer Giovanni Caboto (a.k.a. John Cabot). Learn about the wildlife and history of the trail, or look into lodging and dining along the way. You'll also find links to local whale-watching operators.

www.cabottrail.com

Hikenet

This non-commercial site focuses on the sheer enjoyment of exercising outdoors, rather than pushing yourself to the limits of endurance. Check out the decidedly low-key collection of links, tips, trail reviews, and clubs.

members.aol.com/hikenet/index.html

Hiking and Walking

A great guide for backpackers, with a much-needed emphasis on the foot. A large section is devoted solely to boot and shoe reviews and invites readers to contribute evaluations of their own. Tips to help treat aching feet and backs are another welcome addition to this site.

www.teleport.com/~walking/hiking.html

Newfoundland Backcountry

Here's a guide to the glorious scenery and hiking trails of the western side of the Rock. You can read up on the fauna of the area while listening to midi files of traditional Newfoundland tunes.

www.stemnet.nf.ca/~cpelley/homepage.htm

Trailmonkey

A collection of worldwide hiking and mountain biking destinations, coupled with informative articles and reviews.

www.trailmonkey.com

Trans Canada Trail

This planned path of approximately 16 000 km will wend its way through every province and territory of the country, to be used for walking, cycling, horseback-riding, cross-country skiing, and snowmobiling. Visitors to this web site can help fund the trail's construction at the bargain-basement price of only $40 per metre.

www.tctrail.ca

OUTDOORS — PADDLING

All About Canoes

This multimedia dedication to all things canoe has branched out from its original history-themed page to include feature articles on outdoor activities, wilderness art, and other naturalist sites.

www.canoe.ca/AllAboutCanoes/home.html

Canada Canoe Pavilion

Aside from the usual facts about the history of the boat and its significance in Canadian history, the Canoe Pavilion invites visitors to participate in the "Grand Challenge," an attempt to create the largest archive of maps, stories, and videos of the lakes and waterways of Canada.

www.wf.carleton.ca/canoe/index.html

Canadian Canoe Association Sprint Racing Division

Those who think that sprint canoe racing is a marginal sport, think again. World champion sprint racer Caroline Brunet was the winner of the Lou Marsh Award for 1999. Read up on team profiles, regatta dates, and general information about the sport at this CCA site.

www.openface.ca/paddle/

Canadian Recreational Canoeing Association

This frequently updated site provides information on any and all paddling activities, including kayaking, sea-kayaking, and canoeing. Readers will find a bevy of feature articles, event news, and expedition opportunities.

www.crca.ca

Canoe Camping Checklist

A handy reminder of things that you may have forgotten to pack for that canoe trip into the wilderness.

www.outdoorclub.org/canoe_camp.html

On-Water Sports

Try this web site for information on kayaking and rafting. There are numerous forums, lessons, tours, links to manufacturers of gear, and safety articles (e.g., how to avoid hypothermia when sea-kayaking). They have even taken the time to set up a message board for lost and stolen boats.

www.viewit.com/wtr/kayak.html

SEE Kayak Directory

A collection of links for sea kayaking equipment, resources, businesses, publications, and discussion groups.

www.seekayak.com

The Adventurers

Follow the travels of well-known paddlers Gary and Joanie McGuffin as they travel over thousands of kilometres of Canada's finest waterways. The site serves the dual purpose of spreading the word on conservation of Ontario's and Canada's forests.

www.adventurers.org

Watersports Resources

Information on kayaking and all other paddling sports, with articles on technique and safety as well as reviews of Canadian waterways.

www.onwatersports.com

Wavelength Paddling Magazine

This free online magazine for kayaking and paddling enthusiasts features pictures, descriptions of destinations, events, classifieds, and a list of related links.

www.wavelengthmagazine.com

OUTDOORS — PARKS

Banff National Park

Canada's first national park offers a wealth of natural beauty, as well as cultural and historical sites. Check out this page to find out about the mountains, glaciers, mineral hot springs, canyons, and a myriad of other attractions to be enjoyed at Banff.

www.worldweb.com/ParksCanada-Banff

L'Anse aux Meadows

The remains of the 1000-year-old Viking settlement at L'Anse aux Meadows, Newfoundland, deserve to be better known; they are the oldest known European settlement in North America. Photos of the archaeological site are available, along with links to the other 11 UNESCO World Heritage Sites in Canada.

parkscanada.pch.gc.ca/unesco/MEAD/Mead_e.htm

National Parks Around the World

If it's a global village, then this site links you to the worldwide garden. Visit this site for information on national parks from Africa, Australia, New Zealand, Europe, Asia, and Latin America.

www.gorp.com/gorp/resource/US_National_Park/intlpark.htm

Parks Canada

Whether you're looking to reserve a camp site or find a seasonal job, the web site for Parks Canada has all the connections you'll need. There's also a large section of the site devoted to ecosystem conservation and environmental resources.

parkscanada.pch.gc.ca

Protected Areas of the World

This web page created by the United Nations lists every area protected for environmental reasons in the world. For a country with the second-largest land mass in the world, Canada has surprisingly few conservation zones and sanctuaries for wildlife. Find out more at this site.

www.wcmc.org.uk/data/database/un_combo.html

OUTDOORS — SCOUTING

ScoutDocs

A lo-fi collection of straight-text files dealing with training and development of scouts in Canada. Includes links to scouting organizations worldwide.

www.csclub.uwaterloo.ca/u/lkmorlan/ScoutDocs/

Scouts Canada

Check out this youth development organization's official home page and learn about their mission, programs, contact details, events, and more.

www.scouts.ca

The Girl Guides of Canada

The Girl Guides of Canda provides a non-competitive, non-judgmental learning environment for girls of all races, creeds, and colours. This site has information on every aspect of the Girl Guides program in this country for the curious parent.

www.girlguides.ca

OUTDOORS — SCUBA

British Columbia Scuba Diving Information

Plumb the depths of this web site dedicated to west coast scuba divers. Visitors can read dive site reviews, dive logs, and trip reports, as well as look up dive charters and related reading material.

www.clever.net/kerry/scuba/main.htm

Canadian East Coast Diving

Look up everything you need to know about scuba diving in Nova Scotia, New Brunswick, Newfoundland, and P.E.I.

www.chebucto.ns.ca/Recreation/EastCoastDive

Confessions of a Mortal Diver

A text-only account of one person's experience with the consequences of decompression sickness. A sobering counterpoint to poor training and over-reliance on dive computers.

diver.ocean.washington.edu/bendstory.html

Diving in Ontario

Scuba diving (an acronym for Some Come Up Barely Alive?) is alive and well in Ontario if this page is any indication. Aside from the usual information related to scuba activities in the province, visitors will want to bookmark this page for the government's official policy on the retrieval of sunken logs.

www.onramp.ca/~adb/ontdive/Ontario.html

NAUI Worldwide

An excellent site promoting diving safety across Canada and around the world. Visitors will find resources for beginner divers, as well as trip guides, links to equipment sites, and an easy-to-read dive table.

divemar.com/naui.html

Nova Scotia Diving

Check out this site for information on diving clubs and organizations, news, details on shipwrecks and other dive sites, a photo gallery, and links to diving-related businesses.

www.chebucto.ns.ca/Recreation/EastCoastDive/ns.htm

SCUBA Diving Safety Page

Something to read before taking the big plunge. This site covers emergency rescue plans and assorted scuba safety issues.

media.vbs.vt.edu/SCUBA/safety/

Worldwide Diving Encyclopedia

A gerneral interest site for those searching for scuba information on the inernet. Start with the searchable directory or link to resources through a useful map. Includes sections devoted to conservation and travel destinations.

divefree.net

OUTDOORS — VOLKSSPORTING

International Federation of Popular Sports

Global volkssporting information available in English, German, and French.

www.ivv.org

Volkssport Ontario

Volkssports are free, non-competitive, and are for fitness, fun, and friendship. This Ontario organization has year-round events listed at this address and clubs across the province. But what, pray tell, is volkssporting? Find out here.

www.ncf.carleton.ca/~ao877

Walklist

An automated e-mail service that connects you to information on walking and volksmarching activities.

www.ava.org/walklist.htm

RECREATION AND LEISURE

Academy of Leisure Sciences

Spend some time with this group of scholars and intellectuals who've dedicated themselves to the advancement of leisure sciences. Based at the University of Alberta, this page provides biographies of academy members and discussions on important leisure-related issues. Topics covered include everything from "Leisure Apartheid" to "The State of Children's Play."

www.eas.ualberta.ca/elj/als/als1.html

Leisure Studies

Not laid-back at all, this site devotes itself to an intense examination of research and sholarship on leisure and recreation. How hard could it be? Find out here.

www.gu.edu.au/school/lst/services/lswp/

Leisure Stuff

A testament to one man's quest for self-improvement and subsequent struggle with his waistline. Look here for speed-reading, accelerated learning tests, and other mental exercises to try in your spare time.

www.familystuff.com/leisure001.htm

Society for Laziness, Effortlessness and Procrastination

A quickly expanding community of slackers and would-be deadbeats populates this informal web site. Just don't expect regular updates.

www.cs.mcgill.ca/~raven

World Leisure and Recreation Association

Though the goal of the World Leisure and Recreation Association is to discover and foster those conditions best permitting leisure to serve as a force for human growth, development, and well-being, it still seems like an excuse for a whole lot of people to sit around in hammocks. Judge for yourself at the WLRA web site.

www.worldleisure.org

SKATEBOARDING

Ed Templeton

Join the blood-sucking internet machine today by signing up for Ed's e-mail news service. Even though the popular "Kill Ed" game is no longer with us, this skater's web site is still chock full of mindless entertainment for fans.

www.edtempleton.com

Nothing

A comprehensive list of personal skate pages, manufacturer links, online magazines, and internet mail-order services.

www.geocities.com/TimesSquare/Labyrinth/3626/nothing.html

Skate Source

An independent collection of all things related to skateboarding. Skate Source has all the pictures, news, games, profiles, links, trick tips, and product reviews for the online thrasher.

www.skatesource.net

Skateboard.com

With a URL like this, how can it be ignored? The largest skateboarding site on the web has more to offer than this small space will allow for description. Let's just say that the ever-changing articles, tips, videos, and up-to-the-minute coverage of pro events will keep you well informed.

www.skateboard.com

Skateboarding in Canada

A nice lo-fi independent site covering all the necessaries for skaters in our fair country. Twenty-two different sections covering everything from moves to videos, links to 18 different skate parks, and resources for skaters of all skill levels make this site well worth a visit.

home.earthlink.net/~jay540/index.html

Skateboarding.com

Brought to you by the creators of *TransWorld Skateboarding Magazine*, this site may very well be the web's largest and most comprehensive resource for skateboarders. Aside from the archive of articles from the last several years, visitors will find plenty of skate-related shenanigans to keep them occupied for many months.

www.skateboarding.com

Skater Girls

Enough of the rampant misogyny that plagues the sport of skateboarding! Hear from skaters who are not obnoxious adolescent males at this all-female web site. A very positive vibe and a very informative site for young girls.

www.globalserve.net/~gord/skatergirls.htm

Villa Villa Cola

A great online zine produced by and for female skaters. Features include event reviews, creative writing, tour info, online art, and a section of relevant links.

www.angelfire.com/hi/villavillacola/

SKYDIVING

Canadian Formation Skydiving Team

Yes, Canada has a formation skydiving team and their web site gives detailed information on each jumper (for identification purposes), as well as the rules and regulations of the sport. Includes links to the elusive Skydive! Team Canada home page.

cpu2161.adsl.bellglobal.com/TeamCanada/FS/index.shtml

Canadian Sport Parachute Association

Incorporated in 1956, the CSPA promotes safe, enjoyable sport parachuting through cooperation and adherence to self-imposed rules and recommendations. If you're planning to throw yourself out of a plane in the near future, stop here first for safety and equipment information.

www.cspa.ca

Dropzone

Dropzone is *the* source for online news from skydiving organizations around the world. The site provides gear reviews, information for beginners, morbid humour, and an online auction for hard-to-find equipment.

www.dropzone.com

Skydiving Statistics

A sobering collection of facts and stats on the sport of skydiving, culled from listservs all over the world. Example: the death ratio per 100 000 jumps is approximately 1.4. Pretty good odds!

www.afn.org/skydive/sta/stats.html

Tak's World

Tak's World is a lo-fi homage to skydiving that's endearing as well as informative. Read one of his action-packed accounts of falling out of a plane or visit the web cam to see what Tak's up to today.

www.TaksWorld.com

The Dead Mike Home Page

Hear the incredible story of Mike Vederman, a skydiver who survived a 100-foot fall onto a concrete runway. Fourteen surgeries and months of rehabilitation later, Mike is attempting a comeback to the sport. Visitors can follow his progress and hear the A&E documentary on the accident at this site.

www.deadmike.com

SPORTS

shift

Sports for Women

After decades of enduring crappy equipment and learning the Egyptian Water Dance in gym class while the boys played b-ball, women are finally starting to get some respect. While Sports for Women does all the usual stuff—scores, athlete profiles, a chat area—its focus is estrogen-powered athleticism. The site places special emphasis on the upstart WNBA league, capturing the spirit of the players and showing the world girls can play ball. But if soccer or even boxing is more to your liking, Sports for Women won't dissapoint.

www.sportsforwomen.com

shift

Wall Street Sports

Sports fans think they know it all; now they've got a chance to prove it. Wall Street Sports is an online combination of the stock market and the sporting world that lets would-be tycoons buy and sell shares in athletes. Highly recommended for competitive sports buddies looking for bragging rights.

www.wallstreetsports.com

SPORTS — AMATEUR

Canadian Olympics Association

Though not as active during non-Olympic years, the Canadian Olympics Association's web site contains athlete profiles and news concerning the Canadian sports community.

www.coa.ca

Olympic Almanac

Summaries of major events, competition results, and interesting stories from all of the summer and winter Olympics.

infoplease.lycos.com/ipsa/A0114094.html

Science and the Olympics

Read a history of how science has influenced the games from ancient Greece to the modern-day competition. Special bonus: how a computer can help your high jump.

whyfiles.news.wisc.edu/019olympic

Sport Canada

A branch of the federal Department of Canadian Heritage, Sport Canada seeks to strenghten and celebrate our country's athletic achievements. Their site provides background on programs and policies, links to major events, sports facts, and Olympic results.

www.pch.gc.ca/sportcanada

SPORTS — AUTO RACING

Canadian Association for Stock Car Auto Racing (CASCAR)

Though the design of their web site would seem to indicate a paucity of fans relative to the adoring throngs that follow NASCAR events, CASCAR is a thriving organization in Canada that provides the same high-decibel entertainment boasted by other racing leagues. Fans will find all the information on races, drivers, and standings at the official CASCAR site.

www.cascar.ca

CART Online

The official site of CART racing is a comprehensive collection of updates, articles, results, standings, audio and video files, and previews of upcoming race locations.

www.cart.com

Formula1.com

The definitive site for Formula 1 racing fans, this site has all the usual statistics, standings, and results, but also provides live feeds for streaming audio and video of races.

www.formula1.com

Le Musée Gilles Villeneuve

Before spikey-haired Jacques, there was the great Gilles Villeneuve. Read all about his many Grand Prix victories at this site that keeps his memory alive.

www.villeneuve.com

NASCAR Online

The official site of NASCAR Racing provides fans with results, standings, and all the indside coverage that anyone could possibly need. Peek into the Garage section for a detailed look at the crews, or check out the statistics on the various race tracks around the circuit.

www.nascar.com

SLAM! Motorsports

All the latest in the world of auto racing from a Canadian perspective. Brought to you by the mighty Canoe.

www.canoe.ca/SlamMotorsports/home.html

The Jacques Villeneuve Site

Why does the web site for a Formula One race car driver have a cartoonist in residence? I have no idea either, but you can view new cartoons and information on Jacques's latest escapades at this site.

www.jacques.villeneuve.com

Vintage Automobile Racing Association of Canada

As the name implies, this association organizes races of vintage automobiles divided up into different classes. New members are welcome and events are posted at this site.

www.varac.ca

SPORTS — BASEBALL

Amateur Baseball Umpire

This site, created by amateur umpire Brent McLaren, is an in-depth archive of information. Included are a regular newsletter, articles on umpire mechanics and style, and an introduction to signals.

www.superaje.com/~brenmcla

Baseball Canada

The governing body of amateur baseball in Canada has set up a seviceable web site to impart their frequently updated news items and feature articles. You'll also find official rules and heavy-hitting line-up of links.

www.baseball.ca

Baseball: The Game and Beyond

A great site for baseball trivia and history. Includes interesting articles on the finer points of being an umpire and an extensive section devoted solely to the world of baseball physics.

library.thinkquest.org/11902/

Canadians in the All-American Girls Professional Baseball League (1943-54)

Read about the Canadians who slugged it out in the professional women's baseball leagues of the 1940s and 50s.

www.dlcwest.com/~smudge/index.html

ESPN SportsZone Major League Baseball Information

Baseball nuts can get their fill here, one of the top five sports sites online.

espnet.sportszone.com/mlb

Major League Baseball

The official home of major league baseball has more scores, photos, player profiles, and statistics than anywhere else on the internet. Just don't expect any insightful commentary. For some reason, everything about this site is wildly positive.

www.majorleaguebaseball.com

Montreal Expos

Fans won't get a hint of the financial troubles the Expos are experiencing at this flashy site. With the difficulty the team has been having in securing a television broadcast deal, this site may very well be one of the best places to take in an Expos game away from the park.

www.montrealexpos.com

Negro League Baseball History

A well-designed site dedicated to the memory of the players in the short-lived Negro Leagues. Read up on the history of the league, or peruse essays and profiles on the great Jackie Robinson or Satchel Paige.

www.negroleaguebaseball.com

Official Site for Major League Baseball

The benign organization that runs major league baseball teams or an evil empire bent on world domination? You be the judge.

www.majorleaguebaseball.com

PCBaseball.com

Fans of the desktop diamond will find reviews of the latest baseball video games as well as downloadable games for the PC.

www.pcbaseball.com

Rules of Baseball

A detailed, searchable breakdown of the rules of Major League Baseball that will give the definitive answer to any diamond-based dispute.

www.majorleaguebaseball.com/u/baseball/mlbcom/headquarters/rulesfront.htm

Strike Three

An engaging site featuring original articles on the latest issues in baseball.

www.strikethree.com

The Science of Baseball

Kids and adults will enjoy this online look into the various scientific aspects that affect a player's performance. Test your reaction speed, read about how weather can affect the game, or go through the finer details of hitting home runs.

www.exploratorium.edu/baseball

Toronto Blue Jays

Game summaries, statistics, press releases, history, and more photos than you can shake a baseball bat at—all are here at the Toronto Blue Jays' home page.

www.bluejays.ca

TSN Baseball

Look to this site for great commentary on the state of baseball in Canada. Fans will also find game previews, summaries, and a detailed injury report.

www.tsn.ca/mlb

SPORTS — BASKETBALL

Barry Smith's Basketball Reviewmarks

Witness the majesty of over a kabillion web links for all things pro-basketball. Okay, there are only 1190, but still! Mr. Smith was kind enough to review each and every one of them so you can avoid the turkeys.

www.watsonsports.com/index.htm

Basketball Canada

Find out all the news, scores, and updates for the Canadian men's basketball team. Along with detailed game summaries and player biographies, visitors will find all the requisite links and contact pages.

www.basketball.ca

Canadian Wheelchair Basketball Association

Begun in the early 1940's, the sport of wheelchair basketball has flourished and become a vibrant, national league. Read all about the history and current competitions for this fast-paced sport.

www.cwba.ca

CNN/SI NBA Statistics

Number crunchers can use this site to sort the top players by fouls, points, assists, rebounds, or any number of specicific stats that are tallied from game to game.

www.cnnsi.com/basketball/nba/stats

ESPN SportsZone NBA Information

The latest news, articles, polls, scores, and hoopla surrounding the NBA.

espnet.sportszone.com/nba

National Basketball Association (NBA)

League highlights and links to broadcasting sites for all the games.

www.nba.com

NBA Canada

Get the Canadian perspective on the NBA with Canuck player profiles, articles by players from the Raptors and Grizzlies, and local television broadcast schedules.

www.nba.com/canada

Officiating.com

Referees and players of basketball will both appreciate this site, which gives the definitive word on the rules of the game.

www.officiating.com

shift

Remember the ABA

The ABA (American Basketball Association) may only have lasted from 1967 till 1976, but the memories of huge afros, wild clothing, and those red, white, and blue balls live on forever. Jump back in time and revisit the glory days of the funkiest sports league that ever walked in size-15 Converse All Stars.

www.remembertheaba.com

The Association for Professional Basketball Research

An in-depth guide to the history of the game in general, and pro leagues in particular. This site includes a rundown of every NBA draft from 1947 to the present, a history of team logos, and links to every major professional and amateur league on the web.

hometown.aol.com/bradleyrd/apbr.html

Toronto Raptors

With Vince Carter in the lineup, Toronto now has a team that can win and, eventually, contend for a championship. Check out all the latest news on the team at this site.

www.nba.com/raptors

TSN Basketball

Up-to-the-minute coverage of professional basketball is provided by this site that features highlights, scores, polls, complete playoff summaries, and, of course, video highlights of the most interesting stories and most exciting plays.

www.tsn.ca/nba

Vancouver Grizzlies

Though the Grizzlies have missed the playoffs yet again, they have been making improvements ... slowly. Watch their progress from the team's official web site.

www.nba.com/grizzlies

Vince Carter

All the photos, highlight videos, and statistics on the greatest player in the country, Toronto Raptor Vince Carter. Air Canada, flight #15 now boarding ...

www.vincecarter.com

Women's National Basketball Association (WNBA)

Find out about the professional women's basketball league that is flourishing south of the border. Follow the links to team pages or read the latest league news.

www.wnba.com

SPORTS — CURLING

Canadian Curling Association

This web site includes contact information for the association, an online gift shop, TV listings, and info on major competitions like the Labatt Brier and the Scott Tournament of Hearts.

www.curling.ca

CBC Curling

Yes, they are better known for their hockey coverage, but there are few who offer comparable coverage of the sport of curling. All the latest news as well as sections devoted to the men's and women's national teams.

cbc.ca/sports/curling/

Curling's Premiere Directory

Aside from links to the usual broadcasting sites, this page provides connections to every single club, team, and competition in Canada. Includes resources for equipment and the finer points of making ice.

www.curling.com

International Curling Information Network Group

Here's a global view of the sport, which offers detailed information on equipment, the history of curling, and rules of the game for the uninitiated.

www.icing.org

Labatt Brier

The official page for the "big freeze"—arguably the biggest event of its kind in Canada.

www.brier2000.com

TSN Curling

Those who don't have cable can at least enjoy the web presence for TSN, by far the finest purveyor of curling coverage on the tube. The tradition continues on the web with current stories that other sites will not have until several days later.

www.tsn.ca/curling

SPORTS — CYCLING

Atlantic Canada Cycling Home Page

Representing one of the most beautiful and cycle-friendly destinations in the world, this web site will allow travellers to organize their tour of the Maritimes with relative ease. For those of us who are too lazy to peddle, there's even a virtual tour.

www.atl-canadacycling.com

Bike to Work

Here's one possible option for reducing fossil fuel emissions in urban areas. Those who commute via bicycle will find plenty of company at this web address. Look up commuter tips, equipment for bikers, and links for global events like Bike to Work Week.

www.biketowork.com

Canadian Cyclist

The home page for the print version of the same name, *Canadian Cyclist* provides a selection of recent articles, classifieds, bicycle dealers, and subscription information.

www.canadiancyclist.com/default2.html

Cyber Cycle

Aside from the regular links to equipment, events, and publications, Cyber Cycle provides a great deal of information on nutrition and training for those who take cycling a little more seriously.

library.thinkquest.org/10333

Girl Groove

Girl Groove is the online source for women and bicycles. Unusual? Perhaps, but with gender-specific features that promote healthy exercise and fighting world hunger, how can you complain? Bonus: the "Grease Monkey" section is as gear-savvy as it is entertaining.

www.girlgroove.com

MTB Info

An all-in-one resource for mountain bikers on the web, MTB Info has tips for riding and tricks, trail guides, racing information, a beginner's manual, and an online bike doctor for advice on repairs.

www.mtbinfo.com

Science of Cycling

Another great site that takes visitors into the hows and the whys of sport. This page explains everything from aerodynamics and human power to frames and the power of the wheel.

www.exploratorium.edu/cycling

The Boy Cyber Cycle

Read up on the men's national cycling team at this web site that provides pictures, competition news, information on the Calgary track scene, and more.

www.spots.ab.ca/~gluzmand

The British Columbia Mountain Bike Directory

Check out the trail database, post comments on the message board, browse through bike shops, look for clubs, and more at the B.C. Mountain Bike Directory.

www.openroad.ca/bcmtbdir/

Tortoise's Cycling Page

Mr. Tortoise provides a decent listing of cycling resources on the web, including links to periodicals and stores. Those new to the sport will appreciate the explanations of various kinds of cycling, including recumbent bikes, BMX, and endurance racing.

www.turbotortoise.com

Uncle Lou's Bicycle Information

Turn to Uncle Lou for advice on independent bicycle dealers across the country, sorted by region. Helpful charts of mountain bikes allow rapid comparison of brands and prices.

persweb.direct.ca/gamiller

Victoria Wheelers Cycling Club

Know the difference between a rear derailleur and a down tube? An interactive bike anatomy tool will sort it out for you. This well-maintained site provides items of interest for those who know "speed is everything." A handy section calculates your gear ratio for you.

www.islandnet.com/~see/vwcc/index.htm

WHO Helmet Initiative

Find all the resources you will need to scare your children into wearing their helmets while cycling. Spinal injury anyone? Brought to you by the World Health Organization.

www.sph.emory.edu/Helmets/

SPORTS — EQUESTRIAN

Canadian Driving Society

Get all the equestrian news and links straight from the horse's mouth. The CDS site provides members with event news, member services, and e-mail contacts.

www.cadvision.com/Home_Pages/accounts/norwest/cds/index.html

Canadian Pony Club

Aside from the usual events and club information that this site offers its members, there are a number of games and quizzes geared toward kids who were actually lucky enough to get a pony for their birthday.

www.ebtech.net/ponyclub

Equestrian Connection

Covering the national and international scene, Equestrian Connection is an engaging look at horseback riding and racing. Read about the different disciplines, find out results from recent events, take advantage of the many chat rooms, or browse the EquiMarket classifieds.

www.equestrian-connection.com

Equine Online

A useful collection of related links, including a job database, an international events calendar, and a glossary of equine terms.

www.equineonline.com

International Museum of the Horse

A staggeringly large web site that covers the evolution of the relationship between horses and humans. Features online exhibits and a visual art gallery.

www.imh.org

Ontario Trail Riders Association

Here's a web site for Ontario members of the horsey set who want to preserve trails and bridleways before they disappear due to development. Consult a trail rider's handbook that discusses environmental awareness and includes a code of ethics.

www.csolve.net/~newdawn/otra.htm

SPORTS — FENCING

Canadian Fencing Federation

Rattle sabres with your fencing peers at this web site full of news and information on the sport. Look up the latest competition results, read competitor profiles, or browse through the events calendar.

www.fencing.ca

Fencing Encyclopedia

A detailed breakdown of fencing terms and techniques including diagrams of all eight foil parries. En garde!

www-personal.usyd.edu.au/~mprince/fencing/encyclopedia.shtml

Fencing Online

An international look at the sport, focusing on world championships and Olympic events. Visitors will also find a history of the sport and a description of the differences between classical and modern techniques.

www.fencing.net

His True Art of Defense

An interesting look at a fencing manual written by Italian fencing master Giacomo di Grasse in 1594.

www.kismeta.com/digrasse.html

The Noble Science

A detailed, illustrated timeline of the development of fencing, from classical to Renaissance and Elizabethan swordplay to Baroque styles.

people.clarityconnect.com/webpages/ifv/noble.html

SPORTS — FIELD HOCKEY

Field Hockey Canada

Hockey without ice?!? Ice hockey's less publicized cousin has a web presence as well.

www.cyberus.ca/~fieldhockey

Field Hockey's Home

A daily updated site that covers every aspect of world competition. Sections on coaching, umpiring, and archived news are yours to explore, along with a bevy of related links.

www.fieldhockey.com

Fieldhockey Training

A great site to help keep players in shape, brought to you by field hockey aficionado Remco Hartgers. Includes online training clinics coupled with video examples to help improve your game.

www.fieldhockeytraining.com

SPORTS — FOOTBALL

AFL Official Site

Newcomers to Australian rules football will want to check out this site for a much-needed explanation of the game, as well as standings and news items from the league.

www.afl.com.au/home/default.htm

B.C. Lions

Vancouver's feline footballers. Show Lions' pride by stopping by for news, team facts, and merchandise, or checking out the fans' corner and the dance team. The Beast must feast!

www.bclions.com

CFL Fun Facts Page

The first Canadian football game to be played "under the lights" was on October 29, 1930, at Ulster Stadium in Toronto between Oshawa and Balmy Beach. Would you have known that if you hadn't just read it? Of course not, so bone up on your CFL trivia at this site.

www.conway-sports.com/wally

CIAU.ca

A great page that covers every conference in Canadian university football. Fans will find all kinds of news items, updates, and even a detailed account of the CFL's university draft.

www.ciau.ca/football/default.asp

Edmonton Eskimos

The storied Eskimos have all the standard material on their web site: player roster and statisitics, ticket and tailgate party info, an especially active program of events, and schedule information with TV coverage notations for away games.

www.esks.com

ESPN SportsZone Canadian Football League Information

An American TV station covering the CFL? You have to see it here to believe it!

espnet.sportszone.com/cfl

Hamilton Tiger-Cats

What with the conspiracy to deny Hamilton an NHL franchise, Steeltown sports fans will have to settle for the Tabbies for the foreseeable future, and that's not too shabby. Their site has all the usual features: news, player profiles, ticket info, a fan forum, and merchandise.

www.tigercats.on.ca

KFFL

Don't be fooled by the full name of the site: Kahnawassee Fantasy Football League. This hidden gem will help you win your football pool with a free and meticulously updated "Hot Off the Wire" feature, which gives you 11th-hour news on trades, injuries, squabbles, rumours, and arrests. News is submitted from all over the place by loyal readers, just in time for you to submit your starters for Sunday. Don't tell your friends about this one. Whoops, we just did!

www.kffl.com/fantasy

Montreal Alouettes

The on-again off-again CFL franchise appears to be solidly on again. Follow their exploits at this site with statistics, news, game results, ticket info, a quiz, and details on the "Adopt an Alouette" program, which enables the athletes to visit local high schools.

www.alouettes.net

NCAAFootball.net

Fans of American college football will find everything they need at this official site. Head here for photos, updates, and standings.

www.ncaafootball.net

NFL Europe

Those imperialist devils are at it again! It wasn't enough that everyone is choking back Big Macs and singing the praises of Mickey Mouse, oh no—they had to go and start an American-style football league in Europe! Find out the standings and read about the league's struggling teams at the official site.

www.nfleurope.com

NFL.com

The official home of the NFL on the web links to every team page, provides frequently updated news items, and features video clips and live audio feeds for games. Available in Spanish too.

www.nfl.com

Sports & Recreation

Saskatchewan Rough Riders

Now the only Rough Riders left standing in the CFL. Their site includes all the features you'd expect from the Western division mainstays: the schedule, team history, roster info, ticket office, wallpaper, news updates, and more.

www.srfc.sk.ca

The Canadian Football League

Somehow the CFL refuses to be tackled and keeps driving forwards for extra yardage, thanks in large part to loyal fans across the country. This site has more than the most rabid of the lot could want: news, stats, records, the rule book, Grey Cup memories, roster updates, video highlights, player profiles, and the Pigskin Challenge, which gives you a chance to win a trip to the final.

www.cfl.ca

The CFL in America

Other football leagues come and go in the U.S., and the NFL sacks them all for a loss. Here's a tribute to the American adventure of the CFL from 1993 to '95. From the successful Baltimore Stallions to the lowly Las Vegas Posse, the teams are all here with photos, logos, and records.

www.geocities.com/colosseum/sideline/7586/index.htm

Toronto Argonauts

This is the official page of the Toronto Argonauts. Check here first for schedules, ticket information, promotions, stats, cheerleaders, and merchandise. Aaaarrr-gooоos!

www.argonauts.on.ca

Winnipeg Blue Bombers

With the late, lamented Jets long gone, the Bombers are just about the only game in town. Everything for the fan is here: schedules, ticket information, merchandise, the Blue Lightning, and let's not forget Buzz the Boomer. Go Big Blue!

www.bluebombers.com

SPORTS — GENERAL

Canadian Sport

Here's a good springboard for anything on sports in Canada, with links by sport, a jobs section, and news. Also centralizes hard-to-find links and contact information related to coaching, halls of fame, national sports centres, phys ed. programs, and more.

www.canadiansport.com

CanThrow

Stop destroying your best dinner ware and learn how to throw the discus! The CanThrow web site is your source for news and training tips for discus, javelin, hammer, shot put, and anything else you might toss in the air.

canthrow.com

Chris Creamer's Sports Logo Page

Mr. Creamer's collection of new and old sport team logos will allow you to decorate you desktop with team emblems for every sports organization from the National Hockey League to the Hawaii Winter Leg Baseball League. Four hundred thousand rabid sports fans can't be wrong!

members.tripod.com/~emblems

The Canadian Lacrosse Association

Despite what Don Cherry will tell you, lacrosse is Canada's official, national sport, with a greater fan base than hockey in some areas of the country (sacrilege!). Check up on the national team and provincial lacrosse associations at this web site.

www.lacrosse.ca

The National Lacrosse League

Though some may be sceptical of the possibilities for the success of a professional lacrosse league, some of these teams have come close to having better attendance than their Major League Baseball counterparts. Not bad for an organization that's only a few years old.

www.be-lax.com/main.php3

SPORTS — GOLF

Bell Canadian Open

There's nothing like being there, but if you can't make it to Glenn Abbey in Oakville, this web site is the next best thing. Check out press releases, live coverage, and player profiles, while imagining that you are on the green.

www.bell.ca/cdnopen

British Columbia Golf Association

The British Columbia Golf Association is the governing body for amateur golf in B.C., and the BCGA web site serves as a valuable source of informaiton for golfers on the west coast. Follow links to other golf associations around Canada and the United States or check up on local tournaments, players, and news.

www.bcga.org

Canadian Golf Tour

Surf to this site for the latest news, results, photos, player profiles, and statistics from the Canadian Tour.

www.canoe.ca/SlamGolfCanTour/home.html

Canadian Ladies Golf Association

The organization responsible for ladies' amateur golf in Canada brings you a fine web site filled with member information, tournament news, and much more.

www.clga.org

CPGA

This is the official site of the Canadian Professional Golf Association, the represenatative body for club and tournament golf professionals in Canada. You'll find lots of news stories about the latest tournament results, golf tips, and a directory of Canadian clubs.

www.cpga.com

Golf Channel

Though some may think that a 24-hour channel devoted to golf is complete overkill, avid fans are said to watch little else. Head here for the net's best source of golf news and an online version of "Academy Live." There are few sites that can match this one for online instruction.

www.thegolfchannel.com

Golf Rounds

Players will appreciate this collection of daily tips and advice from golf pros on how to improve your game. This site also includes a handy search engine to help visitors locate courses in their area.

www.golfrounds.lycos.com/protips/index.html

GolfNet Canada

Tour course profiles, book accommodations for your golf destinations, or even try an online tee time booking system at this web site.

www.golfcanada.com

Legends of Golf

Read up on some of the finest players in the history of the game at this web site. Features such luminaries as Jack Nicklaus, Arnold Palmer, and Lee Trevino.

www.all-legends.com/golf.html

Mr. Golf Etiquette

A great guide for beginners who want to learn how not to offend their fellow players. Example: no fidgeting, talking, wiggling, or otherwise distracting a player who is about to putt.

www.mrgolf.com

Ontario Golf Association

This organization is dedicated to sustaining the growth of golf at the amateur level in Ontario. Read about the tournaments they administer, their junior golf program, and their handicapping system, or check out the directory of Ontario courses.

www.oga.org

Royal Canadian Golf Association

The RCGA has been the governing body of men's amateur golf for over a century. Their site explains amateur status, the rules of golf, and handicapping.

www.rcga.org

Scoretrack

Golfers obsessed with their own personal statistics will want to register for the Scoretrack service. This site allows players to keep track of every possible aspect of their game, at absolutely no cost.

www.freegolfinfo.com/scoretrack/

Slam! Golf

Track all the professional tours at this Slam! Sports site. Detailed coverage includes everything from the Canadian pro and junior tour, to results from Europe and the ever-popular PGA.

www.canoe.ca/SlamGolf/home.html

Virtual Golfer

Don your plus-fours and white shoes and point your browser at Virtual Golfer. You'll find articles, a pro shop, chat rooms, PGA schedules, tips for your game, and course reviews.

www.golfball.com

SPORTS — HANDBALL

Canadian Team Handball Federation

What is team handball? How are the Canadian national teams doing? Find the answers to these and other questions that keep you up at night, at the CTHF web site.

www.handball.ca

Handball Oasis

Those of you who just can't seem to quench your thirst for handball resources on the internet will surely find your fill here. Links are divided into manageable country categories to facilitate consumption.

www.geocities.com/Colosseum/Hoop/9615/

Handball Rules

There's more to it than just swatting a ball with your hand. Read up on the official rules of handball at this illustrated online guide by Luke Wildman.

www.cs.uq.oz.au/personal/bof/Handball/rules.html

Worldwide Handball

Yes indeed, it's the world headquarters of team handball. What would one do with such a site, you ask? Well, report on the standings and competition results of handball competitions all over the globe, of course.

www.handball.gr

Yeah! Handball

A useful collection of links to national teams, events, and competitions from all over the world. Yeah!

www.yeahsports.com/dir/handball/

SPORTS — ICE HOCKEY

A to Z Encyclopedia of Ice Hockey

Set to take over the web as *the* resource for all things related to hockey, this site still has a long way to go in terms of design and content. Bonus points: text is translatable to French, German, Italian, Portuguese, and Spanish.

www.azhockey.com

All Hockey Links

Just as the title suggests, this site is packed with links to hockey sites covering everything from the NHL to leagues in Asia.

www.hockeylinks.com

American Hockey League (AHL)

See the future of the NHL today at the American Hockey League web site! Listen to live cybercasts of AHL games, check statistics, or read up on your favourite teams.

www.canoe.ca/AHL/home.html

Calgary Flames Home Page

Look up all the scores, statistics, and the latest news on the Calgary Flames at their official home page.

www.calagaryflames.com

Canadian Hockey Association

The CHA is the sole governing body of amateur hockey in Canada, with over half a million registered players. Get the official info on our national men's and women's teams, read all about inline hockey, and find out about all the CHA's development programs—for coaches, safety, skills development, officiating, and more. Also, the chat forum gives visitors the chance to sound off on the state of "The Game."

www.canadianhockey.ca

Canadian Hockey League

Read all the news that's fit to print about the teams that make up the CHL. Visitors can browse through the record book and photo gallery or participate in a live online "Puck Chat."

www.canoe.ca/CHL

CTV Sportsnet NHL

Great coverage and commentary on all aspects of the game at this site that includes a fantasy league, archived articles, and fan forums. Holy Mackinaw!

www.ctvsportsnet.com/nhl/index.shtml

Edmonton Oilers

Though the fate of the Oilers, as with all small-market teams, seems to be constantly being questioned, their web site will help fans forget about the club's financial woes. Visitors can read recent news items as well as features on the team's glorious past. Get stats, the schedule, and videos of Rem Murray playing with puppets.

www.edmontonoilers.com

ESPN SportZone NHL Information

A convenient collection of the latest NHL scores, highlights, and news.

espnet.sportzone.com/nhl

Eurohockey

Looking for the site of KKH Katowice from Poland? You'll find it here at this extensive collection of sites for every pro hockey team in Europe.

ehg.pinknet.cz

Faceoff

A great independent site with a perspective often ignored by professional sports media—that of the fan. This site features player and coach quotes (some deliberately funny, some unintentionally so), a 10-year history of all NHL salaries, a feature on mascots, and over 800 links to other hockey sites.

www.surf.to/hockeyzone

Fifty Mission Cap

Titled after the infamous Tragically Hip song of the same name, this site chronicles the story of Toronto Maple Leaf Bill Barilko and the legend of his 1951 Cup-winning goal.

www.interlog.com/~robdm/fifty.html

Hockey Night in Canada

Now any night can be HNIC! This site has got to be bookmarked by any hard-core fan. Check it out for headlines, stats and other stuff for poolies, trivia contests, and yes, *Coach's Corner* in RealVideo.

www.hockey.cbc.ca

Montreal Canadiens

No true hockey fan can resist a peek at the web site for Les Glorieux, even if the current lineup is not exactly up to par. Relive the past with news, player stats, trivia games, and an e-mail club.

www.canadiens.com

National Hockey League Players Association

Fans will find full coverage of contracts (another millionaire?), disputes, playoffs, drafts, and stats, plus video interviews with star players.

www.nhlpa.com

Ontario Hockey Association

The OHA is a hotbed of pro-bound talent. Find links here to various subordinate leagues around the province.

www.ohahockey.org/index.htm

Ottawa Senators

This web site ignores the hoopla surrounding Alexei Yashin's contract disputes and the owner's attempt to procure government funds, and sticks to the success that the Senators have experienced over the last two seasons. Fans will find all the stats, trivia, video clips, and schedule info they are looking for at the Senator's home page.

www.ottawasenators.com

Science of Hockey

Why is ice slippery? Is your reaction speed fast enough to stop a puck? How do you slap a puck 100 miles per hour? Find answers to these and other entertaining questions at this site sponsored by San Fransisco's Exploratorium.

www.exploratorium.edu/hockey

The Hockey Net

Billing itself as the world hockey audiosite, the Hockey Net lets you listen to clips of great players discussing the game. Visitors can listen to comments on current issues or look up archival interviews to discover that all players basically give the same answers to the same questions.

www.thehockey.net

The Internet Hockey Database

A massive archive of statistics, trading cards, and team logos from the different professional leagues.

www.hockeydb.com

The State of Hockey in Canada

An online forum devoted to that most Canadian of preoccupations, the future of pro hockey in our country. With season ticket sales down and stiff competition from U.S. teams with larger markets, will cities like Edmonton and Calgary be able to hold their own? Join in the discussion at the site for this lively debate.

jump.to/hockey

The Women's Hockey Web

With all the interest created during the 1998 Winter Olympics, the prospects for women's hockey have never been better. Begin any search for relevant information here: data on univeristy-, national-, and international-level hockey; camps; tournaments; trading cards; and tons more.

www.whockey.com

Toronto Maple Leafs

Any fan that had to endure the Ballard years is certainly enjoying the current success that the Leafs are experiencing. Look up the team history (skip the '80s), player profiles, the latest news, a virtual tour of the locker room, and an archive of video highlights.

www.torontomapleleafs.com

Vancouver Canucks

While Vancouver seems to be going through a bit of a rebuilding stage, fans can settle for what is offered online as opposed to on the ice. The site offers the usual ticket info, statistics, news, trivia, team history, and photos.

www.canucks.com/canucks/

Zamboni

Never has the much-maligned, oft-ridiculed, resurfacer of ice experienced such a tribute. Follow this extended essay through text and movie files on the history and mechanics of this mighty machine. More of a Zen-like meditation than straight reportage, readers will be scrambling for the $60 000 necessary to buy one.

www.charged.com/issue_o/frost/stories/zamboni/index.html

SPORTS — IN-LINE SKATING

Aggressive Skaters Association

The home page for aggressive inline skaters features membership information and links to other like-minded sites on the web.

www.aggroskate.com

Sports & Recreation

Agressive Skating Online

Inline skating and youth culture form a seamless mix here. See how young skaters keep their trim physiques (apparently by drinking gallons of Yoo-hoo), or click on the area for photos of "nasty injuries and wounds." Definitely not the straight and narrow.

www.3rdimension.com/aso

Hardcore Inline

Easily the best guide to aggressive skating on the web. Includes videos, online tutorials, safety advice, an index of skate parks, and information on professional tours. Also offers a section devoted to a female point of view on the sport.

www.aggressive.com

How to Inline Skate With Your Dog

An online tutorial on how to negotiate skating with an energetic pooch. Not recommended for beginners.

www.caryn.com/francis/francis-blade.html

Roller Sports Canada

Roller hockey, speed skating, and a history of inline sport are all here at the Roller Sports Canada web site. Link to other national web sites for roller sports or discover the key to artistic style when rolling down the track.

www.rollersports.ca

Uncle Derek's Sk8 Page

For those who would rather flip off a ramp than tour around the park, Uncle Derek has provided a nice page of tips and a useful set of links to help with acrobatic feats.

members.tripod.com/~hot_stuff_page/index.htm

SPORTS — MARTIAL ARTS

Beginner's Resource for Martial Arts

If your knowledge of martial arts is limited to a few kung fu movies, you'd do well to check out this online guide to choosing a discipline to follow. This site can help help you decide on the style that's best for you, and provides listings of reputable instruction centres in your area.

www.martialresource.com

Bruce Lee Educational Foundation

The Bruce Lee Educational Foundation is dedicated to the teachings of kung fu film star and Jeet Kune Do master Bruce Lee. Jeet Kune Do is a nonclassical, nontraditional, combat-modified American martial art that uses elements of western boxing and fencing to create an effective form of street combat for self-defence.

www.jkd.com

Judo Information Room

Browse this page's collection of rules, regulations, history, and terms on the sport of Judo. Experience seiryoku-zenyo (maximum efficiency with minimum effort) at this site.

www.actc.nf.ca/jcoffey/sankyo/judoinfo.htm

Martial Arts Resource Page

A noncommercial page whose only priority is to bring visitors the best information on martial arts web resources. Find out information on everything from Aikido to Japanese sword arts, or use the search engine to help you find an appropriate martial arts school.

www.middlebury.edu/~jswan/martial.arts/ma.html

Snow Tigers Martial Arts Association

Dedicated to the development of martial arts in Canada, the Snow Tigers promote authentic instruction and respect for all styles. Visitors will find brief descriptions of the different kinds of martial arts, as well as a list of reputable instructors.

www.bancroft.bancom.net/~wandap

The Martial Arts Network Online

Worth a visit just for the multimedia intro and Flash-enhanced interface, TMAN is a comprehensive resource for events, tips, projects, and martial arts links.

www.martial-arts-network.com

Top Ten Martial Arts Movies

One person's take on cinema's contribution to the world of martial arts. Each movie is reviewed for martial arts content and authenticity, and links to separate sites for each film.

home.rmi.net/~jhaynes/movie.htm

Yang Style Tai Chi Homepage

Tired of destroying your knees by jogging every day? Read up on the low-impact, meditative exercise known as Tai Chi at this web page.

www.chebucto.ns.ca/Philosophy/Taichi/tc-home.html

SPORTS — MUSEUMS & HALLS OF FAME

Aquatic Hall of Fame and Museum of Canada

The Olympics may be over and the pool may be closed but the Aquatic Hall of Fame and Museum will keep the memory of Canada's greatest swimmers and divers alive for posterity. Take a virtual tour of this Winnipeg-based museum and see photos of hall members, displays of aquatic art, and links to other watery web sites.

www.city.winnipeg.mb.ca/parks/recserv/aquahall/INDEX.HTM

Baseball Hall of Fame

Cooperstown, New York, plays host to this most famous of sports shrines. Though visitors to the web site can take a virtual tour and browse the contents of the hall online, nothing is going to beat the experience of actually going there.

www.baseballhalloffame.org

Basketball Hall of Fame

A visit to the web site for the Springfield, Mass., hall is an experience in itself. Check out all the awards, exhibits, inductees, history, and stories that are housed in the offline hall, or just bask in the glory of the vintage photos of 1970's hoops.

www.hoophall.com/index.cfm

Canada's Sports Hall of Fame

Your guide to Canada's greatest athletes provides profiles of them online, along with a colourful history of the Hall itself.

www.inforamp.net/~cshof

Canadian Baseball Hall of Fame and Museum

If you can't visit the hall in St. Mary's (just outside of London, Ontario), you can always check out this web site. Scroll through detailed biographies of inductees, read up on the latest news and events, or follow the links to pro baseball sites in Canada.

www.baseballhof.ca

Canadian Pro-Wrestling Hall of Fame

Bios and pics of all the greats from the pro-wrestling arena, including Mad Dog Vachon, Crybaby George Cannon, Tiger "Tweet Tweet" Tomasso, and, of course, the right honourable Bret Hart.

www.canoe.ca/SlamWrestling/hallofame.html

Hockey Hall of Fame

The relatively new Hall of Fame in BCE Place in Toronto is a classy tribute to hockey's greatest heroes. The web site is much improved and features an extensive online photo gallery that spans a century.

www.hhof.com

International Tennis Hall of Fame

Located in Newport, Rhode Island, in what used to be a private tennis club, the International Tennis Hall of Fame is, undoubtedly, a much more interesting visit offline. Visitors to the web site will have to console themselves with pictures of the grounds and a few, select photos from the Hall's collection of memorabilia.

www.tennisfame.org

The Home Computer Hall of Fame

Okay, admittedly home computers have nothing to do with sports in any way, but didn't you need a break from all that testosterone? Besides, this book is about computers, isn't it? The Home Computer Hall of Fame is available only on the web and is a wicked nostalgia trip through those heady days in the 80s when everyone started buying Commodore 64's. Revisit such classics as the PET2001 or the ever-popular Tandy MC-10.

www.gondolin.org.uk/hchof/

SPORTS — NEWS

CBC Sports Online

CBC provides even-handed, unbiased, detailed summaries of all major sporting events—from the latest in hockey to the results from Olympic events. Also includes an archive of video and audio segments from events covered on television.

cbc.ca/sports

shift

CNN/SI

A collaboration between CNN and *Sports Illustrated*, this is the best all-round sports site on the internet. Analysis of U.S. and world sporting events is superb, while the Javascript scoreboard delivers enough scores and highlights to satiate even the most rabid fan.

www.cnnsi.com

CTV Sportsnet

The most recent addition to the world of online sports coverage, CTV Sportsnet has all the news and views on the world of sport from a distinctly Canadian point of view (in other words, mostly hockey).

www.ctvsportsnet.com

shift

Quokka.com

Bored with baseball? Think the X-Games are not as in-your-face as they used to be? Drop by Quokka.com, the web's premier adventure-sports site, and get the scoop on marathons through the Sahara, mountain climbing in China, and around-the-world solo yacht races. With live video feeds and incredibly comprehensive coverage (you can check mountain climbers' blood oxygen levels), the only thing missing is adrenaline.

www.quokka.com

Slam!

If there is anything happening in the world of Canadian sports then it will be covered by the Canoe Slam! sports section. Statistics, summaries, and opinion pieces abound at this comprehensive sports site.

www.canoe.ca/slam

shift

Sportspages.com

For the true fan, nothing tops the in-depth coverage of a team's hometown rag. Luckily, Sportspages.com has links to hundreds of newspaper sports pages from around the continent, divided by region and sport. Makes being a Broncos fan living in Guelph a little more tolerable.

www.sportspages.com

Sympatico Sports

A decidedly low-key affair, tastefully providing the scores and news items you would regularly find in the sports pages, but without any bells and whistles. A diverse and up-to-date site.

www1.sympatico.ca:80/Contents/Sports

TSN

The Sports Network, Canada's first national television sports channel, brings you all the latest, up-to-the-minute scores and news. Of course you can always search through their broadcast schedule if you're actually planning to get off the computer and switch to TV anytime soon.

www.tsn.ca

SPORTS — ORGANIZATIONS

Athletics Canada

Athletics Canada is the national sport-governing body for track and field in Canada. Their web site keeps visitors abreast of all the results of the latest competitions by Canadian track athletes all over the world.

www.canoe.ca/Athcan/home.html

Canadian Association for the Advancement of Women and Sport and Physical Activity (CAAWS)

Read about all the latest achievements of Canadian women in all major sports. CAAWS not only encourages women to join in to the previously male-dominated world of sport, but to explore all areas of life where women have been discouraged. Bookmark this site for your daughter instead of renewing her subscription to *Seventeen*.

www.caaws.ca

Canadian Centre for Ethics in Sport

You've heard it before, but it bears repeating: it's not whether you win or lose, it's how you play the game. This organization promotes drug-free sport, equity, fair play, safety, and non-violence.

www.cces.ca

Canadian Interuniversity Athletic Union

Visit the internet home of university sports in Canada for athlete profiles and news on every single collegiate sport that falls under CIAU jurisdiction.

www.ciau.ca

Golf Alberta

From the poshest country clubs to the wackiest mini golf courses, they're all here, indexed by region. You can also find out about events, tournaments, and news stories, or peruse the tips on how to improve your game. And for masochists, there's even a page of (cringe) golf humour.

www.golfalberta.com

SPORTS — ROLLER HOCKEY

Inline Hockey Central

It was not enough that hockey could be played on skates on indoor rinks year round. No, the sport of inline hockey had to be created to fill the gap where ice could not be found. This web site is the nexus of inline hockey information in North America.

www.inlinehockeycentral.com

Inline Hockey Network

The source for news on professional roller hockey in North America. Also includes links to information on amateur organizations, collegiate competition, and sites devoted to women's inline hockey groups.

www.inlinehockey.net

Roller Hockey International Statistics Archive

Yes, there are professional roller hockey leagues, and where there is pro sport there will always be someone keeping a tally of statistics. View them at this site that also features an interesting comparison of RHL rules vs. NHL rules.

members.aol.com/rhistats/

Women's Roller/Inline Hockey

Find out the difference between traditional roller hockey and inline hockey, read about world and national competitions, or just find out more about the sport that doesn't put up with sweaty guys.

www.cs.toronto.edu/~andria/inline/

SPORTS — ROWING

About Rowing

A quick and easy overview for general inquiries about rowing. Includes links, race results, training tips, and more!

rowing.about.com/sports/rowing/

Rowing Canada Aviron

This web page is rowing central, playing host to the national teams as well as major clubs across the country. Want to send e-mail to your favourite rower? This is the place to find the address.

www.rowingcanada.org

Rowing Links

Use the handy map of the world to click on the country you'd like to find rowing information about at this definitive collection of links.

www.rowinglinks.com

Rowing Results

Since the big names in sports coverage usually ignore rowing competitions on their commercial web sites, fans will have to make do with other sources of information. You won't be settling for less at this site featuring a searchable database of rowing results from all over the world.

www.rowingresults.com

The Coxswain Cafe

The always-overlooked, but nevertheless essential, coxswain will find solace at this online community's home page. Read articles on technique, scan online resources, or take part in the section for Coxswain Humour.

fly.to/coxswaincafe

Virtual Library — Rowing

A staggering collection of rowing-related events, clubs, equipment information, and general facts. Sections are divided up by country to help with organization, but you'll still find yourself wading through reams of rowing ephemera to reach the subject you're looking for.

archive.comlab.ox.ac.uk/other/rowing.html

SPORTS — RUGBY

National Rugby Post

An online version of the Canadian print publication features select articles and news from the national rugby scene.

www.rugbypost.com

Planet Rugby

A truly international web site, Planet Rugby tackles news items ranging from the Ontario player of the week to the scores in games from the British leagues. The World Cup is the only event that pre-empts this detailed coverage, keeping the focus global rather than local.

www.planet-rugby.com

Rugby Canada

The official site of the Canadian Rugby Union. You'll run into details on the Super League (match results, standings, and a page on each of the 13 teams), the junior and senior national teams, news, links, and a section devoted to coaching, refereeing, and merchandise.

www.rugbycanada.ca/

Rugby Today

Though this site takes a decidedly U.K. slant to its coverage of the sport, fans from around the world will still appreciate the coverage of global competitions. Blessed with a memorable URL, this site is sure to keep fans in the thick of the latest events and scores.

www.scrum.com

Unofficial Repository of Rugby Information

A collection of articles dealing with the sport's history, rules, and coaching, as well as songs and jokes, will be of interest to seasoned fans or the curious sportsman.

www.uidaho.edu/clubs/womens_rugby/RugbyRoot/

SPORTS — SKATING

Canadian Figure Skating Association

You dare to disparage the sport of figure skating? (1) These people have sharp blades on their feet! (2) There are almost 200 000 of them in Canada alone! Think again, as you browse this site full of news, biographies of popular skaters, and amateur programs.

www.cfsa.ca

Elvis Stojko: Heart of a Champion

Though filled with news and photos that will placate the most ardent of fans, this site fails to mention a pivitol moment in Mr. Stojko's career: the day that he trimmed that mullet! Ever since he got rid of the hockey hair, his performance has improved dramatically, though recent photos show that he's getting a little shaggy again. Time for another trip to the barber!

members.aol.com/dgeorge994/elvis

Skateweb Figure Skating Page

Find mountains of information relating to figure skating at this text-heavy page, including: pictures, news stories, articles on technique, scoring, and etiquette.

frog.simplenet.com/skateweb

Slam! Skating

Whether you're looking for the latest from world competitions or just an update on Tonya Harding's most recent court case, the Slam! Skating site will cover it. Includes archived sections for recent Canadian, World, and Olympic competitions, as well as a special tribute to Elvis Stojko.

www.canoe.ca/SlamSkating/home.html

Stars on Ice

Find out when this star-studded extravaganza will be coming to your town or read profiles of the various skaters involved.

www.starsonice.com

SPORTS — SKIING

Canadian Association for Disabled Skiing

CADS has expanded from its modest beginnings to become a cross-country organization with over 4000 members. This web site provides information on joining the association, the latest news from world competition, sponsorship opportunities, and more.

www.canuck.com/cads

Canadian Freestyle Ski Association

Anyone who has ever seen a freestyle skiing event can attest to the sport's appeal. Who would deny that acrobatic moves while flying through the air with only skiis and a helmet is exciting? The national team's web site has a fine balance of informative content and aesthetic charm. Now all they have to do is get freestyle recognized as an Olympic sport.

www.freestyleski.com

GoSki Canada

A useful site that keeps tabs on ski resorts across the country, providing up-to-the-minute snow conditions for those looking to hit the slopes.

www.goski.com/canada.htm

Ski Canada Magazine

The web site for Canada's most-read ski magazine comes complete with listings of all makers and models of alpine skis, sample stories from the print version, and lots of relevant links.

www.skicanadamag.com

Ski Council of Canada

This site keeps skiers across the country informed with a frequently updated site on the state of skiing in Canada. Features include links to hundreds of ski areas, industry information, and the Discover program, which helps make costs affordable for novices.

www.skicanada.org

SkiCentral

Focusing more on North America than just on good ol' Canada, this site has a comprehensive search and site index of all things skiing to be found on the internet. Complete your fantasy desktop with skiing wallpaper and screen savers.

skicentral.com

SkiNet Canada

Canada.com brings you a comprehensive listing of resorts and popular ski areas around the country, listed by region. There are also links to various publications and ski-related sites, as well as a section devoted to the all-important weather forecast.

www.skinetcanada.com

Slam! Skiing

Count on the folks at Canoe to have the latest results and news from the World Cup ski circuit, as well as regional competitions in Canada and abroad.

www.canoe.ca/SlamSkiing/home.html

The Snozone

A great online magazine (and one of the oldest on the internet) that brings readers daily articles on ski conditions and equipment news, with a focus on the Pacific Northwest. Special bonus: these articles read the way skiers talk (sample titles include "Techno Weenies and Techno-Skis" and "Hey! What's with the Weather!").

www.wzone.com/snozone

X-C.com

A decent hombase for cross-country-skiing aficionados. Features organized charts of links to events, clubs, and resorts across the country.

X-C.com

SPORTS — SNOWBOARDING

Boarding for Breast Cancer

Boarding for Breast Cancer (BBC) is a nonprofit, youth-focused awareness and fundraising foundation. The organization spreads awareness about good health practices and the importance of early cancer detection among young people, through sports, music, art, and events. Check out the news on the latest research and fundraising events at the official site.

bbc.chickclick.com

Canadian Snowboard Federation

For a sport that cultivates both a laid-back attitude and a certain edge of rebelliousness, you might not expect the existence of a body that "establish[es] standards of professional excellence in competition, behaviour, coaching, judging and officiating, for snowboarders of all ages and skill levels." You'll even find marketing data here.

www.csf.ca

Frosty Rider Snowboarding Tips

A great site for beginners, this collection of tips, equipment advice, and snowboarding etiquette will give you a push in the right direction.

dynawebdesigns.com/snowboarding/tips/

Ross' Gold

Those who aren't interested in reliving the whole pot-smoking fiasco at Nagano, or know all about Mr. Rebegliati's career, will find something here that no other site provides: Ross as the starring actor in *Austin Powers*! Why? Who knows, but it sure isn't helping his clean-cut image.

home.ipoline.com/~pw20/rossgold.html

Snowboard Central

This online guide to snowboard culture brings you all the music, gear, and lingo you'll need to pose as a bona fide snowboarder. Visit SC University for tips on technique, or go to the "Betty" section devoted to female snowboarders.

www.snowboardcentral.com

Snowboarder Review

A helpful guide to boards and related equipment, Snowboarder Review also provides a tutorial for beginners, online classifieds, tuning techniques, and snow and road conditions for all of North America.

www.snowboarderreview.com

Snowboarding.com

News items, events, equipment listings, board reviews, a picture gallery, and just about everything else that you could want to find at a URL called Snowboarding.com.

www.snowboarding.com

SPORTS — SOCCER

BBC Sport: World Cup 2002

Follow the events leading up to the most coveted of all football championships, the World Cup. Six competition regions covering the whole world make this a truly global sporting event.

www.bbc.co.uk/sport/static/football/competitions/wc_2002_draw.shtml

Canada Kicks

Though popular everywhere in the world except for the northern two-thirds of North America, soccer is slowly gaining acceptance in Canada. Everyone plays this game as a kid, so why do we ignore it as adults? It makes no sense, but those determined to forge a niche for the game of soccer in Canada would do well to stop by its official home on the web.

www.canadakicks.com

Federation Internationale de Football Association (FIFA)

Another great entry point for information on international competition, the official FIFA site has extensive coverage of current and archived events in the global soccer arena.

www.fifa.com

International Soccer Server

One-stop shopping for standings and statistics for European football leagues in a no-nonsense format. Includes one of the most comprehensive collections of links for international soccer sites on the web.

sunsite.tut.fi/rec/riku/soccer.html

SLAM! Soccer: Canadian Soccer News

This site provides the latest news on Canadian-based soccer leagues, as well as updates from major events like the World Cup.

www.canoe.ca/SoccerCanada/home.html

Soccer Canada

This unofficial page for the men's national team features the latest news on international competition, player profiles, and links to other soccer-related sites.

www.soccercanada.cjb.net

SPORTS — TENNIS

Slam! Tennis

All the latest news from international and amateur competition in tennis. Of course, there's the usual attention to Canadian content with a "Canadian Tennis This Week" section.

www.canoe.ca/SlamTennis/home.html

Tennis Canada

Though mainly concentrating on high-profile tournaments such as the Montreal-based Canadian Open, this site provides year-round coverage of amateur and professional tennis in Canada. Look up rankings, competition schedules, and news at this web page.

www.tenniscanada.com

Tennis Elbow

It's estimated that over half of all players over age thirty suffer from lateral epicondylitis in one form or another. Those afflicted will appreciate this page full of tips to help deal with tennis elbow, and those who still have healthy arms can check out the guide on how to avoid it.

www.tennislovers.com/Content/elbow.htm

Tennis Sport Science

Part of the NASA educational outreach program, this web site chronicles the findings of research into the ways that aerodynamics affect tennis. An interesting site for students of physics or the curious player.

muttley.ucdavis.edu/Tennis/

The Women of Tennis

An extensive collection of photos and profiles of almost every player on the pro tour—with special attention paid to Canadian ladies.

www.igs.net/~bmitchell/Tennis/tennis.htm

TSN.ca: Tennis

Check here for coverage of the latest tournaments, as well as current headlines and archived articles on various events. Includes links to the official sites for competitions and a listing of major tennis sites for Canada.

www.tsn.ca/tennis

SPORTS — VOLLEYBALL

Beachmania

The online source for news, events, links, and general inquiries about this sport that's quickly gaining popularity. Beach volleyball fans will appreciate profiles of the most popular players, as well as a detailed guide to catching TV coverage.

www.beachmania.com

Canadian National Volleyball Team

This site provides listings for all the news, events, and organizations that are involved in the sport of volleyball in this country. Brought to you by Volleyball Canada, the national governing body for volleyball and beach volleyball.

www.volleyball.ca

True North Volleyball

The official site for *True North Volleyball Magazine* presents regional news; updates on the national, college, and university teams; and features on beach volleyball.

www.tnvmag.com

Volleyball World Wide

Up-to-date information on amateur, professional, collegiate, and Olympic variations of the sport. Plus FAQs, rules, and general directories.

www.volleyball.org

Volleyball.com

Whether you're a weekend player or a dedicated coach, Volleyball.com has all the best products and information to enhance your game. Get coaching tips, updates from local and itnternational competitions, or post a message at the volleyball forum.

www.volleyball.com

Volleyballstuff.com

Touted as one of the best volleyball sites on the web, Volleyballstuff.com offers coverage of the sport at the CIAU, club, pro, and World League levels—plus, of course, the latest on Team Canada. There are also columns on topics like sport medicine.

www.volleyballstuff.com

SPORTS — WATERSKIING

Water Ski Canada

Read up on the latest news from the pro tour of water skiing or check out the statistics on Canadian national team members. There are also rule books for competition and downloadable software for tournaments.

www.waterski.ca

Waterski Listings

About.com provides this well-organized guide to online waterskiing resources. The most thorough listing of its kind on the web.

waterski.about.com/sports/waterski/index.htm

Waterskier's Web

A great collection of links covering clubs, events, jobs, schools, boats, equipment, and great locations to ski. There are also sections devoted to different disciplines within the sport, such as barefooting, wakeboarding, and slalom.

www.waterski.net

SPORTS — WINDSURFING

A Windsurfer's Guide to Hypothermia

A useful introduction to the warning signs of hypothermia, with tips on how to conserve heat in case you capsize in cold water.

www.walrus.com/~belov/hypothermia.html

Wind-Surf.net

This worldwide network of windsurfers features daily weather conditions from around the globe, live surf-cams, and photos.

www.wind-surf.net

Windsport

Though this site features more links to sponsors than it does to windsurfing resources, there is still plenty to interest windsurfers of all abilities. For beginners, there are tips on technique broken down into various stages of learning. Others will profit from loads of advice on what to look for when shopping for boards.

www.windsport.com

Windsurfer

A great resource for globe-trotting windsurfers, this site contains travel reviews and location guides to help you plan that trip across the ocean. International weather updates and an online tool to calculate wind speeds will also prove useful.

www.windsurfer.com

World Windsurfing Directory

Welcome to the online world o' windsurfing, where you'll find links to the hottest surfing sites from all over the globe. Explore the Paros Islands of Greece or read up on the weather conditions at Pelican Point in Australia.

www.worldwindsurf.com

SPORTS — WRESTLING

Freestyle Wrestling Homepage

Here's a good introductory page for those unfamiliar with Olympic-style wrestling. A brief explanation of the sport is followed by useful articles on training and the rules of the sport, as well as links to clubs and organizations from around the world.

www.dcs.shef.ac.uk/~mlee/social/wrestling.html

Nihon Sumo Kyokai

An English-language web page providing an introduction to the sport of sumo wrestling, along with profiles of the most popular wrestlers, a guide to events, and the latest news items.

www.sumo.or.jp/index_e.html

Slam! Wrestling

The latest news from the world of pro wrestling, including items from more obscure, Canadian leagues. Features an ongoing section with tributes to the late, great Owen Hart.

www.canoe.ca/SlamWrestling

The Web's Best of Amateur Wrestling

A frequently updated independent site that features comprehensive coverage of high school and college wrestling. There are also helpful sections to help fans identify various wrestling moves, collect stamps, and participate in online chats.

www.geocities.com/Colosseum/Sideline/9563/

Wrestling Canada

A far cry from the greased-up world of the WWF and other such "wrestling" leagues, this site for Canadian amateur wrestling has the latest on serious, international competition. Find out about current competitions or check the calendar for upcoming events.

www.wrestling.ca

Wrestling World Magazine Online

All the latest news and rumours from the WWF, WCW, and ECW professional leagues. Includes an archive of news items and match listings, so fans will be sure to not miss a single episode featuring their favourite soap star ... I mean, wrestler.

www.wwmagazine.com

WWF Too Cool Homey Page

The wholesale missappropriation of hip-hop culture "representin'" at this web site is laughably bad. Watch well-greased, overly-muscled, grown men act like b-boys and encourage visitors to check out sections titled "Boo-ya Video" and "Whatsup G?".

www.wwftoocool.com

TRACK & FIELD

All Legends.com: Track and Field

An interesting collection of profiles of mainly American track and field stars.

www.all-legends.com/track.html

Donovan Bailey

Though not the sprinter he once was, Donovan Bailey is taking the slow road to recovery after a nasty tendon injury. There is more here to see than just track results, though, with videos, a fan club, and news about his charity work.

www.donovanbailey.com

Endureplus

A free, online magazine dedicated to news and tips on training for any endurance athlete. Features a great list of links to various Olympic-related sites, as well as useful nutrition information. Did you know that prunes are a great source of anti-oxidants?

www.endureplus.com

Track and Field Links

A collection of global links covering topics such as clubs, athletes, competitions, training, statistics, event pages, and much more.

www.tflinks.com

Track and Field Online

Get involved in live chats with well-known athletes or take advantage of other features at this interactive site. Everything from news on the latest "vitamin supplements" (steroids) to downloadable video clips.

www.trackonline.com

Triathlon Canada

If you want to find facts on the national team, read news stories, or learn about the "Kids of Steel" program, head for this page. Also includes lots of pictures of people with zero body fat.

www.triathloncanada.com

Health & Fitness

AIDS/HIV

AIDS Quilt: The Names Project (Canada)

This is the Canadian branch of the Names Project, started in in San Francisco in 1987 as a memorial to those who've died from AIDS. Though the actual quilt is far too expansive to be seen all at once, this site allows visitors to sort through thumbnail pictures of different panels in the quilt. The Canadian AIDS Quilt is a nationally incorporated, registered charitable organization recognized by the Canadian AIDS Society

www.quilt.ca

Canadian AIDS Society

A coalition of over 100 community-based AIDS organizations across the country, the Canadian AIDS Society works to provide awareness about HIV/AIDS, while enriching the lives of those living with the disease. Visit this site for CAS projects, events, community contacts, and information resources.

www.cdnaids.ca

Canadian HIV Trials Network

The Canadian HIV Trials Network (CTN) is a partnership committed to developing treatments, vaccines, and a cure for HIV and AIDS, by conducting scientifically sound and ethical clinical trials. Visitors to this site can learn more about the program and other available resources.

www.hivnet.ubc.ca/ctn.html

Canadian HIV/AIDS Legal Network

Some articles are available online at this site and others must be requested through the network, but all legal issues regarding HIV/AIDS are covered. A search engine is also provided to help visitors plow through the seemingly endless legalese.

www.aidslaw.ca

Joint UN's Programme on AIDS/HIVS

The official home page of the Joint UN's Programme on AIDS/HIVS. The site provides news of the ongoing fight with an international bent.

www.unaids.org/

The AIDS Resource List

The AIDS Resource List is a comprehensive collection of links and available info on the net. Includes a downloadable "red ribbon" so you can show your support for the fight on your own web page.

www.specialweb.com/aids/

TheBody.com

TheBody.com is a fantastic resource for those with AIDS/HIV. It includes a 35 000 strong document library, with topics ranging from basic info to quality of life to government-related issues. Also a section for "Helping and Getting Help" with information on getting tested for those not sure, or wanting to make sure, but needing more info on the test itself.

www.thebody.com/

BIRTH

Childbirth.org

Everything you need to know about the subject: educating yourselves to be good consumers, knowing your options, and knowing how to provide yourselves with the best possible care are essential to a healthy pregnancy.

www.childbirth.org/

Planned Parenthood Federation

There are extensive licensing procedures that can last years before a person can drive a car, but any fool can become a parent. Warn teenagers and adults alike about what they're getting into or, better yet, teach them about birth control with a trip to this web page.

www.ppfc.ca

The Unofficial Guide to Having a Baby

Experience cyber pregnancy at this site swelling with facts for expectant parents. There's a library, a newsletter, and even conception tips to help you get in a family way.

www.having-a-baby.com

CANCER

Breast Cancer Society of Canada

The BCSC is a charitable organization that funds breast cancer research and prevention programs. Visit this web site for donation and contact information, listings of locations, a history of breast cancer, and more.

www.bcsc.ca

Canadian Breast Cancer Network

The Canadian Breast Cancer Network is a survivor-directed organization created to link together all groups and individuals concerned about breast cancer. The CBCN web site provides educational information, research news, related links, and support group contacts for locations across the country.

www.cbcn.ca

Canadian Cancer Research Group

Formed in 1992 by William and Kathryn O'Neill when their son was diagnosed with brain cancer, the Canadian Cancer Research Group provides specialized advocacy and research services for its clients. This web page contains the background information on the CCRG and the services it provides, as well as an online interview feature for prospective clients.

www.ccrg.com

Canadian Cancer Society

Read chilling statistics about cancer at the web site for the Canadian Cancer Society, or perhaps make a donation that will go towards research for the elimination of the disease.

www.cancer.ca

CHARITY

Child CyberSEARCH Canada Home Page

Child CyberSEARCH Canada is an independent charitable organization that runs Canada's first internet-based missing children agency. This web site provides law enforcement resources, parenting links, and a service that allows parents to register their particular case online.

www.childcybersearch.org

Child Find Canada Online

The Child Find web site works to assist in the search for missing children and advocate for the rights of children in Canada. Visitors will find an online directory of missing kids, as well as preventative safety information at this web page.

www.DISCribe.ca/childfind

Free the Children

An organization that protests child labour around the globe. Includes a varied resource list and annual conference information.

www.freethechildren.org

Kids Help Phone

Online info providing kids with a person to talk to about everything from homework to physical abuse.

kidshelp.sympatico.ca

CHILDREN — CHILD ABUSE

Canadian Society for the Investigation of Child Abuse

The Canadian Society for the Investigation of Child Abuse was formed in 1985 in response to a growing need for a coordinated, professional approach to child sexual abuse investigations. Major activities of the society include training abuse investigators and responding to the needs of abused children—particularly in the area of child witness court preparation.

www.csica.zener.com

Child Abuse Monument

Under construction as of this writing, the Child Abuse Monument promises "to assist with the personal and social healing of the ravages of child abuse."

www.childabusemonument.org/

On the Road to Healing

A resource for victims and survivors of child sexual abuse.

www2.addr.com/~sariaa/onroad/index.html

DEATH

Bereavement Self-Help Resources Guide

The Bereavement Self-Help Resources Guide provides visitors with useful information, links to support groups and services, and connections to other relevant sites. Resources are divided into easy-to-follow subject headings, with all-important categories listed on the opening page.

www.inforamp.net/~bfo/guide/index.html

Canadian Memorial Cremation Foundation

Why a cremation society? This organization feels compelled to provide listings for low-cost cremation services across Canada and the U.S. Find out where to get vaporized after you shuffle off this mortal coil.

www.crremation.org

DeathNET

Help advance the art and science of dying well with a visit to DeathNET. Read the latest how-to suicide information or visit the "Last Rights" information centre at this web site specializing in all aspects of death and dying—with a sincere respect for every point of view.

www.islandnet.com/~deathnet

Find a Grave

Look up the locations and find photographs of the final resting places of just about any remotely famous (and dead) person you can think of. The site approaches comprehensiveness: you'll find Kareem Abdul Jabar's mother and Emile Zola's illegitimate son. Notable oversights include Jimmy Hoffa and Amelia Earhart.

www.findagrave.com

DENTISTRY

Canadian Dental Association

Come see what those crazy dentists are up to when they're not scraping your teeth or prodding your gums. Quick Tip: Reverse your usual brushing pattern to catch the spots you might regularly miss.

www.cda-adc.ca/index.html

Dentistry Now

A comprehensive site about dentistry.

www.DentistryNow.com

Sybertooth

A directory of events in dentistry, including continuing education seminars and dental society meetings. Also, get free "dental" e-mail and access to free dental classifieds.

www.sybertooth.com

The Wisdom Tooth Home Page

The whole tooth and nothing but the tooth. This site offers tons of dental hygiene and health information.

www.umanitoba.ca/outreach/wisdomtooth

DISEASES & CONDITIONS

Alzheimer Society of Canada

The Alzheimer Society of Canada is dedicated to providing support for Alzheimer sufferers and their families, while actively searching for a cure for the disease. Provided at this site is a wealth of information on the treatment of the disease, the latest research, contact information, and more.

www.alzheimer.ca

American Diabetes Association

A resource for diabetics, with good coverage of nutritional information.

www.diabetes.org/default.asp

Arthritis Canada

Arthritis Canada provides links to all other major arthritis information and research groups in Canada, including the Arthritis Society, Arthritis Health Care Providers Association, and the Canadian Arthritis Network.

www.arthritis.ca

Asthma Society of Canada

The Asthma Society of Canada is dedicated to improving the lives of Canadians who have this disorder, while promoting research to find a cure. Visitors can find out how they can get involved in various fund-raisers, use the online resources to learn more about the disorder, or follow a list of asthma-related links.

www.asthmasociety.com

Bloorview Epilepsy Research Program

This program studies drug-resistant seizures in children and tests new therapies designed to control them.

www.utoronto.ca/berp/

Canadian Cardiovascular Society

If you are reading this directory while enjoying a cigarette and neglecting to exercise, you may want to slide over to your computer and visit the Canadian Cardiovascular Society web page. Peruse the latest news on cardiovascular health and then maybe butt out and go for a walk.

www.ccs.ca

Canadian Celiac Association

Celiac disease is a medical condition in which the absorptive surface of the small intestine is damaged by a substance called gluten. A proper, more extensive description of the disease and its treatment can be found at this web site.

www.celiac.ca

Canadian Diabetes Association

This page provides a useful resource for those looking to learn more about this incurable disease. Read the "About Diabetes" section, find information on living with the disease, and take a look at the diabetes dictionary.

www.diabetes.ca

Canadian Lung Association

The Canadian Lung Association's web site features an extensive information base to provide support to any possible visitor. Everything from smoking cessation to flu shots to asthma is covered here for the curious and the health-conscious netizen.

www.lung.ca

Chrohn's and Colitis Foundation of Canada

The CCFC web site provides regular research and medication updates related to colitis and Crohn's disease.

www.ccfc.ca

HepNet

A comprehensive and regularly updated resource on hepatitis and liver health.

www.hepnet.com

Ketogenic Diet

A ketogenic diet "tricks" the body into burning fat stores rather than storing fat. Sound good? It's not to be taken lightly, but some athletes use it for sudden fat loss. The trick is to eat zero carbs and a lot of fat and protein for a few days, making sure to exercise. The caloric intake is about the same, but the body begins to burn fuel by a different mechanism. This is followed by a high-carb "carb-up" period. The diet was originally developed as a means of controlling the symptoms of epilepsy. The site contains recipes, calculation tools, testimonials related to the use of the diet in controlling epileptic seizures, and links to more useful info. Those interested in using the diet for athletics or cosmetic fat loss should read a recent book by Lyle Macdonald. Lyle's nutrition column is called "Nutrimuscle!" and appears at www.cyberpump.com

www.ketogenic.org

Laboratory Centre for Disease Control

Check to see if there are any travel health advisories for your vacation destination, or look up disease prevention and control guidelines at this web page.

hwcweb.hwc.ca/hpb/lcdc/hp_eng.html

Mad Cow Disease

Touted as the "official" page for Mad Cow Disease, this site provides links to over 5000 articles about the illness—if you're actually interested (ugh!).

www.cyber-dyne.com/~tom/mad_cow_disease.html

National Institute of Allergy and Infectious Diseases Home Page (NIAID)

Head to the NIAID site for news, info, publications, and activities. Plus, you can check out cool pictures of ugly microbe-type thingys.

www.niaid.nih.gov/

Pneumonia

Second only to lung cancer as a cause of death due to respiratory illness, pneumonia can be avoided through preventative action. Learn more about the different causes of this disease and the ways to avoid it at this web site by the Lung Association of Canada.

www.lung.ca/pneumonia

The Emerging Infectious Diseases Journal

A peer-reviewed journal published by the National Center for Infectious Diseases, the *Emerging Infectious Diseases Journal* focuses on all the nasty things currently brewing in mosquito-infested swamplands around the world. Ahh, the wonderful world of Escherichia coli ...

www.cdc.gov/ncidod/eid/index.htm

The Journal of Infectious Diseases

Another cybergem of ailments ... ahem ... to die for. The *Journal of Infectious Diseases* covers just about every disease known to man. Published by the University of Chicago Press, it's proof that Chicago really is the home of the blues, if you'll excuse a poor joke.

www.journals.uchicago.edu/JID/home.html

The Rare Genetic Diseases in Children Homepage

If you have children, and you still sleep easy, for the love of all things holy, DO NOT visit this site. The Rare Genetic Diseases in Children Homepage is an exhaustive resource of information on enough diseases to keep a generation of parents awake at night for years to come. Chicken pox are for wusses, anyway.

mcrcr2.med.nyu.edu/murphp01/homenew.htm

Thyroid Foundation of Canada

This organization, with 22 chapters across the country, promotes awareness of thyroid conditions, provides information, and raises funds for research. You'll find news and events, contact information, medical information, and updates on the state of research.

home.ican.net/~thyroid/Canada.html

DISEASES & CONDITIONS — LIVER DISEASES

Canadian Liver Foundation

More than three quarters of the liver will be non-functioning before a person will notice any symptoms of liver damage, so hurry over to this site for information on how to protect yourself. Besides the usual question-and-answer-type service that this site provides, there is also a section for physicians to discuss treatment and updates on the latest research.

www.liver.ca

DRUGS — ABUSE

Addiction Research Foundation

As a part of the Centre for Addiction and Mental Health, the Addiction Research Foundation provides a wealth of information about alcohol, tobacco, and other drugs. Find facts on drug and alcohol addiction, look up info on available courses, browse research papers, or check out the related links.

www.arf.org

Addictions Foundation of Manitoba

The Addictions Foundation of Manitoba's primary mandate is the treatment of alcohol, drug, and gambling addictions. This web site looks at the history and membership of the foundation, and discusses rehab, training, prevention, and education programs offered across the province.

www.afm.mb.ca

Against Drunk Driving

Every 20 minutes someone in Canada becomes a victim of drunk driving. This is a reality that the members of ADD are seeking to change through public awareness and education programs. Check out the facts and find out how you can get involved in the fight against drunk driving.

www.netmediapro.com/add

Alcoholics Anonymous

AA is a nonprofessional, self-supporting, nondenominational, multiracial, apolitical organization open to anyone who wants to do something about his or her drinking problem. The AA web site provides resources designed to answer questions that prospective members may have, and contact info for the chapters located across North America.

www.alcoholics-anonymous.org

Canadian Centre on Substance Abuse

Parents and educators will be interested in the educational resources provided at this web site, while others may want to peruse the support services for drug, alcohol, and gambling addiction. Featured news covers statistics and treatment for addiction, and there's lots of links to related sites.

www.ccsa.ca

Drink Smart

This web site for young people does not discourage underage drinking but rather encourages responsible drinking at any age. Articles and facts about drinking create a base of knowledge that will help kids know when to draw the line.

www.drinksmart.org/index.html

Drug Education and Awareness for Life

Drug awareness information for youth. It never hurts to be told over and over again.

www.deal.org/english

Extreme Attitudes Against Drinking and Driving

Attempts to warn teens against drinking and driving, with the help of a hip band and cool graphics. Hosted by the CBC.

www.extreme.netc.net

Fetal Alcohol Syndrome

This site is partly supported by the Fetal Alcohol Support Network of Toronto and Peel. Fetal Alcohol Syndrome is a devastating affliction that's more common than you might think. The hard-hitting stance taken by the group may not be for everyone: "Many of society's most persistent problems stem from a single source—pregnant women drinking alcohol causing neurological damage to the child. The injured child is unable to meet the demands of parents, family, peers, school, career, adherence to rules, and enters a lifetime cycle of failures. Often the neurological damage goes undiagnosed, but not unpunished."

www.acbr.com/fas/

Mothers Against Drunk Driving

A well-known organization that seeks to eliminate impaired driving, MADD places special emphasis on service to victims. Just by visiting this site you'll be helping spread awareness. Don't get even, get MADD.

www.madd.ca

Substance Abuse Network of Ontario

Meant for both substance abuse workers and the general public, this site provides general information on addictive substances from caffeine to heroin.

sano.arf.org

FITNESS

Active Living Canada

Active Living Canada is a collective of community groups (including nonprofit, private-, and public-sector organizations) whose goal is to provide a broader range of active-living programs and services at the local, regional, and national levels. Find out how you can integrate physical activity into your daily life by using the ActiveSearch, a database of innovative practices, policy documents, planning strategies, public info materials, and more.

activeliving.ca/activeliving/alc.html

Body Break

If you've ever allowed yourself to atrophy in front of the TV on a weekday morning, you've probably been stirred out of your complaisance by the Body Break duo of Hal Johnson and Joanne McLeod. The web site for these Canadian icons provides recipes, fitness tips, nutrition info, and the requisite list of links to other such physically fit pages.

www.bodybreak.com

Canada's Healthy Living Guide

The Healthy Living Guide provides up-to-date research on alternative and complementary medical treatments, as well as info on vitamins, minerals, herbs, sports and fitness supplements, pro-sexual nutrients, and anti-aging formulations. Read the latest articles or dig through the archives at this site.

healthylivingguide.com

Canada's Physical Activity Guide

Take the quiz provided at this Health Canada web site to see if you're getting enough regular exercise. If you're like 63 percent of Canadians, you will then need to take a look at the suggested activities to improve your sedentary lifestyle.

www.paguide.com

Canadian Fitness and Lifestyle Research Institute

Head to this online database for research and surveys on physical fitness in Canada. Apparently, we've been spending too much time in front of the computer, because only one-third of us are sufficiently active.

www.cflri.ca

Keyboard Yoga

Reach nirvana without ever leaving your beloved computer at this site for office-bound workaholic types. Learn basic yoga postures and muscle-kneading techniques to help you relax during the work day. The medium is the massage!

www.ivillage.com/fitness/tools/yoga

YMCA Canada

Look up the programs and activities offered by your community's local YMCA at this site. Take a guided tour of the site, including information about the YMCA movement, associations, the national organization, and their international involvements.

www.ymca.ca

Zone Diet

Dr. Bill Sears developed the Zone or 40-30-30 diet plan based on research on insulin sensitivity and hormone levels. Some feel that they're hungry all the time on the Zone diet, but about 25 percent of the population find extreme success with it—many of the these people have exacerbated their weight problems with high-carbohydrate diets to which they are genetically ill-suited. This site is meant to be an independent source of info on the Zone Diet. Even if Sears's science isn't accepted by many, moderating carb intake and avoiding high-glycemic-index carbs are known strategies in the fitness community and have a solid basis in past treatments for diabetes.

www.he.net/~zone/primer

HEALTH — CONDITIONS

4Allergies.com

4Allergies.com is the 4.com network's page dedicated to all things allergic. A really impressive site jam-packed with info on just about all of life's sniffles and sneezes.

4allergies.4anything.com/

Allergy and Environmental Health Association of Nova Scotia

The AEHA:NS home page tackles the current concern over the effect of natural gas combustion on people with environmental illness, chemical sensitivity, asthma, and allergies. Links to various articles and reports are included to create awareness of this perspective on the natural gas debate in Nova Scotia.

www.geocities.com/RainForest/6847/index.html

drkoop.com

This is one of the most popular sites on the web, so don't make fun of the name. People must really love Dr. Koop—this is a premier destination for health information.

www.drkoop.com

Food Allergies and Intolerances

This complete online resource discusses recipes, blood tests, and more.

www.skyisland.com/OnlineResources/index.html

Help for Headaches

Temples throbbing after too much time in front of the computer screen? You may find some relief at the web site for this nonprofit organization.

www.headache-help.org

Hypothermia Knowledge and Technology Site

A no-nonsense resource offering techniques for overcoming hypothermia.

www.hypothermia-ca.com/

Online Resources for People with Food Allergies and Intolerances

Head here for info, recipes, books, support forums, and more.

www.skyisland.com/OnlineResources/

Sniffles & Sneezes

Allergy and Asthma care and prevention. This is the online version of a quarterly public service newsletter that's been published since 1989. Your host is Louise H. Bethea, M.D., a board-certified allergist/immunologist in private practice in the North Houston area.

www.allergyasthma.com

The Food Allergy Network

Anyone who's experienced the sensation of swelling up like a fleshy balloon after eating the wrong food will appreciate this organization's web site for food allergies and anaphylaxis. Those with slow modems should probably head to the hospital before stopping here.

www.foodallergy.org

The Migraine Association of Canada

Migraine sufferers across the country will appreciate this resource of free information, newsletters, and even a migraine-friendly cookbook.

www.migraine.ca

HEALTH — INDICES

A.D.A.M

This major source of online health and medical info has been building its enormous computerized database since 1990. Now this data is web-friendly.

www.adam.com

Health Promotion Online

The Health Canada site offers a plethora of resources. The "10 Hottest Resources List" is only the beginning: it covers everything from nutrition to childhood and youth. A must-visit for your health search.

www.hc-sc.gc.ca/hppb

Healthy Way

Healthy Way is an online health guide designed specifically for Canadians. Visitors can browse through available resources by province.

healthyway.sympatico.ca

The Global Health Network

The Global Health Network (GHNet) is an alliance of experts in health and telecommunications who are actively developing a health information structure. Look up publications, newsletters, travel advisories, and articles on global health issues at this site.

www.pitt.edu/HOME/GHNet/GHNet.html

The Patient's Guide to Healthcare Information on the Internet

An easy-to-follow index of medical sites on the web. There are pages for medical research, references, resources, current events, and terminology.

www3.bc.sympatico.ca/me/patientguide

Your Hospital at Home

Research any number of medical conditions at this online index or take advantage of the free medical newsletter.

www.yourhospitalathome.com

HEALTH — MAGAZINES

Cannabis Culture

With marijuana gaining acceptance daily as a valid medical treatment, physicians and stoners alike may be interested in this online publication on hemp and pot.

www.cannabisculture.com

Healthy Living Guide Online

The online extension of the newsstand edition of *Healthy Living* magazine, this site hopes to be "the solution to all of your health questions." Effort has been made to recommend only sites that contain accurate information.

www.healthylivingguide.com

HEALTH — ORGANIZATIONS

AIDS Quilt: Canadian Electronic Names

This is the Canadian branch of the Names Project, which was started in San Francisco in 1987 as a memorial to those who've died from AIDS. Though the actual quilt is far too expansive to be seen all at once, this site allows visitors to sort through thumbnail pictures of the different panels in the quilt. The Canadian AIDS Quilt is a nationally incorporated, registered charitable organization that is recognized by the Canadian AIDS Society.

www.quilt.ca

Canadian Institute for Health Information

The CIHI web site organizes its online info by province and categories of health professionals, expenditures, and services. Information that cannot be accessed at the site may be requested through an online order form.

www.cihi.ca

Canadian Medical Association Online

Though mainly a resource for Canadian Medical Association members, there's also a great deal of medical information available for the home doctor. Did you know that tick-borne diseases peak in the summer months?

www.cma.ca

Heart and Stroke Foundation

Here you'll find nutrition tips, preventative medicine for all ages, and links to provincial organizations. A professional and highly useful resource.

www.hsf.ca

John Dossetor Health Ethics Centre

Read articles and essays on issues in the field of bioethics, written by members of the medical profession. The history and programs of the centre are also explained in detail at this web site.

www.ualberta.ca/~ethics/bethics.htm#top

Mayo Clinic Oasis

There's lots of info on cancer and Alzheimer's disease in particular, but the Mayo site also has a lot more. Possibly the most trustworthy and interesting source of updated health info on the web.

www.mayohealth.org

Pest Management and Regulatory Agency

Check out this site for the safest and most effective methods for dealing with household and backyard pests. Everything from bats to earwigs to moles to voles is covered, with extensive background and control data for each.

www.hc-sc.gc.ca/pmra-arla/qpnote-e.html

HEALTH — PUBLIC

Body Mass Index

One of the world's most misleading health indicators, as it takes absolutely no account of body composition (body fat percentage, muscle mass, bone size and density). In any case, you can type in your vitals and get your BMI here. Also available are other pseudo-scientific indices such as "target heart rate" and "waist to hip ratio."

search.onhealth.com/ch1/interactives/mbi/default.asp

Calorie Control Council

If your concept of health requires strict calorie control, then this site is for you. The Enhanced Calorie Control Counter is a handy tool, allowing you to interactively search a big database of food items and their calorie counts. If you're having trouble gaining weight, skip the Big Mac and just scarf down two cans of tuna packed in oil (minus the dressing and other condiments) every day: you'll add 370 calories to your total.

www.caloriecontrol.org

Canada Mortgage and Housing Corporation

For over a decade, the Canada Mortgage and Housing Corporation (a federal agency) has been researching ways to renovate or build housing that is healthy to live in, uses less energy, is good for the environment, and is affordable. Info for buyers and builders is provided—and the case is made that there are financial incentives for healthy housing.

www.cmhc-schl.gc.ca/HealthyHousing

Health Canada

The federal ministry in charge of Canadians' physical well-being has a massive site offering headlines and information on product regulation, diseases and conditions, the health system, and much, much more. A votre sante!

www.hc-sc.gc.ca

Learn CPR

Includes information and training resources for cardio-pulmonary resuscitation, including games, links, and a video (QuickTime) demonstration of CPR.

www.learncpr.org/

Nick's Yellow Fingers Club

Smokers of all ages are invited to sit down, relax, and quit smoking before it's too late at Nick's Yellow Fingers Club. The Dead End Cafe lists the top ten reasons to quit, while Cinema International features the top ten anti-smoking spots on TV, and the Jungle Lounge has the best reasons never to light up in the first place.

www.hc-sc.gc.ca/real/smoking

Quit for Life

An animated and humorous look at the stories of three fictional teens and their trials and tribulations with smoking. At the end of each segment, a help feature gives tips on how to quit.

www.quit4life.com

Quit Smoking Support

Judging by the number of hits this site receives (four every minute), there are thousands of people who want to quit smoking. Join in the discussion group with other aspiring ex-smokers or take advantage of the extensive resources provided.

www.quitsmokingsupport.com

Search and Rescue Society of British Columbia

Find everything you need to know about search and rescue: hypothermia, rope rescue, search dogs, behaviour of lost persons, SAR training, and more.

www.sarbc.org

HEALTH — WOMEN'S

Canadian Women's Health Network

The CWHN web site posts new research, articles, press releases, and information sheets from organizations that may not have their own web sites but are actively involved in women's health. Find out what's new in women's health, follow selected links, or search through the women's health databases at this site.

www.cwhn.ca

LAW — HEALTH

Canadian Foundation for Drug Policy

The Canadian Foundation for Drug Policy supports the reform of Canada's drug laws to make them more effective and humane. Towards that end, the group provides extensive coverage of drug policy in the media, as well as information on Canada's current drug legislation.

www.apothecary.on.ca/~eoscapel/cfdp/cfdp.html

MEDICINE

Active First Aid Online

"Active First Aid Online! is the Internet version of the official PARASOL EMT First Aid book. Written by ambulance paramedics with a total of 40 years experience in pre-hospital care." This is an Australian company, but for once the urgent entreaties to buy are not plastered all over the front page, and there's plenty of information on all sorts of emergencies provided at no charge. Trust the Aussies to be this nice!

www.parasolemt.com.au/afa/index.html

Feet for Life

Pity your much-maligned and oft-forgotten feet! Find out how to treat your tender tootsies well by visiting this page brought to you by the Society of Chiropodists and Podiatrists. What's the cause of most foot problems? Ill-fitting shoes and a lack of visits to this site.

www.feetforlife.org

Foot Web

"Congratulations! You have made the first step in understanding the cause, treatment and self help universe of foot problems. Foot Web has been created as a network and information resource for all foot problems and conditions. We invite you to browse around the various sections of our site." These include finding a foot doctor "from around the world," but unfortunately, the interactive "find a foot doctor map of the world" seems to look a lot like just the U.S.A. Still, there's plenty of information elsewhere on the site regarding all aspects of foot care.

www.footweb.com/

Glebe Apothecary

Find articles on various, mostly minor, health annoyances, like jet lag, bug bites, swimmer's ear, and poison ivy.

www.apothecary.on.ca/articles.asp

Global Medic

Now there's no excuse not to go get that check-up. Take the online health quiz to see what kind of shape you're in, or use the self-care tools and health info provided at this site.

www.globalmedic.com

GYN 101

Prepare for your gynecological exam with advice on choosing a doctor and a useful online quiz.

www.gyn101.com

WebMed—Foot Care

Lycos's association with WebMed brings you this informative document on caring for your feet—for life. It includes such sage advice as: "wash your feet regularly" and "trim your toenails each week or when needed." How exactly could people survive without the internet?

webmd.lycos.com/content/dmk/ dmk_article_1460461

MEDICINE — HOMEOPATHY

AromaWeb

You can dispute the medical benefits that aromatherapy may offer, but anyone who has experienced a massage with essential oils will know that it smells and feels darn good! Research the historical and current methods of treating such ailments as arthritis and insomnia with aromatic oils at this web site.

www.aromaweb.com

British Institute of Homeopathy, Canada

Based on the teachings of Dr. Samuel Hahnemann, the British Institute of Homeopathy trains students in classical and modern methods. This web site provides an intro to the courses offered, as well as a cursory run-down of application, payment, and other necessary administration info.

www.homepathy.com

Canadian Herb Society

This national nonprofit association provides accurate information and networking for herb enthusiasts. Here you'll find news, events listings, and classifieds.

www.herbsociety.ca

Herb Research Foundation

Before you start guzzling kava tea or popping echinacea pills, look up the facts on side effects and proper usage at this site. If there's still room for doubt, you can contact experts in the field of herb research through this web page.

www.herbs.org

Naturopathic Medicine Network

Naturopathy isn't for everyone, but if you're interested in holistic approaches to healing and health, this site provides general information and various directories to naturopathic services.

www.pandamedicine.com

Oxygen and Ozone Therapies

Read the articles at this site designed to inform you on the benefits and techniques for oxygen therapy, which include the use of hydrogen peroxide, ozone therapy, hyberbaric oxygen, stabilized oxygen, and ionization.

www.oxytherapy.com

The Guide to Aromatherapy

The Guide to Aromatherapy, a thorough site from Britain, includes a comprehensive list of oils, a glossary, and a page of ominous warnings like "avoid use in the sun."

www.fragrant.demon.co.uk/

The Toronto School of Homeopathic Medicine

The web site for the Toronto School of Homeopathic Medicine provides info on the courses and training methods of the school, while presenting a useful resource for the homeopathic community. Learn more about the foundation of homeopathic medicine and the principles behind it, and read reviews of different treatments from the patients themselves.

www.homeopathycanada.com

MEDICINE — ACUPUNCTURE

Acupuncture.com

Want to get poked by hundreds of needles? Who wouldn't? Find out the facts about this ancient form of medicine, which has been curing people for thousands of years.

www.acupunture.com

Chinese Medicine and Acupuncture in Canada

This site provides resources and an information exchange for practitioners and students of Chinese medicine, and also provides patients with info on different treatments and the theory behind them. According to a National Academy of Sciences study of 796 Chinese herbal and animal remedies, at least half of these remedies have some kind of scientific basis for their reputed claims.

www.medicinechinese.com

Possible Adverse Effects of Acupuncture

Generally speaking, acupuncture is a safe procedure. Serious complications with acupuncture are rare. Most have occurred because of practitioner negligence, such as blatant violations of sterile procedures. The use of sterilized disposable needles is increasingly common.

webmd.lycos.com/content/dmk/dmk_article_58930

Welcome to Acupuncture Canada

"The natural heath domain" is a good site search engine, with lots of info about acupuncture for Canadians—including where to find an accredited acupuncturist in Canada—all three of them.

www.acupuncture.ca/

Westside Acupuncture & Natural Healing

Acupuncture, herbal medicine, and a *free* online consultation are services offered by this clinic. It's located on the west side of Los Angeles, and just in case you're lumped in with the 99.9 percent of the world that *doesn't* live in L.A., Westside Acupuncture provides a free online consultation in an effort to educate the internet community about the benefits of Oriental medicine.

www.acupuncture.cc/

MEDICINE — DERMATOLOGY

DermWeb

All the dermatology information you could ask for.

www.dermatology.org

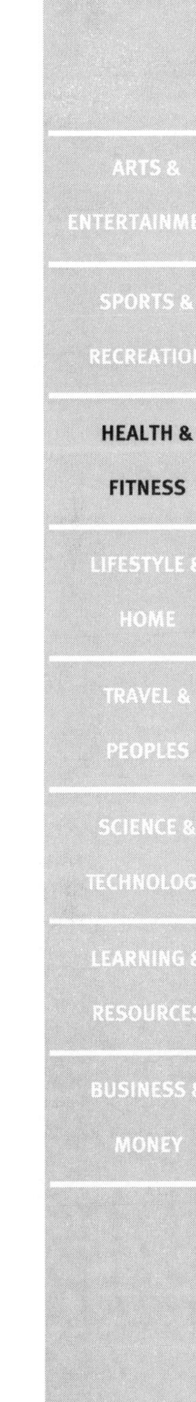

MEDICINE — OPHTHALMOLOGY

Mediconsult.com-Eye

Finally, there's a site like Mediconsult.com-Eye, where you can join in and discuss everything from glaucoma to macular degeneration to cataracts. It's about time, too.

www.mediconsult.com/mc/mcsite.nsf/conditionnav/eye~sectionintroduction

The American Academy of Ophthalmology

The American Academy of Ophthalmology maintains a good site with information for both patients and medical care professionals. Although there's a decided bent toward information in the United States, be sure to check out the International section, where you'll be able to locate member physicians in most countries—with the usual high concentration of info in Europe and the Americas. Don't be too disappointed if you can't find any in Afghanistan, for example.

www.eyenet.org/

MEDICINE — OPTOMETRY

The Canadian Association of Optometrists

The web site for the Canadian Association of Optometrists provides useful Q&A's about eyecare and the nature of optometry.

www.opto.ca

MEDICINE — ORGANIZATIONS

Canadian Anaesthesia List

A resource geared toward professional anaesthetists, the Canadian Anaesthesia List provides a number of related medical discussion groups, anaesthesia departments, and relevant sites.

www.anesthesia.org/professional/can_anes.html

Canadian Anaesthetists' Society

The CAS's web page provides info on the practice of anaesthesia for lay people, while updating anaesthesiologists on news and job opportunities. Warning! Prolonged exposure to this site will induce sleep.

www.cas.ca

Canadian Medical Organizations and Hospitals

A search for medical or institutional info can usefully begin here—follow the links and you'll get what you need eventually.

www.crha-health.ab.ca/othres/canlink.htm

Canadian Red Cross

No longer a blood donation organization in Canada, the Canadian Red Cross still organizes relief efforts for crises in Canada and all over the world. Search through this web site that includes sections for first-aid, abuse prevention, fundraising, publications, and more.

www.redcross.ca

St. John Ambulance

An organization that works to "enable Canadians to improve their health, safety and quality of life by providing training and community service." You can read about their CPR and first-aid training programs, or you can even find out how they descended from the medieval Order of St. John.

www.sja.ca

WebDoctor

Designed by physicians for use by physicians, WebDoctor is an index of medical resources available on the web. It has links to over 10 000 pages and documents, so it's probably a good place to begin looking for medical info. Claims that its links are peer-reviewed by professionals.

www.gretmar.com/webdoctor/home.html

MEDICINE — PHYSICAL THERAPY

Canadian Chiropractic Infosite

The overall philosophy of chiropractic care is to help your body heal itself without drugs or surgery. This site is a guide to spinal afflictions and how manipulation and adjustment by a chiropractor can alleviate your pain. It also helps you locate a chiropractor near you.

www.ccachiro.org/

Dr. Watson's Chiropractic Online

This web site provides a listing of some basic info to settle your curiosity about chiropractic medicine. If there's something you'd like to know about but can't find it here, just e-mail the good doctor.

www3.sympatico.ca/drwatson/index1.html

Ontario College of Reflexology

Improve your foot massages with a number of reflexology-related resources provided at this site.

www.ocr.edu

The Chiropractic Page for Patients

This web site provides those curious about chiropractic medicine with the resources to make an informed decision based on articles and listings of chiropractors across Canada.

www.mbnet.mb.ca/~jwiens/pat.html

The Method

Here's an overview of the Pilates method, a rigorous but low-impact method of physical conditioning based on 34 matwork exercises and apparatus work developed by Joseph Pilates.

www.the-method.com/

Yogaaaahhh

The name of the site says it all: yoga is promoted as a form of relaxation, meditation, and a healthy means of strengthening the body. And the site is so friendly that you'll leave out the "lousy" when you say "I came to this site and all I got was this lousy t-shirt." Non-lousy Yogaaaahhh t-shirts are available.

www2.gdi.net/~mjm/

MEDICINE — SURGERY

Online Surgery

You've heard of webcams, and you've seen surgery performed on TV. Now, you can see webcasts of surgery and post-op interviews. The site owners give away free surgery to selected "qualified candidates," presumably to provide them with an inexpensive source of broadcast material. The most recent recipient received a free otoplasty (ear surgery).

www.onlinesurgery.com/

MENTAL HEALTH

ADDMed Homepage

The ADDMed Homepage offers a wealth of info about the diagnosis and treatment of children with Attention Deficit Disorder. Brought to you by Dr. Anthony Laws, this site provides answers to initial questions that parents may have about the nature and treatment of ADD. Any further queries may be answered through an extensive list of links or by e-mailing Dr. Laws directly.

www.addmed.com

Art Therapy in Canada

Art Therapy is a form of psychoanalysis that facilitates expression and healing through nonverbal means. This site provides an introduction to the field, an Art Therapy newsgroup, and several links to related resources.

home.ican.net/~phansen/index.html

Canadian Association for Music Therapy

Visit the web site for those who wish to sing their cares away. The Canadian Association for Music Therapy's site provides a history of treating illness with music, and lists publications, stats, and other resources for this area of study.

www.musictherapy.ca

Eating Disorder Shared Awareness

A wealth of info on eating disorders, maintained by a support group from Sudbury. Head here for articles and serious info about many aspects of eating, health, body image, and pressures on teens.

www.mirror-mirror.org/eatdis.htm

Internet Mental Health

Born out of the discovery of highly incongruous treatments for mental health disorders in Canada and Japan, this organization works to freely share whatever info they have on mental health with the world. Look up disorders, diagnoses, medications, and related links at this site.

www.mentalhealth.com

LifeMatters

Take action to find well-being in all aspects of your life: health, parenting, nutrition, fitness, and relating. You'll find thoughts on dreams, tai chi, handling kids' aggression, and homeopathy.

lifematters.com

Love & Learn

Become a functional unit. Make your love life work. It's easy: just follow common sense, like not messing around with your significant other's best friend; and marrying for love, and not money. Heck, pretty much anyone could purvey this advice, but sometimes it's important to hear someone else say it. "Mr. Sensitive" is the caring host. Bob Eubanks must be a writer for the site—who says "make whoopee" anyway?

www.loveandlearn.com

shift

Mental Health Net

I'm crazy. You're crazy. We're all crazy, sometimes. Which is precisely why the Mental Health Net remains an invaluable resource. It makes searching easy, even for the stressed-out, strung-out, and freaked-out. Check medical texts or unabashedly honest bulletin boards for the truth about various psycho-chemicals you may be considering for casual consumption. The site provides extensive resources for all the major fin-de-siecle maladies—from anorexia nervosa to sleep disorders to schizophrenia—without preaching or passing judgment. The best thing about Mental Health Net (other than the sheer volume of info it offers): it's resolutely New Age-free, shunning the dumb-downs and chanting exercises prescribed by other self-help sites.

mentalhelp.net

Health & Fitness

Ontario Association for Community Living

This is an organization of persons who have been identified as having an intellectual disability, and their families. Their goal is "that all persons live in a state of dignity, share in all elements of living in the community, and have the opportunity to participate effectively."

www.acl.on.ca

Virtual Psych

Need some pointers on "coping and growing from the challenges of life"? Here's a site that offers advice on topics such as stress, depression, love, spirituality, and workplace issues.

www.virtualpsych.com

MENTAL HEALTH — DISEASES & CONDITIONS

Autism Treatment Services of Canada

Autism Treatment Services of Canada is a national affiliation of organizations that provide educational, management, and consultation services to people with autism and related disorders. This web page provides an introduction to some of those services offered, as well as online resources describing this disability and its popular misconceptions.

www.autism.ca

Borderline Personality Disorder Page

An extensive archive of articles, reports, and reflections on BPD, created and maintained by a former sufferer.

www.golden.net/~soul/borderpd.html

NURSING

Canadian Association of Critical Care Nurses

This regularly updated site provides critical care nurses with info on the latest research, job opportunities, a bulletin board, and links to other nursing sites.

www.execulink.com/~caccn

NUTRITION

Calorie and Fat Gram Chart

A handy reference for data on fat, calories, carbohydrates, protein, cholesterol, and saturated fat content in a list of foods from alfalfa to yogurt.

www.ntwrks.com/~mikev/chart1a.htm

Canola Connection

Whether you're interested in crop forecasts or just want to find out info on nutrition, this site will give you the field of canola facts. Who wouldn't want a recipe for canola-enhanced apricot loaf?

www.canola-council.org

Dieticians of Canada

Dieticians of Canada is an association of food and nutrition professionals committed to the health and well-being of Canadians. Look up consumer info on the foods you buy, or look through the guides provided to see how you can make your daily meals a little healthier. The slogan at this site is "Eat Well, Live Well."

www.dieticians.ca

Supplements On-line

A voluminous source of info on vitamins, herbs, and homeopathic remedies for various health conditions. There's a shopping list option that returns approximate retail prices of products, but the site itself sells nothing.

www.supplementson-line.com

PUBLIC HEALTH & SAFETY

Canada Safety Council

Nationally recognized for its work with children through Elmer the Safety Elephant, the Canada Safety Council covers various commercial, residential, and work-related safety issues. In addition, this site provides listings for training programs, online quizzes, educational information, and links to other safety sites.

www.safety-council.org

Canadian Association of Fire Chiefs

Stop, drop, and scroll on over to the CAFC web site for fire prevention and safety tips.

www.cafc.ca

Canadian Centre for Emergency Preparedness

The CCEP was created to assist communities, governments, and private business to prepare for, prevent, respond to, and recover from manmade or natural disasters. Check this web site for programs such as Critical Incident Stress Management and Bomb Threat Management. The necessary contact information is also provided.

www.ccep.ca

Canadian Centre for Occupational Health and Safety

If you spend a great deal of time surfing the web or using a computer at work, you might want to look into this site's section on carpal tunnel syndrome. Other diseases and disorders related to common working conditions are also listed, along with tips on how you can avoid them.

www.ccohs.ca

Canadian Coast Guard

Our Coast Guard provides a variety of emergency response services around Canada's massive coastal waters. Okay, so it's not *Baywatch*, but ice-breaking and dredging services can be pretty darn interesting!

www.ccg.gcc.gc.ca

Canadian Injured Workers Alliance

The CIWA is a national network of injured workers groups. The web site provides a history of the alliance, postings for current projects, and resources for those seeking aid.

www.ciwa.ca

Emergency Preparedness Canada

This government agency, a sub-unit of the Department of National Defence, provides emergency preparedness resources for individuals, companies, and agencies at various levels of government. The goal of the agency is to ensure that emergency preparedness efforts are coordinated based on the Emergency Preparedness Act.

www.epc-pcc.gc.ca/

Firehall

This web site is dedicated to Canadian fire departments and fire fighters.

www.firehall.com

Sexscape.org

Available seven days a week, from 7:00 p.m. until 8:00 a.m. eastern time, Sexscape.org provides objective and entertaining info about all aspects of sexuality. Check the web site for further details that may not be printed here.

www.sexscape.org

REPRODUCTIVE HEALTH — BIRTH CONTROL

Woman's Guide to Contraception and Responsible Sex

A no-nonsense guide to resources about contraception and safer sex.

www.epigee.org/guide/

SLEEP AND DREAMS

Sleep/Wake Disorders Canada

Most of us can take sleep and wakefulness for granted, but for those who suffer from conditions affecting these fundamental states, there's SWDC, a national voluntary oganization "dedicated to helping people suffering from sleep/wake disorders by distributing information, encouraging research, establishing self-help groups, and acting as an advocate when necessary."

www.geocities.com/HotSprings/1837

SPECIAL NEEDS

The Council for Exceptional Children

"The Council for Exceptional Children (CEC) is the largest international professional organization dedicated to improving educational outcomes for individuals with exceptionalities, students with disabilities, and/or the gifted. CEC advocates for appropriate governmental policies, sets professional standards, provides continual professional development, advocates for newly and historically underserved individuals with exceptionalities, and helps professionals obtain conditions and resources necessary for effective professional practice." 'Nuff said.

www.cec.sped.org/

Lifestyle & Home

ACTIVISM

Canadian Coalition Against the Death Penalty

With the death penalty long since abolished in this country, this group focuses its attention abroad, particularly on what they call the U.S. "injustice system." For example, this organization is involved in a tourist boycott of Texas. The web site also provides information on death row inmates who have requested penpals.

members.tripod.com/~ccadp/homepage.htm

Council for a Tobacco-Free Ontario

Smokers will want to avoid this web page dedicated to the elimination of all tobacco use in Ontario. Contact this organization for info on the chapter in your area at this web site.

www.opc.on.ca/ctfo

Netaid

A fifth of the world's population survive on $1 a day. More than 50 million people have been forcibly displaced from their homes. Seven million children die each year because the poorest countries spend more money on debt than on health or education. That's the bad news.

The good news is that there is an organization like Netaid.org—a "unique effort to use the power of the Internet to create unprecedented economies of scale and connect effective problem-solvers with real resources." Visit the site to see what you can do to help.

www.netaid.org

Safe-Lane

Read up on the efforts by Canada and the international community to address the problem of landmines. Find out what you can do to help in this global humanitarian crisis. The late Princess Di put her weight behind this cause, and the site has a dedication page to her.

www.mines.gc.ca

Lifestyle & Home

AGE GROUPS

GoKewl

A cool site for youth. Includes features, culture, chat, and interactive polls to get the teen take on breaking news items.

www.gokewl.com

Gurl

Check out this lively zine for young girls, with tons of features, gossip, content, free web pages, and giveaways (like soccer gear!). Comes in pretty colours too. Or try gurlnet.com, which brings together content from dozens of gurl zines.

www.gurl.com

Teens Online

Looking for a cyber-pal? Here's a meeting place for teenagers that provides chat forums, free e-mail and web space, movie and music reviews, and a teen zine.

www.teens-online.com

AGRICULTURE — INDICES

Rural Living in Canada

This site acts as a compendium to Canadian non-urban web pages. Look up features on gardening, home care, wood stoves, livestock, antique sales, and much more.

tor-pw1.netcom.ca/%7Ekenruss/rural.htm

ALTERNATIVE

Hempola

You can buy hempseed oil online in a quaint decanter, and it's totally legal! You get the idea that companies that make stuff like this want to be seen as a bit outside the mainstream, however. They also flog watermelon lip balm and massage oil. Aaaah.

www.hempola.com

Ya-Hooka

"The guide to marijuana on the internet." This site aims to be a "portal"—but a portal to what? Meticulously updated news section contains stories like "Bad News: Marijuana Testing Is Coming to the NBA." Under Facts and FAQ's, they offer "How-to Instructions for bongs, joints, vaporizers and cooking, prices, laws, industrial hemp, research..." This group was reportedly quite bummed out when they heard that their first choice for a domain name—Yahoo!—had already been taken by some plucky upstart.

www.yahooka.com

BEER

Beer.com

A site for real beer lovers, complete with photos of beer bellies.

www.beer.com

Big Rock Brewery

This site for the Calgary-based micro-brewery provides fans with contests, product info, trivia games, and words of wisdom from former lawyer and company founder Ed McNally. For devoted beer lovers, there's even a section on investment information.

www.bigrockbeer.com

Canadian Beer Review

What could be a more worthwhile endeavour than the cultivation of beer knowledge? The Canadian Beer Review is a net-based publication dedicated to the discovery, promotion, enjoyment, and review of all things Canadian in beer.

www.canbeer.com

Stephen Beaumont's World of Beer

National and international stories about ales, lagers, pilsners, and stouts from "an unapologetically opinionated" point of view. So there.

worldofbeer.com

The Canadian Beer Index

Stretching from the brewpubs of the Northwest Territories to the micro-breweries of Ontario, this page allows Canadians to track down beer from any part of the country. Search for suds by province or event, and read the latest in beer news at this site.

realbeer.com/canada

BEVERAGES

Absolutly Canadian

Browse through these pictures of the famous Absolut vodka ads with Canadian themes.

web2.kw.lgs.net/~absolut

Coffee Experts

Ah, sweet Java! Read about it, talk about it, and roast it yourself with help from these coffee experts from Victoria. The amphetamine quality of the text at this page would indicate that these are indeed aficionados of the mighty bean.

www.islandnet.com/coffee

iDrink

Any sod can make a G&T, but if you've always wanted to mix an Astronaut, a Buttery Nipple, or a Facist Liver Torture, here's the mixologist's dream come true: thousands of recipes at the click of a mouse.

www.idrink.com

shift

Martinis Online

It's Epicurious for people on a steady—some might say excessive—diet of liquid mirth. The site features tips and hints a-go-go, not to mention fierce arguments about the appropriate use of vermouth. It also includes a liquor cabinet recipe engine: Simply type in what you've got at home and it will spit out a tasty cocktail suggestion. Best of all, you can vote on your favourite libation: at press time, the James Bond Martini was tops, while the White, White Russian held up the rear.

www.martinisonline.com

Vintages

Browse the exceptional selection of wines and spirits at this site brought to you by the LCBO. Then take a look at the catalogue filled with unique and delicious items from around the world. Just don't tell your liver!

www.vintages.com

Wired Java Fanatic

Techniques for making coffee, coffee FAQ's, a glossary, and information on growing and producing this most sublime of berries. Says one beanaholic: "If I were a woman, I would wear coffee as perfume."

www.nwlink.com/~donclark/java.html

CANADIAN STUDIES

Canada Rocks the World

Still not tired of all the tirades about why Canada is such a great country? Then stop by the "That's Canadian?" section of this web site and prepare to burst with national pride. Wow, a Canadian invented the paint roller!

www.geocities.com/SouthBeach/1708/Canada_eh.html

Canadians Among Us

Read biographies on some of the more popular Canadian actors, featuring such thespians as Mike Myers, Pamela Anderson, and Phil Hartman.

moviething.com/bios/canadians/index.html

Conversation Canada

Intergovernmental Affairs has created this web site with the hopes that it will be a place where people come to find out about Canada—learn about our history, browse the Constitution, explore Canadian symbols, or look up information in the bibliography.

198.103.111.55/aia

Symbols of Canada

Feeling insecure about national identity as only Canadians can? Maybe a reminder of our national symbols like the flag, anthem, maple leaf, and beaver is the answer to your angst.

canada.gc.ca/canadiana/symb_e.html

CHILDREN

Baby Name Locator

Having trouble choosing a name for the new addition to your family? This site has a database of over 29 000 names for you to search through. The database provides different spellings and a short description of the name's origin. Visitors can also check to see the most popular names for each decade. The most popular names for the 1990's? Michael and Jessica.

www.homepagers.com/names/index.html

Bigbot.com

This site's dedicated to Transformers, the macho kids' robot toy (robots in disguise, if you want to get technical), and their contemporary counterparts, Beasties. Head here for sounds, icons, screen savers, and cheat codes. Someone forgot to tell us, but these robots must also be some kind of computer game.

www.bigbot.com

Boys and Girls Clubs of Canada

Get your children involved in a local Boys and Girls Club to help promote physical fitness, community values, and learning skills through group activities.

www.bgccan.com

Canadian 4-H Council

A youth organization formed in Manitoba, 4-H is now a Canada-wide council focusing on developing well-rounded, responsible, independent citizens. Some features included on the site are club projects, membership stats, a club history, a trivia quiz, club resources, and a sharing centre.

www.4-H-Canada.ca

Canadian Kids Home Page

Parents will appreciate this collection of links to sites with appropriate children's content. Visitors can browse through a regularly updated list of new sites or search a database of web pages by subject.

www.onramp.ca/~lowens

cbc4Kids

Does this sound familiar: "Mom ... I'm boooored." Try parking them in front of this site, with its sections on time (the past and the future), jokes, the worst songs ever, tongue twisters, science, cute pets, and space. Then put up your feet, curl up with a novel or a cup of tea, and enjoy it while it lasts.

www.cbc4kids.ca

EcoKids Online

Kids can explore the clubhouse at this site for a seemingly endless supply of games and activities designed to educate them about the environment and wildlife. Sponsored by the Friends of the Environment Foundation, EcoKids Online also provides accompanying materials for parents and teachers.

ecokids.earthday.ca

OWL Kids Online

Here's a site from the publishers of *Owl*, *Chickadee*, and *Chirp*, magazines for kids about nature. Send the little ones here to meet the Might Mites (or suggest an adventure for them), try the puzzles, and check out the knock-knock jokes.

www.owl.on.ca

Rebecca's Toad Hall

By Jove! What a toady little site you've found! Read stories, look at pictures, visit the animals in the stables, or follow Mr. Toad's favourite links. Tally ho!

www.thetoadhall.com

Today's Parent

Since kids don't come with an instruction manual, try this site for articles on caring for them, or post your questions via e-mail to be answered by experts.

www.todaysparent.com

CITIZENSHIP

Citizenship and Immigration Canada

Come one come all! Looking to start a new life in a country with one of the highest standards of living in the world? Visit this web site for all the information you need to find out what it takes to become a Canadian citizen.

cicnet.ci.gc.ca

CYBERCULTURE

ArtByte

Now that *Shift Magazine* is becoming popular state-side, the emergence of its clones has begun. Check out this New York-based mag that claims to be a guide for "living in digital culture." Where have I heard that before?

www.artbyte.com

CTHEORY

CTHEORY is an international journal of theory, technology, and culture. Articles, interviews, and key book reviews in contemporary discourse are published weekly, along with theorizations of major "event-scenes" in the mediascape.

ctheory.aec.at

shift

Geek Culture

A lifestyle site dedicated to those not known for having lives, Geek Culture is a funny, fine-looking celebration of all things geeky. To wit: there are comix; regular issues of Mind-Numbing Magazine; frontline testimonies from geeks-for-hire who work as corporate cogs; and geek TV, which features cute, quick-loading animation. There's even a geek-love chat group, which is not as implausible as you might think, given the impressive on-site contributions of girl geeks.

www.geekculture.com

iToke

Just another pot pipe dream or the beginnings of legalized weed? Either way, it'll be interesting to see how this site plays out.

itoke.co.uk

She Bytes!

A grrrly slant on the latest in new media and digital culture, She Bytes! covers everything from IT executives to home design. A tech-savvy Martha Stewart.

www.shebytesmag.com

shift

Urban Legends Reference Pages

A few hours here will make your leg pretty much pull-proof. No longer will your acquaintances flim-flam you with tales of cyanide-laced ATM envelopes and LSD-coated public telephones. Some stories in the archive, which features sections like "Toxin du Jour" and "Cokestore," trace the lineage of the tall tales. All legends are thoroughly examined and debunked, if untrue. Then there are the ones that are true ...

www.snopes.com

DISABILITIES — BLINDNESS

Canadian National Institute for the Blind

A comprehensive resource for those with blind family members, friends, or co-workers, the CNIB web site provides info on Braille resources, events such as white cane week, and a host of other programs for those who have lost their sight.

www.cnib.ca

DISABILITIES — DEAFNESS

Canadian Hearing Society

The Canadian Hearing Society provides services that enhance the independence of deaf, deafened, and hard-of-hearing people, and encourage prevention of hearing loss. Check for regularly updated news features, job opportunities, technical devices, and more.

www.chs.ca

DISABILITIES — ORGANIZATIONS

Ability Online Support Network

This charitable organization connects children with disabilities and chronic illnesses to disabled and nondisabled peers and mentors. What started as a small computer club of just four teens has grown into an expansive network that provides support and up-to-date medical information for disabled kids and their families. This site includes information on connecting to the network and links to healthcare sites.

www.ablelink.org

Association for the Neurologically Disabled of Canada

AND Canada is a charitable organization providing functional rehab programs to individuals with nonprogressive neurological disabilities. The association's web site discusses the different disabilities it provides treatment for, supplies extensive contact information, and offers tips for concerned parents.

www.and.ca

Canadian Abilities Foundation

Ranking people as their most valuable resource, the Canadian Abilities Foundation provides connections to support for families and children with disabilities. Look up available products and services, read the Abilities Magazine, or browse the EnableLink section for online resources.

www.enablelink.org

Canadian Wheelchair Basketball Association

Head here for information in English or French on women's and men's teams, a calendar of events, news items, a directory of members, merchandise, various links in Canada and around the world, and lots more.

www.cwba.ca

CAPS—Canadian Association for People Who Stutter

The objective of the CAPS web site is to provide people who stutter, their family and friends, speech-language pathologists, academics, students, and members of the general public with info on stuttering resources available both in and outside Canada.

webcon.net/~caps

Council of Canadians with Disabilities

The CCD works to provide a voice to influence government policy and legislation concerning disabled Canadians. Find out more about the council's initiatives in areas such as equality and consumer control at this site.

www.pcs.mb.ca/~ccd/

Rick Hansen Institute

This institute within the University of British Columbia is dedicated to finding a cure for paralysis and improving the quality of life for people with spinal cord injuries. Read up on the institute's work, find out about the Canadian Wheelchair Basketball Association, and take a look at the maps and itineraries of Hansen's "Man in Motion" world tour.

www.rickhansen.ubc.ca

Special Needs Education Network

This site provides resources for parents, teachers, schools, and other organizations involved in the education of students with special needs.

www.schoolnet.ca/sne

War Amps

Here you can learn about the history of the organization founded after WWI to provide services for amputees and their families. The War Amps are still going strong with their key tag promotion and more.

www.waramps.ca

EDUCATION — FINANCIAL AID

Canada Student Loans Program

The Canada Student Loans web site provides loan-assessment software, updated news on loan program developments, and links to provincial student loan agencies.

www.hrdc-drhc.gc.ca/student_loans

Canada-US Fulbright Program

The Fulbright Program facilitates exchanges between Canadian and U.S. graduate students and faculty members. Read up on the structure and history of the program or check out award info and funding at this site.

www.usembassycanada.gov/fulbrigh.htm

Studentawards.com

This site provides free access to a database of thousands of scholarships available to Canadian post-secondary students and helps match you with appropriate awards, bursaries, grants, and fellowships. As student debt piles up, tools like this one become indispensable.

www.studentawards.com

shift

The Motley Fool

Getting solid financial advice online is nearly impossible unless you sign on with The Motley Fool and learn to manage your money. Bonus: The site includes a weekly radio show that is (we hope) the only place you'll ever hear John Tesh discuss his financial management strategies.

www.fool.com

FAMILIES

Canadian Adoptees Registry and Classifieds

Created by a birth mother who was reunited with her daughter, the Canadian Adoptees Registry is a starting point for those looking for adopted family members or birth parents. This site provides an online registry and links to other searching pages and government agencies.

www.bconnex.net/~rickm/indes.html

Canadian Parents Online

Get the latest parenting news at this online weekly. There are sections for shopping, community news, and frequently asked questions by age group, as well as seasonal topics such as "Kids and Summer."

www.canadianparents.com

Child and Family Canada

Parents can browse the information at this site by themes ranging from media influence and literacy to nutrition and physical activity.

www.cfc.efc.ca

Family and Children's Resources

Tons o' links to sites and mailing lists about parenting. Plain-looking site that lacks focus (a Toys "R" Us link?), but a useful listing nonetheless.

www.ok.bc.ca/TEN/family/family.html

Lesbian Mothers Support Society

Though new family units are slowly gaining acceptance in Canada, there is still the need for a support network for parents who are not heterosexual couples. Empower yourself with the reference library of books, files of articles and essays, and a collection of videos available for access at this site.

www.lesbian.org/lesbian-moms

No Kidding!

A social club for singles and couples, who, for whatever reason, have not had kids. Includes links to various chapters across North America.

www.nokidding.bc.ca

FOOD

3000 Recipes from Innkeepers

Get the inside scoop with gourmet recipes from the kitchens of some of the finest inns across Canada and the United States.

www.virtualcities.com/~virtual/ons/recipe.htm

4Vegetarians

Are you a vegetarian or vegan? Here's a terrific guide. This site, part of the 4anything.com network, offers resources aplenty, covering healthy eating, veggie kids, ethical shopping, "macromania," and "fruitarianism." Is there anything those 4anything people don't know?

4vegetarians.com

Buffalo Meat

Tired of boring old beefsteak day-in, day-out? Then experience the great taste of Canadian bison! Sample a boneless square chuck cut, a shoulder clod roast, or bison barbecue ribs at the B&E Ranch's web site.

www.ncbison.com

Canadian Egg Marketing Agency

Here's an eggsciting look at the Canadian egg industry! Look up news, recipes, children's activities, and educational info at this web site. Visitors will be dispensed such pearls of wisdom as "eggs are good for you" and "Canadians love their eggs."

www.canadaegg.ca

Canadian Federation of Chefs and Cooks

This web site provides useful education, employment, and consulting resources for the culinary aficionado. Everything from business cards to cooking competitions is covered at this page for Canadian chefs and cooks.

www.cfcc.ca

Cooking.com

A slick, contemporary site with little pizzazz. Nonetheless, quite popular. There are three areas: recipes, shopping, and cook's tips. The site opens on shopping. Clever.

www.cooking.com

EarthSave Canada

Learn about the environmental consequences of your daily food choices at this web site. This organization advocates a move to plant-based diets for better health, environmental sustainability, and compassion towards non-human animals.

www.earthsave.bc.ca

shift

Epicurious Food

Hungry? Conde Nast's venerable megasite can help you with everything from a case of the munchies to planning a ten-course meal. The site features information on countless world cuisines, vegetarian cooking, and how to select seasonal procduce. Double bonus: You can search according to ingredient and access food and drink dictionaries.

food.epicurious.com

Fear Itself

A tribute to spicy food. Check it out for recipes, links, and more.

www.fearitself.com

Filmworks Catering

If you're sitting in front of your computer with a coffee and a few crumbs from yesterday's muffin, probably the last thing you need to see are photos of the hoagies, pizzas, salads, blueberry waffles, melons, and vegetarian back bacon that the actors, directors, and other spoiled brats in the film industry have served up to them while they're working. This is a company that boasts the "most talented chefs in showbiz." The small number of hits at the site may be an indication that we're too busy eating to read about the chefs.

www.filmworks.ab.ca

Food Beverage Canada

This industry association site provides a newsletter, info about trade shows, and the usual fare.

www.foodbeveragecanada.com

Food in Canada

A magazine of insider news and new technology for the food and beverage industry. The online version contains items ranging from updates on the ill effects of genetically modified foods to the possibility of a global beer brand.

www.foodincanada.com

Foodfare

Canada's first internet grocer, they say. Serves the greater Winnipeg area.

www.foodfare.com

FoodTV

Kick your life up a couple of notches! The main draw to this site must be Emeril Lagasse's recipes for dishes such as Monster Bam Steaks, Chili-marinated Double-Cut Pork Chops, Chicago-style Italian Sausage, and Pepper Deep Dish Pizza. Why? Because pork fat rules, baby! This culinary wunderkind with the New York accent (and based in New Orleans) mixes and matches cultures and flavours with ease, one day offering a clever mix called "Creole vs. Acadiana"; the next, a Blues Brunch; and the day after that, inviting you into the Vegetable Patch for dishes such as Grilled Tomato Risotto with Roasted Portobello Mushrooms and Pan Crispy with Fresh Fava Bean and Mushroom Ragout. For the biggest munch-fest of the year, the Super Bowl, sports fans will want to tune in to be schooled in the preparation of ribs suitable for Fred Flintstone-sized appetites. We'd be remiss if we didn't mention that all the other shows and recipes are featured here, as well. They don't archive old recipes, so the best way to go about it is (1) watch show, (2) get hungry, (3) come to web site for recipe, (4) give recipe to someone who can cook, and finally (5) enjoy!

www.foodtv.com

Home Canning Online

Learn how you can enjoy seasonal fruits and vegetables year round with the help of this online magazine. Beginners and experienced canners will be interested in the selection of recipes and home canning tips available at this site.

www.homecanning.com

John's Vegetarian Recipes

A hearty listing of recipes for practising vegetarians or those interested in trying a few dishes. The site conveniently divides recipes into categories such as main dishes, sauces, or spreads, and even provides tips on cooking techniques. Available in English, Spanish, French, and German.

www.interlog.com/~john13/recipes

Maple Syrup

Everything you wanted to know about maple syrup but were afraid to ask is at your fingertips thanks to this site by the Ontario Maple Syrup Industry. Read the history of Canada's coveted elixir or, heck, why not find out how to tap the trees in your own backyard!

www.gov.on.ca/OMAFRA/english/crops/facts/maple.htm

Messy Gourmet

Here's a site for those who like cooking, but not cleaning up. Learn how to make a Hindenburg souffle or hammer and pickle soup, and find out the secret to keeping your recipe clippings stain-free. The Messy Gourmet puts the fun back in cooking.

www.messygourmet.com

Out of the Frying Pan

The queens of cuisine at Out of the Frying Pan serve up a great collection of recipes for those who are tired of eating like students. Get tips on how to grow your own spices, find out about affordable wines and champagnes, and check out the section devoted to new and unusual cocktails.

www.outofthefryingpan.com

Porridge People

"Vegan recipes for every day." Don't worry, you don't have to eat porridge every day; it should be noted, however, that if you got too far from a reliable source of nuts and tofu, you'd be in a real pickle.

www.geocities.com/HotSprings/Sauna/7015

Poutine or What Quebec Does to French Fries

Experiments into unknown realms of French fry cuisine with many poutine links!

www.tx7.com/fries/docs/poutine.html

Savoir Faire

Invite Nik Manojlovich into your home to add a touch of panache to your cooking, entertaining, and home decorating. Look up recipes and tips by keyword or find out when the next broadcast of the *Savoir Faire* television show will be.

www.savoirfaire.ca

The Internet Chef

Welcome to the site for recipes, recipes, and more recipes, courtesy of the Internet Chef. Visitors will find a culinary cavalcade of cooking tips, wine reviews, and online chats for kitchen-related topics.

www.ichef.com

The Monks' Cookbook

Friar Bob takes you to the fryer for recipes such as pumpkin soup and chicken pesto. Peppered with helpful tips and suggestions, these recipes will make you want to thank the almighty for the joy of food.

www.cam.org/~bobrob/monkcook.html

The Peach Tree Network

Browse through online grocery shopping, read up on exotic foods, or participate in a forum for cooking tips and recipes.

www.peachtree.ca

The Recipe Folder

Thank goodness for graduate student procrastination. This is a carefully edited collection of recipes available online—lots of contemporary favourites (baba ghanoush) to go with the old faves (pies and cakes). Let's hope this student received extra credit for an extracurricular job well done.

www.eserver.org/recipes/

Vegetarian Pages

This site intends to be the most definitive internet resource for vegetarians and vegans. Head here for FAQ's, nutrition information, recipes, a list of famous vegetarians (Plato and Michael Bolton together at last), worldwide events, and a directory of restaurants and organizations around the planet.

www.veg.org

FOOD — RESTAURANTS

Canadian Restaurant and Entertainment Network

Look up restaurant and entertainment listings for most major cities across Canada at this site.

webcom.net/~real/rest-tor/canada.html

Restaurant.ca

This site provides eatery listings for Edmonton, Toronto, Halifax, Quebec, Ottawa, Calgary, Montreal, and Vancouver that are searchable by area, price, cuisine, and features (like "open late" "B.Y.O.W." or "wheelchair accessible").

www.restaurant.ca

GENDER

Celebrating Women's Achievements

Each year the National Library celebrates Women's History Month in Canada by honouring the contributions of Canadian women in developing Canada. Read up on present and past years' articles dating back to 1995.

www.nlc-bnc.ca/digiproj/women/ewomen.htm

Cool Women

Read eye-opening tales of cool women from Canada's past and present at this web site's cafe section, or look up profiles in the archives. Post messages to the bulletin board, join the chat room, or send Fe/Mail at this site for Canada's coolest ladies.

www.coolwomen.org

Feminism.com

A clunky site, ill-suited to conveying the aspirations of its founders. Which just goes to show, the revolution will be televised, and it will most definitely need a good webmistress.

www.feminsim.com

Gender Reassignment Surgery in Montreal

These surgeons perform so-called gender reassignment surgery. The site tries to make their institute as attractive as possible to prospective clients, in part with nice photos of Montreal, and in part with a wealth of relevant information. They also adhere to a "Total Quality Concept," meaning that they book your hotel for you and everything.

www.grsmontreal.com

Herstory: An Exhibition

A major feminist project has been archived online with federal government assistance through Canada's Digital Collections initiative.

library.usask.ca/herstory

She's Got the Beat

Here's a lively look at women's roles in the music industry. Fun and personal but with serious subject matter, too. Covers discrimination against female roadies, sound engineers, musicians, etc. Hosted by an energetic woman going under the pseudonym Tammy Whynott.

www.geocities.com/Nashville/4479/lafemme.html

Status of Women Canada

This federal government agency was established to promote gender equality and full participation of women in the economic, social, cultural, and political life of the country.

www.swc-cfc.gc.ca/direct.html

The Field Guide to North American Males

Think of it as a Hinterland Who's Who for women to understand male behaviour—like why they play air guitar. This site offers handy descriptions of over 50 species of boys, along with descriptions of the their plumage, mating calls, sexual and antagonistic displays, courtship rituals, and habitats.

www.fieldguide.com

Wired Woman

A site "where women can learn and share ideas about new media technology in a comfortable and dynamic space." Check out the columns on careers and education, arts and entertainment, and technology—plus changing features of interest to women in the Information Age.

www.wiredwoman.com

Women in Technology International

Resources for women who focus on technology in their careers. "WITI's goal is to empower its constituents by providing access to people and content which are significantly relevant to the issues faced by women in technology." Written by engineers?

www.witi.org

Women's Net

Terrific site that's definitely for grown-ups. Supported by and supporting women's organizations around the world, this page offers a riveting selection of international news updates, features, and academic articles. Recent features include "Lesbian Marriage: Radical or Conformist?"; a heads-up on about the marginalization of women who work flexible schedules due to family demands; a report on electronic networking strategies initially proposed at a 1995 UN conference on the status of women; and a report on some feminists' opposition to 3Com's titillating advertising campaign for its PalmPilot hand-held computer.

www.igc.org/igc/womensnet/

women.com

This women's mega-portal is a bit commercial, but it's very comprehensive—kind of like *Cosmo*, *Business Week*, Sympatico, and Amazon.com all rolled into one.

www.women.com

GENDER — MEN

The Best Man

Many men are thrown into a panic when chosen as the best man for a friend's wedding. This site teaches all the basics of the job using a slick and well-designed interface.

www.thebestman.com

HOLIDAYS

Ceremonial and Canadian Symbols Promotion

Perhaps it's our cynicism about patriotism that makes Canada the greatest country on the face of the earth. Here's the government's propaganda site devoted to Canadian boosterism. You'll find stuff on Canada Day and other holidays and anniversaries, ceremonies and protocol, the monarchy, the Governor-General, and a bunch of quintessentially Canuck symbols like the beaver, the maple leaf, the flag, and the anthem. However, there's no sign of the hockey fight, the mosquito, the stubby, or the donut shop.

www.pch.gc.ca/ceremonial-symb

Sargeant Willie's Halloween Safety Tips for Young People

Before you send the little goblins out on the town, sit them down in front of this site prepared by the Winnipeg Police Department.

www.city.wiinipeg.mb.ca/police/youths/halltips.html

Spirit of the North

The web site for cottagers who don't own cottages! Spirit of the North is Canada's largest cottage rental directory. List your cottage if it's available for rent or browse rental listings by province.

www.spiritofthenorth.com

Valentine's Day Collection

How do I love thee? Let me crunch the numbers ... If you're romantically challenged, check out this site for Valentine's Day crafts, recipes, the history of the day, and tips for keeping roses fresh. You'll also find links that let you send your sweetie an online postcard or even help you compose love letters.

www.ok.bc.ca/TEN/valentine/valentine.html

Wiarton Willie

The site that lets you speak to the little critter beyond the grave! He's apparently still predicting the arrival of spring and receiving e-mail, no less. Not bad for an ex-groundhog. His web site is distinguished by adorable animations and amusing squeaks. Ah, Willie, a nation mourns its loss.

www.wiarton-willie.org

HOME & GARDEN

Benjamin Moore

This attractive site is more than a paint store. It has information for contractors, architects, homeowners, and designers—and it also includes a paint calculator and environmental info. Sure, they're biased, but as these things go, the Moore site is informative, easy on the eyes, and a good resource for anyone who needs to paint.

www.benjaminmoore.com

Better Homes and Gardens Online

From kitchen storage to decorative painting, this major publication can help you do it all for your home, without any help from Martha Stewart.

www.bhglive.com/househome/index.html

Feng Shui Ultimate Resource

Have you identified the prosperity corner of your home where the money energy resides? Standing somewhere between genuine Chinese wisdom and New Age malarkey, Feng Shui may help you grasp the workings of the energies of your living space and garden. And a visit to this site should help you save the hefty F.S. consultant fees.

www.qi-whiz.com

Geomancy.net

The source for Feng Shui research. If you're interested in this decorating philosophy, this site has it all, including customized design to help you access your destiny in your home or office.

www.3dglobe.com/fs/index.html

Home Tips

Itching to know what makes your septic tank tick? Author and host of TV's *The Fix* Don Vandervort offers advice on this and many more topics like mulching mowers, gas heaters, and fibreglass doors. You'll find advice on buying fixtures and other necessities for the home and a section devoted to "dang good ideas."

www.hometips.com

Housenet

Slick site offering loads of stuff on home improvement, decorating, lawns and gardens, sewing ideas, shopping, cooking, car care, and more. Features include a project of the week and a tip of the day.

www.housenet.com

ImproveNet

This company has a database of 600 000 prescreened contractors, designers, and architects for those wanting to make home improvements. A "vertical portal" par excellence.

www.improvenet.com

Natural Handyman

Bushels of home repair info presented with encouragement and humour. If you've spent too much time struggling with "widgets and thingamabobs," go to this site and share the wisdom of this expert putterer, and soon you'll be a Jack—or a Jill—of—all-trades too. The site is also compiling a directory of handypeople—get your contact info in fast.

www.naturalhandyman.com

HOME & GARDEN — GARDENING

Canadian Gardening Magazine

The web site for this popular magazine provides a bounty of gardening tips, seed catalogues, discussion groups, and sites of the week. Links are divided into sections for kids, garden plans, plant finders, and a map of different Canadian geographic zones.

www.canadiangardening.com

Canadian Orchid Congress

With over 20 member organizations, the COC's stated purpose is "to improve the relationship among orchid societies in Canada by meetings devoted to the advancement of knowledge and appreciation of orchids in Canada." The turn of the millennium surely represents an historic opportunity for peace among the fragmented and factionalized orchidophile community. The site contains a list of upcoming shows, vendor information, and tips on growing these undeniably attractive flowers.

www.chebucto.ns.ca/Recreation/OrchidSNS/coc.html

Canadian Rose Society

Tour this site's listings for flower shows, "rosy" links, rose planting tips, recommended roses for Canadian climates, and much more.

www.mirror.org/groups/crs/CdnRoseSoc.html

City Farmer's Urban Agricultural Notes

City Farmer is a valuable resource for those involved in any form of urban agriculture. The site tackles subjects from rooftop gardens, to composting toilets, to air pollution and community development. Read the informative articles or follow a list of related links.

www.cityfarmer.org

Cultivating Canadian Gardens

This online exhibition assembled by the National Library in Ottawa is subtitled "The History of Gardening in Canada." Enriched with illustrations from items in the library's holdings, today's green-thumbed Canadians can enrich their understanding of a long tradition.

www.nlc-bnc.ca/eents/garden

Debbie's Garden Tour

Visit this friendly site for photos of real people's North American gardens. Not up there with the major gardening sites, though.

www.total.net/~pcarrier/gardtour.html

Garden Centre

This friendly and attractive resource offers gardening tips, a landscaping guide, seasonal information, contests, trivia, and a children's area.

www.familygardening.com

GardenCrazy.com

This is supposed to be "the most complete garden centre online," so whip out your trowels and dig up some horticultural information at this web site. There are free seeds, daily tips, weekly articles, and much more.

www.gardencrazy.com

I Can Garden

Looking for cool-weather greenhouse tips or new ways to control dandelions? Then get your hands dirty at this web site that claims to be "the Canadian internet gardening resource." How can you resist a column by garden weasel Art Drysdale?

www.icangarden.com

Jardins de l'Oubli Daylily Garden

There's an online photographic tour available of this private garden of more than 400 cultivators located in Ste. Foy, Quebec.

www.geocities.com/RainForest/Vines/7809

Seeds of Diversity Canada

Did you know there are 37 varieties of eggplant? Two hundred seventy-five varieties of beans? Six hundred seventy-five varieties of tomatoes? Think of the salad! Seeds of Diversity, a "living gene bank," is a group of gardeners from across the country who preserve and exchange rare plant seeds.

www.seeds.ca

HORTICULTURE

Calgary Horticultural Society

Find out everything you need to know about Calgary's unique climate and growing conditions. The web page for the Calgary Horticultural Society (the largest gardening group in Canada) also provides gardening tips and postings for upcoming gardening events.

www.calhort.org

Lifestyle & Home

HOUSING

Appraisal Institute of Canada

With over 5000 members across the country, the AIC is dedicated to serving the public interest by continually advancing high standards for the real estate appraisal profession. Browse a list of public services, check info for students and new candidates, or peruse the appraisal digest.

www.alcanada.com

Cadillac Fairview Corporation

With a collection of high-profile clientele and a portfolio that includes Vancouver's Pacific Centre and Toronto's Eaton Centre, this company may not appeal to the average web-surfer. Billionaire corporations may feel free to browse the Corporations Available service, though, while the rest of us can ogle the accrued wealth.

www.cadillacfairview.com

Canada Lands Company Ltd.

The CLC has the task of governing the development, improvement, and sale of surplus crown land. Check out the listings for available properties in each province or read up on the company's current news and activities.

www.clc.ca

Canada Mortgage and Housing Corporation

Working to provide a competitive mortgage system and maintaining excellence in Canadian housing, the CMHC has created this web site to disseminate info to the public. The site provides recent housing news, advice on buying a home, housing market info, and much more.

www.cmhc-schl.gc.ca

Canada-wide City and County Real Estate Search

Take advantage of this free service that can find a new home for you in any part of the country. Just fill out the specs for the area you are interested in, and wait for the e-mails to arrive.

web.onramp.ca/jpearcy

Movers.ca

If you are moving anywhere in Canada, Movers.ca will give you a free estimate on how much it will cost. Use the interactive space and weight calculator to get an idea of how many kilograms your shipment is going to weigh, and get the estimate based on the weight of your belongings.

www.movers.ca

Multiple Listing Service Online

Maintained by the Canadian Real Estate Association, this site provides access to real estate listings nationwide.

www.mils.ca/mils/home.asp

PM Online

Here's a digital media company that provides info on supplies and services to the property management industry.

www.pm-online.com

Real Estate Institute of Canada

A nonprofit organization for the education and certification of real estate professionals. Search a members directory, get info on courses and seminars, or read the events section and newsletter.

www.reic.ca

Rent Canada

Providing good coverage across the country, this site maintains classifieds for mostly upper-end rental properties handled by various property management firms. For corporate space as well as housing.

www.rentcanada.com

LESBIAN, GAY & BISEXUAL

bi.org

Persons who identify themselves as bisexual are often viewed with suspicion from both sides of the proverbial swinging door. Seen as perverts by the straight world, and as traitors to the cause by many in the gay world, bisexuals need a site like this, an online resource "serving the world's bisexual community." A comprehensive listing of home pages and world links, including newsgroups, mailing lists, organizations, and a "City Bi City guide."

www.bi.org

Canadian Chapters of Parents and Friends of Lesbians and Gays

PFLAG is a support group of friends and family members of persons who have just "come out" as being gay, lesbian, or bisexual. This directory lists the group's local chapters across the country.

www.cglbrd.com/categories/pflag.htm

Equality for Gays and Lesbians Everywhere

An advocacy site for this gay rights organization.

www.islandnet.com/~egale

Gay and Lesbian and Bisexual Vancouver Online

This site makes the top of Excite's listing of Vancouver "Specialty Sites." Attractive, newsy site with a dash of humour. A Vancouver webcam is one thing, but the webmaster webcam? A personal look at a thankless task.

www.gayvancouver.bc.ca/

Gay and Lesbian Youth

Nice source of basic info for gay and lesbian youth, including issues of coming out, discrimination, and the use of the word "queer."

www.campuslife.utoronto.ca/services/sec/big.html

GayCanada.com

GayCanada is the largest and most comprehensive source of Canadian gay, lesbian, and bisexual information on the net. If you're travelling to different areas or just a visitor to this great country and want some info about GLB resources, then this is the site for you!

www.cglbrd.com

Groovy Annie's

Online resource for Canadian lesbians. Includes chat-forums and heaps of links. Groovy, Annie!

www.groovyannies.com

Singing Out!

This web site for a Toronto lesbian and gay chorus features schedule info and pictures from past events.

www.interlog.com/~singout

The Canadian Lesbian and Gay Archives

These archives, created to preserve the history of the lesbian and gay community, contain a selection of archival holdings and library collections. Visitors to this site can search through the records, photographs, monographs, periodicals, and artworks. Those interested are also encouraged to contribute any historically relevant items of their own.

www.web.net/archives

Xtra

The online complement to the newsprint publication that has editions in Toronto, Vancouver, and Ottawa. Xtra offers gays and lesbians "mass media in which to express their sexuality, share information, debate ideas, and advocate actions."

www.xtra.ca

NUDISM

Federation of Canadian Naturists

This group advocates the practice of exposing one's sagging flesh to one's fellow human beings, not for erotic reasons, but because being naked is "natural." As they put it, naturism "embodies freedom, and a unique sense of communion with nature in the purest form." Word has it these people may also be responsible for the infrequently painted houses and poorly edged lawns your Uncle Phil is always ranting about. And they never sweep their sidewalks.

www.fcn.ca

PETS

Adopt-a-Greyhound of Central Canada

Adopt-a-Greyhound is a nonprofit organization dedicated to finding homes for retired racing greyhounds. This site provides answers to commonly asked questions about greyhounds, and supplies info on the adoption process. Though this particular chapter is located in central Ontario, there are links to other greyhound adoption groups in Nova Scotia and southern Ontario.

www.geocities.com/Heartland/Plains/8834

Bow Wow Meow

Stumped on what to name your cat? Don't want to name your dog Spot or Rover? Click on over to BowWow Meow and access their free database of pet names with personality. How about beverage-related names like Chablis, Pepsi, or Kahlua?

www.bowwow.com.au

Boxer Club of Canada

Not a pugilist's home page, but a web site dedicated to the owners and breeders of the Boxer breed of dog. Check upcoming events, read the BCC newsletter, or investigate breed standards at this site.

www.netrover.com/~vjaeger/index.html

Canadian Breeders Directory

A good resource for dog breeders and their customers, this web site provides a database searchable by dog breed. Breeders can add their names to the directory for a nominal fee and visitors can add their favourite dog links to this page.

www.canadianbreeders.com

Canadian Cat Association

The CCA publishes *Cat Fancy*, a regular magazine on pure-bred cats and their breeders. This site provides a run-down of the association's code of ethics, as well as detailed descriptions (with great photos) of different breeds.

www.cca-afc.com

Canadian World Parrot Trust

The CWPT is a branch of the only international conservation organization devoted exclusively to the survival of parrot species in the wild. Read the "Manifesto of Aviculture" for a brief history of this bird-brained hobby.

www.canadianparrottrust.org

Cats in Canada

Feline fanatics can search this database by breed, breeder, or province to find a suitable pet. There are also informative sections for supplies, books, articles, shows, and a featured breed of the week.

www.catsincanada.com

Dogs in Canada

Dogs in Canada is a lively and comprehensive magazine for the canine fancier. Its web site now even has a cats section. Rather than housing feline info under a cat-related domain name, it can be found with the dogs. Curious.

www.dogs-in-canada.com

How to Love Your Dog

Teaches kids pet care. Plus there's cute photos of little furry fellas with names like Buddy and Cody.

Howtoloveyourdog.com

The Budgerigar and Foreign Bird Society of Canada

A well-maintained and informative resource for owners of exotic birds, the Budgerigar and Foreign Bird Society of Canada's web site includes articles, links, pictures, news, and much more.

www.geocities.com/Heartland/Plains/5470

The ErotiCat Homepage

Finally, with the launch of this site, there's "a place to congregate and celebrate the eternal and sensuous beauty of the feline form." Warning: this site contains feline frontal nudity and some rather lurid poetry. Home of the "Sexiest Cat of the Millennium" contest.

homeican.net/~otiss/

The German Shepherd Dog Club of Canada Inc.

This riotously slow web site may lead to a splinter group of left-handed German Shepherds moving their operations to a faster server. In fairness, this club has been around since 1922, so what's a five-minute wait?

juliet.albedo.net/~gsdcc/index.html

RELATIONSHIPS

Dads Can

Though we'd all like to believe that there's an innate quality in men that provides them with the resources for proper parenting, this is rarely the case. Dads Can promotes responsible and involved fathering by supporting men's personal development into fatherhood and healthy fathering patterns in society.

www.dadscan.org

Divorce Magazine

Though some might see this magazine's title as being a tad pessimistic, in a society where almost half of all marriages fail, it's simply pragmatic. Look up info on divorce-related issues of lifestyle, finances, and even (yikes!) dating.

www.divorcemag.com

eCrush

Love, lust, or just checking someone out, eCrush finds out if the feeling is mutual. Sign up and list whomever you have a crush on. If you provide their e-mail, they'll get a message inviting them to register at eCrush because *someone* likes them. If they eCrush you, it's a match. Juvenile? Perhaps, but still intriguing.

www.ecrush.com

StupidBoy

StupidBoy.com is the place for you to tell the opposite sex what it is you've wanted for all these millennia. Scope out the boards for the dish on relationships, sex, "what should I do's," and more! Submit a question to doll, the resident relationship guru, or read what she had to say to other folks in your shoes.

www.stupidboy.com

The Wedding Planner

Even those who cannot take advantage of this Ottawa site's local information will still find useful tips and ideas. Read about the "Couple of the Month," listen to the wedding march, or shop for invitations online.

www.the-wedding-planner.com

RELIGION

Ontario Consultants on Religious Tolerance

This series of essays from a neutral viewpoint describes many different faiths and belief systems (from Agnosticism to Zoroastrianism), and looks at issues associated with religion, such as abortion, suicide, and capital punishment. Other topics include religious wars, religious hatred, morality issues, and cults.

www.religioustolerance.org/ocrt_hp.htm

RELIGION — BAHÁ'Í FAITH

The Baha'i Community of Winnipeg

The Baha'i faith has been practised in Winnipeg since it was first presented in the 1930s. This web page provides information on local events in the Baha'i community, internet resources, contact info, and connections to the Baha'i Web Ring.

www.mts.net/~bahai

RELIGION — BUDDHISM

Buddhism in Canada

A comprehensive collection of Buddhist temples and centres in Canada, this database can be searched by province and city. There are also sections devoted to schools and traditions of Buddhism, special events in Toronto, and links to other Canadian Buddhist web sites.

www.interlog.com/~klima/toronto.html

RELIGION — CHRISTIANITY

Anglican Diocese of Nova Scotia

This web page, online since 1994, provides various related links, info about the diocese, postings for various youth programs, and the bishop's message.

www.chebucto.ns.ca/Religion/AnglicanChurchNS/AnglicanNS-Home.html

Anglicans Online

This page is devoted to theological discussion and encourages its visitors to start here to learn about being Anglican. You'll find numerous religious resources, including liturgy postings, links to dioceses all over the world, a chat room, and a news archive.

novascotia.anglican.org

Campus Crusade for Christ, Canada

Find out about the campaign that is taking Jesus to the world of university students. Visitors to this site can read about the crusade, look up volunteer opportunities, or take advantage of resources for spiritual growth.

www.crusade.org

New Advent

The old edition of the *Catholic Encyclopedia* is now online. The articles are dated, but it's still a valuable source of info on thousands of topics from the Catholic point of view. This page also has other important documents of the Church and links to important Catholic sites, including some with daily news stories.

www.knight.org/advent/

The Bible Magazine Internet Edition

Download the virtual version of *The Bible Magazine* with Acrobat Reader, or follow links to back issues, videos, books, and subscription info at this web site.

www.biblemagazine.com

RELIGION — ISLAM

Canadian Council of Muslim Women

This organization was established to assist Muslim Women in participating effectively in Canadian society and to promote mutual understanding between Muslim women and women of other faiths. Get contact info for the chapters across the country, or browse through the archive of the organization's newsletter.

www.ccmw.com

RELIGION — JUDAISM

B'Nai Brith Canada

Active since 1875, B'Nai Brith brings Jewish men and women together in fellowship to serve the Jewish community through combatting anti-Semitism, bigotry, and racism. The organization's web site keeps visitors informed on current initiatives, departments, volunteer services, and more.

www.bnaibrith.ca

Calgary Jewish Community Council

Find related internet resources, a calendar of events, contact info, and much more at this site.

www.jewish-calgary.com

TorahFax

Updated daily, this service founded by a Montreal rabbi is designed to give the busy professional a chance to learn some Torah in cyberspace.

www.netaxix.ca/torahfax

RELIGION — ORGANIZATIONS

Association of Americans and Canadians in Israel

The AACI is a volunteer organization that acts as an advocate for the over 50 000 North Americans living in Israel. Visit this site for resources such as the AACI Israel job net, regional and branch programming of the association, or information for prospective immigrants.

www.aaci.org.il

Canadian Council of Christian Charities

A charitable organization run mainly by volunteers, the CCCC integrates spiritual concerns of ministry with practical aspects of management. See what kind of programs and services they have to offer at this site.

www.cccc.org

Lifestyle & Home

Canadian Council of Churches

An association of Christian Churches in Canada, the CCC sponsors a number of inter-church activities and common causes. Check out the latest events at this web site.

www.web.net/~ccchurch

Canadian Friends of the International Christian Embassy, Jerusalem

This web site provides a research resource for those interested in topics related to the holocaust, the expansion of dialogue between Christian and Jewish groups, and associated Jewish causes, including wrongful treatment of Jews. Browse sections on Judeo-Christian studies, the Jerusalem Petition, and legal issues, or follow the links to related sites.

www.cdn-friends-icej.ca/index.html

Development and Peace

Links to organizations and initiatives in international development. Offers perspectives on debt relief for Third World nations.

www.devp.org

The Gateway Centre

Why is it that people interested in psychic phenomena, the afterlife, spiritualism, and the like, all have the same taste in fonts? For your information, "Spiritualism" is the "Science, Philosophy and Religion of continuous life based upon the demonstrated fact of communication, by means of mediumship, with those who live in the Spirit World." Nothing here explaining spiritualists' penchant for velvet paintings of Elvis ... maybe they help facilitate communication?

www.nucleus.com/~gateway

World Interfaith Education Association

The Canadian HQ of an international organization that works to promote understanding and respect among different religions. The site provides an intro to WIFEA, its past accomplishments, and its future goals and events.

www.connect.ab.ca/~lfahlman/wifea.htm

RELIGION — OTHER

Pagan Federation International

The Canadian branch of a group founded in Britain to counter misconceptions about Paganism. Whether you're a seeker of the Old Ways or just want some info, thia site provides links to groups across the country, relevant magazines, and academic resources.

www.ncf.carleton.ca/~cq081

Wiccan Church of Canada

Their three stated goals are to help practising Wiccans achieve harmony with the gods, to promote understanding of their beliefs among the general population, and to acquire for Wiccans the same rights enjoyed by mainstream religions. There are currently three temples in the country, located in Ottawa, Toronto, and Hamilton.

www.wcc.on.ca

SENIORS

Age of Reason

If you're over 50 and you don't want to spend the rest of your life in never-ending cyberspace, check out the Age of Reason. Explore links to major Canadian web sites, take a trip through the senior's discount mall, and try your hand at a search engine especially for the silver-haired set. Wherever you want to go today, you can get there from here.

www.ageofreason.com

Canadian Senior Citizens Information and Services Center

This site is a good starting point for senior-oriented info of various kinds. You'll find travel tips, health articles, a directory of seniors clubs and associations, and financial planning info.

www.infoseniors.com

Elderhostel

This is the site of the American headquarters of Elderhostel, the provider of low-cost educational travel for adults 55 and over. (There is a Canadian branch based in Kingston, Ontario, for which there's no web site yet, but the U.S. site offers info on vacations in Canada.) You can search their catalogue of vacations by keywords.

www.elderhostel.org

Fifty-plus.net

A popular destination site for those over 50, maintained by the Canadian Association for Retired Persons (CARP). Head here for news, travel, chat, humour, and more.

www.fifty-plus.net

QEII Geriatric Internet Resources

Features a large number of links to medical and health sites, associations, gerontology journals, Alzheimer's sites, and more.

www.geratrics.halifax.ns.ca

RetireWeb

Specializes in the financial aspects of retirement, from planning and saving to post-retirement choices. Features include annuity and RRIF calculators and info on government programs.

www.retireweb.com

Senior Link

Community-based agency promoting independance and dignity. Offering helping services from meals to "red tape" assistance.

209.237.152.31/

Seniors Computer Information Program

A project of Creative Retirement Manitoba to provide older adults with access to, and help with, computers at various locations in Manitoba. Their web site provides possibly the most comprehensive set of links of interest to Canadian seniors in categories like advocacy, health, housing, finance, legal/consumer, lifestyle, special needs, and more.

www.crm.mb.ca/scip/

SIZE ISSUES

Tall Clubs International

This organization promotes "tall awareness" and provides social activities for its members. There's an annual convention where they choose Miss Tall International, a goodwill ambassador for their organization.

www.tall.org

WINE

Canadian Wine Home Page

CANWINE was started in January 1994 to provide a forum for discussing Canadian wines. It's not a collection of wine snobs—just a friendly group interested in discussing wines made in Canada. The site also lists major wineries and stores all over the country.

www.canwine.com

Canadian Wines, Wineries and Vineyards

This site provides links to wineries and vineyards across the country, with reviews and commentary where possible.

www.vancouver-island-bc.com/canadianwines

Glen's Winey Home Page

A true oenophile, Glen keeps you updated on wine and food events in the Ottawa-Hull area, a locale with one of the highest concentrations of wine-and-cheesers in North America.

www.synapse.net/~wine

Ice Wine

Enough of European wine-makers looking down their red noses at Canadian-made wines! Revel in the beverage that is ice wine, made only with the cold climate we enjoy (?) here in the Great White North. Read a description of the process and theory of ice wine-making at this web site.

www.icewine.com

Inniskillin Wines

Though not one of the oldest wineries in the world, Inniskillin has achieved global fame for its top-rated ice wines. This web site for the Okanagan Valley-based winery provides a comprehensive listing of available vintages, as well as a history of Inniskillin and a virtual tour of the estate.

www.inniskillin.com

OPIMIAN—The Wine Society of Canada

Stop drinking for a moment and step over to the computer to check out this site for the Wine Society of Canada. Read about the latest news, reviews, and tastings, or share information with fellow lushes from across the country. All right, now back to the bottle!

www.opim.ca

Pressing Business

This site claims to be the definitive guide to wine news from southern Alberta. Lists events in Calgary, Banff, and other communities; plus there's a selection of worldwide links.

www.askaway.com/wine.htm

Vintners Quality Alliance

The VQA is an appellation of origin system, by which consumers can identify wines of Canada based on the origin of the grapes they're made from. Read about the history and high standards of the VQA at this site by Inniskillin Wines.

www.inniskillin.com/vinifera/vqa.html

Wine Route

The point of departure for an electronic tour of Ontario Wine Country. It's made up of a calendar of events, a map and explanation of the wine regions of Ontario (Niagara Peninsula, Lake Erie North Shore, and Pelee Island), and a set of links to various wineries.

www.wineroute.com

Travel & Peoples

ALBERTA

Alberta Information

Alberta Information provides a concise introduction to the province. Overviews of historical and recreational information are provided, along with links to more detailed web sites. Visitors are invited to submit digital pictures from their stay in Alberta.

www.cuug.ab.ca/VT

Alberta Prairie Rail Excursions

Take a ride on a fully functional steam train through rural Alberta. Alberta Prairie hosts many steam and diesel one-day excursions that focus on different themes throughout the year, including murder mysteries, live theatre, and wine and cheese specials. The site also includes links to other train-related sites.

www.nucleus.com/~cliffw

Alberta Prairie Rail Excursions

Take a ride on a fully functional steam train through rural Alberta. Alberta Prairie hosts many steam and diesel one-day excursions that focus on different themes throughout the year, including murder mysteries, live theatre, and wine and cheese specials. The site also includes links to other train-related sites.

www.nucleus.com/~cliffw

Alberta South Tourism Destination Region

This part of the province includes such attractions as Fort Whoop-Up and Head-Smashed-In Buffalo Jump. The site includes background and contact information for activities from golf to dinosaurs. Plot your course on a selection of maps, set your itinerary with the help of an events calendar, or order a free travel guide online.

www.albertasouth.com

Alberta Travel Information

This comprehensive travel guide provides links to cities and major attractions across the province. Read travelogues, book tours, or check out connections, including *Vue Weekly,* Edmonton's "urban voice" magazine.

www.travel-library.com/north_america/canada/alberta/index.html

Alberta World Wide Web Sites

Yahoo Canada provides an extensive list of Alberta-related links to cities, business sites, entertainment pages, travel information, and more.

www.yahoo.ca/Regional/Countries/Canada/Provinces_and_Territories/Alberta

Alberta's Heartland Tourism Destination Region

This region emcompasses prairie grasslands, as well as Rocky Mountain foothills, Edmonton, Red Deer, and Lloydminster. Much less extensive than the related site devoted to Alberta South, but still worth a look.

www.comcept.ab.ca/cantravel/heart.html

Calgary Convention and Visitors Bureau

The Calgary Convention and Vistitors Bureau web site provides tourist information and links to various local attractions and accommodations. Plus you can download free Canadian Rockies screen savers.

www.visitor.calgary.ab.ca

Calgary International Airport

Those flying in and out of Calgary will appreciate this advance tour of the local airport, which includes tourist information, an airport map, real-time flight info, and a separate "Space4Kids."

www.airport.calgary.ab.ca

City of Calgary Municipal Government

Job listings, transit information, and tourist features are among the subjects you can check out at this site for the City of Calgary. The extensive FAQ section includes everything from abandoned buildings and hot air balloons to the Calgary zoo.

www.gov.calgary.ab.ca

City of Edmonton

There's more to Edmonton than just a huge mall and a hockey team. Find out what's new and exciting in the Alberta capital at this web site brought to you by the municipal government.

www.gov.edmonton.ab.ca

Discover Alberta

Here's a flashy resource for tourists heading for the wild west. Includes an accommodation search and online booking service. Check out the live web cams, a photo gallery with a virtual postcard service, and interactive maps. A new feature is the online activity search.

www.discoveralberta.com

Eye on Banff

This web cam site takes a picture every ten minutes from the scenic heights of Sulphur Mountain in Banff, Alberta.

www.banffgondola.com/cam

Images of the Canadian Rockies

Spectacular views (without the exhausting climb and the thin air) thanks to QuickTime Virtual Reality. Link to backcountry, cycling, and environment sites.

www.frontrange.ab.ca/Media/

Remington Alberta Carriage Centre

Bring back the time of chuck wagons and Clydesdales, hansoms and horse-drawn hearses, with this online presentation, illustrated with photos of the exhibits. You'll also find background info on horse breeds and an online coupon for those who make the trip to southernmost Alberta.

www.remingtoncentre.com

See Alberta

Yet another major resource of information on Alberta communities, events, attractions, golf courses, campgrounds, accommodation, ski areas, and more. The site's photo galleries include pictures of Banff and the Badlands.

www.seealberta.com

ANTHROPOLOGY & ARCHAEOLOGY

Anthro.net

A vast collection of links to information on ancient civilizations. The What's New area includes job postings, conferences, and articles on anti-malaria drugs.

www.anthro.net

Anthropology Internet Resources

Log on to this useful site of the Western Connecticut State University. Scroll down to connect to journals on Gypsy culture or a language resource site. Or click on specific topics such as Native American or world area studies. Links provide course descriptions, newsletters, articles, and scientific databases.

www.wcsu.ctstateu.edu/socialsci/antres.html

Archaeology in Arctic North America

Here's an in-depth examination of archaeological exploration in Canada's arctic. This site not only provides you with background information on the cultures of the arctic region but, through pictures and video clips, takes you right to the sites themselves.

arts.uwaterloo.ca/ANTHRO/rwpark/ArcticArchStuff/ArcticIntro.html

Archaeology in Nova Scotia

From the Palaeo-Indians to the first permanent European settlers, the Archaeology in Nova Scotia site covers the last 11 000 years of the province's history. Peruse the sections on current archaeology sites, artifacts, underwater expeditions, and clickable maps to European settlers.

www.ednet.ns.ca/educ/museum/arch

ArchNet

This virtual library for archaeology lists museums, academic departments, and publishers worldwide. Link to hundreds of excerpts from books and complete recent articles such as "Did We Pick Dogs or Vice Versa?" The ArchNet Forum discussion list contains a great search feature.

archnet.uconn.edu

Perseus Project Homepage

Ambitious project to assemble resources about the archaic and classical Greek world. The encyclopedia helps with terminology, and the FAQ section is useful to navigate this extensive site.

www.perseus.tufts.edu

Protecting Archaeological Sites Today

This site helps put the latest in global telecommunications in the service of the past. It's an online organization dedicated to the preservation of archaeological, cultural, and historical sites through political action and education. To this end, they conduct e-mail letter-writing campaigns.

home.uleth.ca/geo/jasweb/jasweb.htm

BRITISH COLUMBIA

B.C. Adventure

Anyone West Coast–bound will want to pay a visit to this online tourism resource. Take advantage of their travel planner, recreation, adventure, and great outdoors sections. Send a digital postcard, read the online magazine, buy books from the bookstore, or post a question on one of the bulletin boards.

bcadventure.com/adventure/index.html

B.C. Excite #1

This part of the Excite search engine provides links to travel information on some B.C. destinations different from what you find on most tourism sites. You might become interested in visiting Salmon Arm, Harrison Hot Springs, or Osoyoos!

www.excite.com/travel/countries/Canada/british_columbia

B.C. Excite #2

The best thing about this area of the Excite search engine is that it provides links to dozens and dozens of travel web sites in B.C. Just name your place!

www.excite.com/travel/destinations/north_america/canada/provinces_and_territories/british_columbia

B.C. Highway

Visuals are too busy on this site and the many levels of links make it frustrating to reach the weather information, but other areas are easy to get to. Find the latest information on road conditions, photo-radar locations, and toll rates. Or check out the current highway cams and ski reports.

www.bchighway.com

B.C. Rockies

This tourism-promotion organization focuses on the B.C. side of the Rocky Mountains, with links to golf, adventure tours, family outfits, and more. Check out What's New and vacation specials, or send a virtual postcard. A search listed 39 links to hot springs!

www.bcrockies.com

British Columbia Ferry Information

What are the Nimpkish, the Tachek, and the Tenaka? Find out at the web site for B.C. Ferries. Navigate the sea of information provided, including fares, routes, schedules information, contact numbers, and trip-planning services. You can also make online reservations for selected routes. Welcome aboard!

www.bcferries.bc.ca

British Columbia Travel Information

A good first stop for those travelling to B.C., this site provides general interest information about the province, listings for accommodations, available tour packages, ferry schedules, and more.

www.travel-library.com/north_america/canada/british_columbia/index.html

British Columbia Wine

What could be more pleasant than a day trip into B.C.'s wine country? Well, if you can't make it out there yourself, this site is the next best thing. Read about the history of wine-making in B.C., look up your favourite winery, or try your hand at the wine word-search puzzle.

www.bcwine.com

British Columbia Wine

What could be more pleasant than a day trip into B.C.'s wine country? Well, if you can't make it out there yourself, this site is the next best thing. Read about the history of wine-making in B.C., look up your favourite winery, or try your hand at the wine word-search puzzle.

www.bcwine.com

British Columbia Yellow Pages

Look up jewellery stores, computer dealers, or anything else in a particular area or on a specific street. Then find that location on the map and click on Directions to enter your starting point. You'll receive not only complete details and a route map, but also your estimated travel time. It doesn't get any easier than this.

www.bcyellow.com

Discover Vancouver

This Vancouver site includes sections on entertainment, tourist attractions, shopping, and Hollywood North. The Local Info section is particularly interesting, with pieces on Chinatown, bridges of Greater Vancouver, and the marijuana cash crop. Post a message on the bulletin board or sign up for membership to receive discounts and enter contests.

www.discovervancouver.com/index.shtml

Geo-Images Virtual Reality Panoramas

If you can't afford to go to the real British Columbia, you might have to settle for this collection of QuickTime Virtual Reality images of B.C., the Rockies, and the North.

geogweb.berkeley.edu/geoimages/qtvr/qtvr.html#Canada

HelloBC.com

This site, created by Tourism British Columbia, provides connections to general tourist information for the province, as well as corporate and contact numbers for the ministry. Find trip ideas, search for accommodations, download a free screen saver, or register to use the handy trip planner.

www.hellobc.com

Lighthouses of British Columbia

Check out this online directory of operational stations run by the Coast Guard, as well as automated and decommissioned lighthouses. This site not only has details about the lighthouse locations but also provides e-mail addresses for some of the lightkeepers. And in case you fancy the lifestyle, there's a brief unofficial explanation of the hiring process for B.C. lightkeepers.

fjogwhistle.com/bclights/

SearchBC

Type a keyword at the top of the screen, or scroll down beyond the ads and registrations to reach 15 categories of links, including such topics as Computer, Software & Internet and Travel & Vacations.

www.searchbc.com

Travel.BC

This tourism web site will connect you to useful resources for the different regions of the province, and it claims to have 5000 links! The Islands link provides an easy-to-use distance calculator.

travel.bc.ca

Vancouver International Airport

A trip to the airport can be less of a hassle with a bit of preparation. This site includes guides and maps, instructions on transportation and parking, and other useful tips. The flight information section can be set to e-mail you with updates on your flight.

www.yvr.ca

Vancouver VR

Provides panoramic virtual reality views of the downtown, the airport, and Granville Island. You can also find out how these images are constructed.

hotel.cprost.sfu.ca/vanvr/qt/index.html

CONSUMER ECONOMY

Bizrate

With so many e-commerce companies popping up these days, how do you know which retailers to trust? This site acts like a Better Business Bureau of the online world. Bizrate-affiliated merchants expose themselves to lenthy customer feedback surveys, and major retailers also receive staff reviews.

www.bizrate.com

Canadian Consumer Handbook

This is a publication produced by Industry Canada and provincial consumer affairs departments. Equip yourself with knowledge about everything from landlord/tenant problems to standard cremation practices. You'll also find a directory of consumer organizations in a number of fields. The *Handbook* is downloadable as text or a printable Adobe Acrobat file.

strategis.ic.gc.ca/SSG/ca01136e.html

Consumers Council of Canada

Investigate your consumer rights and responsibilites at this web site. A listing of consumer help lines will give visitors plenty of options for complaining. Also find out how to stop receiving junk mail. There are links to other consumer web sites in Canada and worldwide.

geocities.com/WallStreet/Floor/3105

Directory of Consumer Associations

This section of the Strategis site provides an alphabetical listing of links to many consumer associations across Canada, such as the Canadian Toy Testing Council, Democracy Watch, and the One Voice Seniors Network.

strategis.ic.gc.ca/SSG/ca01010e.html

free.com

There are a lot of sites now that will find free goods, services, and offers on the web. Just goes to show, people like getting free stuff, even if they usually end up paying for it somehow. Head to this site for free trials and samples, and connect to links for many free and almost-free items.

www.free.com

Freebie Stuff

Free downloads, coupons, games, CD-ROMs, and a lot more tech stuff. And—probably appropriate for this and similar sites—free debt-reduction services are offered.

www.freebiestuff.com

FreeClutter.com

Free cash, free e-zines, free movies, free dating service, free everything! The good thing about this site is that you can key in a search word (or words) and locate your specific free item.

freeclutter.snap.com/

It's Freakin' Free.com

If you don't receive enough electronic messages already, sign up to receive weekly updates for free stuff and special offers by e-mail in as many categories as you want. Check out the top 50 free sites for samples, travel guides, and T-shirts, and possibly win a trip to the Caribbean.

www.itsfreakinfree.com

Marketplace

This is the web site of the long-running CBC program that presents news and reviews of products and services from the consumer's point of view. Keeps a listing of product recalls and warnings, and informs you of the latest consumer alerts. Easily view current articles or search the archives.

cbc.ca/consumers/market/

Public Interest Advocacy Centre

This nonprofit organization provides legal and research services on behalf of consumer interests. They have identified the need for vigilance toward the activities of government, big business, and utilities, which sometimes put political and commercial interests ahead of those of the public. Read PIAC publications in areas such as privacy, telecommunications, energy, cable TV and broadcasting, financial services, and e-commerce.

www.piac.ca

Straight Goods

Straight Goods is Canada's consumer and news watchdog. Their mission is "to help you save money, protect your rights, and untangle spin." They have investigative reports, features, forums, archives, and links. If you send in a consumer complaint, they'll try to sort it out for you. Go to the joke of the day and add your own. Or give your opinion in the daily poll.

www.straightgoods.com

Street Cents

This is the online version of the CBC show that aims to help teens become savvy consumers. The site's cool design and straight talk are enough to interest anyone who shops and thinks at the same time. Check out the streeters in RealVideo, or the Bite Me link, where viewers send in their questions about food and the *Street Cents* team investigates.

www.halifax.cbc.ca/streetcents

TechnoFILE

A consumer-friendly publication that gives you the lowdown on the latest home and office technology developments and products in an easy-to-understand way. From PlayStations to DVDs to sports utility vehicles, there's information about any type of technology for the tech-challenged. But then again, you're reading it online, so you can't be that hopeless.

www.technofile.com

The Buyers' Club

A free service for online shoppers, the Buyers' Club offers a no-nonsense connection to common household items, such as kettles, humidifiers, watches, and rechargeable shavers. Also find calculators, phones, and musical instruments. They provide prices in Canadian and U.S. currency. Yeah!

www.thebuyersclub.com/

The Consumers' Association of Canada

CAC is an independent, nonprofit, volunteer-based organization. They inform and educate consumers on marketplace issues and work with government and industry to solve marketplace problems in beneficial ways. Their philosophy is far-reaching. Read about their national program on consumer literacy, and about the food tips project to help close the "wealth and health" gap.

www.consumer.ca

CULTURES

shift

420.com

If you don't already know, 420 is police lingo for marijuana possession. Thus, the groovy webmasters at this site encourage you to smoke a bowl before you eyeball the toons, chat with other heads, post your thoughts on cannabis culture, or take quizzes that determine whether you're baked, wired, or stoned. 'Cause there's a difference, man.

www.420.com

Am Braighe

Celtic culture is alive and kicking thanks to magazines like *Am Braighe* (pronounced Uhm Bri-uh and means "higher ground"), based in Cape Beton, Nova Scotia. Read a sample issue or follow the links to other Celtic sites. Use the Gaelic forum to ask questions about the culture or the language. And you can even learn Gaelic via online tutorials.

www.chatsubo.com/ambraighe

Asian Canadian

This comprehensive Asian Canadian site celebrates how Asian communities continue to enrich Canadian culture. Find information about Asian film festivals, sports, politicians, and much more. And you can check out the law centre and history section, and find many links to other Asian sites worldwide.

www.asian.ca

Biser Balkanski

This Canadian Macedonian internet community provides news, stories, music, history, and other areas of interest. Believe them when they say they've got the internet's largest collection of Macedonian villages. It's a long list with photos and info about the locations.

www.biserbalkanski.com

BlackSearch

This search engine for the black American experience online also contains international links, such as blackgirl international and the International Black Student Alliance.

www.blacksearch.com

Celtic Heritage

This magazine contains feature articles and tall tales about Celtic culture in Canada. Browse the catalogue of available merchandise or find out how to begin tracing your genealogy. From this site, connect to the College of Piping on P.E.I. or gaelic.net.

www.tartans.com/celticheritage

Celtic Music and History

Fiddling raccoons and herring that drown? This site is compiled in Judique, Cape Breton, and dedicated primarily to Scottish heritage. Check out the photo gallery, folktales, and profiles of prominent musicians. In the Resources section, you'll find true/false questions, a word find of Celtic instruments, and a guessing game.

collections.ic.gc.ca/celtic

China.com

This popular portal for all things Chinese can be viewed in multiple languages. Start by reading your Chinese horoscope, then use the web guide to connect to reference links, business and economy sites, and much more.

www.china.com

Cultures.com

This site is devoted to living and ancient cultures, and the promotion of world communication. A variety of information is elegantly presented, and links are provided to encyclopedias of Greek mythology and Meso-American cultures. Become a headhunter in the colossal heads contest!

www.cultures.com

Hot Links

Reach a variety of Canadian and American sites via this page. The sites are not categorized because they are deemed to represent "diversity within diversity" of the black culture. Scroll down the page to read 20 Ways to Know You're Black in Corporate North America.

www.cableregina.com/users/ediversity/links.html

Mennonites in Canada

The Mennonite Historical Society of Canada has set up an interesting site. The encyclopedia section appears to be updated daily. Also included is information about the history, beliefs, and culture. The bibliography and related sites will be useful to those wanting to find out more.

www.mhsc.ca/

Paths of Glory

This substantial site celebrates the accomplishments of Canadians of African heritage. The biographical section covers heroes in every walk of life (politicians, scientists, artists, etc.). Also look for the 400-year-long timeline of events, book and video recommendations, and a fun and games section with Shockwave video.

www.pathsofglory.com

Scots in Nova Scotia

"Come away in" from the tartan screen! Read all *aboot* the history of the Scots in Nova Scotia, the clan system, poetry, and other material on the Highland clearances, events, and more.

www.chebucto.ns.ca/Heritage/FSCNS/ScotsHome.html

Slovaks and Slovakia

A crossroads for Slovak Canadians and their cultural organizations. Pictures, videos, links to the embassy in Ottawa, and a Slovak-English dictionary can all be found here.

www.slovak.com

The Other Metis

Find information on Metis peoples from across North America. This comprehensive, easy-to-use site hopes to reach those who are not represented by the better-known Metis organizations. Link to recent judgments about Metis issues, take a Metis 101 tutorial, or check out the links to Canadian Aboriginal sites in the What's New section.

www.cyberus.ca/~mfdunn/metic

EMBASSIES & CONSULATES

Foreign Embassies in Canada

No bells and whistles on this site, but you will find contact information for all foreign embassies in Canada.

www.usask.ca/sas/isao/country/embassy.html

Foreign Embassies Online

This University of Guelph site includes links to web sites for about 18 embassies and consulates in Canada. Be aware, though, that only some of these links actually work!

www.uoguelph.ca/CIP/embass.htm

Foreign Embassy Web Sites

This import-export consulting group offers a free e-zine and information about international business. Scroll down the home page to find dozens of foreign embassy web sites in Canada.

www.importexportcoach.com/embassies.htm

FIRST NATIONS

Aboriginal Business Canada

Did you know that there are over 20 000 Aboriginal businesses in Canada? Or that by 1996, the proportion of Aboriginal workers aged 15 to 24 who were self-employed was higher than that for all Canadians? This organization provides service and support to Aboriginal business people. Some of the links are confusing, but the information is interesting, and there's a map of which communities are located in each province.

abc.gc.ca

Aboriginal Digital Collections

This is a web site for Industry Canada's pilot program to provide links to Aboriginal sites in many categories, such as art, business, and language. The program pays Aboriginal youth to create web sites featuring significant Canadian Aboriginal material. Find traditional teaching units, the Aboriginal Suppliers Directory, and photo galleries in The Urban Aboriginal Experience Through the Works of Aboriginal Artisans.

aboriginalcollections.ic.gc.ca/e/index.html

Aboriginal Youth Network

This is an online resource created by youth for youth. The site provides a chat room focusing on issues relevant to young Aboriginal Canadians, bulletin boards that post community events across the country, and a weekly Alberta radio show.

ayn-o.ayn.ca

Assembly of First Nations

The AFN allows Canada's Aboriginal peoples to voice their concerns on current issues. Click on the feathers to find current information and news about land rights, residential school issues, job opportunities, health, and much more. Or follow the links to sites for Native newspapers and other media, research papers, and organizations.

www.afn.ca

Background and History of First Nations in Canada

Canadian First Nations have inhabited this land for thousands of years, ever since the first group of hunters crossed over the Bering Strait. This archive provides an overview of that rich and storied past. Click on Publications to download recent articles.

www.inac.gc.ca/pubs/fnic/index.html

Canadian Alliance in Solidarity with the Native Peoples

CASNP works to promote awareness of Native issues, cooperation between Native peoples and non-Native peoples, environmental projects, and justice issues. Browse the CASNP bookstore, add to the resource list, or read the latest press releases.

users.cyberglobe.net/~casnp

Capucine's Native Resources

The links to scores of other Native sites are produced as part of a Mi'kmaq woman's studies at McGill University. Choose from topics such as art, culture, language, nations and tribes, education, and associations. There's a lot of Canadian content here.

www.klingon.org/native/pages/index.html

First Nations Information Project

This site aims to become a portal for online research on business and economic development, community planning, self-government, education, culture, and other issues of interest to First Nations communities. The WebBoard area includes such topics as jobs, events/pow wows, and genealogy.

www.johnco.com/firstnat/index.html

First Perspective Online

This online version of "news of indigenous peoples of Canada" includes a discussion forum, listings of powwows by province, employment ads, commentary, and reader polls.

www.firstperspective.ca

Heritage of Canada's Native Peoples

This part of the CMCC virtual museums web site focuses on indigenous peoples in Canada. Click on links such as biographies, science and technology, and social relations.

www.civilization.ca/membrs/biblio/orch/wwwo6f_e.html#top

Links to Aboriginal Resources

Here you'll find a list of newsgroups and legal issues related to Canadian First Nations groups, as well as links to Aboriginal resources from Canada and all over the world. But be warned: many of these sites are out of date and don't connect. There are also sections dedicated to Aboriginal arts, human rights, the environment, and Aboriginal law and legislation.

www.bloorstreet.com/300block/abori.htm

Turtle Island Native Network

Although B.C.-based, this in-depth site has information and connections from all over Canada and the U.S. The Discussion section lists bulletin boards and chats by specific topics or areas of interest. You won't be disappointed with this comprehensive site.

www.turtleisland.org

GEOGRAPHY

AfriCam

View up-to-the-minute cams at this site, the first virtual game reserve associated with major African and international conservation organizations. Read an EcoNews piece and recent articles about elephants and other wildlife. Send in your cams to win a T-shirt, a watch, or a room at a game reserve lodge, among other prizes.

www.africam.com

Canadian Distances Calculator

The distance between Kapuskasing, Ontario, and Banff, Alberta, is 1717 miles or 2764 kilometres. Use the calculator to find the distance between any two cities in any part of Canada.

www.uvl.ca/mileage.htm

Canadian Geographical Names

Where is Tsiigehtchic? Search this database of Canadian places to find out. Search by geographic name or point coordinates. There are online queries for abbreviations, Canada's newest places, and changes in community names. Link, for example, to general and specific databases of geographic names or to a page of Nunavut news. Or click on through to name origins and geographic terminology.

GeoNames.NRCan.gc.ca/english

Canadian Heritage Rivers System

Check out this site for photographs, maps, and information on the geography, history, natural heritage, and recreational uses of a selection of Canadian rivers.

collections.ic.gc.ca/rivers

Countries of the World

Find information for any country supplied in a handy, comprehensive format. The infoplease.com site offers dozens of guides, almanacs, and information repositories. The miscellaneous sections are really interesting. Did you know that English is the third most widely spoken language in the world after Chinese and Spanish?

www.infoplease.com/countries.html

Geography, Maps, Travel

A short and plain but useful page providing some of the most important links in these three areas. Connect to interactive atlases, travel planners, shots of the earth from space, and currency converters.

www.sil.org/general/areas.html

National Atlas of Canada

From Natural Resources Canada, this site is a good jumping-off point for geographic information of all kinds. Find all kinds of facts about Canada, check out quizzes for schoolkids, or order maps online.

www-nais.ccm.emr.ca/english/home-english.html

Tour Canada from Space

At the site for the Canada Centre for Remote Sensing, you can click on different areas of the map of Canada for aerial topographic maps of specific locales. And read the March 2000 issue of the Remote Sensing newsletter to learn how another remote sensing puzzle was solved.

www.ccrs.nrcan.gc.ca/ccrs/tour/toure.html

HERITAGE

Bluenose

If you can't get enough of Nova Scotia's famous sailing ship that graces our dime, this is the place for you. This history site boasts a good yarn of the sea and a QuickTime video of the great schooner.

trinculo.educ.sfu.ca/hpost_e/ipost2/10-11/default.html

Bluenose II Preservation Trust

Bluenose II is the identical re-creation of the famed *Bluenose* schooner, which was undefeated in a series of races over a period of 18 years. Though the original ship was sold in the 1950s, the Preservation Trust was established to keep the *Bluenose II* as the symbol of Nova Scotia around the world. Read up on the specs and facts of the ship, check out the history of the *Bluenose*, or vist the picture gallery.

www.bluenose2.ns.ca

Canadian Heritage Gallery

"The most extensive collection of historical Canadiana on the Internet." And you'll have fun surfing this well-organized site. Find images by the search feature or by topic. Each image also provides links to other images of similar topic or time period. Check out the placards in the Documents, Posters, and Signs section, or look at some beautiful rivers of the Northwest Territories. The site provides information on how to order reproductions of the paintings and photographs—and, of course, you can order online.

www.canadianheritage.ca/index2.htm

Canadian Heritage Information Network

"Welcome to the gateway to museums, galleries, and heritage information in Canada and around the world." The CHIN/RCIP site has been completely revised and is much improved. Go through a virtual exhibition of musical instruments, for example, or enroll in an online course on collections management or internet training. You can also add your vision for the Virtual Museum of Canada.

www.spiff.rcip.gc.ca/

Canadian Museum of Civilization

Visit online exhibitions or take a virtual gallery tour at this web site. The calendar of events will keep you up to date, and the CyberMentor provides themed resources for teachers, such as the interactive internet project for schools. The puppet collection pages are really cute and include outside links and a QuickTime VR.

www.civilization.ca/cmc/cmceng/welcmeng.html

Diefenbunker

The Diefenbunker may become "Canada's Cold War Museum." Below a farmer's field in the Ottawa Valley, Canada's "secret" bunker quietly began operation in 1961. It was decommissioned in 1994, and there are now tours, events, and a passionate web site. There are general photographs, but you'll have to visit the place itself to walk through the fall-out shelters and see a high school history Cold War project. There are links to other Cold War web sites, including the Weapons archive and FAQs.

www.diefenbunker.ca

Gathering of the Clans

If you have even a drop of Scottish blood in you, you can drop by this site to research genealogy and learn the proud mottos of different Scottish clans. Go to the Pub to send and read messages, or use the Clan Finder to locate clan-specific discussion groups and other links.

www.tartans.com

Great Canadian Questions

At this site, you'll find Canadian heritage and trivia questions origanized by topic. There's also a Tools for Teachers section that includes video debates and discusses learning outcomes.

www.greatquestions.com

InfoSource Databases

Not much to look at, this web site is a directory of federal government heritage databases, from A to Z. There are links to and information about dozens of databases, and many of them are online.

infosource.gc.ca/InfoSource/Info_3/CH-e.html

Pier 21 Society

Pier 21, Halifax Harbour, was for many the door to Canada. Recently transformed into a heritage centre chronicling the immigrant experience, Pier 21 is looking for family stories and memorabilia (including traditional recipes) to add to their exhibits. Learn about war brides and guest children, visit the interactive gallery, and send virtual postcards from this web site.

pier21.ns.ca

The Great Canadian Heritage Project

This is the group that puts together those spots that are "a part of our heritage" for television and movie trailers. Watch the clips, and see what kids' activites, lesson plans, and national events these historians are planning.

www.heritageproject.ca/default.htm

HISTORY

Arctic Dawn: The Journeys of Samuel Hearne

Your guide is beckoning, the day is crisp and clear, and vast, unknown web pages lay before you! The western shore of Hudson's Bay is one of the least populated places in the world today, so imagine how forbidding it must have been in the late 1700s, when Samuel Hearne was explorng the area for the Hudson's Bay Company. Read Hearne's own diaries of his travels and follow the hyperlinks for useful facts and background info.

web.idirect.com/~hland/sh/title.html

Argos

Links to associate sites include "Byzantine Studies on the Internet" and "Materials for the Study of Women and Gender in the Ancient World." This site also provides links to other related searching tools.

argos.evansville.edu

B.C. Archives

Archiving the history of an entire province is a masive undertaking, and the B.C. archives have the listings on their web site to prove it. Visitors will be overwhelmed with the amount of information at their disposal, which includes online searches, exhibitions, maps, and visual records.

www.bcarchives.gov.bc.ca/index.htm

Beaton Institute Archives

The Beaton Institute's mandate is to collect and preserve the social, economic, political, and cultural history of Cape Breton. The Archives' web site provides listings of manuscripts, maps, published materials, audio/video materials, and more.

eagle.uccb.ns.ca/beaton/beaton.html

Bone Snow Knives and Tin Oil Lamps

Culled from the collections of the Museum of Civilization, the Royal Ontario Museum, and the Canadian Heritage Information Network, this display of Native artifacts presents a storied socio-historical document. Visitors will find facts and photos of the objects, as well as a geo-cultural area list.

xist.com/ROM-MCQ

British Columbia History

Check out this site for a comprehensive list of internet resources on B.C. history. If there's something on the web that has anything to do with B.C.'s history, it's probably here.

victoria.tc.ca/Resources/bchistory.html

Canada's National History Society

Explore our nation's culture and history. The CSHS web site provides information on the bimonthly history publication *The Beaver*, background on the Hudson's Bay History Foundation, history awards, and links to related sites.

www.historysociety.ca

Canadian Confederation

This site, produced by the National Library, explores topics such as the territorial evolution of Canada, fears of annexation by the U.S., and the Underground Railroad. Check out the Little-Known Stories link.

www.nlc-bnc.ca/confed/e-1867.htm

Canadian Genealogy and History Links

Type in your name or choose a province and find information about a family. You'll see links to specific and general sites. And if you're looking for cemetary links, this is the place for you. Link to other genealogy, history, and cultural sites, including the "Bob's Your Uncle, Eh!" search engine.

www.islandnet.com/~jveinot/cghl/cghl.html

Canadian Women in History

Read about some of Canada's neglected historical figures, such as Edna Jacques, Agnes Macphail, and Victoria Calihoo. The site also inlcudes famous quotes by Canadaian women, a selection of related topics, and a "Woman of the Week" feature.

www.niagara.com/~merrwill

Diefenbaker Web

The definitive source for fans of Dief. Pay attention while it loads the "creepy Dief" photo (that's what the tag reads before the image comes up when it's loading!) There's a link to a profile site about the *other* Diefenbaker, the dog from the series *Due South*.

diefenbaker.ottawa.com

Early Canadiana Online

Here you'll find a searchable, full-text collection of thousands of books and pamphlets about early Canadian history, from the first European contacts to the late 19th century. The collection is particularly strong in literature, women's history, Native studies, travel and exploration, and the history of French Canada.

www.canadiana.org

Engendering Consent: World War II Posters and the Home Front

A short but interesting page with images of World War II propaganda posters aimed at Canadians on the home front. The "Buy Victoria Bonds" posters are excellent, one with the caption "I'm making bombs and buying bonds."

web.arts.ubc.ca/history/www2prop/prop.htm

Fortress of Louisbourg

This plain-looking but frequently updated site provides you with everything you need to know about this historic Cape Breton landmark.

fortress.uccb.ns.ca

Freedom of Expression in Canada

Read an outline of Canada's shameful history of censorship, including current news items. Scroll down examples of banned materials from 1914 to the present. Here's a fairly recent entry: "March 1994 ... during Freedom to Read Week, Alberta MLA Victor Doerksen calls for the removal from Alberta schools of *Of Mice and Men*." Amazing as it may seem, that book is No. 2 on the Most Frequently Banned Books of the 1990s. The site includes many censorship links.

insight.mcmaster.ca/org/efc/pages/chronicle/chronicle.html

Ghosts of the Klondike Gold Rush

Thar's gold in this here site! Rush on over to a page full of tall tales of the likes of "Diamond Tooth Gertie," "Skookum Jim," and "The Bishop Who Ate His Boots." Try the Pan for Gold Database.

www.gold-rush.org

Great Canadian Scientists

Canadians have 13 Nobel prizes, and 10 of those were for scientists! Read detailed information about the Canadian scientist who dined with orangutans, or the one who fought the battle of the sexes. Take the science quiz or e-mail a question to a scientist.

www.science.ca

Heritage Project

The Heritage Project is a program designed to raise interest in and awareness of Canada's past. You've probably seen their Heritage Minute series on TV, where notable incidents from our history are re-enacted.

heritage.excite.sfu.ca

History Learning and Teaching Page

This University of Victoria site is geared partly to teachers of Canadian history. Features include tips on conducting research, a quiz, a This Day in History section, and a Famous Canadian Quotes section.

web.uvic.ca/hrd/history.learn-teach/canindex.html

History of Coal Mining in Nova Scotia

You'll find a range of historical resources and editorials at this regularly updated site. It includes a coal mining photo album.

eagle.uccb.ns.ca/mining/index2.htm

On This Day

From events of national importance to true banalities, you'll find they all pop up on this page compiled by Sympatico. Provides easily digestible tidbits of history for those with short attention spans. Includes regularly updated Canadian quotes.

www1.sympatico.ca/cgi-bin/on_this_day

Protecting Archaeological Sites Today

This site helps put the latest in global telecommunications in the service of the past. It's an online organization dedicated to the preservation of archaeological, cultural, and historical sites through political action and education. To this end, they conduct e-mail letter-writing campaigns.

home.uleth.ca/geo/jasweb/jasweb.htm

RMS Empress of Ireland

Just so Canadians don't feel insecure (us?), we have our own famous and horrific passenger ship disaster. The *Empress of Ireland* went down in the St. Lawrence in 1914, with over 1000 souls on board. The web site even houses a comparison chart with the better-known *Titanic* and *Lusitania*. The wreck was recently declared Quebec's first underwater heritage site.

www.total.net:8080/~kinder/

The Discovery of Insulin

Here is all you need to know about the discovery of insulin at the University of Toronto in 1921. View photographs and listen to audio clips in the Scrapbook. Link to various diabetes associations and Nobel Prize details.

www.discoveryofinsulin.com/

LANGUAGE

A Web of Online Dictionaries

This site provides links to hundreds of online dictionaries and grammar aids in many, many languages. This is the place to go if you're looking for a Swahili to Russian/Russian to Swahili dictionary.

www.yourdictionary.com

Canadian Languages

This listing of all known languages spoken in our country will have you marvelling at the diversity of it all. There's a lot of interesting info here. For example, there are 20 speakers of Abnaki-Penobscot and 6 000 000 mother-tongue speakers of French in Canada. And the Nova Scotian sign language is nearly extinct. Of the 79 known languages listed for Canada, three are now extinct.

www.sil.org/ethnologue/countries/Cana.html

Canadian Raising and Other Oddities

Listen to RealAudio examples of some of our distinct speech patterns or look up related articles on the subject.

www.yorku.ca/twainweb/troberts/raising.html

History of the English Language

From pre-history to modern Englishes, it's all here! Join the HEL-L discussion list or search the list archive. There are also links for course syllabi/syllabuses and for conferences and workshops.

ebbs.english.vt.edu/hel/hel.html

Language Identifier

Type in a sentence, a phrase, or a word, and this online resource will attempt to identify the language. It might not hit it right on, but you will get the most likely sources to point you in the right direction.

www.link.cs.cmu.edu/dougb/ident-doc.html

Language Sites on the Internet

Find many links to online resources for English grammar, usage, linguistics, dictionaries, and thesauri. There are even some pun sites. You might want to follow the connection to the International Save the Puns Foundation if you're so inclined.

pw1.netcom.com/~rlederer/rllink.htm

Languages of the World

Search the Ethnologue page for information about the world's languages, including alternate names, number of speakers, location, dialects, and linguistic affiliation.

www.sil.org/ethnologue/ethnologue.html

Rivendell Language Dictionaries and Translators

Kajillions of dictionaries for well over 100 languages, a chat group about languages, and the tantalizing offer of free translations. Just enter an English word to find the translation in, say, Bengali.

rivendel.com/~ric/resources/dictionary.html

The Dialectizer

Translate normal English into Redneck, Jive, Cockney, Elmer Fudd, Swedish Chef, Moron, or Pig Latin dialects. That's right. Onfusecay youray iendsfray andyay olleaguescay!

www.rinkworks.com/dialect

The Internet Language Dictionary

If you think "It's all Geek to me!" this site is for you. Sure, you've heard talk of ethernet and WebCrawler, but do you really know what they are? Search a specific word or click on a letter of the alphabet for a list of words and definitions.

www.netlingo.com/

World Wide Words

"World Wide Words is devoted to the English language—its history, quirks, curiosities, and evolution." This site is loads of fun. Updated weekly are sections on turns of phrase, weird words, and pronunciations. They also review online dictionaries. You can receive their newsletter by e-mail. Or send in your own questions about word origins.

www.quinion.com/words/

MANITOBA

City of Winnipeg

This web site provides a detailed look at Manitoba's capital, featuring all kinds of investor and tourist information. There are photos of the downtown, city statistics, contact information, a city history, and more.

www.mbnet.mb.ca/city

Manitoba for Manitobans

The information site by Manitobans for Manitobans, it says. Not all of the links are active yet, but it does connect you to places like Folkorama in Winnipeg. It also lets you see if your dot-com or dot-net or dot-org is available for registration.

www.manitobaweb.com

Manitoba Highway Conditions

Save yourself some hassle and check out construction projects and damage information on your route before you set out into the wilds of Manitoba in the dead of winter.

roadinfo.hwy.gov.mb.ca

Manitoba Now!

A useful resource filled with sports, government, travel, entertainment, and community news for the province. Use the Portage and Main search engine for commercial business listings of local, national, or world interest.

www.manitobanow.com

Travel Manitoba

This site has a very soothing home page. It specializes in events and activities for Manitoba-bound tourists. You'll find a good summary of general information and some links for locating a place to stay. It's available in English, French, and Spanish, and the categories of activities include museums, historic sites, beaches, meetings, performing arts, outdoor adventures, and hunting and fishing. Download a screen saver or send a virtual postcard.

www.travelmanitoba.com

MULTICULTURALISM

Anti-Racist Action

ARA Toronto began in 1992 to combat fascism and show support for a multiracial, multicultural, sexually diverse, liberated, and fun society. Keep up to date with the latest events, read *On the Prowl* newsletter, see and listen to RealAudio interviews, or visit other chapters of the ARA at this informative web site.

www.web.net/~ara

Artists Against Racism

AAR is a nonprofit, international organization dedicated to teaching young people that we are one people, regardless of religion, ethnicity, nationality, or skin colour. The organization uses popular actors and musicians in various media campaigns to promote education against prejudice. Take advantage of this site to learn more about the program or to get involved with AAR in your community.

www.vrx.net/aar

Black Cultural Centre for Nova Scotia

The centre began in 1977 to meet the needs and aspirations of Black communities in the province. At their web site, they provide a taste of the culture with samples of life stories, traditional music, and more.

www.bccns.com

Canadian Centre on Minority Affairs

Devoted to the promotion of social development and public policy initiatives to enhance the quality of life for present and future generations of the Black and Caribbean Canadian community. CCMA sponsors a number of public education and advocacy programs. The site provides a newsleter, press releases, upcoming events, a monthly update, and more.

www.interlog.com/~ccma

Canadian Council for Multicultural and Intercultural Education

The CCMIE is a nongovernmental organization comprising multicultural organizations across Canada. This site offers youth internships, information about March 21 celebrations, etc. Click on the Youth Page, read their journal, or take a quiz to test your knowledge. And there's a glossary of terms in the Resources section.

www.ccmie.com/

Canadian Council for Refugees

CCR is a nonprofit umbrella organization committed to the rights and protection of refugees in Canada and around the world, and to the settlement of refugees and immigrants in Canada. There are links to multicultural organizations across Canada, law-related sites, anti-racism sites, and international NGOs.

www.web.net/~ccr/

Canadian Ethnocultural Council

This umbrella organization is connected to ethnocultural organizations across Canada. They work to "ensure the preservation, enhancement and sharing of the cultural heritage of Canadians, the removal of barriers that prevent some Canadians from participating fully and equally in society, the elimination of racism and the preservation of a united Canada." You can get involved in the organization's activities or link to similar organizations nationwide.

www.ethnocultural.ca/

Chinese Canadian National Council

The CCNC was founded in 1980 with a mandate to promote the rights of Chinese Canadians and to encourage their participation in all fields of society. Check out the Chinese Canadian historical exhibit in the photo gallery, connect with the closest chapter of the council, or read about issues of concern and current projects.

www.ccnc.ca

March 21 Web Site

This government of Canada site will keep you up to date on events and activities planned for the International Day for the Elimination of Racial Discrimination: March 21.

www.pch.gc.ca/march21/

The Inter-Church Committee for Refugees

The ICCR is a coalition of ten Canadian church bodies. Its mandate is to promote an equitable, generous, and compassionate response to refugees by Canadians. Read the bulletins or find out about the latest information and workshops.

www.web.net/~iccr/

NATIONAL UNITY

Canada by Design

A multimedia forum for mutual education and exchange of views, Canada by Design offers a virtual town hall on the future of technology and how it's shaping our country. Add your voice to open forums, travel to virtual communities, or check out the Visionary Speaker Series through detailed transcripts at this site.

www.candesign.utoronto.ca

The Council for Canadian Unity

The CCU's purpose is to educate people on the legal and fiscal structures and the cultural and political nature of our country. Visitors to this site can read articles on the political and cultural state of the nation or check out the Today in History section. There are also comprehensive sections on health, tech news, space, and Hey Martha.

www.ccu-cuc.ca

The Globe and Mail National Issues Forum

The *Globe* does its bit to induce more Canadians to discuss national issues on discussion threads. National unity is one of the many topics, and the messages are current.

www.theglobeandmail.com/hubs/forums.html

The Unity Link

Started in 1995 and kept up to date, this site has all of the latest news on national unity, and actively solicits opinions from the site's visitors. Watch webcast interviews with Charles Taylor, Alexa McDonough, and others; and read all the latest releases.

www.uni.ca/index_e.html

Unity Canada

Here's a site that focuses on the debate on national unity and the most recent Quebec referendum. It includes many stories from the Canadian press on the issue. It's a mostly no-frills site, but you can download the national anthem.

fox.nstn.ca/~gholt/index.html

NEW BRUNSWICK

City of Fredericton

Did you know that Fredericton High School is the oldest high school in Canada (est. 1785) and the largest in the British Commonwealth, with a student population of more than 3000? Well, you would if you paid more attention to this web site for New Brunswick's capital. It features a host of municipal government data, city events, local attractions, and a very cute detailed map.

www.city.fredericton.nb.ca

Greater Moncton Online

If you can eat it, drink it, swap it, listen to it, read it, do it, say it, or go to it, you'll find it on this site. If you can't find it, then it probably doesn't exist in Greater Moncton.

www.greatermoncton.com

New Brunswick Online

Everything the prospective visitor will need to know about the province is on this web page. Link up to airlines and train services, or just browse through listings of popular golf courses. You might want even to download the New Brunswick screen saver when you're planning your visit.

www.new-brunswick.com

Tantramar Interactive QuickTime VR Gallery

There are some pleasant scenes of New Brunswick that let you adjust the viewpoint and zoom in as you scroll around in QTVR.

www.tantramar.com/ti/qtvr_gallery.html

The New Tide of Adventure

This is the official tourism site of New Brunswick. Throw yourself into the fun of the the Bay of Fundy, the site of the greatest tides in the world (up to 14 metres or 48 feet!). Or check out more than 180 other attractions, divided among five scenic driving routes.

www.tourismnbcanada.com/web/english/main.asp

NEWFOUNDLAND

City of St. John's

Visitors to the web site for Newfoundland's capital will find all the requisite municipal, historic, economic, and tourist information. Check out the link to the St. John's Haunted Hike.

www.city.st-johns.nf.ca

Newfoundland & Labrador Ferry Services

This government site provides detailed schedules and maps of the ferry routes to help you plan your trip.

www.gov.nf.ca/ferryservices

Newfoundland & Labrador's Registered Heritage Structures

This site has descriptions and brief histories of 157 registered sites, and images of most of them. Walking tours and town maps are included for those areas with numerous heritage structures. Click on links to read architectural terms or a variety of articles.

collections.ic.gc.ca/tours/

Newfoundland and Labrador Tourism

The emphasis here is on background information on topics such as traditional cuisine, local fauna, folklore, geology, history, and trivia. There's also some practical information such as transportation, maps, and attractions. And there's a great list of FAQs on icebergs: check out this tourist draw before the greenhouse effect melts the polar ice caps.

www.worldplay.com/welcome.html

Newfoundland Outport

Click on a whale tale to enter the different areas of the site. Or go to the Outport Chatter for some "gab." This site is assembled by a couple who've moved to the mainland. They've included humour, yarns, photos, history, and a listing of pubs, restaurants, and clubs elsewhere where Newfoundlanders are likely to meet up.

www.durham.net/~kburt/index.html

Newfoundlinks

A keyword-searchable database of Newfoundland-based web sites—some commercial, some personal, and some for associations. Also, there's a tool for finding Newfoundland e-mail addresses.

pagemaker.ca/db/links.html

NF Interactive

This site calls itself "your guide to Newfoundland on the Net." With this many links to all sorts of categories, it might be right. Check out the great digital galleries of nature photography and lighthouse pictures. There's an amusing Catch-a-Cod game—the last legal way to catch one! There's a daily mystery photo too.

www.nfinteractive.org

Welcome to Labrador!

Labrador represents one of the last serious wilderness areas around. This site does its part to make sure available tourist resources become better known. There's a section on travel tips, and you'll also find a list of museums, maps, and information on ferry service. Take a "magical history tour" of Labrador or view photo-illustrated pages of six different regions.

members.xoom.com/labradorian

Welcome to Newfoundland & Labrador

Travelling to Newoundland? Looking for a job or business opportunities? You'll find maps, classifieds, and search engines. Also find some more unusual items, such as the sheet music for "Ode to Newfoundland" in the Odds and Ends section.

www.nfld.com/

NORTHWEST TERRITORIES

Arctic Circle

With environmental repercussions being felt from pollution farther south, and encroaching industrial development of nonrenewable natural gas and oil resources, inhabitants of the Arctic Circle are facing a threat to their lifestyle never experienced before. This site addresses these issues, and also features sections on history and culture and an Arctic Forum discussion group.

arcticcircule.uconn.edu

Aurora Research Institute

The Institute is based in the Inuvik Research Centre, and is responsible for providing support services for and conducting research activities in the Northwest Territories. This web site also provides links to other research outfits operating in the Canadian north.

www.nwtresearch.com

CanadaEH–Northwest Territories

General information about the Northwest Territories, special events, and stats. There are some pretty cool—and cold—photos in the NWT picture gallery.

www.canadaeh.ca/provinces/northwestterritories/main.html

Canadian Polar Commission

The Commission monitors, promotes, and disseminates information about the polar regions. It informs the public about the importance of polar science to Canada, enhances Canada's international profile as a circumpolar nation, and recommends polar science policy direction to government. Check this web site for workshops, conferences, research, and other endeavours in the polar region.

www.polarcom.gc.ca

City of Yellowknife

Yellowknife is the diamond capital of North America. This virtual city hall provides instant access to Yellowknife's bylaws, taxes, permits, and other miscellaneous municipal government documents.

city.yellowknife.nt.ca

Unbearably Cool

This youth-oriented site is run by the Northwest Territories government. Find out about the plants, animals, and people of the NWT. There's also a special section on the myths and tales of the north. You might want to read about the "Man Who Became a Caribou." You'll also find various links for young people, including arts, sports, clubs, and health.

www.gov.nt.ca/kids/kidshome.htm

NOVA SCOTIA

Cape Breton Island: Atlantic Canada's Masterpiece

Cape Breton Island is located on Atlantic Canada's coast but it's only a click away at this interactive and informative web site. Visitors can take a detailed tour of the island, visit various tourist attractions and resorts, or send postcards to friends. There's also an e-mail directory.

www.cbisland.com

Cape Breton Showcase

This web showcase is designed to seduce the prospective tourist. Check out the displays for breathtaking photos and suggested tourist activities. And if you'd like your vacation to be a little more permanent, there's a section for real estate listings. The Caper's Corner is just for Cape Bretoners, home or away.

www.capebretonisland.com

Destination: Nova Scotia

This is an attractive, comprehensive tourism guide for the province. And you can also read the Nova Scotia factoids or join one of the discussion forums.

destination-ns.com

Explore Nova Scotia

As well as the usual tourist info, this site includes a photo gallery, e-postcards, and, best of all, virtual tours of every area in Nova Scotia.

www.explorenovascotia.com/

Halifax Regional Municipality

This site is a potpourri of basic info on "the major business, cultural, government, and institutional centre of Atlantic Canada." You'll also find links to accommodations and tours.

www.region.halifax.ns.ca

Pictou County Tourist Association

If you've picked Pictou County, N.S., for your vacation this year, you can get all the necessary details at this web site. There's a list of 100 things to do, as well as information on historic attractions, beaches, festivals, lobsters, and ferry schedules. You'll find local business information and a chat area, too.

www.prdc.com/pcta

The Virtual Tour of Antigonish

This site provides a detailed guide to the sights and attractions of this beautiful town between Sydney and Halifax. Here you'll find numerous pictures of the town, informative descriptions of various locales, and the obligatory links and contact info.

www.antigonish.com

Titanic: The Unsinkable Ship and Halifax

This is a reminder that this famous shipwreck is more than just part of Leonardomania. Short of a visit to the bottom of the ocean, Halifax and its museums and graveyards offer the most tangible legacy from the disaster. On this site, read wireless transcript excerpts, right up to the fatal last moments. There are also details about the 150 victims who were buried in Halifax.

titanic.gov.ns.ca

Virtual Nova Scotia

Check out the official tourism web site of the province. Plan your trip with the help of this slick site's information on events, attractions, accommodations, music, scenic travelways, and more. Other features include web poscards, animations, and information in French and German. And to get you in the mood, why not tune in to the weekly *Nova Scotia Kitchen Party* radio show. You'll find details at this site.

explore.gov.ns.ca

NUNAVUT

Nunavut Handbook

Almost all of Canada's population huddles close to the U.S. border, with few of our citizens ever daring to head north of the most-populated provinces. It's time to leave your well-heated home and find out what it's like to experience a serious Canadian winter. Head to Nunavut, Canada's newest territory, and find out what the Great White North truly is.

www.arctic-travel.com

Nunavut Tourism

Find out about the newest Canadian territory. Nunavut has a population of approximately 24 000, and 85% are Inuit. The site bills Nunavut as one of the last great unspoiled wilderness habitats on earth, and the photos confirm it. Wilderness adventures include dog sledding and kayaking. You'll find a bit about the history and government, and links to the planes that fly there. There's also a searchable database of services. The site doesn't just tell you what the weather is; it also advises you about what to wear, and when. Your accommodation could be a first-class hotel or an igloo: you choose.

www.nunatour.nt.ca/

The Government of Nunavut

Read about the history and the new government on this site. (Apparently, some people are not too happy about their anniversary date of April Fool's Day!) Find out about the symbolism used in the flag. Or download the 1999 labour force survey to learn what people actually do up there. To read the site in Inuktitut, download the Nunacom font.

www.gov.nu.ca/

ONTARIO

Attractions Ontario

Hit this web site before you hit the road to Ontario. Visitors can search the site by attraction or destination, browse listings for accommodations, and take advantage of the free coupon book provided by Attractions Canada.

www.attractions.on.ca

Canada's Capital and Its Region

There's a lotta Ottawa here at this site. Take the virtual tour, or head over to the Activity zone for a youth chat area and games.

www.capcan.ca

Cities and Towns of Ontario

This part of the Attractions Ontario site will link you to over a hundred cities and towns in Ontario.

www.attractions.on.ca/a_links.htm

City of Ottawa

Taxes, parking, permits, parks, recreation, culture, city services, and business information are just a few of the available topics at this web site for our nation's capital.

city.ottawa.on.ca

City of Toronto

The City of Toronto web site provides information on the vast number of community activities and services that Canada's largest city has to offer. Since Toronto is the country's most culturally diverse urban centre, this site provides important information in many languages.

www.city.toronto.on.ca

CN Tower

At over 550 metres tall, the world's tallest free-standing structure cuts an imposing figure on the Toronto skyline. Over 20 years old, the tower is still a major tourist attraction, with millions of visitors every year. Check this site for the various activities, lookout spots, and dining facilities at the CN Tower.

www.cntower.ca

COMPASS Cameras

The Ontario Ministry of Transportation has conveniently provided a number of strategically placed web cams in and around Toronto's worst traffic areas. Check this web site for highway conditions before you get in the car.

www.mto.gov.on.ca/english/traveller/compass/camera/cammain.htm

Niagara Falls

Compiled by the Visitor and Convention Bureau, this site advertises the town of Niagara Falls, with shopping, dining, golf, casinos, wedding plans, accommodations, and so much more than just a natural landmark. There's also an illumination schedule for colourful evening viewing. But this site is missing basic information about the Falls themselves, truly one of the natural wonders of the world.

www.niagarafallstourism.com

Northern Life Magazine

This is the site of an online magazine based in North Bay. It features a pictorial history of the city, a classifieds section, and various links. The highlight is probably the loon call.

www.northernlife.com

Old Fort William

Located in Thunder Bay, Old Fort William was the largest fur trading post in the world, and is one of the largest living-history museums in North America. This site has all the practical info you need to plan a visit, plus historical and educational information.

www.oldfortwilliam.on.ca/homepage.html

Ontario Place

Located on the Toronto waterfront, it's an amusement park without all the glitz. Their web site gives practical information on prices, hours, and directions, as well as descriptions of various attractions, such as the H.M.C.S. Haida History Battleship, the Purple Pipeline, the Mega Maza, and the Cinesphere—the first permanent IMAX theatre in the world. The screen is 60 feet wide by 80 feet high: now that's the way a film should be seen! You'll also find details on the annual fireworks competition and concert information.

www.ontarioplace.com

Ontario Postcards

Choose from a variety of snapshots of Ontario towns and landmarks, write a message on the back (just like a real postcard!), and e-mail the whole thing to a friend. Instructions are in English, French, German, Italian, and Ukranian.

204.101.2.101/pcard/

Outside Toronto

There are many suggested excursions and events within two hours of the Mega-city. This web site is updated weekly in the spring and summer.

outsidetoronto.com

PEACE & PEACEKEEPING

Canadian Peacekeepers

A well-maintained page by a veteran of Canadian missions and dedicated to all peacekeeping veterans. Here you'll find a comprehensive set of links to the latest news stories on Canadian peacekeeping and military actions around the world, as well as stories submitted by peacekeepers.

pk.kos.net

Project Ploughshares

This organization promotes disarmament, demilitarization, and the abolition of nuclear weapons. They also produce a report on conflicts happening around the world that don't make the mainstream media's flavour-of-the-week coverage. Why not take the 20-minute peace workout?

www.ploughshares.ca

PRINCE EDWARD ISLAND

Elephant Rock: Its Creation and Transformation

No, it's not an unforgettable kind of popular music, it's a red sandstone formation in northwest P.E.I. that recently lost its trunk in a storm. However, it will live on in the hearts of those who've seen it and also in cyberspace. View the remarkable geological story in words and pictures.

www.elephantrock.org

Folk Songs of Prince Edward Island

Get into the mood of P.E.I. with lyrics, commentary, notation, and RealPlayer audio files of authentic folk songs.

www.peifolksongs.charlottetown.pe.ca/

Prince Edward Island Business & Vacation Guide

All the resources you'd expect from a major portal for tourists to Canada's smallest province. Choose a virtual tour from the many offered, or find out about ferry and Confederation Bridge information, upcoming events, accommodations, business and real estate stuff, and island news. You can also try your hand at a tough quiz or request a visitor information package.

www.peisland.com

QUEBEC

Alliance Quebec

Alliance Quebec is a nonprofit, federally funded organization dedicated to preserving vital and secure English-speaking communities in the province of Quebec. Use this web site to join your local chapter, read about pertinent news issues, or check out related links.

www.aq.qc.ca

BonjourQuebec.com

This site, the Quebec official tourist site, provides a lot of current information from around the province, including weekly reports and a What's Happening Today section. There's a calendar of events, and you can subscribe to their e-zine.

www.tourisme.gouv.qc.ca/index_en.html

Cite Libre

Cite Libre is a magazine of ideas created in 1950 to defend freedom of expression and put an end to "the Great Darkness," which characterized the Duplessis regime in Quebec. Look up this web site for articles, event announcements, and other political rants. There's a bulletin board forum, of course, and they also organize monthly dinners. But can two words be considered a glossary?

www.citelibre.com

Destination Quebec

This is a tourism site for la belle province. It includes information on lodging, restaurants, festivals, transportation, sports, cultural attractions, and much more.

www.destinationquebec.com

Festival de Montgolfieres

Every summer this Quebec festival helps revive the Golden Age of Ballooning. During the festival, a live camera lets those who can't attend in person see all of the creatively shaped balloons via the net. You can also get schedule and program information on the music and comedy acts that appear on the event's stage.

www.montgolfieres.com

Greater Quebec City Region

This is the definitive site for those travelling to Quebec City and environs. The events calendar is actually a slick search engine, and everything but everything is listed.

www.otc.cuq.qc.ca/eng/otc1e.html

Montreal e-Guide

A guide to the city, with a personal slant by a long-time resident. The information is arranged by district and category, such as shopping, club and bar listings, transit deals, family activity ideas, museums and monuments, hotels by price range, and a cheapskates guide. Clearly a labour of love.

www.pagemontreal.qc.ca/meg

POC Communications Virtual Tour

So you'd like to lace up your skates and play for the Habs, but don't want to go through all the training, the years in minors, and the bone-crushing checks to get there. Here's the closest you'll ever get to standing at centre ice of the Molson Centre.

www.poc.ca/en/pqtvr22h.htm

Quebec Tourism

This site opens with a map so you can go directly to a specific area. If you're planning a trip to Quebec, check out this site that organizes information on lodging, dining, culture and entertainment, sports, shopping, and special events on a regional basis.

www.quebectel.com/tourisme/0000ag.htm

Repertory of Virtual Panoramas

The web address may be a bit of a mouthful, but these interactive panoramas of historic Quebec City may well be worth it. See the Basilica, the Chateau Frontenace (of course), and the fortifications of North America's only walled city.

www.tourisme.gouv.qc.ca/anglais/tourisme_a/villes_a/indexvr_a.html

RACE RELATIONS

Canadian Centre for Police-Race Relations

This is a nonprofit national resource centre "where theory, practice and social responsibility converge to promote positive police race relations." They are a practical, prevention-oriented service, and will advise clients across Canada on material relevant to their specific needs. They provide information on current research and organizations, and expert advice on bias-free standards, policies and procedures, cross-cultural and anti-racism training for police officers, and a lot more.

www.ccprr.com/

Canadian Race Relations Foundation

This registered charity is committed to "building a national framework to fight against racism." They provide links to resources and other organizations. In the Activities section, take a quiz to test your knowledge of racism in Canadian history.

www.crr.ca

Equality Today! E-zine

This e-zine is published by Young People's Press and features articles written by youth, aged 14 to 24, on the issues of multiculturalism and anti-racism. Their mandate is wide-ranging: entertainment, politics, educational curriculum. View RealPlayer dramatizations and interviews, take an online tutorial on analyzing race in the media, or add your own message and send a greeting card.

www.equalitytoday.org/

Ontario Black Anti-Racist Research Institute

This web site calls public attention to important cases of discrimination that are before various boards and tribunals in Ontario and across Canada. The site includes many links as well.

www.geocities.com/CapitolHill/2381

RAILROADS AND TRAINS

Canadian National

Check out this site for investor information and customer service updates for business people and travellers. Looking to buy a short-line? You've come to the right place.

www.cn.ca

Canadian Passenger Rail Services

Visitors to this web site can obtain information on timetables, as well as operational and equipment descriptions for all passenger rail services in Canada. You'll also find detailed route maps with bus and ferry connections across Canada.

www.mcs.net/~dsdawdy/Canpass/canpass.html

CP Railway

The Your Track section of the Canadian Pacific Railway web site allows you to create a customized page for quick access to your favourite sections of the site. This is also where verified customers can get access to secure e-business applications.

www.cpr.ca

Prairie Dog Central

Prairie Dog Central is a completely restored and operational locomotive operating between Winnipeg and Gross Isle, Manitoba. All parts of the train pre-date World War I: the coaches are made of wood and the steam engine was first built in 1882. Run by the volunteers of the Vintage Locomotive Society.

www.winnipeg.freenet.mb.ca/pdc/

Via Rail

The site of Canada's passenger rail service offers information on schedules and fares; information for seniors, students, and business travellers; an online photo album; background on Canadian tourist attractions; and even a booking service. Enter the "Win an overnight dream trip" contest.

www.viarail.ca

SASKATCHEWAN

City of Regina

Look up information on history, city services, news, employment, events, and transportation at the web site for the capital of Saskatchewan.

www.cityregina.com

Dinocountry

Eastend, Saskatchewan, is home to Scotty the T-Rex and his dinosaur pals. If the pictures and sound files don't sate your curiosity, there's info on local accommodations in case you want to visit. And there's the brand-new T-Rex Centre that houses the fossil record of the Eastend area, started many years before the discovery of Scotty in 1994.

www.dinocountry.com

MySask.com

The mysask.com web site has incorporated the Yellow Pages site along with business searches, community info, and online shopping links. Club Magic connects you to audio and video multimedia displays. I don't know where they get their quotes, but the one listed on the day I searched this site was "I haven't lost my mind—it's backed up on a CDR somewhere."

www.mysask.com

Saskatchewan News Index

This archive contains full-text newspaper stories dating back to the 1880s. Although it does contain some recent stories, it's mainly a source of historical information. In the Top News Stories, you'll find such intriguing items as "Stubbornness Put Writer on Road to Success" (1969) and "Has the Time Come for Provincial Autonomy?" (1896).

library.usask.ca/sni/

Saskatchewan Tourism

"The city of Estevan in southeast Saskatchewan is Canada's sunshine capital, averaging 2540 sunshine-filled hours each year!" So who needs the Caribbean? Seriously, you'll find this site and its resources a big help if you're going to Saskatchewan.

www.sasktourism.com

Virtual Regina

Pan around and zoom about a full 360-degree view of Regina's skyline from the top of the Hotel Saskatchewan. The next best thing to being there.

www.rreda.com/whatsnew/qtvr_1.html

Virtual Saskatchewan

Read an article by a 92-year-old retired cowboy, find out where to get some saskatoon-berry pie, and read about the mysterious St. Louis ghost train. This online magazine provides tourist and general information about the province, including golf course locations, geographical zones, and local events.

www.virtualsk.com

TRANSPORTATION

Airlines of Canada

Connect to specific airlines or locations, and find cheap flight deals from this site. Also find out a little bit about runways while you're here.

gocanada.about.com/travel/gocanada/library/weekly/aa032999.htm?iam=dp&terms=Transport+Canada

Airlines of the Web

Airlines of the Web is a clearinghouse for airline information, with listings ranging from Air Labrador in Canada to Nippon Airlines in Japan. This site allows visitors to book airline tickets, check the weather at major airports around the globe, or peruse a list of air travel tips. The especially cautious traveller can even look up the specs of particular planes. There's also a handy search function to make sure you've found the lowest fare.

flyaow.com

Canadian Transportation Web

Take care of all of your shipping inquiries at this nonprofit web site. The Canadian Transportation Web provides links to such topics as Canadian and U.S. customs information, air carriers, ocean liners, trucking, and warehousing.

www.cteam.ca/ctw

Greyhound Canada

This very functional site can help you ascertain schedules and fares for any starting point and destination. For those times when your Porsche is in the shop.

www.greyhound.ca

Subways of the World

They're all here! From the Montreal Metro to Vancouver's SkyTrain; from the London tube and Singapore MRT to the Sao Paulo Metro (in Portuguese and English).

www.reed.edu/~reyn/transport.html

Voyageur Colonial Bus Lines

Visit this online source of schedules, fares, maps, and special deals with Voyageur, which runs bus routes in Ontario and Quebec.

voyageur.com/infoe.htm

TRAVEL

Atlantic Explorer TravelMag

Planning a trip to Canada's east coast? The *Atlantic Explorer* will tell you where to eat, where to sleep, and what to do and see. Feature articles on various tourist sites are also included, along with season-specific attractions and information for golf enthusiasts.

www.atlanticonline.ns.ca/travmag

Outpost

Though based in Toronto, this travel magazine has a decidedly global feel. Articles range from reports on exotic locales to a regular health watch for those travelling abroad. For the morbidly occupied traveller, there's even a "10 Ways to Die" section, which is a great deal funnier than it sounds.

www.outpostmagazine.com

TRAVEL — FOR SOMETHING DIFFERENT

An American's Guide to Canada:

This site was written by an American who has been living in Canada since 1992. It was intended to give Americans an idea about just what the heck goes on up here in Canada, eh. You can click on to a transcript of last night's *The National*, for example. In the category of Canadianisms, subtitled "Could you hand me a serviette? I knocked over my poutine," you'll find definitions for terms such as pogey, depanneur, and mintie.

emily.icomm.ca/

Budget Traveller's Guide to Sleeping in Airports

A truly no-frills option for travellers, I suppose this type of travel is picking up since the site boasts well over 800 stories. This site rates the world's airports for safety, comfort, and noise. Visitors can search airport ratings by country or contribute their own story of no-budget accommodation. Singapore's Changi airport, winner of the best airport (to sleep in) award, is apparently so quiet that students study for exams there! The first runner-up is Amsterdam.

www3.sympatico.ca/donna.mcsherry/airports.htm

Canadian Geographic

You can subscribe to the online version, or read a selection of articles from the magazine at this site. Take the GeoQuiz to win a prize. The GeoMaps plot such eclectic information as UFO hot spots, and towns and cities with four or more players in the NHL.

www.canadiangeographic.ca/

Canadian Relocation Systems Encyclopedia

Choose your destination and then follow links to entertainment, rental, public service, and other information on that area. There is even a section that calculates how much you will have to earn in your new city to live the same lifestyle as you did on your old salary in your old city. The Relocation Cafe lists newspapers in each province and how much each costs.

www.relocatecanada.com

Center for Disease Control and Prevention

Sure, this site tells you what vaccinations you need when travelling the world, but it also includes a lot of other useful health information. The Health Topics A–Z section includes information about such diseases as chicken pox, skin cancer, and asthma.

www.cdc.gov/travel

Infohub Specialty Travel Guide

There are hundreds of listings of unique specialty tours in Canada. Hiking, ecotours, dog-sledding, camping—you name it. Click on each item to find tour summaries, itineraries, prices, and other information.

www.infohub.com/TRAVEL/SIT/sit_pages/Canada.html

PassengerRights.com

If you've had a bad experience while travelling, well, you don't have to take it anymore! Voice your complaint on this site. This is a U.S.-based site, but there's a place for you to write your feelings about Canada's airlines, hotels, and bus companies. Your complaint will automatically be sent to the organization or travel supplier. And there's a Whistle Blower section to enable industry insiders to let the cat out of the bag.

www.passengerrights.com/

TRAVEL — HOTELS & INNS

Bed and Breakfast Online

Here you'll find thousands of listings for B&Bs in Canada. Listings include photographs of the location, maps of the area, prices, services, and a description by the owner. Browse the site by geographic location or search for B&Bs in a specific city or town.

www.bbcanada.com

Excite Canada Hotel Chains

Find links to all the major Canadian hotel chains, including Ramada Inn, Canadian Pacific, Eco-Net Canada, Delta, and Radisson.

www.excite.ca/travel/lodgings/hotels_and_motels/hotel_chains/

Hostelling International Canada

Part of the International Youth Hostel Federation and an international nonprofit organization, Hostelling International runs inexpensive, safe, temporary accommodation facilities in many countries around the world, from dorms in big cities to remote cabins. These are the established, "brand name" hostels. Check out the links to do some pre-trip research, to plan transportation, or to look up e-zines and guide books. From those sites, you can view maps, check prices, and book reservations.

www.hostellingintl.ca/

Hostels.com

This site is a terrific resource for all backpackers and budget travellers. It includes a comprehensive, worldwide guide to hostels, general advice on hostelling, bulletin boards, and links to buy cheap tickets, travel books, and gear.

www.hostels.com

International Hotel Chains

Connect to international hotel chains, such as Club Med, Four Seasons, Days Inn, Grupo Sol Melia, and a selection of the "Leading Hotels of the World."

www.abconnect.com/travel/hotels/travel13j.htm

TRAVEL — LOCAL INFO GUIDES

CalgaryPlus

Don't you hate it when you click on a site and it's still under construction? "From rodeo to restaurants," they say CalgaryPlus is on its way. By the time this book is published, it should contain more than just "coming up" sections and ads.

www.calgaryplus.ca/

Citysearch

This site provides links to complete city guides and arts and entertainment guides for many U.S. cities, as well as four Canadian, three Australian, one Swedish, and one Danish city. Find out about local events, jobs, attractions, festivals, movies, and much more.

www.citysearch.com

Go Montreal

Very classy, this site. For example, click on Movies and you receive links to film festivals, production companies, and virtually any organization that has anything to do with film or video in Montreal. There's even a site dedicated to Jackie Chan. You can also link to online publications, financial institutions, and alternative health sites.

www.gomtl.com/eng.html

MapBlast! the World

Zoom in close to maps of cities all over the world. And find the weather while you're at it. Search for local schools, parks, airports, museums, shopping areas, convention centres,... the list goes on.

www.mapblast.com/myblast/index.mb

Montreal.com

All kinds of topics for virtual tourists, real-life visitors, and residents. There are FAQs, links, and articles. The site also includes a chat board/babillard. *Completement bilingue*.

www.montreal.com

MontrealPlus

Bonjour ... a la Montreal. At this official tourist site offered by Tourisme Montreal, you'll find maps and information about accommodations, restaurants, museums, and attractions.

www.montrealplus.ca

My BC

This is a comprehensive portal for British Columbia that offers navigation and search sevices, news, and tons of local event information.

www.mybc.com

My Saskatchewan

"Flat. Bald. Frigid. Don't believe the hype about Saskatchewan. Find out what's really going on." This was the banner ad that got me surfing over to mysask.com. Click on Saskatoon or Moose Jaw, for example, to see when local movies are playing or where to buy an eBook.

www.mysask.com

My Winnipeg

Local events, job postings, weather, and a lot of city stuff, along with international news and your horoscope. View LiveCam movies and photographs of Winnipeg. They seem to have thought of everything.

www.mywinnipeg.com

QuebecPlus.ca

The Quebec government's official tourist site for the city. You'll find history, arts and culture, accommodations, and nearby attractions. Most of the links are in French, but for anglophones, there are nice pictures. The English part of this site is at www.bonjourquebec.com.

www.QuebecPlus.ca

Search! Ottawa-Hull

Did you know that Ottawa has an international jazz festival? You can find out what else the city has to offer at this site with "Ottawa-Hull's most extensive listing of people, businesses, and organizations."

ottawa.canadasearch.com/

SurfOttawa

This site is a bit different from the other local info guides. For example, find the best gas prices for Ottawa or click on the Wedding Planner Site for the Ottawa Valley. There's live chat, and you can also find the usual categories like tourism, business, and the weather.

www.surfottawa.com/

Toronto.com

The terrific "everything site." Here's a reliable source for larger festivals such as Caribana: information is supplied alongside attractive official festival logos. The Community News section here is first-rate, keeping folks updated on blood donor clinics, support groups, and more. If you live here, or plan to come here, put this site on your toolbar.

www.toronto.com

Vancouver Link

Links such as community services, real estate, education, and news make this site of interest to Vancouverites but maybe not as much to those just visiting. Unless you need to know where the nearest fire station is. You can also send special-occasion electronic postcards from this site.

www.vanlink.com/

Vancouver.com

This is another one of those "soon to be up and running" sites, but this one's worth it because it asks you what you want to see on the site when it does appear. Prizes are offered.

www.vancouver.com

Yahoo Canada Cities

Selections from the Lonely Planet Guides and Rough Guides connect you to restaurants, hotels, attractions, etc. There are feature articles, photos, and maps of places such as Sault Ste. Marie, Banff, Halifax, and Niagara Falls. Some are more up-to-date and comprehensive than others.

travel.yahoo.com/destinations/North_America/countries/Canada/

TRAVEL — TRAVELOGUES

Journeywoman

The travel stories of other women travellers provide a lot of information that ranges from the practical to the inspirational. Conveniently divided into topics such as ecotourism, business travel, health advice, travelling alone, and the older adventurer. This site is livened up with interesting quotes and other tidbits. And if you have a travel question, just ask HERmail.net.

www.journeywoman.com

Travel @ the Speed of Light

This is a collection of travel stories, tips, adventures, and archived articles with a distinctly personal tone and a refreshing candour that you won't find in most upscale print travel magazines. The contents are "on-the-edge, off-the-wall travel stories." ... But *please* change the title and pictures of "Trips from a Broad"!

vanbc.wimsey.com/~ayoung

Ucluelet Adventure

Read of one man's travels to, and appreciation of, a place called Ucluelet (Yoo-Kloo-Lett). Read an area history, look at the town's natural features, or check a list of activities and events that has made one travlleler wonder whether he "need ever travel another step." And, yes, it's in Canada.

www.dist.ucluelet.bc.ca

TRAVEL — TRIP PLANNING

AllCanada.com

This site is mostly about fishing and adventure travel throughout Canada.

www.allcanada.com/

Attractions Canada

Step right up and see the sites that Canada has to offer! Thrill to the Attractions Canada seasonal features, swoon at the sight of magnificent Canadian geography, follow the links to parks and historic sites, enter contests, and try the Interactive Zone's quizzes and games.

www.attractionscanada.com

B&B Info Canada

Search using regional maps of Canada or by name or distinctive feature such as best beaches, best food, central location, or best places to ski. It includes photos of the properties, contact info, and prices.

www.bandbinfo.com/index2.htm

Campsource

Search for parks by province or territory; find brochures, maps, and guides; or join a discussion forum. Once you find the parks in the area you want, you can check their facilities, services, rates, locations, and other features. Then check to see if any reviews have been submitted for that particular campground.

www.campsource.com

Can Travel—Western Canada

Planning on a vacation in Alberta or B.C.? Looking for a mountain adventure? You'll need to think about a cabin, guest ranch, or bed and breakfast. You might also want to investigate cultural heritage or alternative destination sites where you're headed. This site could be just what you need.

www.comcept.ab.ca/cantravel

Canada Rentals

Online listings of cottages and chalets for rent across Canada. Includes general details, a specific description of the properties, maps of the area, and prices. The photos are a real plus for anyone who's ever booked a cottage and then been sadly disappointed.

www.canadarentals.com/

Canada's Atlantic Coast

Here's a tourism resource for anyone heading out east for a vacation. Check it out for information on shopping, accommodation, museums, golf, entertainment, festivals, and events in the Maritime provinces.

www.canadacoast.com

Canadian Rockies.net

The Rockies have some of the most spectacular scenery in this country or any other. Check out this travel resource for everything from wedding and convention planners to National Park permit information. Specializes in Banff, Lake Louise, Jasper, Canmore, Kananaskis, and Waterton.

www.canadianrockies.net

Canadian Tourism Commission

This web site finds out your destination and your preferred vacation activities and then supplies you with a list of available packages from various businesses. A useful planning tool but not meant for frugal travellers.

www.travelcanada.ca

Eco-Net Canada

A comprehensive tourism guide. Features include contact info for Canadian embassies abroad and live cams from across the country. Click on maps to find festivals, road conditions, and so on. Also connect with search engines across Canada.

pages.infinit.net/econet/net.html

Explore North

This site offers links, original articles, and other resources to help you plan a visit to the Yukon, Northwest Territories, Nunavut, or Alaska. It's a good place to start for links to standard tourist information such as transportation, tours, and lodgings, as well as history, media, and nature facts.

www.explorenorth.com

GORP Canada

This Canadian section of the Great Old Recreation Pages includes a number of sites across the country, along with photos, attractions, contact info for local organizations, and other links. It focuses mainly on archaeological sites, but covers much more.

www.gorp.com/gorp/location/canada/canada.htm

Great Canadian Parks

View some great photographs and read transcripts from the TV series that explores parks across Canada.

www.interlog.com/~parks/

Greatest Escapes

This travel webzine covers international destinations, but the issue I looked at included an article (with pictures) on "Plowing the Sea Lanes of the St. Lawrence in a Steamboat Replica" and, believe it or not, a gourmet food article on the M.V. Canadian Empress Cruise.

www.greatestescapes.com/

International Student Travel Confederation

This is the site of the organization that administers the International Student Identity Card (ISIC), an internationally recognized card for discounts at all kinds of attractions. This site is a good place to find out where this card will actually get you a discount. There's also information of general interest to the student traveller, and you can get a free e-mail account here.

www.istc.org

Lonely Planet Online

Before you hop on that slow boat to China, head to Lonely Planet Online. The sister site of the popular guide-book series features detailed information on all the major destinations. Be sure to check out the Thorn Tree, the best travel bulletin board on the web. Someone here is bound to know whether your blow-dryer will work in Bangladesh or where it's safe to travel in Egypt.*

www.lonelyplanetonlinel.com

Mapquest

Mapquest is your ideal online road map. The intuitive interface allows you to zoom in and zoom out, to view from ten different levels of detail, from street level to national. It also offers printable driving directions, local city news and events, major points of interest, and links to local hotels, restaurants, and other businesses. Cities in Canada, the U.S., and Mexico are supported to the street level of detail.

www.mapquest.com

Smarter Living

Bargain fares to Canadian and American destinations are out there—you just need to know where to find them. This site seems to tell you how. They have some internet-only prices, last-minutes deals, and a link to the Name Your Price web site. The Smarter Living site also lists car rental and hotel specials.

www.smarterliving.com

Sympatico Travel Canada

Check out this site for all sorts of travel-related subjects. Just for starters, see the booking services, articles, links, or Yellow Pages searches across Canada. You'll also find maps, weather data, currency converters, and forums.

www1.sympatico.ca:80/Contents/Travel/destinations/canada.html

TourWorld

This internet vacation guide is a searchable storehouse of links to resorts, hotels, cottages, fishing sites, camp sites, outfitters, snowmobiling, and more—all over the country.

www.tourworld.com

TransCanada Trail

Completed in 2000, the main trunk of the TransCanada Trail is about 16 000 kilometres in length. About 75% of the trail consists of existing trails, abandoned railway lines, and Crown lands; 25% is "new" trail. It winds through all provinces and territories. You can buy a metre of the trail for $40 and see your name "in lights," or, more specifically, on panels. The Yesteryears section of this web site includes photos of the past along the trail. You can also view and read animated Trail Trivia.

www.tctrail.ca/

Travel Clinics

A list of travel clinics and tropical disease centres. It doesn't cover the entire country, but there are clinics in B.C., Alberta, Saskatchewan, and Ontario. These Canadian clinics all belong to the American Association of Travel Medicine and Hygiene; the site connects from their home page.

www.astmh.org/clinics/cl31.html

Travel Information and Advisory Reports

Brought to you by the Department of Foreign Affairs and International Trade, this page features regularly updated reports on safety, security, health condiditons, and visa requirements for Canadians travelling abroad. Check it out if you're planning a trip to anywhere potentially dangerous.

www.dfait-maeci.gc.c/travelreport/menu_e.htm

Travelocity

Book flights, make hotel reservations, or just do a little research into your destination at this comprehensive travel-planning site. There's an extensive currency converter, so you could find out that 1 Botswana pula = 1.2922 Andorran francs—in case you ever need to know.

www.travelocity.com

YUKON

Canada's Yukon

From dog mushing to fishing to rock climbing, the Yukon has a variety of activities to attract north-bound tourists. Search this site for road trips, adventures, and trail maps, or read up on the history of the Klondike gold rush.

www.touryukon.com

City of Whitehorse

Looking to arrange a dog-sledding vacation? How about a trip into the sub-arctic climate zone? You can set up both at the web site for Whitehorse. You'll also find information about what else there is to see and do, local issues, and employment opportunities. The photo gallery will give you a sense of what to expect. And you'll find out some interesting bits of info by taking the short Yukon quiz.

www.city.whitehorse.yk.ca

Internet Yukon

This is a directory of links to Yukon sites: everything from culture to business to interactive maps. Download files and get internet help, too.

www.Yukon.net/

Yukon Web

This site provides many links to arts, business, a community forum, tourism, government services, education, events, and much more in the Yukon. It's also useful for road conditions, classifieds, weather data, realty listings, links to newspapers, and a directory of holders of Yukon-based e-mail accounts.

www.yukonweb.com

Science & Technology

AGRICULTURE

ACEIS

This is the Department of Agriculture and Agri-Food's electronic information service. Here you can find out about agricultural legislation, inspection procedures, industry information, research, and technology, and connect to databases, articles, and all types of Canadian agencies and associations.

aceis.agr.ca

AgFind

AgFind is an extensive collection of agriculture-related links and search engines. Select one of the databases or search engines, type in a keyword, or choose a link from several categories within general, livestock, and crops, and land topics.

agri-infolink.com

AgriWeb Canada

AgriWeb Canada is a national directory of Canadian agriculture and agri-food information resources available through the internet and other electronic resources. Produced by a team of librarians and other information professionals, this user-friendly database can be searched by subject, geographic region, type of organization, or keyword.

www.agr.ca/agriweb/agriweb.htm

Canadagriculture Online

Brought to you by Canada's largest publisher of farm magazines and newspapers, Canadagriculture is the online source for agri-news. This web site provides classifieds, a careers section, events, a world report, and national agricultural headlines.

www.agcanada.com

Canadian Organic Growers

Increase the biodiversity in your backyard with the help of the online resource library, organic agricultural message board, or other relevant publications and articles that this site provides. You can also link to related sites around the world.

gks.com/cog

eHARVEST/Farms.com

This site is the result of a merger between Farms.com and eHARVEST.com. Developed to encourage the use of agricultural resources on the internet, this site provides news and services ranging from weather and employment to canola and cattle. You can read articles or join the online chat forum.

www.farms.com

FoodNet

Developed by the Food Institute of Canada, FoodNet provides a series of links to policy, regulatory, food safety, trade information, and other sites. You can even click to recipes in the Other Links area.

foodnet.fic.ca

Hemp Nation

Hemp is an environmentally friendly crop that can be used to make paper, textiles, building materials, medicine, paint, detergent, varnish, oil, ink, and fuel. Of course, this is the low-cannabinoids (THC) type of cannabis grown for industrial use. This site links to a newsletter, events, and world organizations.

www.hempnation.com

Sustainable Agriculture

This web page provides links to various sites that focus on sustainable agriculture, including connections to topics such as farming, herbal health, and alternative crop production.

www2.msstate.edu/~dlang/sustaglink.html

The Farm Directory

You can search the database by category or keyword. Or check out their agricultural links to news, agri-business organizations, aquaculture, dairy, horticulture, research sites and companies, soil science sites, universities, weather information, and even entertainment. There's also a classifieds and employment section.

www.farmdirectory.com

ANIMALS & WILDLIFE

Animal Alliance of Canada

The Animal Alliance of Canada is involved in all facets of the animal protection movement, incuding cosmetic product testing, endangered and protected species, and pet overpopulation. They work on local, national, and international educational and legislative advocacy initiatives to protect animals and the environment. Check the compassionate shopping list to make sure you're not using products that have been tested on animals, or find out how you can do volunteer work for the Alliance.

www.animalalliance.ca

Aquatic Environments

Click through this site to see pictures and find out general information on Canada's invertebrates, fish, amphibians, reptiles, birds, and mammals. Take the reptile and amphibian test, or connect to references and links in each field.

www.aquatic.uoguelph.ca/animal.htm

Canadian Animal Network

You're sure to find information on all of your pets at this site, which covers dogs, cats, fish, reptiles, amphibians, and other wildlife. The Canadian Animal Network offers discussion groups, a library of frequently asked questions, pet show listings, and animal health news. There's also an interactive photo contest. You can either submit your picture or vote on those already submitted.

www.pawprints.com

Canadian Endangered Species

This site highlights a different endangered species each week. Information is provided on the history of the species, why it is endangered, where it lives and, most importantly, how it can be saved.

www.geocities.com/Heartland/Flats/8400

Canadian Nature Federation

CNF is a nonprofit organization with a naturalist's perspective. Their main programs focus on conservation of wildlands and seas, endangered species, birds, and community education. This web site includes FAQs (find out the difference between naturalists and naturists—there's a big difference!), news and alerts, and a very long species-at-risk list.

www.cnf.ca

Canadian Wildlife Federation

Since 1962, the CWF has advocated the protection of Canada's wild species and spaces. Representing over half a million members and supporters, the CEF is now Canada's largest nonprofit, nongovernmental conservation organization. Their scope is very broad, covering everything from oceans to turtles to tips and techniques for attracting wildlife to your backyard. Find out about the CWF's latest initiatives or access a variety of educational materials at this site.

www.cwf-fcf.org

Canadian Wildlife Service

Educate yourself on the finer points of wildlife conservation at this site. The CWS is part of Environment Canada, and it handles federal government wildlife matters, such as the protection and management of migratory birds, nationally significant habitat and endangered species, and other national and international wildlife issues. This site includes programs, publications, and a Kid's Zone.

www.cws-scf.ec.gc.ca

Ducks Unlimited Canada

Pretty ducks, pretty web site. Ducks Unlimited Canada is a private, nonprofit organization dedicated to the conservation of wetlands for the benefit of North America's waterfowl, wildlife, and people. After all, Canada supports one quarter of the world's wetlands, 80 percent of which have been drained or converted because of agricultural and urban expansion. On this site, you'll find out about the organization's research and education, habitat programs, and careers. You can also check out the silent auction or the Wild Things section with sample video clips.

www.ducks.ca

Fauna Foundation

It's time to "meet the chimps!" This organization provides a retirement home for abused farm and domestic animals, as well as chimpanzees formerly used in biomedical research. Current articles cover information from around the world.

www.faunafoundation.org

Hinterland Who's Who

There's a lot of information about many species at this site. It's like a very detailed field guide to Canadian birds and animals, including habitats, breeding, illustrations, and reading lists. View the Canada lynx or the red-throated hummingbird, among many others.

www.cws-scf.ec.gc.ca/hww-fap/index.html

Humane Society of Canada

This web site features information about campaigns, pets, and wildlife, among other things. Each area also connects to archived articles and information.

www.humanesociety.com

Society for the Prevention of Cruelty to Animals

The SPCA is a group of nonprofit, nongovernment organizations committed to putting an end to animal suffering, and they work with the public, government, industry, the scientific community, educators and the media toward this end. At this page, you can connect to many, but not all, of the various regional SPCAs. Their sites vary, from the comprehensive Ontario SPCA site to the more modest Charlotte County and Fredericton sites. The full URL is <dir.yahoo.com/Regional/Countries/Canada/Science/Biology/Zoology/Animals__Insects__and_Pets/Organizations/Humane_and_Rescue_Societies/Society_for_the_ Prevention_of_Cruelty_to_Animals/>

dir.yahoo.com/Regional/Countries/Canada/Science/Biology/Zoology/Animals__Insects__and_Pets/Organizations

Sounds of the World's Animals

Each language expresses animal sounds differently. Did you ever think about that? Well, on this site you can explore the sounds of the world's languages through the sounds of the world's animals. So listen to how a hyena's laugh is interpreted differently in Africaans and English; or to a cat's meow in many languages, from Albanian to Ukranian.

www.georgetown.edu/cball/animals/animals.html

Species at Risk in Canada

This site runs down the list of endangered birds, fish, mammals, reptiles, and plants in an attempt to create awareness of Canada's species that are close to extinction. You can search by location or species. You can also plot the species on maps or click on a specific species for general information.

www.speciesatrisk.gc.ca/Species/

Wildlife Habitat Canada

There are many lovely paintings of birds at this site, some by Robert Bateman. WHC is a national, nonprofit, conservation organization that works to find effective solutions to complex environmental problems facing wildlife habitat.

www.whc.org

World Wildlife Fund Canada

The WWF is more than just "save the pandas." Check out their web site for details on how to minimize your exposure to hormone-tampering chemicals, how to reduce your ecological footprints, and how to join this conservation organization. There's also a big section for kids, as well as connections to WWF sites throughout the world.

www.wwfcanada.org

BIOLOGY

Applied Biology

Learn how a tree frog or a sea snail can help people suffering from pain so severe that even morphine isn't enough. Everything you need to know about biotechnology—careers, ethical issues, applied biology, and chronicles of the early days of the "biotech revolution." The photo gallery contains well over a hundred detailed illustrations.

www.accessexcellence.org/AB/index.html

BIOTECanada

BIOTECanada is the national organization that promotes a better understanding of biotechnology and how it contributes to improving quality of life. This site contains position papers, as well as information on food, health, and the environment. Members of the biotechnology community in Canada will be interested in the resources and regular newsletter.

www.biotech.ca

Biotechnology Research Institute

BRI maintains advanced facilities to carry out research in molecular biology and biochemical engineering. The BRI web site provides access to current research, publications, employment opportunities, training, and other related links.

www.bri.nrc.ca/irbgenen.htm

Canadian Biodiversity Information Network

The CBIN is part of Environment Canada, and its goal is to provide as much information on Canadian biodiversity as possible, from all sectors. Link to a variety of sites on education, management tools, indigenous communities, and sustainable development.

www.cbin.ec.gc.ca/cbin/html

Canadian Bioethics Society

Stop! Don't splice that gene until you have visited the web site for the Canadian Bioethics Society. Read reports, find out about jobs, get conference information, check out bioethics links, and more.

www.bioethics.ca

Canadian Biological Server

Scroll down past the image of a goose and goslings to find nationwide links to biology sites, listed federally and by province.

www.uregina.ca/science/biology/liu/bio/can-bio.html

Canadian BioScience Index

This web site focuses on the legislation, policies, funding, and resources of the Canadian government in biological and biomedical sciences. Connect to government agencies, legislation, policy, and programs, as well as nongovernmental organizationss and other links.

www.home.golden.net/~rieger/index.html

Canadian Botanical Conservation Network

Those unfamiliar with the CBCN's work promoting biodiversity will still marvel at the pictures of botanical gardens and arboreta. Look up current projects sponsored by the CBCN or simply look at the endangered plant cams.

www.rbg.ca/cbcn

Digital Learning Centre for Microbial Ecology

Teaches about germs and other neat stuff (for students from age 7 to 107, they say). Includes the Microbe Zoo: Go on a safari to learn about microscopic organisms and their habitats. There are also news articles and lists of resources by title and media type, as well as links to other educational web sites.

commtechlab.msu.edu/sites/dlc-me/index.html

The Virtual Embryo

This University of Calgary site is dedicated to developmental biology. Features include online tutorials and modules keyed to textbooks. Search the virtual library of developmental biology by subject, organisms, organization, or journal. Where else can you see a picture of a transgenic *Xenopus laevis* tadpole expressing the green fluorescent protein gene under control of the cytomegalovirus promoter?

www.acs.ucalgary.ca/~browder

COMPUTER SCIENCE

ANSI Code Page

What can you do when you're inputting along and suddenly come to a crashing halt at a character unreproducible on the basic keyboard. Here's a chart of those difficult-to-remember ANSI codes for diacriticals.

www.fotonija.com/Products/CodePages/ANSI/CpANSI.htm

Association for Computing Machinery

ACM is an international organization dedicated to advancing the arts, sciences, and applications of information technology. This site provides links to receive their free publications and many other materials, and connections to chapters, special interest groups, conferences, a digital library, and more.

www.acm.org

Canadian Society for Computational Studies of Intelligence

The CSCSI site is hosted by the Centre for Systems Science at Simon Fraser University. Find connections to workshops, conference information, and journals, and links to related organizations nationwide and worldwide.

cscsi.sfu.ca

Centre for Research on Computation and Its Applications

CERCA (Centre de recherche en calcul applique/Centre for Research on Computation and Its Applications) specializes in applied scientific computation, and carries out interdisciplinary research and development projects through contracts with companies and organizations. This site offers a variety of listservs and information on conferences.

www.cerca.umontreal.ca/welcome.html

Computer Science Departments at Universities Across Canada

The title pretty much says it all. Links are provided.

www.cs.uwindsor.ca/users/c/cacs/university.html

Excursions in Computer Science

You can start with a Beginner's Guide to HTML. Or follow a history of computer science, with activities on everything from Pythagoras and Turing to Newton and Euclid. You can even check out excursions in entropy and artificial life for fun.

jeff.cs.mcgill.ca/~godfried/teaching/ecs-web.html

Glossary of Java-Related Terms

For web site designers who've progressed beyond HTML but have not yet mastered Java, this nifty applet-driven interface lets you enter any term you need defined right on the one page, so there's no waiting for your browser to find any links. You can print the glossary or submit a new term and explanation to be added to the list. You can also connect to Java online support, news, case studies, and discussions.

java.sun.com/docs/glossary.html

The Collection of Computer Science Bibliographies

They say there are more than a million references here (mostly to journal articles, conference papers, and technical reports), and the 1200 bibliographies are updated monthly from their original locations. There's also a list of major changes to the collection in reverse chronological order, and you can find out which bibliographies have been added or updated within the last two weeks.

liinwww.ira.uka.de/bibliography/index.html

COMPUTERS — GENERAL

Computer Recycling

This web page lists Computers for Schools organizations across Canada that facilitate the donation of used computer hardware to schools or students that need them.

www.microweb.com/pepsite/Recycle/Can.html

Free Online Dictionary of Computing

Type in a word or phrase, check the contents, or click on a random search and see what comes up to increase your jargon vocabulary.

wombat.doc.ic.ac.uk/foldoc/index.html

reBOOT Canada

reBOOT Canada is a nonprofit charity providing computer hardware, networking, and technical support to charities, nonprofits, and people with limited access to technology. They provide services for a cost, but at much less than the regular cost.

www.reboot.on.ca

Seniors Computer Information Program

This site provides links to many organizations of interest to seniors across Canada. Search by topic, geographic location, or keywords, or check out the Selected Sites of Interest. Join the "We're off our rockers" web discussions or hook up with a CyberPal anywhere in the world.

www.mbnet.mb.ca/crm

COMPUTERS — GRAPHICS

Free Graphics

Everything from backgrounds and fonts to animated graphics and tutorials. It's all free. There's even a separate section at the top for graphics to use for upcoming holidays.

www.freegraphics.com

Free Guides

This site is produced by the Virtual Church Hall. The Beginner's Guide to Computer Graphics is a *very* basic guide. How basic? Well, they show the difference between bitmap and vector formats, and talk about dpi's and colour. The Web Graphics link discusses formats: you know, GIFs, JPEGs, and PNGs, and background and inline images.

www.cc-art.com/guides.html

Knowledge Hound Computer Graphics

This is the computer graphics part of the Knowledge Hound site. Click on a subtopic and you might find graphic tips, tutorials, or a graphic portrayed and explained in great detail, including images of the different levels of backgrounds used to get just the right lighting.

216.15.142.170/topics/compgrap.htm

COMPUTERS — INFORMATION TECHNOLOGY

CanadaIT

This site provides one-stop shopping for information on IT–based companies, events, deals, and news. You can also access specific information according to your location within Canada.

www.CanadaIT.com

Canadian Information Processing Society

There are connections to local chapters, special interest groups, and affiliated organizations worldwide.

www.cips.ca/default.asp

CIT Infobits

Infobits is an electronic service of the University of North Carolina's Center for Instructional Technology. Each month they select articles about information technology and instructional technology. The titles in the archives include "Avoiding the Pitfalls of Electronic Publishing," "The Social Life of Information," and "If John Dewey Were Alive Today, He'd Be a Webhead."

www.unc.edu/cit/infobits/bitjanoo.html

CNET.com

Tech news, virus alerts, hardware and software reviews, downloads, auctions, stock quotes, games, jobs ... the list goes on.

www.cnet.com

Digital Doomsday

For those concerned with freedom of speech and privacy rights on the internet, this is the equivalent of the original Atomic Doomsday Clock and other similar "countdown" clocks.

www.catalaw.com/doom

Great Microprocessors of the Past and Present

From the very first, the Intel 4004 in 1971, to the many competing smart chips of the present day. This site is for history-of-technology buffs, but it might interest anyone.

www.cs.uregina.ca/~bayko/cpu.html

My Desktop

This page is filled with tips and hints for computer users. Find HTML FAQs, reviews of new software and hardware, downloads, an e-mail newsletter, and a lot more.

www.mydesktop.com

COMPUTERS — PUBLICATIONS

Andover.net

Here is a comprehensive network of web sites catering to programmers and engineers. You can link to such sites as the Andover News, Open Magazine, and the Internet Traffic Report. There's a section of online tools and features, including a free font of the day, an animated banner maker, and even a cartoon of the day.

www.andover.net

CanadaComputes.com

Read the headlines and reviews, and find out about industry trends and careers. Or link to local compute.com publications.

www.canadacomputes.com

Science & Technology

Computer Graphics World

The online version of *Computer Graphics World* brings you daily updates and news from the industry, as well as access to five years of editorial archives. Check the calendar of events for the next industry-related conference or read the product reviews. You'll find classified ads and a subject search, and you can submit your own graphics for their gallery.

cgw.pennwellnet.com/home/home.cfm

Computer Magazines

This web page will link you to quite a few computer magazines, from *Byte* to *MacUserWeb* to *Windows Sources*. Lots of good techie and no-too-techie stuff here.

www.abacom.com/innomagi/online/computng/cmagazin.htm

Computer Watch

Computer Watch is a syndicated column by Richard Morochove that runs in *The Toronto Star*'s Fast Forward section on technology, as well as nine other Canadian publications. The column focuses on technology developments of interest to home and small business computer users. It features interviews, news, and reviews of new computer products. The columns are posted at this site a few weeks after the original publication date. You can read older columns by date or search the archives for specific topics.

morochove.com/watch

Computing Canada

This site is definitely up to the minute. Check out all the news, reviews, events, and lists of user groups across Canada. Of special interest is the Benchmark section, where each month the test lab writes about the best products in the industry.

www.plesman.com/cc/

MultiMediator

It calls itself Canada's multimedia guide. This site will connect you to associations, news and information, resources, events, newsgroups, jobs, a newsletter, and more. And, as they put it so eloquently, "This guide is guaranteed to turn you into a jargon-dropping cyber-wiz in no time flat. Pocket protector optional."

www.multimediator.com/info/index.shtml

ZDNet

ZDNet is a well-integrated monster network of online computing information. Don't miss their "incredibly useful site of the day." Popular features include daily news updates, contests, reviews, publications, and a help area for your maddening computer problems. There's also a software library.

www.zdnet.com

COMPUTERS — USER GROUPS

Apple User Groups

This page is part of the Apple web site, and if you click on Canada you'll receive a list of several groups across the country.

www.apple.com/usergroups

Association of Canadian Linux Users Groups

This association, or CANLUG, is here to help with a support system that stretches from B.C. to the Maritimes. The site provides articles and tips for people new to the LINUX operating system, as well as links to other LINUX user groups, newsgroups, and distributors of the necessary software.

www.oclug.on.ca/Aboutcanlug.html

Association of Personal Computer User Groups

Interested in finding out more about computer user groups worldwide? Head over to the APCUG home page for information on different computer user groups in your area.

www.apcug.org

Canadian Macintosh User Groups (MUGs)

This page contains a list of Mac user groups by province and territory. It also supplies connections to Macintosh news, newsletters, and worldwide MUGs.

tdi.uregina.ca/~mugors/links/mugs-can.html

The Classic Computer Club

Everyone who still pines for tape drives and 64K memory will find a friend at the Classic Computer Club. This web site offers information and forums for vintage computer systems from the '70s and '80s, such as the Amiga, Collecovision, and Texas Instruments' TI99/4A.

www.chebucto.ns.ca/Technology/Classic/CCC.html

User Group Newsletters

If there isn't a user group in your area, check out this site with links to user group newsletters worldwide. You can locate a newsletter by category, or type in a keyword to see what comes up. Some of the newsletters are very detailed with plenty of graphics to keep you amused.

easyrsvp.com/ugnotw

User Groups in Canada

Several dozen user groups across the country. This list includes groups that focus on PC, Mac, Unix, OS/2, and others.

www.easyrsvp.com/ugotw/old/ugca.htm

ENERGY

Canada's Greenfuels

Find out more about ethanol and biodiesel at this site for alternative fuels. The Greenfuels site provides facts, research, related publications, retail directories, and other news on options to oil-based gasoline.

www.greenfuels.org

Canadian Coalition for Nuclear Responsibility

Here's a collection of links to various articles concerned with handling nuclear weapons, waste, reactors, nonnuclear alternatives, and the scary accident possibilities in nuclear reactors. But it's not all seriousness and gloom: there's also a photo gallery and a laugh page.

www.ccnr.org

Canadian Sustainable Energy

Head here for information on how to use energy in the most intelligent and environmentally friendly ways possible. The site discusses different types of energy (such as solar, wind, and co-generation) and includes links to organizations in each category, as well as information about publications, news, and events.

www.newenergy.org

Canadian Wind Energy Association

The global wind energy potential is roughly five times current global electricity use. Canada's installed wind turbines result in about 1.5 watts per capita for the country, compared with Denmark, for example, which has 122 watts per capita. See how our country could be making better use of our wind resources.

www.canwea.ca

Earth Energy Society of Canada

This web site explains what earth energy is (a ground-source heat pump) and how it differs from other heating energy. View an animated Flash demo of how it works, or read information about how it can be used in residential, commercial, and school areas.

www.earthenergy.ca

Energy Council of Canada

The ECC is a nonprofit organization and member of the World Energy Council. It focuses on enhancing the effectiveness of national energy policy. Members are government departments, agencies, and energy-related associations. This site provides information about conferences, publications, and projects.

www.energy.ca

Energy Probe Research Foundation

Energy Probe Research Foundation is one of Canada's largest independent think tanks. From this page, you can connect to Probe International, the Environmental Bureau of Investigation, or to Energy Probe, which is a nonprofit organization active in the fight against nuclear power. Energy Probe focuses on resource conservation, economic efficiency, and effective utility regulation. On their site (www.energyprobe.org), read about current issues and campaigns, news, publications, and how to become a volunteer.

www.e-p-r-f.org/eprf/index.html

Natural Resources Canada

NRCan is a federal government department specializing in energy, minerals and metals, forests, and earth sciences. The energy section of this web site includes news, sector and technology information, and specific info on provincial and territorial emmissions. The Kids section includes games, ask the experts, and general information.

www.nrcan.gc.ca

Office of Energy Efficiency

The OEE, part of Environment Canada, provides energy efficiency tips and tools for home, business, and cars. This site also lists energy efficiency workshops for energy consultants, driving instructors, building managers, and others.

oee.nrcan.gc.ca

Residential Energy Efficiency Database

Check out REED for such topics as indoor air quality (from radon to dust mites), energy-efficient housing construction, insulation, electricity conservation tips, and more. A thorough visit to this site is the right thing to do—and it could save you money too.

www.its-canada.com/reed

Solar Energy Society of Canada

SESC is a nonprofit organization that promotes the increased use of solar and other renewable energies in Canada. It focuses on education, technical development, and public policy. The web site provides news, events, and links, and invites you to share your solar stories for posting on the site.

www.solarenergysociety.ca

The vertical side tab reads "Science & Technology".

The Canadian Nuclear FAQ

This site contains an unofficial and privately maintained list of Frequently Asked Questions regarding CANDU reactors and nuclear power generation in Canada. Learn about the SLOWPOKE reactor, or what nature tells us about nuclear waste disposal. There are images that go along with almost every question. For example, view a 3D layout of a CANDU reactor plant or a map of Canadian nuclear sites.

www.ncf.carleton.ca/~cz725

ENGINEERING

Canadian Association for Earthquake Engineering

Curious about the concept of overstrength in seismic design? Check the CAEE web site for earth-shaking projects and investigations in your part of the country. Search the database by researcher, project, or project topic.

cee.carleton.ca/CAEE/index.html

Canadian Association of Technicians and Technologists

The CCTT is a federation of provincial professional societies represetning the interests of engineering and applied science technologists and technicians. See what the CCTT is doing to promote its members at this web site.

www.cctt.ca

Ergonomics in Teleoperation and Control Laboratory (ETC-Lab)

This University of Toronto unit undertakes applied and basic research on ergonomics and human factors. The site contains updates on research and useful resources related to the field. You'll also find MPEG demonstration videos here.

vered.rose.utoronto.ca/

ENVIRONMENT

Acid Rain and Water

This section of Environment Canada's site provides a regularly updated section about acid rain. It contains case studies, a Kids' Corner, and a list of resources.

www.ec.gc.ca/acidrain/index.html

Canada's Aquatic Environments

Dive into this educational web site that promotes awareness of wetlands, rivers, lakes, and oceans. Paddle your way around marine animals and float past plants at this extensively illustrated site. You can also play some of the games, such as "Which Bird Am I?"

collections.ic.gc.ca/acquatic

Canadian Centre for Pollution Prevention

Cut down your car's emissions or research environmentally friendly dry-cleaning methods at this site. Any questions about pollution control may be directed to the CCPP's help line. A regular newsletter is also available, and you can order their free publications.

c2p2.sarnia.com

Canadian Council of Ministers of the Environment

Do you have concerns about the state of our nation's environment? Send your comments straight to your elected representatives courtesy of this web site.

www.mbnet.mb.ca/ccme

Canadian Environmental Assessment Agency

This group promotes and conducts research in matters of environmental assessment and encourages the development of environmental assessment techniques and practices. Read their five-year review, or find out information about their public consultations, publications, and training.

www.ceaa.gc.ca

Canadian Nature Federation

The CNF is a nonprofit organization dedicated to the preservation of Canada's endangered species and their habitats. Learn more about the federation's initiatives toward wildlife preservation or read up on the CNF-sponsored research and browse the *Nature Canada* magazine.

www.cnf.ca

Climate Change Calculator

Estimate your personal CO2 emissions with the online climate change calculator. It's a downloadable interactive software tool designed to raise people's awareness of the greenhouse gases they produce through their daily activities and lifestyle choices.

www.climcalc.net

Critical Ecoregions Program

The clickable map on this page guides visitors around North America by ecosystem rather than government border. Learn about the environmental problems in your area, and find out how to help with initiatives to restore ecological health to the planet.

www.sierraclub.org/ecoregions

David Suzuki Foundation

Well-known television personality David Suzuki is responsible for a variety of environmental initiatives. This foundation works to establish a bottom-line that is rooted in the Earth and its life-support systems rather than the global economy. This site includes environmental news from around the globe, as well as conservation programs that can be adopted into our everyday lives. There are also FAQs, action alerts, and ad campaigns; and you can read a weekly article by Suzuki.

www.davidsuzuki.org

Earth Day Canada

April 22 may be Earth Day, but this web site will help you do something for the planet year-round. It includes resources to help you organize a community event like the thousands that already take place across the country. The site also contains a good section for kids.

www.earthday.ca

Ecological Monitoring and Assessment Network

This is a coordinated initiative whose purpose is to "set up a national network of representative sites for monitoring ecological functions over long periods of time." Read the EMAN headlines or check out the range maps or the movie. You can also sign up to be a Frogwatch Canada volunteer.

www.cciw.ca/eman-temp/intro.html

Elements Online

This is a lively environmental magazine provided in both official languages. Browse the magazine or view the content by theme. There's also a kids' section, which includes things that they can do to help save the environment. And you can join one of the discussion forums to have your say.

www.elements.nb.ca

EnviroLink

EnviroLink is a nonprofit organization that provides comprehensive, up-to-date environmental resources online. It unites hundreds of organizations and volunteers around the world with millions of people in more than 150 countries.

www.envirolink.org

Environment WWW Virtual Library

A searchable index of over 1000 environmental resources arranged alphabetically and by category. You'll also find links to other environmental indices. Unlike many links on the web, these sites are verified on a regular basis.

www.earthsystems.org/Environment.shtml

Environmental Industry Virtual Office

This web site connects the diverse members of Canadian industry associations dealing with the environment.

virtualoffice.ic.gc.ca

Environmental News Network

The ENN provides a mix of international news and information about the planet, including environmental news, live chats, interactive quizzes, daily feature stories, forums for debate, audio, and video. They say that they try to present information from all sides. You can search through a 10 000-article archive to gain the information you need to make up your own mind.

www.enn.com

Evergreen Foundation

Mission: to connect urban Canadians to their natural environment. An example of their work is the Learning Grounds program, which transforms barren concrete schoolyards into dynamic learning environments. In the Common Grounds Program, shared public space is transformed; and with Home Grounds, Canadians learn how to restore and enhance their own individual environments.

www.evergreen.ca

Friends of the Earth Canada

The Canadian site for this large international environmental group focuses on climate change, mining, ozone, and toxins. Read about clean air, real food, and eco-offices, among other campaigns.

www.foecanada.org

Go for Green

Go for Green is an active living and environment program designed to encourage outdoor physical activity that protects, enhances, or restores the environment. Find out more about this organization's projects at this web site full of suggested activities.

www.goforgreen.ca/home_e.html

Great Lakes Information Network

The four E's—economy, environment, education, and ecosystem—are covered on this interesting site. It's operated by a broad-based advisory board and in particular the Great Lakes Commission.

www.great-lakes.net

Great Lakes Kids

Great Lakes Kids/Les enfants des Grands Lacs provides games, quizzes, and activities for 8- to 14-year-olds. This Environment Canada site educates children about pollution and endangered species of the Great Lakes area. It also provides environmentally friendly activities to keep them interested and active.

www.on.ec.gc.ca/greatlakeskids/

Science & Technology

Greenpeace Canada

Find out about Greenpeace Canada's current campaigns. Play "Save the Whales" on the Kid's page, learn about the organization's projects, or make a donation through this web site. There are 130 000 Greenpeace members in Canada.

www.greenpeacecanada.org

International Institute for Sustainable Development

ISSDnet is the online presence of a Winnipeg-based organization that realizes that "business as usual is no longer an option." They confront important environmental and economic issues, such as climate change, international trade, natural resource depletion, and other policy questions. Check out their international internship opportunities, or order books from this site.

iisd.ca

National Renewable Energy Laboratory

This U.S. lab site includes news and events, and listings of national and international initiatives. In the easy-to-use databases, you can search for photos, documents, and general information. The Clean Energy Basics section clearly explains renewable energy and efficiency.

www.nrel.gov

PlanetDiary

This site provides a regular update of environmental, meteorological, and astronomical events on our planet. The calendar tells you what phenomena you can expect to happen on a particular date, and also gives some historical information about things that happened around that date in past years.

www.phschool.com/science/planetdiary/index.html

Pollution Probe

This leading environmental organization specializes in research, education, and advocacy in pollution-related subjects. They have concentrated on fighting for clean water and clean air, and more recently on topics such as children's health and indoor pollution.

www.pollutionprobe.org

Project Green

The web site of this nonprofit, nongovernmental organization features an online store of environmentally friendly products, from composters to pipe wrap.

www.projectgreen.ca

Right to Quiet Society

This association for soundscape awareness and protection presents a hefty list of specific goals, from the tighter regulation of flight paths to the banning of "acoustic deterrent devices" from fish farms. Learn about hearing hazzards and some pretty inventive strategies to cut down on noise. Guaranteed to contain zero streaming audio.

www.quiet.org

Sierra Club of Canada

The Canadian offshoot of this prominent environmental organization has been going strong for over 30 years. The Sierra Club focuses on loss of animal and plant species, deterioration of the planet's oceans and atmosphere, the presence of toxic chemicals, destruction of wilderness, and population growth and overconsumption. This site also offers an annual report card on the status of the commitments made at the Earth Summit in 1992 in Rio de Janeiro.

www.sierraclub.ca

Tree Canada Foundation

Like Kermit says, "It's not easy being green/Having to spend each day the colour of a tree...." And what do we do for trees in return? Well, the Tree Canada Foundation educates Canadians on the economic, environmental, and aesthetic importance of trees, and provides tips on how we can help them. With their partners, they have helped to plant over 70 million trees in Canada in seven years.

www.treecanada.ca

GOVERNMENT — ONTARIO

Environmental Commissioner of Ontario

This watchdog may not have the wholehearted backing of the government, but the commissioner's office is still active and the web site is updated regularly.

www.eco.on.ca

Government of Ontario Home Page

Ontario's open for business, says a smiling Mike Harris as he invites you into the increasingly high-tech government web site. Much useful info is available at this site, but other info is hard to find and will require a phone call, or ten, to track down.

www.gov.on.ca

GOVERNMENT — PRINCE EDWARD ISLAND

Government of P.E.I.

Explore election results, trip planners, job listings, interactive maps, media info, provincial symbols, and anything else you can think of about P.E.I. at this site.

www2.gov.pe.ca

GOVERNMENT — QUEBEC

Government of Quebec Home Page

A slick, state-of-the art site from head to toe, covering everything from tourism and business, to culture and "Quebec dans le monde." Just what you might expect from the hippest bureaucracy in Canada. Comes in French, English, and Spanish flavours.

www.gouv.qc.ca/

GOVERNMENT — RESEARCH LABS

Directory of Canadian Laboratories

This is a comprehensive resource to Canadian research and innovation. You'll find research centres, expertise networks, and technology indices.

strategis.ic.gc.ca/SSG/te01152e_pro04.sgml

INTERNET — COMMUNITY NETWORKS

Canadian Free-Nets and Community Networks

From Commox Valley to Cape Breton, find listings for free networks across the country at this site.

www.freenet.mb.ca/othersys/freenets/canada.html

shift

ChickClick

Don't hate ChickClick because it was Lilith Fair's official community sponsor. Love it because it launched Shewire and provides links to thirty-one "girl sites that don't fake it." ChickClick also links to must-read discussions like "Blossoming Britney: Did She Get a Boob Job?" (The consensus: Yes.)

www.chickclick.com

shift

Disgruntled Housewife

Men speak their minds in locker rooms, women at Disgruntled Housewife. The free-for-all results in biting censure recommendations for Bill Clinton—"He must be made to grow a little baby mustache and wear his hear in a mullet for one month"—and gems like "The Dick List," a database of the world's lousiest ex-boyfriends.

www.disgruntledhousewife.com

Excite Communities

Something of an alternative to web sites, in the sense that many Excite communities have become popular destinations for sharing information on topics of every shape and size. The site also doubles as a virtual office with the ability to store any type of document for shared viewing, have threaded discussions, control member access, and make the site private. Free and enormously useful.

www.excite.com/communities

Great Plains Free-Net

Nothing "free" is really free, but members of this group join for their own reasons: community spirit, and access to a network of like-minded people and voluntary organizations. This "free" network is supported by voluntary membership dues.

www.gpfn.sk.ca

Hell.com

It's easily the web's least friendly destination. A members-only playground for some of the net's top designers, Hell.com refuses to be indexed by search engines and takes great pains to scare off casual surfers. Follow the caustic instructions however, and you'll receive e-mailed invitations to cutting-edge online art and design events.*

www.hell.com

RemarQ

RemarQ is a compilation of Usenet and e-mail listservs available in a convenient, browser-based format. Discussion groups run the gamut from cars to travel, and the site features a daily list of the top 50 message boards.

www.remarq.com

Site Central

Netscape may give Geocities a run for its money with this service offering users free home pages with 11MB of web space. The service is attractively packaged and offers many different tools and features to spice up your site, and there's no requirement to post Netscape advertising. There is, however, a tempting offer of cash in exchange for an AOL banner on your site.

home.netscape.com/sitecentral/index.html

Suite101.com

An early web community, Suite101 has evolved into a modern portal covering all areas of interest on the web. Semi-volunteer ediotrs provide visitors with a guide to useful categories of web content. On par with any other major portal, but with a communal sensibility.

www.suite101.com

⇧shift

The Avatar Teleport

Avatars—2D or 3D digital representations of people—are the new standard of cool in online communication. At the Avatar Teleport, you can build a digital body double, take a course at Avatar University, and go trekking through the net's finest virtual worlds. Because e-mail is so passe.

www.digitalspace.com/avatars/index.html

Webgrrls

The international networking community for women in or interested in new media and technology. They currently have eight Canadian chapters, all with web sites: London, Mississauga, Montreal, Niagara Region, North of Toronto, Nova Soctia, Ottawa, Toronto, and Vancouver.

www.webgrrls.com

Webring

Webring is a free ad banner exchange service whereby cheesy, small-time sites can recommend other cheesy, small-time sites. Those looking to present an upscale and independent feel to their page may want to avoid this mode of traffic direction, but fan sites and other sites that depend on a community of appreciation will find Webring quite useful.

www.webring.com

Yahoo! Clubs

A popular alternative to private web sites, Yahoo! Clubs offers a range of features, such as threaded discussions and the ability to post photos. The most important aspects of the site: free and easy to use.

www.clubs.yahoo.com

Yahoo! Geocities

Now under the banner of the all-powerful Yahoo!, Geocities is still one of the most popular sources for free web space on the internet. Few restrictions apply, aside from the unavoidable Yahoo! logos and banner ads.

geocities.yahoo.com/home

INTERNET — GENERAL

20 Questions on How the Net Works

Helpful starting point for those who've never used a browser before. Brought to you by CNET.

coverage.cnet.com/Content/Features/Techno/Networks/?dd

Ask the Surf Guru

Answers to all those pesky little questions that make online life confusing, like "What is a wav. file?" and "How do I clear my History folder?"

www.zdnet.com/yil/content/surfschool/guru/gurutoc.html

Bunny's Free Stuff for Canadians

Never before has a Bunny given so much away, with the possible exception of Easter. Kajillions of links to sites that give away things at no charge. A random sampling of the compiled treasures includes magazines, votive candles, baby formula, screen savers, carbo gel mix, a molasses cookbook, cat food, and motivational posters.

www.microtec.net/bunny/freestuf.html

ClNet

ClNet is really a network of web sites, keeping visitors up to date on the fast-paced world of technology. The news section offers strong coverage of the business side of the tech sector, and inside information is provided by Skinny duBaud's "Rumor Mill." Other essentials related to this site include Shareware.com and Download.com, possibly the two best sources for free software for Mac or PC.

www.cnet.com

Canada's Digital Collections

Explore this online archive of Canada's history, featuring political figures, major events, photographs, timelines, and much more.

collections.ic.gc.ca

Community Access Program

The Community Access Program (CAP) is a government initiative, administered by Industry Canada, that aims to provide Canadians with affordable public access to the internet and the skills they need to use it effectively. Under CAP, public locations like schools, libraries, and community centres act as on-ramps to the Information Highway and provide computer support and training.

cap.ic.gc.ca

Cybersurf

Free internet access? Well, only if you're in Calgary, Edmonton, or Vancouver, but worth looking into. Special software is required, and plenty of advertising awaits.

www.3web.net www.cybersurf.net

Deja.com

Formerly a handy collection of usenet newsgroups, the e-commerce boom seems to have propelled Deja.com into the world of online shopping. Rather than joining in on the virtual mall free-for-all, this site provides an understated guide for comparative shopping and consumer reviews, acting as a kind of watchdog for online shoppers. The usenet groups are still there as well, but they're no longer the main focus of the site.

www.deja.com

shift

Disinformation

Disinformation is the web's central nervous system of marginal culture, be it conspiracy theory gossip or apocalyptic prophecies. Read mini-profiles of the freaks that make civilization so interesting or behold Disinformation creator Richard Metzger's slightly eerie web show, *The Infinity Factory.* But what really makes the site worth a visit are the Yahoo!-like indexed links pages that rate web sites in the same way that movies are reviewed.

www.disinfo.com

Download.com

One of the foremost sources for shareware and freeware on the internet, Download.com provides software for PC, Mac, Linux, Windows CE, and PalmPilot operating systems. Browse through categories that include games, multimedia & design, business, and education.

www.download.com

Fork in the Head

Tired of the endless stream of banal text and graphics that you're constantly being subjected to on the internet? It's time to fight back! This site lets you send a "fork-a-gram" to disappointing web pages. You'll also find tips on how to improve your own web space so as to avoid the dreaded utensil. Stick a fork in us, we're done.

www.forkinthehead.com

Formerly Useless Pages

Yes, someone has taken on the job of chronicling the vast wasteland of useless web space that is the internet. Not only are these obscure gems inane and uninteresting, but they have been abandoned by their creators. Oh, the pathos of "How to Use Nose Drops" or "The Online Pregnancy Test." When will the suffering end?

www.go2net.com/useless/useless/retired/retired-steve7.html

Free Email Addresses

Why bother with Hotmail when there are over 1000 other providers of web-based e-mail access? This site provides the listings for all of those sites. How about your name @youpy.com or @catsrule.garfield.com? The selection is seemingly limitless, and each includes a description of the service's features, as well as some tips on how to maximize the potential of your service.

www.emailaddresses.com

Gator

Now that you've got so many internet resources at your fingertips, maybe you should snap up Gator. This free piece of downloadable software simplifies filling out online forms and remembers account numbers, login names, and passwords for you.

www.gator.com

Geek Culture

Guess what? Being shunned is now a marketable commodity. The Geek Culture site ensures that even "normal" people can feel like part of the information revolution by accessorizing their life with the trappings of geekdom (download the screensaver, buy the shirt!). Strangely, there's no mention of the downside of geek life here ... For that real geek feeling, maybe the site owners should offer to call you names, refuse to dance to "Stairway to Heavan" with you, or give you wedgies in the locker room.

www.geekculture.com

Gibson Research Corporation

Got a DSL line or a cable modem? Lucky you. If you want to stay lucky, you need a firewall to render your computer invisible to hackers and data theives. Not worried? Visit the Gibson Research Corporation's site and run Shields Up!, a series of diagnostics that will tell you exactly how vulnerable your computer is to outside attacks.

www.grc.com

Learn the Net

Another great site for internet neophytes. Learn the Net has info on topics like e-mail, web publishing, doing business online, and newsgroups. Available in English, French, Italian, German, and Spanish.

www.learnthenet.com

MaxPlanet

Yet another Yahoo!-type portal with all the subject headings and categories visitors have come to expect. One feature that sets it apart: the ability to translate English to five other languages.

www.maxplanet.com

Science & Technology

MSN Canada

Compared to portals offering similar coverage, the Canadian version of Microsoft's home page is anemic and uninspired. Made up mostly of content from other sites, visitors are better off going straight to the source rather than dallying with this has-been middleman.

www.msn.ca

Network Solutions

In 1995, the U.S. government awarded this company the lucrative monopoly on the registration of generic, top-level domain names .com, .net, and .org. The monopoly has come to an end, but Network Solutions is still scheming to maintain its hold over the business. General consensus takes a dim view of NSI's high registration fees and poor customer service, and with plenty of other options, their time may have come and gone.

www.networksolutions.com

OASIS

The Organization for the Advancement of Structured Information Standards (OASIS) is on a mission to implement uniform SGML, XML, HTML, and CGM codes related to information processing. Sound dull? The development of XML (eXtensible Markup Language) as an extension to the internet document protocol HTML promises to make web searches a whole lot easier. No longer will *The Economist* be mistaken for the word economist, for example, because a category would be built into its description in a manner similar to library indexing.

www.oasis-open.org

Register.com

A supposedly friendlier domain name registrar, Register.com was the first out of the gate when NSI's monopoly ended. Unfortunately, the service is just as costly.

www.register.com

Snowball

It seems that every age group is no longer significant without being co-opted into a media-friendly moniker. Welcome to Snowball, the site built by and for Generation i (those who grew up with the internet). Though it may sound gimmicky (well, really, what doesn't?), this is a great collection of pop culture geared towards the younger crowd. Notable if only for the fact that it exposes kids to the almighty ChickClick group.

www.snowball.com

Sympatico

Like it or not, this is one of the best Canadian start pages available. Users do not have to subscribe to the Sympatico internet service, and for quality portals with a Canadian focus, this one is in the top ten.

www.sympatico.ca

The Subtle Art of Trolling

Troll: As a verb, it's the practice of trying to lure other internet users into sending responses to carefully designed, incorrect statements or similar "bait" (Source: www.whatis.com). For example, you wander into the alt.religion discussion group and announce that "God is dead," just to get a reaction. That's not very subtle. As a troller, your mission is to devise ever-subtler traps. As a trollee, your job is to stay cool and not be goaded into responding. This site offers advice for both.

www.altairiv.demon.co.uk/troll/trollfaq.html

Truly Canadian Web Site Club

This club provides links to more than 200 members' sites, all of which are more or less Canadian in content. Organized by province, the list includes some highly specialized topics such as "The Family History of Terry and Val Hvidston" or "Hillbilly Country." Head to the Canada-wide section for sites that may be of more immediate use.

www.island.net/~renada

Tucows

One of the most popular shareware sites on the internet, Tucows is packed with cheap applications for the serious user. The home page divides all the files by platform (Linux, Macintosh, and various incarnations of Windows), and then visitors are directed to a the site geographically closest to them for faster download times. There's also a rating system used to review available files.

www.tucows.com

Winfiles

Made for those with Windows difficulties, Winfiles will walk users through almost any problem with the popular user interface. There's also a generous selection of shareware, freeware, commercial demos, and hardware drivers available at this web site.

www.winfiles.com

ZDnet Downloads

Another large bank of shareware and freeware in heaps of categories, with more extensive descriptions and reviews than most similar sites. Includes a handy listing of relevant software news items.

www.zdnet.com/downloads

INTERNET — POLICY

Anonymizer.com

It's an Orwellian world of information infiltration according to Anonymizer.com. Find out how this web page can help ensure your privacy while you surf the net. If you don't believe them, go to the "what we already know about you" section for a chillingly accurate breakdown of your computer system and internet connections.

www.anonymizer.com

Canadian Information Highway Advisory Council Archive

In a world where the internet is supposed to represent freedom of expression, Canada has led the way in terms of trying to legislate it into submission. Browse through this organization's reports, questionnaires, studies, news releases, biographies, and other documents related to information control.

strategis.ic.gc.ca/SSG/ih01015e.html

Electronic Frontier Canada

An organization that fights against internet censorship, the EFC's own description of its mission is "to ensure that the principles embodied in the Canadian Charter of Rights and Freedoms remain protected as new computing, communications, and information technologies are introduced into Canadian society." A straightforward, no-nonsense site.

www.efc.ca

TERLA

TERLA's mandate is to ensure that Canadian writers, photographers, illustrators, journalists, and other creators of online content are properly compensated by the companies that use their work. Anyone involved in the industry will want to stop by and consider taking out a membership.

www.terla.com

INTERNET — RESEARCH

100 Hot Sites

Using a secret method to measure the number of weekly page hits, 100hot.com ranks web site popularity in various categories. The real attention-grabber is the 100 top sites list, but by not revealing their method for calculating the rankings, this must be viewed with scepticism. The ranking tends to be friendly to 100hot's owner, go2net.

www.100hot.com

4a2z

The user-friendly portal for 4anything.com. Join their e-mail newsletter service or take advantage of their Yahoo!-inspired web search.

www.4a2z.com

shift

Ask Jeeves

The search engine for dummies. Simply ask butler Jeeves a question and the site's propietary algorithm will look for pages that answer said query directly. Broad questions work best—"Is there a God?" for example—but the engine will also handle narrowly focused queries surprisingly well.

www.askjeeves.com

Britannica Internet Guide

A web guide compiled by Britannica editors? Yes, it's true and the site carries on the high-quality tradition that one would expect from the name. Check out this human-edited guide for detailed reviews of worthwhile sites.

www.britannica.com

shift

FAST

When there's a problem, throw a bunch of PhDs at it. At least that's what Fast Search and Transfer (a.k.a. FAST) is doing. In conjunction with Deli, this Oslo, Norway-based company has hired more than 20 eggheads from across the world to rewrite web-search algorithms in order to make query results more precise. Although FAST's database tracks only 300 million pages at the moment, it gets bonus points for comprehensive MP3 and FTP engines.

www.alltheweb.com

Femina

This search engine is a massive storehouse of links to female-friendly sites—by, for, and about women.

www.femina.com

shift

Google

Another meta-engine with a wacky name. Using mathematical formulas, Google rates a site's utility in part by how many web pages link to it. When searching for a company or a product, click on "I'm feeling lucky" and you'll be transported directly to the official site (most of the time, at least).

www.google.com

Science & Technology

Infospace

Yet another player in the internet directory business, with a useful Canadian version. It's particularly strong on city guides, classifieds, white and yellow pages, as well as government directories. The Canadian Business Finder is an effective tool for tracking down that elusive service.

www.infospace.com/canada/

Internet FAQ Consortium

This site offers a searchable database of Usenet FAQ's. Hundreds of newsgroups have compiled their Frequently Asked Questions archives here for easy searching.

www.faqs.org

Magellan

One of several edited guides to what's on the web. Owned by Excite, Magellan presents a directory-style web search with recommended sites highlighted with a red star.

magellan.excite.com

Mamma

A metasearch engine with a look and feel similar to Metacrawler. Mamma searches several different engines and returns the results.

www.mamma.com

Metacrawler

AltaVista? Hotbot? Excite? Too many search engines! Stop wasting time checking several different sources, when Metacrawler will query several leading search engines at once, and return the results in a easy-to-read format.

www.metacrawler.com

Onelook

A middle-weight contender in the battle of the research tools, suffering only from the site's specificity. Those looking for lexical resources or dictionaries would do well to check out this site.

www.onelook.com

Open Directory Project

This project aims to be the largest human-edited guide to the web. An interesting effort, it's shepherded by some toilers at Netscape, who have quietly gained a good reputation over the years for their idealism (originally, the site was called NewHoo, a thinly veiled jab at the world's biggest internet directory). It may not be the biggest yet, but it is impressive and constantly improving. Visitors will appreciate the stripped-down, no-banners aesthetic of the site, which is happily free of all advertising.

www.dmoz.com

PC Data Online

This site offers a free listing of the top 1500 most-visited sites overall. Some information is broken down by demographic category, and more detailed accounts are available for paid subscribers.

www.pcdataonline.com

Raging Search

Tired of everything-but-the-kitchen-sink portals? Raging Search, the newest search engine on the block, is as bare-bones as they come: a search window and a button. AltaVista, which operates the site, claims Raging is 20 percent faster than the competitors and that its 350-million-item index is free of dead and redundant links. Maybe, but so far it's no match for Google.

www.raging.com

Refdesk

Some folks like their info in a consistent format, in digestible morsels. If you're one of these people, then Refdesk isn't for you. If, on the other hand, you have a voracious appetite for just about anything, and actually like sifting through a jumble of different formats and search metaphors, then Bob Drudge's monster research site is right up your alley.

www.refdesk.com

shift

SavvySearch

SavvySearch is a metasearch engine, meaning it doesn't index the web itself but rather runs search terms through a number of engines, idexes, and databases. It will enlist the help of the regular engines—Yahoo! Lycos, and AltaVista—as well as site-specific databases such as online encyclopedias and entertainment reference sources like the Internet Movie Database. Plus, you can customize SavvySearch by selecting any of a hundred different engines, indexes, and databases you want it to query.

www.savvysearch.com

Search Engine Showdown

Billing itself as "The Users' Guide to Web Searching," this site by Greg Notess could also be called the "Battle for the Planet of the Search Engines." It's packed with stats about useful things like which engine produces the most dead links (if you hadn't noticed yet, it's poor old AltaVista).

www.searchengineshowdown.com

Search Engine Terms

The good people who run the I-Search Discussion list have built this useful glossary of terms relating to all aspects of search engines. They've even provided translations in French, Italian, German, Spanish, Dutch, and Serbian.

cadenza.org/search_engine_terms/

shift

Search Engine Watch

Here's the scenario. You've just posted your snazzy new web page—one of 600 million or so on the internet—and want browsers to check it out. That means registering the site with search engines and web indexes like Yahoo! While it sounds easy, it's actually wrought with difficulty because you won't get any traffic if you didn't register your site properly with the major engines. Look no further than Search Engine Watch, the best reference tool for learning to manipulate the internet's Boolean gatekeepers. This site will be of interest to grizzled and neophyte surfers alike, as it explains the disparate methods engines use to reference and chronicle pages. It also provides alternative search methods for specific needs, as well as status reports, search engine news, and histories of all the existing engines.

www.searchenginewatch.com

Search Voyeur

Watch what other people are searching for on the Magellan directory at this site that refreshes every 10 seconds. Metacrawler offers a simlar tool, called Metaspy.

voyeur.mckinley.com/cgi-bin/voyeur.cgi

Switchboard

Switchboard offers search and directory tools, as well as some clever tricks such as roaming access to your browser bookmarks. Every one of these tools is available somehwere else, but this site is attractively packaged and includes several search tools for finding everything from online businesses to old school mates.

www.switchboard.com

Top Ten Links

This is a directory of different categories, each listing the top ten web sites for that topic. The ratings are based on user votes, but the methodology, while undoubtedly objective, is somewhat murky.

www.toptenlinks.com

Topica

Topica lists hundreds of specialized e-mail discussion groups and makes signing up as easy as pointing and clicking. Try "YogaForever" or "Charley Stough's BONG Bull" if your inbox isn't full enough already.

www.topica.com

Yahoo Suck!

It seems that certain lawyers have no interest in this site. For those who feel that monster site Yahoo! is too stingy about what it includes in its directory, Yahoo Suck! offers an alternative listing in the form of a look-alike site. You may find some interesting, "below the radar" offerings here.

www.yahoosuck.com

Yep

A search engine that goes to the trouble of rating sites by popularity and quality. Includes software that will display reviews of sites as you search.

www.yep.com

INTERNET — RESOURCES

shift

1001 Winamp Skins

Winamp became the net's hottest MP3 player for one reason: Its skin, or graphical interface, can be changed without affecting its functionality. At 1001 Winamp Skins, you can emblazon your copy of Winamp with fake wood panelling, a sultry picture of Lara Croft, or, um, somewhere around 999 other skins.

www.1001winampskins.com

4anything.com

These megalomaniacs registered thousands of domain names beginning with the number 4 and have used them to create a fairly comprehensive directory of internet information. For example, 4email.com is a detailed and carefully edited resource guide to everything to do with e-mail: netiquette, free providers, hoaxes, and searches. A particular strength is the site's city guides, featuring 4Toronto.com, 4Montreal.com, and 4Vancouver.com.

www.4anything.com

Babel Fish

Pinching it's name from the popular *Hitch Hiker's Guide to the Galaxy* series, this site attempts to replicate the fabled fish's powers on the net. Visitors can cut and paste text into the site's window and receive translations into a number of different languages.

babelfish.altavista.com/cgi-bin/translate?

Canadian Flag Clip Art Gallery

Patriotic web designers will want to access this collection of over 200 images of or related to the Canadian flag. There are also links to a Proud to Be Canadian Web Group and a Proud to Be Canadian Chat Room for other Canuckish nattering.

canflag.ptbcanadian.com

shift

Cool Archive

Want to give your tired home page a new look? At Cool Archive, you can take your pick from more than 950 fonts, 4000 icons, and 1000 clip-art images. Get additional help from a logo generator and the sound library. Before leaving, take the "Ten Sites That Bite" tour to ensure you're not making any fatal design decisions.

www.coolarchive.com

Crayon

Does online news seem too impersonal? Create your own virtual newspaper using input from over 1000 different sources at Crayon.

www.crayon.net

Excite (the other one)

This is a group of web designers, animators, poets, and scholars who provide professionally designed online content. Located in Vancouver, this group's web site provides an interesting showcase for their wares.

www.excite.sfu.ca

Internet Baglady

Here's a collection of free resources for web authors. As Baggie herself says, you don't have to be a rocket scientist, rich, or a programmer to create compelling content.

www.dumpsterdive.com

Internet.com

Internet.com does a great many things very well. Among them, acquiring new web sites for its online portal. In 1999 it purchased mydesktop.com, a tech newsletter run by three teenagers, for over a million dollars. Dozens of the most important industry publications are housed here, and quickly evolving fields like consulting and e-commerce are well covered.

www.internet.com

PGP International

Worried about your privacy? Visit the PGP International home page and fret no more. PGP (Pretty Good Privacy) is nearly unbreakable public domain encryption software for your e-mail. Version 6.5.3 is now available for Windows, Macintosh, and Linux. The PGP download wizard helps you access the latest freeware PGP version.

www.pgpi.com

shift

Screen Savers a2z

Okay, so you don't need another screen saver. Don't let that stop you from checking out a2z, which claims to have the net's largest collection of useless imagery. Of particular interest are an earnest Donny and Marie Osmond saver and some hard-to-find Mac savers that don't require AfterDark.

www.ratloaf.com

shift

Shareware.com

You wouldn't buy a car without test-driving it. So why would you purchase software if you haven't played with it for a week or two? At Shareware.com, you'll find a repository of more than 250 000 files, all allowing you to try before you buy. Entries are separated into everything from PC and Mac sections to Atari and Amiga.

www.shareware.com

Sitelaunch

For the individual webmaster who wants tricks of all kinds, with a focus on tips for promotion and advertising. A friendly site, not oriented to big business concerns, Sitelaunch is a great starting point for beginners in web design.

www.sitelaunch.net

The Box Network

Tired of feeling superior? Drop by the Box Network for a nice shot of humility as you browse this collection of search engines, directories, and archives built for only the most seasoned netizens.

astalavista.box.sk

The Canuck Site of the Day

Check out the day's Canadian web page or search the archives for sites dating as far back as the previous year.

www.maplesquare.com/canuck

shift

The GNOME Project

It's the ultimate chameleon. GNOME (pronounced "GUH-nome") is a graphical interface that can mimic Windows, the Mac operating system, and pretty much anything else you tell it to. It runs atop Linux in the process, transforming Linus Torvald's hackers-only curiosity into the most user-friendly operating system on the planet. The GNOME Project features 256 core programmers, all of whom share unblinking dedication to copyrighting the opposite of copyright (as in go ahead and steal it). Their work is free to download and is open source—meaning anyone can view and alter the source code. And because it runs on Linux (rhymes with cynics) GNOME is faster, more powerful, and less likely to crash than any other OS.

www.gnome.org

Traffick —The Guide to Portals

Portals are indispensable news sources. They are purveyors of free entertainment and helpful tools. They are an infinite number of things to an infinite number of people. Traffick helps you get a grasp on just what some of those infinite things might be, with articles and reviews on major portal sites. Including a partnership with Aboutportals.com, this is the best place to stop before settling on Yahoo! or MSN.

www.portalhub.com

shift

Webfree

At last, the definitive reason why Macs will always be cooler than PCs. Webfree, a Mac-only control panel developed by programmer Steve Falkenburg, reads HTML codes as web pages load, while blocking blinking text, GIF animations, cookies, and—best of all—banner ads.

www.falken.net/webfree/

INTERNET — SEARCH ENGINES AND INDICES

Canadian Personal Home Page Directory

Use this search engine to look up any personal home page in Canada by surname, city, and province, or add your web site to the directory.

bltg.com/people

INTERNET — WORLD WIDE WEB

Featherweight Sites

Tired of bloated, ungainly web pages that take forever to load? So are these people, who started the 5k Award for Excellence in Web Design and Production. Take a look at these sites and revel in what can be done with a mere 5 kilobytes of space. Small is beautiful.

www.sylloge.com:8080/5k/home.html

Futurelog

Futurelog is the mother lode of technological punditry: a running index of predictions about the brave new world to come, ranging in tone from breathless and uncritical ecstasy to the most cynical pessimism you can imagine. Check out Bruce Sterling's predictions about life in 2035.

www.gyford.com/futurelog

Looking Good in 2010

IDEO, the firm that designed the sexy, streamlined Palm V, has taken a guess at what sorts of toys the geek who has everything will be playing with a decade from now. This article has lots of snappy renderings of digital pens, artificially intelligent personal assistants, featherweight phones that perch delicately inside your ear, roll-up LCD screens ... Gee, if our stationery looks this good, we might not have to worry about war, famine, and disease at all.

www.businessweek.com/2000/00_10/b3671021.htm

Rotten.com

The soft, white underbelly of the net, eviscerated for all to see. Rotten.com collects images and information from many sources to present the viewer with a truly unpleasant experience.

www.rotten.com

shift

Slashdot

The subhead says it all: "News for Nerds. Stuff that matters." Slashdot, the open-source community's town hall, is frequented by Linux heads and copylefting programmers (meaning they don't protect their source codes). Slashdot's members come to read and debate articles about *Tron* remakes, Microsoft's misadventures, and everything else of burning importance to geeks. Many of the featured articles are reprinted from other sources, but no one seems to care. Jon Katz, who writes for the likes of *Shift* and *Rolling Stone*, is a regular contributor, as is Rob "CmdrTaco" Malda, Slashdot's founder.

www.slashdot.org

The Future Gets Fun Again

Wired magazine's first issue of the millenium, which focused entirely on gee-whiz technological predictions for the coming decade, is now available online. As is usual for *Wired*, the selection of articles ranges from hard science to whimsy to outright crap, often within the span of a single article.

www.wired.com/wired/archive/8.01

The Industry Standard

If you really want to know the dirt about what's happening in the online universe, the Standard is essential reading. This is a deep-content site: not only does it present in-depth articles on the latest online trends, there's a Metrics section with enough stats about online growth to satisfy the most meticulous of researchers.

www.thestandard.com

Web Informant

Consultant David Strom keeps you up to date on trends and happenings online. Includes articles such as "Surfing on Company Time" and "A Plea to Return to Single Tasking." Added cred: Strom has also written a book on internet messaging (Prentice-Hall, 1998).

mappa.mundi.net/inform/

Whatis.com

What is Whatis.com you may ask? A giant guide to help you negotiate the impenetrable tech jargon that plagues the internet, making life confusing for the average surfer. Find out what ExploreZip Virus and Extensible Markup Language are or get a pithy description of ARPANET, the little acorn (the early internet, intended for military applications) that grew into a mighty virtual oak.

www.whatis.com

Wired

Wired provides an indispensable source of current high-tech and internet-related news. At its site, you'll find a collection of clever zine articles, interviews, tutorials, job listings, gossip, and serious news geared toward those who are likely to read it in the wee hours of the morning, still buzzed with too much java. Though ostensibly for the netizen who is already well informed, *Wired* has plenty to offer the casual reader. The Webmonkey section is a popular resource for webmasters, pitched at an intermediate level. Though now owned by Lycos, this site has yet to demonstrate any adverse effects from the new partnership.

www.wired.com

World Wide Web Consortium (W3C)

Created in October 1994 by web-inovator Tim Berners-Lee "to lead the World Wide Web to its full potential by developing common protocols that promote its evolution and ensure its interoperability," the W3C now has more than 400 member organizations around the world.

www.w3.org

INTERNET TOOLS

Alexa

Alexa is a companion tool that can be set up to work with your browser. Get information about any site you visit, including rough measures of site traffic, written reviews by visitors, a ranking system based on votes, and links to related sites. A handy tool for spying on the competition.

www.alexa.com

shift

Copernic

This PC software is available for free download, allowing customizable metasearching in four categories (Web, Newsgroups, Email, and Buy Books) across more than 100 site-specific search engines, such as CNET's Search.com. Copernic compiles them according to relevance, and dumps duplicate hits. To really go hog-wild, cough up some cash and buy the full version, which refines your searches in 18 specific areas, ranging from recipes to tech news.

www.copernic.com

Country Digraphs

A directory of the nation-specific suffixes used in web addresses (Canada's is ca). Browsable by country or by digraph.

www.theodora.com/country_digraphs.html

Disabling Cookies

Tired of having your browser keep track of your every move on the internet? Instructions for turning off cookies can be found at the junkbusters web site.

www.junkbusters.com/ht/en/cookies.html#disable

Efax

Those reticent to spend the money on an expensive fax machine will appreciate this free fax service. Efax assigns you your own personal fax number and can route voice mail and faxes to your e-mail account. The catch? Toll-free numbers cost extra.

www.efax.com

Finding Information on the Internet

Flummoxed by this new-fangled gadget called the internet? Know someone who is? Here's an online tutorial produced at UC Berkeley that explains the internet, world wide web, Netscape, and other applications.

www.lib.berkeley.edu/TeachingLib/Guides/Internet/FindInfo.html

Freedom

Zero Knowledge Systems of Montreal has created online anonymity software for those worried about their personal internet security. Also includes headlines and news items relevant to internet privacy issues.

www.freedom.net

Freeservers

Small businesses and beginners in the world of web page creation can take advantage of this site's offer of free web space. Freeservers will give anyone 30MB of web space in exchange for banner advertising that they select. Upgrade pricing for expanded services is reasonable, but as with any free lunch, there will be restrictions as to what can and cannot be placed on your web page.

www.freeservers.com

Internet Subject Directory

Having trouble with search engines and their random responses to search terms? Look for it the old-school way with this straightforward subject directory. Not a completely comprehensive list, but still a good start.

www.albany.edu/library/internet/subject.html

Librarians' Index to the Internet

As the storage of knowledge moves from print to digital form, librarianship is transforming into "information science." Here's an example of the fruit of this electronic shift: a directory of sites in every subject area, selected and evaluated by professional librarians. An attempt at providing a virtual card catalogue for the internet.

lii.org

Looksmart

A directory-style guide to web content, similar to Yahoo! but with slightly more comprehensive subject directories. A straightforward resource.

www.looksmart.com

Mail.com

Yet another source of free e-mail on the internet? Of course! Just like Hotmail, Excite Mail, and pretty much every other web site on the net, Mail.com is a web-based e-mail service. The difference? Most of these free services, like Canada.com and Ehmail.com, are hosted by this site. So why not go right to the source?

www.mail.com

mylook.com

Customize your own preferences at this site that surveys the web and collects articles based on your specific needs.

mylook.com

Neoplanet

Hotbot/Lycos's answer to Internet Explorer and Netscape, Neoplanet is a free web browser that combines e-mail, instant messaging, chat, web directory, search engine, and user-created communities all into a single application. Not the most popular option so far, but it's still nice to know that there are serviceable alternatives.

lycos.neoplanet.com

Net Floppy

Believe it or not, NetFloppy was created in response to Apple's decision to ship the iMac without floppy drives. This service allows users to store their important data on its servers on a 3 Meg virtual floppy. Those wary of just who these "guys in white coats" are and what they're able to do with your private documents will justifiably be interested in exploring other options, or maybe even buying an external drive. An interesting service nonetheless.

www.netfloppy.com

Netscape Navigator Plug-ins

For a complete list of available plug-ins, visit the Netscape Browser Plug-ins page. For a list of the plug-ins currently installed in your copy of Navigator, type "about: plugins" in the browser's Location window.

home.netscape.com/plugins

Opera

If you're a no-nonsense power-user type who's not afraid to tinker with the default settings of your software, or if you're fed up enough with the never-ending Netscape/IE wars to want to become a no-nonsense power-user type, Opera is for you. Why bother? Find out here.

www.opera.com

Palm Gear HQ

Here's a one-stop spot to buy fax, e-mail, and web software for your Palm.

store.yahoo.com/pilotgearsw/faxemail.html

SmartUpdate

With recent versions of Navigator and Communicator, Netscape has intorduced a service called SmartUpdate. When you visit the SmartUpdate page, the site can automatically detect which version of the Netscape browser you're using and what components are missing.

www.netscape.com/smartupdate

The Source for Java Technology

Developed by Sun Microsystems, Java is the application that allows computers to communicate with each other no matter who built them. Find out about Java at this site or visit Gamelan, the Official Java Directory, at www.gamelan.com.

java.sun.com

Web Accessories for IE5

If all the extra options for IE5 still aren't enough to satisfy your need for gadgetry, check out the web accessories available on this page.

www.microsoft.com/windows/Ie/WebAccess/default.asp

Web Site Garage

This assemblage of savvy web site management and tracking tools includes a browser snapshot, which provides a comprehensive review of how your pages look to people using 18 different browsers.

websitegarage.netscape.com

MATHEMATICS

Canada/U.S.A. Math Camp

This is a camp for mathematically talented students from around the world. From this site you can fill in an application to attend the five-week summer camp, complete a qualifying quiz, and link to such interesting student math sites as Math in the Movies and a Famous Curves Index.

www.mathcamp.org

Canadian Mathematical Electronic Services

The Canadian Mathematical Electronic Services aims to expand the electronic services available to Canadian research mathematicians, mathematics educators, and students. Take advantage of the available resources or check out sections on research and employment.

camel.cecm.sfu.ca

Canadian Mathematical Society

This society aims to promote and advance the discovery, learning, and application of mathematics. Check out the site for membership information and listings of math-related activities, projects, and reports.

camel.cecm.sfu.ca/CMS

Electronic Games for Education in Math and Science

Math and science can be fun! Check out the E-GEMS site for educational tools masquerading as games. Or is it games masquerading as educations tools? No matter.

taz.cs.ubc.ca/egems/home.html

MacTutor History of Mathematics

For math buffs, this site contains a cool chronology of various math discoveries, early astronomy, and biographies of important mathematical innovators. The site is provided by the University of St. Andrew's in Scotland.

www-groups.dcs.st-andrews.ac.uk/~history/

Mathematics WWW Virtual Library

As well as providing links to online mathematics resources, this site includes a newsletter, computer support, and job resources.

euclid.math.fsu.edu/Science/math.html

The Math Forum

This site contains discussion groups for students, teachers, parents, and others interested in math education. There are links to libraries and other research resources, and a features section that includes Ask Dr. Math and an internet newsletter. You can also search the internet mathematics library.

forum.swarthmore.edu/

MULTIMEDIA

Audionet Canada

Tired of plain old TV? Check out Audionet for live radio and television broadcasting simultaneously from the same web site! Choose shows by category or search through the archives for programs you've missed.

www.audionetcanada.com

Beyond Geography

Check out this independent site for the latest on new media and audio in Canada. Here you'll find web-based artwork, documentation of installations, and a selection of audio art pieces. Vist a powwow or link to "liquidation fiction" web audio.

www.culturenet.ca/ifva/beyond

Multimedia Authoring Web

"Programming by non-programmers" is what this authoring site is all about. It's a resource collection of pointers to internet sites for those who develop multimedia. It contains over 900 resources, and you can search by category or keyword.

www.mcli.dist.maricopa.edu/authoring/about.html

Multimedia Centers on the Internet

This page provides links to sites about authoring, graphics, scanning, and various other multimedia information. Most of the resources are American, but some are Canadian or international.

www.library.nwu.edu/media/resources

MultiMediator

This Canadian site includes general information about the multimedia industry: what's new, publications, awards, jobs, and a calendar of events within Canada and around the world.

www.multimediator.com

newMEDIA

Find out about Canada's international multimedia showcase and conference. They showcase digital technology from creative applications to deliver across all media platforms. This site has general information on the yearly show, and specific conference information.

www.infopreneur.com/newmedia2000

Wired

You won't find news discussions in MP3 on many sites, but you will find it on this site, which covers "news of the digital world," along with stock quotes and articles on business, politics, culture, and technology. Their other products include the HotBot search engine and the HotWired web site.

www.wired.com

PARANORMAL

Canadian Scientific Paranormal Investigations

If you thought Canada was exempt from weird sightings, well you were wrong. The CSPI aims to scientifically explain such sightings. They'll be happy to receive your e-mails of personal experiences, videos, or recorded sounds of anomalies. Join the discussion forum or read about their recent investigations.

www.ghrs.org/cspi

Experience the Paranormal

Join the paranormal chat room at this site. Download the "Nessie" screen saver from the Lake Monsters section, or connect to such topics as Ghosts & Poltergeists, Big Foot, and Miscellaneous Phenomena.

www.phoenixgate.com/paranormal.html

Mysteries of Canada

Everything is not as it seems in Canada after all. Read short tales of adventure and the unexplained from across the land. Marvel at the Treasure Pit of Oak Island, the Creature of Lake Memphremagog, and the Mad Trapper of Rat River. You can search for stories by region, author, or keywords.

www.mysteriesofcanada.com/

Strange Magazine

This online magazine covers a variety of feature articles, as well as departments such as the Anomaly Pages, Book Reviews, Haunts, and First Person, where you can send in your own weird encounters by e-mail.

www.strangemag.com

The Skeptics Society

The organization is for "anyone curious about controversial ideas, extraordinary claims, revolutionary ideas, and the promotion of science." Join the discussion forums, read *Skeptic Magazine*, view the news articles and archives, or send in your psychic one-liners. You can order books such as *Why People Believe Weird Things*.

www.skeptic.com

X-Chronicles

Here's the site for the internet radio show hosted by Rob McConnell. Try the X-game, read about supernatural phenomena in the X-zine, or check out one of the 170 links.

www.xzone-radio.com/Chronicles

PHYSICS

Canada's National Laboratory for Particle and Nuclear Physics (TRIUMF)

Interested in pondering the properties of subatomic particles? TRIUMF (Tri-University Meson Facility) is in just such a business, where their meson factory (one of three in the world) mass produces pions, the lightest of the mesons, by the billions every second. To find out just what the heck all this means, visit this web site.

www.triumf.ca

Help for Physics Students

A solid starting place for any physics-related questions you may have, this site includes heaps of links—including hundreds of links to humour sites alone. Check out the feature articles such as "Is It Worth Running in the Rain?" and "Big Bang in a Test Tube."

www.dctech.com/physics/student_help.html

Physics Online

Many of us suffered through high school physics, but there must be some who enjoyed it. For those who miss it, here's a B.C.-based site offering various resources related to high school physics, including photos from an annual Balsa Bridge Building Contest.

www.ndrs.org/physicsonline/index.htm

PhysicsWeb

This site provides global news and information about physics. Check out the feature articles, Physics in Action section, calendar of events, job banks, and many other online resources—especially the TIPTOP link (The Internet Pilot TO Physics).

physicsweb.org

The Light Bullet

This page provides a fairly straightforward introduction to light and laser physics. If visitors are not interested in text on light bullets and solitons, there are some cool-looking movies and stills demonstrating their properties.

www.sfu.ca/~renns/lbullets.html

SCIENCE — GENERAL

Canada-Wide Science Fair

This is an annual event sponsored by the Youth Science Foundation (YSF) Canada. It involves around 500 participants, and many other delegates. Scroll down to a specific year, and click to see information and the on-site virtual fairs.

www.reach.net/~grants/

MAD Scientist Network

More than 700 scientists have signed up to answer questions on the Mad Scientist web site. So maybe the stereotype is true! Ask a question, search the archives, go to the MAD labs for demonstrations, or take a trip through the digital images of the Visible Human Project. The MAD library of links is searchable by category or keyword.

www.madsci.org

The Virtual Science Centre

This web site is filled with fun items, such as a dinosaur simulator and an internet science quiz. The site is provided by the Singapore Science Centre, and it is a mirror site for information on the latest Mars missions and for online dictionaries. You'll also find a Virtual Science Centre Search Engine, and connections to science exhibit activities, international science organizations, and educational resources.

www.sci-ctr.edu.sg/vsc.html

SCIENCE — MAGAZINES

Astronomy Magazine

Check out the news and sky events, or take the astro quiz at this online version of *Astronomy* magazine. You can also check the archives by recent articles, recent monthly issues, or a keyword search.

www.kalmbach.com/astro/

Discovery Channel Online Canada

This lively site for science, technology, and nature buffs is perfect for younger readers. By the way, when they talk about "full frontal," they mean the brain.

www.exn.ca

Nature

This is an international weekly journal of science. You must register to read the current special-feature articles, but it's free. There's a section on jobs and careers, and you can also connect to other *Nature* journals (genetics, biotechnology, medicine, etc.).

www.nature.com/nature

Science

Browse articles and summaries in *Science* magazine. You can search by various functions within the magazine, and across multiple science journals. There's also a good section of essays that examine the interaction between science and society, written by people inside or outside the scientific community. Each article is provided in summary and full text, and there are links to debates about the content of the article. You can also submit your own response.

www.sciencemag.org

Science Magazines for Kids

From this location, you can link to the sites of four science magazines: *Canadian Rockhound: Junior Rockhound Magazine*, *Dragonfly*, *OWL Kids*, and *Yes Mag*. There's a lot of colourful, interactive science stuff for kids on these pages.

public-library.calgary.ab.ca/cya/klsmags.htm

Science News Online

This is a weekly science newsmagazine with current and archived feature articles and news. There's also a connection to an archive search at the Smithsonian Institute, which houses a collection of some of the magazine's photographs taken between 1926 and the present.

www.sciencenews.org/

ScienceDaily

This online magazine contains articles selected from news releases submitted by leading universities and other research organizations around the world. Read the features, or search the news by topic or keyword. There are discussion groups, links, and pictures/sites/talks of the day.

www.sciencedaily.com

Scientific American

One of the great features of this online magazine is the Ask the Experts section. You can also view past answers by category. Read current and past interviews and feature articles (including illustrations and links to subtopics). Or click on and read the very first issue—from August 28, 1845.

www.sciam.com

Yes Mag: Canada's Science Magazine for Kids

This magazine's site is a collection of quizzes, puzzles, articles, reviews, and projects for children. There's a listing of kids' science camps, as well as a section for parents and teachers.

www.islandnet.com/~yesmag

SCIENCE — ORGANIZATIONS

Canadian Association for Girls in Science

CAGIS members meet regularly to explore science with women who have chosen careers in science and technology fields. This site includes experiments, optical illusions, a word-search, and connections to the different chapters across Canada.

publish.uwo.ca/~cagis

Canadian Science Writers' Association

The Canadian Science Writers' Association is a national alliance of professional science communicators in all media. Read the latest issue of *Science Link*, their quarterly newsletter, or check out the job board.

www.interlog.com/~cswa

Community of Science

Formerly the Canadian Community of Science, this international organization works with 400 000 scientists and scholars to help them find funding and promote their research. Check out the other services this organization provides, read their online news and events, or search the Commerce Business Daily database.

www.cos.com

Science Organizations

This web page lists links to science organizations around the world, including NASA.

www.spocom.com/science/orgs.htm

Science Organizations Around the World

This page provides links to science organizations including government ministries, agencies that fund science and engineering research and education, and nongovernmental organizations. Search by geographical area or click to global and regional organizations.

www.nsf.gov/sbe/int/map.htm

Science Organizations on the Internet

This web page lists links to science centres, museums, and other science organizations on the internet. Scroll down the page or search by letter, then click to the Virtual Science Centre main pages.

www.sci-ctr.edu.sg/sciorg/sc_onnet.html

The Aging Research Centre

As the largest segment of the world's population gets older, there will undoubtedly be more interest in how to slow down the aging process. Visit the ARC's web site for a fountain of youthful news and genetic research projects, or look into getting yourself cryogenically frozen in the hopes that future scientists will figure things out.

www.arclab.org

SCIENCE, TECHNOLOGY & SOCIETY

Birth and Crisis of Scientific Paradigms

This history-of-science site features Aristotle, Galileo, Descartes, Newton, and Leibniz.

www.bdp.it/~pspsooo1/Paradigmi/enascita.html

Charlotte Science Resource Page

The Charlotte Science Resource Page aims to promote science literacy. Science lovers can browse this web site by its convenient groupings into energy, forest ecology, and human environments. There are also listings for scientists and their work on the web, as well as curriculum suggestions for teachers.

www.swifty.com/apase/charlotte/corepage.html

shift

Discovery Channel Online

If you feel out of the loop whenever someone mentions time, space, or matter, you should check out the Discovery Channel's site. Discovery Online has some slick, yet smart, interactive features, along with video from its TV programs and updates of science stories in the news.

www.discovery.com

Globetechnology.com

Here you can read archived articles from the Technology section of the *Globe and Mail*. The site covers a wide range of topics, including Tech News, Tech Alert, Events, and searches.

www.globetechnology.com

Junk Science

Junk science is defined as "bad science used to further a special agenda." The implied existence of a perfect world of objective science notwithstanding, it seems as if bad science comes from many sources, and this site has it covered. Link to the Trash Talk Forum to "debunk the junk."

www.junkscience.com

The Why Files

Visit this site for a scientific look at current events, complete with explanations of glossed-over scientific jargon found in the mainstream media. Past articles are archived to maximize this site's research appeal.

whyfiles.news.wisc.edu

SPACE & ASTRONOMY

Apollo Lunar Surface Journal

Find out about different Apollo missions and the astronauts who were on them. It's not often you'll get chills listening to a RealAudio file, but you will when you hear some of these recordings.

www.hq.nasa.gov/office/pao/History/alsj/frame.html

Astronomy and Astrophysics WWW Virtual Library

Connect to Canadian university departments and other groups and institutes in the field.

www.bilkent.edu.tr/pub/DataSources/bySubject/astro/departments-and-groups-canada.html

Astronomy and Space Links

Whether you're an amateur or a pro, if you're looking for space-related newsgroups or lists, you'll find quite a few here. There are also many other links to general astronomy and space sites around the world, including professional research, amateur research, and star parties.

www.skypub.com/resources/links/links.shtml

Astronomy in Your Face

View photos, movies, and animation from several galleries at this web site. There are answers to space questions, a glossary of terms, and time conversion tables, among other features. You can also link to a solar system simulator and other space-in-your-face sites.

www.sorgeweb.com/astronomy/index.htm

Astronomy Picture of the Day

Each day a different image or photograph of the universe is featured, along with a brief explanation written by a professional astronomer. The archive goes back to mid-1995, and you can search it by keyword. Also check out the glossary to help you understand what you're seeing.

antwrp.gsfc.nasa.gov/apod/astropix.html

Canadian Astronaut Office

Have you got what it takes to boldly go where only a few Canadians ever have? Here you can read about Canada's astronaut training program, inform yourself about missions, or examine our nation's role in the development of space technology.

www.space.gc.ca/csa_sectors/human_presence/en/canastronauts/index_en.htm

Canadian Astronomy Data Centre

The CADC is responsible for collecting data from a number of observatories and telescopes, including the fabled Hubble space telescope. Visitors can browse the various archives and get news and updates from this web site.

cadcwww.dao.nrc.ca

Canadian Space Agency

Kids can play space games, read space jokes, or ponder their future in space. Adults might want to enter the KidSpace too, and they can also read about news, research, training, and events, and connect to the different sectors of the agency.

www.space.gc.ca

Kennedy Space Center Video Feeds

Want to view some launch pads? These cameras will take you there, and you can set the updates to refresh every 45 seconds to 180 seconds. Click on the information below the pictures to read background information about each location.

www.ksc.nasa.gov/shuttle/countdown/video/video.html

shift

Liftoff to Space Exploration

It's a bird. It's a plane. It's ... space junk. Yes, aside from providing scientific articles on the space program and the cosmos, this NASA site lets visitors follow such celestial tidbits as the paths of orbiting satellites, spacecraft flight schedules, and the facts on what it's like to live in zero gravity.

liftoff.msfc.nasa.gov

NASA

The first FAQ on the National Aeronautics and Space Administration site asks, "Why NASA?" Well, this site explores that question in great detail and explains everything that NASA does. There are such sections as NASA for Kids, Space Science, Earth Science, Multimedia Gallery, News, and NASA television. And this site also connects you to related sites. By the way, if you're thinking about exploring space or working for NASA, they warn you to avoid black holes and drugs.

www.nasa.gov

Nasaquest.com

This web page provides hundreds of links to such sites as observatories and astronomical societies, backyard astronomy sites, meteorite pages, sky calendars and plotters, and several Native star knowledge pages.

www.nasaquest.com

Sat Passes

Why get caught out on a cold night looking for the MIR space station in vain? This site tracks satellites and spacecraft as they pass over many Canadian and American cities.

www.bester.com/satpassses.html

Space Programme

This site offers space news articles from a variety of sources, including CNN, the *Economist*, the *New Zealand Herald*, space.com, newswire, and businesswire. They also provide many links to related space sites.

www.space-photos.com/

Space Science Program

This site is put together by the Canadian Space Agency. Discover what physiological changes occur to humans in the weightlessness of space. Explore the stars from telescopes in space. View high- or low-resolution photos in the Image Gallery. Or read the up-to-the-minute news releases.

www.science.sp-agency.ca

The Nine Planets

This multimedia tour of our solar system is very impressive. It provides an overview of the history, mythology, and current scientific knowledge of each of the planets and moons. Each section includes text and photos, some have sounds and movies, and most provide references to additional related information. Vote for your favourite planet.

www.seds.org/billa/tnp/

The Space Page

This web page connects you to a great deal of space-related material, from satellite pictures of the earth and maps of the planets, to the *Lunar Base Quarterly* and places to make your reservation for a ticket to space (it will cost you about $96 000 for a three-hour tour).

www.chebucto.ns.ca/~adw/space.html

Windows to the Universe

If you're looking for visuals of space, you'll find them at this site. View in low-, medium-, or high-resolution modes. Each section takes you to a variety of images, general information, and links. Check off beginner, intermediate, or advanced content levels, and you'll receive different info. You'll also find activities, Ask a Scientist, and related resources sections throughout the site.

http://www.windows.umich.edu

SPACE & ASTRONOMY — CLUBS

Amateur Astronomy Clubs and Organizations

Scroll down this page to find Canadian clubs: These links are all active too! You'll also find links to other amateur astronomy clubs worldwide.

www.science.mcmaster.ca/HAA/

Astronomical Societies

Astronomical societies worldwide are listed on this page, from Agrupacio Astronomica de Sabadell in Spain to Wycombe Astronomical Society in Buckinghamshire, England.

www.stsci.edu/astroweb/yp_society.html

Astronomy Clubs in Canada

Astronomy clubs in Canada, listed by province. Contact address information is given, and most have web sites or at least e-mail addresses.

www.kalmbach.com/astro/SpacePlaces/CanadaClubs.html

Canadian Astronomical Society

Check out the listings for observatories and research centres across Canada and around the world. You'll also find information on CASCA membership and upcoming meeting dates.

www.casca.ca

Students for the Exploration and Development of Space (SEDS)

Here's the site for the Canadian section of SEDS, a student-volunteer-run organization that promotes awareness of the peaceful exploration and development of space. The site offers quizzes, contests, and information about the SEDS scholarship.

www.seds.ca

SPACE & ASTRONOMY — OBSERVATORIES

Canada-France-Hawaii Telescope

CFHT is a joint project of the National Research Council of Canada, Centre National de la Recherche Scientifique of France, and the University of Hawaii. The CFHT is located atop a 4200-metre-tall dormant volcano. There are schedules, tools, references, and news bulletins for observers. Take a virtual tour of the CFHT or access the galaxy of astronomy resources.

www.cfht.hawaii.edu

Dominion Radio Astrophysical Observatory

This is a National Research Council of Canada web site. The observatory operates the seven-antenna Synthesis Telescope (ST), the 26-meter Telescope, and the 10 cm Solar Flux Monitor. See photos of these items and take a virtual site tour (movie with sound). You can also check out the FAQs, sky-gazing notes, newsletters, and some interesting articles, such as "Probing the Invisible Universe."

www.drao.nrc.ca

Liquid Mirrors

Liquid mirrors? They're pretty much what they sound like, starting from the idea that liquid "could, in principle, be used as the primary mirror of a telescope." The centre of this technology is at the Universite Laval. View the astronomical image gallery or link to references and related sites.

wood.phy.ulaval.ca/lmt/home.html

Space Places in Canada and the U.S.

This web page will link you to museums, planetariums, and observatories in North America. It also contains a section on astronomy clubs.

www.kalmbach.com/astro/SpacePlaces/SpacePlaces.html

TELECOMMUNICATIONS

BBM Bureau of Measurement

BBM is a not-for-profit, broadcast research company responsible for monitoring radio and television ratings for Canadian advertisers. Check out the top programs list or a variety of news, membership, and contact information. You can also read the latest analyzed data about radio listeners and TV watchers. Or read the latest issue or download archived editions of *In Sync*.

www.bbm.ca

Canadian Radio-Television and Telecommunications Commission (CRTC)

You hear about the CRTC often enough these days, what with debates about the regulation of new technologies and so on, so why not head over to their web site for the scoop? The CRTC is an independent agency responsible for regulating Canada's broadcasting and telecommunications systems. The FAQs answer such interesting questions as "How does a song qualify as Canadian?" "What can I do about those junk faxes I keep receiving?" and "Where do I find out about upcoming public hearings so I can take part?"

www.crtc.gc.ca

Canadian Telecommunications Consultants Association

The CTCA is Canada's only professional association of independent telecommunications consultants. Those seeking assistance in this field may consult the CTCA's online directory of registered members. You can also check out their newsletter archive.

www.ctca.ca

Emergency Telecommunications

Ever wonder who takes charge when there's a major emergency in Canada? This Industry Canada site will tell you. They give advice and assistance to federal departments and agencies. They also handle emergency broadcast services, priority access for dialing, and other general preparedness tasks.

hoshi.cic.sfu.ca/ic

Media Awareness Network

Click on the remote control on this page to take you into the main body of the site. Read such articles as "Web Awareness: Knowing the Issues" and try the web literacy game "CyberSense and Nonsense: The Second Adventure of the Three CyberPigs."

www.media-awareness.ca

Telecommunications Online

What does it take to become a hot technology? This question and others are tackled in the online version of *Telecommunications* magazine. There are international and American versions here. Industry links to many associations, forums, and other sites are also provided.

www.telecoms-mag.com

The Telecommunications Standards Advisory Council of Canada

This organization focuses on standards in information technology and telecommunications. The web site provides links to Canada-wide standards organizations, working groups, committees, and international resources.

www.tsacc.ic.gc.ca

Learning & Resources

COMMUNICATIONS

Canada's Community Access Program

Industry Canada's Community Access Program works with rural Canadian communities to take advantage of new communication technologies. Examine the different programs that might be useful for your town at the CAP web site. Download signs and posters or link to more general Canadian sites.

cap.ic.gc.ca

Communications Research Centre

CRC is a major research facility of Industry Canada. Find out about the latest info on multimedia technology as well as objectives and careers.

www.crc.doc.ca

HyperMedia

HyperMedia is a working group at U of T's McLuhan Program designed to explore web architecture and interface design, including tangible media, augmented realties, and bio-interface technologies. Examine the group's latest projects at this web site.

www.mcluhan.utoronto.ca/hypermedia

McLuhan Program in Culture and Technology

Marshall McLuhan was investigating how electronic media and new technologies affect our world long before the popularity of personal computers and the internet. Visit this site to find out about the institute that bears his name and continues his explorations into the social ramifications of living in a wired world. The McLuhan Program offers continuing education courses for non–U of T students, as well as a variety of lectures and events designed to educate people in the use of new technologies.

www.mcluhan.utoronto.ca

Who Was Marshall McLuhan?

"The medium is the message." Learn about the man behind the catchphrase at this anecdote-filled site.

www.beaulieuhome.com/McLuhan/default.htm

CRIME

Canadian Criminal Justice Resource Page

An extensive list of web-based criminology-related resources, this site ranges in content from juvenile delinquency to media sites to university graduate programs. Begin at the helpful "Starting Points" section to send you on your way.

members.tripod.com/~BlueThingy/index.html

CAVEAT Home Page

CAVEAT is an organization that works to contribute to the creation and maintenance of a just, peaceful society through public education, changes to the justice system, and ensuring the rights of victims. Find out more about the struggle against violence or offer your support at this web site.

www.caveat.org

Crime Prevention

Read this sobering and hypertext-peppered essay on the state of crime prevention in Canada.

www.bconnex.net/~cspcc/crime_prevention

CRIME — CRIME PREVENTION

National Crime Prevention Centre

The focus of this organization within the Department of Justice is to deal with crime before it happens, rather than through reactive measures after the fact. This site includes details on local initiatives (sorted by province) that share this goal.

www.crime-prevention.org

CRIME — LAW ENFORCEMENT

Officer Down Memorial Page

An online memorial site dedicated to all Canadian law enforcement officers who have given their lives in the performance of their duties. A grim reminder of the dangerous jobs these men and women perform across the country every day.

www.odmp.org/canada

Royal Canadian Mounted Police

See what the Mounties have been up to lately. Check out a scary "wanted" line-up, find out about organized crime, or even look into joining up.

www.rcmp-grc.gc.ca

DISABILITIES

Attention Deficit Disorder FAQs

This is one of the most comprehensive online resources available on this common disorder.

www3.sympatico.ca/frankk/contents.html

EDUCATION

shift

PBS Online

All the science, history, politics, and culture you could ever want, minus the pledge-week guy to make you feel guilty. This site is jam-packed with film clips and information from public broadcast staples. But what really makes it worth bookmarking is the bounty of web-specific articles on everything from the theory of relativity to the history of China.

www.pbs.org

Postgraduate Pages

A nice resource from the University of South Australia. Head here for research advice, tips on how to write a thesis, how to succeed in graduate school, and other sound advice, which, as a typical graduate student, you likely won't take. For the antidote to this page, we recommend Matt Groening's classic *Life in Hell* description of graduate school. D'oh!

www.library.unisa.edu.au/postgrad/

The Educator's Toolkit

While not dedicated solely to teaching exceptional children, the Educator's Toolkit is an invaluable resource for teachers of all disciplines. Included is a list of links for teachers faced with the rewarding challenge of teaching exceptional children.

www.eagle.ca/~matink/

EDUCATION — ADULT & CONTINUING

Athabasca University

Canada's leader in distance education, Athabasca University provides BA, MA, and certificate programs. Students can sign up for programs year-round and are able to complete them at their own pace. This web site provides a useful guide and intro to the university's courses and available services.

www.athabasca.ca

Ecole Virtuelle School

Take courses in high-tech computer training from the comfort of your own desktop. The Ecole Virtuelle School provides training in both French (duh—who would've guessed) and English.

www.virtuelle.org

Older Adults and Learning Technology Project

Created in the wake of a 1997 conference, this site publishes some of the results in areas such as recommendations for buying a computer and glossaries of computer and internet terms. You'll also find links to online learning resources and contact info for other older adults' education providers.

www.crm.mb.ca/scip/oalt

The Banff Centre

The Banff Centre is an educational and developmental resource for Canadian artists and managers. This site provides information on conferences and events.

www.banffcentre.ab.ca

UBC Distance Education & Technology

This branch of UBC offers courses and certificate programs for those living in remote areas of the country, or for people who cannot fit their lives into a university schedule. Check the course offerings and registration info at this web site.

det.cstudies.ubc.ca

EDUCATION — CAREER & VOCATIONAL

Adler School of Professional Psychology

The ASPP offers courses leading to a Master of Arts degree in Counselling Psychology. The degree is fully accredited and is recognized in Ontario by the Ministry of Training and Education, the College of Psychologists, the Ontario Psychological Association, and other professional organizations. Find info on entrance requirements, courses, and duration of the program, as well as a description of counselling services offered by the school.

www.adlerontario.com

Canadian Academy of Private Investigation

Sign up gumshoes! At the CAPI students can get everything they need to become fully trained private eyes. Explore this site for course information, application forms, and links to similarly inquisitive sites.

www.cadvision.com/Home_Pages/accounts/capi/capi.html

Canadian Coast Guard College

Head to Cape Breton for a career in the Canadian Coast Guard. Find out about the training involved in the protection of the coastline that is longer than any other nation's.

www.cgc.ns.ca

Canadian Forces College

If you're a Canadian officer looking to further your education, then this is the site for you. Browse course descriptions, read military news, look up government sites, or use the handy search tools at this web page.

www1.cfcsc.dnd.ca

Gemmology World

Here's a site for professional gemmologists—those who identify and evaluate gemstones—or people curious about the field.

www.cigem.ca/211.html

Homeopathic College of Canada Home Page

Providing an overview of programs for aspiring homeopaths and promising to uphold professional standards. FYI, you can also phone them at 1-888-DRHOMEO.

www.homeopath.org

The College of Piping and Celtic Performing Arts of Canada

This Maritime educational centre has been actively promoting and preserving Celtic culture and heritage by offering instruction in traditional Celtic disciplines. Known for an annual concert featuring east-coast band Great Big Sea, the college hosts a number of P.E.I. musical events and gives detailed descriptions of them at this web site.

www.piping.pe.ca

EDUCATION — INDICES

Canadian Education on the Web

Here you'll find a comprehensive collection of education-related sites, including links to subjects such as private schools, independent institutions, community colleges, and jobs in education.

www.oise.utoronto.ca/~mpress/eduweb.html

Canadian University Phonebooks

Up-to-date listings for all campuses across Canada.

www.physics.mcmaster.ca/resources/CanUniv.html

CollegeNET

CollegeNET lets applicants complete, file, and pay for their admission applications entirely through the internet. Though each application is available through the specific university's home page, CollegeNET provides a collection of over 250 schools in one convenient location.

www.collegenet.com

Edge Post-Secondary School Finder

You'll rule with this cool school tool.

www.schoolfinder.com

Go Higher!

This studious site provides a terse tour of post-secondary institutions. Look up information on registering, finances, housing, and careers, or pose any questions you have to the discussion group.

www.gohigher.net

Scout

"Surf smarter, not longer" proclaims Scout, a tool for education professionals, or really anyone with interests in academic fields. No doubt a big problem with the net is its bewildering mass of info. Take advantage of this service, which filters online resources for the education community in thousands of subject areas. Allows you to find the best of the net without the hassle.

scout.cs.wisc.edu/index.html

EDUCATION — INTERNATIONAL

Canadian Bureau of International Education

Canadians looking to study overseas or residents of other countries looking to study here should investigate the services offered at this site.

www.cbie.ca

Canadian Institute for Teaching Overseas

The CITO was created to facilitate the exchange of Canadian and American teachers to foreign countries. Visitors to the site can look up information on teaching abroad, recruitment, consulting, and TESL certificate courses through distance education.

www.nsis.com/~cito/CITO.html

Study Abroad

This is an American-oriented online reference for study-abroad programs, but with thousands of such programs listed, many are sure to be of interest to Canadians. You can search by academic subject area or by country.

www.studyabroad.com

EDUCATION — K-12

Cable in the Classroom

Focusing on television's potential to educate rather than conciliate, Cable in the Classroom offers a range of youth-oriented instructional programming. The web site for this nonprofit organization provides lesson plans, a regular magazine, contact information, and more.

www.cableducation.ca

Children's Literature Web Guide

The CLWG is an attempt to gather together and categorize the growing number of internet resources related to books for children and teens. This site rates the best books from the last year, lists award winners and bestsellers, and provides enough links to make any book-buying decision difficult.

www.ucalgary.ca/~dkbrown

Community Learning Network

The CLN is a telecommunications network maintained by the Open School, a service within the Open Learning Agency. Kindergarten to Grade 12 teachers will appreciate the online resources designed to help integrate information technology into the classroom.

www.cln.org/cln.html

Education World

A learning site for educators. Expansive and attractive resource.

www.education-world.com/

Green and Growing Environmental Education Project

A teacher's guide related to food, agriculture and sustainable development. Don't forget to tell the grownups!

www.GateWest.net/~green

Kinder Art

Boasting the largest collection of free art lessons on the internet, Kinder Art proves to be a great resource for any parent or teacher looking to keep kids occupied. Subjects range from architecture to slushy design, with a selection of art trivia, articles, kits, and magazines to be used as backup.

www.kinderart.com/lessons.htm

Mr. G's Applied Technology Site

Good old Mr. G provides lesson plans for science and technology-based studies. Educators can download step-by-step visuals, find out about suggested careers in science and technology, or simply browse the lesson designs.

www.coaltyee.nisa.com/at/at.htm

Saskatchewan Education

Here's an uncommonly attractive and useful site with many resources for educators, including some definitive perspectives on early childhood education and resource-based learning. Take your time—there's lots here.

www.sasked.gov.sk.ca/k/index.html

The Brainium

Focusing on Grades 4 through 8, the Brainium provides interactive science education through the use of educational games, activities, and animated adventures. Sample the preview section or look up info on how to become a member at this site.

www.brainium.com

The Green Group's Eco-Pals Program

The Green Group is responsible for providing environmental programming to school-aged children. Their Eco-Pals program teams up different classrooms across the country, in order to communicate and produce environmental programs locally.

www.greengroup.com

EDUCATION — ORGANIZATIONS

AIESEC

AIESEC is an international exchange program that allows Canadian students to work abroad. The international Traineeship Exchange Program sends one Canadian student abroad for every foreign student brought to Canada, with exchanges lasting anywhere from two to eighteen months. The AIESEC web site lists companies and communities that are involved in the program, and provides info on applying for an exchange of your own.

www.ca.aisec.org

Alberta Correctional Education Association (ACEA)

The ACEA is dedicated to the academic, vocational, and personal development of offenders, and the professional enhancement of the association's members. The site gives curious citizens detailed info about the ACEA, and provides a message board and newsletter for members.

www.tellusplanet.net/puhlic/acea/

Association of Canadian Community Colleges

The ACCC is a volunteer organization designed to promote communication and interaction between community colleges across the country, while promoting these schools to prospective employers. Visitors to the web site will find descriptions of the association's programs, postings of recent news events, and a list of other ACCC web sites.

www.accc.ca

Association of Universities and Colleges of Canada (AUCC)

It's one-stop shopping for future students at the AUCC site. Visitors can check the school's stats on everything from scholarships to faculty, or follow the links to every university in Canada.

www.aucc.ca

Humanities and Social Sciences Federation of Canada

Created by an amalgamation of the former Canadian Federation for the Humanities and the Social Science Federation of Canada, this federation came into being on April 1, 1996. It currently represents 54 learned societies, 69 universities and colleges, and over 24 000 scholars and graduates active in the study of languages, sociology, literature, religion, geography, psychology, anthropology, history, philosophy, classics, law, economics, education, linguistics, women's issues, industrial relations, and international development. Known for an annual congress that was in the past nicknamed the "Learneds" (or the "Stupids" depending on who you ask).

www.hssfc.ca

The Association for the Promotion and Advancement of Science Education (APASE)

In a world where gloabal communications and cloned sheep are commonplace events, scientific knowledge becomes increasingly more important. APASE promotes science literacy for children and adults through various educational programs and events. Check out the association's parent and teacher resources, online activities for kids, and a list of events and publications.

www.apase.bc.ca

EDUCATION — PROGRAMS

Canada's Schoolnet

Schoolnet is an organization dedicated to connecting Canada's schools to the internet. Check out Schoolnet news and cool sites, online learning resources, and info on connecting your school to the web at this site.

www.schoolnet.ca

Canada-US Studies

This resource provides info on Canada-U.S. relations and business consulting, as well as links to Canadian universities and other relevant sites.

phoenix.som.clarkson.edu/~canweb

Canadian Association for Girls in Science

It's time to break the stranglehold that young boys have kept on the subject of science. Thanks to the CAGIS, that may soon happen through programs that encourage young women to take on the challenges of the scientific world. Try the Brain Snacks, duck into the Laboratory, or see what kind of careers are out there.

publish.uwo.ca/~cagis

Encounters With Canada

A youth exchange program.

www.encounters-rencontres.ca

Group of Ten Student Exchange Program

A little-known undergraduate exchange program organized among ten of Canada's most prominent universities.

admin1.intlcent.ualberta.ca/GOTSEPinfo/gotsep.html

Ryerson School of Interior Design

One of only two accredited four-year interior design programs in Canada.

www.ryerson.ca/programs/interior.html

EDUCATION — STUDENT

Campus Access

An info and resource centre for Canadian university and college students. The site discusses academic, social, and professional topics, including high school students going on in their studies, student businesses, teaching English abroad, and graduate and professional schools.

www.campusaccess.com

Canadian Federation of Students

With over 400 000 members, this organization is one of the largest lobby groups in the country. It represents university and college students' interests nationwide, coordinating campaigns for an accessible, high-quality, post-secondary education system.

www.cfs-fcee.ca

Egyptian Student Association in USA and Canada

An interesting guide to organizations across North America.

www.esana.org/esa.html

Learning & Resources

The Actuarial Students' National Association

Founded in 1989, the ASNA has grown to include 85 percent of actuarial students in Canada. Their goal is to provide representation for the student body at the same level as the professional societies, while promoting and demystifying actuarial science.

www.fortunecity.com/campus/electrical/15/

EDUCATION — TECHNOLOGY

EvNet

This research and consulting group evaluates instructional technologies on behalf of universities, colleges, schools, and other educational organizations. The site contains many resources, as well as information about an annual conference.

www.socserv2.mcmaster.ca/srnet/evnet.htm

EMPLOYMENT

B.C. Agricultural Labour Pool

This web site connects agricultural employers in B.C. with prospective employees. Job seekers can search employment listings and apply for jobs, and employers can post job vacancies.

www.agri-labourpool.com

Canada Job Bank

Search for jobs in any part of the country with this national employment listing. Job searches are broken down by province and can be explored by title or by date posted.

jb-ge.hrdc-drhc.gc.ca

CanadaWorkInfoNet

CanadaWorkInfoNet provides a variety of employment-related resources for people looking for work or looking to improve their training. Look up info on jobs, education, self-employment, financial help, and job trends at this site.

www.workinfonet.ca/cfn/english/main.html

Canadian Career Development Foundation

CCDF works in partnership with various organizations to improve career prospects for individuals all over the country. Browse this web site's resources, training information, and career links to see how they can help you.

www.ccdf.ca

Canadian Career Page

If you're unemployed or looking to change jobs, you'll appreciate the job postings, career fair listings, news, and links provided at this page. With over 250 000 hits per month, this site is bound to have the latest info.

www.canadiancareers.com

Canadian Jobs Catalogue

Each month, the CJC opens up a different industry or occupation-specific category, with free direct links to the sites contained in it. For a nominal fee, those looking for employment may also gain access to the site's entire job listings.

www.kenevacorp.mb.ca

Canadian Medical Placement Service

This resource allows medical professionals to find and post practice opportunities. Looking for a new career?

www.cmps.ca

Canadian Resume Centre

Post your resume to this site where 25 million potential viewers might see it. The site is also a free service for employers to find resumes according to their hiring criteria.

www.canres.com

CareerMosaic

"Where employers and job seekers go first." It's the leading employment site on the net, with the possible exception of the Monster.com group of sites. Apparently this site records more than 4.4 million visitors per month.

www.careermosaic.com

Charity Village

Here's an excellent source of employment opportunities at a wide variety of nonprofit organizations. The ads tend to include a good selection of management positions, and you can also find volunteer opportunities.

www.charityvillage.com

Electronic Labour Exchange

According to them, "The ELE is an exciting job matching service offered by Human Resources Development Canada."

www.ele-spe.org

GlobeCareers.com

A newer-generation job-hunting site packed with current articles and resources.

www.globercareers.com

Human Resources and Development Canada Job Bank

This national job bank run by HRDC is also available in French. Like so many government sites, it loads rather slowly, and at present, the job postings annoyingly don't give the name of the employer. Nevertheless, its size alone makes it worth a visit.

jb-ge.hrdc-drhc.gc.ca

Job Search Canada

If you had to pick just one place to start your online job search, this would not be a bad choice. It includes loads of links to job banks, advice, and much more. A short description accompanies all of the links, so you don't waste time connecting to inappropriate sites.

jobsearchcanada.about.com/mbody.htm

Monster Board

This is one of the best-known employment sites in both English and French, with a good-sized cache of want ads. You can personalize your own account, research companies, post your resume, and search the jobs by keyword, location, and category.

www.monster.ca

Monster Talent Search

This huge job exchange focuses on "free agents" and those wanting to hire them. Known for its great television advertising campaigns.

www.monster.com

National Graduate Register

The NGR is for both students and graduates. It includes resources for both job seekers and employers, including a resume database. It's a free service, but registration is required for several federal programs.

ngr.schoolnet.ca

New Media Recruiting Services

A visually interesting site, although a somewhat annoying interface, geared to matching positions and personnel in the field of new media. Divided into permanent and temp jobs, you can apply via e-mail for any listing—as if they'd ask you to send it in by regular post.

www.newmediars.com

OnSite Human Resource Assistance

This program gives employers salary-free, entry-level, professional employees, and gives EI recipients a chance to continue to receive benefits while getting valuable work experience.

www.epi.ca

Opportunities 45+

An employment site for older workers with disabilities, funded by Human Resources Development Canada.

www.opportunities45.org/

Public Service Commission of Canada Federal Job Site

Check out this database of jobs open to the public, featuring links for students and a service that alerts you by e-mail if an appropriate position becomes available.

jobs.gc.ca/home_e.htm

Work in Culture

This Ontario site features three main sections: Cultural Careers Council Ontario; CHRIS (Cultural Human Resources Information Services), which offers info, counselling, and assistance; and Training Resources and Databases, which is searchable. Events listings are also included.

www.workinculture.on.ca

Youth Resource Network of Canada

Check out this site for one of the best sources of what the feds offer for youth. Sections include career self-assessment, training and education, job opportunities, job search techniques, and self-employment.

www.youth.gc.ca

EMPLOYMENT — ORGANIZATIONS

Co-op Japan

The Co-op Japan Program specializes in developing work placements and internships in Japan and Asia for Canadian university students and recent graduates. This web site also offers career services for companies interested in employing graduates with international work experience.

cjp.coop.uvic.ca

Work in Culture

This Ontario site features three main sections: Cultural Careers Council Ontario; CHRIS (Cultural Human Resources Information Services), which offers info, counselling, and assistance; and Training Resources and Databases, which is searchable. Events listings are also included.

www.workinculture.on.ca

GENEALOGY

Acadian Genealogy Home Page

Created and maintained by Yvon L. Cyr of Ontario, this page is a cornucopia of Acadian facts and observations. Search through thousands of genealogy links, browse through selected books and music, or make a request for Yvon to research your Acadian roots.

www.acadian.org

Ancestry.com

A partly free, partly fee-based conglomerate of genealogy databases. Together, they add up to hundreds of millions of names.

www.ancestry.com

British Columbia Cemetery Finding Aid

Not a site for choosing your final resting-place, the B.C. Cemetery Finding Aid is designed to help people find names of relatives in order to trace their family history. This genealogical resource lists over 344 000 internments for visitors to sort through by surname, given name, cemetery, and region.

www.islandnet.com/bccfa/homepage.html

Canada GenWeb Project

An important site for the collection and distribution of Canadian genealogical data. Every province and territory has a sub-site within GenWeb offering resources and links. An invaluable tool for family research that promises to keep growing. It even has a section to help kids get started on researching their genealogy.

www.rootsweb.com/~canwgw

Canadian Genealogy and History

Look up a genealogy site from your province or suggest a site to add to this directory of historical links. There are also sections for archives, cemeteries, and organizations to help visitors delve into their family's past.

www.islandnet.com/~jveinot/cghl/chgl.html

Family Search

Although an American site, this massive genealogical database is potentially useful to anyone searching for their ancestors. It's sponsored by the Mormons and is reportedly one of the heaviest traffic sites on the entire internet.

familysearch.org

Ontario Cemetery Finding Aid

No this isn't the site you go to if you've got a body on your hands, but rather it's a family history research tool. Its database consists of the surnames, cemetery names, and locations of over 2 million internments from several thousand cemeteries, cairns, memorials, and cenotaphs in the province.

www.islandnet.com/ocfa

GOVERNMENT — ALBERTA

Alberta Health

Explore Alberta's health system at this site. Here visitors can get detailed information on the internal operations of the province's health system, as well as up-to-date health news.

www.health.gov.ab.ca

Government of Alberta Home Page

This is an off-the-shelf-looking portal page. Albertans, visitors to Alberta, and researchers will want to keep this site on their toolbar, as it's bursting with info and frequent updates, including a monthly "What's Hot" section, which is also archived in case you want to check out what was hot after it's cooled down a bit.

www.gov.ab.ca/index1.html

GOVERNMENT — BRITISH COLUMBIA

B.C. Forest Service

The B.C. Forest Service is the steward responsible for the province's unreserved public forestland, covering two thirds of B.C. Look up the Forest Practices Code, check fire bulletins, or fill out a comments and questions form at this site.

www.for.gov.bc.ca

B.C. Government Directory

Your tool to track down anyone in the B.C. government. You can search by name or organization.

www.dir.gov.bc.ca

B.C. Legislative Assembly

The price of freedom is eternal vigilance, and sometimes vigilant citizens take this to mean that they must read detailed accounts of the goings on in their provincial legislature. This site provides those very reports for B.C., as well as various postings on the bills, orders of the day, and budget appraisals for protectors of freedom in that province.

www.legis.gov.bc.ca

Government of B.C.

The Stellar's Jay, a "saucy and intelligent bird" welcomes you to this government web site, which offers news updates on major developments in the province's economic fortunes, and the usual directory of departments.

www.gov.bc.ca

GOVERNMENT — DOCUMENTS

Government Information in Canada

This isn't just a listing of government departments, it's actually a librarians' publication that can help you find info in the labyrinthine world of bureaucracy. This site hasn't been updated in a while—just when we need them most, have the editors deserted us?

www.usask.ca/library/glc

GOVERNMENT — FEDERAL

Atomic Energy of Canada Ltd.

Boasting a source of energy that produces virtually no greenhouse effect, the AECL page is here to convince you to go nuclear! Check out the company profile, products, and services, or send your children to the Kids' Zone.

www.aecl.ca

Bank of Canada

Whether you want to use the Inflation Calculator or to check exchange rates, the BOC site provides a range of easily accessible resources. Included at the site are savings bond info, a currency museum, and a listing of unclaimed accounts.

www.bank-banque-canada.ca

Canada Information Office

This resource of web links wraps up Canadian government, tourism, education, news, historical facts, and heritage into one convenient package.

www.infocan.gc.ca

Canada's Parliament

You may never go to Ottawa, but that doesn't mean you can't sit in on Canada's Parliament. Contact your local MP, have a nap in the Senate, check out the projected order of business, or get familiar with Canada's past and present prime ministers. Hockey fans take note: you can e-mail Senator Frank Maholovich!

www.parl.gc.ca

Connecting Canadians

This government initiative is to make Canada "the most connected country in the world." A leading-edge, comprehensive effort.

www.connect.gc.ca/en/100-e.htm

Environment Canada: Freshwater Web Site

A useful resource dealing with water quality.

www.ec.gc.ca/water

Fax the Feds

"The Canadian Internet activist web site." Provides fax numbers for all federal cabinet ministers and MPs, so you can give any of them a piece of your mind, anytime. You can run for office, but you can't hide.

www.net-efx.com/faxfeds

Government of Canada

Searches for official government sites start here. Like the government, the site is organized into departments.

canada.gc.ca/main_e.html

Governor General

Who is Adrienne Clarkson, anyway? And why does she keep handing out medals and awards? Find out about the Queen's representative in Canada, or how to get a congratulatory message from the Queen herself at the GG's home page.

www.gg.ca

Natural Resources Canada

NRC tracks everything from forests, energy, and mines, to floods, forest fires, and landslides. Visit this site for a wealth of info on Canada's landmass and resources.

www.nrcan.gc.ca/home/default.htm

Prime Minister's Web Site

With this web site, it's no longer necessary to sneak past the sleeping Mountie at 24 Sussex Drive for a visit with the PM. Now you can browse through an online photo album of our PM or listen to clips of his speeches. You can send the PM an e-mail, and get an electronic acknowledgement in return. Best of all, you don't have to worry about Mrs. Chretien lurking behind the door with a frying pan!

pm.gc.ca

Privacy Commissioner of Canada

This office seeks to safeguard Canadians' right to privacy. It acts as an ombudsman for anyone having difficulty accessing personal info under the Privacy Act, and also monitors the federal government's role in collecting said info.

www.privcom.gc.ca

Royal Canadian Mint

Numismatic nirvana.

www.rcmint.ca

The British Monarchy

In case anyone needs reminding, Canada is a constitutional monarchy, which makes our head of state Queen Elizabeth II, not the prime minister. And now that the Queen Mum has brushed up on her HTML and Java skills, we can all tune in to the official site of those crazy British royals.

www.royal.gov.uk

Veterans Affairs Canada

The internet might be a glimpse of the future, but sites like this one ensure that the past is not forgotten, either. Extensive options include a virtual reality tour of Vimy Memorial Park, views of medals and decorations, and RealAudio files of veterans' recollections and war songs.

www.vac-acc.gc.ca

GOVERNMENT — MANITOBA

Manitoba Government

The premier's message, tourism info, business news, and a virtual tour of the legislative building.

www.gov.mb.ca

GOVERNMENT — NEW BRUNSWICK

Government of New Brunswick Home Page

This page greets you with some backpackers enjoying the sunshine, a photo of the planet Earth, and a shot of a semiconductor chip—surely a signal that New Brunswick is lean, mean, and open for business in the global economy, and a darn nice place to raise a family.

www.gov.nb.ca

GOVERNMENT — NEWFOUNDLAND

Government of Newfoundland and Labrador

A schooner, a lighthouse, the premier's message, and info related to tourism and business in this, the friendliest Rock in the world. A link for the provincial budget is also prominently displayed at this site.

www.gov.nf.ca/

GOVERNMENT — NORTHWEST TERRITORIES

Government of the Northwest Territories

This well-organized site welcomes you to Canada's north and provides prompt news updates.

www.gov.nt.ca

GOVERNMENT — NOVA SCOTIA

Government of Nova Scotia Home Page

Warm, attractive site, covering Nova Scotia from Antigonish to Yarmouth.

www.gov.ns.ca

GOVERNMENT — SASKATCHEWAN

Government of Saskatchewan

No identity crisis here: stylized wheat graphic and big green text lead you to a well-organized directory of info about Saskatchewan and all of its public goings-on.

www.gov.sk.ca

GOVERNMENT — YUKON

Yukon Territory

All things Yukon—ish.

www.gov.yk.ca

GOVERNMENT AGENCIES

shift

The CIA World Factbook 1999

After World War II, the U.S. started three government-wide intelligence projects. True, you're not going to get your hands on many joint Army-Navy intelligence studies, but you can console yourself with the countless charms of *The CIA World Factbook*, which contains facts and maps for every country in the world.

www.odci.gov/cia/publications/factbook

HUMAN RIGHTS

Canadian Human Rights Foundation

Learn about the various programs, publications, and activities of this nongovernmental organization.

www.chrf.ca

Canadian Human Rights Tribunal

Discover the history of the Tribunal, and read up on past decisions and currently active cases.

www.chrt-tcdp.gc.ca

OneWorld

OneWorld's mission is to promote "human rights and sustainable development by harnessing the democratic potential of the internet." By bringing issues of injustice to light, they hope to effect positive change. Read spotlighted articles and other news stories from around the world.

www.oneworld.org

INDICES

A Short Dictionary of Scientific Quotations

If your efforts at pomposity could use an injection of insight from real scientific legends, look no further.

naturalscience.com/dsqhome.html

A Web of Online Dictionaries

Go to this site for online reference material, which indexes web-based dictionaries and thesauri from Afrikaans to Xhosa. It's all here.

www.facstaff.bucknell.edu/rbeard/diction.html

Acronym Finder

How many acronyms could they possibly have on file? Try 98 600.

www.AcronymFinder.com

Bartlett's Quotations

Spice up that essay with a few snappy quotes from the likes of Shakespeare, Alexander Pope, Erasmus, Montaigne, and many more.

www.cc.columbia.edu/acis/barltleby/barttlett

BestPlaces.net

A comparison of the best places to live. Hundreds of U.S. cities are covered in detail, and some data is also available for 1700 other cities.

bestplaces.net

Dictionary.com

This site offers hundreds of interactive online dictionaries. It's faster than leafing through the paper versions and it gives you hundreds of language translation dictionaries that you are unlikely to have on your shelves.

www.dictionary.com

eHow

Instead of letting your parents, your spouse, or the local library tell you how to live, you can try eHow. Step-by-step info on how to do just about anything: from composting and buying a house, to grooming your pet or asking someone on a date. Can life really be this easy?

www.ehow.com

Encyclopaedia Britannica Online

Users are asked to pay five dollars a month for "the premier web encyclopaedia." Some may pay. Most will go elsewhere and get the info for free—even if Britannica is the best.

www.eb.com

t shift

Encyclopedia.com

Finally, a freebie encyclopedia that's nearly as comprehensive as the venerable—and pricey—Britannica Online. Encyclopedia.com has more than 14 000 entries from the third edition of the Columbia Electronic Encyclopedia, and while it's not as grandiose as the leather-bound British tomes of learning, you'll feel better knowing that a fact is an awful thing to pay for.

www.encyclopedia.com

Encyclopedia.com

If it's encyclopedic knowledge you seek, this site is for you—and it's free.

www.encyclopedia.com

Essay Depot

Professors be warned. Sites like this provide essay search engines and other academically illicit wares. They don't try to hide it, either: "We organize our papers in categories so you'll have no trouble with that much-needed paper."

www.essaydepot.com

Infotrieve Online

A library services company offering full-service document delivery, databases on the web, and a variety of tools to simplify the process of obtaining published literature. They boast "the best free Medline on the web." Vital for searching out published medical studies.

www3.infotrieve.com

LibWeb

You probably won't need to look any further. A healthy international list of libraries, including most Canadian university libraries.

sunsite.berkeley.edu/Libweb/

Research-It!

A big page with search boxes for various dictionaries, maps, thesauri, and more.

www.itools.com/research-it/

Robot Wisdom

It's hard to describe what it is: it most resembles Refdesk.com. The author uses artificial intelligence to scour the web for news. He also has various pages that may be described as "smart portals"—guides to a lot of good stuff to read, without all the junk.

www.robotwisdom.com

Roget's Thesaurus

The definitive tool for finding just the right word.

www.thesaurus.com

The Alternative Dictionaries

A compendium of hundreds of dictionaries of slang and local dialects, including a dictionary of Quebecois slang, which is admirably concise.

www.notam.uio.no/~hcholm/altlang/

The English Server

Careful you don't get lost in this wonderfully comprehensive archive of full-text books and periodicals available online. The clean, contemporary design is a tip-off that this site is well maintained.

eserver.org/

The Thomas Register of American Companies

Canadian companies can also join this index of thousands of businesses across North America. Membership is free and exposure is unlimited.

www2.thomasregister.com

Webopaedia

What is a webopaedia, you ask? Look it up here.

www.webopaedia.com

INSTITUTES

The North-South Institute

This is the leading organization in the country involved in research and analysis of Canada's foreign policy and in international development issues. The web site presents news, events, press releases, and details of research projects in progress.

www.nsi-ins.ca

INTELLIGENCE

Canadian Security Intelligence Service

No joke, this is the web site for the real-life Canadian spy agency CSIS. For an organization that is supposed to be in charge of national security and international espionage, this site is surprisingly user-friendly, offering public reports, contact numbers, and even employment opportunities.

www.csis-scrs.gc.ca

STRATNET

Based at the University of Calgary, STRATNET is a research tool for academics, students, researchers, government officials, and others interested in strategic studies, security, international relations, and politics.

www.stratnet.ucalgary.ca

LAW

Access to Justice Network

Democracy is alive and well here at AJN, where all kinds of judicial, legal, and legislative resources are at your disposal. Take a gander at the Canadian Charter of Rights and Freedoms, check out Quebec's Civil Code, or peruse suggested lesson plans for schools at this politically charged site.

www.acjnet.org

BC Civil Liberties Association

The oldest continuously active civil liberties association in Canada, this organization seeks to defend and extend civil liberties and human rights in B.C. and across the country. They are active in such causes as patients' and prisoners' rights, access to information, freedom of speech, and discrimination issues.

www.bccla.org

Canadian Bar Association

Though it seems implausible that all lawyers in Canada would be able to come to an agreement, the CBA purports to be the voice "of and for all members of the profession." Come read through the fine print of member news, events, and links at this site.

www.cba.org

Canadian Civil Liberties Association

This nonprofit, nongovernmental organization lobbies for civil liberties such as freedom, the the right to privacy, and equality before the law. Their web site posts position papers, lists events, and solicits new members.

www.ccla.org

Canadian Institute for Environmental Law and Policy

This independent research and education organization was created to provide leadership in the development of environmental law and policy that promotes the public interest and the principles of sustainability. Check out this site for publications on environmental law and info on government agendas in each province.

www.web.net/cielap

Canadian Intellectual Property Office

Got a brilliant invention that will save the planet or at least make millions of dollars? If so, check out the web site of the folks who look after patents, trademarks, copyrights, and industrial design.

cipo.gc.ca

Canadian Law Resources on the Internet

A collection of legal links, including sections for research centres and laws of the internet.

mindlink.net/drew_jackson/mdj.html

Canadian Law Schools

Browse through these links to Canadian law schools via a stylish map of the country or by a text list.

www.canadalawschools.org

Canadian Lawyer Index

A site designed to help you find a lawyer from a database of over 55 000. Also supplies similar listings of court reporters, appraisers, TM and patent agents, private investigators, and members of related fields. Packed with features including legal classifieds and a section that lets you file a complaint against a judge or lawyer in Canada.

www.canlaw.com

Canadian Legal FAQs

Compiled by the University of Alberta, these FAQs are divided up by national or provincial relevance, and by topic.

www.extension.ualberta.ca/legalfaqs

Canadian Legal LEXPERT Directory

Look up the leading Canadian law firms and lawyers in over 50 practice areas across the country.

www.lexpert.ca

Canadian Legal Resources on the WWW

In addition to having an extensive list of legal resources grouped by province and category, there are useful search engines for the page itself and for the entire web.

www.mbnet.mb.ca/~psim/can_law.html

Centre for Public Law Research

The CRDP web site aims to make Quebec and Canadian laws more accessible. Among the legal documents of interest at this site, the Civil Code of Quebec and the Quebec Charter of Personal Rights and Freedoms deserve special mention.

www.droit.umontreal.ca/en

Copyright and Fair Use

A broad-based, searchable resource on copyright in the U.S. put together by Stanford University Library.

fairuse.stanford.edu/

Copyright Canada

The National Library provides a superb overview of the latest information related to copyright, including legislation, reports, and organizations dealing with the issue.

www.nlc-bnc.ca/window/copyrt/copye.htm

Department of Justice of Canada

Canada's Department of Justice web site houses the laws of Canada and other useful info.

canada.justice.gc.ca

ElectricLawyer

No, it's not a new twist on the Frankenstein story, but a web site devoted to legal matters. There's lots of info for lawyers who want to expand their business onto the net, and clients who want online services. Read about security issues of interest to legal professionals or the latest legal news.

www.electriclawyer.com

Federation of Law Societies of Canada

It may take a bit of searching, but if you want to know about the legal profession in Canada, or if you're doing an exhaustive search on a legal issue such as copyright, you'll find this to be a useful network of sites and resources. Brought to you by the 13 law societies in Canada.

www.flsc.ca

Kosovo and Yugoslavia – Law in Crisis

Law professors around the world have declared war on NATO. Dozens of experts contend that NATO's military action in Yugoslavia was a contravention of international law and a "humanitarian hypocrisy." Their collective wisdom and ongoing exchanges are recorded here.

jurist.law.pitt.edu/kosovo.htm

Legal Research on International Law

The starting point on the internet for looking up issues on international law is hosted by the University of Chicago Law School. Lawyers may be used to digesting copious amounts of text, but to follow all the links at this site and absorb even a fraction of what you've found would require a lifetime.

www.lib.uchicago.edu/~llou/forintlaw.html

QUICKLAW

Legal eagles take note: this site claims to be Canada's largest legal database provider, with over 1100 searchable databases and bulletin boards of full-text judgments from all court levels and many administrative tribunals in Canada, as well as full-text databases of legislation, tax, and news.

www.qlsys.ca/quicklaw.html

Supreme Court of Canada

The web site of the highest court in the land lets you search for judgments dating back to 1989, read about the history of the institution, see pictures of the court building, link to their library, and much more.

www.scc-csc.gc.ca

Virtual Canadian Law Library

At present, the format of the library is merely a list of links, but the authors intend to adopt a searchable Yahoo-style format in the near future. For now, try it out anyway.

www.droit.umontreal.ca/doc/biblio/en/

LAW — CONSTITUTIONAL

The Solon Law Archive

An online database of Canadian constitutional documents, as well as links to related documents for other countries. From the Charter of Hudson's Bay and the Constitutional Act of 1867, through the Statutes of Westminster to the Meech Lake Accord and beyond.

www.solon.org

LAW — IMMIGRATION

U.S. Immigration Law FAQs for Businesses and Professionals

Thinking of contributing to Canada's brain drain? A private law office has put together a bunch of FAQs for those interested in working or living south of the 49th parallel. Get details on visas, green cards, citizenship, and more.

www.grasmick.com/canimfaq.htm

LIBRARIES

Alliance of Libraries, Archives, and Records Management Index

ALARM offers educational and developmental opportunities for people working in the information resources sector. This web site provides a list of useful marketplace contacts and a mailing list to facilitate communication among members.

www.mbnet.mb.ca/~alarm/

Canadian Library Index

Look up library web pages by province or see if your library's catalogue is listed in HYTELNET or webCATS.

www.lights.com/canlib

Libraries Today

This site outlines a history of Canadian libraries and librarians, with a slight emphasis on the province of Ontario. Browse through photo archives or link up to various library history study groups via this web page.

www.uoguelph.ca/~lbruce

National Library of Canada

Browse through the online presence of our national library, which holds a copy of everything printed in Canada. Even rare publications are housed here.

www.nlc-bnc.ca

shift

Refdesk.com

Okay, so it's owned by Bob Drudge, as in the father of Matt, and it's really nothing more than a long links page. Still, the more than 16 000 links cover everything from dictionaries to currency converters. And it's organized perfectly to get you to the fact you needed to know, like, yesterday.

www.refdesk.com

shift

The Internet Public Library

Experience the joys of the Dewey Decimal system once more, with no risk of fines or need to shush. The Internet Public Library has more than 9000 complete texts online, including the works of leading white guys like Shakespeare and Chaucer. It also links to How Things Work, a site that covers everything from buying a puppy to medieval European history.

www.ipl.org

U.S. Library of Congress

Hardly Canadian, but worth mentioning as one of the great repositories of info in the world. Mounts online exhibitions on American history and themes, and is a good source of copyright law info.

www.loc.gov

Virtual Canadian Law Library

At present, the format of the library is merely a list of links, but the authors intend to adopt a searchable Yahoo-style format in the near future. For now, try it out anyway.

www.droit.umontreal.ca/doc/biblio/en/

LITERACY

ESL Flow

This site links many online resources for ESL in one clever package.

www.homestead.com/ESLflow/

National Adult Literacy Database

NALD is a Fredericton-based umbrella organization for literacy groups around the country. It provides program models, data, and ideas for community, school, and government literacy groups. The web site provides contact info, a resource catalogue, documents, and more.

www.nald.ca

TOEFL.org

Offers resources for those studying for the test of English as a Foreign Language.

www.toefl.org

LOTTERIES

Canadian Lotteries

Although also present on a host of portal sites, at the Canadian Lotteries web site you can look up last night's numbers from any lottery result in the country.

www.canada.com/lotteries

Lottolore

Wondering if you're a millionaire? This site provides winning numbers for all national and provincial lotteries in Canada. Now you can check to see if your old tickets left lying around were winners. You could be sitting on a fortune.

www.lottolore.com/home.html

MILITARY

Canadian Air Force

An online resource for info on the current whereabouts and activities of Canada's Air Force.

collections.ic.gc.ca

Communications Security Establishment

The CSE is an organization that provides information technology security to the government. Read up on the various programs that they are currently working on.

www.cse.dnd.ca

D-Net

Even a snappy title like D-Net cannot hide the fact that Canada's Department of National Defence is not quite as action-packed an outfit as they would have us believe. Sections about Canadian military heroes and reports from the latest peacekeeping missions help to jazz up our military's image, but one just can't get over the fact that there are only three thirty-year-old subs in our entire navy.

www.dnd.ca

Defense Advanced Research Projects Agency

This is where the internet was born. Come see what they're working on now.

www.arpa.mil

Department of National Defence—Recruiting

If you're really stuck for a job, there's always the army, navy, or air force. Also check out this site for details on subsidized education through the military.

www.recruiting.dnd.ca

MILITARY — NAVY

Royal Canadian Air Cadets

The unofficial web site of an organization that claims a national membership of almost 25 000 young men and women. Find info on training and flight safety, a squadron directory, and related links.

www.aircadet.com

Royal Canadian Sea Cadets

This organization for 12- to 19-year-olds is free to join. Activities include seamanship, swimming, first aid, sailing, band, and sports.

www.seacadet.com

The Royal Canadian Navy

Hey sailor, why not drop by the Canadian Navy web site and check out their career information section? You may also want to look up the history of the Navy in Canada, or check out the detailed descriptions of the operating fleet.

www.dnd.ca/navy/marcom/cdnnavy.html

MILITARY — ORGANIZATIONS

Canadian Air Aces and Heroes

Yes, there were other Canadian Air Aces besides Billy Bishop. Visit this web site for listings of Canada's top pilots from WWI, WWII, and Korea. You'll also find sections dedicated to biographies, medals, and an extensive bibliography.

www.accessweb.com/users/mconstab

The Black Watch of Canada

The home page of the Canadian branch of the Royal Highland Regiment, with battle honours, contact info, and music. Nemo me impuni lacessit!

www.blackwatchcanada.com

The Books of Remembrance

These contain the names of Canadians who fought in wars and died during or after them. If unable to make the journey to the Peace Tower in Ottawa, where they are kept, visitors to this web site can search through a database of names contained in the books or read about the books' history.

www.schoolnet.ca/collections/books

The Canadian Institute of Strategic Studies

Established in 1976, the CISS has gained wide recognition as the nation's foremost source of independent info and research on a broad range of issues affecting Canada.

www.ciss.ca

NEWS & MEDIA

22Online

Forget Mansbridge. Tune out Lloyd. Sayonara CNN. Here's all the news, sports, showbiz, and business news you'll ever need from the same perspective as the TV show *This Hour Has 22 Minutes*.

www.22online.com

22Online

Forget Mansbridge. Tune out Lloyd. Sayonara CNN. Here's all the news, sports, showbiz, and business news you'll ever need from the same perspective as the TV show *This Hour Has 22 Minutes*.

www.22online.com

shift

Ad Critic

At Ad Critic, you can watch all your favourite commercials and learn what the critics have to say. Bonus: the cartoon spoof of Budweiser's "Wazzzzup!" Super Bowl spot.

adcritic.com

shift

BBC Online

Despite a national bent toward tradition, the Brits have marched into the cyber age with the most comprehensive news site on the internet. BBC Online takes full advantage of its parent company's massive global resources to complement the expected British news with constantly updated coverage of world events. The site features news in text form and a regional audio and video broadcasts from the BBC World Service. Finishing touches include English lessons for readers and a news ticker that links your desktop to the BBC's breaking coverage.

www.bbc.co.uk

Canada.com

Brought to you by the Southam chain of newspapers, Canada.com provides a powerful search engine based web site and a free e-mail service. You'll find various useful features on the site, as well as links to all the Southam-backed dailies.

www.canada.com

Canadian News

Those interested in online news without an American angle should check out this page, which has links to all the major Canadian dailies and provides special sections for weather and computer news.

www.wj.net/rborek/cannews.html

CANOE—Canadian Online Explorer

A partnership between the Sun Media newspaper chain and BCE Media Investments, CANOE has become *the* site for Canadian news and information. There are immediately available headlines as well as quick links to exclusive online editions of all of the Sun Media dailies.

www.canoe.ca

Critical Mass

They say we can truly buy the world, but who would want it? Are we watching as the internet chokes on its own success, and turns into television? These and other questions are bandied about on this web zine for communications issues, which serves a heady mix of neo-Luddite alarmism and tech-savvy reportage.

hoshi.cic.sfu.ca/~cm

Dolomite

Self-described as guide for "skimming uberculture," Dolomite is a collection of articles and essays culled from the depths of the alternative press. Features run the gamut of subjects from mullet hairdos and prose poetry to Noam Chomsky and Sun Ra, with a healthy dose of hypertext in every byte.

www.dolomite.net

shift

Drudge Report

Along with a show on Fox, Matt Drudge was recently given a morning spot on ABC Radio. A sad comment on the state of online journalism? Perhaps. Although he did break the Lewinsky thing, should a peddler of rumour, gossip, and hype be the web's most famous member of the press corps? Who cares. Drudge continues to prove that the little guy can take on any media Goliath in infospace.

www.drudgereport.com

Flipside

Flipside is an alternative daily web publication that takes on the same issues covered by national publications such as the *National Post* and the *Globe and Mail*, but provides a point of view that these supposedly unbiased institutions of journalism ignore. When was the last time a major paper gave intelligent criticism on Mike Harris's destructive social policies? They won't, but *Flipside* certainly will.

www.flipside.org

Media Awareness Network

Evil forces would gladly manipulate you toward their darker purposes, but thanks to groups like this, you can be cured of media ignorance. Discover more about how our fast-evolving media culture subtly shapes and informs our perceptions.

www.media-awareness.ca

shift

Media Channel

The preferred news source and community centre for those reluctant to buy into network hype. Added cred: endorsed by Walter Cronkite.

www.mediachannel.com

shift

MSNBC

With zip-code-specific news, weather, sports, and a worldwide network of contributors and wire sources, MSNBC has up-to-the-minute information that's as narrow or as broad as you want. Click any region on its world map and MSNBC will give you local news from local sources.

www.msnbc.com

shift

Pitchforkmedia

A great source for album and concert reviews or general music news that lets its readers get in on the critique. You mean, if we, like, review these albums, we, like, get them for free? Dude!

www.pitchforkmedia.com

shift

The Obscure Store and Reading Room

The Obscure Store provides links to all the offbeat news of the day, from mysteriously exploding condiment jars to cops who solve parking shortages by simply painting new spaces. It also includes links to tech-business news and daily gossip.

www.obscurestore.com

NEWS & MEDIA — MAGAZINES

shift

The Onion

The Onion is one of the few voices of reason left in the modern-day quagmire of journalism. With fake stories skewering everything from consumerism ("New Crispy Snack Cracker to Ease Crushing Pain of Modern Life") to general stupidity ("American People Ruled Unfit to Govern"), *The Onion* is leagues more insightful than any *USA Today*-ified news report.

www.theonion.com

NEWSPAPERS

Calgary Herald Online

Check out the online version of this Calgary paper for world headlines and a host of local business, sports, and entertainment news.

www.calgaryherald.com

Canadian Jewish News

This frequently updated resource focuses on national and foreign news relevant to the Jewish community in Canada. The web site is presented in a newspaper style, with sections such as sports, travel, and arts.

www.cjnews.com

eye.NET

The online presence of the popular tabloid entertainment magazine owned by Torstar ... a competitor to *NOW Magazine*.

www.eye.net

Halifax Chronicle-Herald

Read highlights of major east coast news at this web site.

www.canoe.ca/ChronicleHerald/home.html

Montreal Gazette

Check out extensive coverage of major news issues at the web site for this Southam-owned daily newspaper.

www.montrealgazette.com

National Post Online

The launch of Conrad Black's national newspaper in 1999 has spawned an allied web site that's sure to be a major online source of news.

www.nationalpost.com

Northern News Services Online

This site features stories from *Deh Cho Drum*, *Inuvik Drum*, *Kivalliq News*, *Yellowknifer*, and *News/North*. Includes a classified section.

www.nnsl.com/

Nunatsiaq News

An online version of both the Nunavut and Nunavik editions of this newspaper rolled into one.

www.nunatsiaq.com

Regina Leader-Post

The online version of Saskatchewan's largest daily newspaper. You'll find all the news, regular columns, classifieds, and hockey draft sweepstakes (in season).

www.leader-post.sk.ca

Saskatoon StarPhoenix Online

One of three Hollanger group newspapers in Saskatchewan. This web site features a news sampler and classifieds.

www.saskstar.sk.ca/

Sun Newspapers

Follow the links from this web site to any of the Sun dailies across the country.

www.canoe.ca/PlanetSun

The Globe and Mail

This web site reflects the paper's colourful history and national concerns. There is, of course, a diverse and varied coverage of the daily news available for consumption by the intenet surfer.

www.globeandmail.com

The Ottawa Citizen

All the sections you've come to expect from the capital's best-known paper, plus a few more.

www.ottawacitizen.com

Toronto Star

Though ostensibly a news source for the Toronto area, the online version of one of Canada's largest daily papers is filled with items of interest to a national audience. The online archive of back issues may also be of interest to those conducting research on the web.

www.thestar.com

Vancouver Province

The online version of the newspaper. Of special interest for its B.C.-related news stories, classifieds, and standard newspaper fare, it also has national and international news.

www.vancouverprovince.com

Winnipeg Free Press

Read local, national, and international news highlights from the pages of this Manitoba daily.

www.mbnet.mb.ca/freepress/summary.htm

Young People's Press

YPP is a national news service for youth, with articles published in over 200 newspapers and a weekly section in the *Toronto Star*. Young writers can send in article suggestions via this site or read features by people of their age group.

www.ypp.net

NEWSPAPERS — ALTERNATIVE

buzzON

A collection of arts and entertainment events and news for the province of P.E.I. This site has extensive listings for leisure events, theatre, art, and even karaoke.

www.isn.net/buzzon/

Disinformation

Serve yourself a healthy dose of conspiracy and news topics that are much maligned by the mainstream media. With section titles like "The Revolution," "The Conspiracy," "Apocalypse Now," and "Orgasmatron," there's got to be something interesting going on at this site.

www.disinfo.com

Montreal Mirror

Here's your essential guide to what's happening on the Montreal scene. The online version of this alternative weekly offers you a chance to post rants, sample reviews and listings, and digest articles on various topics.

www.montrealmirror.com

NOW Online

NOW has been telling Torontonians what's going on in their city for years. Entertainment listings and of course the classifieds will be mostly of interest to those in the TO vicinity, but the music, book, and movie reviews should be of wider interest.

www.nowtoronto.com

Salon.com

This alternative newsmagazine contains features ranging from technology news and movie reviews to a section titled "Mothers Who Think." By former *San Francisco Chronicle* writers and editors, Salon.com dispenses incisive political commentary in a daily e-zine format.

www.salon.com

Shewire

It's a news site that believes girl power isn't about the Spice Girls alone. From the politics of Lilith Fair to the entertainment value of Elizabeth Dole, Shewire dishes up a sassy estrogen-fuelled perspective on the news of the day—everything a grrl could ask for.*

shewire.chickclick.com

Suck

Not even Canada is safe from the razor-sharp wit and sarcasm of this daily e-zine. Suck has tweaked the nose of such cultural icons as Celine Dion, the MacKenzie brothers, and (gasp!) Jean Chretien. Perhaps it's just disheartening to see Americans doing a better job of making fun of us than we usually do.

www.suck.com

The Drudge Report

The source for insider entertainment and political news, the Hollywood-based Drudge Report receives over 20 million hits per month.

www.drudgereport.com

The Georgia Straight

Vancouver's news and entertainment weekly serves up a slick dish of reviews, events, and opinion pieces in the online version of this newspaper.

www.straight.com

The Onion

Though *The Onion*'s headlines are completely fictitious and satirical, they have a way of stirring up as much interest and controversy as real news items. Check out the section for a book created by the web site, aptly titled *Our Dumb Century.*

www.theonion.com

shift

Wired News

While the print magazine continues to go the way of glossy shrines to capitalism, the web newswire remains dedicated to exploring the ways in which technology is changing the lives of ordinary people. Content here ranges from the most recent developments in medical technology to *Star Wars* news. And there's a superb ongoing series on MP3 and the music industry.

www.wired.com

NEWSWIRES

BBC World News

World-class news site with breaking news and audio feeds.

news.bbc.co.uk/worldservice/

Canada NewsWire

A corporate online news services that provides public relations services to corporations across the country. View press releases from all over Canada or check out this site's many other features.

www.newswire.ca

Daily Message

Not as silly as it sounds, considering folks can choose to have the "Windows Tip of the Day" mailed to them instead of just reading the Help files. If your tastes run to the less serious, you can also get quotes, sports facts, and horoscopes for daily inspiration.

www.dailymessage.com

Science Daily

If you want your science news fresh, this is the place to go.

www.sciencedaily.com/

Sympatico NewsExpress

A major site for up-to-the-minute news stories taken from the CP and Reuters newswire services.

newsexpress.sympatico.ca

The Canadian Press

Though news from the CP wire service is only made available on a subscription basis, the casual reader can still check out selected headlines at this site.

www.cp.org

PHILANTHROPY & SOCIAL SERVICE

Canadian Centre for Philanthropy

The CCP is a national charitable organization dedicated to advancing the role and interest of the charitable sector for the benefit of communities across the country.

www.ccp.ca

Habitat for Humanity Canada

An independent nonprofit program that provides houses for families in need. They rely on donations of labour and material, which, coupled with no-interest loans and the labour of the family to be housed, result in new or renovated homes. Best known due to the involvement of former U.S. President Jimmy Carter.

habitat.ca

Labatt People in Action

This program funds employment for students with registered charities, allowing organizations to improve their communities and young people to gain work experience.

www.lpia-ltao.com

OXFAM-Canada

One of the most prestigious of all relief agencies at work in the developing world, they focus on health security, food security, and democratic rights. Current campaigns explained on their site include fair wages for coffee farmers, an OXFAM Visa card, education programs, and Kosovo.

www.oxfam.ca

United Way of Canada

This is the web page of the prominent network of community organizations. There is a directory of branches and info on how to make a donation or get involved.

www.uwc-cc.ca

Variety Club of B.C.

This international group has raised $650 million for disabled and disadvantaged children since its inception in 1927. The B.C. chapter is highly active in funding and supporting a variety of projects.

www.variety.bc.ca/

VolNet

Part of the federal government's initiative to get Canada connected. This organization makes available computer equipment, skills development programs, and support to voluntary organizations.

www.volnet.org

PHILOSOPHY

Canadian Philosophical Association

Wax metaphysical with your intellectual peers at this site for students and teachers of philosophy. Among the ontological oddities on this page are CPA publications, online resources, and the humorously titled "Jobs" section.

www.acpcpa.ca/framee.htm

PHONE NUMBERS

555-1212.com

Comprehensive utility for looking up phone numbers, area codes, country codes, and related info. Look up your own phone number and prepare to be creeped out. More and more international info is becoming available.

www.555-1212.com

Area Code Look

Got a phone number but no area code? You can find it here. Search by city, state, number, or country.

www.555-1212.com/aclookup.html

Canada 411

Search this database of over 10 million telephone listings and postal codes by name or by business.

www.canada411.com

Canada YellowPages.com

Look up Canadian and American businesses, browse through the classifieds, and more.

www.canadayellowpages.com

POLITICS

Canada Speaks

If you're more familiar with speeches by American presidents than by Canadians, why not check out some historical orations by our own prime ministers?

collecitons.ic.gc.ca/canspeak

Canada West Foundation

The CWF conducts research and education on the economy and impact of the west and north of Canada within a national and international context. Look up research projects, read the current news, or explore CWF publications at this site.

www.cwf.ca

COAT – Coalition to Oppose the Arms Trade

By organizing events and publishing pamphlets, booklets, and a magazine, COAT participates in public education campaigns to raise awareness and encourage people to pressure their governments for change in arms trade policies.

www.ncf.carleton.ca/coat

Enter Stage Right

The definitive page for arch-conservatives provides in-depth information. If you want to probe Stockwell Day's psyche, there's an article here for you.

www.enterstageright.com/

Federation of Canadian Municipalities

Nice-looking, professional web site.

www.fcm.ca

Forum for Young Canadians

This professional-looking web site greets you with a slick interface and the grinning face of Jean Chretien. Each year the forum brings together a group of bright young Canadians so they can learn about the mechanics of government.

www.forum.ca

Historic Moments in Canadian Politics

A picture is worth a thousand words. And these thousand words aren't worth hearing. If you're still interested, this modest pictorial site offers an uncommonly evocative look at selected moments in Canadian history with the use of carefully chosen photos of events and a bit of narrative.

www.planetcast.com/historic-moments

The Fraser Institute

"Tax Freedom Day" is the gimmicky device that entices you to read other reports produced by this Conservative think tank.

www.fraserinstitute.ca

Viscount Richard Bedford Bennett Anti-Disinternment Web Site

Truth is stranger than fiction. There's a proposal afoot to disinter the PM of the 1930s, R.B. Bennett, and bring his remains to Canada from England, apparently to create a tourist attraction. The goal of this really quite elaborate web site is to discourage the macabre repatriation. Consider making this your home page.

www.omalko.com/bennett-rip.htm

Webactive

An attractive and comprehensive site for political activism and protest.

www.webactive.com

POLITICS — ORGANIZATIONS

C.D. Howe Institute

An independent, nonprofit economic- and social-policy research institution that's regularly cited in newspapers across Canada. Check out the institute's available publications or search the extensive archive of related press.

www.cdhowe.org

Canadian Food for the Hungry

CFH is a nonprofit charitable organization providing emergency relief and life-changing, sustainable development. Browse through the organization's programs on child development and emergency aid, and find out how to make a donation at this web site.

cfh.ca

POLITICS — PARTIES

Bloc Quebecois Party

They want to split up the country. Find out who's leading the party today or view topics up for discussion—as if they have anything else to discuss.

blocquebecois.org

Green Party

Sort of akin to the little electric-powered engine that could, this party has big ideals and big hopes for Canada's future. The Green Party advocates a move toward sustainability instead of unchecked growth—an idea whose time has come.

green.ca/index-e.htm

Liberal Party of Canada

There's more to this political party than just choking and pepper-spraying protesters. Read Liberal policy and propaganda at this, their official web site.

www.liberal.ca

Natural Law Party

Ah, bless the Natural Law Party. Read about this party's plan to bring peace and prosperity to Canada through the ... ahem ... scientifically proven method of "Yogic Flying."

wwww.natural-law.ca

New Democratic Party of Canada

Canada's only left-wing federal presence. Read all about the party and international socialist issues.

www.ndp.ca

Postal Code Lookup

What do you think this does?

www.candapost.ca/cpc2/addrm/pclookup/pclookup.shtml

Progressive Conservative Party of Canada

On the verge of imploding or exploding since Jean Chretien's Liberals' landslide victory in the early 90s, this party—one of the oldest in Canada—has been reduced to only a handful of seats in Parliament. However, fear not, right-wingers, Joe Clark is at the wheel once again.

www.pcparty.ca

The Canadian Alliance

All political parties have sections for recruitment and donations on their web sites, but only the Canadian Alliance has stooped to the annoying inclusion of the dreaded pop-up window asking for money. Finally, they are now offering the web site in French, as well as in English. In the midst of a leadership race as of this writing, Canadians can only shiver with anticipation as to the outcome.

www.canadianalliance.ca

POSTAL INFORMATION

shift

Mapquest

If you ask "Where am I?" with the frequency of Dorothy, you need Mapquest. Clean, comprehensive city and highway maps take you pretty much door to door. If they don't, consult the route finder for directions.

www.mapquest.com

POVERTY

The Great Depression

This page focuses on what life was like for the poor during the time of severe economic crisis in Canada. Focuses on urban poverty in Canada and gets into detail. Compiled by Grade 11 students at Point Grey Mini School in Vancouver, an alternative school.

www.arpp.sfu.ca/pgm/depress/greatdepress.html#lowcls

PSYCHOLOGY

Adlerian Psychological Association of British Columbia (APABC)

The APABC is a nonprofit, accredited educational organization offering training in Adlerian psychology. Programs include Masters degrees in graduate studies, parent study groups for tots and teens, and family counselling. The APABC provides speakers and workshop leaders for the education, medical, and business communities, and may be contacted through this site.

www.adler.bc.ca/

Canadian Food Inspection Agency

Visit this site for the latest news on food health concerns in Canada. Browse detailed reports on the agency's various inspection procedures or look up fact sheets on topics ranging from consumer awareness to animal disease.

www.cfia.acia.agr.ca

Canadian Journal of Behavioural Science

Check out this site for articles in current and back issues of the *Canadian Journal of Behavioural Science*. There are also updated links to current events in the world of psychology, and outline info for those interested in submitting an abstract to the *Journal*.

www.cpa.ca/ac-main.html

Canadian Psychological Association

Along with info aimed at established members, the CPA web site presents useful information for students, as well as career postings. Follow links to other psychological sites or use the handy search engine to find what you need here.

www.cpa.ca

REFERENCE — CANADIAN INDICES

A Bag of Rubber Hammers

If you're feeling as fine as frog's hair, you'll feel even better after a trip to this site of collected colloquialisms. Browse the compiled wisdom from P.E.I. and other parts of Canada, or add your own peculiar phrase to this growing encyclopedia of expressions ... but don't let the screen door hit you on the way out!

www.gov.pe.ca/bag

APlus Research

This scary site for high school and post-secondary students gives you a step-by-step guide on how to write an A+ paper. Sadly, technique wins out over inspiration, genius, and pacing the quad at 4:00 a.m., clutching a half-empty bottle of red wine. Why didn't someone tell us this before?

ipl.org/teen/aplus/

Canadian Communities Atlas

An in-depth and vibrant look at our country's geography, this site provides an up-close look at the human, physical, and economic layout of the land. Full-colour photos and maps await those interested in everything from plate tectonics to urban geology.

CGDI.GC.CA/ccatlas

Canadian Government Information

This site provides comprehensive listings for any federal, provincial, or municipal government pages in Canada.

www.nlc-bnc.ca/cangov/egovinfo.htm

Canadian Information by Subject

This site is an information service developed by the National Library of Canada to provide links to info about Canada from resources around the world. The subject arrangement is in the form of a "Subject Tree" based on the structure of the Dewey Decimal Classification System.

www.nlc-bnc.ca/caninfo/ecaninfo.htm

Canadiana Resource Page

Everything stereotypically Canadian (the lyrics to "The Maple Leaf Forever") and some oddities (a croquet page?) populate this site for Canuck-themed links.

www.cs.cmu.edu/Unofficial/Canadiana/

How Stuff Works

Voted 1998 Cool Site of the Year, How Stuff Works can tell you how gears work, or what makes the inside of your fridge cold. For curious minds from 6 to 106.

www.howstuffworks.com

Learn2

Want to know how to do all those things they don't teach in school and your parents never told you? Visit this site for advice on everything from fixing a leaky faucet to cleaning fish. This site covers all the "simple" things you never learned and are now too embarrassed to ask about. Finally, men will not only know how to tie a tie, but they'll also be able to press their own pants.

www.learn2.com

Sources Select Online

A serious research tool for journalists and others, this site mainly offers a searchable directory of over 5000 contacts from over 1000 companies and organizations offering expertise. Other resources include a directory of members of Parliament, and contact info for foreign embassies in Canada and our own embassies abroad.

www.sources.com

Sympatico Tools

Here's a useful listing of some of the best online tools for finding stuff. You could make this your start page—less advertising, no news, just all the handy lookup tools you need to find just about anything online.

www1.sympatico.ca/Tools/tools.html

The Canadian Resource Page

Here's a collection of links covering everything from science and technology, to arts and entertainment, to Canadian-oriented news groups.

www.cs.cmu.edu/Unofficial/Canadiana/README.html

The Virtual Gramophone

The National Library of Canada has made a selection of historical recordings from their archives. Search the database by artist or song title, and download RealAudio versions of songs dating back to the late 1800s.

www2.nlc-bnc.ca/gramophone/src/home.htm

Wayfarers Canadian Achievers

Here you'll find an illustrated encyclopedia of great Canadian accomplishments. Includes entries for things (e.g., the canoe), people (e.g., Chief Dan George), organizations (e.g., the National Film Board), and corporate achievers (e.g., Dofasco Inc.).

www.schoolnet.ca/collections/wayfarers/

RESEARCH — INSTITUTES

Angus Reid Group

Check out this site for a smattering of polling data for free consumption. Of particular interest is the Angus Reid/*Economist* comparison of quality-of-life ratings for 29 countries.

www.angusreid.com/

Environics Research Group

A useful source of information on past Environics opinion polls. Frequent coverage of political issues and party popularity.

erg.environics.net/

URBAN STUDIES

Disaster Recovery Institute Canada

Provides info about disaster recovery, as well as details about an annual conference. Topics covered include emergency response, business continuity, and emergency health care. Of particular importance to those who work in municipal government.

www.dri.ca

Metropolis Project

This is the Canadian site of an international forum for research and policy on migration and cities. Contains a virtual library on immigration and integration.

canada.metropolis.net

WEATHER & CLIMATE

Atmospheric Environment Service

This is the source for weather information and climate research in Canada. Check out major weather events from the last few years or get a daily forecast at this site.

www1.tor.ec.gc.ca/

Daily UV Index and Calendar

Learn all about ultraviolet rays and ozone depletion at this daily update of conditions for different areas of the country. The site provides a handy graph that helps make sense of the reading, while also listing tips on how to protect your skin while out in the sun.

www1.tor.ec.gc.ca/uvindex

El Nino: A Canadian Perspective

The definitive Canadian resource for this much-hyped weather system.

www1.tor.ec.gc.ca/elnino

Environment Canada Weather

The same content as weatheroffice.com, but some prefer the format at this site. Less commercialized. Updated hourly.

weather.ec.gc.ca/

Weather Network Online

This is the web presence of the Weather Network TV channel. Access a forecast of any Canadian city, or check out the weather in U.S. and international areas. Other features include the chance to ask an expert a question.

www.theweathernetwork.com

WeatherOffice.com

This site maintained by Environment Canada provides cross-country forecasts and conditions, and has interesting features such as current satellite shots, a map of lightning activity, and road reports. You can also check out the Green Lane for environmental news and links.

www.weatheroffice.com

Business & Money

BUSINESS — AUCTIONS

Auction Guide

Connect to online and offline auctions all over the world from this site. It links to Canadian sites and even provincial ones within Canada. Or search the directory to find a specific auctioneer.

www.auctionguide.com

Bargoon

This auction service allows you to sell or buy stuff where you live. The cities covered have rapidly expanded from just Halifax and Toronto, to include Vancouver, Calgary, Edmonton, Regina, Winnipeg, Ottawa, Montreal, Charlottetown, and St. John's—and New York and Boston, too.

www.bargoon.com

Bid.com

You can get some Loonie Deals on the Canadian section of this site or go to the American part for more selection. Hey! I see a 900 MHz cordless phone starting at a bid of $1! Now that *is* a loonie deal.

www.bid.com

Bid4geeks

On the Bid4geeks site, hi-tech talent (and even whole teams of people) can offer itself for sale in a silent auction. It may be useful for well-funded startups who want to acquire a whole team of web designers, for example. And many toilers in the tech field might be interested to find out if they're worth a bit more than they thought. Messages in the discussion forum suggest adding a separate area on the site for other types of geeks, such as doctors, plumbers, teachers, and lawyers. So maybe they'll expand.

www.bid4geeks.com

BidStream

"One click. Unlimited auctions." Choose your weapon, er, I mean auction site, by category, sub-category, or keyword. The Power Search function allows you to specify things like your highest and lowest bid, fixed price items, ending date, ascending/descending order, and the number of items returned per page. Then go!

www.bidstream.com

eBay Canada

All of the categories of the original site seem to be here, but from this site you can choose items located in Canada or specified as "seller will ship to Canada." There's a Canadian chat spot, too. And if this doesn't satisfy you, surf over to the main eBay site at www.ebay.com.

pages.ca.ebay.com/index.html

uBid

Talk about bargains! How about a four-night cruise to the Bahamas with a starting bid of $9? In fact, a lot of items start at $9, even some computer equipment. Can you resist those flashing icons? "2 hours left!" "45 minutes left!" And for those who simply must buy something right away, there's a link to Auctions Closing This Hour. This site seems to cover all the usual auction site categories, too.

www.ubid.com

BUSINESS — COMMERCE

AnyWho

This U.S. site allows you to search for any American business across the country without having to enter a specific city or state.

anywho.com

Bplans.com

The new economy has spawned new markets and new ideas, but implementing them seems to be some kind of magic restricted to savvy entrepreneurs. For help in crossing the divide between clueless and savvy, look at sample business plans here. There are also online books, free for browsing, and a panel of experts online.

www.bplans.com/index1.html

Business by Name

This very basic site has only one function: searching for businesses. Just key in a business's name, the province, and, if you like, a city. You then receive the contact information, its location on a map, and the opportunity to click on similar businesses in the area. There are also links to the same service for the U.K. and the U.S.

www.infospace.com/info.infobel/canadabiz.htm

Canada411

The great thing about this search site is that you don't have to specify a city or province. It will search for a business's name across the entire country and provide the complete address and phone number.

canada411.sympatico.ca

CNNfn

Produced by the massive CNN news company, CNNfn is a valuable resource for Canadian investors and financiers to keep abreast of American and international business news.

www.cnnfn.com

Ethics in Action

This site deals with awards for B.C. and Ontario businesses that exhbit corporate social responsibility. Balancing profits and responsibility may not be easy, but those who do can experience enhanced brand image and reputation, improved financial results, and increased loyalty from customers and employees. You can link to nomination forms for the next round.

www.ethicsinaction.com

Strategis

This is Industry Canada's tool for business information on the internet. There are links to hundreds of resources on consumer information, e-commerce services, business directories, information on licenses and regulations, economic analysis and statistics, research and technology, and much more. This should be one of your very first stops for all commerce-related questions.

strategis.ic.gc.ca

BUSINESS — CREDIT UNIONS

Credit Union Central of Canada

The CUCC provides credit unions with such services as strategic planning, central financial facilities, new product and service offerings, national services, system advocacy, and international relations. The site includes a branch and ATM locator, live cams of their meetings, and online order forms.

www.caseybyte.com/cucc/index.htm

Credit Unions Canada

This is a short list of credit unions and related web sites for all of Canada. Click on the link to reach your provincial site.

www.cuets.ca/links/crunion.htm

Business & Money

BUSINESS — E-COMMERCE

Canadian Institute of Tourism and Electronic Commerce

CITEC seeks to help the Canadian tourism industry benefit from new and emerging electronic commerce opportunities. They provide workshops, training, and evaluations, and they represent the Canadian tourism industry at various international technological forums. The FAQ section explains the basics of becoming e-literate and provides links to sites for specific help, such as how to get funding and find guides.

www.citec.ca/

Electronic Commerce Canada Inc.

ECC is a voluntary organization composed of executives from the public and private sectors. They share information, discuss ideas, and conduct seminars. Some topics addressed by ECC include streamlining processes, interconnectivity, electronic funds transfer, security, electronic document management, workflow processing, bar coding, imaging, smart cards, voice response, and networking.

www.ecc.ca/

Electronic Commerce Council of Canada

The ECCC is a nonprofit voluntary standards organization that works to enhance the efficiency and effectiveness of industries. The ECCC provides education and standards documentation, and maintains international barcode registration for an annual fee. The ECCnet part of the site appears to provide customer and product databases.

www.eccc.org/

BUSINESS — MAGAZINES

Adbusters

You won't find any paid ads in this publication, but the award-winning magazine is flourishing anyway. (Well, it does have uncommercials and spoof ads.) *Adbusters* is "a not-for-profit, reader-supported, 60 000-circulation magazine concerned about the erosion of our physical and cultural environments by commercial forces." So join in on TV Turnoff Week, Buy Nothing Day, or one of the other campaigns.

www.adbusters.org

Adnews Online

Adnews Online is a daily publication of the latest in advertising and marketing news. Search through the archives for past articles, skim through the headlines, or browse through related marketing and advertising sites at this electronic magazine with over 23 000 subcribers.

www.adnews.com

Arts Business Exchange

Focusing on the business end of the arts world, ABX coverage ranges from general news pieces to reports on the state of the arts market. Also available are a number of business resources, a regular e-mail newsletter, and postings for announcements and jobs.

www.ffa.ucalgary.ca/artbusiness/homepage.html

Benefits Canada

Specializing in employee benefits and pension investments, *Benefits Canada* also covers other business-related issues. Sample the latest issue of the magazine at their web site.

www.benefitscanada.com

BusinessWeek Online

You'll need to buy a subscription to access the full magazine part of this site, but there are still many areas to access for free. Read feature articles and the sections about technology, small business, global business, and careers. You can also access stock quotes.

www.businessweek.com

BusinessWoman Canada

There are more than 700 000 women-led firms providing jobs for 1.7 million Canadians, and they are creating new jobs at four times the rate of the average firm. This magazine is about mentoring, role models, and success stories. *BusinessWoman Canada* celebrates these women through interviews and articles on health, technology, finance, and more.

www.businesswomancanada.com/

CanadaOne

This is a free online magazine for small businesses in Canada. It also connects to a Canadian business directory, Canadian-specific business resources, a technology centre, and business tools. There are interesting articles and reviews, and you can send questions to an expert and read the other Q&A's.

www.canadaone.com/ezine/index.html

Canadian Telecom

This is an independently owned and operated bi-monthly publication produced for managers of voice and data communications. Read articles about the application of communications technology to business.

www.cdntele.com

CCN Disclosure

Formerly Canadian Corporate News, CCN Disclosure delivers news electronically to the media and the financial community worldwide. There are media and industry links, of course, and you can search the news by category, organization name, or stock symbol.

www.cdn-news.com

Financial Post

If you're a financial news junkie, you won't want to miss this site, packed with stock quotes and articles about RRSPs, taxes, small business, and all that.

www.canoe.ca/FP

Marketing Online

Portions of the print version of *Marketing Magazine* can be accessed without charge via the internet. Its articles focus on the business of marketing, advertising, and media. You'll find job listings, events, discussion areas, and a searchable calendar.

www.marketingmag.ca

Realm

"You create the work you want," says *Realm*. This is the online version of the print magazine about careers and entrepreneurship aimed at young Canadians. Head here for inspiration, strategy tips, articles, a discussion forum, and more.

realm.net

Refresher Publications

This site offers three main options. The CEO Refresher is a monthly newsletter on contemporary topics in creative leadership, competitive strategy, and performance improvement. Words and Wisdom is a collection of great sayings, offering food for thought for management types. Now You're Cooking offers thought about food via recipes and memories.

www.refresher.com

Report on Business

The online version of the *Globe and Mail* publication provides analysis for the businessperson who wants more than just the headlines. Includes archived issues back to 1997.

www.robmagazine.com

Small Business Canada

The *Small Business Canada* magazine includes online articles on topics such as communication, finance, accounting, the internet, marketing, and a review of products. There is a discussion forum, and you'll find links to other internet resources for small businesses.

www.sbcmag.com/

BUSINESS — NONPROFIT

Better Business Bureau

This page will link you to BBB sites all over Canada. Read business and consumer alerts, file a complaint, or search for information about a specific company. You can also connect to the BBB system in the United States.

www.bbb.org/bureaus/canadian.asp

Canadian Nonprofit Resource Network

Those looking to make a difference can drop by this web site for volunteer listings, free training programs, available grants, and links to other not-for-profit programs represented around the web.

www.waterlooregion.org/cnrn

Charity Village

This award-winning site supports the 175 000 registered Canadian charities and nonprofit organizations, and the millions of professionals, staffers, volunteers, and donors. You'll find news, resources, and information about volunteers and jobs. Some destinations are accessible only by people actually working and volunteering in the nonprofit sector.

www.charityvillage.com/

iComm

iComm is a nonprofit internet service provider that donates its services to other nonprofits, community organizations, and charities all over the world. At this site, you can find out how to apply for the service and how to help the organization with their work, through donations and other methods.

www.icomm.ca/

Idealist

Idealist is a project of Action Without Borders. You can search 20 000 nonprofit and community organizations in 140 countries by name, location, or mission. There's a job bank and there are also links to resources, jobs, news sites, and volunteer opportunities. You'll also find tools for nonprofits and a calendar of events.

www.idealist.org/

reBoot Canada

reBOOT Canada is a nonprofit charity providing computer hardware, networking, and technical support to charities, nonprofits, and people with limited access to technology. They provide services for a cost, but at much less than the regular cost.

www.reboot.on.ca

Web Networks

Web Networks offers the internet public "a doorway to progressive Canadian issues, people, and organizations." This is an online community of more than 3500 Canadian nonprofits and social activists. It's been around since 1987.

community.web.net/

BUSINESS – ORGANIZATIONS

Atlantic Canada Opportunities Agency

The ACOA provides a vareity of services for businesses in Atlantic Canada to further their goal of improving the region's economy. The ACOA web site provides business information, links to financial help, a list of related business news, a hot topics section, and more.

www.acoa.ca

Canada Business Service Centres

CBSCs are located in every province across the country and are designed to cultivate and nurture new businesses through information distribution and access to government programs. Learn more about these services or follow the links to the Canada Business Service Centre in your province.

www.cbsc.org

Canadian Federation of Independent Business

This is a large national organization that represents small business. The web site includes news on legislation of interest to business (especially budgets), their current activities, a section for youth, information on banking and insurance, and, for members only, a daily mandate page to vote on various issues.

www.cbif.ca

Canadian Franchise Association

This site is for people who own or are thinking about purchasing a franchise in Canada, and the organization's members are "united by a common interest in ethical franchising." Because there is much to learn if you are considering such a purchase, the organization provides various resources to help you out. Find out about *Franchise Canada* magazine, the Franchise Show, and seminars across the country.

www.cfa.ca

Canadian Marketing Association

Tired of receiving junk mail and all of those unsolicited calls? Take your name off the list at the Canadian Marketing Association web site. They must receive many requests for this because it's the first question on their FAQ page. And when people receive outstanding, unbelievable offers, the CDMA says that the rule of thumb is "if it sounds too good to be true it probably is." Wise advice.

www.cdma.org

Canadian Standards Association

This is the place to ask all of your questions about product standards. CSA International develops standards in many areas, including electrical, environmental, communications, and health care. Go to the Audits & Investigations section for current and previous product recalls.

www.csa.ca

Canadian Women's Business Network

This site offers articles, news, internet tools, an online business directory, and more. There's also a series of links covering everything from search engine tips and postal codes to breast cancer and worldwide holidays.

www.cdnbizwomen.com

Canadian Youth Business Foundation

This web site is a strong advocate for young "go-getters." Their focus is on financing for starting a business, but they also offer resources, business guides, and expert opinions.

www.cybf.ca

Conference Board of Canada

This independent, non-policy-presciptive body comprises Canadian business, government, and public-sector organizations with an interest in the Canadian economy, public policies, and organizational practices.

www.conferenceboard.ca

Women Business Owners of Canada

WBOC is a not-for-profit national business association that represents the interests and concerns of women entrepreneurs across Canada. In the Partners and Resources section, you'll find links to women's business organizations across the country, and to government and nongovernment organizations that help business owners. You can also find out about business plans, international organizations, and more. Members have access to networking opportunities, a newsletter, advocacy, and a bulletin board. WBOC is also creating a database of Canadian women-owned businesses.

www.wboc.ca

Young Entrepreneurs Association

YEA is a not-for-profit organization, Canada's only national peer support group for young (under 35) entrepreneurs in the early stages of building their business. YEA's Newsroom was still under development, but it should be working by the time of publication of this book. It will provide tools to allow the media to connect quickly with several hundred of Canada's young entrepreneurs. News and information about YEA members' businesses will be available here.

www.yea.ca/

YouthBusiness.com

This site from the Canadian Youth Business Foundation will link you to gazillions of resources, discussion forums, internet tools, and online mentoring programs.

www.youthbusiness.com

ECONOMIC DEVELOPMENT

Aboriginal Economic Development Program

This programs provides long-term employment and business opportunities for Canada's Aboriginal citizens by giving them the means to effectively manage their own skill-development programs, economic institutions, and business enterprises. Get all the details at this site.

www.cbsc.org/nb/display.cfm?BisNumber=2753&Coll=Federal_Bis

Canadian Business Map

This site is a geographic outline of major areas of business interest in the country. Categories include research and development, exporting from Canada, investing in Canada, company directories, Canadian industry statistics, and an aboriginal business map. Connect to financial templates, calculators, and other online business tools.

strategis.ic.gc.ca/scdt/bizmap/index_js.html

Canadian Career Development Foundation

CCDF is a charitable foundation that works to strengthen and support the career development profession for Canadians. This organization sees this focus as pivotal to Canada's social and economic advancement. They approach economic development from the perspective of people's career development in today's rapidly changing labour market.

ccdf.ca

Canadian Centre for Policy Alternatives

The CCPA is an independent, nonprofit research organization, founded in 1980 to promote research on economic and social policy issues from a progressive point of view. Download the Alternative Federal Budget to read some insights that you don't often get to hear about.

www.policyalternatives.ca/

Human Resources Development Canada

HRDC's mission is to enable all Canadians to participate fully in the workplace and the community. There are links to labour market information, services for employers and entrepreneurs, legislation, and HRDC sites across the country. Click to job banks, newspaper classifieds, and newsgroups.

www.hrdc-drhc.gc.ca/common/home.shtml

Sustainable Business.com

At Sustainable Business.com, they believe that the Environmental Revolution is on its way. Opportunities do and will exist for people to start up new businesses or revise older businesses; many of the world's largest organizations have changed to eco-friendly practice. This site includes an online magazine, help for green businesses to find resources, Green Dream Job listings, and links to databases, books, and more.

www.sustainablebusiness.com/

The Business Climate Across Canada

Get a province-by-province look at economic performance and business incentives across Canada from this About.com page. Link to economic development departments in each region, and find industry profiles, databases, and business facts.

canadaonline.about.com/newsissues/canadaonline/library/weekly/aa102297.htm?iam=dp&terms=economic+development+canada

The Canadian Council on Social Development

The CCSD develops and promotes progressive social policies inspired by social justice, equality, and empowerment. They deal specifically with issues such as income security, employment, poverty, and government social policies. You can be added to their e-mail list to keep informed about current information and upcoming events.

www.ccsd.ca/

The International Development Research Centre

Based in Ottawa, the IDRC is a public corporation created by the Canadian government to help communities in the developing world find solutions to social, economic, and environmental problems through research. Find online databases and an online magazine, and you can join their mailing list.

www.idrc.ca

ECONOMICS

Canadian Economics Association

The Canadian Economics Association seeks to advance economic knowledge through study and research, publications, and free and informed discussion of economic questions. At their site you'll find news, activities, and links to such resources as an employment exchange, a directory of economists, and a grants database.

economics.ca

Economics Departments, Institutes, and Research Centers in the World

This site provides lists of economics institutions and associations on the web. You can search by country or continent, by areas, fields, and functions, or by a keyword search. There are almost 200 links for Canada alone.

ideas.uqam.ca/EDIRC/index.html

IDEAS

An acronym for "Internet Documents in Economics Access Service." This service provides a series of working papers (i.e., articles not yet published in journals) in the field of economics.

ideas.uqam.ca

The Canadian Centre for Policy Alternatives

Visit the site of this nonprofit organization that promotes research on economic and social policy from a progressive point of view. Browse through their publications, take a look at their alternative federal budget, or peruse the latest news.

www.policyalternatives.ca

FINANCE & INVESTMENT

BankruptcyCanada.com

Bankrupt and browsing the internet? BankruptcyCanada.com provides information on all aspects of insolvency, including business and personal bankruptcy, proposals, and choosing a trustee. You can hear RealAudio comments on personal bankruptcy and business proposals. You can also e-mail questions to a trustee in your province. Link to personal finance sites, calculators, and insolvency software systems.

www.BankruptcyCanada.com/

Bay-Street

This site offers various resources geared toward individual investors: Canadian and U.S. tech and headline news, and annotated guides to online brokerages, weekly stock prices, jobs, and more.

www.bay-street.com

Bloomberg

This is the big one in finance and investment sites, offering investment information from around the world, market data and analysis, top headlines, interest rates, tips, tools, and a lot more.

www.bloomberg.com

Brill's Mutual Fund Interactive

This is the place to find all the tools a mutual fund investor will need. The site covers news, quotes, portfolios, charts, and fund screening, and you can sign up to receive the free weekly newsletter.

www.brill.com

CA-Xchange

If you're desperately seeking a chartered accountant, look no further than the CA-Xchange! Non-accountants can search the members directory, but this site mainly provides news and service to CA-Xchange members. Features include accounting software comparisons and an accounting discussion forum.

www.cax.org

Canada Stockwatch

"No hype, no ads, just the facts." But you must pay for this service, and this web site offers a free trial subscription to tempt you. Check out the news, RealTime quotes, market statistics, charts, and information on all public Canadian companies. They also cover Canadian and American stock markets.

www.canada-stockwatch.com

Canada WealthNet

Covering everything from stocks and commodities to mutual funds and real estate, Canada WealthNet keeps vistors up to date on financial news.

www.nucleus.com/wealthnet

Canadian Financial Network

This time-saving service brings together and categorizes over 6000 quality online financial resources (mostly free), and describes them in sufficient detail so that you can hang up your surfboard and get down to business...

www.canadianfinance.com

Canadian Investor

Allied to the TV show of the same name, this site offers many of the usual—and several unusual—resources for the Canadian investor. Listen to an audio file of the TSE week-in-review, peruse hot stock picks from the TV show and Investor Radio, or listen to top financial stories.

www.canadian-investor.com

Canadian Stock Market Reporter

Here's a good source of regularly updated stock quotes and company information. Also offers subscriptions to Ferguson Fractal, a tool for market predictions based on chaos theory.

Canstock.com

Canoe Money

Read up on all of the latest business and finance news from a Canadian perspective. Find out the latest about funds and stocks, have money chats, or join forums. The Tool Box includes a glossary of financial terms along with the Top Ten Terms.

www.canoe.ca/MoneyNews/home.html

Carlson Online Services

Carlson Online provides resources such as press releases, reports, 15-minute delayed quotes, charts, and other fundamental data to keep investors informed. Search by industry group, exchange, stock symbol, name, index, and so on. The basic service is free but can be upgraded to a more detailed service for a subscription fee.

www.fin-info.com

CBS Market Watch

This comprehensive site includes sections on market data, portfolios, mutual funds, personal finance, and discussions. The tools, headlines, and industry news areas round out the content.

cbs.marketwatch.com

CNN Financial Network

The CNNfn site provides world stock market indexes updated every three minutes. But that's not all. Other sections include news, retirement planning, deals and debuts, and consumer information.

www.cnnfn.com/markets/world_markets.html

Credit Institute of Canada

Read the program outline and career opportunities for those training in credit and financial management. The Credit Institute's program is available by correspondence through a number of Canadian universities listed at this site. They've added a student study group forum.

www.creditedu.org

Downside

In a cryptic parody of the popular Silicon Valley business report upside.com, this site graphically illustrates their view: "We're gonna party like it's 1929." Hey, they could be wrong. Click on Misery Row for a gallery of overhyped stocks.

www.downside.com

E*Trade Canada

Visit this site to look up stocks and mutual fund quotes, invest, or simply hone your trading skills. There's also a newsletter and occasional live chats.

www.canada.etrade.com

Ethical Funds

If you want to ensure that your money is not made at the expense of other people's well-being, head over to Ethical Funds for detailed background info on popular stocks. Check out their list of different fund and bond portfolios, read about their principles and criteria, and click on Daily Performance Highlights to see how your ethical funds are doing.

www.ethicalfunds.com/index.html

FinanceWise

Start financial explorations with this free search engine of indexed web pages for financial services. The site also includes a banking and finance job search and financial headlines.

www.financewise.com

FreeRealTime

Fill out some routine forms at FreeRealTime and you'll have access to real-time quotes for listed stocks on all U.S. exchanges, wihtout paying a fee. If you don't want to fill in the forms, you'll still get the 15-minute-delay quotes.

quotes.freerealtime.com/frontpage/

Fund Library

Here's a comprehensive online source of information on mutual funds. Every fund sold in Canada is discussed here, and you'll also find tools, a weekly ReadAudio Mutual Fund Minute, and *The Screeming Capitalist* articles, both current and archived.

www.fundlibrary.com

Fund Watch Online Services

This capable guide to mutual funds and related tax information is regularly updated. Link to a net-worth calculator or to many mutual fund company sites.

www.fundwatch.ca

Business & Money

FundMonitor

This is the web site of leading mutual fund analyst Duff Young, the best-selling author and *Globe and Mail* columnist. Here you can register for access to FundMonitor's company research. You can also join a discussion forum, check out Young's seminar schedule, or post a question in the Ask an Analyst section.

www.fundmonitor.com

GlobeFund

There are mutual fund online forums, tools for new investors, a glossary, and a searchable database of articles at this site. Maybe most useful of all in this confusing and competitive marketplace are the powerful search tools Fund Selector and Fund Filter. For example, you can find all Canadian no-load funds with a given performance over a given period.

www.globefund.com

GlobeInvestor

This site, sponsored by the *Globe and Mail*, provides quotes, articles, news, and a database of financial information on Canadian companies. Globe Portfolio is a new free service that allows you to keep track of your stocks and mutual funds, and to compare yours to major indexes. You can also add other investments, such as your bonds, GICs, real estate, and even your jewellery, to this portfolio tool. You'll also find a Quote Pal and other tools.

www.globeinvestor.com

Gordon Pape

This site provides news and RealAudio mutual fund tips from CBC financial guru Gordon Pape. You'll also find full-text transcripts from the regular *Pape's Notes* radio broadcasts and updated book excerpts.

www.gordonpape.com

ilmoney

"Canada's personal finance web site" lets you track a portfolio, trade online, get market snapshots and stock quotes, consult a library, check out the latest business news, and much more. Search for topics, tools, or quotes and rates, or join a discussion group.

www.imoney.com

Investment.com

Check out this site for news, in-depth articles, tools, up-to-the-minute mortgage rates, and snap quotes. Link to auctions, stocks, or insurance sites. The domain name investment.com was reportedly acquired for an amount in the low six figures.

www.investment.com

Next Great Stocks

Some investors draw on their years of valuable experience in the financial community. Some utilize in-depth company profiles. Some employ advanced forecasting formulae. Some use tea leaves. And others still will try Next Great Stocks. You can even be added to a mailing list to receive the next great picks *before* they show up on this web site.

www.nextgreat.com

Oanda

Converting your loonies into greenbacks is easy, but what about rupees, patacas, or Mongolian tugriks? This online currency exchange calculator can perform calculations based on the exchange rate of the day, or from any day from the past few years. Several languages are available, and results can be printed in a handy conversion table.

www.oanda.com

Quicken Canada

This major portal for financial stuff features a portfolio tracker, and mortgage and car loan locators. There's also a lot of information on stocks and markets, RRSPs, mutual funds, taxes, insurance, and more. Amateurs can learn the basics with a stock market simulation game. In the What's New section, go to a Risk vs. Returns Chart or e-mail fund cards to friends.

www.quicken.ca

RetireWeb

It's never too early to start planning for your retirement. This site is easy to use, and specializes in the financial aspects of retirement, from planning and saving to post-retirement choices. Features include annuity, RRIF, and other calculators, and information on government programs.

www.retireweb.com

RRSP.org

This site promises "everything that you need to know about Registered Retirement Savings Plans, without the sales pitch." Check out the suggestions on many aspects of retirement, tax, and estate planning; follow the links to mutual fund companies; try out the mortgage calculator; and read the book reviews.

www.rrsp.org

Silicon Investor

The internet's premier financial discussion site. View discussions for free, or pay for a pricey lifetime memberhsip for posting privileges. Remember to register with an alias you can live with, as sacrcastic members may twist your nickname around if they disagree with you about their favourite stocks.

www.siliconinvestor.com

Small Investor Protection Association

Visit the Brokers Hall of Shame and Investor Alerts at this Canadian web site. Bring your broker and investor complaints here too. This national nonprofit organization provides guidance to consumers and investors, and works toward changing legislation and tightening enforcement powers in the financial services industry. They also provide links to other investor information sites.

www.sipa.to

Stock Detective

Read about Stinky Stocks and the Red Light District. Find out how to tell the difference between a real stock analysis and a paid promotion. This page of the FinancialWeb site warns visitors about the latest schemes and scams in the financial world.

www.financialweb.com/editorial/stockdetective/

Stockformation.com

"Your virtual stock market analyst," Stockformation.com provides articles and stock ideas by Canadian analysts. They focus on technology and smaller-cap stocks. There's an IPO Centre, Most Actives section, and much more easy-to-find information. And you can head to the Jobs area if you are an analyst or investment journalist looking for a career change.

www.stockformation.com

Stockgroup.com

This web site provides quotes, news stories, and profiles of small and micro-cap companies for investors.

www.smallcapcenter.com

The Armchair Millionaire

This site provides live chats and message boards that are useful for beginning mutual fund investors. Messages from new investors receive responses from more experienced ones. The site also features portfolio strategies and "fundamentals" of investing.

www.armchairmillionaire.com

The Motley Fool

The Motley Fool's mission is to educate, to amuse, and to enrich. This popular how-to site about investing has evolved into a major cultural phenomenon. Popular features include a risky growth portfolio, and the Dogs of the Dow, which teaches you how to invest in "the cheapest" Dow Jones Industrial Average components. Go to the Fool's School for investing basics, then read through their 13 steps to become completely Foolish.

www.fool.com

The Social Investment Organization

Here's the site of a national nonprofit organization that promotes socially responsible investment. They produce a newsletter and industry reports and maintain an extensive directory.

www.web.net/~sio

The True Cost of Mutual Fund Fees

This page was put together by the U.S. magazine *Smart Money,* but the page can still be useful for Canadians worried about the corrosive effect of management fees on their mutual fund investments. An interactive tool gives you graphic evidence of where your dough's really going. Key in a symbol to get a stock snapshot.

www.smartmoney.com/si/tools/fundfees/

FINANCE & INVESTMENT — EXCHANGES

Canadian Dealing Network Inc.

CDN is Canada's organized over-the-counter stock market. It's essentially a network of securities dealers who trade unlisted stocks over the telephone.

www.investcom.com/page/canadn.html

Canadian Venture Exchange (CDNX)

Canada's small-capital stock exchange was formed as a result of a merger of the Vancouver Stock Exchange and the Alberta Stock Exchange. Historical ASE and VSE information is included in a separate section. Search by industry, ticker symbol, or company name. Check out the bookshelf, IPOs, and links, or view a Breakfast with the Market webcast.

www.cdnx.ca

International Federation of Stock Exchanges

This web site provides contact information and connections to member and nonmember stock exchanges around the world. It also lists market holidays, and contains a calendar of events and the *Focus* newsletter.

www.fibv.com

Montreal Exchange

The Montreal Exchange was founded in 1874 and was the first institution of its kind in Canada. Now it's home to derivatives trading and a small-cap market; its large caps have moved to Toronto. Visit the virtual floor and find all the investment information you need about equity, options, and futures.

www.me.org

Toronto Stock Exchange

All trading of large capitalization stocks now resides on the Toronto Stock Exchange. It has over 1300 listed companies' stocks, proprietary derivatives, indexes, and market information. And there's a lot to do on the TSE site, including a contest that lets you manage a fantasy online trading account worth a cool $100 000. Remember: buy low, sell high.

www.tse.com/challenge.html

Winnipeg Commodity Exchange

If you're already dealing in commodities, you probably won't be intimidated by the long disclaimer on the home page: "None of the information provided is intended, in any way whatsoever, to induce the purchase or sale of any futures or options contract traded on WCE." You're on your own. But then, in the risky market of options and commodities, you probably knew that.

www.wce.com

Winnipeg Exchange

Common and preferred stocks and debentures are currently listed on the WSE. Some securities are exclusively listed on the Winnipeg Exchange, while others are interlisted with other exchanges.

www.wse.com

FINANCE & INVESTMENT — PUBLICATIONS

Business 2.0

Business 2.0 calls itself "the magazine of business in the Internet Age." Not surprising, considering the title. This magazine is devoted to e-commerce in all of its forms: e-business, marketing, technologies, investing, and net statistics. Don't forget to check out the regular Get a Life section, about how the Internet Age affects your mental and physical health.

www.business2.com

Ka-Ching

Ka-Ching describes itself as providing information and resources to help women manage their financial lives. This guide includes columns and articles, as well as calculators, games, message boards, and chat sessions. Regular topics include Your Money, Your Business, Your Career, and Your Family. Meet some very interesting women in the Like Minds section.

www.ka-ching.com

MoneySense.ca

This Canadian magazine web site includes everything in the spending and saving categories—from investments and careers to holidays and family. It also includes calculators and other Quicken tools. You can look up stocks by symbol, too.

moneysense.ca

The Canadian Ethical Investment Web Site

This site is a companion internet resource to *The Canadian Ethical Money Guide*. It explains what ethical investments are and how they compare financially to other investments. Find out which funds screen the companies they invest in according to social or environmental criteria. You'll also find useful links to other ethical investment sites.

www.web.net/ethmoney

TheStreet.com

TheStreet.com is published entirely online. It combines free insights on market happenings, discussion forums, and a comprehensive Investing Basics area with a paid service that includes daily columns, tools, and a portfolio tracker.

www.thestreet.com

INSURANCE

Insurance Bureau of Canada

A source of general information on home, auto, and business insurance in Canada, from the industry association. Also find safety and loss-prevention tips and discussions about legal and regional issues.

www.ibc.ca

Insurance Canada

Provides information on inusrance for the benefit of consumers and industry professionals. There's a directory of providers nationwide and a section devoted to industry news and events.

www.insurance-canada.ca

INTERNATIONAL ECONOMY

Canadians in the World

Compiled by the Department for Foreign Affairs and International Trade, this site chronicles the history of Canada's international relations. Examines the global economy, culture, sports, Canada and the UN, and more.

www.canschool.org/menu-e.asp

Canadians in the World

Compiled by the Department of Foreign Affairs and International Trade, this site chronicles the history of Canada's international relations. It examines the global economy, culture, sports, Canada and the U.N., and other topics. The links provide information about Canada's specific participation in other international organizations.

www.canschool.org/menu-e.asp

International Economy Resources

This page provides links to resources and sites dealing specifically with the international economy. These links include an emerging markets directory, economic data, world business resources, and international economy institutes.

www.forworld.com/economy/resources/intl.htm

LABOUR

Canadian Labour Congress

With over 2.3 million members across the country, the CLC is a force to be reckoned with in the realms of social and economic justice. Look up the latest projects, campaigns, and boycotts; send e-mail to the president; or use the handy feature at this site to fax your MP about labour issues that concern you.

www.clc-ctc.ca

Guide to Canadian Labour History Resources

The National Library of Canada has put together this resource to connect you to sites about unions, labour documents, statistics, and labour history.

www.nlc-bnc.ca/services/ewebsite.htm

International Confederation of Free Trade Unions

For an international perspective on labour, the ICFTU has 215 affiliated organizations in 145 countries and territories on five continents. There are many appalling work situations in the world that we never hear about in the news, but there's really no excuse with sites like this one on the internet. Search the site for information by date, subject, country, and type. Also in French and Spanish.

www.icftu.org

International Development

This page of the Web Networks site links you to information and organizations working for economic and social development around the world. Connect to regional news feeds and international development conferences and organizations.

community.web.net/international/

LabourNet Canada

The LabourNet web site promotes computer communications as a medium for building international labour solidarity. There are LabourNets that focus on specific areas of the world. The Canada site includes a streaming video interview on web activism and labour activism in Canada.

www.labournet.ca

Our Times

Check out the online version of Canada's independent labour magazine for feature articles and photos from each issue and a table of contents for the current issue. You can submit an article online.

ourtimes.web.net

The International Labour Organization

This is a United Nations specialized agency that seeks to promote social justice and internationally recognized human and labour rights. Check out the What's New section or search by location or by topic, such as child labour. A features section will link you to an encyclopedia of occupational health and safety, among other sites.

www.ilo.org

UnionNet

This page of the Web Networks site links you to labour organizations, news, and conferences across Canada.

community.web.net/unionnet

SMALL BUSINESS INFORMATION

Business Development Bank of Canada

Canada's small business bank's web site provides a starting point for budding entrepreneurs looking for financing. Visit this site for the requisite contact and service information, as well as facts on loans for electronic commerce and student business loans.

www.bdc.ca

CanadaOne

This web site calls itself "Canada's small business hub." It provides a search engine specially geared to find sites of interest for Canadian businesses, a business directory, great articles such as "E-Commerce Basics" and "Getting Terrific Trade Show Results," and events listings.

www.canadaone.com

Garage.com

This is a meeting place for tech entrepreneurs and venture capitalists, so they can find each other and fall in love. The two-day seminar for startups is called "Boot Camp."

www.garage.com

GoSoloCanada.com

This site for small and new (first 5 years) businesses offers information on subjects like registering your business and going public, plus e-business help and space. Information, directories, articles, and business forms are included.

www.gosolocanada.com

Venture

The CBC TV show that tracks the ups and downs of the Canadian entrepreneur in his or her native habitat. All of their seasons on the air (*Venture* began in 1984) provide a wealth of case studies about people starting, growing, and sustaining businesses. Nothing ventured, nothing gained.

www.tv.cbc.ca/venture

TAXES

Canada Customs and Revenue Agency (Revenue Canada)

How many of you knew that Revenue Canada has a new name? This is everyone's favourite government department, and the site offers information on taxation for business and individuals, quick reference FAQs, contact information, and details on telefile, efile, and now netfile.

www.rc.gc.ca

Canadian Taxpayers Federation

This taxpayers advocacy group acts as a watchdog on government spending. Sign online petitions, read up on the latest studies, or buy a "Tax Me, I'm Canadian" T-shirt. There's a lot of stuff about gas taxes, and you can add information about gas prices in your community. Link to political parties, federal organizations, and all of the right-wing money institutes.

www.taxpayer.com

Tax Tip of the Day

Provided on the web site of accounting giant KPMG, this page features daily doses of avoidance advice.

www.kpmg.ca/tax/tip_main.htm

TaxWeb

From this page you can access several tax calculators. For example, choose RRSP Savings, enter your income and RRSP contribution, and you'll find out, by province or territory, your tax savings.

www.tax.ca/taxtools/home/taxtoolshome.cfm?p=-1&c=-1

TRADE

Canada China Business Council

A nonprofit, private-sector organization, the CCBC was created to promote business relations between Canada and China. Vist this web site for information on investment opportunities in China, member services, and related events.

www.ccbc.com

Canadian International Trade Tribunal

The tribunal is an administrative body operating within Canada's trade remedies system and reporting to Parliament through the Minister of Finance. Visit this site for information on trade-related issues such as appeals, dumping and subsidizing, procurement, and safeguards.

www.citt.gc.ca

Export Source

Navigate the confusion of different departments and save time (which, as we all know, equals money) on your search for information about foreign trade. For both export-ready and new-to-export Canadian businesses, it brings trade information from many federal departments together into a single web site. Get the goods on foreign markets, trade stats, financing, export missions, trade shows, and the logistics of delivery.

exportsource.gc.ca

International Federation for Alternative Trade

IFAT is a global network of 143 fair-trade organizations in 47 countries. They work to improve the livelihoods and well-being of disadvantaged people in developing countries and to change the unfair structures of international trade. Find out about their current educational, networking, conference, and lobbying activities.

www.ifat.org

North American Free Trade Agreement

This is it, the downloadable PDF file of NAFTA, brought to you by the Canadian Department of Foreign Affairs and International Trade. You'll find it all here: who, what, where, why, when, and how.

www.dfait-maeci.gc.ca/nafta-alena/menu-e.asp

Universal Currency Converter

Like Onanda, this site performs up-to-the-minute currency conversions. While it has fewer features and functions, the interface is extremely straightforward.

www.xe.net/ucc

World Trade Organization

The first article's headline reads "Mike Moore hails EU-China agreement." But, alas, it's not the Mike Moore of *TV Nation* fame. No, this is the official site of the WTO. "Is it a dictatorial tool of the rich and powerful? Does it destroy jobs? Does it ignore the concerns of health, the environment and development?" they ask in the section on 10 Common Misunderstandings About the WTO.

www.wto.org

TRADE — ASSOCIATIONS

Alliance of Manufacturers and Exporters Canada

The Alliance works to improve the competitiveness of Canadian industry and to expand export business. Read articles on Canada's current business climate or join to visit the members-only site. There are links to the provincial divisions of the Alliance.

www.palantir.ca/the-alliance

Canadian Advanced Technology Alliance

The CATA*Alliance* is a national trade organization that focuses on the provision of business services that conserve and leverage member resources. They have resource centres across the country, and their members ranked personal income taxes as their number one advocacy concern.

www.cata.ca

Canadian Association of Petroleum Producers

Find out about industry news, issues, and related sites at the Canadian Association of Pretroleum Producers web site. CAPP member companies are responsible for 95 percent of all natural gas and crude oil in Canada.

www.capp.ca

Canadian Booksellers Association

Check out the best-selling Canadian books, as well as industry news, advocacy issues, convention postings, bookstores, and author tours.

www.cbabook.org

Canadian Environmental Industry Virtual Office

This web site connects members of Canadian industry associations dealing with the environment. It provides sources of information, services, and advice on human resources, research and development, domestic and international markets, and investment and financing. There are also links to quite a few environmental job banks.

virtualoffice.ic.gc.ca

Media Trade Associations

From this web page directory of media associations, you can link to organizations such as the Canadian Association of Broadcasters, the Canadian Community Newspaper Association, and the Canadian Magazine Publishers Association, as well as to provincial organizations.

www.newsdirectory.com/assoc/na/ca/

Organic Trade Association

OTA is a national association representing the organic industry in Canada, the United States, and Mexico. The site includes a publications list, information about events and news releases, and links to industry sources and specific country associations.

www.ota.com

Retail Council of Canada

Here's an organization that serves, promotes, and represents the Canadian retail industry. The site includes articles, a calendar of events, pricing accuracy guidelines, research, and government information.

www.retailcouncil.org

White Pages Canadian Trade Associations

Link to national and provincial trade associations from this web page.

206.184.157.225/in/americas/canada/tradeassociations.htm

Worldwide Trade Associations

This page will link you to a variety of Canadian trade associations, or you can select one of the links to dozens of other countries to find out about their associations.

www.firstworldwide.com/ta/can.htm

SUBJECT INDEX ▶

WEB SITE INDEX ▶

C

D

E

F

G

H

O

P

Q

R

S

T